Professional NT Services

Kevin Miller

Wrox Press Ltd. ®

Professional NT Services

Published by Wrox Press Ltd. 30 Lincoln Road, Olton, Birmingham, B27 6PA
Printed in USA
ISBN 1-861001-30-4

Trademark Acknowledgements

Credit

Author
Kevin Miller

Editors
Jon Hill
Tim Briggs

Index
Seth Maislin

Cover
Andrew Guillaume

Technical Reviewers
Bob Beauchemin
Richard Grimes
Sing Li
Claus Loud
Christophe Nasarre
Anil Peres-da-Silva
Marc Simkin
Mark Stiver

Layout/Design
Frances Olesch

About the Author

Kevin Miller works for Microsoft Corporation as a Consultant in the Southwest District MCS practice in Phoenix, Arizona. He is a Microsoft Certified Solutions Developer, has an MBA in Technology Management, and an undergraduate degree in Philosophy. Kevin works with a variety of Fortune 500 clients, helping them to architect and develop systems using the latest Microsoft technologies. When he is not working, Kevin enjoys four wheeling and camping in the back hills of Arizona and Colorado, traveling, reading, and relaxing by the pool with his wife, Vicki, and dog, Jenny.

Dedication

To my best friend in the whole world, my wife Vicki. Now we can reclaim those many hours.

Acknowledgements

I won't forget that day about a year ago when I got this crazy idea that the world needed a book on NT service programming and wrote to Dave Maclean at Wrox, outlining my idea in a paragraph. Within only a few hours, emails were flying and I was writing an outline. Little did I realize, then, how difficult the task would be in its entirety. I thought that I could write, but I had no idea what a naïve belief that was, or what I was truly in for. This has been one of the truly demanding journeys of my lifetime.

First, I'd like to thank my wife, Vicki, for all the love, support, and advice she gave me during this long, difficult project. I would also like to thank her for putting up with all those hours that I was in the office, door closed, when I could have been spending time with her. In many ways, this book is the fruit of her labors as well as of mine – there certainly would have been no book if she had not pushed me forward on those many occasions when I felt like I could not continue. Her way of encouragement always focused on the positive – it was never the "get in there and go to work" variety (which she knows would not have worked), it was always more a gentle reminder of my long-time desire to do something like this. Now, we just have to recapture some of the months that we were apart.

Next, I'd like to thank my technical editor at Wrox, Jon Hill, whose precision and care kept the book from becoming a jumbled mess of confusing thoughts, and who worked the same long hours I did at the end to keep the schedule up. I can certainly write a grammatically correct sentence, even a paragraph, but clearly expressing thoughts through a chapter that's scores of pages long is much more difficult; it requires help from a specialist like Jon. Every time I thought I could 'get away' with a poorly worded or unclear statement, Jon called me on it. The end result, I think, is a much better experience for the reader.

Furthermore, my gratitude to the many technical reviewers who read the book along the way, and kept me honest when I expressed an unjustified opinion. Their excellent commentary and suggestions helped to make the final product much better than it would otherwise have been. I'd also like to thank John Franklin, managing editor at Wrox, who had a consistent vision for the book in the marketplace and sent me many words of encouragement to keep me going.

I'd like to thank my mother, Sharon, and my Aunt Peggy, for helping to give me the character I do have. And, for never telling me that there were things I could not do. I'd also like to thank the teachers and professors I've had along the way who taught me the few things that I know, including how to work hard when I need to. Among them, I'd particularly like to thank Mr. Howard, who did what a great teacher would do, push me forward when I needed to go further.

Finally, to my faithful dog, Jenny, who spent a lot of hours under the desk keeping me company.

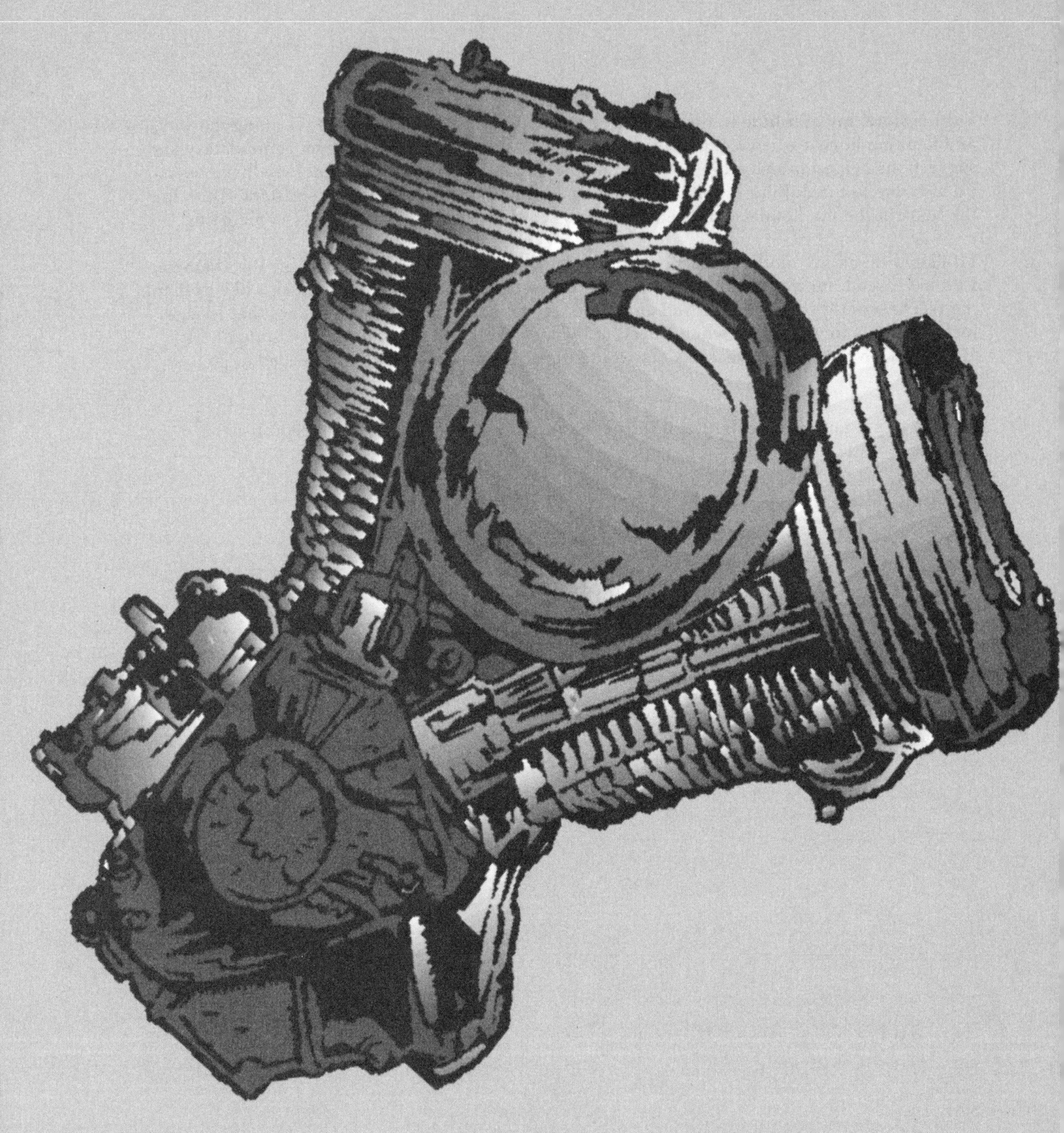

Table of Contents

Introduction

When we need to learn something new (particularly a new programming technology), we often seek out a book for information. When we pick up that book, we are hoping – perhaps unconsciously – to have three questions answered:

- How do I make the technology work?
- Where and when is the technology appropriate?
- How do I fashion the engineering techniques I now know into an elegantly designed solution to my problem?

There are many computer books on topics right across the board that give you plenty of the 'how', but very little practical advice on where and when to use that knowledge to solve real problems. This book sets its sights on the lofty goal of meeting all three needs.

More importantly than just describing how to write NT services, this book is about service *design.* To me, design is 'engineering with intention', where the goal of that intention is solving the problem at hand. Put another way, good design is about understanding when, where and how to use particular engineering principles to solve a problem.

It is the aim of this book to provide you with enough information to know not only *how* to write services, but also *when* it is appropriate to use in your software system. I'll do that by showing you how to think of your software system in terms of **usage patterns**. From there, you will be able to tell whether any of the usage patterns in your system indicate a need for an NT service.

Who is this Book for?

This book is aimed at two types of programmer:

- C/C++ Windows programmers who need to write server applications that perform user-independent tasks.
- Client/server developers who want to use services as part of a multi-tiered system architecture. This may be with an NT web server, or as a broker of business or supplementary services for use by lighter client development environments such as Visual Basic, VBScript, or Active Server Pages. If you're this type of developer, you'll want your service to perform well in networked, multi-client scenarios.

In both cases, your goal is high-performance services that have good administration, security, and feedback mechanisms. This implies that you are a C/C++ developer who has experience programming with Win32. You should also have a basic understanding of multithreaded programming under NT, and of COM and DCOM, if you want your service to serve up COM objects.

The book will also be of interest to:

- Senior or architectural developers in medium to large projects – programmers who can influence the design and architecture of the software system being built.
- People in small development teams in which a handful of programmers do everything, and where each new round of code addition can affect the architecture.

If you fall into one of these categories, the important sections of the book will be the ones that focus on the design of NT services, and their place in the architecture of a system. You might not be writing services at the moment, but you need to know when you might want to use them, and their implications should you decide so to do.

What this Book Covers

Treatment of the topic of writing NT services has been sketchy and scattered across a variety of places in the existing literature. This book is aimed at bringing that wide range of material together in an organized way and teaching not just the principles, but their practical application. Briefly, here's what we'll cover together:

- How to write services and the applications that support them
- How to configure NT to run services
- Where to put services in your software system architecture, if at all
- How to create a service that meets your engineering goals elegantly

Note that one thing this book won't *cover is writing hardware device drivers implemented as services.*

Usage Patterns

Ultimately, this book is about showing you how to implement robust NT service designs that coherently fit the system architecture of which they are a part. At the heart of this teaching motif is the **usage pattern**.

The term 'usage pattern' borrows from the concept of the **design pattern** first introduced in the book *Design Patterns* by Gamma et al (Addison-Wesley ISBN 0-201-63361-2, 1995). A design pattern is a way to solve classic software design problems using specific, patterned design motifs or architectural layouts of code. Our term 'usage pattern' refers not to a way of thinking about code design, but rather to a way of *using* particular software components as part of a functioning system. Under this regime, then, services have a set of rôles (usages) that they can play in a software system.

The goals of the usage pattern technique are threefold:

- To introduce you to the various usages that services have in a software system
- To train you to be able to spot where a usage pattern fits into a software system's architecture
- To provide specific examples for the implementation of those patterns

In this book, I use code samples and snippets to show basic code structures for the concepts, and I use usage patterns to illustrate design issues. As we move through the book, I will introduce an example/sample of each of the major classes of usage pattern. By the end of the book, you will have specific code and design experience with all of the major usage patterns.

Synopsis

On a first reading, this book should be read from front to back, as individual chapters are not intended to be references to discrete topics that can be considered in isolation. I have tried not only to cover the basic 'how' in a sensible order, but also to tell a design story in usage patterns that are dispersed throughout the book. (Of course, the book will remain useful to those who want to refresh their memory of the details of a particular usage pattern at a later date.) That said, here's a summary of what's in store for you in the pages to come:

The first four chapters deal with the fundamentals of NT services. In Chapter 1, we'll examine the basic theory and structure of services, and how the different architectural components of a system interconnect. We will also survey at some length the specific usage patterns for services. Chapter 2 looks at the bare-bones service architecture and code structure. By the end of this chapter, you will understand what distinguishes a service from other types of executable objects in NT, and you'll have seen all the code required for a trivial service implementation.

In Chapter 3, we'll look at what needs to be done to install a service, for use both by hand and in code, and I'll demonstrate the theory by getting our example service up and running. Once that's done, we'll look at controlling the operation of a service through code. In Chapter 4, to complete this section of the book, we'll design and build a generic C++ class and a set of macros for service implementation, and then use them to implement our first and simplest usage pattern, the **Monitor**.

Chapter 5 broadens the discussion a little to introduce the NT event log, itself a service, which your service should use to report errors and other status information. I'll explain how to add event-logging functionality to our C++ service class, and hence to any service you create from it, ultimately adding that capability retrospectively to the Monitor usage pattern implementation. After that, Chapter 6 returns to our main theme, introducing Microsoft Message Queue as a means of implementing another resource pattern, the **Agent**.

In order to be robust and usable in real-life environments, NT services need appropriate security. Chapter 7 outlines the basics of NT's security architecture, and how we can programmatically control security from inside our services. This chapter also focuses on the complexities of service run models, security impersonation, and the various ways a service can interact with the user.

Chapters 8 and 9 form something of a pair, the first of them introducing the concept of **resource pooling** by way of ODBC's implementation of the technique. We'll then discuss expanding and improving on that implementation through the **Quartermaster** usage pattern, in which a service pre-initializes database connections to make database query functions more efficient on large client/server or internet systems. Then, in Chapter 9, I'll show you how to use the Active Template Library to create services that can host COM objects, and use the Quartermaster implementation of the previous chapter to demonstrate the **Business Object** pattern.

With the coverage of our major usage patterns now complete, in Chapter 10 I'll talk about how to debug and tune your services – two topics that introduce a number of issues that are different from when you're writing ordinary applications. Next, Chapter 11 shows you how to write administration programs for your services. It discusses both control panel applets and a new architecture that has become a major part of service control with the NT 4.0 Option Pack – the Microsoft Management Console.

Finally, in Chapter 12, I'll reprise all the design issues that have raised their heads in the preceding chapters and provide you with a checklist for developing your own services, covering issues like control, communication, security, and threading. I'll even tell you when a service might *not* be appropriate.

BackOffice Logo Compliance

If you follow the recommendations in this book regarding service design, the services you create will be well on their way to being **BackOffice Logo compliant**. This important certification proves that you are properly using a range of NT features to make your services secure, robust, scalable, and easy to administer. The full logo compliance requirements are available on the Web at http://www.microsoft.com/backoffice/designed/how.htm.

What You Need to Use this Book

In order to compile and run *all* the samples in this book, you will need the following tools:

- Visual C++ 5.0 compiler with Service Pack 3
- Visual Basic 5.0 with Service Pack 3
- Windows NT 4.0 Server and Workstation with Service Pack 3
- NT 4.0 Option Pack
- The January 1998 Platform SDK
- SQL Server 6.5 with Service Pack 4
- The ODBC 3.5 SDK
- Two machines connected to a network

However, not all the examples require all the tools, and it's in the nature of these things that the requirements tend to increase towards the end of the book. It's certainly possible to do useful service development on a single NT Workstation machine, and Chapters 1-5, 8, 10 and 12 need no more than a single computer running NT Workstation 4.0 with Service Pack 3, and a copy of Visual C++ 5.0.

Conventions Used

We use a number of different styles of text and layout in the book to help differentiate between the different kinds of information. Here are examples of the styles we use, and an explanation of what they mean:

These boxes hold important, not-to-be-forgotten, mission critical details that are directly relevant to the surrounding text.

Background information, asides and references to information located elsewhere appear in the text like this.

- **Important words** are in a bold font
- Words that appear on the screen, such as menu options, are in a similar font to the one used on the screen – the File menu, for example
- Keys that you press on the keyboard, like *Ctrl* and *Delete*, are in italics
- All filenames are in this style: `Quartermaster.cpp`
- Function names look like this: `GetResourceHandle()`
- Code that's new, important, or relevant to the current discussion will be presented like this:

```
int main()
{
   cout << "Professional NT Services";
   return 0;
}
```

- Code that you've seen before, or isn't directly relevant to the matter at hand, looks like this:

```
int main()
{
   cout << "Professional NT Services";
   return 0;
}
```

Tell Us What You Think

We've tried to make this book as accurate and enjoyable for you as possible, but what really matters is what the book actually does for you. Please let us know your views, either by returning the reply card in the back of the book, or by contacting us via e-mail at `feedback@wrox.com`

Source Code

All the source code from the examples in this book is available for download from the Wrox Press web site:

http://www.wrox.com
ftp://ftp.wrox.com
ftp://ftp.wrox.co.uk

Errata & Updates

We've made every effort to make sure there are no errors in the text or the code. However, to err is human and as such we recognize the need to keep you, the reader, informed of any mistakes as they're spotted and corrected.

While you're visiting our web site, please make use of our *Errata* page, which is dedicated to fixing any small errors in the book, or offering new ways around a problem and its solution. Errata sheets are available for all our books – please download them, or take part in the continuous improvement of our tutorials and upload a 'fix' or pointer to the solution.

For those without access to the 'net, call us on **1-800 USE WROX** and we'll gladly send errata sheets to you. Alternatively, send a letter to:

Wrox Press Inc.,
1512 N Fremont, Suite 103
Chicago,
IL 60622-2567
USA

Wrox Press Ltd,
30, Lincoln Road,
Olton,
Birmingham,
B27 6PA
UK

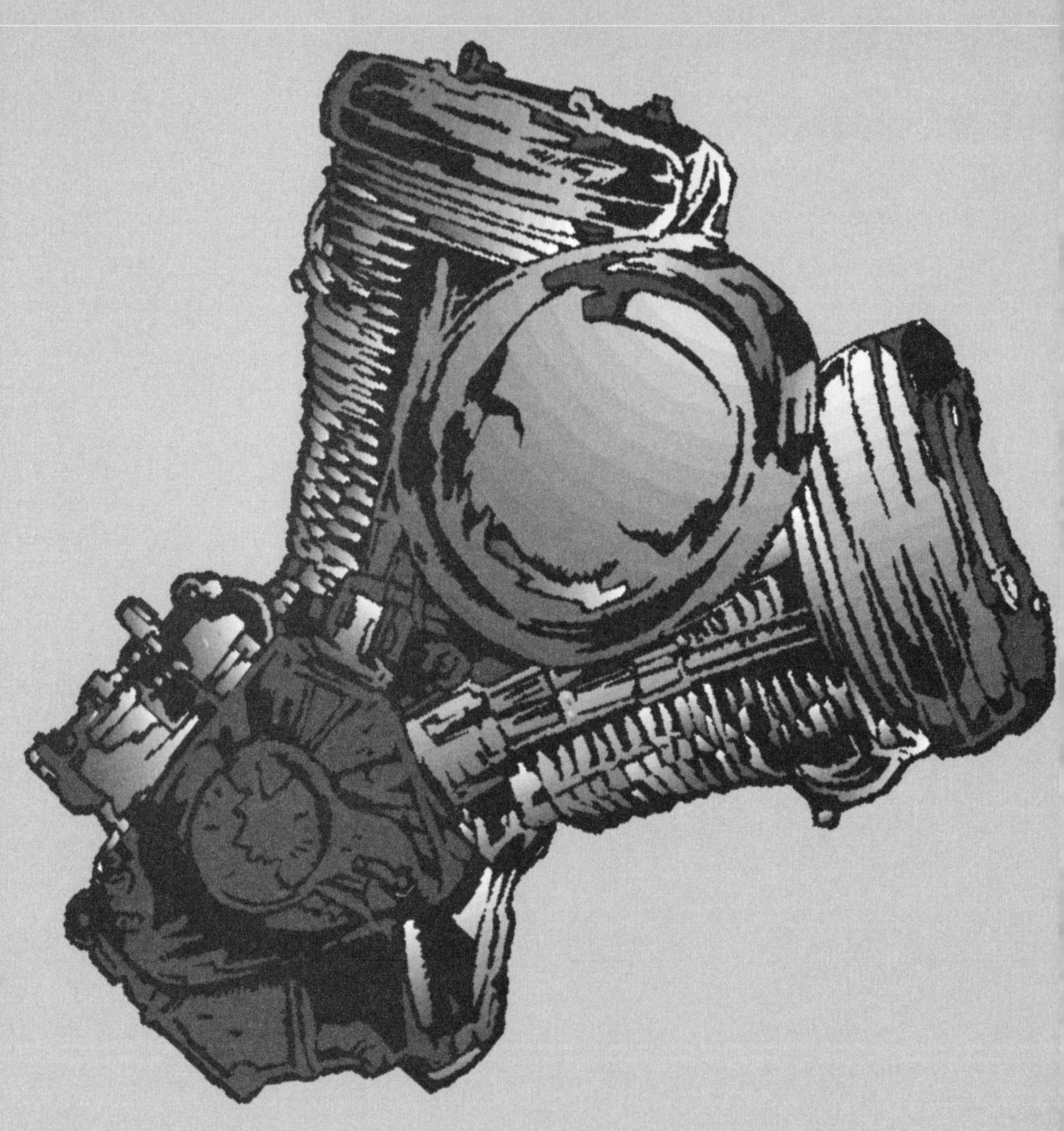

1

Understanding NT Services

In principle, NT services are very easy to understand. As with so many simple ideas, however, what makes them complex is knowing when and how to use them well. The goal of this chapter is for you to get a better handle on what services are, what they can do, and what other types of system resources they interact with.

It is important to be aware from the very beginning that 'services' actually come in two flavors: **Win32-based services** and **driver services**. Win32-based services are server applications, while driver services implement NT hardware drivers; device drivers are typically interesting only to the special group of people who write hardware interfaces. The topic of this book is exclusively services of the Win32-based variety, so every time I mention 'services' from this point on, you can assume I'm talking about Win32-based services.

What are NT Services?

Since you're reading this book, there's a good chance that you know what an NT service is already. Still, to make sure that we're all talking about the same thing, let's start with a definition that captures the essence of the term, and then fill in the details afterwards.

> **An NT service is an executable program (`.exe`) that runs as a background task, and whose lifetime is controlled by the Service Control Manager (SCM). Services may be run at system startup, or may be started (via the SCM) by the interactive user, or by a process that a user is running.**

The key to understanding what services are is to understand that their lifetimes are controlled by a core Windows NT component known as the **Service Control Manager** (SCM), affectionately called 'the scum'. You'll discover more about the SCM later on in this chapter; suffice it to say for now that, based on instructions you give when you install your service, the SCM decides when to load your service and then handles the details of launching the process that contains it, when needed. No user interaction is required.

This model differs from the usual way in which executables load and run. Generally, when an executable program loads, it is in response to the request of a user who has just double-clicked an item in a program group or in Explorer. Alternatively, the program might load because another executable that is already running has launched it programmatically. The ability of a service to live independently of individual client, user, or call requests is the key to some of the important things it can do in your system.

In the next chapter, you'll learn that the basic service infrastructure will take us about 25-30 lines of boilerplate C++ code to implement. In fact, you can make any old `.exe` a service with just a few extra lines of code. If that were all there is to it, I could end this book in under 50 pages! What on earth is the rest of the book about?

The thing is that a service is the model of a **server application**. It is not so much the 'service' part of a service that is important, but the fact that when you write one, you accept the burden of responsibility to make it perform well and to be a good NT citizen. Furthermore, if you write a non-trivial service, it will usually have more than one client or perform some relatively critical system function. The expectations and the risks are proportionately higher than in a stand-alone application, because bad networking and threading design manifest themselves *n*-fold when your component is doling out resources to tens or hundreds of simultaneous clients. In a sense, a good portion of this book is about good *server applications* rather than services, or at least the principles that apply equally to both. Services are the quintessential server applications, and that's why we use them to shine light on the topic of writing excellent server applications that integrate tightly into the NT environment.

Why Write NT Services?

Now for the big question: who cares about NT services? The motivation for writing a service might not be so obvious as it is for using other programming technologies, like MFC or COM. Like many programmers, you may have thought that NT services were components written only by the guys at Microsoft for core operating system features, or for BackOffice products like SQL Server. "NT services are for systems engineers to disable, enable, restart, and troubleshoot when something goes wrong," you might say, "but who would need one for the everyday running of their software system?"

In fact, NT services are useful in all types of client-server system architectures, and occasionally in non client-server architectures as well. As you'll see, services are for real systems – systems that you are writing right now for your clients or for your company. They are just what the doctor ordered for a whole array of system design opportunities. The kinds of work that services can do can be divided into three general categories:

- Tasks that can't or shouldn't involve the interactive user, either because they run in the background or because they require some privileged security access.
- Monitoring some critical OS function.
- Providing some kind of resource to other machines on a network, or doing work on behalf of other machines on a network. This category contains most of the interesting and sophisticated usage patterns we'll examine in this book.

Usage Patterns for Services

I described what usage patterns are in the introduction. It's time for us now to take a look at the specific usage patterns that NT services fit.

Possible Scenarios for Usage Patterns

Let's brainstorm for a few moments. Imagine you have a tool that allows you to perform actions independently of the interactive user, and to maintain state independently of user calls. If you had that kind of tool, when might you use it?

Here are a few possibilities. This is probably not a comprehensive list, and it may even be redundant in a couple of places, but it will help us to get our minds thinking about the patterns that services fit.

> *When I mention service architectural designs and the usage patterns they relate to, I'll speak of the usage pattern 'fitting' the service design, or the service design 'fitting' the usage pattern. This is because to be a design is not to be a pattern; designs* match *or* fit *patterns – they are not patterns themselves.*

You might use a service when...

Your object needs a lifetime or a persistent state independent of whether a client is connected to it.
Consider a simple case. Perhaps your software system is for a grocery store chain (XYZ Stores) that has 1,000 stores throughout the United States. The CFO of the chain wants to be able to know, at a moment's notice, what daily sales totals are for the whole chain. A plausible use for a service might be to connect to each store periodically and gather the total sales number from the main sales data server at the store, before summing those totals. This service would probably be located on an NT server at the central office. When the CFO wishes to see the data, he launches a client application that connects to the service and obtains the summarized data.

Maybe it's a dumb thought experiment, maybe not, but it points out a couple of important capabilities a service has, namely:

- The ability to be working on a processing task whether or not anyone is connected to it (in this case, gathering data from data servers).
- The ability to store state information (in this case, the stores it is connecting to, when it last gathered information from them, as well as their individual sales numbers) independently of whether an interactive user is working with the application. This state information can 'outlive' the connections of individual clients, because the life of the process is controlled by the SCM.

Your object needs a job to get done when no one is around to run the job.
Certainly, you could give the CFO an application that performed these tasks on demand, but they may not be happy having to wait while your software connects to 1,000 stores over the company WAN and gathers data. In this case, it would probably be better to be doing the data gathering in advance, and have it ready for them when they ask for it. Your service is now a background task that does work without being specifically asked by a user to do so.

You need to share a central resource (like data, or a modem pool) among many clients.
Let's use our grocery store chain example again. Once they find out the CFO has access to real-time sales data, all the executives (about 100 of them) want the application as well. Does it make sense to have each client application running the query against 1,000 sales databases across the WAN, all to arrive at the same result? Of course not. It makes more sense to let a service gather and assemble the data, feeding the compiled information to each client on request. The service, then, is taking on the role of sharing a central resource – namely, the data it has painstakingly gathered – with many clients.

Initialization is time-consuming and you want your object to be in a waiting state when a client asks for work to be done.
This scenario is pretty self-explanatory. Perhaps the initialization of the resources your object will need is time-consuming – for instance, it may have to initialize many database connections or compile lots of data before it can handle the first request. It makes sense to have an **automatic startup** service (a service that starts automatically after boot-up) do this work and wait for clients with the initialization work already done, rather than have the first client incur the time penalty.

You need a scalable gateway to another resource.
You have an application that occasionally needs to connect to a database, look for some data, run a few business rules on the data, and use the result as input to other user functions. For each of 1,000 clients, for example, such a function would run perhaps 500 times a day. The data on which the function is run is different each time, however, so results cannot be cached. Let's also say that making a fresh connection to the database takes about 1.5 seconds, much longer than it takes to look up the data and run the business rules, which takes about 0.3 seconds. At first blush, you have two options:

- Saving database connections by connecting to the database afresh every time, incurring the 1.5-second penalty each time the operation runs.
- Holding the database connection open for the entire time the application is open, burdening the database server with an additional 999 connections to manage, even though the total time *you* spend running this function is only 150 seconds per day.

Neither is very palatable, is it? But wait, there's a third option! You could write a service that holds open a pool of a few database connections (say, 10), all pre-initialized and waiting, and uses them on behalf of each connecting client. The response time is almost as good as what you would get from running the database calls from inside the client processes, but without causing the undue strain of many connects and disconnects on the database server. You've just improved the scalability of a scarce resource – database connections – dramatically, by using a service as a gateway.

Let's be clear about scalability here. Systems that are designed for scalability are able to grow their client base or throughput without reprogramming or redesign, but simply by adding more hardware. In other words, in a scalable system there is a linear relationship between the number of clients the system can serve and the hardware resources required to support those clients while still keeping a fixed client response time.

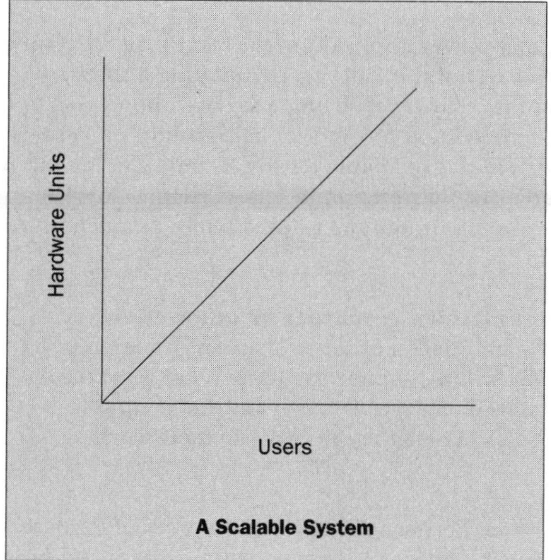

A Scalable System

In a *perfectly* scalable system, this linear relationship proceeds out to infinity.

In a non-scalable system, each additional client requires a disproportionately (and increasingly) large amount of extra hardware to run:

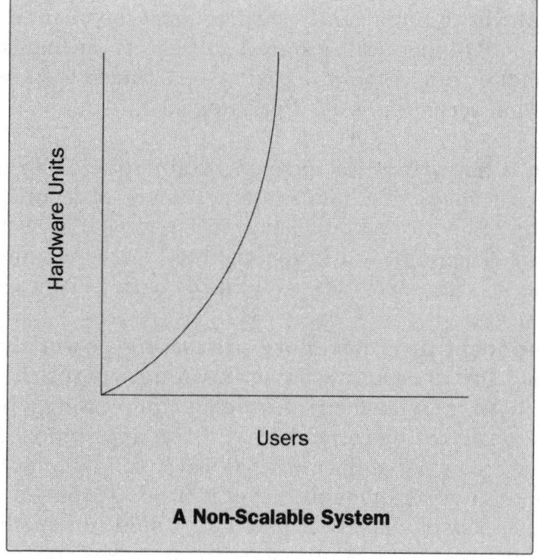

A Non-Scalable System

For example, if you can handle 500 users with a one-second response time on your system on a single processor server, you should be able (in theory) to achieve the same performance for 1,000 users with two processors, 2,000 with four, and so on. This presumes that both your software and your hardware are scalable. In reality, NT systems are not perfectly scalable; the fourth processor can only net about 90% of the work the first processor could do alone. If, however, your service is only capable of doing 20% more work with two processors than it could with just one, you know it is not scaling well.

Nothing about the intrinsic act of writing a service (or any server application) makes it scalable. Only efficient use of threads and other resources, and effective use of the CPU by partitioning a software system into a group of cooperating components can do that. However, being a service allows your object the *opportunity* to be a good NT server citizen by allowing it to run as a background process controlled by the SCM, which is more than a standard Win32 executable has by default. Let me put it this way: if your component is going to dole out resources or information to lots of clients simultaneously, it should begin life as a service. As we move through the book, I'll talk in much more detail about making services scalable.

You need a 'switchboard' for connecting clients to unknown resources or other clients.
Imagine a scenario where clients need to connect to one another in order to share information or resources. Those clients don't know in advance who they will be connecting to, or what resources they will need. They only know how to find the switchboard. A service can act as that central switchboard, connecting clients with the resources or other clients they need to do their work.

You need a load balancer for other resources.
This scenario is a more refined version of the previous one. Perhaps the shared resources of the last example are 'unknown' to the client because you *want* the client to be independent of where and how they run. Your service merely delegates a task to the resource that is most capable of handling the request. Maybe it 'intelligently' decides what the client needs, or perhaps it just allocates the least busy of a pool of identical resources on several machines. In either case, it provides an additional layer of indirection so that the client doesn't need to know where to look for what it needs – it contacts your service as a third party agent.

Location is important for ease of administration or ease of upgrade.
Sometimes, for ease of administration, reasons of security, or ease of upgrade, you need your server application to be located on a central server. That server might even be locked in a closet somewhere. The point is that you need to be able to administer it easily from a remote location. A service has all these facilities, so it makes sense to house your component inside one.

The component provides more processing power than can reasonably be given to each client, and the processing power gain outweighs the cost in network latency.
Sometimes, an individual client *could* do a processing job, but the job would be much faster on a higher-performance machine. Perhaps your application does extremely complex, multidimensional data analysis on a set of data in a database, then applies business rules to that analysis. The application is not run frequently, but it is run periodically by hundreds of users. The business rules and the complex data analysis functions would run much faster on a large multiprocessor server than on the client machines. In this case, it makes sense to move the complex functions off the client and onto the powerful machine.

Does this *need* to be an NT service? Not necessarily; it could be a simple distributed COM object run on a remote machine (the powerful server). The point here is that complex data work or business-tier services are not, in themselves, a compelling reason to use a Win32 service in your architecture. Infrequently-used components, ones that don't require persistent state, or components whose initialization is quick and dirty are reasonable candidates for vanilla COM or DCOM servers. In short, to want to create a service you need some other good reason as well as this, like one of the other scenarios in this section.

Identifying Usage Pattern Categories

There are a million specific examples of the scenarios above. However, the important thing for us is to discern *patterns* from the scenarios, so let's narrow them down into categories, bringing together the various types of usage pattern into the list below.

Monitor

The **Monitor** can be used to monitor the status of system services, resources, or even clients.

Agent

The **Agent** does background work that needs to get done without a client user. It can also do intensive processing work to prepare resources in advance of an incoming client.

Quartermaster (or Resource Pooler)

The **Quartermaster** hands out pre-initialized resources to clients. These resources can be database connections, worker threads, etc. The Quartermaster can also help manage resources more effectively by using them on behalf of clients.

Switchboard

The **Switchboard** makes the location of resources irrelevant to the client. The client simply contacts the switchboard for resources, and the latter then connects the client to the proper resource.

A variation on the design of the switchboard is that it can assist in making the system scalable by breaking up processing work among several other objects and coordinating their activities. This removes the burden of load balancing from the client, who simply contacts the switchboard with a request. The switchboard assembles the 'least used' resources, asks them to do the work, and then returns a result to the client.

Business Object

An 'industrial strength' **Business Object** differs from a typical in-process COM DLL in that it runs inside a service, providing a combination of rules, data, and calculating power upon request by a client. Business Objects are appropriate for services when you need intensive calculation strength, fault isolation, or when the Business Object has intensive pre-initialization work to do before it can get started.

Features of NT Services

In this section, we'll take a quick look at several important features of NT services, and at how certain basic system components interact with them. This section will also serve as an explanatory overview of the other chapters in the book, providing a context for the information to come.

The Service Control Manager (SCM)

What is the purpose of the NT Service Control Manager? It has five main roles:

- It accepts requests for the installation and removal of services.
- It accepts **control requests** and routes them to the proper services. Control requests are messages that the SCM sends to a service to tell it to take some action, like pause or stop.
- It starts 'automatic startup' services at boot time.
- It maintains a database of installed services.
- It maintains a volatile database of the status of running services, which it can enumerate when requested to do so. However, the SCM does *not* periodically 'poll' running services for their status. It actively queries service status only when a program makes a control request for it.

First and foremost, the purpose of the SCM is to launch services and manage their lifetimes. It does this by interacting with the **services database**, which is really just an area in the system registry. The registry path to this database is `HKEY_LOCAL_MACHINE\SYSTEM\CurrentControlSet\Services`.

Beneath this key are subkeys for each installed service. These keys hold such information as the start type, the name of the executable that houses the service, the service's dependencies, the service type, and several other things. We'll get to the intricacies of the keys in this path in Chapter 3.

API calls to the SCM control most of what gets written to the services database. API calls also are used to command the SCM programmatically to control a service by starting, stopping, pausing, or restarting its operation. *All* service executables are spawned by the SCM, either because an application asked the SCM to do so programmatically, or because the service was installed as automatic startup. Even the Services control panel applet is just a shell application that talks through the SCM to instruct a service.

> *The Service Control Manager is implemented such that any machine can access the SCM of any other machine on a network if it has the appropriate permissions to do so. This allows NT services to be administered and controlled remotely.*

At this juncture, it is important to point out that the NT operating system has *two* implementations of SCM-like functionality. The first is the NT SCM, which handles the operations listed above for Win32 services. The NT SCM is implemented in `Services.exe`. The *other* Service Control Manager is implemented in `RPCSS.exe`; this implementation handles RPC networking connection and control services and, since RPC is the underlying mechanism for DCOM, those same operations for COM/DCOM. Appropriately, this is called the COM SCM, and we'll be covering it in more detail in Chapter 9. For now, just be aware that even though these two things have the same name, they don't perform the same rôle.

Startup Options

I took care not to say as part of the definition above that services are started at the time the operating system is loaded. That's often true, but services can actually be configured to start at any time. The three options available to you are:

- **Automatic startup** at system startup time. When the Windows NT splash screen has appeared but the hard disk is still whirring, these types of services are being loaded.
- **Manual** (or **demand**) **startup** services are triggered by the user or administrator. They require a programmatic start request to be supplied to the SCM.
- Setting a service's type to **disabled startup** allows the user or administrator manually to prohibit a service from starting.

Manual startup services take two forms depending on whether the request comes from a client application or from COM. To start a service manually using a non-COM client, you have to take care of the programming details with a `StartService()` call inside your client; this call instructs the SCM to start the service. On the other hand, if your service hosts a COM object and is not started when the object is required, the COM SCM will start it as either a local or a remote service, depending on the settings in the `HKEY_CLASSES_ROOT\AppID` key in the calling machine's registry.

The tool that system administrators usually use to configure services and check their status is the Services control panel applet, pictured below:

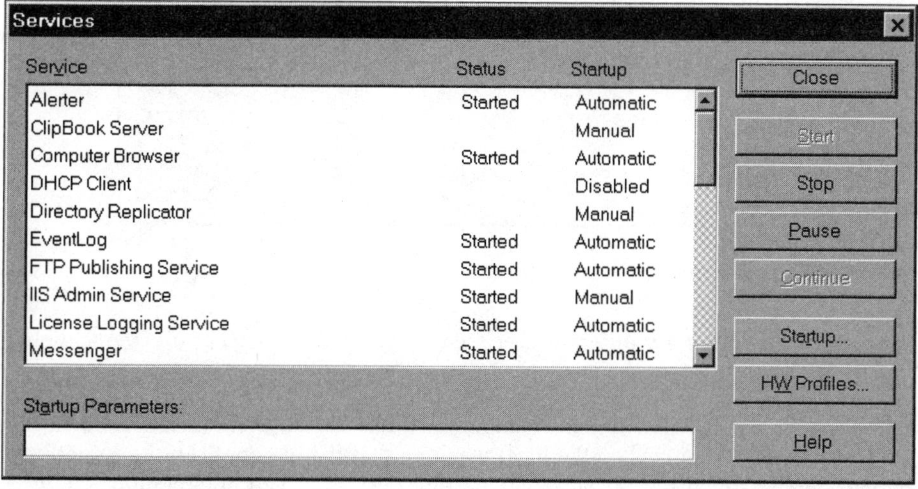

As you can see from the bottom of the figure, services can have startup parameters too, just like a regular NT executable. However, these are *not* the same as command line parameters for the service executable itself, because the SCM controls the service startup.

Dependencies

Any service can be set to have **dependencies** on other services. If, for instance, Service A uses RPC to communicate with clients, then it is dependent on the Remote Procedure Call service being started. By specifying this dependency during installation, NT will guarantee that Service A does not try to start before the RPC service starts. NT uses a non-trivial set of rules to determine the order in which to load services at boot time, so that the timing is always right. When we discuss service control functions in Chapter 3, we will look more closely at setting up dependencies.

Hardware Profiles

Hardware profiles can also change what services are loaded. With each hardware profile you set up, you have the ability to enable or disable a particular service. This does not change the service's startup type, its dependencies, or other service configuration details, only whether or not it is enabled for each particular hardware profile. For example, the Computer Browser service is not really needed on a hardware profile with no network adapter, so its startup type could be set to 'disabled' under that profile.

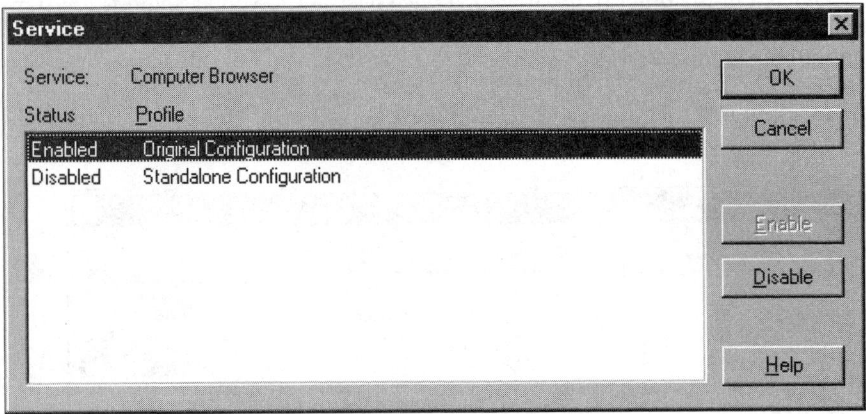

Security

Services are capable of running under different user security contexts, as well as (of course) being able to use the base security calls that are available to all Win32 applications.

By default, services run in a privileged system account known as LocalSystem (the 'System Account'), which gives services rights to resources on the local machine that regular applications do not have. However, running a service under the LocalSystem account also restricts it to operations on the machine on which it is installed; LocalSystem has no rights to go off the server and perform secure operations on the network.

Alternatively, a service can run under a specific user account (either on the local machine or in the domain) if you provide a password for that account. Running the service as a specific user allows the service to use any network resources to which that account has access. However, the user account must be assigned certain security privileges to be allowed to run a service, and still others to be allowed to do the same things LocalSystem can do.

Services themselves can be secured with **access control lists** (ACLs). They can also impersonate incoming client callers, although the issues and caveats involved with this are somewhat intricate, and we'll look at them later. Services can check access rights, enforce security on their objects using security descriptors, and secure private objects. In short, they can do any of the things a standard application can do. We'll get into much greater detail about impersonation and security in Chapter 7.

User Interfaces

This is perhaps a controversial subject, but there is a broad consensus among people who do a lot of NT service work: *services should not have windows or consoles that provide feedback to the user.* Furthermore, any tools that may be needed to administer a service should be written as separate executables that expose configuration options and run in the context of the interactive user.

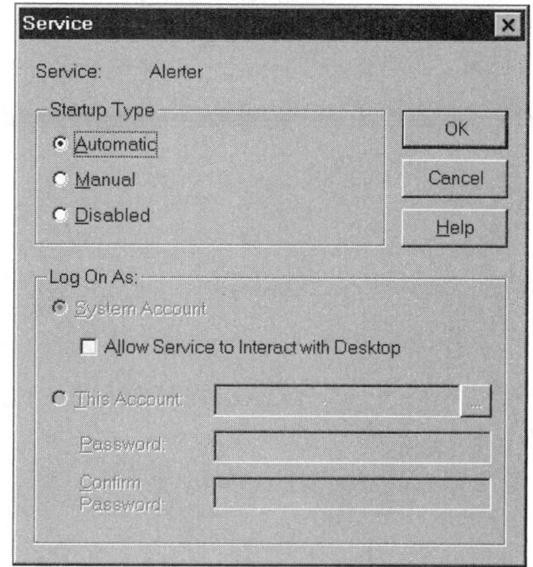

In the Services control panel applet, you may have noticed that a service can be set so that it can interact with the desktop user. That does *not* mean it should be. Imagine a service running on a secured server locked in the bottom of a salt mine somewhere in Utah. The service encounters an error and displays a message box, which halts the service until someone presses OK. There's more to the 'interactive' setting than that, but you get the picture.

We'll talk more about why the service executable itself should (almost) never have user interface features later on, although I'll show you how to do it anyway, because it prompts an interesting discussion on several security issues.

Remote Installation and Administration

To be part of an effective client-server architecture, a service should be capable of being administered remotely. A service does this by storing all of its configuration information in the registry.

The Services control panel applet is easy to use, but it's limited to working with services that are on the same machine. To administer remote services, you must use the Server Manager application in the Administrative Tools group of an NT server, or use the `SC.exe` tool that comes in the Platform SDK. SC is a very useful tool that we will discuss in more detail in the next chapter.

You can also use the `WinMSD.exe` tool (shown below) to view the state of services on remote machines, but unfortunately you can't use it to start and stop services.

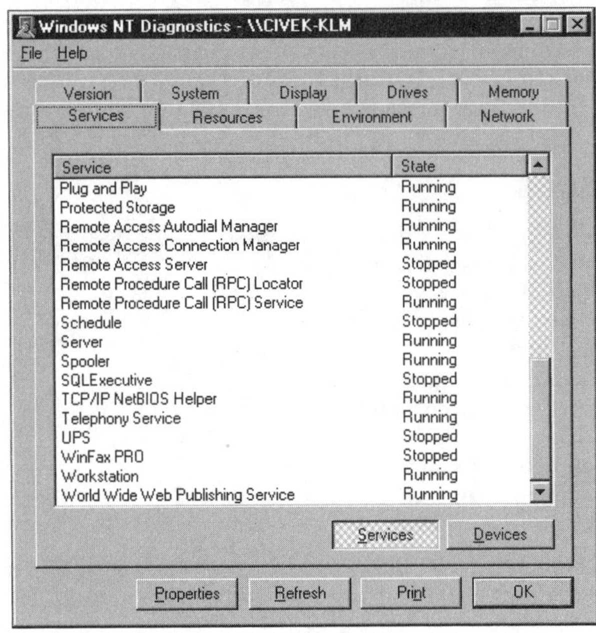

The Event Log

Since a service usually has no user interface, how should it report interesting incidents that happen during its lifetime to the system administrator or user? It must make entries in the **NT application event log**. Instead of each service creating a different file in which to record errors, the creators of NT decided to create a unified mechanism and API that all applications that need to perform logging can use. Your service should take advantage of the event log by feeding it status or error information.

Services that use the event log also support remote administration, since the Event Viewer allows administrators to view events on remote machines.

Event Viewer - Application Log on \\FANDANGO

Log View Options Help

Date	Time	Source	Category	Event	User	Computer
1/28/98	10:41:15 AM	MSSQLServer	Server	17055	N/A	FANDANGO
1/28/98	10:41:15 AM	MSSQLServer	Server	17055	N/A	FANDANGO
1/28/98	10:41:12 AM	MSSQLServer	ODS	17056	N/A	FANDANGO
1/28/98	10:41:12 AM	MSSQLServer	Kernel	17055	N/A	FANDANGO
1/28/98	10:41:12 AM	MSSQLServer	Kernel	17055	N/A	FANDANGO
1/28/98	10:41:12 AM	MSSQLServer	Kernel	17055	N/A	FANDANGO
1/28/98	10:41:01 AM	MSSQLServer	Server	17055	N/A	FANDANGO
1/28/98	10:41:00 AM	MSSQLServer	Server	17055	N/A	FANDANGO
1/28/98	10:40:54 AM	SQLExecutive	Service Control	101	N/A	FANDANGO
1/28/98	10:40:51 AM	MSSQLServer	Kernel	17055	N/A	FANDANGO
1/28/98	10:40:43 AM	MSDTC	SVC	4097	N/A	FANDANGO
1/28/98	10:40:42 AM	MSDTC	CM	4156	N/A	FANDANGO
1/28/98	10:40:42 AM	MSDTC	CM	4156	N/A	FANDANGO
1/28/98	10:40:07 AM	Autochk	None	1001	N/A	FANDANGO
1/28/98	10:20:44 AM	MSSQLServer	Server	17055	N/A	FANDANGO
1/28/98	10:20:44 AM	MSSQLServer	Server	17055	N/A	FANDANGO
1/28/98	10:20:41 AM	MSSQLServer	ODS	17056	N/A	FANDANGO
1/28/98	10:20:41 AM	MSSQLServer	Kernel	17055	N/A	FANDANGO
1/28/98	10:20:41 AM	MSSQLServer	Kernel	17055	N/A	FANDANGO
1/28/98	10:20:41 AM	MSSQLServer	Kernel	17055	N/A	FANDANGO
1/28/98	10:20:31 AM	MSSQLServer	Server	17055	N/A	FANDANGO

Performance Feedback

Each service has unique characteristics that indicate how effectively it is doing its work. By exposing that performance data to the system, applications such as Performance Monitor can display it to the system administrator, who can then tune the system or the service to achieve higher performance. The performance data structures are hideous, but they're worth knowing so that you can give your service this professional feature.

Conclusion

That's it! A service is a simple thing to understand, but it presents a wide range of opportunities to your system architecture. At this point, we can get a clearer look at how all the system components fit together with services. The graphic below shows their interaction, which may look confusing at first, but it will become clearer over the course of the book.

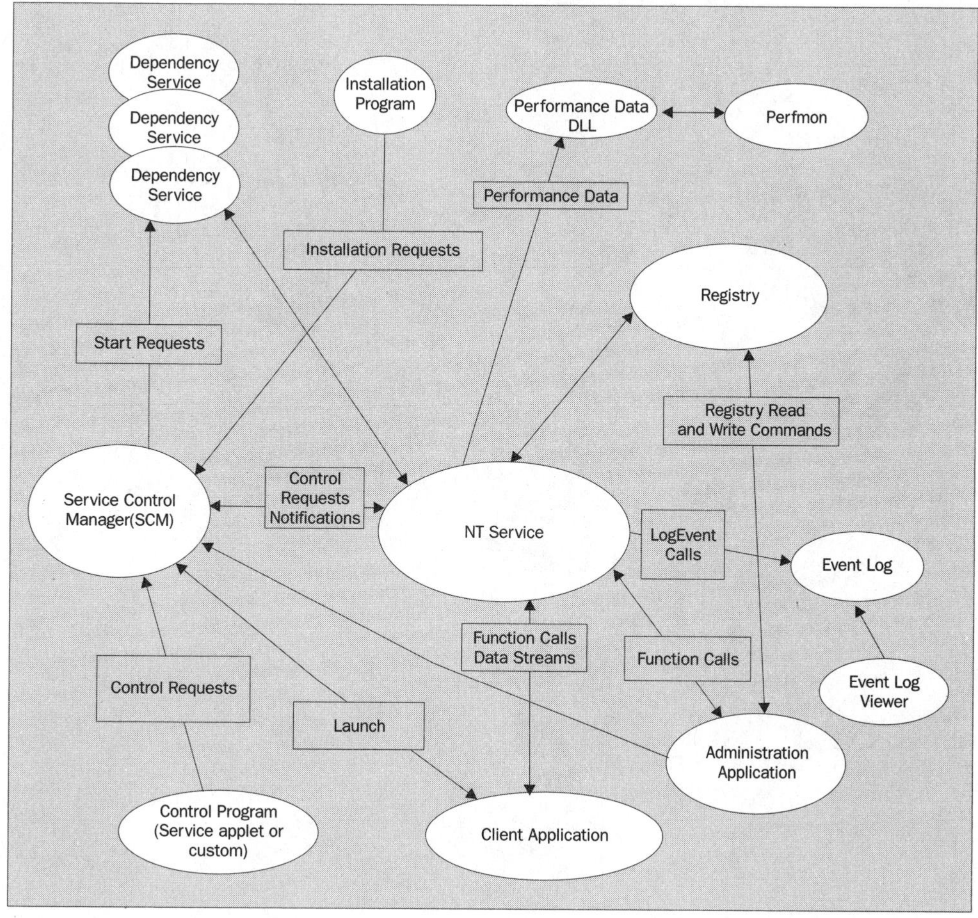

You should now have a better understanding of where and how services can be used in your software system architecture, but if it's not yet completely clear, never fear! We're going to deal with the usage patterns we've identified by means of specific examples, and we'll write code to implement them as we progress through the book.

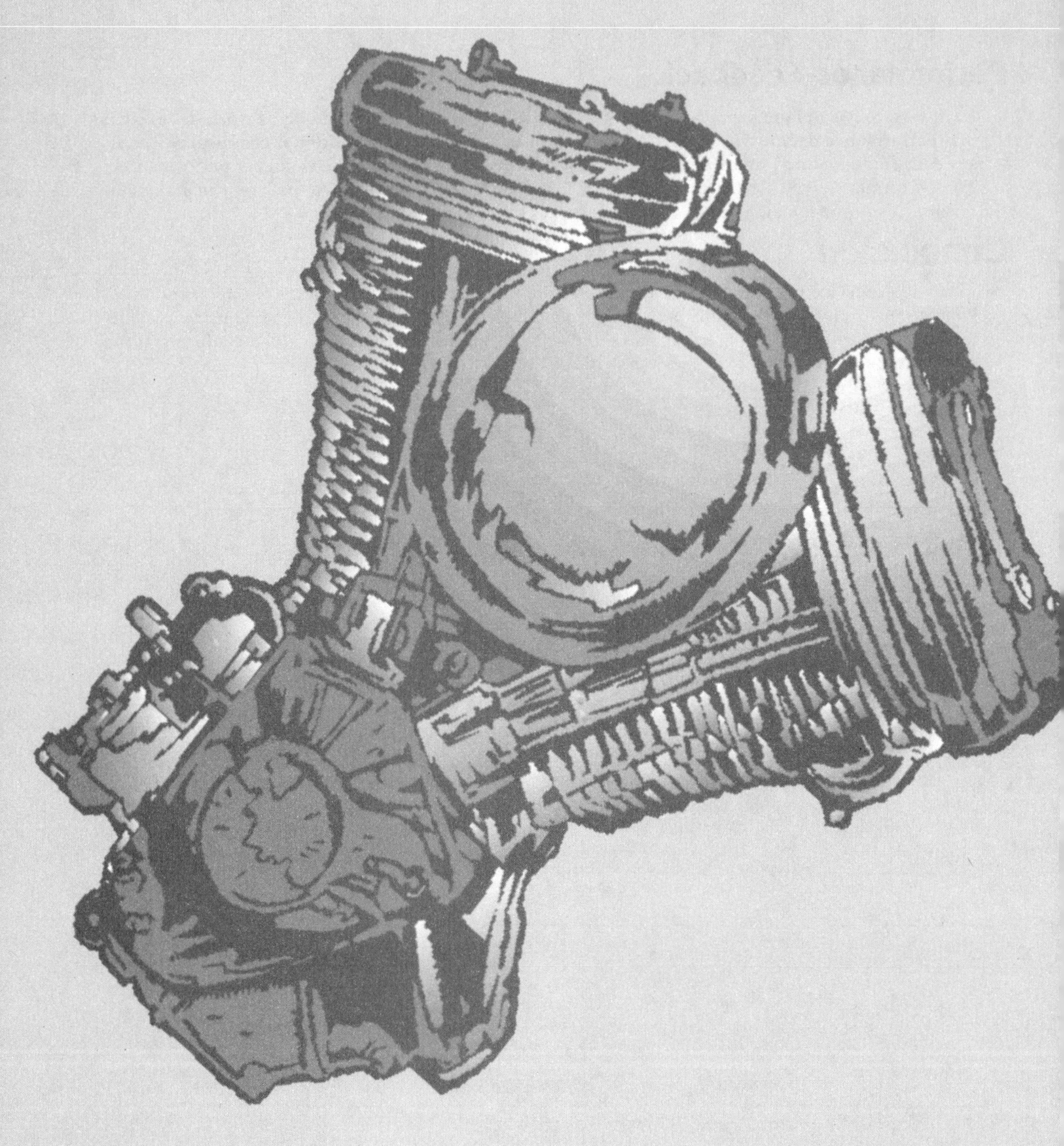

2

Service Processes

It's time to delve into some code! In this chapter, we'll work with the Win32 APIs that support service development. We'll examine the 'duties' of services – how NT, the SCM, and client programs are expecting them to behave and feed back information. Throughout this chapter, I'll show you generic code examples to illustrate concepts. In Chapter 3 we'll look at installing and configuring services, and then in Chapter 4 we'll have the chance really to apply what you've learned when we build a C++ class that implements a service, and look at a live example.

Three Types of Service Executable

Before getting started with services themselves, let's clarify exactly where they fit into the grand scheme of things. There are three types of executables that interact with services or with the SCM.

- **Service processes** are the things we've been talking about so far: the executables that implement the scenarios outlined in the last chapter. Creating service process executables will be the major topic of this chapter.
- **Control executables** issue commands to services, via API calls to the SCM. The `StartService()` function, for example, instructs the SCM to start a service. The SCM then acts on behalf of the control executable to perform the requested operation. The Services control panel applet can certainly be considered a control executable (though it is *also* a configuration executable, see below), as can *any* process that starts or stops a service, such as a service management or administration application. If you're a SQL Server buff, the SQL Service Manager application can be considered a control executable because it can start, stop, and pause the different services that SQL Server uses.
- **Configuration executables** request installation, removal, modification, etc. of service processes by making requests to the SCM through API calls. These calls make changes to the services database in the system registry. A configuration executable is usually used to make the SCM calls that install a process as a service or change the configuration of an existing service.

Service processes will be the topic of discussion for the remainder of this chapter, and we'll move on to look at control and configuration executables in Chapter 3.

Internal Architecture of Services

To give you a context for the information to be presented in this chapter, I want first to describe briefly what happens to a service during its lifetime. When the SCM receives a request to start a service, it first determines whether the process that houses the service is already running. Because most service processes house only one service, this is usually not the case, so the SCM launches the process and its `main()` function executes. From there, the service calls a function that connects the main process thread to the SCM, which will use that thread to call into the service when it needs. This function also names the main processing function for the service that is to be started.

The SCM now has the main process thread, called the **dispatcher**, and the name of the service's main processing function, which is usually called `ServiceMain()`. The dispatcher then creates a new thread on which to call this function, and proceeds to call it. Inside *that* function, the service makes a call that registers the **control handler** for the service, which is the function that the dispatcher thread will call when the SCM passes it a control request (a request to stop, pause, or continue, for example) from another process.

Next, the service sends back **status information** to the SCM that tells it about what state the service is in, what control requests it will accept, and so forth. After initializing, the service tells the SCM (via status information) that it is running. The service's main processing function is now in command, doing what it does best: servicing clients, spawning worker threads, or whatever. The dispatcher thread just sits there in a loop waiting to receive a control request from some process that it can pass on to the service's control handler.

When it gets a request, the dispatcher passes it on to the control handler to do what is necessary to inform the service that it should stop, pause, continue, etc. When the service has completed that action (or while it is working on it), the service posts back more status information to let the SCM know about it.

Eventually, when the service has stopped (because it was instructed to do so), it lets the SCM know by sending back yet more status information. When the dispatcher thread realizes that *all* the services in the process have stopped, it exits its loop and allows the primary thread to fall back through to processing in the `main()` function, from which it eventually returns to close the process. The following diagram should help to make all these interactions clearer:

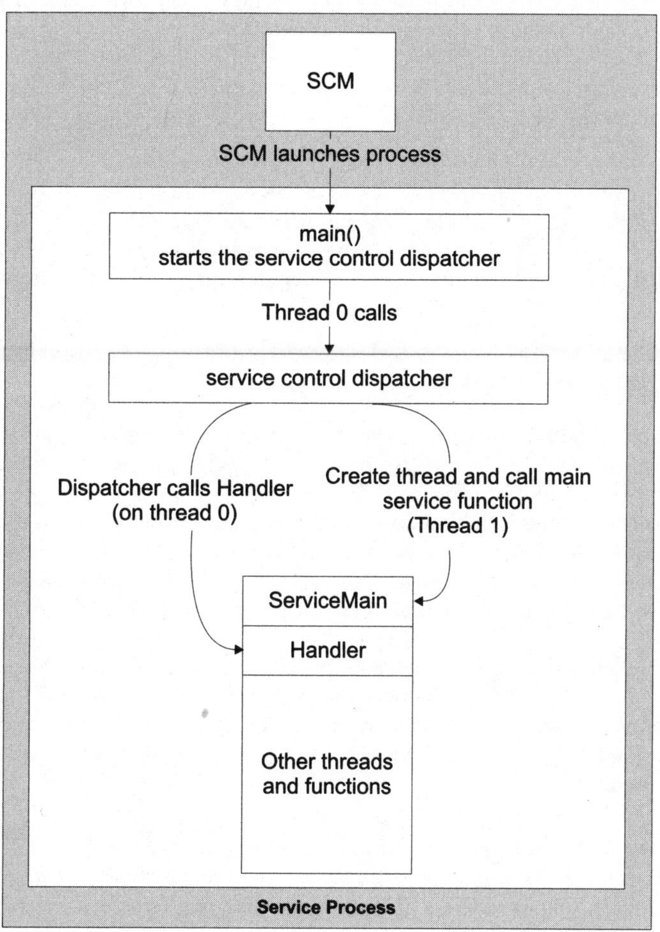

Services in Action

A Win32 service has several duties to fulfill in order to interact properly with the SCM. The most important of these are to implement the three critical functions I mentioned above: `main()`, `ServiceMain()`, and `Handler()`. Aside from these major duties, there are a few other minor ones, which are included in the list below. We'll take each of these topics in turn in this chapter. A service executable must:

- Implement `main()`
- Connect the main thread to the SCM by calling `StartServiceCtrlDispatcher()`
- Implement `ServiceMain()` for each service in the process
- Set up a handler for each service in the process to deal with requests for start/stop/pause/continue
- Spin off thread(s) to do work, if necessary
- Feed status information back to the SCM

At this point, don't worry if you still haven't quite grasped all of the concepts and the terminology. We're going to march through each of these requirements in detail.

main

Like most console-style applications, execution of the service starts off in the `main()` function. `main()` has at least one major responsibility: to call the Windows API function `StartServiceCtrlDispatcher()` immediately, in order to hand over the process's main thread to the service control manager. The dispatcher creates a new thread to execute the `ServiceMain()` function for the service, and holds onto the main thread to dispatch requests to the running services in the process.

Multiple Services in a Process

Each Win32 service process can contain one or more services, running on separate threads. Processes that contain more than one service are responsible for registering and implementing separate `ServiceMain()` and `Handler()` functions for each service they expose. If the service process *is* shared among two or more services, then you should carefully consider how you want to initialize common resources. The general rule is that you should allocate and initialize shared resources in `main()` *before* calling `StartServiceCtrlDispatcher()`. This makes sense because you have no way of knowing which service in a shared service process will get started first.

However, if the initialization of shared resources takes *too* long (more than two minutes, according to my tests), the SCM will believe that the service is unresponsive and produce an error. If shared resource initialization will take a while, you should spin off another thread to do the initialization and immediately call `StartServiceCtrlDispatcher()` from `main()`, so that the service can properly report its status to the SCM.

> *Of course, if you do that, you'll need to make sure that you re-synchronize the initialization thread with `ServiceMain()` so that a race condition doesn't develop. Don't forget that your shared resources will be accessed by more than one thread, so remember to synchronize access to the common data structures your services will be sharing!*

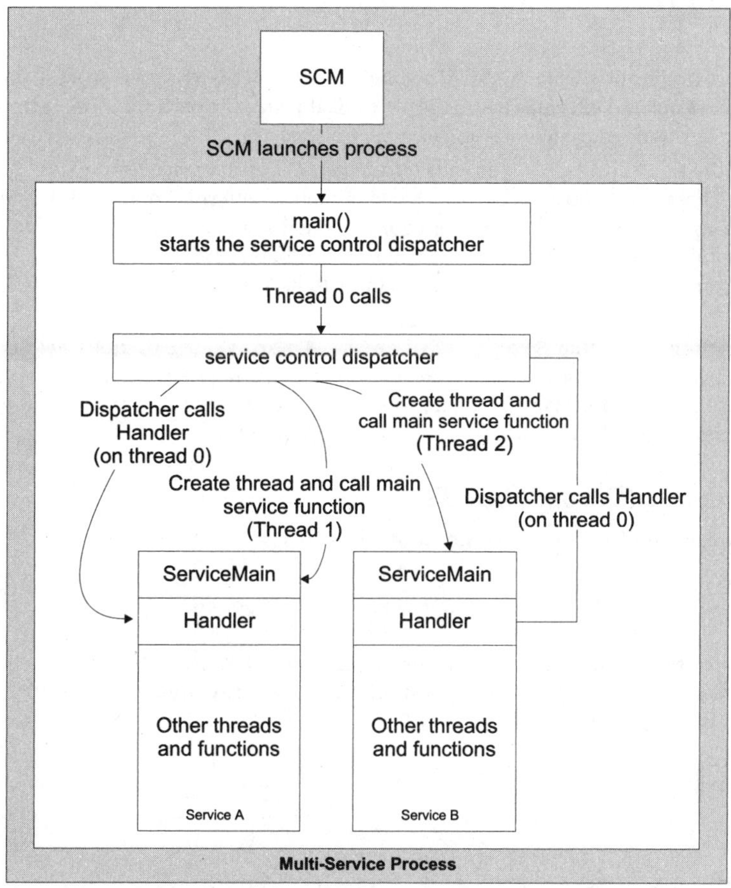

If the service does not share a process, all initialization work should take place in `ServiceMain()` for two reasons. First, doing so allows the service to respond more quickly to the SCM by calling `StartServiceCtrlDispatcher()`. Second, the main thread is not going to be doing the work of your service – all service operations will be carried out by (or dispatched to worker threads by) the thread that runs `ServiceMain()`. The initialization that's needed to support service functions should be performed in the thread that requires it whenever possible – this is just a good design principle.

The Service Control Dispatcher

Each time the SCM receives a request to start another service in your shared service process, the dispatcher spins off a new thread, which it uses to run the implementation of `ServiceMain()` for the requested service. It then uses the thread that it has taken over for the use of the dispatcher to invoke `Handler()` for the service when it receives an incoming control request.

Technically, what happens is this. `StartServiceCtrlDispatcher()` sits inside a loop waiting for one of two things:

- A control notification from the SCM to one of the services inside the process. In this case, the thread goes out and executes `Handler()` to deal with the notification request for the service, then returns back to the dispatcher loop when it's finished.
- One of the `ServiceMain()` threads terminates. When a service terminates, `StartServiceCtrlDispatcher()` decrements an internal counter of the number of running services in the process. If this counter equals 0, the dispatcher returns control to `main()` and the process finishes and terminates. If the counter is still non-zero, `StartServiceCtrlDispatcher()` returns to its loop.

A key point to remember is that `StartServiceCtrlDispatcher()` does *not* get called when a service is started, only when *the service process that contains the service is loaded.* So, when a client asks the SCM to start the second service in a shared service process, the already-running dispatcher creates an additional thread to run its `ServiceMain()` function.

The StartServiceCtrlDispatcher Function

The function declaration for the dispatcher looks like this:

```
BOOL StartServiceCtrlDispatcher(LPSERVICE_TABLE_ENTRY lpServiceStartTable);
```

The one parameter to this function is a pointer to an array of `SERVICE_TABLE_ENTRY` structures. The structure itself is quite simple, but the last entry in the array must contain `NULL` values to indicate the end of the table:

```
typedef struct _SERVICE_TABLE_ENTRY
{
   LPTSTR                     lpServiceName;
   LPSERVICE_MAIN_FUNCTION lpServiceProc;
} SERVICE_TABLE_ENTRY, *LPSERVICE_TABLE_ENTRY;
```

`lpServiceName` points to a `TSTR` (a Unicode string; see the box on the next page) that names the service, which should be no more than 256 characters in length. The parameter is ignored when the service doesn't share a process.

`lpServiceProc` is a function pointer to the named service's implementation of `ServiceMain()`. Remember that each service in a service process needs its own implementation of a `ServiceMain()`-like master function.

If you want or need to find the service-related APIs, they are all declared in the `winsvc.h` *header file.*

A Quick Look at main

The implementation of `main()` for a single-service process is incredibly simple. It just has to initialize the `SERVICE_TABLE_ENTRY` array, and then start the service control dispatcher. In fact, it's so straightforward that we can have a good stab at guessing what it will look like already:

```
int main()
{
   // Perform any necessary initialization

   SERVICE_TABLE_ENTRY svcTable[] =
   {
      {_T("MyService"), ServiceMain },
      {NULL, NULL}
   };

   if(!StartServiceCtrlDispatcher(svcTable))
      ErrorHandler();

   return 0;
}
```

`TCHAR`, Unicode, and Windows NT

If you are uninitiated in the ways of `TCHAR` and Unicode, and you're wondering about that `_T()` macro above, here's a quick primer.

Unicode is a multi-byte character set that maps the characters in many of the world's alphabets into a single 16-bit space. All the API calls in Windows NT are implemented in Unicode, so you should use Unicode when you write Windows NT applications. The reason for this is that NT has *two* versions of every API function that takes a string parameter: one with a name ending with `W` to denote the wide character set, and one ending in `A` for ANSI strings. The native call is the '`W`' function, while the '`A`' function simply ends up calling the '`W`' function. Using ASCII therefore makes for an extra function call, and has additional string conversion (and memory) overhead.

To use Unicode in your application, `#include <TCHAR.h>` in your precompiled header or source file. Then, `#define _UNICODE`. If you now use `TCHAR` instead of `char` when you use string or character functions, the preprocessor will translate all the `TCHAR`s in your application into `wchar_t` datatypes, which are the wide character types you'll need. If you don't define `_UNICODE`, it simply maps them to `char` types. Windows 95 doesn't support Unicode, but if you use `TCHAR`s then you can construct your application such that it will also run under Windows 95 simply by not defining `_UNICODE`.

When you want to use string literals in Unicode, use the `_T()` macro, which will take care of translating strings by prefixing them with `L`. If `_UNICODE` is not defined, the macro has no effect.

When you're using Unicode, you need to think about string functions and string manipulation differently. For instance, when you would otherwise use a common string function like `strncmp()`, you should instead use `_tcsncmp()`, which is the equivalent function that works with `TCHAR` types. There is a list of the function mappings in the Win32 SDK documentation. While the `_UNICODE` preprocessor will go some way to helping you by mapping these functions properly, you need to be careful when using expressions like `sizeof(szBuffer)`, which must become `(sizeof(szBuffer) / sizeof(TCHAR))`.

The Service Thread

When the service control dispatcher receives a request to start a particular service, it spawns a thread to execute the `ServiceMain()` function for that service. `ServiceMain()` is the 'master' function for a service, and serves the same role for a service that `main()` does for a process: it is the entry point, where work starts.

Each service in the service process has its own `ServiceMain()` function. As you can probably tell by the syntax of the `StartServiceCtrlDispatcher()` function, though, it doesn't actually have to be named '`ServiceMain`'. It can be called anything you like, so long as it has the proper parameters and you pass the function pointer to `StartServiceCtrlDispatcher()`.

ServiceMain

The work of `ServiceMain()` is significantly more complex than for `main()`. `ServiceMain()` has several responsibilities:

- Register the control handler function for the service
- Notify the SCM that it is starting
- Break out (and use) any start parameters sent by the control process
- Initialize any resources, feeding back its status to the SCM at reasonable time intervals
- Get itself into a state to do whatever work it does (receive RPCs, listen on sockets, etc.)
- Notify the SCM that it is running
- Wait for a stop signal from the control handler
- Clean up resources and terminate

The prototype for the function is quite simple:

```
void WINAPI ServiceMain(DWORD dwArgc, LPTSTR* lpszArgv);
```

`lpszArgv` points to an array of pointers to argument `TSTR`s. The first element in the array is the name of the service, and any elements following it are strings passed to the service by the process that requested the SCM to start it. `dwArgc` indicates the number of elements in the arguments array. Note that this argument array is different from the command-line arguments that `main()` receives, which are arguments to the *executable*. These are arguments to the *service itself*.

Registering the Control Handler

The immediate duty of `ServiceMain()` is to set up the control handler for the service. The control handler is called from the dispatcher thread (the main thread seized by the SCM when you started the dispatcher, and which is now idly waiting for notifications) whenever a client application sends a control request to the SCM. The control handler registration routine tells the dispatcher which service function to call when it receives such a request.

You have to make sure to call `RegisterServiceCtrlHandler()` within one second of `ServiceMain()` starting. Otherwise, the SCM will assume that an error has occurred. The service will probably continue on, initialize, and function properly, but the service control process you used to start the service will indicate to the user that the service had an error, when really it was just too slow in registering the handler. Usually, the effect of this is that you'll see a message along the lines of, "The service is not responding to the control function," which is confusing to users because they are then never really sure if the service worked. In any case, it makes the service look unreliable. `RegisterServiceCtrlHandler()` therefore should be the first call you make inside the `ServiceMain()` function.

RegisterServiceCtrlHandler

To register the control handler, you use the following API call:

```
SERVICE_STATUS_HANDLE RegisterServiceCtrlHandler(
                                        LPCTSTR            lpServiceName,
                                        LPHANDLER_FUNCTION lpHandlerProc);
```

The syntax of `RegisterServiceCtrlHandler()` is similar to that of `StartServiceCtrlDispatcher()`. Basically, it identifies to the SCM the name of the service and the address of the callback function the control dispatcher should call when it receives a control notification destined for that service.

In the first parameter, `lpServiceName`, you identify the service by name, using a `TSTR`. In the second parameter, `lpHandlerProc`, you pass the address of the handler function. Like `ServiceMain()`, the handler function can be named anything you like, as long as it follows a particular parameter signature. We'll talk more about the control handler later in this chapter.

The return value of this function is a 32-bit handle of type `SERVICE_STATUS_HANDLE` that uniquely identifies the service. When the service notifies the SCM of changes in its state, it must use this handle. The service may need to set the status from more than one thread, so you may wish to save this handle in a global variable. Don't worry about closing the service status handle; the SCM takes care of it when the service terminates.

`RegisterServiceCtrlHandler()` must be called before the first status notification call, because the control handler must be in place to field control notifications by the time the service specifies the types of requests it will accept. You also need the handle that is returned from this function to be able to send status requests at all. Once the handler has been registered with the SCM, the SCM uses the name/function pointer structure in its own internal list of handler functions. When a control request comes in for a particular service, the SCM uses this information to look up the pointer to the handler function that will service the request.

Sending Service Status to the SCM

One of the most important responsibilities of `ServiceMain()` is to return status information to the SCM on a regular basis during the initialization, running, and shutdown phases of its lifetime.

Service States

A service is always in one and only one state. The SCM knows what a service is doing and what it can do at a given time, based on the state that it's in. A service spends most of its lifetime (hopefully) in a 'running' state, but it also spends some time moving in and out of other states. In fact, a service can be in any one of seven possible states, listed in the table below.

State	Description
SERVICE_STOPPED	Service is not running.
SERVICE_START_PENDING	Service is initializing but not yet running.
SERVICE_STOP_PENDING	Service is de-initializing but not yet stopped.
SERVICE_RUNNING	Service is fully operational.
SERVICE_CONTINUE_PENDING	Service is restarting after a pause but not yet running again.
SERVICE_PAUSE_PENDING	Service is pausing.
SERVICE_PAUSED	Service is not stopped, but is not fully functioning. Service chooses how to implement the pause operation.

Two of these states are important for `ServiceMain()` initialization processing: `SERVICE_START_PENDING` and `SERVICE_RUNNING`. `SERVICE_START_PENDING` tells the SCM that the service is trying to initialize, so the SCM should not generate an error due to a lack of response. Once initialization is concluded, the service should send `SERVICE_RUNNING` to let the SCM know that it is in a fully operational state and was initialized properly. The other states are important for responding to control requests from the SCM; we will see how they work presently.

> *On a point of terminology, we say that a service is in a particular* ***state****, but that it sends* ***status*** *information (about its state and other things, such as which control requests it accepts) to the SCM.*

SetServiceStatus

`SetServiceStatus()` is one of the most important functions your service will use, so let's examine it in some detail. The service should call this function anytime it needs to let the SCM know what it is doing or what state it is in. For instance, when a service is being started, the SCM needs to know that the service heard its request to start and is performing the task. The service would use `SetServiceStatus()` to tell the SCM that it was, for instance, in a `SERVICE_START_PENDING` state. Here's the prototype:

```
BOOL WINAPI SetServiceStatus(SERVICE_STATUS_HANDLE hServiceStatus,
                             LPSERVICE_STATUS      lpServiceStatus);
```

The first parameter, `hServiceStatus`, is the handle returned from the `RegisterServiceCtrlHandler()` function that you conscientiously saved. The second parameter is a pointer to a `SERVICE_STATUS` structure, which is a typical Win32-style beast, as you can see below:

```
typedef struct _SERVICE_STATUS
{
    DWORD dwServiceType;
    DWORD dwCurrentState;
    DWORD dwControlsAccepted;
    DWORD dwWin32ExitCode;
    DWORD dwServiceSpecificExitCode;
    DWORD dwCheckPoint;
    DWORD dwWaitHint;
} SERVICE_STATUS, *LPSERVICE_STATUS;
```

Let's look at each of the members of this structure in turn, as they are all very important and require proper explanation.

dwServiceType

The first member of the structure is `dwServiceType`. This member is a bit flag consisting of four possible service type values, along with a fifth value that can be ORed with the first two to indicate that the service interacts with the desktop. These type values should match the ones used in the call to the API function `CreateService()`, which installs the service into the services database, and which we'll explore in the next chapter.

`dwServiceType` **Value**	**Meaning**
`SERVICE_WIN32_OWN_PROCESS`	A Win32 service that runs in its own process.
`SERVICE_WIN32_SHARE_PROCESS`	A Win32 service that runs in a process with other services.
`SERVICE_KERNEL_DRIVER`	An NT device driver.
`SERVICE_FILE_SYSTEM_DRIVER`	An NT file system driver.
`SERVICE_INTERACTIVE_PROCESS`	A flag that can be ORed with either of the two Win32 service flags to indicate that the process can interact with the desktop.

dwCurrentState

This member indicates the state you are setting the service to with the SetServiceStatus() call. Set this member to any of the seven states indicated in the service state table above.

dwControlsAccepted

This member lets the SCM know the types of control messages the service will accept whenever a control executable calls ControlService(). There are five different control requests that a service can receive and choose to process:

- SERVICE_CONTROL_STOP
- SERVICE_CONTROL_PAUSE
- SERVICE_CONTROL_CONTINUE
- SERVICE_CONTROL_INTERROGATE
- SERVICE_CONTROL_SHUTDOWN

Of these, the first four can be sent by ControlService().

ControlService() *is the SCM API function that allows a client program to send a control request through the SCM to a service. Chapter 3 will discuss this function in more detail.*

By setting the dwControlsAccepted member, the service lets the SCM know what types of control messages it can handle. The different flag values for dwControlsAccepted are shown in the table below. These values can be ORed together to create the combination of calls that the service supports.

dwControlsAccepted **Value**	**Meaning**
SERVICE_ACCEPT_STOP	Service accepts SERVICE_CONTROL_STOP requests
SERVICE_ACCEPT_PAUSE_CONTINUE	Service can handle PAUSE/CONTINUE requests in a meaningful way
SERVICE_ACCEPT_SHUTDOWN	Service will be notified when a system shutdown occurs

By default, all services *must* accept and process the SERVICE_CONTROL_INTERROGATE control request. The service should respond to this request by returning the current status.

Accepting Stop Requests

If a service sets SERVICE_ACCEPT_STOP, then it can be stopped from external service control programs such as the client application, the Services control panel applet, or any of the other utility tools available to control services. Depending on what a service does, though, it may choose *not* to be stopped by external programs. Several system-provided services do not accept stop requests – they simply run whenever the system is running. Look at the EventLog service in the screenshot below, for example. This service does not accept SERVICE_CONTROL_STOP, so the button for the Stop command is disabled in the Services applet.

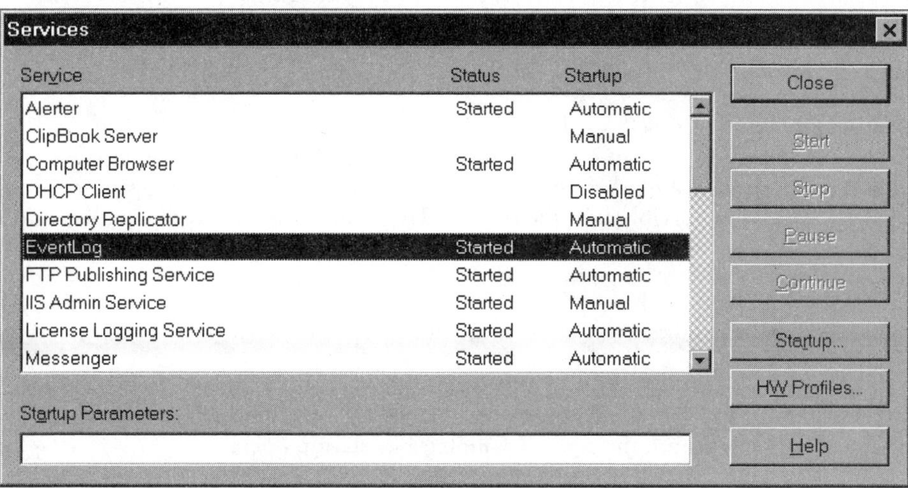

Accepting Pause/Continue Requests

A service can choose to accept `SERVICE_CONTROL_PAUSE` and `SERVICE_CONTROL_CONTINUE` requests by adding the `SERVICE_ACCEPT_PAUSE_CONTINUE` flag to the `dwControlsAccepted` mask. Again, whether the service chooses to be capable of pausing is entirely up to the service, and is determined by what rôle the service performs. For some services, pause/continue makes sense. For others, it doesn't.

For example, take a look at the Net Logon service in the screenshot below. From the enabled buttons, you can tell that it accepts pause requests. What 'pause' means for Net Logon is not that it blocks all network requests or throws out existing connected users, but that it stops accepting *new* logon requests. What a service does to implement pause is entirely its own concern.

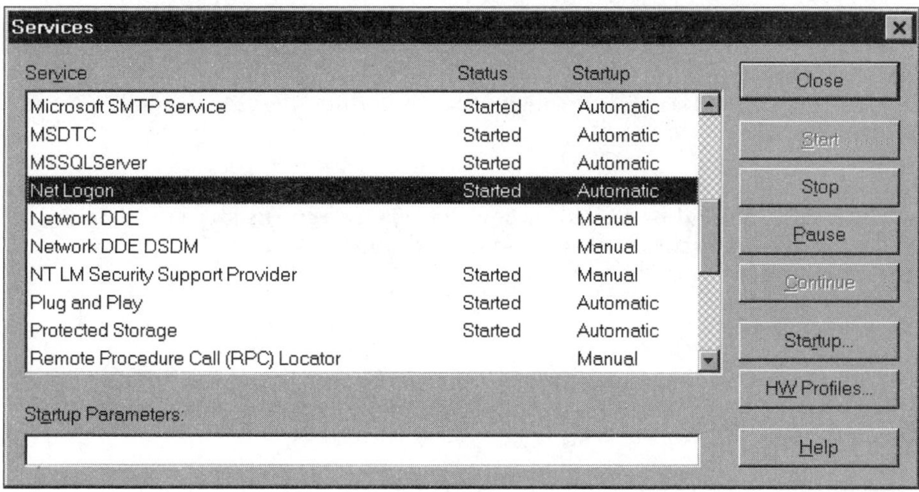

Services that don't accept stop requests probably shouldn't accept pause/continue requests, either. At least, I can't think of a good reason to make a service able to pause without also making it able to stop.

Accepting Shutdown Notifications

The service can also accept notifications from the system that it (the system) is shutting down. Some services need to do a quick cleanup of persistent data structures, etc., so that they are not corrupted in situations where the system forcibly kills the service. They can do that by accepting this notification. We'll talk in more detail about what to do if you need to process this notification in the section called *The Control Handler*, later in this chapter.

Be aware that the controls your service should, or will, accept can differ over the course of its lifetime, which is why you are allowed to set the `dwControlsAccepted` member each time you update the SCM with `SetServiceStatus()`. For instance, when your service first starts, it sends the `SERVICE_START_PENDING` notification to the SCM. It's quite conceivable that you would not want to accept stop requests until the service completes its startup operation.

dwWin32ExitCode

This member of the structure indicates a Win32 error code that the service can use to return information about *why* it failed when starting, stopping, or during operation. When the service is functioning normally, it should set this member to `NO_ERROR`. Alternatively, the service can return an error code that's specific to itself by setting this member to `ERROR_SERVICE_SPECIFIC_ERROR`. This indicates that the `dwServiceSpecificExitCode` member contains the unique error code.

dwServiceSpecificExitCode

This member contains an error code unique to the service. This value is completely ignored unless `dwWin32ExitCode` is set to `ERROR_SERVICE_SPECIFIC_ERROR`.

dwCheckPoint

The checkpoint member allows the service to indicate increments of completion during a lengthy `START_`, `STOP_`, `PAUSE_`, or `CONTINUE_PENDING` operation. For instance, if the start operation is going to take, say, 20 seconds, the service might send back `SERVICE_START_PENDING` status notifications five times during the initialization process. Each time it sends a new `SERVICE_START_PENDING` status, it should update the `dwCheckPoint` member by 1 to tell the SCM that it is still alive.

> **`dwCheckPoint` should be set to 0 when the service returns any of the non-pending states (`SERVICE_RUNNING`, `SERVICE_STOPPED`, or `SERVICE_PAUSED`).**

dwWaitHint

The final member of the SERVICE_STATUS structure specifies the amount of time in milliseconds that the SCM or the service control process can expect to wait before receiving the next status update with a changed dwCheckPoint or dwCurrentState member during a pending operation. When this amount of time has passed and the SCM has not been notified of another status change, it will assume that an error has occurred. This member should be 0 unless you are sending one of the SERVICE_XXXX_PENDING states back in dwCurrentStatus. How long the wait hint should be depends on the individual service and on the amount of work being done between calls to SetServiceStatus(). We'll see many examples of this as we move through the book.

From what we've discussed so far, you can imagine that the following would be a reasonable way of calling SetServiceStatus() for an initial SERVICE_START_PENDING status:

```
SERVICE_STATUS ss = { SERVICE_WIN32_OWN_PROCESS,
                      SERVICE_START_PENDING,
                      0,
                      NO_ERROR,
                      0,
                      1,
                      5000 };

SetServiceStatus(g_hServiceStatus, &ss);
```

Note that since you'll be using the SERVICE_STATUS_HANDLE, *that was returned from* RegisterServiceCtrlHandler(), *many times, it should be stored in a global variable.*

Parameters to ServiceMain

The parameters to ServiceMain() get passed through from the StartService() call issued from a control program. Be aware that these are *not* the command-line parameters passed to main(); they are parameters passed to a specific service when it's started. I won't say much about the parameters to ServiceMain(), simply because they are not very frequently used. If you think about it, it would be rather unusual for a service to need to customize how it operated based on flexible start-up information. Typically, configuration issues for production services should be handled with registry settings rather than parameters.

That said, there is at least one type of usage pattern that *might* make use of parameters: the Monitor. Perhaps you have a monitoring service to watch activity on a certain directory on your server's hard disk. You probably want to have some flexibility about the directory that you're watching, so that it can be changed each time you start the service (without having to hack into the registry each time or use an administration program). Short of creating a separate user interface program to help you configure it, a simple start parameter might fit the bill.

Completing Initialization

By now, the service has sent its first `SERVICE_START_PENDING` status back to the SCM and is working on initialization. Usually, initialization comprises a lot of little steps, in which case the initialization function should just be peppered with lots of `SetServiceStatus()` calls with updated checkpoints and wait hints. Sometimes, though, even a single step in the initialization process (say, a lengthy database query) can make the SCM wait too long. In these situations, consider spinning off an additional thread to do the initialization work, then call `WaitForSingleObject()` on the thread handle with a timeout of a few seconds. If the wait expires, post another pending status to the SCM and loop back around. When the thread finally signals, move on and post the `SERVICE_RUNNING` status.

The Running Service

After dealing with the preliminary initialization, the service should indicate to the SCM that it is now functioning normally by calling `SetServiceStatus()` with the `SERVICE_RUNNING` state. Now begins the **running phase** of the service's lifetime. In most cases, a service will go into a processing loop at this point, suspending itself in order to wait for one of the following:

- **A work request.** This can take different forms. In one, the service can do some type of work on a timed basis (every five minutes, for example). In another, a request can come in from a client (such as an RPC, or on a socket or named pipe). When the processing loop has completed the work, it loops back and waits for the next thing to happen.
- **A notification that the SCM demands a change in state: stop, pause, continue, shut down, etc.** When the processing loop receives a control notification, it processes it and loops around again, as above, to wait for the next work request or control notification. If the notification is a stop request, then the service exits its processing loop, notifies the SCM that it is stopping, de-initializes its resources, and exits `ServiceMain()`.

How the running phase is written is clearly one of the core issues in service development. Of course, how the service handles the processing it needs to do in its running phase varies widely depending on what the service does – in our terms, depending on what usage pattern it fits.

Handling an Error in ServiceMain

If, during the initialization or running phase of the service, an error occurs that requires the service to stop (you can't get access to a file handle you need, for instance), try to make sure that the thread cleans up any resources it is using. If the cleanup process is lengthy, send the `SERVICE_STOP_PENDING` state to the SCM. When the service has finished cleaning up, send out a `SERVICE_STOPPED` state. Also, set the `dwWin32ExitCode` or `dwServiceSpecificExitCode` member of the `SERVICE_STATUS` structure to show why the service failed, so that the user gets something more specific than the generic error message, "Error 2140: An internal Windows NT error occurred." from the Services control panel applet.

If the service returns a `SERVICE_STOPPED` status to the SCM with a non-zero `dwWin32ExitCode` member, the SCM records an entry with an ID# 7023 in the system event log. In the text of the message it records the Win32 error description.

Terminating ServiceMain

When `ServiceMain()` receives notification that it should stop, it should immediately let the SCM know that it is working on it by calling `SetServiceStatus()` with the `SERVICE_STOP_PENDING` state. It should then begin to wait for work requests to finish up, and to handle de-initialization details. If de-initialization will take a long time, it should send `SERVICE_STOP_PENDING` several times, incrementing the `dwCheckPoint` member at logical intervals. When it has cleaned up, it should again call `SetServiceStatus()`, this time with the `SERVICE_STOPPED` state. `ServiceMain()` should then return.

When `ServiceMain()` returns, the process's main thread, which is sleeping in `StartServiceCtrlDispatcher()`, wakes up and decrements the running service counter. When that counter reaches zero, the process terminates.

ServiceMain in Code

The preliminaries aside, let's take a quick look at a skeletal implementation of `ServiceMain()`. The 'work' of this service is cheesy indeed: it simply writes out to the event log every ten seconds that it is 'doing work'. Still, at least it shows the proper structure of calls and notifications to the SCM. Don't worry – we'll see how to write services that do *real* work in later chapters.

For now, it is important that you ignore one thing in this code, and that's the way that `ServiceMain()` decides when its work is complete and that it should terminate. In this sample, it simply waits on a stop event that is set in the control handler. This is not always (or even usually) the best choice – just remember that your service will have a mechanism so that it somehow knows when to terminate. The difficulties and issues surrounding termination, control of services, and proper feedback to the SCM will be clearer after an extensive analysis in the next section.

```
void WINAPI ServiceMain(DWORD argc, LPTSTR argv[])
{
   // Set up the SERVICE_STATUS structure
   SERVICE_STATUS ss = { SERVICE_WIN32_OWN_PROCESS,
                         SERVICE_START_PENDING,
                         0,
                         NO_ERROR,
                         0,
                         1,
                         5000 };

   // Register the control handler
   g_hServiceStatus = RegisterServiceCtrlHandler(g_ServiceName, Handler);
   if(!g_hServiceStatus)
   {
      // Signal error and return
   }

   // Let the SCM know I'm working on starting
   if(!SetServiceStatus(g_hServiceStatus, &ss))
   {
      // Signal error and return
   }
```

```
    // Do some initialization
    HANDLE hStopEvent = CreateEvent(NULL, FALSE, FALSE, g_pszStopEvent);

    // Let the SCM know I'm still initializing
    ss.dwCheckPoint++;
    if(!SetServiceStatus(g_hServiceStatus, &ss))
    {
       // Signal error and return
    }

    // Finish up initializing

    // Notify the SCM I am running
    ss.dwCheckPoint = 0;
    ss.dwCurrentState = SERVICE_RUNNING;
    ss.dwControlsAccepted = SERVICE_ACCEPT_STOP;

    if(!SetServiceStatus(g_hServiceStatus, &ss))
    {
       // Signal error and return;
    }

    // Put myself in a state to do my work
    DWORD dwWait;
    while(true)
    {
       PrintEvent(_T("Doing my work"));

       // Wait for a signal to stop
       dwWait = WaitForSingleObject(hStopEvent, 10000);
       if(WAIT_OBJECT_0 == dwWait)
       {
          PrintEvent(_T("Got the Stop Event"));
          break;
       }
    }

    // Let the SCM know I am stopping
    ss.dwCurrentState = SERVICE_STOP_PENDING;
    ss.dwCheckPoint = 1;
    ss.dwWaitHint = 2000;

    SetServiceStatus(g_hServiceStatus, &ss);

    // De-initialize resources - Do the steps necessary to stop
    CloseHandle(hStopEvent);

    // Let the SCM know I have stopped
    ss.dwCurrentState = SERVICE_STOPPED;
    if(!SetServiceStatus(g_hServiceStatus, &ss))
    {
       // Signal error
    }
}
```

The Control Handler

The last function that we have to implement in our service is the control handler. You already have a pretty good insight into what the control handler is up to because of its close ties with ServiceMain(), but there are some subtleties of its interaction with ServiceMain() that bear closer analysis.

The control handler's job is to process incoming control requests from the SCM. The handler receives notifications that the SCM wants the service to take some action based on a request from a service control program. The handler then responds to those 'requests' by taking real actions. The actions that the handler takes differ from service to service. In other words, a pause request, for example, can mean something very different for service A than it does for service B.

Service Control Requests

Let's start out by getting a better understanding of what the SCM expects from a service when it sends a control code. From there, we'll be able to tell how to design our handler so that it meets those expectations.

The matrix below shows what the action of the service control manager will be in any of the seven service states when any of the five possible control requests are sent:

	Stop	Start	Pause	Continue	Interrogate
STOPPED	3	1	3	3	3
RUNNING	1	4	1	1	1
PAUSED	1	4	1	1	1
STOP_ PENDING	2	4	2	2	1
START_ PENDING	1	4	2	2	1
PAUSE_ PENDING	1	4	1	1	1
CONTINUE_ PENDING	1	4	1	1	1

(1) Sends the request to the service if it accepts it. Otherwise, the SCM returns ERROR_INVALID_SERVICE_CONTROL.
(2) The control cannot be sent to the service while it is in this state. The SCM returns ERROR_SERVICE_CANNOT_ACCEPT_CTRL.
(3) Service is not active. The SCM returns ERROR_SERVICE_NOT_ACTIVE.
(4) Service is already started. The SCM returns ERROR_SERVICE_ALREADY_RUNNING.

From the matrix, you can see that the SCM may allow a couple of rather strange control requests to reach your service that it must be prepared to handle:

- The SCM will send a stop request through to the service when it is in any of the XXXX_PENDING states (except STOP_PENDING)
- The SCM will send through a pause or a continue request to a service that is already PAUSE_PENDING or CONTINUE_PENDING
- The SCM will send through a continue request to a RUNNING service
- The SCM will allow you to stop a PAUSED service

If your service isn't careful about how it implements the control handler, some of these conditions can lead to unexpected or undefined behavior that may not seem that problematic at first. I'll talk about how to code around these conditions shortly.

User-Defined Control Requests

In addition to the normal control requests, which are in the range 0-127 and are reserved for the SCM, the range of DWORDs from 128 to 255 is reserved for the developer to use. User-defined codes can allow the control program or client to request customized actions from the service, using ControlService() as the inter-process communication mechanism.

```
#define SERVICE_CONTROL_USER_BEEPIFYOUREHAPPY 0x00000080
```

This hypothetical symbol defines a custom request that asks the service to do, well, something pretty obvious. In handling the custom request, the control handler should not bother to return any status information unless it causes an 'official' change in state, like stop, pause, or continue. It should simply do its work and carry on.

The Handler Function

Now that you understand a little bit about what controls can be sent and when, let's look at the structure of Handler() more closely. Once again, your handler function can be called anything you like, but it needs to have the following signature:

```
void WINAPI Handler(DWORD fdwControl);
```

fdwControl can be any one of the following values, repeated here for your convenience, or any user-defined control code the service has set up.

Value	Meaning
SERVICE_CONTROL_STOP	Request the service to stop
SERVICE_CONTROL_PAUSE	Request the service to pause
SERVICE_CONTROL_CONTINUE	Request the service to continue

Value	Meaning
SERVICE_CONTROL_INTERROGATE	Request the service to update its status information immediately
SERVICE_CONTROL_SHUTDOWN	Request the service to perform cleanup tasks because the system is shutting down
SERVICE_CONTROL_USER_XXXX (128-255)	Request the service to perform a service-defined task

The Handler in Code

Let's examine what a handler function that accepts all of the above control requests might look like:

```
#define SERVICE_CONTROL_USER_BEEPIFYOUREHAPPY 0x00000080

SERVICE_STATUS_HANDLE g_hServiceStatus;
DWORD g_state = 0;

void WINAPI Handler(DWORD dwControl)
{
   SERVICE_STATUS ss = { SERVICE_WIN32_OWN_PROCESS,
                         SERVICE_RUNNING,
                         SERVICE_ACCEPT_STOP |
                            SERVICE_ACCEPT_PAUSE_CONTINUE |
                            SERVICE_ACCEPT_SHUTDOWN,
                         NO_ERROR,
                         0,
                         0,
                         0 };

   // Keep an additional control request of the same type
   //  from coming in when you're already handling it.
   if(g_state == dwControl)
      return;

   switch(dwControl)
   {
   case SERVICE_CONTROL_STOP:
      g_state = dwControl;

      // Do what it takes to stop
      break;

   case SERVICE_CONTROL_PAUSE:
      g_state = dwControl;
```

```
            // Do what it takes to pause
            break;

        case SERVICE_CONTROL_CONTINUE:
            g_state = dwControl;

            // Do what it takes to continue
            break;

        case SERVICE_CONTROL_SHUTDOWN:

            // Do what it takes to shutdown
            break;

        case SERVICE_CONTROL_USER_BEEPIFYOUREHAPPY:

            // Do what it takes to beep if I'm happy
            break;

        default:

            // Return a normal status on an interrogation
            SetServiceStatus(g_hServiceStatus, &ss);
        }
    }
```

I'm going to take a wild guess and say that you're incredibly disappointed with this code. It doesn't have any vegetables! It doesn't tell you how to implement handlers for these control requests at all. In fact, about all this code does is return valid status information to the SCM when it receives the `SERVICE_CONTROL_INTERROGATE` request.

Let's move forward and look at some real-life issues that we have to deal with when implementing a control handler, shall we?

Designing a Control Handler

The reason the above code is so generic is that it is not exactly clear what you should do in `Handler()`. The way that most control handler functions are naïvely implemented skirts many of the more difficult issues, such as inter-thread communication, potential race conditions, and so forth. The fact is, that how you implement the control handler is tightly coupled with the type of work your service is doing – that is, what usage pattern it fits. There is no generic, perfect solution; in fact, sometimes there are only tolerable trade-offs, which is why the code above shows only the barest of structure. Let's explore some of the issues, and then look at the available options.

First of all, remember that the control handler is run on the process's `main()` thread, which was taken over by the SCM and the service control dispatcher. The service itself (that is, `ServiceMain()`) runs on the special thread that was created by the SCM. The control handler has somehow to ask the service's thread to interrupt the work it might be doing and execute the requested control, and that is the crux of the matter.

The rule that all services should live by is this: the handler should delegate the work of processing the control notification to the service thread. Only the service thread knows what it means, in a given context, to stop, pause, or continue its operation. The fate that befalls the handler, then, is to dispatch information to the service thread that lets it know one of these operations is pending, and then quickly move on. This means that we have to solve (properly) the age-old problem of communicating and synchronizing work requests between multiple threads. How should the control handler ask the service thread to stop, to pause or to continue? These questions do not always have straightforward or trivial answers.

The control handler should delegate the work of processing the control notification to the service thread because only it knows what it means to stop, pause, or continue its operation in any given context.

The issues get more complex still if the process has more than one service, because in this case there is only one thread to make control handler calls for all the services in the process. Thus, hefty control handler work and slow processing is not a good thing, since it may block other handler requests from performing, under the SCM's strict time constraints.

Stopping, Pausing, and Continuing

If we adhere to our above rule and let the handler function merely be a vehicle for *forwarding requests* to the service thread, which then get handled in the context of the work being done there, that means we have to implement some kind of inter-thread communication mechanism. This mechanism must allow the handler thread to queue up requests to the service thread in the order received, so that the service can then process the requests in the proper order. You have, of course, the usual options:

- Events
- Asynchronous procedure call queues
- Window messages
- Sockets
- I/O completion ports

Which option you use depends upon two things: what your service does, and what the meanings of stop, pause, and continue are for your service. In short, it depends on the usage pattern the service fits. The different usage patterns in this book will give us the opportunity to try out several of the available mechanisms on particular problems.

Handling Stop

We've talked about 'stop' before. When your handler function notifies the service that it should stop, the service should probably respond by:

- Not accepting any more client requests
- Allowing the work of the existing clients to complete
- De-initializing the service and ending the service thread

The `ServiceMain()` function I presented earlier in this chapter handled 'stop' by waiting for an event to get set in the handler routine. How your service will do it depends, again, on what the service is up to.

Handling Pause/Continue

Pause/continue functionality doesn't make sense for every service. Situations where pause/continue *does* make sense are usually implemented like this:

Client programs connect to the service and ask for work to be done on their behalf. What does a pause operation really mean in such a scenario? Usually it does *not* (or at least *should* not) mean that the service stops servicing the requests of clients that have already connected and are waiting for an answer from the service. This could potentially cause many clients to time out and produce errors. What a pause probably *should* mean in this scenario is that the service stops accepting *new* connections and new requests for work, but allows existing queued requests to finish – much like the Net Logon service we looked at earlier in the chapter.

What Not to Do

You will run into some services out there, as well as some sample code, which imply that pause/continue semantics should be implemented, like the code below, by calling `SuspendThread()/ResumeThread()` on the service thread:

```
...
case SERVICE_CONTROL_PAUSE:
   g_state = dwControl;

   // Do what it takes to pause
   SuspendThread(hServiceThread);
   break;

case SERVICE_CONTROL_CONTINUE:
   g_state = dwControl;

   // Do what it takes to continue
   ResumeThread(hServiceThread);
   break;
...
```

Let me say unequivocally that this is hardly ever the right choice. In the first place, it totally hangs up existing clients. Clients of a paused service should at least be able to complete their request, not get cut off at the knees. In the second place, our control combination chart earlier shows us that the SCM expects to be able to call 'stop' on a paused service. If the control handler suspended the main service thread when it paused, how is the service thread going to handle a stop request? By resuming the thread, then stopping it? The results are simply undefined. By calling `TerminateThread()`? You should know better! When `SuspendThread()` *is* the right choice, it is the right choice only in the context of the simple, contrived, do-nothing sample in which it is being shown. It is practically never the right thing to do in a real-life scenario. Enough said.

Returning SERVICE_XXXX_PENDING Statuses

Now that we know where to handle the actual processing work of stopping, pausing, and continuing the service, how do we send information back to the SCM to tell it that we are doing that work? When, and from where, do we send the various `SERVICE_XXXX_PENDING` status updates with `SetServiceStatus()`? That's a good question. To get an idea of the answer, let's consider the intuitively reasonable answer, and then see what problems it has.

That intuitive answer is to send the very first `PENDING` notification from the handler function, as shown below, and then notify the service thread that it should do the actual operation and pick up the pieces:

```
void WINAPI Handler(DWORD dwControl)
{
   SERVICE_STATUS ss = { SERVICE_WIN32_OWN_PROCESS,
                         SERVICE_RUNNING,
                         SERVICE_ACCEPT_STOP |
                             SERVICE_ACCEPT_PAUSE_CONTINUE |
                             SERVICE_ACCEPT_SHUTDOWN,
                         NO_ERROR,
                         0,
                         0,
                         0 };

   // Keep an additional control request of the same type
   //  from coming in when you're already handling it.
   if(g_state == dwControl)
      return;

   switch(dwControl)
   {
      ...

   case SERVICE_CONTROL_PAUSE:
      g_state = dwControl;

      ss.dwCurrentState = SERVICE_PAUSE_PENDING;
      ss.dwCheckPoint = 1;
      ss.dwWaitHint = 20000;
      SetServiceStatus(g_hServiceStatus, &ss);

      // Notify the main thread you want to pause...
      HANDLE hEvent = OpenEvent(EVENT_ALL_ACCESS, FALSE, g_pszPauseEvent);
      SetEvent(hEvent);

      break;

      ...
   }
}
```

Notice the 20 second wait hint that I put in this code. This satisfies the immediate feedback needs of the SCM by giving it an instant status update. It then posts a request to the service thread asking it to pause. But, since the pause request may take a while for the service thread to handle, it tells the SCM that it may take up to 20 seconds (an arbitrary number) to actually get around to the next change of state or checkpoint update. Seems reasonable, doesn't it?

The Problem

The problems with this methodology are twofold:

- The handler doesn't really know how long it will take to update the state of the service
- It exposes the service to a potential race condition

First, the handler's assumption that the service will be able to respond to the pause request in the arbitrary amount of time supplied in the handler status update is meaningless. The handler really has no idea how much time it will take, and should not make assumptions on behalf of a thread it has no control over.

Second, there's a subtle (or perhaps not so subtle) race condition. Suppose that my handler posts the `SERVICE_PAUSE_PENDING` status, and then packs off the work to be done to the service thread, as above. Suppose further that the pause takes 15 seconds. Then, someone using the `SC.exe` tool comes along and issues a continue request. (This is possible with `SC.exe` because unlike the Services applet, it doesn't stop you from issuing new control requests while it is waiting for one to complete. See Chapter 3 for how to use this tool.) Your handler immediately responds with a state of `SERVICE_CONTINUE_PENDING`. The service thread gets control back and finishes the pause operation, sending back `SERVICE_PAUSED`. Then it receives and finishes the continue request and sends back `SERVICE_RUNNING`.

The status series reported to the SCM could be `SERVICE_PAUSE_PENDING`, `SERVICE_CONTINUE_PENDING`, `SERVICE_PAUSED`, `SERVICE_RUNNING`, which really doesn't make any sense. You have a race condition, because depending on how long the 'pause' operation takes, it might or might not complete before the service responds to the SCM with a `SERVICE_CONTINUE_PENDING` status. In these cases, the results can be undefined. Lots of services actually report this series.

The Solution(s)

The solution to these problems is not so clear. If you post *no* status update information from the control handler, then the immediate feedback the SCM gets is that nothing happened. For instance, if you don't set the status to `SERVICE_PAUSE_PENDING` in the example above, the immediate status that's returned to the SCM by the `Handler()` function is `SERVICE_RUNNING`, which clearly is not what the service is up to, either.

You could try putting *all* the status update code into the `Handler()` function, and have it wait for the service thread to set an event telling it that the requested work is complete. This could work for single-service processes, but remember that in multi-service processes, all services share one thread for handler processing. Blocking that thread could be bad news.

Finally, you could refuse to accept control requests when your service is in any of the `PENDING` states. That is, when you set the initial `PENDING` notification in the handler, you could change the `dwControlsAccepted` member of the `SERVICE_STATUS` structure and tell the SCM that you will no longer accept stop or pause/continue requests. This keeps the service thread from getting interrupted by further SCM requests while it is processing the one it is on. This effectively serializes access to the control-processing parts of the service. This is a pretty good solution, but as the matrix earlier in the chapter shows, the SCM would like to be able to send, for instance, 'pause' requests to a service in the `SERVICE_CONTINUE_PENDING` state. Simply not accepting certain notification requests undercuts what the SCM thinks it ought to be able to do.

Here's a summary of the options. None of them is perfect. In each service you write, you have to pick the one that you think is most palatable in the circumstances:

- Live with the race condition. If you're using the Services control panel applet to administer services, the consequences are not that great because it blocks until each individual request is complete. For someone sending requests from an application that does not block on each request, the race condition can be more worrisome.
- Accept that the SCM will get an initial notification that is not really accurate.
- Have `Handler()` block until it has been notified that the operation it requested from the service is complete.
- Do the `PENDING` notification immediately, in the handler, and do not accept stop or pause/continue while the service thread is processing outstanding control requests.

Multiple Requests to the Same Handler

If you use the `SC.exe` tool, you can stop or pause a service twice in a row. This can lead to confusing or undefined behavior if you don't think it through. The code in the `Handler()` function earlier in this section makes sure it *doesn't* send the same request to the service thread many times in a row by simply storing it in a global variable and comparing it to the new request. The code is reprinted below for convenience:

```
// Keep an additional control request of the same type
// from coming in when you're already handling it.
if(g_state == dwControl)
   return;
```

Shutting Down

By default, all services have 20 seconds to close out when the system begins a shutdown. After that, the system begins to kill any services that are still open forcibly, by calling `TerminateProcess()` on them. So, if a forcible kill is going to leave the service in an unusable state by corrupting data structures that get written to disk, etc., then the service should respond to this message by performing the absolute minimum number of operations it needs to do to prevent permanent damage. Remember that this is *not* a 'stop' operation. In principle, we don't care about finishing current clients' work-in-progress because we are shutting down.

If your service has persistent data structures that would be corrupted by a `TerminateProcess()` call, handle the message as quickly as possible. Otherwise, ignore this notification altogether. By the way, the amount of time that services have before they are forcibly terminated can be changed in the `HKEY_LOCAL_MACHINE\SYSTEM\CurrentControlSet\Control\WaitToKillServiceTimeout` registry key. The value is in milliseconds.

If you choose to handle shutdown notifications from the system and they are going to take a long time, set status with stop pending and a wait hint so the system knows what you're up to.

Putting It All Together: A Functioning Service

So far, we've explored some of the issues you have to consider when writing a service. Let's look now at the source code for a complete, albeit incredibly basic, service process. This code will take into consideration each of the issues we've talked about so far. The service doesn't really do anything except attempt to simulate an incoming work request every 2 seconds by writing, "Doing my work – it takes 2 seconds" to the application event log. A few things to note:

- The sleep function is a little hokey. I use it to simulate real work that actually ties up the thread for 2 seconds.
- I've added a function to do the `SetServiceStatus()` calls a little more cleanly.
- The service uses three events that get signaled from the handler function. There's one for each of stop, pause, and continue. The meaning of pause, for this service, is that the "Doing my work..." line doesn't get printed to the event log. The processing loop simply waits for one of these events to get signaled and handles it if it does.
- The service does very little real error checking, though it does call an error reporting function a couple of times that writes errors out to the event log.

To begin, here are the `main()` and `ServiceMain()` functions, which have changed very little in form from the samples I presented earlier in the chapter. There are a few calls to helper functions, and three events (to handle stop, pause and continue) instead of just one, but otherwise they should be familiar to you:

```
#define _UNICODE
#define UNICODE

#include <windows.h>
#include <TCHAR.h>

void WINAPI ServiceMain(DWORD argc, LPTSTR argv[]);
void WINAPI Handler(DWORD dwControl);

int ErrorPrinter(const TCHAR* pszFcn, DWORD dwErr = GetLastError());
void LookupErrorMsg(TCHAR* pszMsg, int cch, DWORD dwError = GetLastError());
void PrintEvent(const TCHAR* psz);
void SendStatus(DWORD dwCurrentStatus,
                DWORD dwCheckpoint = 0,
                DWORD dwWaitHint = 0,
                DWORD dwControlsAccepted = SERVICE_ACCEPT_STOP |
                                           SERVICE_ACCEPT_PAUSE_CONTINUE,
                DWORD dwExitCode = NO_ERROR);

const TCHAR* const g_ServiceName = _T("MyService");
SERVICE_STATUS_HANDLE g_hServiceStatus;

HANDLE g_hEvents[3];
DWORD g_state = 0;
DWORD g_status = 0;
```

```
int main()
{
   SERVICE_TABLE_ENTRY svcTable[] =
   {
      { const_cast<TCHAR*>(g_ServiceName), ServiceMain },
      { NULL, NULL }
   };

   if(!StartServiceCtrlDispatcher(svcTable))
      ErrorPrinter(_T("StartServiceCtrlDispatcher"));

   return 0;
}

void WINAPI ServiceMain(DWORD argc, LPTSTR argv[])
{
   // Register the control handler
   g_hServiceStatus = RegisterServiceCtrlHandler(g_ServiceName, Handler);

   if(!g_hServiceStatus)
   {
      ErrorPrinter(_T("RegisterServiceCtrlHandler"));
      return;
   }

   // Let the SCM know I'm working on starting
   SendStatus(SERVICE_START_PENDING, 1, 5000, 0);

   // Do some initialization
   g_hEvents[0] = CreateEvent(NULL, FALSE, FALSE, _T("StopEvent"));
   g_hEvents[1] = CreateEvent(NULL, FALSE, FALSE, _T("PauseEvent"));
   g_hEvents[2] = CreateEvent(NULL, FALSE, FALSE, _T("ContinueEvent"));
   bool bRun = true;

   // Notify the SCM I am running
   SendStatus(SERVICE_RUNNING);

   // Put myself in a state to do my work
   DWORD dwWait;
   while(true)
   {
      if(bRun)
      {
         PrintEvent(_T("Doing my work - it takes 2 seconds"));
         Sleep(2000);
      }
```

```
        // Wait for a signal to stop
        dwWait = WaitForMultipleObjects(3, g_hEvents, FALSE, 0);
        if(WAIT_OBJECT_0 == dwWait)
        {
           PrintEvent(_T("Got the Stop Event"));
           break;
        }
        else if(1 == dwWait - WAIT_OBJECT_0)
        {
           PrintEvent(_T("Got the Pause Event"));
           bRun = false;

           // Let the SCM know I am paused
           SendStatus(SERVICE_PAUSED);
           ResetEvent(g_hEvents[1]);
        }
        else if(2 == dwWait - WAIT_OBJECT_0)
        {
           PrintEvent(_T("Got the Continue Event"));
           bRun = true;

           // Let the SCM know I am running again
           SendStatus(SERVICE_RUNNING);
           ResetEvent(g_hEvents[2]);
        }
     }

     // Let the SCM know I am stopping
     SendStatus(SERVICE_STOP_PENDING, 1, 2000);

     // De-initialize resources - Do the steps necessary to stop
     for(int i = 0 ; i < 3 ; i++)
     {
        CloseHandle(g_hEvents[i]);
     }

     // Let the SCM know I have stopped
     SendStatus(SERVICE_STOPPED);
  }
```

Next comes `Handler()`, which now makes calls to `SetEvent()` in order to handle the controls requests it receives. The other change from its earlier form is that, instead of calling `SetServiceStatus()` itself, it delegates responsibility to the helper function `SendStatus()`, also listed here:

```
  void WINAPI Handler(DWORD dwControl)
  {
     // Keep an additional control request from coming in when you're
     // already handling it.
     if(g_state == dwControl)
        return;
```

```
    switch(dwControl)
    {
    case SERVICE_CONTROL_STOP:
       g_state = dwControl;

       // Notify the main thread you want to stop...
       SetEvent(g_hEvents[0]);
       break;

    case SERVICE_CONTROL_PAUSE:
       g_state = dwControl;

       // Notify the main thread you want to pause...
       SetEvent(g_hEvents[1]);
       break;

    case SERVICE_CONTROL_CONTINUE:
       g_state = dwControl;

       // Notify the main thread you want to continue...
       SetEvent(g_hEvents[2]);
       break;

    default:
       // Return current status on interrogation
       SendStatus(g_status);
    }
 }

 void SendStatus(DWORD dwCurrentStatus, DWORD dwCheckpoint,
                 DWORD dwWaitHint, DWORD dwControlsAccepted, DWORD dwExitCode)
 {
    g_status = dwCurrentStatus;
    SERVICE_STATUS ss = { SERVICE_WIN32_OWN_PROCESS,
                          g_status,
                          dwControlsAccepted,
                          dwExitCode,
                          0,
                          dwCheckpoint,
                          dwWaitHint };

    SetServiceStatus(g_hServiceStatus, &ss);
 }
```

Finally, here are the other three functions used by this sample. `PrintEvent()` and `ErrorPrinter()` send diagnostic and error information respectively to the NT event log, while `LookupErrorMsg()` just helps `ErrorPrinter()` out a little. Don't worry about how these functions work just at the moment; we'll be looking at all aspects of event logging in Chapter 5.

```
int ErrorPrinter(const TCHAR* psz, DWORD dwErr)
{
   TCHAR szMsg[512];
   LookupErrorMsg(szMsg, sizeof szMsg / sizeof *szMsg, dwErr);

   TCHAR sz[512];
   const TCHAR* rgsz[] = { sz };
   wsprintf(sz, _T("%s failed: %s"), psz, szMsg);

   HANDLE hes = RegisterEventSource(0, _T("My Service"));
   if(hes)
   {
      ReportEvent(hes, EVENTLOG_ERROR_TYPE, 0, 0, 0, 1, 0, rgsz, 0);
      DeregisterEventSource(hes);
   }
   return dwErr;
}

void LookupErrorMsg(TCHAR* pszMsg, int cch, DWORD dwError)
{
   if(!FormatMessage(FORMAT_MESSAGE_FROM_SYSTEM,
                                          0, dwError, 0, pszMsg, cch, 0))
      wsprintf(pszMsg, _T("Unknown: %x"), dwError);
}

void PrintEvent(const TCHAR* psz)
{
   const TCHAR* rgsz[] = { psz };

   HANDLE hes = RegisterEventSource(0, _T("My Service"));
   if(hes)
   {
      ReportEvent(hes, EVENTLOG_INFORMATION_TYPE, 0, 0, 0, 1, 0, rgsz, 0);
      DeregisterEventSource(hes);
   }
}
```

You now have all the code you need for a simple service, and you can either type it in from the listing above, or download it from the Wrox web site (http://www.wrox.com). It's just a straightforward console application that consists of a single source file – I called mine `simplesvc.cpp`.

It shouldn't take you long to realize, though, that this can't be *everything* you need to do to create an NT service. You might have created an executable, but NT can't possibly know that you intend it to be used as a service until you tell it so, and that's going to be our subject for the next chapter.

Summary

In this chapter, I hope, that along with the rudimentary basics of writing a service, I have given you some insight into the more complex issues that you'll need to think about. While services are quite easy to write, *how* you write them makes a difference. How to handle the control notifications from the SCM in a reasonable way is the problem, and how you solve that problem has a great deal to do with what the service is doing. One of the reasons I will present such a wide variety of usage patterns in this book is so that you will be able to explore the different ways to handle control requests.

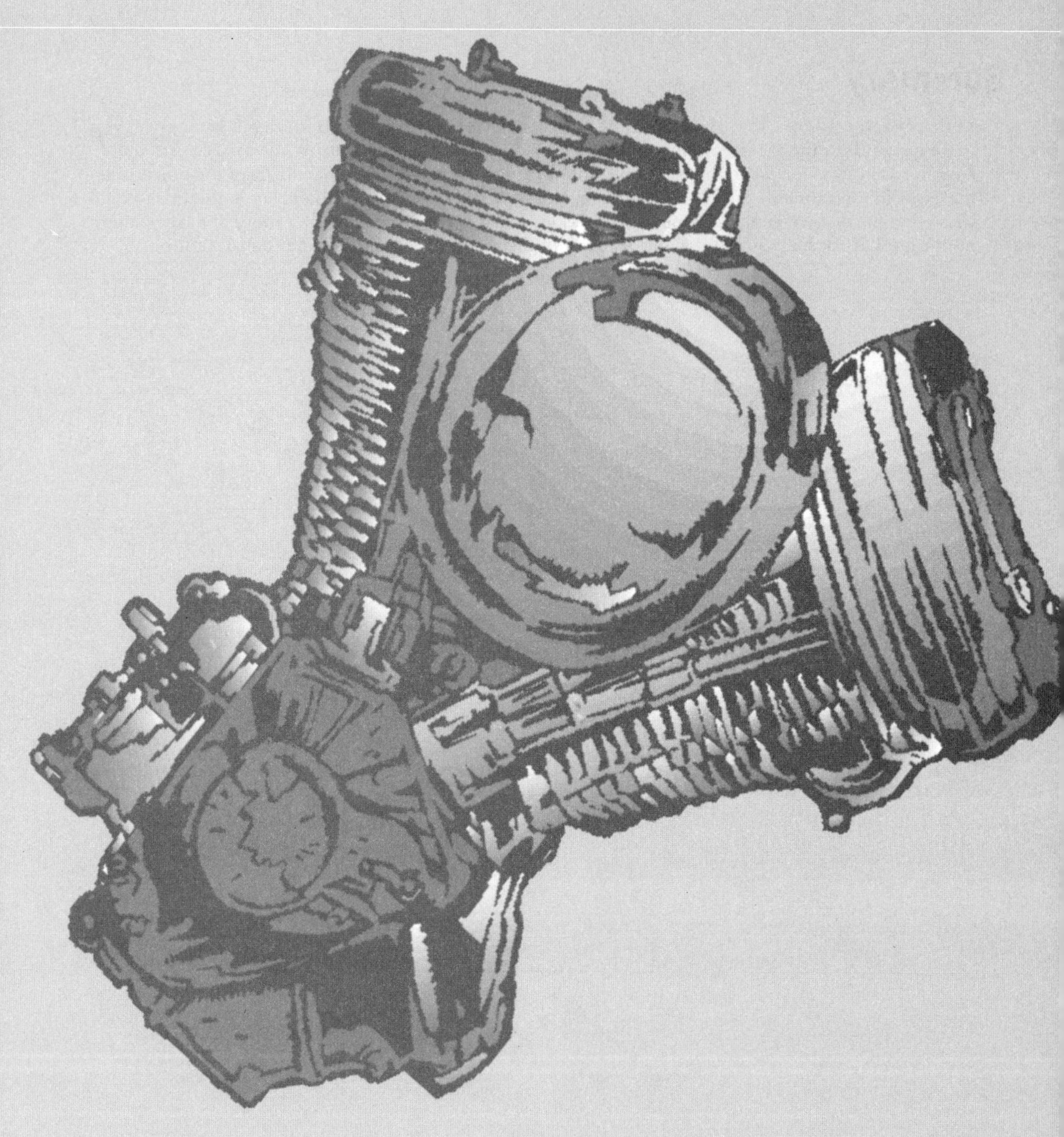

3

Controlling and Configuring Services

If you typed in (or downloaded) the code at the end of the last chapter, you're probably wondering a couple of things. "How do I make it work?" "How does NT know my executable is a service?" These are good questions, because nothing in that code tells NT to treat your new executable as a service. To see what I mean, try running a service process that hasn't been installed. The command will hang for about 30 seconds and then return, making the following entry in the application event log:

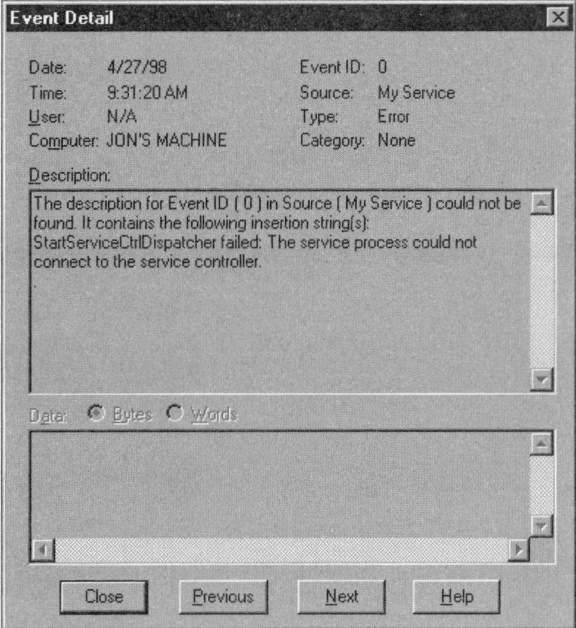

The answer to all these questions is that you use Win32 API calls to command the SCM to install, configure, and control the service executables you write, as well as to query the SCM about other services that may be installed on the system. This chapter will show you how to interact with the SCM and make those calls.

If you struggled through the issues with `Handler()` at the end of the last chapter, the three major sections that make up this one should come as a refreshing change.

- The first of them covers the calls you might make from a service *configuration* process to install or alter settings on a service.
- The second covers the types of calls you might make from a service *control* process to start, stop, pause, continue, or make other requests.
- The last major section will cover a handy command-line tool known as SC, which allows you to perform all the service configuration *and* control operations on any service, on any machine on the network to which you have access permission.

We won't be looking at those functions that have to do with setting or retrieving security configurations in this chapter – I'll save those for Chapter 7.

The Services Database

For a service to be recognized as such by Windows NT, it has to be registered in the **services database**, which is an area in the registry that contains important information about *all* the services installed on the system. When you call the SCM APIs to request a configuration change to a service, what those calls actually do is manipulate these registry entries. The services database is located at the following registry key:

```
HKEY_LOCAL_MACHINE\SYSTEM\CurrentControlSet\Services
```

When you add your service to the database by calling the `CreateService()` API function, a new subkey is created beneath this, containing named values that hold various pieces of information about how the service is to start, where the executable that runs it is housed, etc. All of these bits of information are important, so we're going to look at each of them in detail shortly.

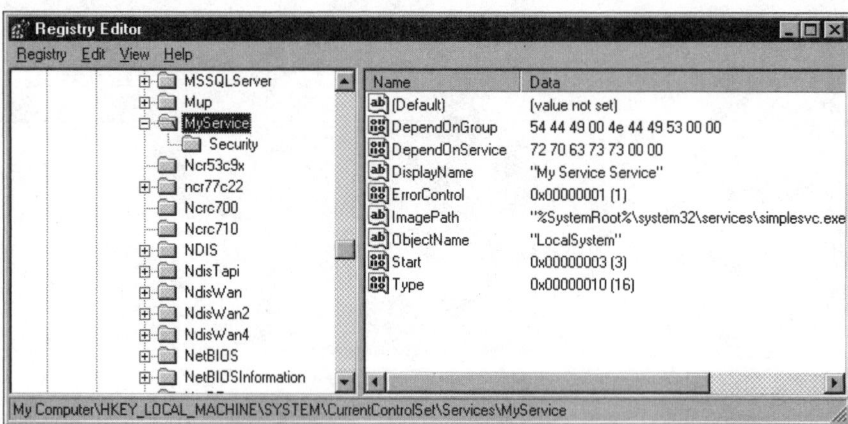

SCM Service Records

At some time during system startup, the configuration information about each service is read from the database in the registry. At that time, the SCM creates a record for the service and puts it into a structure called the **service record list**, which is the 'volatile database' I referred to in Chapter 1. A service record contains the following information about the service:

Service name
Service start type
Service status structure
  type
  current state
  accepted control codes
  exit code
  checkpoint
  wait hint
Dependency list

The SCM uses this data structure to return information quickly to the various API functions that query it about services (such as `QueryServiceStatus()` and `EnumDependentServices()`, which we'll see later on).

Storing Private Configuration Data

The services database is also where you could store configuration data that's specific to a particular service. For instance, if my service needed a number of time-out configuration parameters, I might add a subkey called Timeout to the MyService key, and then add named values beneath that subkey. However, this is not the only choice. Some sources at Microsoft recommend the above, while others suggest putting data like this beneath a key called `HKEY_LOCAL_MACHINE\SOFTWARE\CompanyName\AppName`. I'd say that either is acceptable, provided that you have a good reason for doing one or the other.

The SCM won't touch any registry entries other than those beneath the root of MyService and under its Security subkey. However, a call to `DeleteService()` will remove the MyService key and *everything* beneath it, including any subkeys you add. We'll discuss more about custom registry entries when we come to talk about writing your own administration tools in Chapter 11.

Backup and Security on the Database

The services database is always backed up by the system. After each successful boot, the system saves a copy of the current services database in the following registry key:

```
HKEY_LOCAL_MACHINE\SYSTEM\ControlSetXXX\Services
```

In the above, `XXX` is a numerical value stored in the following key:

```
HKEY_LOCAL_MACHINE\SYSTEM\Select\LastKnownGood
```

The system will restore the previous copy of the database if any changes to the active one cause the boot to fail, or if the user elects to boot up using the 'Last Known Good' option when the OS first loads. Usually (and in contrast to device driver services), a Win32 service won't be the cause of a failed boot. However, if you install a service with a critical error control level, configure it to start up automatically, and then the service fails, NT will invoke the last known good configuration on reboot.

> **The services database is a secured area of the registry. Only members of the local Administrators security group are allowed to view or modify these entries directly from the Registry Editor.**

Locking the Services Database

Before doing configuration work on the services database, a configuration program should acquire the lock on it. When the services database is locked, no other program can change the configuration of (or execute start operations on) *any* service. The lock essentially serializes access to the services area of the registry. It prevents the SCM from starting a service while that service is being reconfigured, and it prevents multiple programs from trying to reconfigure a service at once. Only one process can own the lock at any given time.

To obtain the lock, you use the `LockServiceDatabase()` function.

```
SC_LOCK LockServiceDatabase(SC_HANDLE hSCManager);
```

This returns an `SC_LOCK` handle if the function is successful in acquiring the lock, or `NULL` if it isn't. You must acquire the lock before you call functions like `ChangeServiceConfig()` or `SetServiceObjectSecurity()`. A service configuration program should also acquire the lock before using registry functions to reconfigure a service manually, or to change its private settings. If the database is locked, a call to `StartService()` to start *any* service will fail.

When you've finished working with the service database and want to release the lock you've acquired, you call the `UnlockServiceDatabase()` function with the `SC_LOCK` handle that was returned from `LockServiceDatabase()`.

```
BOOL UnlockServiceDatabase(SC_LOCK ScLock);
```

If a process that owns a lock terminates, the SCM automatically releases the lock. Finally, you can call `QueryServiceLockStatus()` to find out whether the SCM database is currently locked.

```
BOOL QueryServiceLockStatus(SC_HANDLE                    hSCManager,
                            LPQUERY_SERVICE_LOCK_STATUS lpLockStatus,
                            DWORD                        cbBufSize,
                            LPDWORD                      pcbBytesNeeded);

typedef struct _QUERY_SERVICE_LOCK_STATUS
{
   DWORD  fIsLocked;                  // Zero if unlocked
   LPTSTR lpLockOwner;                // Name of user who locked database
   DWORD  dwLockDuration;             // How long it has been locked
} QUERY_SERVICE_LOCK_STATUS, *LPQUERY_SERVICE_LOCK_STATUS;
```

Opening the Service Control Manager

To interact with the services database programmatically, you have to go through the service control manager. When you open the SCM on a particular machine, what you're really 'opening' is a window onto the services database for that machine. To open a connection to the SCM, you use the OpenSCManager() function, prototyped below:

```
SC_HANDLE OpenSCManager(LPCTSTR lpMachineName,
                        LPCTSTR lpDatabaseName,
                        DWORD   dwDesiredAccess);
```

The first parameter is the name of the machine on which you want to open the services database. Again, all these parameters are TSTRs, so you can use either Unicode or ANSI strings. If the pointer is NULL or an empty string, the SCM on the local computer is used. The second parameter is the name of the SCM database to open. It should always be set to SERVICES_ACTIVE_DATABASE or to NULL, which defaults to the same thing. The winsvc.h header defines a SERVICES_FAILED_DATABASE option as well, but the option is undocumented and should not be used.

Access Rights

The final parameter to OpenSCManager() specifies the type of access you are requesting. The table below lists the available rights you can request.

dwDesiredAccess **Type**	**Meaning**
SC_MANAGER_CONNECT	Allows connection to the SCM. This is implicit in calling the OpenSCManager() function.
SC_MANAGER_CREATE_SERVICE	Allows calling the CreateService() function to add a new service to the database.
SC_MANAGER_ENUMERATE_SERVICE	Allows EnumerateServiceStatus() to be called to query the status information of services.

Table Continued on Following Page

dwDesiredAccess **Type**	**Meaning**
SC_MANAGER_LOCK	Allows a lock to be acquired on the services **database**.
SC_MANAGER_QUERY_LOCK_STATUS	Allows lock status information to be retrieved from the database.
SC_MANAGER_ALL_ACCESS	All of the access rights above.
GENERIC_READ	Combines STANDARD_RIGHTS_READ, SC_MANAGER_ENUMERATE_SERVICE, and SC_MANAGER_QUERY_LOCK_STATUS.
GENERIC_WRITE	Combines STANDARD_RIGHTS_WRITE and SC_MANAGER_CREATE_SERVICE.
GENERIC_EXECUTE	Combines STANDARD_RIGHTS_EXECUTE, SC_MANAGER_CONNECT, and SC_MANAGER_LOCK.

The STANDARD_RIGHTS_XXXX *rights that appear in the table map to combinations of the standard object security rights that apply across all NT objects. We'll be looking at all aspects of NT security in Chapter 7.*

The system checks the security access token of the process that's calling OpenSCManager() against the access list in the security descriptor associated with the service control manager before granting the requested access. By default, all processes are permitted SC_MANAGER_CONNECT, SC_MANAGER_ENUMERATE_SERVICE, and SC_MANAGER_QUERY_LOCK_STATUS access to all service control manager databases. However, only processes that run under an account with the rights of the Administrators group will be able to acquire a handle that's capable of being used in calls to CreateService() or LockServiceDatabase(). The key thing to remember is to make sure you request SC_MANAGER_CREATE_SERVICE rights if you'll need to be able to install a new service with this SCM handle.

Return Values

OpenSCManager() returns a handle of type SC_HANDLE, which the calling process will later use to make configuration and/or control calls to the service. If the function fails, this handle is set to NULL, and you can call GetLastError() to retrieve the error code. The most common error is ERROR_ACCESS_DENIED, which occurs when the process calling the function does not have the security rights to obtain the access it is requesting. This usually happens when the process requests CREATE rights from a non-administrative account.

Closing SCM and Service Handles

After you are finished using a service control manager handle, you should close it by calling the CloseServiceHandle() function. You should also use the same function to close any handles that were opened with OpenService() or CreateService(), which we'll discuss shortly. The system will automatically close any open SCM or service handles when the process exits, but you're a good programmer, and you should close them in any case.

```
BOOL CloseServiceHandle(SC_HANDLE hSCObject);
```

Installing a Service

Installation of a service should happen in one of two places: in an official installation or setup program that's shipped with the service, or using a -install command line parameter to the executable that houses the service. (You could also use a -regserver and -unregserver pair of command-line parameters to install the service and be consistent with COM rules.) It's also possible to use the SC.exe tool to install a service, but you should only use this for testing, not as a means to install your commercial-grade service.

Once you've opened the SCM, as we discussed in the last section, you can begin to do some work on individual services. Take a look at the CreateService() call below. It creates a new entry in the services database for the service you're installing, and it allows you to set a number of configuration options that we'll discuss shortly:

```
SC_HANDLE CreateService(SC_HANDLE hSCManager,
                        LPCTSTR   lpServiceName,
                        LPCTSTR   lpDisplayName,
                        DWORD     dwDesiredAccess,
                        DWORD     dwServiceType,
                        DWORD     dwStartType,
                        DWORD     dwErrorControl,
                        LPCTSTR   lpBinaryPathName,
                        LPCTSTR   lpLoadOrderGroup,
                        LPDWORD   lpdwTagId,
                        LPCTSTR   lpDependencies,
                        LPCTSTR   lpServiceStartName,
                        LPCTSTR   lpPassword);
```

The SC_HANDLE returned by the function is a handle to the service you're creating, which can subsequently be used to perform other operations on the service. When you are finished with it, you should close this handle with the CloseServiceHandle() function.

Example of Installing a Service

Let's look at a quick example of how to install a service. The code below forms a structure onto which we'll add more functionality as we move through the chapter; for now it includes a couple of functions that are just enough to get us started. As presented, the call to `CreateService()` in the `Install()` function adds an entry to the services database for the simple service we built at the end of the last chapter. Once you've seen the service up and running with the arbitrary set of configuration options used here, we'll move on to look at what they mean and what other options are available.

```
#define _WIN32_WINNT 0x400
#define UNICODE
#define _UNICODE

#include <windows.h>
#include <iostream>
using namespace std;

#ifdef UNICODE
   #define _tcout wcout
   #define _tostream wostream
#else
   #define _tcout cout
   #define _tostream ostream
#endif

#include <TCHAR.h>

void Install();
void Remove();
void Config(BOOL bAutostart);
void Display();
void GetConfig();
void Status();
void Dependencies();
void Start();
void Control(DWORD dwControl);

DWORD ErrorPrinter(const TCHAR* pszFcn, DWORD dwErr = GetLastError());

const int MAX_SERVICE_NAME = 256;
LPCTSTR g_service = _T("MyService");
LPCTSTR g_display = _T("My Service Service");
LPCTSTR g_binary = _T("%SystemRoot%\\system32\\services\\simplesvc.exe");

int main()
{
   TCHAR* pszCmdLine = GetCommandLine();
   CharLowerBuff(pszCmdLine, lstrlen(pszCmdLine));
```

```
    if(_tcsstr(pszCmdLine, _T("-install")))
        Install();
    else if(_tcsstr(pszCmdLine, _T("-remove")))
        Remove();
    else if(_tcsstr(pszCmdLine, _T("-auto")))
        Config(TRUE);
    else if(_tcsstr(pszCmdLine, _T("-demand")))
        Config(FALSE);
    else if(_tcsstr(pszCmdLine, _T("-display")))
        Display();
    else if(_tcsstr(pszCmdLine, _T("-showconfig")))
        GetConfig();
    else if(_tcsstr(pszCmdLine, _T("-status")))
        Status();
    else if(_tcsstr(pszCmdLine, _T("-depends")))
        Dependencies();
    else if(_tcsstr(pszCmdLine, _T("-start")))
        Start();
    else if(_tcsstr(pszCmdLine, _T("-stop")))
        Control(SERVICE_CONTROL_STOP);
    else if(_tcsstr(pszCmdLine, _T("-pause")))
        Control(SERVICE_CONTROL_PAUSE);
    else if(_tcsstr(pszCmdLine, _T("-continue")))
        Control(SERVICE_CONTROL_CONTINUE);

    return 0;
}
```

The code above really just sets up `main()`, which performs simple command-line parsing to route the request to the proper function. The real meat is in the `Install()` function, which opens the SCM, creates the service in the services database, and then closes the handles it has opened before exiting gracefully:

```
void Install()
{
    SC_HANDLE hSCM = NULL;
    SC_HANDLE hService = NULL;

    hSCM = OpenSCManager(NULL, NULL, SC_MANAGER_CREATE_SERVICE);
    if(!hSCM)
    {
        ErrorPrinter(_T("OpenSCManager"));
        return;
    }
```

```
    hService = CreateService(hSCM,
                             g_service,
                             g_display,
                             GENERIC_READ,
                             SERVICE_WIN32_OWN_PROCESS,
                             SERVICE_DEMAND_START,
                             SERVICE_ERROR_NORMAL,
                             g_binary,
                             NULL,
                             NULL,
                             NULL,
                             NULL,
                             NULL);

    if(!hService)
    {
       ErrorPrinter(_T("CreateService"));
       CloseServiceHandle(hSCM);
       return;
    }
    else
    {
       _tprintf(_T("%s Created\n"), g_service);
       CloseServiceHandle(hService);
    }

    CloseServiceHandle(hSCM);
    return;
}

DWORD ErrorPrinter(const TCHAR* psz, DWORD dwErr)
{
    LPVOID lpvMsgBuf;
    if(!FormatMessage(FORMAT_MESSAGE_FROM_SYSTEM |
                         FORMAT_MESSAGE_ALLOCATE_BUFFER,
                      0, dwErr, 0, (LPTSTR)&lpvMsgBuf, 0, 0))
    {
       _tprintf(_T("%s failed: Unknown error %x\n"), psz, dwErr);
    }
    else
       _tprintf(_T("%s failed: %s\n"), psz, static_cast<LPTSTR>(lpvMsgBuf));

    LocalFree(lpvMsgBuf);
    return dwErr;
}
```

If you compile up the source code that I've presented so far (you'll probably have to change the path name in the `g_binary` variable to match the location of the service executable), you'll be able to install our simple service by typing `svcconfig -install` on the command line. After you've done that, you'll find that a new service called **MyService** is visible in the Services control panel applet, and you can use the latter to start, pause, continue, and stop the service. The only real work that goes on is to print a message to the event log every two seconds, so bring up the event log and have a look:

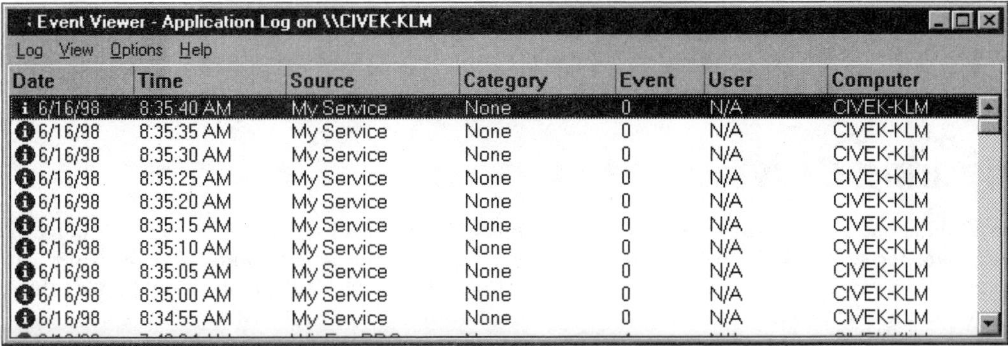

If you open up one of these entries, you'll see something like the dialog below. Furthermore, if you've performed some manipulation of the Pause, Continue and Stop buttons, there will be other events containing descriptions that confirm those actions.

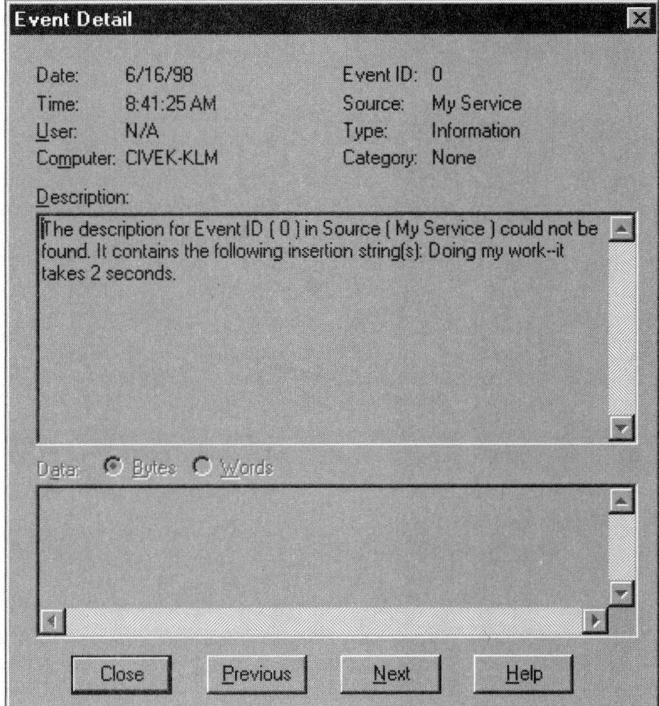

When you're done playing around with the service, remember to stop it so that the application event log doesn't get filled up with your events.

Configuring Services

When I talk about 'configuring' a service, I really mean any operation that adds or changes any of the critical characteristics of that service, such as its security, its dependencies, and so forth. A service configuration program changes the characteristics of an *installed* service, which is any service that's registered in the services database. To make a configuration change to the services database, you must do the following:

- Open the SCM on the machine where the service resides
- Create or open the service you want to change
- Change the service configuration
- Close the handle to the service
- Close the handle to the SCM

Service Configuration Information

I've shown you a very simple example of how to install a service, but I skirted right round the details of the parameters to the `CreateService()` function. We now need to have a proper discussion about what all those installation options are. If you remember (and in case you don't), the prototype of `CreateService()` looks like this:

```
SC_HANDLE CreateService(SC_HANDLE hSCManager,
                        LPCTSTR   lpServiceName,
                        LPCTSTR   lpDisplayName,
                        DWORD     dwDesiredAccess,
                        DWORD     dwServiceType,
                        DWORD     dwStartType,
                        DWORD     dwErrorControl,
                        LPCTSTR   lpBinaryPathName,
                        LPCTSTR   lpLoadOrderGroup,
                        LPDWORD   lpdwTagId,
                        LPCTSTR   lpDependencies,
                        LPCTSTR   lpServiceStartName,
                        LPCTSTR   lpPassword);
```

Apart from the handle to the SCM that was returned by an earlier call to `OpenSCManager()`, the things you can specify at installation time are:

- The short name of the service
- The long name (or display name) of the service
- The access rights you have to the service being created
- The type of the service
- When to start the service
- What to do if the service fails to start
- In what executable the service is housed
- The group the service will be loaded with
- What other services the service will depend upon
- The name and password of the account the service will run under

Let's examine each of these and their impact in greater detail.

Service Names

There are two types of service names: short names and display names. The **short name** is used to label the registry subkey that contains the service's configuration information. It is also used in calls to `OpenService()`. Short names should not contain spaces, and (obviously) should be quite short. The **display name** is used to describe the service in more detail, and can contain spaces and more characters (up to 256 of them). The display name is the one shown by the Services control panel applet, and is also the name used in the NT `net start` command to start a service.

For example, the display name of IIS's web server is, "World Wide Web Publishing Service", but the short name (under which it is stored in the registry) is W3SVC. By the way, the SCM will preserve the cases of the names you enter, but string comparisons are always case insensitive.

Service Types

The types of services we are writing – Win32 services – can be of two possible types: `SERVICE_WIN32_OWN_PROCESS` and `SERVICE_WIN32_SHARE_PROCESS`. Each of these can be ORed with a third flag, `SERVICE_INTERACTIVE_PROCESS`. When you're specifying the service type in the `CreateService()` call, it should be the same as the one you specified in the `SetServiceStatus()` calls of the service code itself, which we saw in the last chapter. However, as far as I can tell, there are no detrimental ramifications to getting this out of sync, except of course that the service would be returning inaccurate status information.

Access Rights

Just as it was when we were opening the SCM, it's possible to specify in the `dwDesiredAccess` parameter what rights we have to make changes to the configuration of the service to which we're acquiring a handle. However, the flags are different for `CreateService()` than they are for `OpenSCManager()`, so let's run through them.

Desired Access Flag for CreateService()	Meaning
SERVICE_ALL_ACCESS	Includes STANDARD_RIGHTS_REQUIRED in addition to all of the access types listed in this table.
SERVICE_CHANGE_CONFIG	Enables the ChangeServiceConfig() function to change the service's configuration.
SERVICE_ENUMERATE_DEPENDENTS	Enables the EnumDependentServices() function to enumerate all the services dependent on the service.
SERVICE_INTERROGATE	Enables the ControlService() function to ask the service to report its status immediately.
SERVICE_PAUSE_CONTINUE	Enables the ControlService() function to pause or continue the service.
SERVICE_QUERY_CONFIG	Enables the QueryServiceConfig() function to query the service configuration.
SERVICE_QUERY_STATUS	Enables the QueryServiceStatus() function to ask the SCM about the status of the service.
SERVICE_START	Enables StartService() to start the service.
SERVICE_STOP	Enables ControlService() to stop the service.
SERVICE_USER_DEFINED_CONTROL	Enables the ControlService() function to specify a user-defined control code.
STANDARD_RIGHTS_REQUIRED	*Maps to the following rights*
DELETE	Enables calling of the DeleteService() function to delete the service from the services database.
READ_CONTROL	Enables calling of the QueryServiceObjectSecurity() function to query the security descriptor of the service object.
WRITE_DAC | WRITE_OWNER	Enables calling of the SetServiceObjectSecurity() function to modify the security descriptor of the service object.

Generic Access Rights	Meaning
GENERIC_READ	Combines STANDARD_RIGHTS_READ, SERVICE_QUERY_CONFIG, SERVICE_QUERY_STATUS, and SERVICE_ENUMERATE_DEPENDENTS.
GENERIC_WRITE	Combines STANDARD_RIGHTS_WRITE and SERVICE_CHANGE_CONFIG.
GENERIC_EXECUTE	Combines STANDARD_RIGHTS_EXECUTE, SERVICE_START, SERVICE_STOP, SERVICE_PAUSE_CONTINUE, SERVICE_INTERROGATE, and SERVICE_USER_DEFINED_CONTROL.

Service Start Phases

From Chapter 1, you know that Win32 services can either be started automatically by the operating system when it boots up, or on demand when a service control process (such as `net.exe`) calls the `StartService()` API. The time when the operating system starts a service is known as its **start phase**. The chart below indicates the possible start phases for each service, specified in the `CreateService()` call:

dwStartType Value	Meaning
SERVICE_BOOT_START	The OS loader loads the service. This is only for driver services that are required to boot the OS, such as SCSI.
SERVICE_SYSTEM_START	Device drivers required for system operation have this value, and are loaded before the logon screen.
SERVICE_AUTO_START	For Win32 services that should be running before a user gets the chance to log on. These begin to load around the time the WinLogon dialog appears.
SERVICE_DEMAND_START	The service is started on a StartService() request, or when another service depends on it.
SERVICE_DISABLED	The service will not start, and any service that depends on it won't start either.

When Do Services Really Start?

Sometimes it's important that a service be able to specify *precisely* when the operating system will load it. If service A uses some capability that service B has, for instance, then A needs to be sure that B is loaded by the operating system before A is. When a service really starts *within* a particular start phase is determined by a combination of a number of configuration settings that you need to tweak rather carefully to achieve the results you want:

- Load-ordering group.
- Tag order within the load-ordering group.
- Service dependencies.
- Group dependencies.

Load-ordering groups

Within each start phase, the single factor that has the most impact on when a service is loaded relative to other services in the same phase is whether it is a member of a **load-ordering group**. If a service declares itself to be a member of a load-ordering group, by having a named value called `Group` in its `HKEY_LOCAL_MACHINE\SYSTEM\CurrentControlSet\Services\MyService` key, then it will be started before *all* services that aren't members of a load-ordering group. NT will start (or, at least, attempt to start) all the members of the group before moving on to the next group. Furthermore, all the groups within the phase will be started in the order specified in the registry key called:

```
HKEY_LOCAL_MACHINE\SYSTEM\CurrentControlSet\Control\ServiceGroupOrder
```

This key contains a value type that's simply a list of group strings:

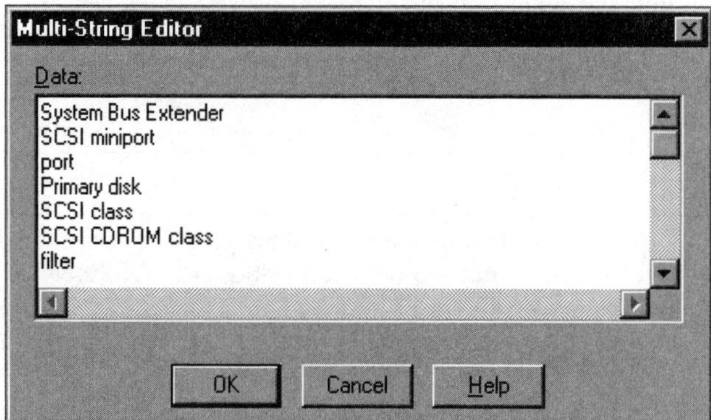

To summarize, NT uses the following algorithm to determine when to start what:

- Start services in the groups in the load-ordering group list.
- Start services in any groups that are not in the group list. The load order for groups that are not in the group list is undefined.
- Start services that are not in a group. The loading sequence for services not in a group is undefined.

Tag Order

Within each load-ordering group, you can further specify when individual services are loaded by using a **tag order** value. The order is specified using a tag value (a `DWORD`) attached to the service itself in the `HKEY_LOCAL_MACHINE\SYSTEM\CurrentControlSet\Services\MyService` key, under the `Tag` named value. Then, you must make an entry under the name of the load-ordering group in the following key:

```
HKEY_LOCAL_MACHINE\SYSTEM\CurrentControlSet\Control\GroupOrderList
```

The first entry in each named value is the number of tag values in the group, and the order of the following entries specifies the loading sequence of the various values, which must therefore be unique within a given load-ordering group. The screenshot shows how these entries look:

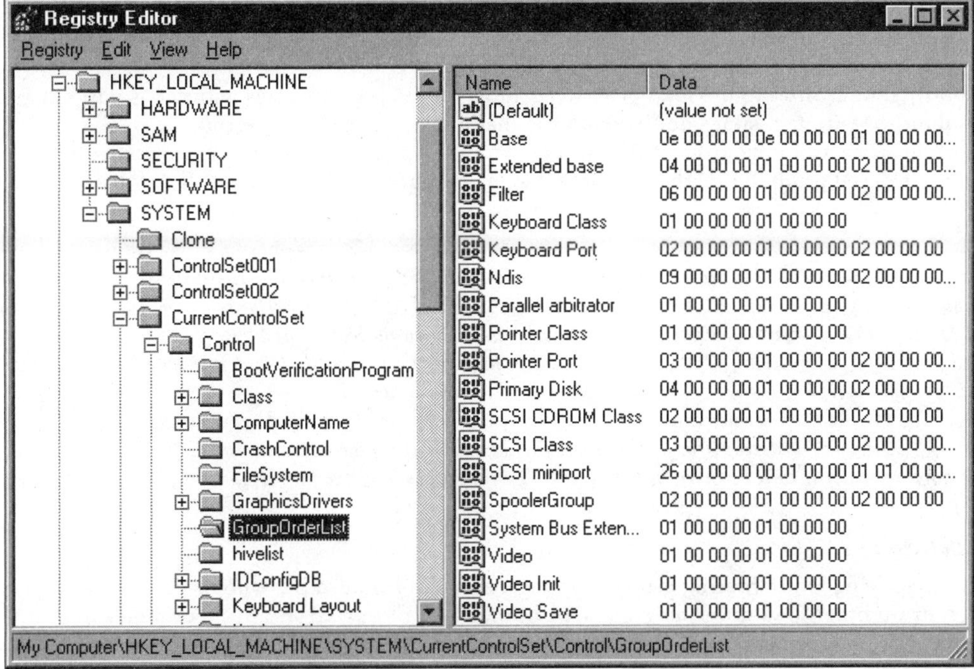

If you expand out the data for one of the named value entries, such as `Pointer Port`, you can see how this works:

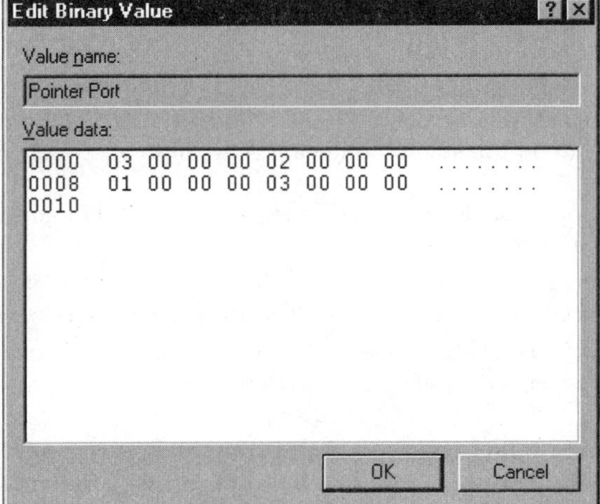

The first data item contains the number of items in the list (that is, the number of services that are members of the load ordering group). In this case, it's 3. After this comes the ordered list of tag values and when they load – 2, 1, and 3, in that order. The configurations of the individual entries in the `GroupOrderList` have to be set up and maintained by you with a separate registry call that manipulates the `REG_BINARY` value. Although you set a particular service's tag value using the service installation API, the actual loading order is *not* automatically configured by those API calls.

Tag values follow similar rules to the load-ordering groups themselves: services within a group but without tag values (or with tag values not listed in the loading sequence for the group, above) are loaded *after* all the services in the group *with* valid tag values. The loading sequence for individual services in a tag-ordered group but without a tag value, or in a group with no tag-ordering list, is undefined.

> *The Win32 SDK documentation states that tags are only evaluated for kernel and file system drivers with* `SERVICE_BOOT_START` *or* `SERVICE_SYSTEM_START` *start types, but it is difficult to say if this is accurate. Experiments I have done seem to indicate that tags are evaluated for* `SERVICE_AUTO_START` *groups and Win32 services as well. The definitive answer is not yet clear, but the* `Serial` *service seems to give us a hint. It is a* `SERVICE_AUTO_START` *service that uses a tag vector value to specify its load order in the* `Extended Base` *load-ordering group. However, this behavior is undocumented, and it is therefore hard to say if it will be there in the future. It is probably best not to rely on it.*

Service Dependencies

In addition to specifying load-ordering groups and tags, services can also be configured to *depend* on other services, or on other load-ordering groups, or both. The `lpDependencies` parameter to `CreateService()` is an array of null-separated names of services or load-ordering group names that should be doubly null-terminated. If you specify a group name as a dependency, you must preface the name with the `SC_GROUP_IDENTIFIER` character. However, this character is just a + sign, so it's usually easier simply to use that.

For example, passing the string `+TDI\0+NDIS\0RPCSS\0\0` would specify that your service depended on the load-ordering groups `TDI` and `NDIS`, and on the `RPCSS` service. When you make a service depend on others, the following rules and consequences apply:

- Services that depend on other services will not start until all other services in the dependency list have started.
- If the service is type `SERVICE_DEMAND_START` and it has service dependencies in its dependency list, the system will start each of the services it depends on before starting it.
- If the service has a dependency on a load-ordering group, the service will not start until *at least one* of the services in the group has started.

The screenshot below depicts `LanmanWorkstation`, an auto-start, `WIN32_SHARE_PROCESS` service that depends on group `TDI`, but not upon any individual services. It is also a member of the load-ordering group `NetworkProvider`. The consequence of this configuration is that `LanmanWorkstation` will not load unless one of the services in `TDI` is loaded.

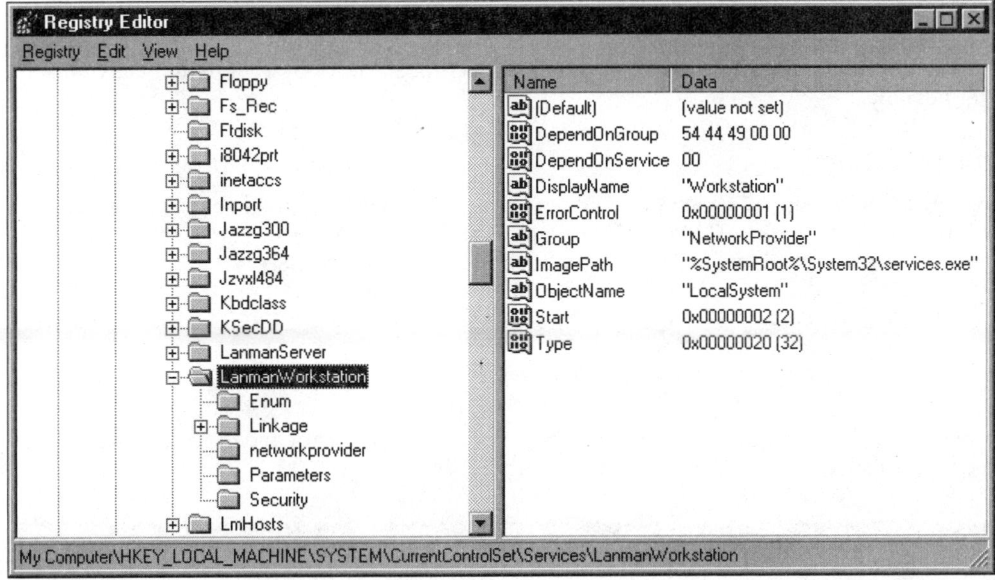

Dependencies take precedence over both the load-ordering group and the start phase mechanisms. What this means is that if, for instance, Service A is an auto-start service that has a higher-ranking tag value than services C, D, and E, and it also has the demand-start Service B listed in its dependencies, then Service B will be started out-of-phase with the auto-start services. Furthermore, B will be started before Services C, D, and E, even though they are defined in a specific order in A's load-ordering group.

A Few Words on Load Groups and Dependencies

Now that we've discussed the issues of how to load services in the right order and how to set up their interactions with other services, I can reveal that what you need to do in real life is almost never extremely complex. Most of the Win32 services you will write won't have convoluted interactions with other services. If the service will use RPC, for instance, you just need to make sure to specify `RPCSS` as a service dependency. This will guarantee that the RPC service is started and functioning before your service begins to run or make RPC calls. In turn, this ensures that the service does not begin to make RPC library calls that might generate errors if the RPC service were not initialized.

Consider a different case. If the service you are writing is intended to be auto-start, and part of a suite of many services in your software system, you may want to make it part of a load-ordering group. For sets of auto-start services, use groups and tags to specify orders and dependencies that will bring in 'stray' demand-start services, and help to handle the errors that might occur if other services are not started. As a general rule, dependencies are not so much for specifying complex load-ordering chains as they are for making sure that your service doesn't go ahead with an undefined operation just because some service it depends on failed to start. Instead of proceeding with an operation that will be undefined, the SCM simply won't start your service.

The permutations are endless, and you may need to do some experimentation. Rather than leave it to chance, though, figure out a combination of groups and dependencies that guarantees consistent results every time. The best advice I can give you is to keep it as simple as possible – use specific service dependencies rather than complex combinations of load-ordering groups and tag values whenever possible.

Error Control Level

By specifying an **error control level** in the `dwErrorControl` parameter, you can decide how the SCM will react to your service if it fails to start while the machine is starting up. As far as we're concerned, the error control levels are important only to services with start type `SERVICE_AUTO_START`. There are four possible error control levels: `SERVICE_ERROR_IGNORE`, `SERVICE_ERROR_NORMAL`, `SERVICE_ERROR_SEVERE`, and `SERVICE_ERROR_CRITICAL`.

- `SERVICE_ERROR_IGNORE` means that the system will log the error in the event log, but continue starting the remaining services.
- `SERVICE_ERROR_NORMAL` means that the system will log the error and display the following, familiar dialog box, and then continue starting the remaining services.

- `SERVICE_ERROR_SEVERE` means that the system will log the error and then restart the system using the last known good configuration. If the system is already using the last known good configuration, it will continue starting the remaining services.
- `SERVICE_ERROR_CRITICAL` means that the system will log the error and then restart the system using the last known good configuration. If the system is already using the last known good configuration, the system boot will fail.

Clearly, `SERVICE_ERROR_SEVERE` and `SERVICE_ERROR_CRITICAL` are too harsh for use by Win32 services. These codes should only be used in situations where device drivers fail to start. Any Win32 service you write that uses the `SERVICE_AUTO_START` start type should specify `SERVICE_ERROR_IGNORE` or `SERVICE_ERROR_NORMAL`.

Service Executable

This configuration option simply specifies the fully qualified path to the `.exe` file that contains the service in question.

Account and Password

Finally, it's possible to specify the user name and password of the account under which a service will run. Names sent to the `lpServiceStartName` parameter should be of the form `Domain\User`, or, if it's a local machine account, just `.\User` or `User`. If you use a particular account, that account must have the 'Log on as a service' user right, assigned in User Manager application. If you don't specify any particular account, the service will run under the LocalSystem account. If you set an account other than LocalSystem, you must also give the password to the user account. Don't worry, though: the account password will be encrypted and stored in a secure area of the registry. If you change the password for the account the service is using, you'll need to call `ChangeServiceConfig()` to reset the storage with the new password. We'll cover accounts and security contexts in much greater detail in Chapter 7.

Changing Service Configuration

To change the configuration of a service, you must first obtain a handle to it. As you know, `CreateService()` returns just such a handle, but it's rather more likely that you'll want to change a service's configuration some time after you installed it, when that handle has long since been closed. Instead, you can obtain one by using `OpenService()`, which is prototyped below:

```
SC_HANDLE OpenService(SC_HANDLE hSCManager,
                      LPCTSTR   lpServiceName,
                      DWORD     dwDesiredAccess);
```

`OpenService()` takes three arguments: the handle to the SCM you held onto earlier, the short service name, and the access rights that you want. The access rights flags are identical to those available in `CreateService()`.Just remember that, to be able to call `ChangeServiceConfig()`, you must make sure to specify at least the `SERVICE_CHANGE_CONFIG` or `GENERIC_WRITE` access flags.

The ChangeServiceConfig Function

To make a change to any of the configuration options of a service, you call `ChangeServiceConfig()`. Aside from a different ordering of the parameters, calls to this function look almost identical to calls to `CreateService()`:

```
BOOL ChangeServiceConfig(SC_HANDLE hService,
                         DWORD     dwServiceType,
                         DWORD     dwStartType,
                         DWORD     dwErrorControl,
                         LPCTSTR   lpBinaryPathName,
                         LPCTSTR   lpLoadOrderGroup,
                         LPDWORD   lpdwTagId,
                         LPCTSTR   lpDependencies,
                         LPCTSTR   lpServiceStartName,
                         LPCTSTR   lpPassword,
                         LPCTSTR   lpDisplayName);
```

The only real difference between this function and CreateService() is that it doesn't allow you to alter the service's short name. Typically, you'll call this function specifying new values for the configuration settings you want to change, but passing SERVICE_NO_CHANGE to the dwServiceType, dwStartType, and dwErrorControl parameters if you are not going to change them, and passing NULL to any other parameters you don't want to change. If this function fails, it returns FALSE and you can call GetLastError() to retrieve one of several possible error codes.

> **If you change the configuration of a service that is running, the changes do not take effect until the service is stopped, except for changes to lpDisplayName, which are effective immediately.**

Example of Changing a Service's Configuration

The following code sample contains Config(), a function for changing the start type of a service. Passing TRUE will make the service auto-start; calling it with a FALSE argument makes the service revert to demand start.

```
void Config(BOOL bAutostart)
{
   SC_HANDLE hSCM = 0;
   SC_HANDLE hService = 0;
   SC_LOCK hLock = 0;
   DWORD dwStartType = 0;
   BOOL bRet = FALSE;

   hSCM = OpenSCManager(NULL, NULL, GENERIC_READ | GENERIC_EXECUTE);
   if(!hSCM)
   {
      ErrorPrinter(_T("OpenSCManager"));
      return;
   }

   hLock = LockServiceDatabase(hSCM);
   if(!hLock)
   {
      _tprintf(_T("Service Configuration could not be changed\n"));
      CloseServiceHandle(hSCM);
      return;
   }

   hService = OpenService(hSCM, g_service, SERVICE_CHANGE_CONFIG);
   if(!hService)
   {
      ErrorPrinter(_T("OpenService"));
      UnlockServiceDatabase(hLock);
      CloseServiceHandle(hSCM);
      return;
   }
```

```
    dwStartType = (bAutostart) ? SERVICE_AUTO_START : SERVICE_DEMAND_START;
    bRet = ChangeServiceConfig(hService,
                               SERVICE_NO_CHANGE,
                               dwStartType,
                               SERVICE_NO_CHANGE,
                               NULL,
                               NULL,
                               NULL,
                               NULL,
                               NULL,
                               NULL,
                               NULL);

    if(bRet)
       _tprintf(_T("Changed Service Configuration Successfully\n"));
    else
       ErrorPrinter(_T("ChangeServiceConfig"));

    CloseServiceHandle(hService);
    UnlockServiceDatabase(hLock);
    CloseServiceHandle(hSCM);
    return;
}
```

You can see that the `Config()` function calls the `LockServiceDatabase()` API before it calls `ChangeServiceConfig()`. As I explained earlier, this serializes access to the service database and prevents any confusion that could arise from multiple processes attempting to modify it at the same time.

Removing a Service

When you remove a service, it is marked for deletion by the SCM. It is not actually deleted until all outstanding handles to the service are released (with `CloseServiceHandle()`) and the service is stopped. The SCM makes no effort to stop the service; it is content to wait until it stops or until the system next restarts, to remove it. Deleting a service means that its key in the registry, as well as all the subkeys beneath that key, are removed.

```
BOOL DeleteService(SC_HANDLE hService);
```

Deletion is accomplished using the `DeleteService()` function, which takes a handle to a service obtained previously by a call to `OpenService()` or `CreateService()`. The service must have been opened with appropriate rights to be capable of being removed. `DeleteService()` returns a `BOOL` that indicates success or failure. If the call fails, `GetLastError()` will tell you the reason.

Example of Removing a Service

Deletion is simple; let's look at an example that implements the `Remove()` function for the configuration program we began earlier:

```
void Remove()
{
   SC_HANDLE hSCM = NULL;
   SC_HANDLE hService = NULL;
   BOOL bSuccess = FALSE;

   hSCM = OpenSCManager(NULL, NULL, SC_MANAGER_CONNECT);
   if(!hSCM)
   {
      ErrorPrinter(_T("OpenSCManager"));
      return;
   }

   hService = OpenService(hSCM, g_service, DELETE);
   if(!hService)
   {
      ErrorPrinter(_T("OpenService"));
      CloseServiceHandle(hSCM);
      return;
   }

   bSuccess = DeleteService(hService);
   if(bSuccess)
      _tprintf(_T("%s Removed\n"), g_service);
   else
      ErrorPrinter(_T("DeleteService"));

   CloseServiceHandle(hService);
   CloseServiceHandle(hSCM);
   return;
}
```

As you can see, most of this function is error checking. It just gets a handle to the SCM, and then a handle to the service in question. If those two operations were successful, it marks the service for deletion, tidies up, and returns. What could be easier than that?

Querying Services

In addition to *changing* the configuration of services, there's a whole variety of functions that you can use to obtain specific information about particular services, or about services *en masse*. These functions are handy for providing status information to a user through the service's interface program.

Service Name Functions

The simplest of the service information functions, `GetServiceDisplayName()` and `GetServiceKeyName()`, simply obtain the display name from the short name, and the short name from the display name, respectively. The prototypes for these functions are given below, and they're extremely simple to use.

```
BOOL GetServiceDisplayName(
      SC_HANDLE hSCManager,
      LPCTSTR   lpServiceName, // The service's short name
      LPTSTR    lpDisplayName, // Empty buffer to receive the display name
      LPDWORD   lpcchBuffer);  // In: size of display name buffer
                               // Out: length of display name
```

```
BOOL GetServiceKeyName(
      SC_HANDLE hSCManager,
      LPCTSTR   lpDisplayName, // The service's display name
      LPTSTR    lpServiceName, // Empty buffer to receive the service name
      LPDWORD   lpcchBuffer);  // In: size of service name buffer
                               // Out: length of service name
```

These functions both return the desired name in an 'out' parameter buffer (parameter 3), along with the size of the buffer in parameter 4. If you haven't allocated enough space in the buffer to return the name, the function returns `FALSE` and the buffer comes back empty. The `lpcchBuffer` parameter will contain the actual number of characters in the requested name, minus the terminating `NULL`. So, just as you have to do with many Win32 API functions that return string buffers, you should allocate a reasonable amount of space that works in most cases, and then handle an insufficient buffer space error by calling the function again with the right buffer size. However, the service name is never larger than 256 (`MAX_SERVICE_NAME`) characters, so this value always works as an initial buffer size.

Example of Using GetServiceDisplayName

Here's another function to plug into the configuration program that we've been putting together during the course of the chapter. This one will handle the `-display` command line option by outputting the display name of the service.

```
void Display()
{
   SC_HANDLE hSCM = 0;
   BOOL bRet = FALSE;

   TCHAR lpBuf[MAX_SERVICE_NAME + 1]; // Long name can't be longer than this
   DWORD cchBuffer = MAX_SERVICE_NAME + 1;

   hSCM = OpenSCManager(NULL, NULL, GENERIC_READ);
   if(!hSCM)
   {
      ErrorPrinter(_T("OpenSCManager"));
      return;
   }
```

```
    bRet = GetServiceDisplayName(hSCM, g_service, lpBuf, &cchBuffer);
    if(bRet)
       _tprintf(_T("The display name is: %s\n"), lpBuf);
    else
       ErrorPrinter(_T("GetServiceDisplayName"));

    CloseServiceHandle(hSCM);
    return;
}
```

Retrieving Service Configuration Information

The `QueryServiceConfig()` function returns a structure that contains all the service configuration information we've looked at in the previous sections. This is the same configuration information that you set with calls to `CreateService()`, or change with `ChangeServiceConfig()`.

The function returns the current state of the *registry entries* for a service, not the configuration of the currently running state of the service. In other words, if the configuration has been changed with `ChangeServiceConfig()` but the service has not yet been restarted, `QueryServiceConfig()` will return the state the service will be in when it is restarted, with the exception of the display name, which is always up-to-date. The service handle passed as the first parameter must have at least `SERVICE_QUERY_CONFIG` access.

```
BOOL QueryServiceConfig(
      SC_HANDLE                hService,
      LPQUERY_SERVICE_CONFIG lpServiceConfig, // Address of config structure
      DWORD                    cbBufSize,       // Size of lpServiceConfig
      LPDWORD                  pcbBytesNeeded); // Address of variable for bytes
                                                //  needed if it fails


typedef struct _QUERY_SERVICE_CONFIG
{
   DWORD  dwServiceType;
   DWORD  dwStartType;
   DWORD  dwErrorControl;
   LPTSTR lpBinaryPathName;
   LPTSTR lpLoadOrderGroup;
   DWORD  dwTagId;
   LPTSTR lpDependencies;
   LPTSTR lpServiceStartName;
   LPTSTR lpDisplayName;
} QUERY_SERVICE_CONFIG, LPQUERY_SERVICE_CONFIG;
```

The only (slightly) tricky aspect of using `QueryServiceConfig()` is allocating the buffer size for the `LP_QUERY_SERVICE_CONFIG` structure. Since this function also retrieves the strings pointed to by the `LPTSTR` members of this structure (not just the pointers themselves), the function can fail for lack of space. If this happens, the buffer is returned empty and `pcbBytesNeeded` tells you the amount of memory needed for the function to succeed. You have the usual options: set the buffer to a reasonable size (say, 1024, or `_MAX_PATH`) and be prepared to call it again if it fails, or allocate the buffer to exactly the right size by letting the first call fail and to find out precisely what size to allocate next time around.

Example of Using QueryServiceConfig

Here's another function for your collection. Protected by the usual error checking, this one calls `QueryServiceConfig()` and then outputs all the information it returns:

```
void GetConfig()
{
   SC_HANDLE hSCM = 0;
   SC_HANDLE hService = 0;
   BOOL bRet = FALSE;

   LPQUERY_SERVICE_CONFIG pqscBuf = {0};
   DWORD dwBytesNeeded = 0;

   hSCM = OpenSCManager(NULL, NULL, GENERIC_READ);
   if(!hSCM)
   {
      ErrorPrinter(_T("OpenSCManager"));
      return;
   }

   hService = OpenService(hSCM, g_service, SERVICE_QUERY_CONFIG);
   if(!hService)
   {
      ErrorPrinter(_T("OpenService"));
      CloseServiceHandle(hSCM);
      return;
   }

   // Obtain the number of bytes needed
   bRet = QueryServiceConfig(hService, 0, 0, &dwBytesNeeded);

   // Allocate the proper size
   pqscBuf = (LPQUERY_SERVICE_CONFIG)LocalAlloc(LPTR, dwBytesNeeded);
   if(!pqscBuf)
   {
      ErrorPrinter(_T("LocalAlloc"), TRUE);
      CloseServiceHandle(hService);
      CloseServiceHandle(hSCM);
      return;
   }

   // Call with the right amount
   bRet = QueryServiceConfig(hService, pqscBuf,
                            dwBytesNeeded, &dwBytesNeeded);
   if(bRet)
   {
      _tcout << _T("Service Configuration for ") << g_service << endl;
      _tcout << _T("Display Name: ") << pqscBuf->lpDisplayName << endl;
      _tcout << _T("Type: 0x") << pqscBuf->dwServiceType << endl;
      _tcout << _T("Start Type: 0x") << pqscBuf->dwStartType << endl;
      _tcout << _T("Error Level: 0x") << pqscBuf->dwErrorControl << endl;
      _tcout << _T("Binary path: ") << pqscBuf->lpBinaryPathName << endl;
```

```
        _tcout << _T("Load Order Group: ") << pqscBuf->lpLoadOrderGroup << endl;
        _tcout << _T("Tag ID: ") << pqscBuf->dwTagId << endl;
        _tcout << _T("Dependencies: ") << endl;

        if(pqscBuf->lpDependencies)
        {
            TCHAR* pszDepend = 0;
            int i = 0;
            pszDepend = &pqscBuf->lpDependencies[i];
            while(*pszDepend != 0)
            {
                _tcout << pszDepend << endl;
                i += _tcslen(pszDepend) + 1;
                pszDepend = &pqscBuf->lpDependencies[i];
            }
        }
        _tcout << _T("Login Under: ") << pqscBuf->lpServiceStartName << endl;
    }
    else
        ErrorPrinter(_T("QueryServiceConfig"));

    LocalFree(pqscBuf);
    CloseServiceHandle(hService);
    CloseServiceHandle(hSCM);
    return;
}
```

A slightly unusual aspect of this code is the loop that enumerates through the list of dependencies, if the service has any. The `lpDependencies` member is actually just a character array, but it is doubly null-terminated, as you may recall from our earlier discussion about `CreateService()`. It contains as many null-terminated strings as there are dependencies in the dependency list. To walk the string and extract the individual entries, you have to go through it character by character, looking for the `NULL` that separates one substring from the next.

Retrieving Service Status

It's also possible to find out the *current* status of a service. To do so, you use the `QueryServiceStatus()` function, which returns a `SERVICE_STATUS` structure full of status information. This is the same `SERVICE_STATUS` information your services fill using `SetServiceStatus()` (remember Chapter 2?) whenever they change state.

It is important to note that this function simply asks the SCM to return the cached status information it has on the service. That is, it returns the cached entry in the service record list, which I discussed in the section on the service database earlier. Calling this function is *not* the same as calling `ControlService()` (discussed later) with a `SERVICE_CONTROL_INTERROGATE` request, which actually asks the service to update the SCM's cached status information with its current status. In other words, be aware that the information returned from `QueryServiceStatus()` can be out of sync with the real state of the service, if the service is in the middle of changing states when it is called. Once again, to use this function, you need to have opened the service handle with `SERVICE_QUERY_STATUS` access.

```
BOOL QueryServiceStatus(SC_HANDLE        hService,
                        LPSERVICE_STATUS lpServiceStatus);

typedef struct _SERVICE_STATUS
{
   DWORD dwServiceType;
   DWORD dwCurrentState;
   DWORD dwControlsAccepted;
   DWORD dwWin32ExitCode;
   DWORD dwServiceSpecificExitCode;
   DWORD dwCheckPoint;
   DWORD dwWaitHint;
} SERVICE_STATUS, *LPSERVICE_STATUS;
```

Example of Using QueryServiceStatus

The way this function works should come as no surprise to you – essentially, it just calls and displays the information returned by `QueryServiceStatus()`:

```
void Status()
{
   SC_HANDLE hSCM = 0;
   SC_HANDLE hService = 0;
   BOOL bRet = FALSE;

   SERVICE_STATUS ss;

   hSCM = OpenSCManager(NULL, NULL, GENERIC_READ);
   if(!hSCM)
   {
      ErrorPrinter(_T("OpenSCManager"));
      return;
   }

   hService = OpenService(hSCM, g_service, SERVICE_QUERY_STATUS);
   if(!hService)
   {
      ErrorPrinter(_T("OpenService"));
      CloseServiceHandle(hSCM);
      return;
   }

   bRet = QueryServiceStatus(hService, &ss);
   if(bRet)
   {
      _tcout << _T("Service Status for ") << g_service << endl;
      _tcout << _T("Type: 0x") << ss.dwServiceType << endl;
      _tcout << _T("Current State: 0x") << ss.dwCurrentState << endl;
      _tcout << _T("Controls Accepted: ") << ss.dwControlsAccepted << endl;
      _tcout << _T("Win32 Exit: ") << ss.dwWin32ExitCode << endl;
```

```
        _tcout << _T("Service Exit: ") << ss.dwServiceSpecificExitCode << endl;
        _tcout << _T("Checkpoint: 0x") << ss.dwCheckPoint << endl;
        _tcout << _T("WaitHint: 0x") << ss.dwWaitHint << endl;
    }
    else
        ErrorPrinter(_T("QueryServiceStatus"));

    CloseServiceHandle(hService);
    CloseServiceHandle(hSCM);
    return;
}
```

EnumServicesStatus

A further possibility is to walk the list of service record entries and gather the status information on every service in a particular SCM database; you can do this using the API function `EnumServicesStatus()`. The function allows you to specify the type and state of the services you want to look at. It returns an array of `ENUM_SERVICE_STATUS` structures filled with information about the service types you requested.

```
BOOL EnumServicesStatus(
  SC_HANDLE              hSCManager,
  DWORD                  dwServiceType,       // Type of service to enumerate
  DWORD                  dwServiceState,      // State of service to enumerate
  LPENUM_SERVICE_STATUS lpServices,      // Ptr to enum service status buffer
  DWORD                  cbBufSize,     // Size of enum service status buffer
  LPDWORD                pcbBytesNeeded,      // Pointer to bytes needed
  LPDWORD                lpServicesReturned, // Ptr to no of services returned
  LPDWORD                lpResumeHandle       // Pointer to next entry
);

typedef struct _ENUM_SERVICE_STATUS
{
   LPTSTR         lpServiceName;
   LPTSTR         lpDisplayName;
   SERVICE_STATUS ServiceStatus;
} ENUM_SERVICE_STATUS, *LPENUM_SERVICE_STATUS;
```

`dwServiceType` allows you to specify what type of services you wish to enumerate, and can be set to either `SERVICE_WIN32` or `SERVICE_DRIVER`. `dwServiceState` allows you to specify whether the function returns running services, stopped services, or both. It accepts `SERVICE_ACTIVE`, `SERVICE_INACTIVE`, or `SERVICE_STATE_ALL`.

The `lpServices` parameter points to an array of `ENUM_SERVICE_STATUS` structures, which in turn contain the short and long names of each service, as well as a `SERVICE_STATUS` structure that contains their state information from the service record list. `lpServicesReturned` returns the number of service entries this call has returned.

Now, this is where it gets tricky. Just like the buffer that's filled by `QueryServiceConfig()`, it's hit or miss as to whether the buffer has enough space. If the function returns `FALSE` and `GetLastError()` returns `ERROR_MORE_DATA`, then the next parameter (`pcbBytesNeeded`) returns the number of bytes required to return the *remaining* service status entries. Also, the last parameter, `lpResumeHandle`, returns the next service entry to be read when the follow-up call to `EnumServicesStatus()` is made.

The best way of dealing with this potentially messy situation is a technique that I'll demonstrate in code in the next section. The first time you call `EnumServicesStatus()`, pass in 0 for `lpResumeHandle`. If your call runs out of memory for the data it needs, then you set the `lpServices` buffer to the size returned in `pcbBytesNeeded`, and specify whatever `lpResumeHandle` value was received back from the previous call. Then call the function again. Love those Win32 data structures!

EnumDependentServices

Finally in this section, it's also possible to enumerate the services that depend on the specified service to run; in other words, the function lists the services that a given service must start *before*. This is a service-by-service operation, so it takes a handle to a particular service rather than to a SCM database. You can also specify whether you want the function to return running, stopped, or both types of dependent services.

```
BOOL EnumDependentServices(SC_HANDLE              hService,
                           DWORD                  dwServiceState,
                           LPENUM_SERVICE_STATUS  lpServices,
                           DWORD                  cbBufSize,
                           LPDWORD                pcbBytesNeeded,
                           LPDWORD                lpServicesReturned);
```

The function is practically identical to `EnumServicesStatus()` in its overall semantics. The `lpServices` array returns the services in reverse starting order, so the first entry in the array is the last to be started. This order allows you to stop the specified service properly, if necessary, by walking the list of its dependencies and closing each dependent service in turn.

Example of Using EnumDependentServices

This sample demonstrates the technique of making two calls that's required to use not only `EnumDependentServices()`, but also the `EnumServicesStatus()` function we discussed above. The first call, which is used to establish how big the `lpServices` buffer needs to be, also serves a check that there are any dependent services at all. If there aren't, there's no point in going any further.

```
void Dependencies()
{
   SC_HANDLE hSCM = 0;
   SC_HANDLE hService = 0;
   BOOL bRet = 0;
```

```
DWORD dwBytesNeeded = 0;
DWORD dwServicesReturned = 0;
LPENUM_SERVICE_STATUS pessBuf = {0};

hSCM = OpenSCManager(NULL, NULL, GENERIC_READ);
if(!hSCM)
{
   ErrorPrinter(_T("OpenSCManager"));
   return;
}

hService = OpenService(hSCM, g_service, SERVICE_ENUMERATE_DEPENDENTS);
if(!hService)
{
   ErrorPrinter(_T("OpenService"));
   CloseServiceHandle(hSCM);
   return;
}

// Find out how much to allocate
bRet = EnumDependentServices(hService,
                             SERVICE_STATE_ALL,
                             0,
                             0,
                             &dwBytesNeeded,
                             &dwServicesReturned);
if(dwBytesNeeded == 0)
{
   _tprintf(_T("No services are dependent on %s\n"), g_service);
   CloseServiceHandle(hService);
   CloseServiceHandle(hSCM);
   return;
}

// Allocate the proper size
pessBuf = (LPENUM_SERVICE_STATUS)LocalAlloc(LPTR, dwBytesNeeded);
if(!pessBuf)
{
   ErrorPrinter(_T("LocalAlloc"), TRUE);
   CloseServiceHandle(hService);
   CloseServiceHandle(hSCM);
   return;
}

bRet = EnumDependentServices(hService,
                             SERVICE_STATE_ALL,
                             pessBuf,
                             dwBytesNeeded,
                             &dwBytesNeeded,
                             &dwServicesReturned);
if(bRet)
{
   LPENUM_SERVICE_STATUS pess = 0;
   _tcout << _T("Services dependent on ") << g_service << endl;
```

```
        for(int i = 0 ; i < dwServicesReturned ; i++)
        {
           pess = &pessBuf[i];
           _tcout << pess->lpDisplayName << endl;
           _tcout << _T("   Current State: 0x");
           _tcout << pess->ServiceStatus.dwCurrentState << endl;
        }
     }
     else
        ErrorPrinter(_T("EnumDependentServices"));

     // Clean up
     LocalFree(pessBuf);
     CloseServiceHandle(hService);
     CloseServiceHandle(hSCM);
     return;
  }
```

NT 5.0 Changes to Configuration APIs

Windows NT 5.0 Beta 1 has revealed a couple of noteworthy additions to the services API. There are two new functions – `ChangeServiceConfig2()` and `QueryServiceConfig2()` – that slightly extend the configuration options.

ChangeServiceConfig2

The new `ChangeServiceConfig2()` function is aimed at providing both additional help information to the new administration tools, and a mechanism for greater reliability of services. In NT 5.0, the SCM is able to take a variety of actions when it detects that a service is no longer running but was not properly stopped. This API function allows the service to instruct the SCM on what action it should take if a service dies unexpectedly. It looks like this:

```
BOOL ChangeServiceConfig2(SC_HANDLE hService,
                          DWORD     dwInfoLevel,
                          LPVOID    lpInfo);
```

The first parameter is the kind of standard service handle that you're familiar with by now. However, you can set the second to either `SERVICE_CONFIG_DESCRIPTION` or `SERVICE_CONFIG_FAILURE_ACTIONS` to denote which of two new structures is being passed in the third parameter.

One option for that parameter, `SERVICE_DESCRIPTION`, contains a single member – a string of up to 1024 bytes – that explains the purpose of the service. This description will be used by the new Services MMC snap-in that will be available in NT 5.0. The other possibility for the third parameter is a `SERVICE_FAILURE_ACTIONS` structure, shown below:

```
typedef struct _SERVICE_FAILURE_ACTIONS
{
   DWORD       dwResetPeriod;
   LPTSTR      lpRebootMsg;
   LPTSTR      lpCommand;
   DWORD       cActions;
   SC_ACTION* lpsaActions;
} SERVICE_FAILURE_ACTIONS, *LPSERVICE_FAILURE_ACTIONS;
```

This structure is built to represent the action the SCM should take if a service terminates without reporting a status of `SERVICE_STOPPED` to the service controller. For details of its members and the values they can take, you should consult the online documentation.

QueryServiceConfig2

`QueryServiceConfig2()` simply allows you to query the SCM for the information that was set in the `ChangeServiceConfig2()` function. Its prototype looks like this:

```
BOOL QueryServiceConfig2(SC_HANDLE hService,
                         DWORD     dwInfoLevel,
                         LPBYTE    lpBuffer,
                         DWORD     cbBufSize,
                         LPDWORD   pcbBytesNeeded);
```

Used in the same fashion as the other 'query' functions we've looked at, `QueryServiceConfig2()` allows you to pass in a request for one of the two possible information types, and a buffer in which to hold it.

At the time of writing, I know of no other changes to the service API functions.

Service Control

As I mentioned at the beginning of the last chapter, a **service control executable** sends requests to a service asking it to start, stop, pause, continue, update the SCM with new status information, or respond in some specific way to a custom command.

Calls to service control functions almost always take place in a separate executable from the one the service is in. They can be part of a custom administration program, such as the SQL Service Manager, which is responsible for starting, stopping and pausing SQL Server-related services. Alternatively, service control functions can be called from inside a client. For instance, if a client of an RPC server service finds itself unable to connect, it can assume that the service is not yet started, and attempt to start the service itself.

Another scenario could be where one service needs to start another service on the fly. A service can start and control other services, itself acting as a service control program. Finally, service control operations can always be requested by the generic applications you're already familiar with, such as the Services applet.

What remains for us to discuss about service control is actually quite easy, not least because I talked about control handling *inside* the service at length in Chapter 2. Basically, service control boils down to two operations: 'starting' and 'everything else'. This is handled by two functions: `StartService()` and `ControlService()`.

Starting Services

You already know that Win32 services will be launched at system startup if they are of type `SERVICE_AUTO_START`. If a service is of type `SERVICE_DEMAND_START`, then it is started on the fly, when it is needed. A demand-start service can be started *implicitly* by being a dependency of another service; in that case it will be started by the system before the other service is started. A service can also be started *explicitly* through a control program using `StartService()`.

The StartService Function

The `StartService()` API is quite simple. All it really requires is a handle to a service that was obtained by a call to `OpenService()` or `CreateService()`, and opened with a `SERVICE_START` or `GENERIC_EXECUTE` access request. Calls to this function are non-blocking, as you are probably aware – at least unconsciously. They do not wait for the service to actually start, which as you know may take several seconds. `StartService()` returns as soon as it gets notified from the service control dispatcher (`StartServiceCtrlDispatcher()`) that the `ServiceMain()` thread for the service was successfully started. At this instant, the SCM sets the default status for the service to `SERVICE_START_PENDING`, the controls accepted to none, the checkpoint to 0, and the wait hint to 2. So, be aware that if your control program or client needs to know that the service is actually *running* before it starts making calls that depend on the service, it should call `QueryServiceStatus()` until it receives a status of `SERVICE_RUNNING`.

```
BOOL StartService(SC_HANDLE hService,
                  DWORD      dwNumServiceArgs,
                  LPCTSTR*   lpServiceArgVectors);
```

The other two parameters are there to enable the sending of startup arguments to the service. These arguments are the ones used as input parameters to `ServiceMain()` that the service gets the opportunity to parse out and use. When the array of argument strings (`lpServiceArgVectors`) comes into `ServiceMain()`, the first one is always the short name of the service. However, you *don't* have to send that from `StartService()` – it gets tacked on by the SCM later. So: either put `NULL` in the second and third parameters if you are not interested in sending arguments, or send just the special arguments; don't send the name as the first argument.

If the function fails, it can return a variety of error codes via `GetLastError()`, some of which may be interesting to you. They are summarized below, straight out of the Win32 API documentation.

`StartService()` **Error**	**Meaning**
ERROR_ACCESS_DENIED	The specified handle was not opened with `SERVICE_START` access.
ERROR_INVALID_HANDLE	The specified handle is invalid.

Table Continued on Following Page

StartService() **Error**	**Meaning**
ERROR_PATH_NOT_FOUND	The service binary file could not be found.
ERROR_SERVICE_ALREADY_RUNNING	The service is already running.
ERROR_SERVICE_DATABASE_LOCKED	The SCM database is locked.
ERROR_SERVICE_DEPENDENCY_DELETED	The service depends on a service that does not exist or has been marked for deletion.
ERROR_SERVICE_DEPENDENCY_FAIL	The service depends on another service that has failed to start.
ERROR_SERVICE_DISABLED	The service has been disabled.
ERROR_SERVICE_LOGON_FAILED	The service could not be logged on.
ERROR_SERVICE_MARKED_FOR_DELETE	The service has been marked for deletion.
ERROR_SERVICE_NO_THREAD	A thread could not be created for the service.
ERROR_SERVICE_REQUEST_TIMEOUT	The service did not respond to the start request in a timely fashion (i.e. within 2 minutes).

Example of Using StartService

This function demonstrates both of the activities I described above. After performing the simple task of calling `StartService()`, it goes into a loop waiting for the service to report the `SERVICE_RUNNING` state. If something goes wrong at this point, it outputs the contents of the `SERVICE_STATUS` structure as a diagnostic aid.

```
void Start()
{
   SC_HANDLE hSCM = 0;
   SC_HANDLE hService = 0;
   BOOL bRet = 0;
   DWORD dwOldCheck = 0;

   SERVICE_STATUS ss;

   hSCM = OpenSCManager(NULL, NULL, GENERIC_READ);
   if(!hSCM)
   {
      ErrorPrinter(_T("OpenSCManager"));
      return;
   }

   hService = OpenService(hSCM, g_service,
                              SERVICE_START | SERVICE_QUERY_STATUS);
```

```
if(!hService)
   {
      ErrorPrinter(_T("OpenService"));
      CloseServiceHandle(hSCM);
      return;
   }

   if(!StartService(hService, 0, NULL))
   {
      ErrorPrinter(_T("StartService"));
      CloseServiceHandle(hService);
      CloseServiceHandle(hSCM);
      return;
   }

   // Optionally, make sure service is running before continuing...
   bRet = QueryServiceStatus(hService, &ss);
   if(!bRet)
   {
      ErrorPrinter(_T("QueryServiceStatus"), TRUE);
      CloseServiceHandle(hService);
      CloseServiceHandle(hSCM);
      return;
   }

   while(SERVICE_RUNNING != ss.dwCurrentState)
   {
      dwOldCheck = ss.dwCheckPoint;
      Sleep(ss.dwWaitHint);

      bRet = QueryServiceStatus(hService, &ss);
      if(!bRet)
      {
         ErrorPrinter(_T("QueryServiceStatus"), TRUE);
         CloseServiceHandle(hService);
         CloseServiceHandle(hSCM);
         return;
      }

      // Service changed state or did not increment in time, so break
      if(dwOldCheck >= ss.dwCheckPoint)
         break;
   }

   if(SERVICE_RUNNING == ss.dwCurrentState)
      _tcout << g_service << _T(" started successfully.") << endl;
   else
   {
      _tcout << g_service << _T(" start unsuccessful: ") << endl;
      _tcout << _T("Current State: 0x") << ss.dwCurrentState << endl;
      _tcout << _T("Win32 Exit: ") << ss.dwWin32ExitCode << endl;
      _tcout << _T("Service Exit: ") << ss.dwServiceSpecificExitCode << endl;
      _tcout << _T("Checkpoint: 0x") << ss.dwCheckPoint << endl;
      _tcout << _T("WaitHint: 0x") << ss.dwWaitHint << endl;
   }
```

```
        CloseServiceHandle(hService);
        CloseServiceHandle(hSCM);
        return;
    }
```

Using StartService Inside a Service

It is possible to use `StartService()` to start a service from inside another service, with the restriction that the latter cannot call `StartService()` while it's initializing. In other words, a service can't call `StartService()` until it has fed back a status of `SERVICE_RUNNING` to the SCM.

The reason for this constraint is clear if you think about what you already know about the SCM and how it works. Starting a service causes the SCM to request the one and only lock on the services database (using `LockServicesDatabase()`). If a service is being started, then the SCM holds the lock. So, if the service tries to start another service *while it is starting*, what is it doing? It's asking the SCM to request the database lock and start another service. The call to `StartService()` inside the service blocks, waiting for the SCM to request another lock, which in turn blocks the starting of the outer service from completion.

Another important thing to do when starting one service from inside another is to ask, "Why am I doing this?" If the outer service depends on the inner service for its basic operations, then it should probably register the inner service as a dependency and let the SCM do the work of starting it at the right time. On the other hand, there may be scenarios where it makes sense to start one service inside another. For example, suppose that a rarely used function in the outer service requires another service to do some work. You might not want to start the inner service by default, because it may never get called and would just be tying up resources. In such a scenario, it may make sense just to start the inner service when and if the rare function is called.

As always, what you do will depend on how your services are used in your system. Just remember not to call `StartService()` from within a service whose status is not yet `SERVICE_RUNNING`.

Controlling Services

If `StartService()` handles the delivery of the service 'baby', then `ControlService()` handles everything from birth until death. Like `StartService()`, a call to `ControlService()` is not blocking. As soon as the `Handler()` function returns from its processing of the control request, the call is complete. Again, this doesn't mean the requested action has been *performed* by the service, just that the `Handler()` function has returned, presumably after notifying the service to do what was requested of it. If the control program needs to make sure that the request has actually been accomplished before continuing with its work, it should call `QueryServiceStatus()` until it gets the answer you're waiting for from the service.

The ControlService Function

Like `StartService()`, `ControlService()` operates on one of those perennial service handles obtained from `OpenService()` or `CreateService()`. Naturally, the handle has to be opened with the type of access you need for the operation that will be requested: `SERVICE_STOP`, `SERVICE_PAUSE_CONTINUE`, `SERVICE_INTERROGATE`, or `SERVICE_USER_DEFINED_CONTROL`. `GENERIC_EXECUTE` is also a handy access right to request, because it gives you all of the rights listed above.

The function also takes a DWORD that specifies the control you are requesting: SERVICE_CONTROL_STOP, SERVICE_CONTROL_PAUSE, SERVICE_CONTROL_CONTINUE, SERVICE_CONTROL_INTERROGATE, or any service-defined control code in the range 128-255. Remember that you *can't* send SERVICE_CONTROL_SHUTDOWN from this function – if you try, you'll get an ERROR_INVALID_SERVICE_CONTROL return code, because only the system can notify the service of a shutdown. Finally, ControlService() takes a pointer to a SERVICE_STATUS structure that gets filled by the SCM when the function returns. It reflects the most recent status given to the SCM by the service; in other words, it reflects the information in the SCM's service record entry for that service.

```
BOOL ControlService(SC_HANDLE        hService,
                    DWORD            dwControl,
                    LPSERVICE_STATUS lpServiceStatus);
```

The function returns a BOOL to indicate success or failure, and GetLastError() reveals the error code if it fails:

ControlService() **Error**	**Meaning**
ERROR_ACCESS_DENIED	The specified handle was not opened with the necessary access.
ERROR_DEPENDENT_SERVICES_RUNNING	The service cannot be stopped because other running services are dependent on it.
ERROR_INVALID_SERVICE_CONTROL	The requested control code is not valid, or it is unacceptable to the service.
ERROR_SERVICE_CANNOT_ACCEPT_CTRL	The requested control code cannot be sent to the service because the state of the service is STOPPED, START_PENDING, or STOP_PENDING.
ERROR_SERVICE_NOT_ACTIVE	The service has not been started.
ERROR_SERVICE_REQUEST_TIMEOUT	The service did not respond to the start request in a timely fashion.

One of the most interesting of these is ERROR_DEPENDENT_SERVICES_RUNNING, which informs you that it is not possible to stop the service because other services that depend upon it are running. This makes it obvious that stopping a service is not something you can just do willy-nilly. The only *safe* way to stop a service generically is to use EnumDependentServices() and stop the interdependent services in the proper order, as described in the last section. Of course, if it is your service and you already know the services that depend on it, you can just manually stop them in order yourself. If you attempt to use the Services applet to stop a service that other services depend on, you will be presented with a dialog that informs you of the other service(s) that will also be stopped, in the proper order.

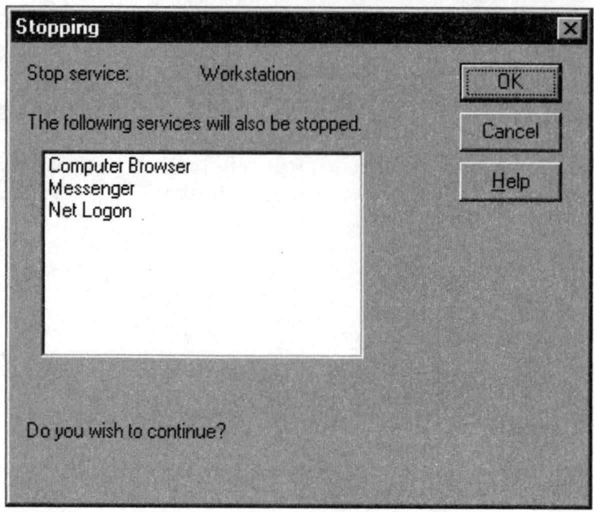

Example of Using ControlService

The final code sample in this chapter implements `Control()`, a function that wraps the `ControlService()` API and outputs the `SERVICE_STATUS` information that describes the state of the service after the requested control code has been issued.

```
void Control(DWORD dwControl)
{
   SC_HANDLE hSCM = 0;
   SC_HANDLE hService = 0;
   BOOL bRet = 0;

   SERVICE_STATUS ss;

   hSCM = OpenSCManager(NULL, NULL, GENERIC_READ);
   if(!hSCM)
   {
      ErrorPrinter(_T("OpenSCManager"));
      return;
   }

   hService = OpenService(hSCM, g_service, GENERIC_EXECUTE);
   if(!hService)
   {
      ErrorPrinter(_T("OpenService"));
      CloseServiceHandle(hSCM);
      return;
   }
```

```
    bRet = ControlService(hService, dwControl, &ss);
    if(bRet)
    {
        _tcout << _T("Service Status for ") << g_service << endl;
        _tcout << _T("Type: 0x") << ss.dwServiceType << endl;
        _tcout << _T("Current State: 0x") << ss.dwCurrentState << endl;
        _tcout << _T("Controls Accepted: ") << ss.dwControlsAccepted << endl;
        _tcout << _T("Win32 Exit: ") << ss.dwWin32ExitCode << endl;
        _tcout << _T("Service Exit: ") << ss.dwServiceSpecificExitCode << endl;
        _tcout << _T("Checkpoint: 0x") << ss.dwCheckPoint << endl;
        _tcout << _T("WaitHint: 0x") << ss.dwWaitHint << endl;
    }
    else
        ErrorPrinter(_T("ControlService"));

    CloseServiceHandle(hService);
    CloseServiceHandle(hSCM);
    return;
}
```

Sending User-Defined Control Requests

The request handler mechanism is a reasonable way to do simple inter-process communication between a client or control program and a service. The `Handler()` function is roughly akin to a Windows message handler for the service – it's there to handle standard 'messages', or control requests, as well as custom ones. If the client or control program needs to request that the service should go into some special state or change configuration in some way, a user-defined control request is a reasonable way to do it.

A word of caution, though. Remember our rules about how the `Handler()` thread and the service thread interact: any type of control request you send should be able to be handled quickly and communicated *asynchronously* to the service thread. A user-defined request is not the place to handle detailed processing work or client communications; it is only for a request the service thread can perform asynchronously – like a state change or a request to read some changed configuration data, for instance.

In Chapter 11, on administration tools, I'll show you how to use a user-defined request to notify the service that someone has dynamically changed a service configuration parameter from an administration program.

The SC.exe Tool

Now that I've shown you the programmatic ways to configure and control services, let's look at the easy way: the `SC.exe` tool, which comes as part of the Platform SDK. It is installed as part of the full setup, or it can be decompressed individually.

SC is a command line tool that allows you to perform any of the service control and configuration functions we have talked about in this chapter, as well as to feed back accurate status information about a service. SC is a testing and debugging tool (rather than an end-user tool like the Services applet or `Net.exe`), and it offers several distinct advantages:

- It allows you to work with services on different machines, which the Services control panel applet will not.
- It shows finer-grained status information than the Services applet or `Net.exe`, whose feedback on status is not usually very accurate (or even consistent). Both of these tools will show the status on a service that is hung in start pending, for instance, as running. If a service hangs while stop pending, Net reports it as running, and the Services applet reports it as stopped.
- SC returns the *full* status structure. It returns the checkpoint information, the wait hint, the 'controls accepted' information, and the exit codes.
- It allows you to do installation and configuration changes (with *all* the available options) from the command line rather than by writing registry or configuration code in an application. For development, this is more convenient than writing your own program for installation or configuration.
- It makes `ControlService()` and `StartService()` calls in non-blocking fashion, unlike the Services applet or `net`. This keeps with the asynchronous character of these calls and demonstrates how they would really look if called from code.
- You can write batch files that repeatedly call control functions on the service for testing, to make sure it behaves properly.

To reiterate, SC is for testing and playing around with a service, or for administrative scripting in a large systems management framework, not for shipping as the installation program for a commercial-grade service. When it comes time to ship your service, write an installation program and a control or administration program for it.

Using SC

SC supports *all* the options for controlling and configuring services, so understandably its command-line interface can be a bit tricky. Let's look at a help list of its commands, then I'll show you how to do a few common operations.

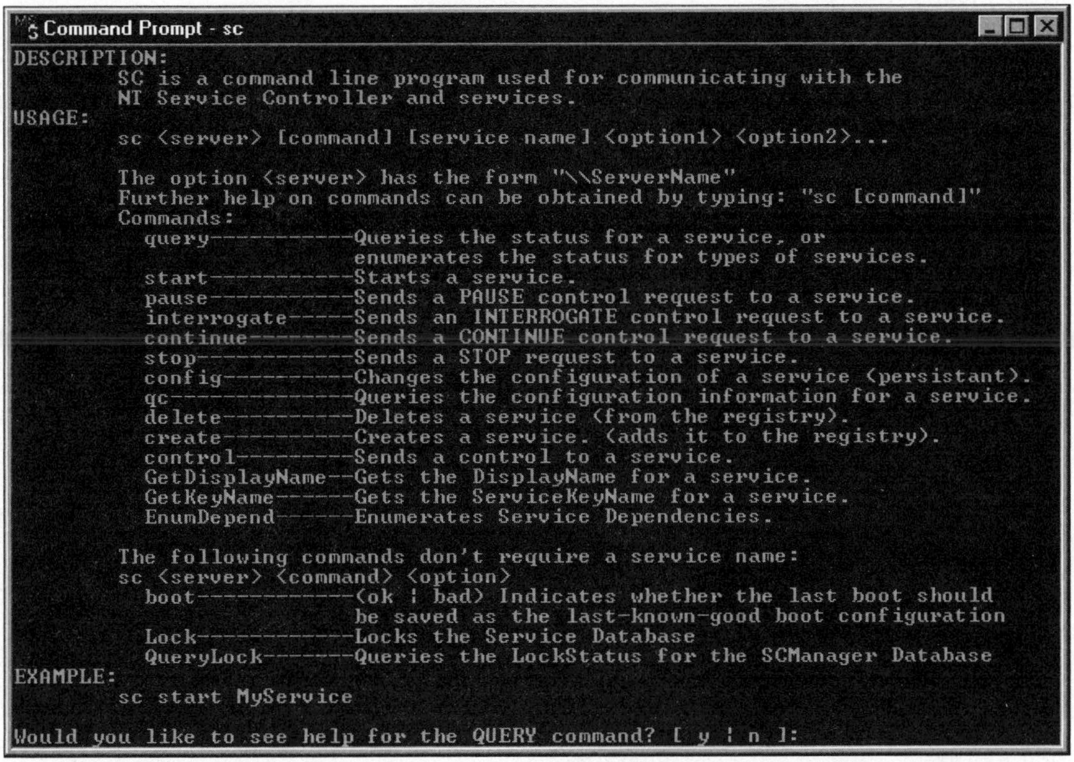

```
Command Prompt - sc
DESCRIPTION:
        SC is a command line program used for communicating with the
        NT Service Controller and services.
USAGE:
        sc <server> [command] [service name] <option1> <option2>...

        The option <server> has the form "\\ServerName"
        Further help on commands can be obtained by typing: "sc [command]"
        Commands:
          query-----------Queries the status for a service, or
                          enumerates the status for types of services.
          start-----------Starts a service.
          pause-----------Sends a PAUSE control request to a service.
          interrogate-----Sends an INTERROGATE control request to a service.
          continue--------Sends a CONTINUE control request to a service.
          stop------------Sends a STOP request to a service.
          config----------Changes the configuration of a service (persistant).
          qc--------------Queries the configuration information for a service.
          delete----------Deletes a service (from the registry).
          create----------Creates a service. (adds it to the registry).
          control---------Sends a control to a service.
          GetDisplayName--Gets the DisplayName for a service.
          GetKeyName------Gets the ServiceKeyName for a service.
          EnumDepend------Enumerates Service Dependencies.

        The following commands don't require a service name:
        sc <server> <command> <option>
          boot------------(ok | bad) Indicates whether the last boot should
                          be saved as the last-known-good boot configuration
          Lock------------Locks the Service Database
          QueryLock-------Queries the LockStatus for the SCManager Database
EXAMPLE:
        sc start MyService

Would you like to see help for the QUERY command? [ y | n ]:
```

As you can see, it has all the common operations. The usual way to call SC is simply to type something like:

```
SC \\servername query messenger
```

The server name is optional, and you can leave it out if you're running the command on the local machine. To receive more specific help on any command, simply type 'SC' followed by the command name, like so:

```
SC query
```

SC Examples

`create` is probably the most difficult of the commands, because there are so many possible parameters to `CreateService()`. Examine the screenshot below:

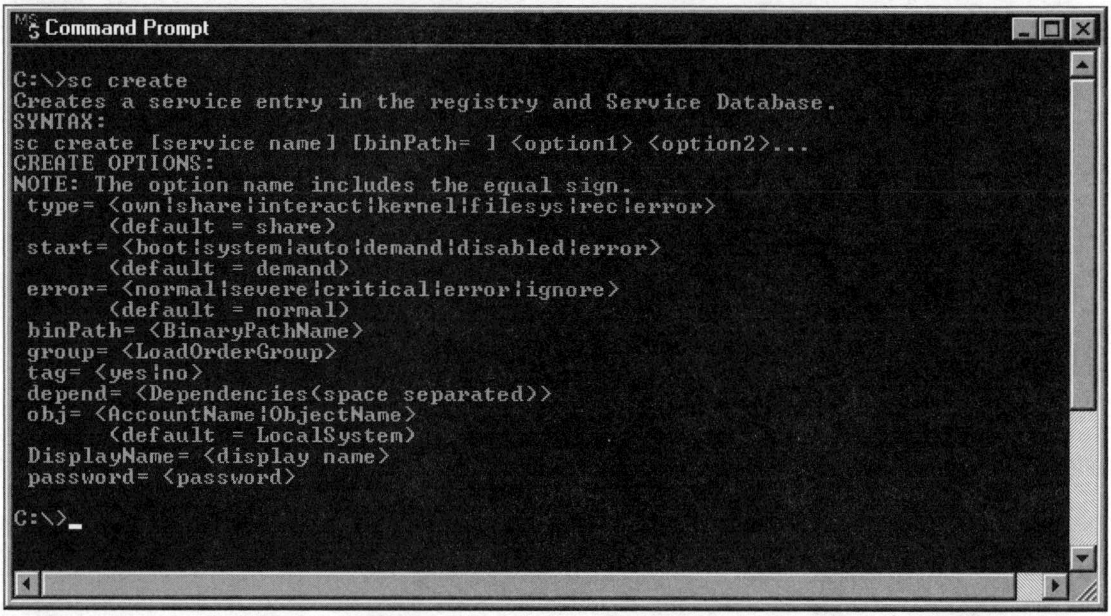

```
Command Prompt

C:\>sc create
Creates a service entry in the registry and Service Database.
SYNTAX:
sc create [service name] [binPath= ] <option1> <option2>...
CREATE OPTIONS:
NOTE: The option name includes the equal sign.
 type= <own|share|interact|kernel|filesys|rec|error>
       (default = share)
 start= <boot|system|auto|demand|disabled|error>
       (default = demand)
 error= <normal|severe|critical|error|ignore>
       (default = normal)
 binPath= <BinaryPathName>
 group= <LoadOrderGroup>
 tag= <yes|no>
 depend= <Dependencies(space separated)>
 obj= <AccountName|ObjectName>
       (default = LocalSystem)
 DisplayName= <display name>
 password= <password>

C:\>_
```

Here's an example of a **`create`** operation:

```
sc \\servername create MyService binpath= c:\winnt\system32\myservice.exe
type= own start= auto depend= "+TDI rpcss"
```

It's not too hard, once you've figured out that each optional parameter is separated by a space, and each parameter name must be *exactly* "`paramname= paramvalue`". The equals sign and the space between it and the value are important. You can also see that the only required parameter is the binary path of the executable. All the others have reasonable defaults or accept null values.

Once you've mastered `create`, the rest of the options are pretty easy. Here are some more examples for your enjoyment:

```
sc query type= service state= active
sc query myservice
sc enumdepend rpcss
sc config myservice start= auto
sc interrogate myservice
sc start myservice
sc stop myservice
```

Summary

Apart from a couple of fairly nasty structures, that wasn't too bad, was it? Now you know how to write a service, how to install it, and how to work with it. With that under your belt, we can move on into more interesting topics. In the next chapter, we'll develop a set of C++ classes that implement much of the plumbing code for services for us, as well as conveniently encapsulating the administration functions you just learned about.

At this point, we have covered most of the functions in the services API, with the exception of a couple that we'll need to look at when we come to discuss security in Chapter 7.

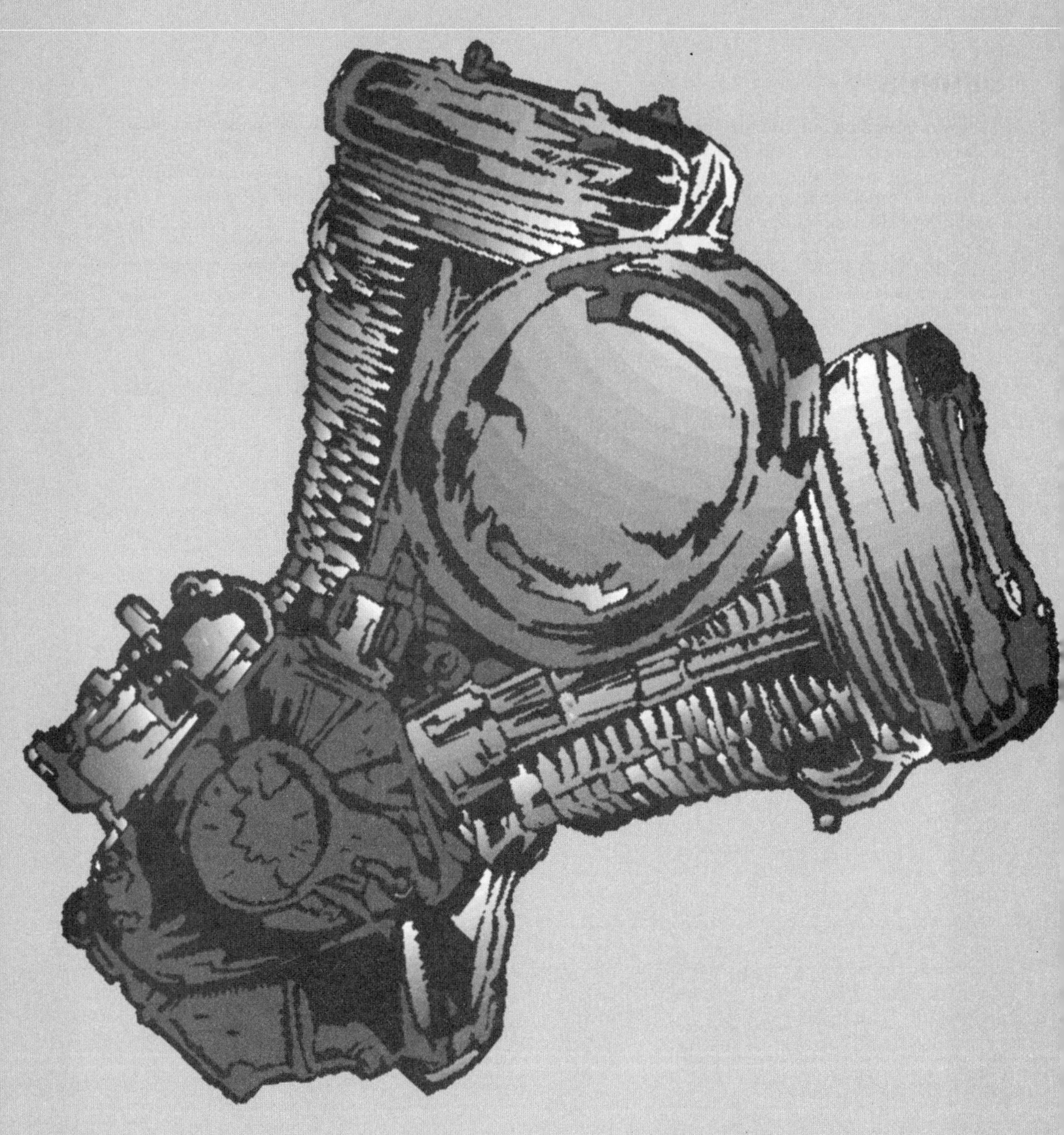

4

Building Supporting Service Classes

Now that you know the basics both of how to write a service and how to support its installation and configuration, let's focus on writing some C++ classes to support these operations. In the first part of this chapter, we'll develop classes to support the service executable, the service itself (remember that a single executable can contain more than one service), and the installation and configuration of the service. In the second part, we'll apply these tools to the simplest of the usage patterns we identified in Chapter 1: the Monitor.

The Service Class

Let's launch right into what we want our class to be able to do. A little consideration reveals a number of important design goals that we should place on our service class. In no particular order, we need to make sure that:

- Creating a service is almost as easy as adding a class
- The class handles easy problems easily, but scales up well for harder problems
- It allows more than one service to be used in a single service executable
- Generic Win32 API service calls are isolated from the user of the class, whenever possible
- The user of the class can focus on implementing the mechanism to do the work, rather than on handlers and other service plumbing
- Entry points into the class are clear to the user
- The class is flexible enough to be changed by the user when necessary

In writing my class, I've tried to make sure that it is generic enough to be applicable to a wide variety of situations, but that it be fairly easy to use straight off. As a result, it is probably over-engineered for very simple services, but it's robust enough to remain useful when the project scales up in size and complexity. In short, it's an implementation that tries to handle the simple case and the more complex case with the same tools. Those tools may be overkill for what the bare minimum implementation for a simple service might be, but they still work well even you're dealing with that situation.

Service Building Revisited

First, let's remind ourselves what we need to build a service. Do you remember our short list of things to do from Chapter 2? Here is a slightly rephrased version of that list to direct us as we write our class:

- Implement `main()`
- Connect the main thread to the SCM using `StartServiceCtrlDispatcher()`
- Implement `ServiceMain()` for each service in the process
- Set up a handler for each service in the process to handle requests for start/stop/pause/continue gracefully, and feed back status information to the SCM
- Implement a mechanism to do the work
- Exit gracefully when instructed

The implementation of `main()` won't be part of the class itself, but it is the necessary starting point for the service, so it's where you will *set up* the classes and call the necessary member functions and macros to get the service started. The rest of the work (the last five points above) takes place inside the C++ class (actually, inside a class you will write that *derives* from the class we'll develop here). I've called the service class `CService`.

C++ Coding Issues

One of the central issues that will drive how the design goals above get implemented in the class architecture is working around C++ conventions to make them fit with an API that was designed for use with C.

ServiceMain and Handler

The biggest issue is that two major APIs, `StartServiceCtrlDispatcher()` and `RegisterServiceCtrlHandler()`, both require pointers to functions that are used by the SCM as callbacks. This means that the functions whose pointers you pass must conform to the calling convention expected by the operating system, namely `WINAPI`. In short, this means that the functions that implement `ServiceMain()` and `Handler()` *cannot* be simple member functions of the service class, which of course you would like them to be for simplicity and encapsulation. This single implementation issue causes some strange (not to mention annoying) convolutions in the architecture. In order to work around it, I created the functions that implement `ServiceMain()` and `Handler()` as static member functions of the `CService` class.

Unlike regular class members, static members of a class do not have access to the implicit `this` pointer. So, in order for them to call other, non-static member functions, and access class data, we need to carry around an *explicit* version of the `this` pointer of the class we want to work on. My service class does this by creating a static `CService` pointer that's set to `this` in the constructor. The static member functions can then use the pointer to call the non-static member functions of the class. In the `CService` class, the static implementations immediately call true member functions that are implemented inside the class to do all the work.

Multiple Services

Unfortunately, this solution has side effects of its own. Having a single, static pointer to `this` means that there can be only one instance of the `CService` class at any time. This cuts us off from our design goal of being able to have multiple services in a single executable. In order to work around this, I made `CService` an abstract base class that doesn't implement either of the static functions for `ServiceMain()` or `Handler()`.

Consequently, to use `CService`, you must derive from it and use a couple of macros that implement the underlying static functions. To me, this seemed a tolerable trade-off, since you'd have to derive from the class to get real work done in any case. In order to have more than one service in the executable, you must derive another class from `CService` – that is, a second derivation with a different name. Again, this didn't seem like too much of a constraint, since it's most unlikely that you'd want two identical services in the process anyway.

Other Design Considerations

A couple of other design issues about the `CService` class are worth mentioning:

- How to handle communication between the main service thread and the dispatcher thread
- Data consistency

Inter-thread Communication Mechanism

You'll remember from Chapter 2 that one of the biggest issues we have to consider in service design is how to implement a proper communication mechanism between the thread that's running the service (on `ServiceMain()`) and the thread that's dispatching control messages received by the SCM. As I said then, the mechanism you choose depends mostly on what the service is doing.

In designing my service class, I chose to implement a communication mechanism based on Win32 kernel events. This might not be the optimal technique for all the possible usage patterns, but versatility was foremost in my mind, and it will never let you down performance-wise. Among the other options open to me, posting messages between threads was a possibility, but using events saved me from the chore of implementing a message pump for each thread. I could also have chosen to roll a variety of homemade mechanisms, such as global structures with locks, but this would have been more work than was really necessary.

In my scheme, the `Handler()` function sets an event when it receives an incoming control request, and there is a different event for each request type. The main service thread spawns a 'watcher' thread when it first launches, whose sole purpose is to wait for any one of these control events to signal. Because of the demands on thread functions, this will also be declared as static and call 'real' class members, in the same manner as the `Handler()` and `ServiceMain()` functions. When an event signals, the main service thread then calls one of the member functions that are implemented in the class derived from `CService` to perform the service-specific work that is required by the control request. For the derived class, this usually means setting a flag and waiting for the derived class's main processing loop to respond to the control.

For instance, if the control message is PAUSE, then Handler() sets the pause event. The watcher thread, which is waiting for *any* control event to get set, breaks out of its wait state and calls the OnPause() function of the class derived from CService. This function sends a PAUSE_PENDING status to the SCM, does whatever 'pause' means for the service in question, and waits for the service's main processing loop to signal another event indicating that it has accepted and processed the control request. After that, the pause function sets the service status to PAUSED. Thus, the watcher thread effectively blocks, waiting for the main service thread to signal that it has implemented the control, and then resumes waiting for events. However, the dispatcher thread can still receive notifications from the SCM, and the notification events will be serialized and handled properly by the watcher thread.

Consistency of Class Member Data

Another design consideration drives the architecture of the class: some parts of the code will execute on the main service thread (the ServiceMain() thread), and some parts will execute on the dispatcher thread that executes Handler(). So, access to member data that both threads touch will need to be protected. Furthermore, in my implementation, the third thread (the 'watcher' thread) also touches a few member variables of CService, so access to those members must be protected as well. I used the Interlocked...() family of functions and a class-scope critical section to keep data consistent.

Code Structure

It's about time we started going through the code for the CService class. As we do so, I'll keep pausing to clarify any sections that are unorthodox, contain subtleties, or have interesting effects.

CService Class Interface

Let's begin by looking at the interface of the CService class, which I placed in a file called cservice.h. As you can see from the listing below, it's a sizable class with a number of things going on. Give it a quick once-over, and then I'll describe how it works.

```
#define STATE_NO_CHANGE 0xffffffff
#define NUMEVENTS 4
#define MAX_SERVICE_LEN 256

//////////////////////////////////////////////////////////
// CService Class
//////////////////////////////////////////////////////////
/* Each service derives from this to do its own
   work. The application must instantiate the derived
   service class one and only one time. */
//////////////////////////////////////////////////////////
class CService
{
public:
   CService(LPCTSTR szName, LPCTSTR szDisplay, DWORD dwType);
   ~CService();

   DWORD   GetStatus()       { return m_dwState; }
   DWORD   GetControls()     { return m_dwControlsAccepted; }
   LPCTSTR GetName()         { return m_szName; }
   LPCTSTR GetDisplayName()  { return m_szDisplay; }
```

```
    // All derived class static ServiceMain functions are delegated to me
    void ServiceMainMember(DWORD argc, LPTSTR* argv,
                       LPHANDLER_FUNCTION pf, LPTHREAD_START_ROUTINE pfnWTP);

    // All derived class static handler functions are delegated to me
    void HandlerMember(DWORD dwControl);

protected:
    // Wraps calls to RegisterServiceCtrlHandler()
    bool SetupHandlerInside(LPHANDLER_FUNCTION lpHandlerProc);

    // Launches a thread to look for control requests
    virtual void LaunchWatcherThread(LPTHREAD_START_ROUTINE pfnWTP);
    virtual DWORD WatcherThreadMemberProc();

    void SetStatus(DWORD dwNewState,
                   DWORD dwNewCheckpoint = STATE_NO_CHANGE,
                   DWORD dwNewHint       = STATE_NO_CHANGE,
                   DWORD dwNewControls   = STATE_NO_CHANGE,
                   DWORD dwExitCode      = NO_ERROR,
                   DWORD dwSpecificExit  = 0);

    DWORD ErrorHandler(const TCHAR* pszFcn,
                       bool         bPrintEvent     = true,
                       bool         bRaiseException = true,
                       DWORD        dwErr           = GetLastError());

    void PrintEvent(const TCHAR* psz, bool bError = TRUE);

// Overrideables
protected:
   virtual void PreInit();     // If you override, call the base class version
   virtual void Init();
   virtual void DeInit();      // If you override, call the base class version
   virtual void ParseArgs(DWORD argc, LPTSTR* argv);
   virtual void OnPause();
   virtual void OnContinue();
   virtual void OnShutdown();
   virtual void HandleUserDefined(DWORD dwControl);

   virtual void Run() = 0;
   virtual void OnStop() = 0;

// Attributes
protected:
    CRITICAL_SECTION m_cs;

    // Status info
    SERVICE_STATUS_HANDLE m_hServiceStatus;
    DWORD m_dwState;
    DWORD m_dwControlsAccepted;
    DWORD m_dwCheckpoint;
    DWORD m_dwWaitHint;
```

```
    // Tracks state currently being worked on in Handler
    DWORD m_dwRequestedControl;

    // Control Events
    HANDLE m_hEvents[NUMEVENTS];
    HANDLE m_hWatcherThread;

    TCHAR m_szName[MAX_SERVICE_LEN + 1];
    TCHAR m_szDisplay[MAX_SERVICE_LEN + 1];
    DWORD m_dwType;

    enum EVENTS { STOP, PAUSE, CONTINUE, SHUTDOWN };
};
```

The very first things to notice here are the two pure virtual functions, `Run()` and `OnStop()`. They are *always* specific to the service in question – *you* must say how your service runs, and how it stops. These pure virtual functions are your reminder that you must derive a class from `CService` in order to use its functionality.

The next thing you'll notice is that there are several virtual functions that can be overridden by the derived class. In the implementation of `CService`, most of these are just empty stubs, but a couple of them have functionality in the base class, and you should call the base class versions if you choose to override them. I could have chosen to make the control request worker functions (`OnPause()`, `OnContinue()`, `OnShutdown()`, and `HandleUserDefined()`) pure virtual as well, but then the derived class would be forced to provide empty stubs for them even if it didn't accept all these controls. Instead, I chose to make them virtual functions with empty bodies. That way, they can be overridden if the particular service requires it, or do nothing otherwise.

Following on, the class contains two functions for implementing the 'watcher' thread that watches to see if any control requests have been made. `LaunchWatcherThread()` handles the creation of the watcher thread, while `WatcherThreadMemberProc()` is the function to which the static watcher thread function (which you'll see in *Derived Class Macros*, below) is delegated. The handle to this thread is stored in the member `m_hWatcherThread`.

`m_hEvents` is an array of handles to the different kernel events that get signaled by `Handler()` when a control request comes in. Currently, there are four events, one each for `STOP`, `PAUSE`, `CONTINUE` and `SHUTDOWN`. A simple enumeration, `EVENTS`, keeps their array positions straight so that you can refer to them by name.

Finally (at least for the purposes of this quick overview), there are also functions for doing boilerplate work like updating status with the SCM (`SetStatus()`), handling error conditions, and outputting strings to the NT event log.

Derived Class Macros

As I mentioned in *C++ Coding Issues*, there are some inelegant kludges that need to be implemented in order for `CService` to work as a class, and yet still be able to pass pointers to its versions of `Handler()` and `ServiceMain()`, and to the function that runs on the watcher thread. You'll remember that to work, these must all be static functions. Causing additional trouble is the fact that each static function needs a separate implementation and a separate name, in case we want to derive from `CService` multiple times to have more than one service in our process.

To handle these messy details, I decided to encapsulate the work in two macros, `DECLARE_SERVICE()` and `IMPLEMENT_SERVICE()`. The former should be put inside the declaration of the class derived from `CService`. It adds the static declarations for the three required functions, as well as a pointer to the static `m_pThis` member, which will hold the derived class pointer. The implementation of `DECLARE_SERVICE()` is shown below, and should be placed in the file that holds the `CService` class definition:

```
#define DECLARE_SERVICE(class_name, service_name) \
public: \
    static class_name##* m_pThis; \
    static void WINAPI service_name##Main(DWORD argc, LPTSTR* argv); \
    static void WINAPI service_name##Handler(DWORD dwControl); \
    static DWORD WINAPI service_name##WatcherThreadProc(LPVOID lpParameter);
```

As input, the macro takes the name of the class you're declaring, and the 'official' name of the service – that is, its short name. Using that information, it adds static function declarations that are unique to the new derived class. For example, `CMyService`, derived from `CService`, might implement a service named `MyService`. This macro would create static functions for the service named `MyServiceMain()`, `MyServiceHandler()`, and `MyServiceWatcherThreadProc()`.

For the implementations of these functions, there is a macro called `IMPLEMENT_SERVICE`, which should be used at the top of the CPP file for your derived class. Here's its definition, which of course must also be added to the `CService` definition file.

```
#define IMPLEMENT_SERVICE(class_name, service_name) \
class_name##* class_name::m_pThis = NULL; \
void WINAPI class_name::service_name##Main(DWORD argc, LPTSTR* argv) \
{ \
    m_pThis->ServiceMainMember(argc, argv, \
                    (LPHANDLER_FUNCTION)service_name##Handler, \
                    (LPTHREAD_START_ROUTINE)service_name##WatcherThreadProc); \
} \
void WINAPI class_name::service_name##Handler(DWORD dwControl) \
{ \
    m_pThis->HandlerMember(dwControl); \
} \
DWORD WINAPI class_name::service_name##WatcherThreadProc(LPVOID lpParameter)
\
{ \
    return m_pThis->WatcherThreadMemberProc(); \
}
```

As we discussed earlier, the implementation of the static `MyServiceMain()` function calls the base class `ServiceMainMember()`, passing in the function pointers for both `MyServiceHandler()` and `MyServiceWatcherThreadProc()`. This is so that `ServiceMainMember()` can do the work of registering the handler and starting the watcher thread.

Both `MyServiceHandler()` and `MyServiceWatcherThreadProc()` simply call the non-static class member functions that have the real functionality in them, both of which are implemented in the `CService` base class.

My final trio of macros won't actually come into their own until later in the chapter, but I present them here to complete the listing of cservice.h. BEGIN_SERVICE_MAP, SERVICE_MAP_ENTRY(), and END_SERVICE_MAP form a convenient way to simplify the procedure of creating the array of SERVICE_TABLE_ENTRY structures and calling StartServiceCtrlDispatcher() that's common to every service executable's main() function. You'll see the macros in action when we come to implement the Monitor pattern a little later on.

```
// For implementing a service process
#define BEGIN_SERVICE_MAP \
SERVICE_TABLE_ENTRY svcTable[] = {

#define SERVICE_MAP_ENTRY(class_name, service_name) \
{_T(#service_name), class_name::service_name##Main},

#define END_SERVICE_MAP \
{NULL, NULL}}; \
StartServiceCtrlDispatcher(svcTable);
```

CService Class Implementation

Hopefully, that gives you a good start for understanding what's really going on in CService, and what you'll have to do in the classes you derive from it to make them work. We'll go through the implementation itself in some detail below, but keep a couple of things in mind as we do so. First, all static functions delegate their work to true class member functions; the static functions merely serve as stubs to humor the operating system on the callback problem. I have tried to hide these static functions in macros so that you don't have to worry about doing too much with them. Second, all work starts and ends in ServiceMainMember(), which handles all service thread processing for the service. Before we get to the code, here's a quick sketch of the flow of calls in the classes:

```
Thread 0
  main()
    CDerivedService created
    Macros set up SERVICE_TABLE_ENTRY and invoke StartServiceCtrlDispatcher()

    Thread 1
      CDerivedService::DerivedServiceMain()
        CService::ServiceMainMember()
          CService::PreInit() (and/or override)
          CService::SetupHandlerInside()
            RegisterServiceCtrlHandler()
                        (registers CDerivedService::DerivedServiceHandler())
              CService::HandlerMember()
          CDerivedService::ParseArgs()
          CDerivedService::Init() (or override)
          CService::LaunchWatcherThread()

          Thread 2
            CDerivedService::WatcherThreadProc()
              CService::WatcherThreadMemberProc()
                CDerivedService::OnStop, OnPause, OnContinue, OnShutdown

          CDerivedService::Run()
          CService::DeInit (and/or override)
```

Now, let's move through the code in the same order as it is run in a real, starting service.

CService Construction

First things first. The constructor accepts three parameters: the short name of the service, the display name, and the type of service it is. Of course, the function that calls the constructor (`main()`) will actually create an object of the *derived* class, but that will delegate construction duties to the base class.

```
#include "precomp.h"
#include "cservice.h"

CService::CService(LPCTSTR szName, LPCTSTR szDisplay, DWORD dwType)
                                                    : m_dwType(dwType)
{
   m_hServiceStatus = NULL;
   m_dwRequestedControl = 0;

   // Control Events
   m_hWatcherThread = NULL;

   m_dwState = 0;
   m_dwControlsAccepted = 0;
   m_dwCheckpoint = 0;
   m_dwWaitHint = 0;

   // Initialize event handles to NULL
   for(int i = 0 ; i < NUMEVENTS ; i++)
      m_hEvents[i] = NULL;

   // Copy string names
   _tcscpy(m_szName, szName);
   _tcscpy(m_szDisplay, szDisplay);

   // Set up class critical section
   InitializeCriticalSection(&m_cs);
}
```

In this function, variables are initialized and the kernel event array members are set to `NULL`. Also, the critical section for the class is initialized. Once the constructor has been called, you have a functional class.

The next thing that happens is that the service control dispatcher gets started in `main()` (you'll see this in detail when we discuss implementing a service later in the chapter), which starts the *derived* class's `MyServiceMain()` function. In turn, this immediately calls the base class `ServiceMainMember()` function, shown next.

ServiceMainMember

`ServiceMainMember()` is where all the service's work starts and finishes. As you can imagine, it's a pretty busy function, so let's look at it first, and then discuss it.

```
void CService::ServiceMainMember(DWORD argc, LPTSTR* argv,
                        LPHANDLER_FUNCTION pf, LPTHREAD_START_ROUTINE pfnWTP)
{
   DWORD dwErr = 0;

#ifndef _DEBUG
   __try
   {
#endif

      PreInit();
      SetupHandlerInside(pf);
      ParseArgs(argc, argv);
      LaunchWatcherThread(pfnWTP);
      Init();
      Run();

#ifndef _DEBUG
   }
   __except(dwErr = GetExceptionCode(), EXCEPTION_EXECUTE_HANDLER)
   {
      if(m_hServiceStatus)
         SetStatus(SERVICE_STOPPED, 0, 0, 0, dwErr, 0);
   }
#endif

   DeInit();
   SetStatus(SERVICE_STOPPED, 0, 0, 0, dwErr, 0);
}
```

This function accepts the original service arguments as parameters, as well as pointers to the static functions (in the derived class) that implement `Handler()` and `WatcherThreadProc()`. We'll need these later in order to start those threads.

Notice that `ServiceMainMember()` is also the root of all exception handling in the service. Since pretty much *all* other functions get spawned from this one, it is the logical place to implement this feature. I used Win32 structured exception handling, because it is a more natural fit in this scenario than native C++ exception handling. All of the important functions for initializing and running the service are placed inside a `try` block. If any of those functions raises an exception, the handler in the `except` block gets the error code and then stops the service, sending that code in the final `SetStatus()` call. Any function in the derived or base class can raise an exception on any error it detects simply by calling `ErrorHandler()` with the `bRaiseException` parameter set to `true`. (You'll see how this works when we talk about `ErrorHandler()` a little later on.)

Whether you should raise an exception is usually determined by the question of whether the service can continue functioning normally if a particular error occurs. If it can't, you should raise an exception. Also, notice that the `try` and `except` blocks are sectioned off and taken out if the service is in debug mode. This is because you won't be able to break into the service and debug it using `DebugBreak()` if exception handlers are active – they even catch user breakpoints!

We'll be looking at the use of `DebugBreak()` *and many other aspects of debugging services in Chapter 10.*

We're going to go through each of the individual functions called by `ServiceMainMember()` separately, in order. Notice, though, that the final call is always to send notice to the SCM that the service has stopped. This should always be the last call in any `ServiceMain()` implementation, because calls after it just don't get executed – the `ServiceMain()` thread is terminated.

PreInit

The first call that `ServiceMainMember()` makes is to `PreInit()`, which is where any initialization that needs to occur *before* the service control handler is registered should go. Since the four control events that `Handler()` will signal are needed before it can be launched, this is a natural place to initialize these events.

```
void CService::PreInit()
{
   // Initialize Events
   for(int i = 0 ; i < NUMEVENTS ; i++)
   {
      m_hEvents[i] = CreateEvent(NULL, FALSE, FALSE, NULL);
      if(!m_hEvents[i])
         ErrorHandler(_T("CreateEvent"));
   }
}
```

`PreInit()` can also be overridden by the derived class in order to perform any custom initialization of this kind that you need – just be sure to call the base class function inside your `PreInit()` override.

SetupHandlerInside

Next, `ServiceMainMember()` calls `SetupHandlerInside()`, which does the work of calling `RegisterServiceCtrlHandler()` for the service. `SetupHandlerInside()` is supplied with the function pointer that was passed into `ServiceMainMember()` from the derived class, thanks to our helpful `IMPLEMENT_SERVICE()` macro.

```
// Register the control handler for the service
bool CService::SetupHandlerInside(LPHANDLER_FUNCTION lpHandlerProc)
{
   m_hServiceStatus = RegisterServiceCtrlHandler(m_szName, lpHandlerProc);
   if(!m_hServiceStatus)
   {
      ErrorHandler(_T("RegisterServiceCtrlHandler"));
      return false;
   }

   SetStatus(SERVICE_START_PENDING, 1, 5000);
   return true;
}
```

The function also sends a quick 'pending' status update to the SCM, just to keep it from timing out while the service is doing additional initialization work.

LaunchWatcherThread

After ServiceMainMember() calls ParseArgs(), which may or may not have any work to do, depending on whether the derived class has implemented a function to parse out special service arguments, the watcher thread is launched with a call to LaunchWatcherThread(). Like ServiceMain() and Handler(), each derived class needs its own watcher thread implementation, so this function takes a pointer to the derived-class-specific MyServiceWatcherThreadProc() that was originally set up in the IMPLEMENT_SERVICE macro, and whose pointer was passed into ServiceMainMember() as the fourth parameter.

```
void CService::LaunchWatcherThread(LPTHREAD_START_ROUTINE pfnWTP)
{
   DWORD tid = 0;

   m_hWatcherThread = (HANDLE)_beginthreadex(0, 0,
               (unsigned (WINAPI*)(void*))pfnWTP, 0, 0, (unsigned int*)&tid);
   if(!m_hWatcherThread)
      ErrorHandler(_T("_beginthreadex"));
}
```

This function simply starts the thread using the CRT-safe _beginthreadex() function. The rather unpleasant casts in the call are just there to cast the parameters to the proper types.

Finishing ServiceMainMember

We're finally getting to the end of initialization. The next function that ServiceMainMember() calls is Init(), which has no base class implementation, and is there for your derived class to use as it wishes. Any initialization that needs doing right before the service starts should be done here, and there is obviously no need to call the base class implementation if you choose to override Init().

Last, ServiceMainMember() calls Run(), which is implemented solely by your derived class. We'll look at a 'real' Run() function later in the chapter, but just know for now that the processing of ServiceMainMember() stops right here until the service stops (that is, Run() terminates).

HandlerMember

Aside from sitting in Run() doing its work, what else does your service do? It handles requests for stop, pause, continue, etc., right? Since we registered a derived class static function with the SCM as the service control handler, that function, which just calls the base class member function HandlerMember(), gets called by the dispatcher (main()) thread whenever a control request arrives.

```
void CService::HandlerMember(DWORD dwControl)
{
   // Keep an additional control request of the same type
   // from coming in when you're already handling it
   if(m_dwRequestedControl == dwControl)
      return;

   switch(dwControl)
   {
   case SERVICE_CONTROL_STOP:
      m_dwRequestedControl = dwControl;
```

```
            // Notify the service to stop...
            SetEvent(m_hEvents[STOP]);
            break;

        case SERVICE_CONTROL_PAUSE:
            m_dwRequestedControl = dwControl;

            // Notify the service to pause...
            SetEvent(m_hEvents[PAUSE]);
            break;

        case SERVICE_CONTROL_CONTINUE:
            if(GetStatus() != SERVICE_RUNNING)
            {
                m_dwRequestedControl = dwControl;

                // Notify the service to continue...
                SetEvent(m_hEvents[CONTINUE]);
            }
            break;

        case SERVICE_CONTROL_SHUTDOWN:
            m_dwRequestedControl = dwControl;

            SetEvent(m_hEvents[SHUTDOWN]);
            break;

        case SERVICE_CONTROL_INTERROGATE:
            // Return current status on interrogation
            SetStatus(GetStatus());
            break;

        default: // User Defined
            m_dwRequestedControl = dwControl;
            HandleUserDefined(dwControl);
        }
}
```

For each of the common request types, `HandlerMember()` just signals one of the events in the event array and updates the `m_dwRequestedControl` member with the type of request it is working on. If the request from the SCM is a simple interrogation, then the function returns current status information.

The default case is a user-defined control request. If an 'uncaught' request type comes in, the base class assumes that the request is defined and implemented by the derived class, so it doesn't touch it. Instead, it sends it through to `HandleUserDefined()`, which can be overridden in the derived class to check the control type value and act accordingly. This mechanism also works if there are multiple user-defined types – the overridden `HandleUserDefined()` would simply switch on the `dwControl` parameter and do whatever work it needed for each custom type.

The Watcher Thread

Of course, the real work of handling control requests happens in the watcher thread.

```
DWORD CService::WatcherThreadMemberProc()
{
   DWORD dwWait = 0;
   bool bControlWait = true;

   // Wait for any events to signal
   while(bControlWait)
   {
     dwWait = WaitForMultipleObjects(NUMEVENTS, m_hEvents, FALSE, INFINITE);

      switch(dwWait - WAIT_OBJECT_0)
      {
      case STOP:
         OnStop();
         bControlWait = false;
         break;

      case PAUSE:
         OnPause();
         ResetEvent(m_hEvents[PAUSE]);
         break;

      case CONTINUE:
         OnContinue();
         ResetEvent(m_hEvents[CONTINUE]);
         break;

      case SHUTDOWN:
         OnShutdown();
         bControlWait = false;
         break;
      }
   }
   return 0;
}
```

The watcher thread just does a `WaitForMultipleObjects()` call, waiting for any of the events in the `m_hEvents` array to signal. If any of them do, it determines which one signaled, and calls the appropriate function (which will be implemented by the *derived* class) to do whatever work the service requires to handle the request. The watcher thread blocks on the `OnStop()`, `OnPause()`, `OnContinue()`, or `OnShutdown()` call waiting for it to return. This can take as little or as much time as the service needs.

The great thing about this mechanism, and the reason why it is designed this way, is that the *control handler* shouldn't block waiting for the service to implement the control. Using the 'watcher' mechanism, the control handler just sets an event and then becomes available to the SCM again. The watcher thread is the one that blocks waiting for the service to act on a request. Implementing control handling in this fashion goes a long way towards solving most of the handler implementation problems I outlined at the end of Chapter 2.

Lastly, notice that the watcher loops back around to service more requests if the control it handles is 'pause' or 'continue'. If it handles stop or shutdown, then presumably the service is terminating and no more control requests will be sent, so the watcher thread can terminate as well. Later on, in the *Monitor* section, I'll show you a real life example of implementing `OnStop()`, `OnPause()`, and `OnContinue()`.

SetStatus

I've already made a couple of calls to the `SetStatus()` function in the code I've presented so far. It simply sends a status update to the SCM by preparing a `SERVICE_STATUS` structure and wrapping up the call to `SetServiceStatus()`.

```
void CService::SetStatus(DWORD dwNewState, DWORD dwNewCheckpoint,
                         DWORD dwNewHint,  DWORD dwNewControls,
                         DWORD dwExitCode, DWORD dwSpecificExit)
{
   // The only state that can set Exit Codes is STOPPED
   // Fix if necessary, just in case not set properly.
   if(dwNewState != SERVICE_STOPPED)
   {
      dwExitCode = S_OK;
      dwSpecificExit = 0;
   }

   // Only pending states can set checkpoints or wait hints,
   // and pending states *must* set wait hints
   if(dwNewState == SERVICE_STOPPED ||
            dwNewState == SERVICE_PAUSED || dwNewState ==SERVICE_RUNNING)
   {
      // Requires hint and checkpoint == 0
      // Fix it so that NO_CHANGE from previous state doesn't cause nonzero
      dwNewHint = 0;
      dwNewCheckpoint = 0;
   }
   else
   {
      // Requires hint and checkpoint != 0
      if(dwNewHint <= 0 || dwNewCheckpoint <=0)
      {
         ErrorHandler(_T("CService::SetStatus:
            Pending statuses require a hint and checkpoint"), true, true,0);
      }
   }

   // Function can be called by multiple threads - protect member data
   EnterCriticalSection(&m_cs);

   // Alter states if changing
   m_dwState = dwNewState;

   if(dwNewCheckpoint != STATE_NO_CHANGE)
      m_dwCheckpoint = dwNewCheckpoint;

   if(dwNewHint != STATE_NO_CHANGE)
      m_dwWaitHint = dwNewHint;
```

```
    if(dwNewControls != STATE_NO_CHANGE)
       m_dwControlsAccepted = dwNewControls;

    SERVICE_STATUS ss = { m_dwType, m_dwState, m_dwControlsAccepted,
                          dwExitCode, dwSpecificExit,
                          m_dwCheckpoint, m_dwWaitHint };

    LeaveCriticalSection(&m_cs);

    if(!SetServiceStatus(m_hServiceStatus, &ss))
       ErrorHandler(_T("SetServiceStatus"));
}
```

This function takes a variety of optional parameters, but the only one that's really required is dwNewState, to set the service's new state. The other parameters' defaults are supplied in the prototype, reprinted below:

```
    void SetStatus(DWORD dwNewState,
                   DWORD dwNewCheckpoint = STATE_NO_CHANGE,
                   DWORD dwNewHint       = STATE_NO_CHANGE,
                   DWORD dwNewControls   = STATE_NO_CHANGE,
                   DWORD dwExitCode      = NO_ERROR,
                   DWORD dwSpecificExit  = 0);
```

The function also self-corrects some common oversights that you might make when setting status information. First, only STOPPED statuses can have a non-zero dwExitCode or dwSpecificExit. These will be automatically set properly if the state is not STOPPED. Other problems compensated for include having a non-zero wait hint or checkpoint on a STOPPED, PAUSED, or RUNNING state, or a zero wait hint or checkpoint on a PENDING state.

The reason for the self-correcting work that this wrapper function does is to make setting statuses as easy as possible. It also keeps you from having to remember to clear the wait hint and checkpoint out when sending, for instance, a STOPPED status after a PENDING status – you can just send SetStatus(SERVICE_STOPPED) and let the defaults for the rest of the members kick in as STATE_NO_CHANGE, safe in the knowledge that they will be cleared and corrected by the wrapper.

Since this function could conceivably be called by any of the three threads (the watcher, ServiceMain(), or the dispatcher), it protects changes to the class members using the class critical section.

ErrorHandler

The ErrorHandler() function takes care of all errors in the service, printing them out to the event log if you require it and/or raising an exception to terminate the service process if you indicate that the error is severe enough to do so by passing true to the bRaiseException parameter. This exception is then caught by the exception handler in ServiceMainMember() and the service is stopped, as we discussed earlier.

If you don't pass in an error code in the fourth parameter, dwErr defaults to the return value of GetLastError(). Furthermore, if you pass in zero for this parameter, it is assumed that you have raised a custom, service-specific error. In that case, it will just print out the error string you send and avoid looking up the error message. You can still raise an exception, though.

```
DWORD CService::ErrorHandler(const TCHAR* psz, bool bPrintEvent,
                             bool bRaiseException, DWORD dwErr)
{
   LPVOID lpvMsgBuf;
   TCHAR sz[512 + 50];                    // Max message len + pre-string

   if(dwErr != 0)
   {
      if(!FormatMessage(
       FORMAT_MESSAGE_FROM_SYSTEM | FORMAT_MESSAGE_ALLOCATE_BUFFER, 0,dwErr,
       MAKELANGID(LANG_NEUTRAL, SUBLANG_DEFAULT), (LPTSTR)&lpvMsgBuf, 0, 0))
      {
         wsprintf(sz, _T("%s failed: Unknown error %lu"), psz, dwErr);
      }
      else
      {
         wsprintf(sz, _T("%s failed: %s"), psz, (LPTSTR)lpvMsgBuf);
      }

      LocalFree(lpvMsgBuf);
   }
   else
   {
      // This is a custom error that is application-specific
      wsprintf(sz, _T("%s\n"), psz);
   }

#ifdef _DEBUG
   OutputDebugString(sz);
#endif

   if(bPrintEvent)
      PrintEvent(sz);

   if(bRaiseException)
      RaiseException(dwErr, EXCEPTION_NONCONTINUABLE, 0, 0);

   return dwErr;
}
```

If you want, the error string for any error can be printed out to the NT event log by passing `true` in the `bPrintEvent` parameter. You'll usually want to do this, so that you can trace where the service failed. Have a look at `PrintEvent()`, below:

```
// Sends the error/event to the event log
void CService::PrintEvent(const TCHAR* psz, bool bError)
{
   const TCHAR* rgsz[] = { psz };

   HANDLE hes = RegisterEventSource(0, GetDisplayName());
```

```
    if(hes)
    {
        WORD dwEventType =
                        bError ? EVENTLOG_ERROR_TYPE : EVENTLOG_INFORMATION_TYPE;
        ReportEvent(hes, dwEventType, 0, 0, 0, 1, 0, rgsz, 0);
        DeregisterEventSource(hes);
    }
}
```

I've managed to sneak in rudimentary use of the event log as an error handling and reporting device for the service class. Don't worry about the mechanism for now; we'll be covering the event log in Chapter 5 – there are a few more subtleties to it than just the `ReportEvent()` function. In the meantime, please allow me to press on without further explanation.

Stopping the Service

Once the service has indicated that it is stopping by returning from the `Run()` function, `ServiceMainMember()` begins the shutdown sequence. It calls `DeInit()`, which is a function that can be overridden in the derived class to do cleanup work. If you choose to override it, make sure to call the base class implementation, which waits for the watcher thread to signal and then closes its handle. It then closes the handles on all of the events in the `m_hEvents` array.

```
void CService::DeInit()
{
    // Wait for the watcher thread to terminate
    if(m_hWatcherThread)
    {
        // Wait a reasonable amount of time
        WaitForSingleObject(m_hWatcherThread, 10000);
        CloseHandle(m_hWatcherThread);
    }

    // Uninitialize any resources created in Init()
    for(int i = 0 ; i < NUMEVENTS ; i++)
    {
        if(m_hEvents[i])
            CloseHandle(m_hEvents[i]);
    }
}
```

Last of all, in the class destructor, all that happens is that the critical section is de-initialized:

```
CService::~CService()
{
    DeleteCriticalSection(&m_cs);
}
```

Overrideable Functions

To complete the `CService.cpp` file, the following functions can optionally be overridden in the derived class, but they have no implementations in the base class:

```
void CService::Init()
{}
```

```
void CService::OnPause()
{}

void CService::OnContinue()
{}

void CService::OnShutdown()
{}

void CService::HandleUserDefined(DWORD dwControl)
{}

void CService::ParseArgs(DWORD argc, LPTSTR* argv)
{}
```

Precompiled Headers

It won't have escaped your attention that the implementation file contained a `#include` for `precomp.h`; as you'll doubtless have guessed, this is just a precompiled header file that you should incorporate in your project in the usual way. The file contains a few definitions and includes that are required throughout the source code, and looks like this:

```
#define _WIN32_WINNT 0x403 // NT4 sp3
#define UNICODE
#define _UNICODE

#include <windows.h>
#include <process.h>

#include <iostream>
using namespace std;

#ifdef UNICODE
   #define _tcout wcout
   #define _tostream wostream
#else
   #define _tcout cout
   #define _tostream ostream
#endif

#include <TCHAR.h>
```

Service Configuration and Control

Available in the source code for this chapter on the web site is another class called `CServiceConfig`. You can add this class to configuration and control programs to automate most of the common configuration tasks for services. To use it, simply construct an object of type `CServiceConfig`, passing in the short name and display name of the service you want to work with. Then, call the various functions to do the work. The code mirrors what you learned in the last chapter, though it has been re-packaged in a handy class.

CServiceInstall, a more concise alternative to CServiceConfig, is also available with the source code. It has only two main functions – Install() and Remove() – which handle the work of installing and removing the service to and from the services database.

The Install() function just opens the SCM and calls CreateService() with the parameters you require. Most of the parameters are defaulted to the common installation options for services, to make using the function as easy as possible.

```
void Install(DWORD dwType        = SERVICE_WIN32_OWN_PROCESS,
             DWORD dwStart       = SERVICE_DEMAND_START,
             LPCTSTR lpDepends   = NULL,
             LPCTSTR lpName      = NULL,
             LPCTSTR lpPassword  = NULL);
```

```
void CServiceInstall::Install(DWORD dwType, DWORD dwStart,
                              LPCTSTR lpDepends, LPCTSTR lpName,
                              LPCTSTR lpPassword)
{
   SC_HANDLE hSCM = NULL;
   SC_HANDLE hService = NULL;

   if(IsInstalled() == TRUE)
      return;

   hSCM = OpenSCManager(NULL, NULL, SC_MANAGER_CREATE_SERVICE);
   if(!hSCM)
   {
      ErrorPrinter(_T("OpenSCManager"));
      return;
   }

   TCHAR szFilePath[_MAX_PATH];
   GetModuleFileName(NULL, szFilePath, _MAX_PATH);

   hService = CreateService(hSCM,
                            m_service,
                            m_display,
                            SERVICE_ALL_ACCESS,
                            dwType, dwStart,
                            SERVICE_ERROR_NORMAL,
                            szFilePath,
                            NULL,
                            NULL,
                            lpDepends,
                            lpName,
                            lpPassword);
   if(!hService)
      ErrorPrinter(_T("CreateService"));
   else
      _tprintf(_T("%s Created\n"), m_service);

   CloseServiceHandle(hService);
   CloseServiceHandle(hSCM);
   return;
}
```

To use `Install()`, just create a stack-based instance of `CServiceInstall`, passing in the service name and display name. Then, use the variable to call the install function, like so:

```
LPTSTR szName = _T("Monitor");
LPTSTR szDisplay = _T("Ping Monitoring Service");
CServiceInstall si(szName, szDisplay);
si.Install();
```

If you don't have the source code to hand, a final option is to install the service via a quick modification to the service configuration example of the previous chapter – all you need to do is tweak the global variables `g_service`, `g_display` and `g_binary` appropriately.

The Monitor Usage Pattern

As I've explained, in order to make use of these classes, you'll have to derive a class from `CService` and come up with something for it to do. A project that fits the Monitor usage pattern is the perfect place for us to see our new classes in action.

The Monitor is a simple pattern, responsible for implementing any usage that requires a component to be on the lookout for the status of an external resource, or for the occurrence of some external event. It has several variations on the same central theme of 'keeping track of something' and notifying someone, or some other software component, that the thing being kept track of is available, unavailable, changing state, or whatever.

There are probably countless specific variations on Monitor, but here are three. You can monitor:

- A job's completion status
- A connection
- The status/availability of some resource

If we're going to implement Monitor as a sample, then we'd better pick something useful to monitor. Let's choose a really simple case that allows us to focus on using the `CService` tools, rather than on a complex problem domain. Imagine that I'm a network administrator who wants to know *immediately* if a TCP/IP server that many clients on my network connect to suddenly becomes unavailable. I need to know whether the server connection is down so that I can react as quickly as possible. Perhaps I could have it page me so I can get it fixed before too many users notice the outage.

How might I do this? A service, you say? A service that polls the server every so often to see whether it's available and warns me if it isn't? Right on.

Design of Monitor

The design of Monitor is actually quite simple. Most implementations will simply do one of two things – they will either wait *passively* for the monitored entity to tell the monitor something has happened, via a message notification or other event, or they'll *actively* hit the resource, connection, or job to discover its status.

The scenario I've described is a case of active monitoring, since we can't feasibly wait for the monitored server to tell us (over the network) that it is no longer functioning properly! So, in terms of design, this version of the Monitor has to try the connection periodically to see if it is active. In short, the running portion of the service will sit in a `while` loop and periodically 'ping' the server, sleeping between pings to save processor time. Every time the Monitor pings, it will indicate via the event log whether the ping was successful.

The Monitor service itself will take three parameters, which are passed in the `StartService()` call. First, it will accept the IP address of the server you want to ping; second, it will take the cycle time, in seconds, between pings of that server; third, it will accept the number of the port you wish to ping (FTP, WWW, or whatever). The defaults for the second and third parameters are 5 seconds and the FTP service (port 21) respectively.

To avoid having to write a user interface for adding and deleting 'watched servers', which is not in the scope of this chapter, this particular implementation is rather boring – it only deals with one server. We'll revisit the Monitor when we come to look at administration tools in Chapter 11, and add that functionality by writing a separate UI program for the service.

It should go without saying that this implementation is a *lousy* use of the event log. It would be far preferable to write *un*successful pings to the event log, and then notify (probably page) the system administrator when a ping is unsuccessful. Short of writing TAPI code to dial a pager, though, this is a reasonably good sample solution. Just remember to stop the service when you're done playing with it!

main Execution

The `main()` function of a process that uses our service classes will actually be quite simple. It just needs to create an instance of each of the service classes it wants to use, passing in the service's short name, display name, and type as parameters to the constructor. Then, it uses the `SERVICE_MAP` family of macros to set up an entry for each service. This sets up a `SERVICE_TABLE_ENTRY` structure for each service that the process contains, and starts the service control dispatcher. At that point, the services are off and running. Here's the code for this project's `main()` function.

```
#include "precomp.h"
#include "cmonitor.h"
#include "cserviceinstall.h"

int main()
{
   LPTSTR szName = _T("Monitor");
   LPTSTR szDisplay = _T("Ping Monitoring Service");

   // Process command line
```

```
    TCHAR* pszCmdLine = GetCommandLine();
    CharLowerBuff(pszCmdLine, lstrlen(pszCmdLine));
    if(_tcsstr(pszCmdLine, _T("-install")))
    {
       CServiceInstall si(szName, szDisplay);
       si.Install();
       return 0;
    }
    else if(_tcsstr(pszCmdLine, _T("-remove")))
    {
       CServiceInstall si(szName, szDisplay);
       si.Remove();
       return 0;
    }

    // Good place to step in and debug
    // DebugBreak();

    // Create the object instance
    CMonitor Monitor(szName, szDisplay, SERVICE_WIN32_OWN_PROCESS);

    // Set up an entry for the one service and go
    BEGIN_SERVICE_MAP
       SERVICE_MAP_ENTRY(CMonitor, Monitor)
    END_SERVICE_MAP

    return 0;
}
```

As you can see, the first thing the `main()` function does is to check to see if the process is being called with either an `-install` or a `-remove` parameter. If it is, then it creates an instance of the `CServiceInstall` class, passing in the service name and display name, and calls the `Install()` or `Remove()` function on it, respectively. At that point, the service is installed or removed, and the process exits.

If the service is actually starting, an instance of `CMonitor` is created, passing in the service name, the display name, and the type of service. (The type should match the one you passed in your call to `CServiceInstall::Install()`.)

Next, I use the `BEGIN_SERVICE_MAP`, `SERVICE_MAP_ENTRY()` and `END_SERVICE_MAP` macros to do the work of setting up the `SERVICE_TABLE_ENTRY` array and calling `StartServiceCtrlDispatcher()`, which is what gets the service running. Simply add a `BEGIN_SERVICE_MAP`, add as many `SERVICE_MAP_ENTRY()` entries (passing the class name and service name, which *must* match the service name you passed to the `CDerivedClass` constructor in a multi-service process) as the process has services, and finish off with an `END_SERVICE_MAP` macro. That's it: the service is started!

Code for the Monitor

`CMonitor` is quite easy to implement now that we have the `CService` class as a base. The code below simply declares overrides for the required pure virtual functions `Run()` and `OnStop()`, as well as for `OnPause()`, and `OnContinue`, and `ParseArgs()`. We'll also need derived class implementations of `Init()` and `DeInit()` in order to set up an additional kernel event, and to start up and close down the Sockets library. (Remember to add `ws2_32.lib` to the project's link libraries for the Sockets calls.) It also adds a few data members to handle the work of the class itself, and an additional function, `Ping()`, to do the pinging against the server. First, the header file, `CMonitor.h`:

```
#include "cservice.h"

class CMonitor : public CService
{
public:
   CMonitor(LPTSTR szName, LPTSTR szDisplay, DWORD dwType);
   virtual void Run();

DECLARE_SERVICE(CMonitor, Monitor)

protected:
   DWORD Ping();
   virtual void OnPause();
   virtual void OnContinue();
   virtual void OnStop();
   virtual void Init();
   virtual void DeInit();
   virtual void ParseArgs(DWORD argc, LPTSTR* argv);

//Attributes
   HANDLE m_hPauseNotifyEvent;

   CHAR m_pingAddress[25];
   DWORD m_nCycleTime;
   unsigned short m_nPort;

   bool m_bPause;
   bool m_bStop;
};
```

The class also has a single kernel event, `m_hPauseNotifyEvent`, which will get signaled when the `Run()` function wants to instruct a control handler that it has responded to a request. Don't worry – this will make more sense very shortly!

CMonitor Initialization

Let's begin at the beginning. Here's the top of the class implementation file, `CMonitor.cpp`. Notice first that the `IMPLEMENT_SERVICE()` macro we discussed in the previous section is used to set up all the awkward static functions that will be needed as callbacks and thread routines.

```
#include "precomp.h"
#include "cmonitor.h"
#include <winsock2.h>

IMPLEMENT_SERVICE(CMonitor, Monitor)
```

Next, the `CMonitor` constructor simply calls the base class constructor and then initializes its own members. The most critical thing, though, is something that you must remember to do in the constructors of all classes that you derive from `CService`: ensure that you set `m_pThis = this`. Assigning the `this` pointer to the static `m_pThis`, declared by the `DECLARE_SERVICE()` macro, ensures that the static functions point to the right class.

```
CMonitor::CMonitor(LPTSTR szName, LPTSTR szDisplay, DWORD dwType) :
                    CService(szName, szDisplay,dwType)
{
   m_pThis = this;

   m_bPause = false;
   m_bStop  = false;

   m_hPauseNotifyEvent = NULL;

   m_nCycleTime = 0;
   m_nPort = 0;
}
```

ParseArgs

The next time we need to pick up in the execution series is `ParseArgs()`, which is called by the base class `ServiceMainMember()`. By overriding this function, we can parse out the service parameters and obtain the IP address, ping rate, and port to ping.

```
void CMonitor::ParseArgs(DWORD argc, LPTSTR* argv)
{
   if(argc > 1)
   {
      // For the first argument, convert it to a regular LPSTR so it can be
      // used inside the sockets calls
      long lconv = (lstrlenW(argv[1]) + 1) * 2;
      char lpa[25] = "";
      WideCharToMultiByte(CP_ACP, 0, argv[1], -1, lpa, lconv, NULL, NULL);
      memcpy(m_pingAddress, lpa, lconv);

      // Get the cycle time and convert to milliseconds - default of 5000
      m_nCycleTime = (argc > 2) ?
                        (DWORD)((_ttol(argv[2]) * 1000)) : (DWORD)5000;

      // Set the port to 21 (FTP) if no port given
      m_nPort = (argc > 3) ? (_ttol(argv[3])) : 21;
   }
   else
   {
      ErrorHandler(_T("Invalid IP address as argument to StartService:
                                    Service Stopping"), TRUE, TRUE,0);
   }
}
```

This function checks to see if there's more than one argument (remember that the first argument is always the service name), and if there is, it gets the first one. However, the incoming string is Unicode, and we'll need a regular `LPSTR` for the Sockets call later on, so we have to go through some convolutions to convert the string from its wide format to a 'slender' format. After that, we set the two other members (`m_nCycleTime` and `m_nPort`) to the appropriate parameter values.

Init

The next derived class function to be called by `ServiceMainMember()` is `Init()`, which simply sets up the `m_hPauseNotifyEvent` and initializes the Sockets library.

```
void CMonitor::Init()
{
   // Set up event that lets handlers know a ctrl request has been processed
   m_hPauseNotifyEvent = CreateEvent(NULL, FALSE, FALSE, NULL);
   if(!m_hPauseNotifyEvent)
      ErrorHandler(_T("CreateEvent"));

   // Initialize Sockets library
   WSADATA wsaData;
   if(WSAStartup(MAKEWORD(2, 2), &wsaData) == SOCKET_ERROR)
      ErrorHandler(_T("WSAStartup"));
}
```

Run

Once initialization is complete, it's run time! The `Run()` function is where the service will spend most of its time, sleeping for the period set in `m_nCycleTime`, then waking up to ping the requested server.

```
// The main processing logic belongs in this overridable
// All start, running, and stop code here
void CMonitor::Run()
{
   SetStatus(SERVICE_RUNNING, 0, 0,
             SERVICE_ACCEPT_STOP | SERVICE_ACCEPT_PAUSE_CONTINUE);

   bool bPauseSent = false;
   DWORD dwErr = NO_ERROR;
   while(true)
   {
      // I'm not stopped or paused
      while(!m_bStop)
      {
         // Do some work
         Sleep(m_nCycleTime);
         if(m_bPause && !bPauseSent)
         {
            // Pausing; SetEvent message received
            SetEvent(m_hPauseNotifyEvent);
            bPauseSent = true;
         }
         else if(!m_bPause && bPauseSent)
         {
            // Continuing; SetEvent message received
```

```
                SetEvent(m_hPauseNotifyEvent);
                bPauseSent = false;
            }
            else if(!m_bPause)                     // (!m_bPause &&!bPauseSent)
            {
                // I'm running as usual, so ping
                dwErr = Ping();
                if(dwErr != NO_ERROR)
                   break;

                PrintEvent(_T("Successful Ping"), FALSE);
            }
        }

        // Stopped, so exit
        SetStatus(SERVICE_STOP_PENDING, 2, 5000);
        break;
    }
}
```

The first thing this function does is to tell the SCM that it is running. Then, it moves into its run loop, sleeping, then checking the state of its `m_bPause` and `m_bStop` members. When the service is stopped, it sends a status to let the SCM know that it has stopped.

Control Handling

In order to deal with control requests, the `Run()` function needs simply to check the state of a couple of member variables to see whether it should stop or pause its activities. When the loop in `Run()` has actually responded to the incoming request, it sets an event that the `OnPause()` and `OnContinue()` implementations are waiting for: `m_hPauseNotifyEvent`. These latter functions simply reset the status wait hint and checkpoint every few seconds, while waiting for the `Run()` function to indicate that it has executed the request (that is, paused or continued). If you start the service with a decent ping time (say, 30 seconds), and then pause and continue it, you can see the wait hint in action.

OnPause and OnContinue

Let's take a brief look at `OnPause()` and `OnContinue()` (which, you will remember, are called by the watcher thread). Unsurprisingly, they both have similar structures.

```
void CMonitor::OnPause()
{
   DWORD dwCheckPt = 1;
   SetStatus(SERVICE_PAUSE_PENDING, dwCheckPt, 6000);

   // Remember, this function is called by the thread watching for handler
   // notifications. The ServiceMain thread (Run) could be reading this value
   InterlockedExchange((LPLONG)&m_bPause, (LONG)true);

   // Wait for the Run loop to signal that it has received the pause request
   while(WaitForSingleObject(m_hPauseNotifyEvent, 5000) == WAIT_TIMEOUT)
   {
```

```
        dwCheckPt++;
        SetStatus(SERVICE_PAUSE_PENDING, dwCheckPt, 6000);
    }

    SetStatus(SERVICE_PAUSED);
    ResetEvent(m_hPauseNotifyEvent);
}

void CMonitor::OnContinue()
{
    DWORD dwCheckPt = 1;
    SetStatus(SERVICE_CONTINUE_PENDING, dwCheckPt, 6000);

    // The ServiceMain thread could be reading this value
    InterlockedExchange((LPLONG)&m_bPause, (LONG)false);

    // Wait for the Run loop to signal it has received the continue request
    while(WaitForSingleObject(m_hPauseNotifyEvent, 5000) == WAIT_TIMEOUT)
    {
        dwCheckPt++;
        SetStatus(SERVICE_CONTINUE_PENDING, dwCheckPt, 6000);
    }

    SetStatus(SERVICE_RUNNING);
    ResetEvent(m_hPauseNotifyEvent);
}
```

First, they send a 'pending' status update to the SCM. Then, they modify the m_bPause member variable value using an atomic InterlockedExchange() call. This is important, because the calls to OnPause() and OnContinue() (and OnStop()) are actually made on the *watcher thread.* However, those values are being read in Run() on the *main service thread*, and therefore any updates to them must be atomic.

Next, the functions sit in a WaitForSingleObject() call, awaiting the signal from the Run() loop that it has received and acknowledged the 'pause' or 'continue' request (which it does by signaling the m_hPauseNotifyEvent event). Every 5 seconds, they break out of the loop to give the SCM a 'pending' status update and increment the checkpoint. When the wait is finished, it sets the status to either PAUSED or RUNNING, appropriately.

OnStop

OnStop() is much shorter, because it just sets a pending status equal to however long the Run() loop sleeps for, updates the m_bStop member variable that the Run() loop will break its cycle on, and returns.

```
void CMonitor::OnStop()
{
    SetStatus(SERVICE_STOP_PENDING, 1, m_nCycleTime);
```

```
        // The ServiceMain thread could be reading this value
        InterlockedExchange((LPLONG)&m_bStop, (LONG)true);
    }
```

Ping

When `Run()` isn't responding to control requests, it is working – that is, pinging the requested server. It does that by calling the `Ping()` function, which sets up a socket and attempts to connect to the server. If it receives an error, it prints an error to the event log and returns. Otherwise, it returns a success code and `Run()` makes an event log entry indicating that fact.

```
    DWORD CMonitor::Ping()
    {
        // Set up socket structures and try to connect
        DWORD dwErr = NO_ERROR;

        SOCKADDR_IN saDestAddr = {0};
        SOCKET sSocket;
        unsigned long destaddr;

        destaddr = inet_addr(m_pingAddress);
        memcpy(&saDestAddr.sin_addr, &destaddr, sizeof(destaddr));
        saDestAddr.sin_port = htons(m_nPort);
        saDestAddr.sin_family = AF_INET;

        sSocket = socket(AF_INET, SOCK_STREAM, 0);
        if(INVALID_SOCKET == sSocket)
           return ErrorHandler(_T("socket"), TRUE, TRUE, WSAGetLastError());

        if(connect(sSocket, (LPSOCKADDR)&saDestAddr,
                                            sizeof(saDestAddr)) == SOCKET_ERROR)
        {
           dwErr = ErrorHandler(_T("socket connect"),
                                                TRUE, FALSE,WSAGetLastError());
        }

        if(closesocket(sSocket) == SOCKET_ERROR)
           return ErrorHandler(_T("closesocket"), TRUE, TRUE, WSAGetLastError());

        return dwErr;
    }
```

De-initialization

Lastly, `DeInit()` is overridden in the derived class to close the event and clean up the Sockets library. With this function, the implementation is complete, and we can move on to seeing whether it works!

```
    void CMonitor::DeInit()
    {
        CService::DeInit();
```

```
    if(m_hPauseNotifyEvent)
        CloseHandle(m_hPauseNotifyEvent);

    WSACleanup ();
}
```

Trying Out Monitor

Let's get the Monitor running! Either assemble the code presented in the chapter so far, or compile the project you've downloaded from the Wrox web site. Then, execute `svcclass.exe` with the `-install` command-line parameter, like so:

```
svcclass -install
```

Next, open up the Services applet, and you should see the Ping Monitoring Service:

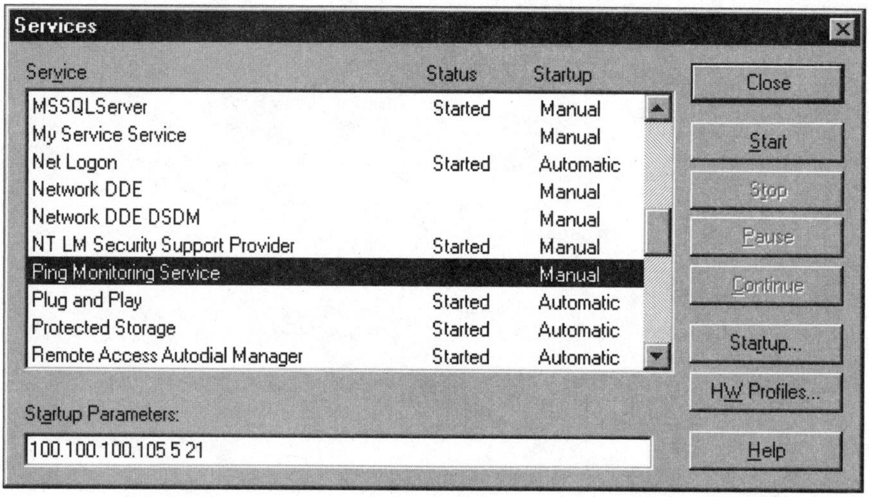

In the Startup Parameters box, enter the IP address of a machine you can access, the time (in seconds) that you want the service to wait between pings, and the port number you want to ping. The IP address is not optional; the other parameters default to 5 seconds and to port 21 (FTP), respectively. Click Start, and you'll notice that you can pause and continue this service as well:

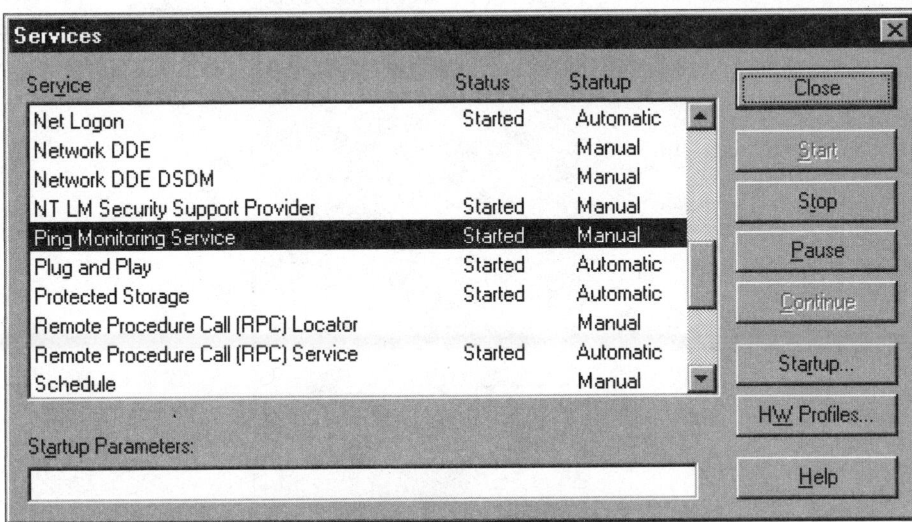

After five seconds (or whatever you specified), the service will begin making entries in the event log. Open up the Event Viewer application and take a look:

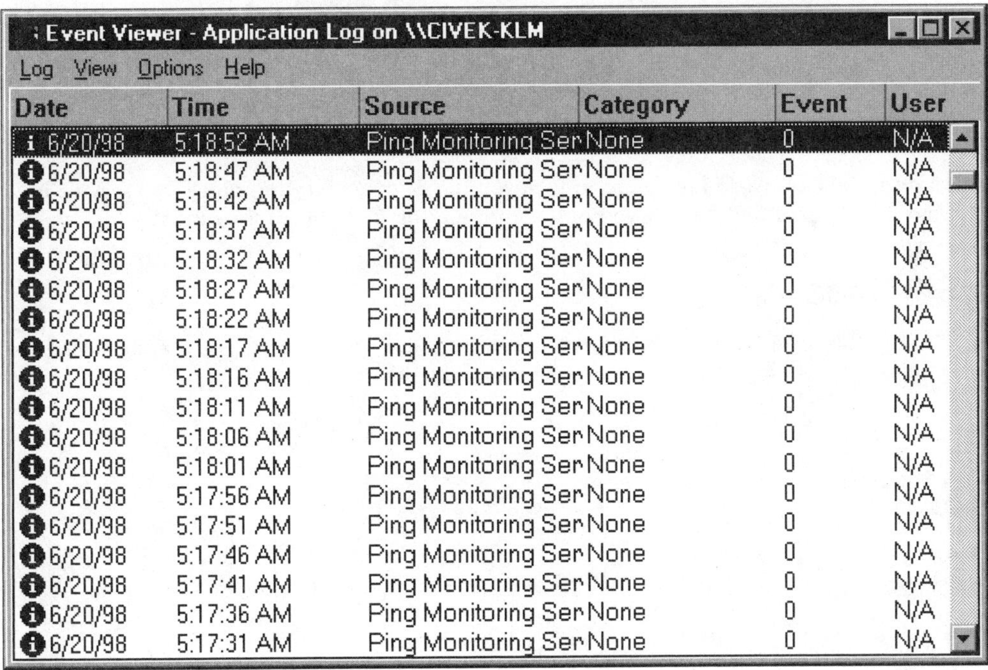

Every five seconds, the service makes an entry in the log that reads like this:

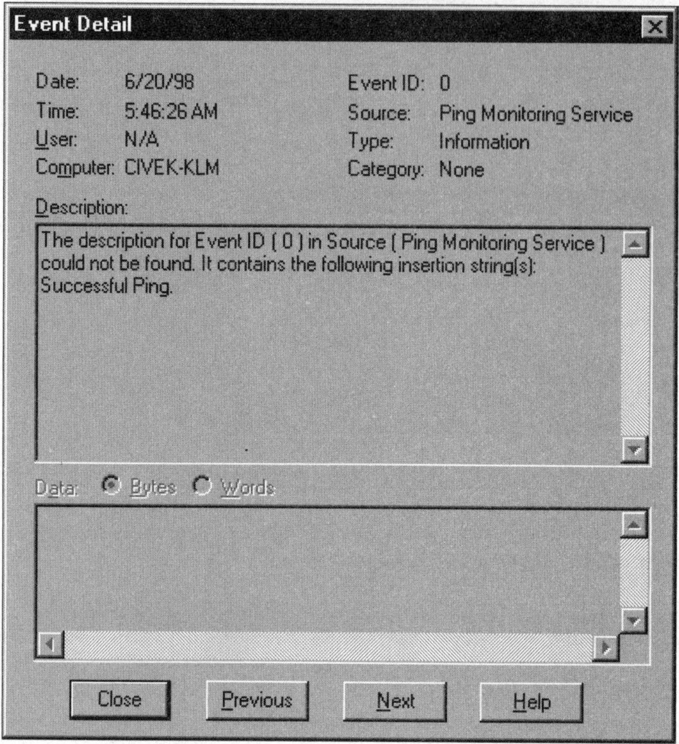

Ignore the first part of the message for now, and focus on the Successful Ping part – the service is working as it should. Chapter 5 will show you how to tidy up the first part of the output.

Multiple Services

If you wanted to use this infrastructure to implement multiple services in a process, it's easy using the `SERVICE_MAP` classes! Just change `main()` to something like this:

```
int main()
{
    LPTSTR szName = _T("Monitor");
    LPTSTR szDisplay = _T("Ping Monitoring Service");

    LPTSTR szName2 = _T("Monitor2");
    LPTSTR szDisplay2 = _T("Ping Monitoring Service Two");

    // Process command line
    TCHAR* pszCmdLine = GetCommandLine();
    CharLowerBuff(pszCmdLine, lstrlen(pszCmdLine));
    if(_tcsstr(pszCmdLine, _T("-install")))
    {
```

```
        CServiceInstall si(szName, szDisplay);
        si.Install(SERVICE_WIN32_SHARE_PROCESS);

        CServiceInstall si2(szName2, szDisplay2);
        si2.Install(SERVICE_WIN32_SHARE_PROCESS);
        return 0;
    }
    else if(_tcsstr(pszCmdLine, _T("-remove")))
    {
        CServiceInstall si(szName, szDisplay);
        si.Remove();

        CServiceInstall si2(szName2, szDisplay2);
        si2.Remove();
        return 0;
    }

    CMonitor Monitor(szName, szDisplay, SERVICE_WIN32_SHARE_PROCESS);
    CMonitor2 Monitor2(szName2, szDisplay2, SERVICE_WIN32_SHARE_PROCESS);

    BEGIN_SERVICE_MAP
        SERVICE_MAP_ENTRY(CMonitor, Monitor)
        SERVICE_MAP_ENTRY(CMonitor2, Monitor2)
    END_SERVICE_MAP

    return 0;
}
```

Note that the `SERVICE_WIN32_SHARE_PROCESS` argument to the `CServiceInstall::Install()` call is absolutely necessary – otherwise, each service will run in a separate copy of the `svcclass.exe` process. Here's what it looks like in the Services applet:

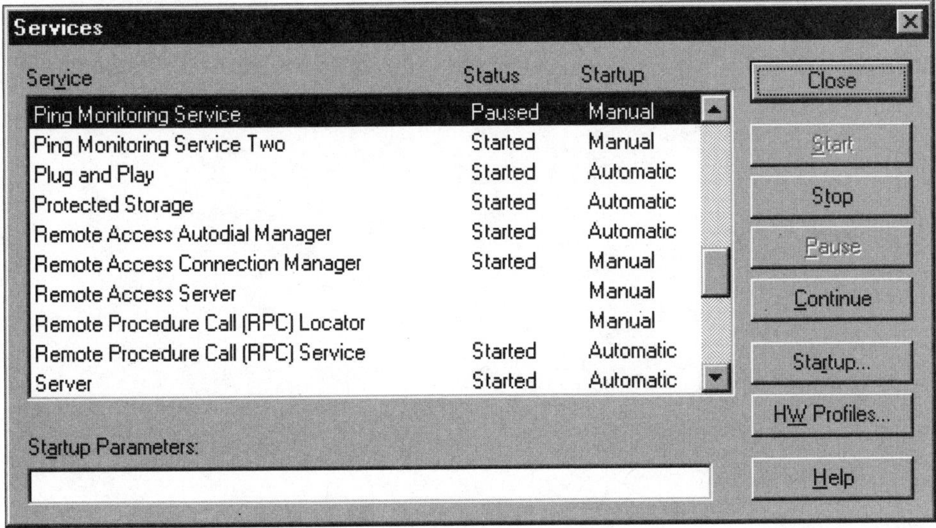

As you would expect, the two services Ping Monitoring Service and Ping Monitoring Service Two can be started, paused, etc. completely independently of one another.

Summary

This chapter has provided you with some useful tools that you can employ to proceed into more hazardous terrain, without having to rewrite the same old infrastructure code over and over again.

The `CService` class should provide a simple, yet flexible, model upon which to base the more complicated usage patterns to come. And that's just what we'll do, after a look at how services can interact with the Event Log.

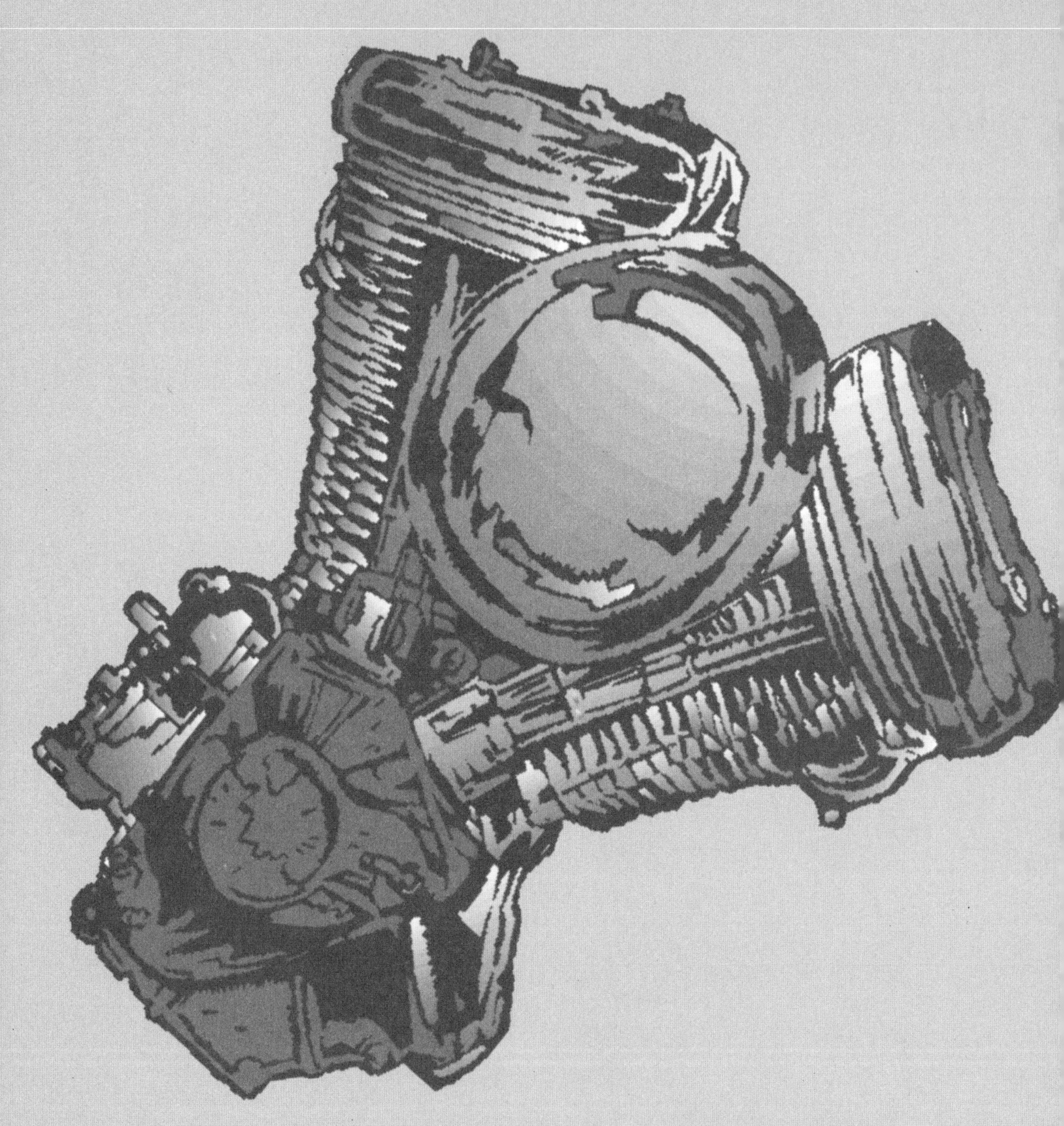

5

The Event Log

This chapter marks a temporary change of direction, in that it focuses on a tool that supports service development, rather than a particular service. We're going to look at the **event log**, a system service that we know all about as NT *users*, but for which rather fewer of us have actually written code in order to integrate it into NT applications.

In this chapter, you'll learn exactly what the event log *is*, how to put events into it, and good etiquette regarding what types of events and information you *should* put into it. Lastly, we'll put together a C++ class that can be added to our existing library of classes, to help automate the task of reporting events.

What is the Event Log?

The event log is itself an auto-start service, of type `SERVICE_WIN32_SHARE_PROCESS`. It's actually part of `Services.exe`, the executable that houses the SCM. Its purpose is to provide a central reporting facility where various system components, device drivers, and Win32 services can return error conditions and detailed error information to NT systems administrators and users. The idea behind the event log is that it's a standard repository for errors, so that individual service writers don't need to invent their own error logging facilities, complete with their own separate log files. Imagine the nightmare if every service registered on your system (there are about 180 on mine) needed to maintain its own separate log file of error events!

In addition, the event log has a number of other strings to its bow. For a start, it is capable of recording and displaying messages using a localized language. This allows service developers to sell their applications in the international marketplace, and have errors and events sent to the event log in the user's own language. Second, the event log allows you to store information *about* the error that you're logging. For example, if the error the service encounters is a bad data structure, you can tell the user that, and then actually record the structure in the log. This is a boon for companies that write commercial-grade services, and whose customer support departments may be thousands of miles from the customer who has the error. Finally, the event log also records security audit events that have been triggered by the system.

Structure of the Event Log

Administrators and users both use the Event Viewer application to view the contents of the event log. The log itself is divided into three 'sub-logs': application, system, and security.

- The **application log** is the repository for events registered by server applications, including Win32 services. All the services that we'll focus on in this book will use the application log.
- The **system log** is for the events that are registered by drivers and boot services. This log records errors and information related to hardware and boot-up failures.
- The **security log** tracks the occurrence of events that are being audited by the security auditor. For instance, if you place a security audit on the successful reading of a particular file, then the security log will record when the file is read.

Event Viewer - Application Log on \\CIVEK-KLM

Log View Options Help

Date	Time	Source	Category	Event	User	Computer
10/17/97	2:06:36 PM	Java VM	None	8192	N/A	CIVEK-KLM
10/17/97	2:06:33 PM	Java VM	None	8192	N/A	CIVEK-KLM
10/17/97	2:06:28 PM	Java VM	None	8192	N/A	CIVEK-KLM
10/17/97	2:04:17 PM	Active Server Page:	None	3	N/A	CIVEK-KLM
10/17/97	1:54:57 PM	Active Server Page:	None	3	N/A	CIVEK-KLM
10/16/97	6:53:03 AM	Active Server Page:	None	3	N/A	CIVEK-KLM
10/14/97	6:33:12 PM	Active Server Page:	None	3	N/A	CIVEK-KLM
10/14/97	6:50:26 AM	Active Server Page:	None	3	N/A	CIVEK-KLM
10/13/97	7:07:29 AM	Active Server Page:	None	3	N/A	CIVEK-KLM
10/11/97	6:32:50 PM	Ping Monitoring Ser	None	0	N/A	CIVEK-KLM
10/11/97	6:32:20 PM	Ping Monitoring Ser	None	0	N/A	CIVEK-KLM
10/11/97	6:31:50 PM	Ping Monitoring Ser	None	0	N/A	CIVEK-KLM
10/11/97	6:31:20 PM	Ping Monitoring Ser	None	0	N/A	CIVEK-KLM
10/11/97	6:30:50 PM	Ping Monitoring Ser	None	0	N/A	CIVEK-KLM

Information Stored in the Log

As the figure above shows, the log stores several pieces of information for each event. Taking Date, Time, User, and Computer as read, let's explore the nature of each of the other pieces of data in turn.

Event Type

Every event in the log is associated with a single **event type**, which indicates its importance or severity level. The small icons at the extreme left of the Event Viewer window show the type of the event, and there are five different kinds:

- Informational event types are used to demarcate important, usually non-recurring, occurrences in the life of a service or a server application. An informational event could, for example, indicate that a particular service started successfully or responded to a control request like 'pause'.
- Warning event types are used to log problems that don't cause the service to stop working completely or to lose data, but which may indicate a more severe problem over the long term.
- An error event usually indicates a severe problem that caused a service either not to start, or to cease performing its most crucial functions. It can also indicate loss of data.
- Audit success/failure event types are for security events, and are therefore only recorded in the security log. Unsurprisingly, they crop up when an audited access attempt succeeds or fails.

Source

The **source** is usually the name of the server application or service that is recording the event. However, it's possible for a service to register more than one source, if it makes sense to break the service's events up into more than one logical grouping. Each source that uses the event log should be registered via the registry and an API call that we'll talk more about shortly.

Category

Categories are logical, numerical groupings of events that can be used to sort the events for a single source into sub-groups. The Event Viewer application allows the user both to filter out and to find events by category. Each event source can define its own, unique category types by using a category message file, but most system components that use the event log do not do so – this is why the entry in the Category column is usually None.

Event ID

The **event ID** is a numerical value that tags each unique event that's sent to the log. After you've registered an event **message file** for your service in the registry, you can simply send the event ID to the event log to report the event. The log itself will then look up the actual description in the message file in order to display the event text in the viewer. An event ID is unique in a particular source. We will look in detail at how to create and use event IDs in the section entitled *Three Steps to Event Logging,* below.

Description

Each event ID is associated with a **description**. You can see the description associated with an event ID by looking at the Event Detail dialog in the Event Viewer (see below). The description string should help the user to understand exactly what went wrong, and so to remedy the problem. When the user wants to view the information about an event, the description gets looked up in the event message file for the source. In the screenshot below for the Java VM, the component has not properly registered its event message file in the registry. This is evidenced by the statement, "The description for Event ID (8192) in Source (Java VM) could not be found."

Furthermore, each event description is *localized*. The actual text that gets displayed for the event ID differs according the locality of the NT operating system the user is using. For that reason, you should avoid using cultural colloquialisms, even if the text is to be translated.

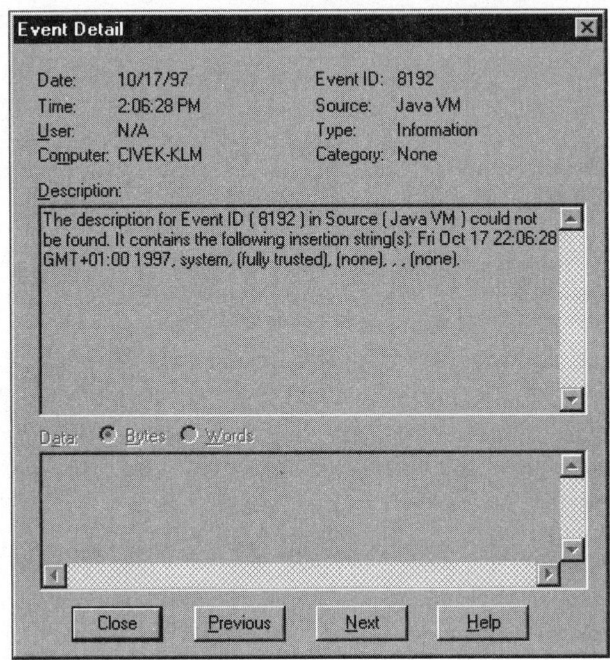

Event Data

Finally, an event can store and display raw **data** that gives greater insight into the specific problem the service is having. This data is displayed in the lower pane of the Event Detail dialog. The data could be a raw dump of an offending data structure, or a detailed diagnostic information buffer that gets filled when the service has an error. In any case, the event description should include information about what the data in the data pane actually *is* enclosed in parentheses. For instance, if the service failed while calling `SetServiceStatus()`, the description might read, "SetServiceStatus() failed. (The SERVICE_STATUS structure is the event data)." Event data takes up room in the event log, so it should only be provided when it will actually be useful to the user or to a technician in debugging the problem. Furthermore, event data is only viewable by the Event Viewer in its binary format – to do more, you'll have to write your own log viewer, which I discuss briefly at the end of the chapter in *Other Operations on the Event Log*.

How Event Logging Works

Before we proceed, there are a few main concepts and artifacts of event logging that you need to grasp in order fully to understand the discussion that follows.

- A **message script** is a text file that holds information about all the messages a particular project is able to write to the event log. It contains the mappings between the **message strings** themselves, and **message IDs** (numerical values). It also contains mappings between the category IDs and their descriptions. We will cover this in detail in the section called *Writing Message Scripts.*
- A **message file** is a DLL (or an EXE) that contains the descriptions of the various messages.
- The **message compiler**, also known as MC, is a small utility program that creates several files from the message script. These are used to build the message file DLL. MC yields a header file containing error constants, a resource script, and one `.bin` file containing description string resources for each language you've decided to support. The `.bin` file(s) and the `.rc` file become part of a Visual C++ project that creates a resource DLL. The `.h` file becomes part of your main project, so that you can refer to the message IDs by symbolic constant rather than by number.

An overview of the build process is shown in the diagram below.

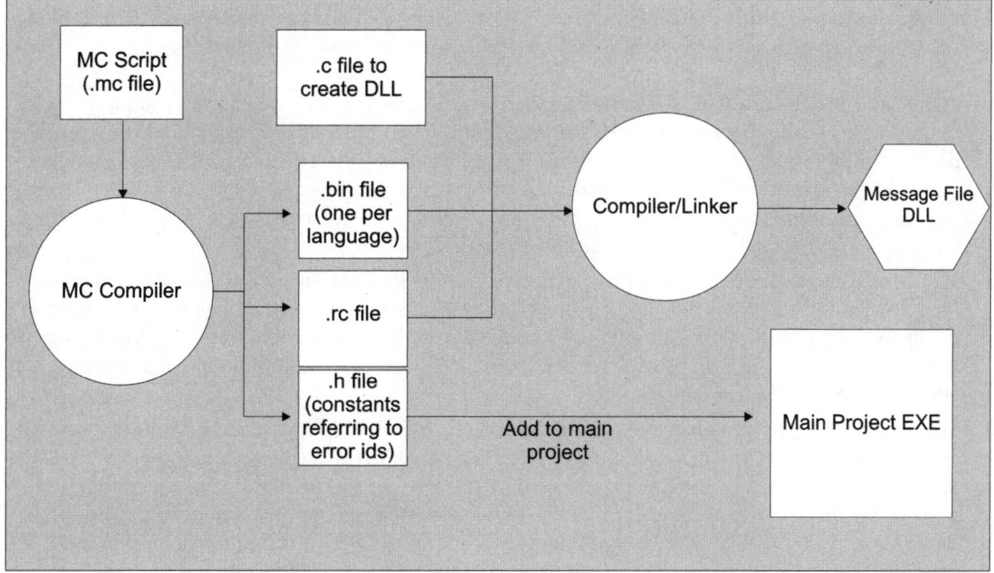

Three Steps to Event Logging

That's enough of the theoretical side of the event log. Let's move on to look at the process of building an event log message file, and hooking up an application to use the event log. To do it right, we need to carry out three basic steps:

- Build the message script and create the message file
- Add a key to the registry to register the event message file
- Generate event messages by calling the event log API functions

Creating the Message File Resource

To create the resource DLL or EXE that contains the message descriptions, we first have to create a message script.

Why use a Message Script?

Strictly speaking, it isn't *necessary* to create a message script in order to write events to the event log. As you saw in the `CService::PrintEvent()` function of the last chapter, it's quite possible to get something into the log by calling the `RegisterEventSource()` and `ReportEvent()` functions. However, there are several good reasons why you *should* write a message script:

- **Language independence.** If you use a message script, each of the messages is uniquely tagged numerically with an error number ID (message ID). When it needs to display the event message description, the Event Viewer will use the `FormatMessage()` API to read the description string based on the error number. That description string will then be displayed in the Event Viewer, in the language of the locale (presuming that you've written the description message in alternative languages and shipped them as part of the resource, of course).
- **Efficient use of space.** As you can imagine, recording event types by number rather than by a long description string (that could conceivably be repeated several times) saves a lot of space in the event log's data file. When the Event Viewer actually needs to show the string (because a user has chosen to view the event detail), it uses `FormatMessage()` to look it up in the module containing the message string resource.
- **It's a clean way to develop new error constants.** When the message script runs through the MC compiler, one of the generated output files is a handy error header file that contains `#define` statements for the values of all your new error codes. By specifying them in your message script, you can set the severity and facility bits for each error code (see below), and even provide descriptions (which will appear as comments in the header file). In fact, the structure of the familiar `winerror.h` file suggests quite strongly that MC was used to create it.
- **It's professional.** As you saw in the event log entries created by the Monitor pattern example at the end of chapter 4, if you don't use a message file, the Event Viewer will not be able to look up the description of the message anywhere. As a result it will display the annoying message, "The description for Event ID (nnnn) in Source (abcde) could not be found." This just doesn't look professional in a server application you're using in a real software system.

In short, using a message script and the message compiler to generate your error messages is a cool way to get language independence, efficiency, organization, and full integration into the operating system's error handling functionality in one fell swoop. Message files are great, and you should use them!

Win32 Error Codes

Win32 error codes are `DWORD` values that describe several pieces of information about an error that's been generated, based on the values of various bit positions within the `DWORD`. Error codes in this format are returned by `GetLastError()` any time a Win32 API call generates an error. Any exception code raised by `RaiseException()` should also adhere to this format.

In addition to a numeric exception code, each error has a **severity** and a **facility code**. The severity bits indicate whether the code represents success, an error, information, or a warning. Facility codes are 'error categories', or subdivisions of errors, that the application can make to group its error codes together. They are therefore defined by the programmer.

The structure of an error code `DWORD` is divided up like this:

Bits 31-30 **Severity**	**29-28** **Flags**	**27-16** **Facility Code**	**15-0** **Exception Code**
00 = Success	Bit 29: 0 = Microsoft 1 = Customer	Defined by Programmer	Defined by Programmer
01 = Informational			
10 = Warning	Bit 28: must be 0		
11 = Error			

When you're constructing your own error codes, it's necessary to fill out all four fields of the `DWORD`, although the MC compiler makes it easier by allowing you to state the severity and facility codes by name rather than by manipulating the individual bits. It also takes care of setting the customer bit if you use its `-c` command-line option. The next section outlines this process.

Writing a Message Script

The whole process of writing a message script begins when you decide what messages you want your application to send to the log, the numbers you want to give them, and the severity and facility codes you want them to have.

Once you've decided what events your service will show the world through the event log, you can begin to construct the message script. (In truth, this is likely to be an ongoing process as you write your application, though it depends on the rigor of the design process you are working under.) This is just a text file that you can start off by copying from samples, or cutting and pasting from other places – the message script that's available in this chapter's materials on the web site is as good a place as any. The default filename extension for a message script is `.mc`.

The basic format of entries in the message script has a `keyword = value` syntax. Spaces around the = sign are ignored, as is the case of the keyword. The value can be a number, a string, or a file name. Comments are allowed using the semicolon (`;`) syntax that's used in `.ini` files; these comments will be transferred to the `.h` file after compilation. If you actually want to write comments *directly* to the header file, use `;//`, and then write the comment's text.

The Header Section

The script itself has a header section and a body section. The header section can contain the following keywords, although none of them is mandatory – they'll be set to default values if you leave them out.

`MessageIdTypedef=name`
This symbol indicates what type each numeric message ID value will be cast to in the `.h` file that the MC compiler generates. They won't be cast to anything if this identifier is left out. Usually, you'll set this keyword to `DWORD` so that the message values will be typecast in the standard Win32 style.

`SeverityNames=(name=number:symbolicname)`
Severity values occupy the two highest bits of a 32-bit message code. The standard severity bits for Win32 messages are defined below. This keyword allows you to diverge from the usual Win32 severity names and values if you choose, but the most convenient option (which you can choose simply by not using this keyword) is just to use the standard Win32 severity types:

```
Success=0x0
Informational=0x1
Warning=0x2
Error=0x3
```

`FacilityNames=(name=number:symbolicname)`
Using this keyword, you can define your own facility codes and give them numbers and symbolic constants. Facility codes occupy the low order 12 bits of the high 16 bits of a 32-bit message code, allowing for 4096 facility codes. The first 256 are reserved for use by the system software. If you don't put anything here, the codes are left with the standard facilities:

```
FacilityNames=(System=0x0FF
               Application=0xFFF)
```

`LanguageNames=(name=number:filename)`
When you come to defining the messages themselves, you specify what language they are in by using the `Language` keyword, as you'll see shortly. The `LanguageNames` keyword in the header section defines the possible names and values that are allowed when you do so. Each language name has a number that is the Language ID tag that's used in the resource table, and a filename that's the name of the binary (`.bin`) file that will contain the message text strings for the language. For each language in which you plan to ship your software, you should create an additional language name and a message string written in that language. If you don't supply any language name, the following value will be assumed:

```
LanguageNames=(English=0x1:MSG00001)
```

However, I recommend that you insert your own definition, and use the real NT language identifier for English:

```
LanguageNames=(English=0x409:MSG00409)
```

To construct other language names (LANGIDs) search under language identifiers in Visual Studio.

Any new names defined in a `.mc` file that don't override any of the built-in names will be added, allowing you to support custom languages.

The Body Section

After the header section, the real fun begins. You get to write one descriptive section, or **message definition section**, for each error message. A message definition begins with one or more of the following keywords.

`MessageId=`*`number`* or `MessageId=+`*`number`*
The message ID is a 16-bit value that's required to mark the beginning of each new message definition. You have three options for specifying values:

- If no value is present for the message ID, then the value used will be the last value used for the particular facility type it is in, plus one
- If the value is specified as `+`*`number`*, then the value used will be the last value used for that facility, plus the number after the + sign
- If there is a specific numeric value, that will be the value used

Frankly, I'd recommend simply starting with `0x1` and putting no values for the message IDs that follow. The compiler will auto-increment and take care of assigning subsequent values.

`Severity=`*`severityname`*
`Facility=`*`facilityname`*
These are optional keywords that allow you to assign specifically the severity and facility codes you set up above in the header area. If these are not specified, they default to the values specified in the *previous* message definition section. For this reason, you should generally try to group together related severity and facility codes.

`SymbolicName=`*`symbolicconstantname`*
This keyword is a C-style symbolic constant name that you can associate with the final Win32 message code that gets output by the compiler. Ultimately, this code is the result of ORing together the message ID and the severity and facility codes. The constant will get written out to the `.h` file that gets generated, like so:

```
#define MYAPP_SYMBOL ((MessageIdTypedef)0xE0020001)
```

After the message definition keywords, you lay out the description string for each message. You write one message description for each of the languages you are supporting. The description string for each language begins with the keyword `Language=` and then, on the very next line, the description string begins. When you are through describing the error, place a single period (`.`) on the line following the description. You can then begin the description for the next supported language, or begin the next message definition section.

```
Language=languagename
Your Message Text Here
.
```

Within the text of the message, blank lines and whitespace are preserved as part of the output. You can also use a number of different formatting characters to refine the output of the description string. The most important of these formatting sequences is the `%n` sequence, in which *n* is a value between 1 and 99. It allows you to use the `ReportEvent()` API to send strings that will be inserted into the actual text of the message at runtime, in the order they occur in the array of insertion strings that this function accepts as a parameter. For instance, `%1` means, 'Insert the first string in the array', and so on. The proper use of insertion strings requires that they be language neutral, so they're usually filenames, system codes, or numerical data. For example:

```
Invalid IP address %1 as argument to StartService: The service failed to
start.
```

To reiterate, it is *very* important that you terminate *each* language entry for a particular message ID with a decimal point, like so:

```
MessageID=0x1
SymbolicName=MY_MESSAGE
Language=English
A message in English.
.
Language=German
Eine Mitteilung auf Deutsch.
.
```

Several other formatting sequences are also supported; this list is straight from the SDK documentation:

Sequence	Description
`%0`	Terminates a message text line without a trailing newline. This can be used to build up long lines, or to terminate the message itself without a trailing newline.
`%%`	Outputs a single '`%`' symbol in the formatted message text.
`%n`	Outputs a hard line break when it occurs at the end of a line.

Sequence	Description
%r	Outputs a hard carriage return, without a trailing newline.
%b	Outputs a space in the formatted message text. Used to ensure that there is the appropriate number of trailing spaces in a message text line.
%t	Outputs a tab in the formatted message text.
%.	Output a single period in the formatted message text. Can be used to get a single period at the beginning of a line without terminating the message text definition.
%!	Outputs a single exclamation point in the formatted message text. This can be used to get an exclamation point immediately after an insert without it being mistaken for the beginning of a `printf` format string.

Message Script Example

The following is a sample message script that uses a good number of the keywords introduced above, and therefore serves as an example of what a script that conforms to all the rules listed above might look like. As we progress, I'll demonstrate how a `.mc` script such as this one becomes a message file, and how you then use that file from your code.

```
MessageIdTypedef=DWORD

SeverityNames=(Success=0x0:STATUS_SEVERITY_SUCCESS
               Informational=0x1:STATUS_SEVERITY_INFORMATIONAL
               Warning=0x2:STATUS_SEVERITY_WARNING
               Error=0x3:STATUS_SEVERITY_ERROR
              )

FacilityNames=(System=0x0:FACILITY_SYSTEM
               Runtime=0x2:FACILITY_RUNTIME
               Stubs=0x3:FACILITY_STUBS
               Io=0x4:FACILITY_IO_ERROR_CODE
              )

LanguageNames=(English=0x409:MSG00409)
LanguageNames=(Testian=0x90AA:MSG090AA)

MessageId=0x1
Severity=Informational
SymbolicName=LOGTEST_GENERIC
Language=English
%1
.
Language=Testian
%1
.
```

```
MessageId=
Severity=Error
Facility=Runtime
SymbolicName=LOGTEST_WIN32_ERROR
Language=English
%1
.
Language=Testian
%1
.

MessageId=
Severity=Error
SymbolicName=LOGTEST_MULTISTRING_ERROR
Language=English
Logtest reported the following Error: Number %1, %2
.
Language=Testian
Error following the reported Logtest: Number %1, %2
.

MessageId=
Severity=Error
SymbolicName=LOGTEST_ERROR
Language=English
Logtest write operation failed in file %1.
.
Language=Testian
File in failed operation write Logtest %1.
.

MessageId=
Severity=Informational
SymbolicName=LOGTEST_INFO_1
Language=English
The logtest was successful.
.
Language=Testian
Successful was logtest the.
.

MessageId=
Severity=Error
SymbolicName=LOGTEST_ERROR_WITH_DATA
Language=English
Logtest operation failed (The LOGTEST_DUDLEY structure is the event data.)
.
Language=Testian
Failed operation Logtest (Data event the is structure LOGTEST_DUDLEY the.)
.
```

> **Message IDs with only an insertion string**
>
> **Notice that the script's first two entries simply accept an insertion string and contain no other description. I always have a message ID with no description, so that I can print out various generic text messages whenever I want to. This prevents me from having to make up an event ID and getting the annoying, "The description for Event ID (nnnn) in Source (abcde) could not be found," message.**
>
> **For the same reason, I always have a generic message ID for printing out Win32 error messages as well. I simply build an insertion string with the Win32 error number and description, and send it to the event ID for the generic Win32 error.**

Building the Message Resource

Once you have a usable message script (I used the one above and called it `logtest.mc`), there are two ways to go. You can:

- Build a separate message DLL that contains the generated message resource strings
- Build the message resource into the EXE that contains the service

How to choose one method over the other? Well, use the same rationale that you would employ to decide whether you would put the resources into the executable of *any* application you're writing. Do you need to abstract out the resources for some reason? Do you want to laden down the executable with error description strings, or is the executable so large that the overhead of extra strings is minor?

Building the Message Resource into a DLL

I nearly always put the message resource strings in a DLL. This keeps the service EXE file lean, and prevents it from loading the error text descriptions (for which it has no use) into the process space of the service. Instead, it allows the Event Viewer to load a small, discrete DLL from which to retrieve the string resources when it needs to display error message detail.

My preferred way of building the resource DLL that contains the message strings for my project is to make the message DLL project a sub-project of the main service. This is because I usually need to add and change error messages and strings throughout the life of the project, and adding it as a sub-project allows me simply to change the message script, recompile, and immediately have access to the new error constants in my main project.

For simplicity in this demonstration, I'm going to forgo using a service and instead send events to the event log from an ordinary executable – the steps involved in creating the message DLL are exactly the same. Start off by creating a Win32 Console Application with a name of your choice (we'll add functionality that simulates a service to this project later). Then...

- Create a sub-project of your project. It should be of type Win32 Dynamic-Link Library. I called mine `EventLogMsg`.
- Create or add your message script (`.mc`) file to the sub-project. Your project structure should look something like the one in the screenshot below:

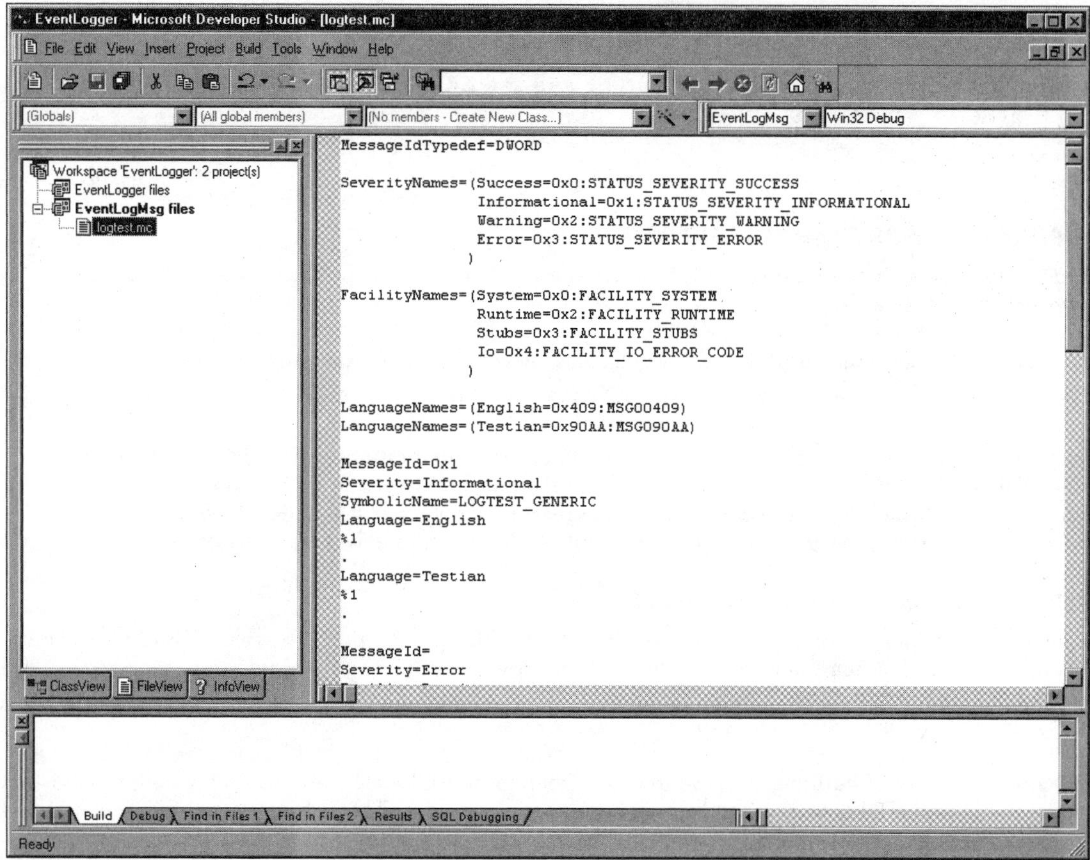

Compiling the Message Script

We need to have a quick discussion about the message script compiler. `MC.exe` is a simple program that comes with the Platform SDK. It interprets the contents of the message script, and builds the files you need to create the message resources.

To use MC to compile a message script, you can do the following:

- Create a new Tools menu item with the command and arguments shown in the screenshot below. I prefer doing this to adding a custom build step, because it becomes part of the Tools menu forever, rather than you having to add a custom build step to each new project. The (slight) drawback is that you have to remember to run the command manually when you change the `.mc` script file.

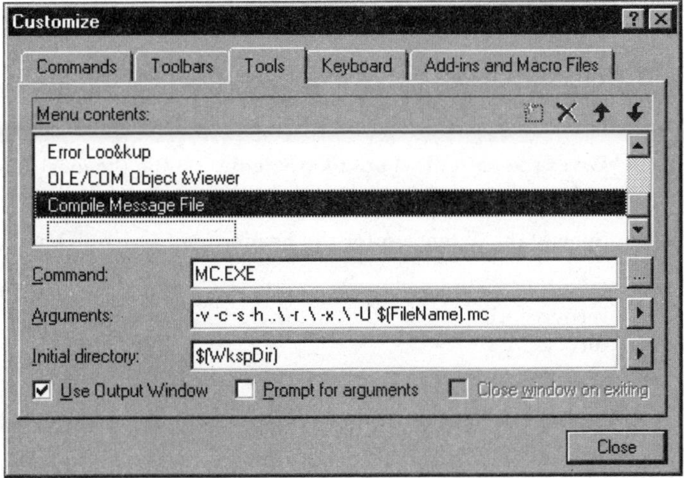

- Execute the command on the file. With the arguments set up as above, the following will happen:
    - The `.h` file that gets generated will appear in the directory *above* the current project directory. In other words, it's in the main project, where the symbols for the messages will be needed.
    - The `.rc` file is generated in the current directory.
    - The `.bin` file(s) are generated in the current directory, and they will be in Unicode (as denoted by the `-U` flag).

MC and its Arguments

Here's a list of some of the more interesting arguments to MC, together with an explanation of their meanings. For complete help, use the `MC -?` command from the command line.

```
MC [-?vcdwso] [-m maxmsglen] [-h dirspec] [-e extension] [-r dirspec]
   [-x dbgFileSpec] [-u] [-U] filename.mc
```

Argument	Meaning
`-?`	Help.
`-v`	Gives verbose output.
`-d`	Use decimal for message values.
`-s`	Insert symbolic name as first line of each message in the header file output.
`-m maxmsglen`	Generate a warning if the size of any message exceeds `maxmsglen` characters.
`-h pathspec`	Gives the path of where to create the `.h` file (header). The default is the current directory.
`-e extension`	Specify the extension for the header file from 1-3 characters.
`-r pathspec`	Gives the path of where to create the `.rc` file, and the binary message resource files (`.bin`) that file includes. The default is the current directory.
`-x pathspec`	Gives the path of where to create the `.dbg` file. The debug symbol file can be used like any other symbol file to help out the debugger while you are debugging.
`-u`	Input file is Unicode.
`-U`	Messages output into the `.bin` file should be Unicode.
`Filename.mc`	The name of the message script to compile.

Building the Resource

Once the message script is compiled, you can make use of the files that it generates in your main project, and build the message resource string DLL. To continue on:

- Add the `.h` file to the precompiled header file (or separately to each source file in which you need error constants) for the main project. This gives you access to all the handy symbolic constants you just created, so that you can invoke errors in your service by symbolic name, not by number.
- Add the `.rc` file to the sub-project. This `.rc` file contains references to the `.bin` resource files.
- Add a `.c` file to the project with a bare-bones stub for `DllMain()`, as shown below, so that your message file DLL has an entry point.

```
#include <windows.h>

__declspec(dllexport) BOOL WINAPI DllMain(HINSTANCE hInstance,
                                          DWORD     dwReason,
                                          LPVOID    lpReserved)
{
    return 1;
}
```

- When you're ready, build the sub-project to generate the DLL.

Building the Resource into the EXE

As I explained above, you can adjust the build process slightly and build the message string resource right into the EXE file that contains the service. To do that, follow these steps:

- Add your `.mc` file to the main service project. Don't create a separate sub-project.
- Modify the arguments to the `MC.exe` compiler to put the `.h` file in the same directory as the `.mc` file. In other words, change the `-h` argument, as follows:

```
MC -v -c -s -h .\ -r .\ -x .\ -U $(FileName).mc
```

- Compile the message script as above.
- Add the `.rc` and `.h` files to the project.
- Build the project when ready, and the resource will be part of the service executable.

Remember that having to load the service executable in order to get at the descriptions for the message strings causes a lot of extra overhead for the Event Viewer. There are very few circumstances in which I would use this method.

Registry Setup

The last thing that you need to do in preparation for using the event log is to add appropriate registry entries so that the Event Viewer knows where to find the message resources when someone wants to view them. The changes are actually quite simple; they all go beneath the following key:

```
HKEY_LOCAL_MACHINE
    SYSTEM
        CurrentControlSet
            Services
                EventLog
                    Application
                        MyService
                    Security
                    System
```

A separate key for each service you write goes underneath the `Application` key. Beneath that subkey, there are five possible name-value pairs:

Name	Meaning
`CategoryMessageFile`	If you are using event categories, this entry contains the full path for the category file. If not, leave this value out altogether. This path is usually the same as the one entered in the `EventMessageFile` entry, though it could be different. The value is of type `REG_EXPAND_SZ`.
`CategoryCount`	The number of categories contained in the `CategoryMessageFile`. The value is of type `REG_DWORD`.
`EventMessageFile`	The full path of the DLL or EXE that contains the resource for the message identifiers and strings. This will be either your message DLL or the service executable itself. You can list more than one file here, separated by semicolons, if you desire. The value is of type `REG_EXPAND_SZ`.
`ParameterMessageFile`	The path to the parameter message file. When it exists, this file is used as the source for the parameters (such as `%1`) in the event description strings contained in the event message files. However, this is rare because the parameters to the event description strings are typically set by the service itself. The value is of type `REG_EXPAND_SZ`.
`TypesSupported`	The bitmask of supported message types that the service can generate. This is a combination of `EVENTLOG_ERROR_TYPE`, `EVENTLOG_WARNING_TYPE`, and `EVENTLOG_INFORMATION_TYPE`. The value is of type `REG_DWORD`.

Of the possible values, only `EventMessageFile` and `TypesSupported` are required. The screenshot below shows what the registry will look like after the appropriate keys have been added.

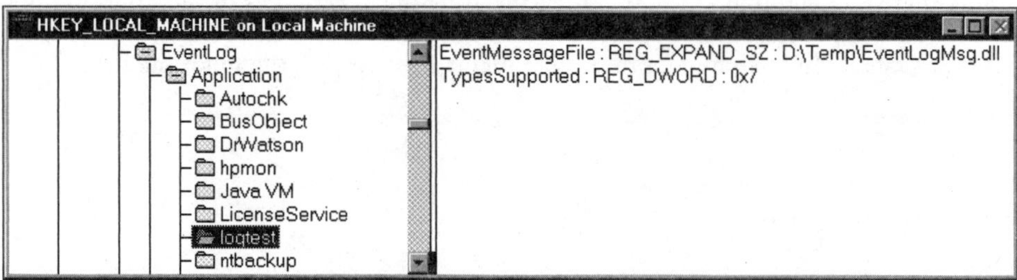

To enact the changes to the registry, at least for a shippable product, you should add code to your setup program to make the appropriate entries in the registry (or otherwise script in the changes). You'll need to have Administrator privileges to make the update. I'll demonstrate how to add the keys programmatically in the sample that we're currently constructing, but first there's another matter to address.

Writing Events to the Log

To write to the event log and use the message resource, you use three basic functions. In case you were worried, writing to the log is an atomic operation for the operating system – that is, the write operation is guaranteed to succeed completely, or to fail.

Opening the Log for Writing

To write an entry to the log, you must first open it. You do that with the `RegisterEventSource()` function:

```
HANDLE RegisterEventSource(LPCTSTR lpUNCServerName,
                           LPCTSTR lpSourceName);
```

The first parameter to `RegisterEventSource()` is the UNC name of the server to whose event log you wish to write. To write to the local machine's log, you can pass `NULL`. The second parameter is the name of the event source you registered in the preceding section; it is the exact name of the registry key you added beneath

```
HKEY_LOCAL_MACHINE\SYSTEM\CurrentControlSet\Services\EventLog\Application
```

Typically, the event source name will be the name of your service, though that's not an absolute requirement – you just have to make sure that you call `RegisterEventSource()` with the same name you set up in the registry above. The function returns a handle to the event log if successful, or `NULL` if unsuccessful.

Writing the Entry to the Log

Now, you're ready to write to the log. To do that, use the `ReportEvent()` function:

```
BOOL ReportEvent(HANDLE    hEventLog,
                 WORD      wType,
                 WORD      wCategory,
                 DWORD     dwEventID,
                 PSID      lpUserSid,
                 WORD      wNumStrings,
                 DWORD     dwDataSize,
                 LPCTSTR*  lpStrings,
                 LPVOID    lpRawData);
```

`ReportEvent()` takes a variety of parameters, some of which you'll use less frequently than others. The first parameter is the handle to the event log that you registered above with `RegisterEventSource()`, while the second parameter is assigned one of the following event type constants, which describe the type of the event:

```
EVENTLOG_ERROR_TYPE
EVENTLOG_WARNING_TYPE
EVENTLOG_INFORMATION_TYPE
```

These values match those that make up the bitmask in the `TypesSupported` value you added to the registry.

The third parameter, `wCategory`, is the category ID of one of the categories you set up back when you created the message script. This value should be `NULL` if you're not using message categories for your service. The fourth parameter, `dwEventID`, is the symbol for the message ID you want this event to be mapped to. This is the ID that the Event Viewer will match to your message resource to display the full error description when requested to do so by someone examining the event in the log. It's the symbol that was generated and put into the `.h` file you referenced in the project.

In the fifth parameter, `lpUserSID`, you can send a Windows NT security identifier to the event log to record which user's request caused the event you are logging. This facility is handy in situations where you might wish to record the SID of the user who was calling into the service – it's particularly useful in the client/server usage patterns we'll investigate later in the book. For services without clients, such as Monitor, you can just pass `NULL`.

The sixth parameter is the number of insertion strings that you will be passing in the eighth parameter, `lpStrings`, which is an array of constant `TSTR`s. Remember that these are the strings that will be inserted, in order, into the parameters (`%1`, `%2`, etc.) that were part of the message descriptions in your original message script (`.mc`) file. If you don't have any insertion strings for this particular message, you can pass zero to the sixth parameter and `NULL` as the value for the `lpStrings` array.

The seventh parameter, `dwDataSize`, is the size of the data that will be coming in the ninth parameter, which is a simple `void` pointer to a memory location. Using this feature, you can pass in any data you wish that might later be useful in debugging the cause of the message you are logging, as long as the data is less than 8Kb in size. As mentioned in an earlier section, you should indicate in the message description what the data being sent actually is.

`ReportEvent()` returns a `BOOL` to indicate whether it succeeded. You can call `GetLastError()` to determine why it failed if you need.

Closing the Log

The final step in the process is to close the log after you've finished writing to it. This is easy enough to do – you just call the `DeregisterEventSource()` API function:

```
BOOL DeregisterEventSource(HANDLE hEventLog);
```

The argument you supply should be the handle of the log you opened. A word of caution, though: you should not leave the log open for long periods of time. When you need to log an event, open the log, write the event, then close the log immediately. Don't open the log and keep the handle for later use.

The CEventLog Class

Unfortunately, there's no good way to automate or encapsulate the steps involved in creating a message script, but we *can* make the act of writing events to the log a tad easier by wrapping the necessary steps up into a simple C++ class.

The `CEventLog` class provides several different ways to call `ReportEvent()`, wrapped up in overloaded functions so that you can exclude data, insertion strings, or categories, depending on what you need for the particular call. Below is the header file for the class, which you can add to the console application project you created earlier in the chapter:

```
// EventLog.h file
// CEventLog Class - Implements event logging functions

class CEventLog
{
public:
   CEventLog(LPCTSTR pszSource, LPCTSTR pszServerName = NULL);
   ~CEventLog() { }

   // Simple Version
   bool LogEvent(DWORD    dwEventID,
                 WORD     wEventType  = EVENTLOG_ERROR_TYPE,
                 WORD     wCategory   = 0,
                 PSID     lpUserSid   = NULL);

   // Does anything version
   bool LogEvent(DWORD dwEventID,
                 LPCTSTR* lpStrings   = NULL,
                 WORD     wNumStrings = 0,
                 LPVOID   lpRawData   = 0,
                 DWORD    dwDataSize  = 0,
                 WORD     wEventType  = EVENTLOG_ERROR_TYPE,
                 WORD     wCategory   = 0,
                 PSID     lpUserSid   = NULL);

   // Single String Version
   bool LogEvent(DWORD    dwEventID,
                 LPCTSTR  lpString,
                 WORD     wEventType  = EVENTLOG_ERROR_TYPE,
                 WORD     wCategory   = 0,
                 PSID     lpUserSid   = NULL);

   // Multiple String Version
   bool LogEvent(DWORD    dwEventID,
                 LPCTSTR* lpStrings,
                 WORD     wNumStrings,
                 WORD     wEventType  = EVENTLOG_ERROR_TYPE,
                 WORD     wCategory   = 0,
                 PSID     lpUserSid   = NULL);

   // Send Data Version
   bool LogEvent(DWORD    dwEventID,
                 DWORD    dwDataSize,
                 LPVOID   lpRawData,
                 WORD     wEventType  = EVENTLOG_ERROR_TYPE,
                 WORD     wCategory   = 0,
                 PSID     lpUserSid   = NULL);
```

```
    // Log a Win32 error
    bool LogWin32Error(DWORD    dwEventID,
                       LPCTSTR szString    = NULL,
                       DWORD   dwErrorNum = GetLastError());

    bool RegisterLog(LPTSTR szPath);

private:
    HANDLE  m_hes;
    LPCTSTR m_pszSource;
    LPCTSTR m_pszServerName;

    void Register()
    {
       m_hes = RegisterEventSource(m_pszServerName, m_pszSource);
    }

    void Deregister()
    {
       DeregisterEventSource(m_hes);
    }

// Event Types are one of the following
    // EVENTLOG_ERROR_TYPE;
    // EVENTLOG_WARNING_TYPE;
    // EVENTLOG_INFORMATION_TYPE;
};
```

Moving on to the implementation, the constructor accepts both a source name and the name of the server on which the events are to be logged. By default, the server name is `NULL`, which means 'log to the local machine'.

```
// File EventLog.cpp Implements the CEventLog class

#include "precomp.h"
#include "eventlog.h"

// Construction
CEventLog::CEventLog(LPCTSTR pszSource, LPCTSTR pszServerName)
{
   m_hes = NULL;
   m_pszSource = pszSource;
   m_pszServerName = pszServerName;
}
```

LogEvent Functions

Simple it may be, but this class does the trick. To use it, just call one of the overloaded versions of `CEventLog::LogEvent()`, of which there are five, or `LogWin32Error()`, which prints out a generic Win32 error to the log. Registering and de-registering the event source are also handled in each call to one of the logging functions, which are described below.

- A 'simple' version, which takes an event ID and, optionally, a type, a category ID, and a SID.

```
// Simple Version
bool CEventLog::LogEvent(DWORD dwEventID,    WORD     wEventType,
                         WORD  wCategory,    PSID     lpUserSid)
{
   Register();
   bool b = ReportEvent(m_hes, wEventType, wCategory,
                             dwEventID, lpUserSid, 0, 0, NULL, NULL);
   Deregister();
   return b;
}
```

- A 'complex' version, which takes an event ID and, optionally, any of the other parameters in any combination.

```
// Does anything version
bool CEventLog::LogEvent(DWORD dwEventID,    LPCTSTR* lpStrings,
                         WORD  wNumStrings,  LPVOID   lpRawData,
                         DWORD dwDataSize,   WORD     wEventType,
                         WORD  wCategory,    PSID     lpUserSid)
{
   if(wNumStrings == 0 && lpStrings != NULL)
      return false;
   if(lpStrings == NULL && wNumStrings != 0)
      return false;

   Register();
   bool b = ReportEvent(m_hes, wEventType, wCategory, dwEventID, lpUserSid,
                        wNumStrings, dwDataSize, lpStrings, lpRawData);
   Deregister();
   return b;
}
```

- A 'single string' version, which takes an event ID and allows you to send a single insertion string without worrying about creating an array of one string. It does not accept data.

```
// Single String Version
bool CEventLog::LogEvent(DWORD dwEventID,    LPCTSTR  lpString,
                         WORD  wEventType,   WORD     wCategory,
                         PSID  lpUserSid)
{
   const TCHAR* rgsz[] = {lpString};

   Register();
   bool b = ReportEvent(m_hes, wEventType, wCategory, dwEventID,
                                    lpUserSid, 1, 0, rgsz, NULL);
   Deregister();
   return b;
}
```

- A 'multiple string' version, which takes an event ID and *multiple* insertion strings. It does not accept data.

```
// Multiple String Version
bool CEventLog::LogEvent(DWORD dwEventID,    LPCTSTR* lpStrings,
                         WORD wNumStrings,   WORD     wEventType,
                         WORD wCategory,     PSID     lpUserSid)
{
   Register();
   bool b = ReportEvent(m_hes, wEventType, wCategory, dwEventID,
                                lpUserSid, wNumStrings, 0, lpStrings, NULL);
   Deregister();
   return b;
}
```

- A 'data only' version, which takes an event ID, a `void` pointer to data, and a 'size of data' parameter. It does not accept insertion strings.

```
// Send Data Version
bool CEventLog::LogEvent(DWORD  dwEventID,   DWORD    dwDataSize,
                         LPVOID lpRawData,   WORD     wEventType,
                         WORD   wCategory,   PSID     lpUserSid)
{
   Register();
   bool b = ReportEvent(m_hes, wEventType, wCategory, dwEventID,
                                lpUserSid, 0, dwDataSize, NULL, lpRawData);
   Deregister();
   return b;
}
```

- A 'log Win32 error' function, which accepts an event ID and a Win32 error number, and outputs the error to the event log, along with its description string.

```
// Log a Win32 error
bool CEventLog::LogWin32Error(DWORD dwEventID,
                                        LPCTSTR szString, DWORD dwErrorNum)
{
   LPVOID lpvMsgBuf;
   TCHAR szErrorDesc[1024];
   if(!FormatMessage(FORMAT_MESSAGE_FROM_SYSTEM |
                        FORMAT_MESSAGE_ALLOCATE_BUFFER,
                     0, dwErrorNum,
                     MAKELANGID(LANG_NEUTRAL, SUBLANG_DEFAULT),
                     (LPTSTR)&lpvMsgBuf, 0, 0))
   {
      if(szString != NULL)
         wsprintf(szErrorDesc,
```

```
                _T("Function: %s returned Win32 Error: %d, Unknown Error"),
                szString, dwErrorNum);
      else
         wsprintf(szErrorDesc,
                _T("Win32 Error: %d, Unknown Error"),
                dwErrorNum);
   }
   else
   {
      if(szString != NULL)
         wsprintf(szErrorDesc,
               _T("Function: %s returned Win32 Error: %d Description:%s"),
                szString, dwErrorNum, lpvMsgBuf);
      else
         wsprintf(szErrorDesc,
                _T("Win32 Error: %d Description: %s"),
                dwErrorNum, lpvMsgBuf);
      LocalFree(lpvMsgBuf);
   }

   const TCHAR* rgsz[] = { szErrorDesc };

   Register();
   bool b = ReportEvent(m_hes, EVENTLOG_ERROR_TYPE, NULL, dwEventID,
                                             NULL, 1, 0, rgsz, NULL);
   Deregister();
   return b;
}
```

RegisterLog

Finally, there is also a function called `RegisterLog()`, which puts the proper entries for setting up the event log into the registry. This is the method for programmatic manipulation of the registry I mentioned earlier, and it looks like this:

```
bool CEventLog::RegisterLog(LPTSTR szPath)
{
   HKEY hk;
   DWORD dwData;
   TCHAR szBuf[256];
   TCHAR szKey[256];
   wsprintf(szKey, _T("SYSTEM\\CurrentControlSet\\Services\\
                     EventLog\\Application\\%s"),
         m_pszSource);

   // Does the key already exist?
   if(RegOpenKey(HKEY_LOCAL_MACHINE, szKey, &hk) == ERROR_SUCCESS)
      return true;
```

```
    if(RegCreateKey(HKEY_LOCAL_MACHINE, szKey, &hk) != ERROR_SUCCESS)
       return false;

    _tcscpy(szBuf, szPath);

    // EventMessageFile subkey
    if(RegSetValueEx(hk, _T("EventMessageFile"), 0, REG_EXPAND_SZ,
     (LPBYTE)szBuf, ((_tcslen(szBuf) + 1) * sizeof(TCHAR))) != ERROR_SUCCESS)
       return false;

    // TypesSupported
    dwData = EVENTLOG_ERROR_TYPE |
             EVENTLOG_WARNING_TYPE | EVENTLOG_INFORMATION_TYPE;

    if(RegSetValueEx(hk, _T("TypesSupported"), 0, REG_DWORD, (LPBYTE)&dwData,
                                              sizeof(DWORD)) != ERROR_SUCCESS)
       return false;

    RegCloseKey(hk);
    return true;
 }
```

Using CEventLog

In order to show how to use the class, I've created a simple executable (*not* a service) that uses the different permutations of `CEventLog::LogEvent()`. Here's the simple `main()` function that generates all the events:

```
#include "precomp.h"
#include "EventLog.h"

int main()
{
   CEventLog log(_T("logtest"));

   // **Change to your path**
   log.RegisterLog(_T("c:\\temp\\EventLogMsg.dll"));

   // Simple write
   log.LogEvent(LOGTEST_INFO_1, EVENTLOG_INFORMATION_TYPE);

   // Single string write
   log.LogEvent(LOGTEST_ERROR, _T("c:\\dummy.txt"));

   // Win32 error write
   log.LogWin32Error(LOGTEST_WIN32_ERROR, NULL, 1234);
```

```
    // Data Write
    struct LOGTEST_DUDLEY
    {
       int  d1;
       char name[25];
    } dummy = {51, "ABCDEFGHI"};

    log.LogEvent(LOGTEST_ERROR_WITH_DATA, sizeof(LOGTEST_DUDLEY), &dummy);
    return 0;
 }
```

The final file you need to add to the project, `precomp.h`, is the same as it was in the last chapter, but for two changes: you don't need to include `process.h`, and you certainly should include `logtest.h`. Then, with everything compiled and functioning correctly, you'll be able to generate events like these. Here's the output of a couple of the more interesting ones, as seen when viewed by the Event Viewer:

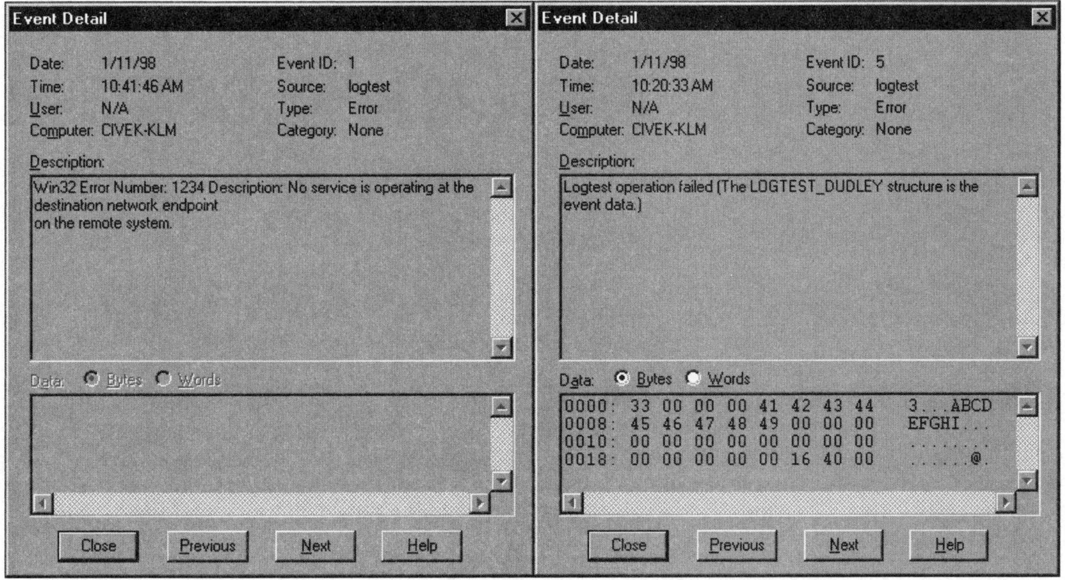

Note that if you had the Event Viewer open before the new message DLL was registered, you'll need to close and reopen it before this will work. The Event Viewer examines the registry just once, when it is first run, and it won't recognize any changes you make until it is relaunched.

Converting the Monitor

In order to demonstrate these concepts further, we can convert the Monitor pattern sample from the last chapter to use the new CEventLog classes for event logging.

Monitor.MC

The MC file contains a couple of simple events. One is the 'successful ping' message that is presently called from CMonitor::Run() every time Ping() returns successfully. It now becomes an official event log message called MONITOR_PING_SUCCESSFUL.

```
MessageIdTypedef=DWORD

LanguageNames=(English=0x409:MSG00409)

MessageId=0x1
Severity=Informational
SymbolicName=MONITOR_PING_SUCCESSFUL
Language=English
The address was successfully pinged.
.

MessageId=
Severity=Error
SymbolicName=SERVICE_WIN32_ERROR
Language=English
%1
.
```

The other message in the file is a generic one for Win32 errors, and you'll see how it works in a moment.

Registering the Message File

After following the steps outlined earlier in the chapter to compile the message script, create the message DLL, and get the error message header file into the main monitor project, you can begin to modify main(), CService, and CMonitor to accommodate the new event logging functionality. main() comes first:

```
CharLowerBuff(pszCmdLine, lstrlen(pszCmdLine));
if(_tcsstr(pszCmdLine, _T("-install")))
{
   CServiceInstall si(szName, szDisplay);
   si.Install();

   CEventLog log(szName);
   log.RegisterLog(_T("D:\\Temp\\MonitorMsg.dll"));

   return 0;
}
```

This addition calls RegisterLog() when the service is installed to put the proper entries into the registry. The screenshot below shows the result.

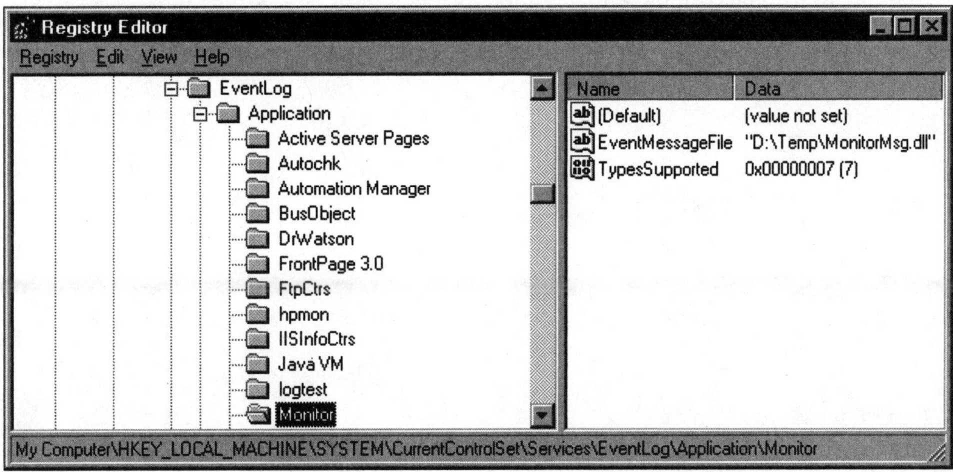

Error Handling Modifications

The next modification is to change ErrorHandler() so that it uses the CEventLog class when it needs to output Win32 errors to the registry.

```
DWORD CService::ErrorHandler(const TCHAR* psz, bool bPrintEvent,
                             bool bRaiseException, DWORD dwErr)
{
   if(bPrintEvent)
   {
      CEventLog log(m_szName);
      log.LogWin32Error(SERVICE_WIN32_ERROR, psz, dwErr);
   }

   if(bRaiseException)
      RaiseException(dwErr, EXCEPTION_NONCONTINUABLE, 0, 0);

   return dwErr;
}
```

You can see that the function is radically simpler than it was. Furthermore, you can remove the PrintEvent() function completely, as it is no longer needed. When a derivative of CService (like CMonitor) needs to print to the event log, it will simply use one of the LogEvent() functions of a CEventLog object created locally on the stack.

Run Modifications

To see an example of the above, look at the modified version of `Run()`, which now calls `LogEvent()` directly on a `CEventLog` object. It uses the `MONITOR_PING_SUCCESSFUL` symbolic constant when logging the event, rather than sending the string in its entirety.

```
        else if(!m_bPause)                  // (!m_bPause && !bPauseSent)
        {
           // I'm running as usual, so ping
           dwErr = Ping();
           if(dwErr != NO_ERROR)
              break;

           CEventLog log(m_szName);
           log.LogEvent(MONITOR_PING_SUCCESSFUL, EVENTLOG_INFORMATION_TYPE);
        }
```

Seeing the Results

Compile the service, and run the executable with the `-install` option. If you ran the service in the last chapter, you might need to remove the service using `-remove` first. Now, start the service, giving it an IP address, and you'll see the following results:

Event Viewer - Application Log on \\CIVEK-KLM

Log View Options Help

Date	Time	Source	Category	Event	User
6/21/98	4:42:50 PM	Monitor	None	1	N/A
6/21/98	4:42:45 PM	Monitor	None	1	N/A
6/21/98	4:38:04 PM	Monitor	None	1	N/A
6/21/98	4:37:59 PM	Monitor	None	1	N/A
6/21/98	4:37:54 PM	Monitor	None	1	N/A
6/21/98	4:37:49 PM	Monitor	None	1	N/A
6/21/98	4:37:44 PM	Monitor	None	1	N/A
6/21/98	4:37:39 PM	Monitor	None	1	N/A
6/21/98	4:37:34 PM	Monitor	None	1	N/A
6/21/98	3:57:21 PM	logtest	None	5	N/A
6/21/98	3:57:21 PM	logtest	None	1	N/A
6/21/98	3:57:21 PM	logtest	None	3	N/A
6/21/98	3:57:21 PM	logtest	None	4	N/A
6/21/98	3:56:50 PM	logtest	None	5	N/A
6/21/98	3:56:50 PM	logtest	None	1	N/A
6/21/98	3:56:50 PM	logtest	None	3	N/A
6/21/98	3:56:50 PM	logtest	None	4	N/A
6/21/98	3:56:26 PM	logtest	None	5	N/A

If you now view the details of one of these events, you'll see something like the dialog below:

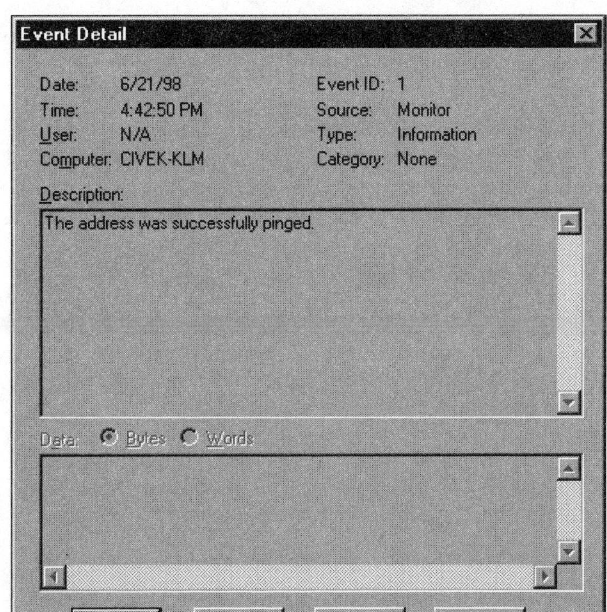

It's as simple as that. Notice that now the Event ID is 1 (rather than 0), and the description reflects what was in the `Monitor.mc` script. Better still, there isn't that annoying preface message, and the string, "The address was successfully pinged," doesn't take up any space in the event log file – it is only loaded from the message file DLL when the viewer needs to display the string that goes along with Event ID = 1.

Other Operations on the Event Log

Needing to read events from the event log is much rarer than the need to write them, mainly because we already have a handy event log reader in place: the Event Viewer. Sometimes, though, it might be appropriate to create your own event log reader as part of an administration program for a service. The custom log reader would show only log entries pertaining to the service, and might also interpret the event log data (which usually just shown in binary in the Event Viewer) into something more meaningful to the user or administrator.

If your application needs to read the event log, there's a set of APIs that performs all types of operations on it, including reading entries, clearing it, and so on. For the sake of completeness, I'll touch briefly upon these functions here.

Reading Records from the Event Log

First of all, you need to open the event log you wish to read from. You do that with a call to OpenEventLog(), which looks like this:

```
HANDLE OpenEventLog(LPCTSTR lpUNCServerName, // Server name
                    LPCTSTR lpSourceName     // Source name);
```

The value of the source name parameter can be Application, System, or Security, or the name of a custom log file that you have created. (I'll discuss custom log files shortly.)

After retrieving the event log handle, you call ReadEventLog() actually to go through the log file and read out event records.

```
BOOL ReadEventLog(
            HANDLE hEventLog,
            DWORD  dwReadFlags,                  // Read method
            DWORD  dwRecordOffset,               // Where in file to start from
            LPVOID lpBuffer,                     // Buffer to put the data into
            DWORD  nNumberOfBytesToRead,         // Buffer size
            DWORD* pnBytesRead,                  // Actual bytes read
            DWORD* pnMinNumberOfBytesNeeded // Bytes needed for next record
);
```

In the dwReadFlags parameter, you pass one of the following values:

Value	Meaning
EVENTLOG_FORWARDS_READ	Read in forward chronological order
EVENTLOG_BACKWARDS_READ	Read in reverse chronological order
EVENTLOG_SEEK_READ	Start from the record specified in dwRecordOffset
EVENTLOG_SEQUENTIAL_READ	Proceed from where the last call left off

The function returns zero or more EVENTLOGRECORD structures in the buffer pointed to by lpBuffer, and they vary in size from record to record because of the size of embedded data, string length, etc. The EVENTLOGRECORD structure is quite large, containing *all* the data for each record, so I won't reproduce it here. Please refer to the Win32 API documentation for more information.

ReadEventLog() will return as many *whole* EVENTLOGRECORD structures (no partial entries) as will fit into the size of buffer it was given, and a count of the actual number of bytes read. If the buffer is too small to read *any* log entries, the function fails and returns a value in the pnMinNumberofBytesNeeded parameter. You can iterate the calling of this function until there are no more entries remaining (pnMinNumberOfBytesNeeded is 0).

Other Event Log Functions

There are several other operations that you can perform programmatically on the event log. I've listed the ones that you may find useful in the table below:

Function	Description
BackupEventLog()	Saves the event log to a backup file without clearing it
ClearEventLog()	Clears the event log
GetNumberofEventLogRecords()	Returns the number of records in the log
GetOldestEventLogRecord()	Retrieves the record number of the oldest entry
NotifyChangeEventLog()	Sets an event object passed in as a parameter to signaled when a new event is written to the specified log
OpenBackupEventLog()	Opens a handle to a backup log

Whatever operations you might perform on an event log, you should always call `CloseEventLog()` after you've finished with it.

Adding a Custom Event Log

It's also possible to add your own custom event log to the mix, to supplement Application, System, and Security. To do so, you need to add an additional key to the registry beneath the `EventLog` key. You can do this by hand, by `.reg` file script, or programmatically; it's up to you:

```
HKEY_LOCAL_MACHINE
    SYSTEM
        CurrentControlSet
            Services
                EventLog
                    Application
                    MyLog
                        MyService
                    Security
                    System
```

When you do that, a value called `Sources` will automatically be added beneath the new log (`MyLog`) that contains a mapping of all the source names you add beneath it. You also need to specify the `File` value, which contains the path to the filename you want the events to be stored in. This file should have a file extension of `.evt`. Optionally, you can also add `MaxSize` and `Retention` `DWORD`s as additional values, to set those parameters on your custom log. Then, just add your source name beneath that new key and proceed like you always have.

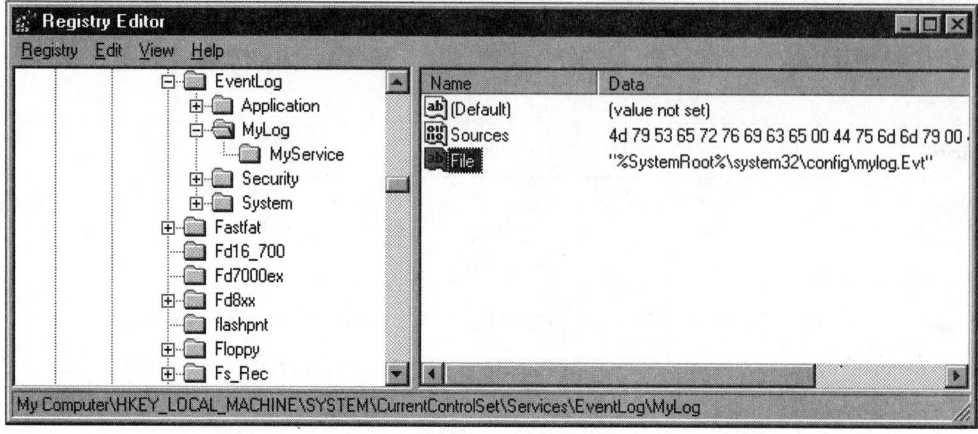

The effect of doing this will be that you now have all the advantages associated with using the standard Win32 API to do event logging, but within the confines of your own private storage area that does not consume space in the other log files. This can be beneficial when you need to log large amounts of data or events in your service, but don't want to tie up the application log. It also affords privacy, since the event viewer is only capable of reading the three standard logs. If you use a custom log, you will need to create your own viewer for it, which is one good reason why you might need the broader logging APIs we discussed in the last section.

Other Techniques

There are a couple of other handy ways to use the event log. For example, one thing you can do to make debugging easier is to have a variable level of event logging, based on whether your service is a debug build or a release build. When you're developing a service, you might find it helpful to know when you call a particular function, or the contents of a particular memory structure. If you find that information helpful for debugging, there's no need to rip it out when you go to release – just surround the logging code with an `#ifdef _DEBUG` statement so that the unnecessary code is taken out during a release build:

```
#ifdef _DEBUG
   CEventLog log2(_T("logtest"));
   log2.LogEvent(LOGTEST_ERROR_WITH_DATA, sizeof(LOGTEST_DUDLEY), &dummy);
#endif
```

In other words, you can use logging in the same way you use `assert()` – to check the state of your assumptions, and to let you know if they are not what you expected. When you get ready to release, the extra logging is just compiled out.

Another technique you can use is to create a registry entry or service parameter to 'tune' the level of event logging that the service does. When your service starts, you can read the value of the registry entry or parameter and set a global variable to a certain logging level. Then, based on the value of that variable, you can choose whether to log a particular event.

```
if(bVerbose)
{
    CEventLog log2(_T("logtest"));
    log2.LogEvent(LOGTEST_ERROR_WITH_DATA, sizeof(LOGTEST_DUDLEY), &dummy);
}
```

Of course, this won't keep your release build free of logging code, but it will allow your customers to 'ramp up' the amount of information they get about what the service is doing in a production environment. This can be a boon for solving production support problems.

Summary

The event log features of NT are quite powerful. They provide a universal data structure and set of APIs that developers can use to build logging functionality into their applications. They are especially important for services, since events tend to be the only way a service communicates with the people administering it.

However, since the event log is being used many different processes, it's important that your service uses it consistently and appropriately. To that end, here are a few guidelines for good event log etiquette:

- The log should *only* be used for events that are on the **error path** of the service. It should not be used as a generalized trace facility, or as a logging mechanism for recurring work processing events – at least, not in a released or production environment. (In short, the Monitor sample is a *bad* use of the event log.)
- If you *do* use the log for tracing, you should make sure that it is only for short periods of time – e.g., during debugging or performance tuning.
- The log *can* be used for certain major non-error events, such as for logging that the service started successfully, or changed to the 'paused' state, etc. Such events should be of the informational type.
- Descriptions should be localized and devoid of cultural colloquialisms.
- Event data should only be used when it provides useful information. Writing data structures to the log consumes a lot of space.

6

Microsoft Message Queue and the Agent Usage Pattern

Ever since Windows' inception, a noticeable omission from its networking features has been the ability for applications that are not running simultaneously, or are disconnected by an unreliable or intentionally unconnected network, to be able to communicate.

As you know, in the typical client-server model, a client application issues a request for a remote procedure to execute somewhere on a server. The thread on the client that issues the request remains waiting and blocked until the server returns the result, or until the network mechanism on which the call is carried times out. We say that these types of requests are **synchronous**. Many networking protocols and subsystems also have the notion of an **asynchronous** request, in which the client issues the request, goes on its merry way, and is contacted again later, via a callback mechanism, when the work is done. Typically, asynchronous requests are used when:

- The operation the client requests requires time-intensive processing on the server
- It *really is* possible for the client to go on doing other work without the result being returned

Both of these models, however, presume that the client and the server are running together, at the same time, and that the network between them is still functioning throughout the synchronous or asynchronous call. If the server, the client, or the network between them dies, the request and any results that may have been processed are lost forever.

Enter **Microsoft Message Queue (MSMQ)**. MSMQ provides that long-needed mechanism on Windows platforms whereby a client and a server (or, more appropriately, a consumer and a provider) can communicate with one another whether or not they're both running at the same time, and regardless of the reliability of the network on which they communicate.

MSMQ does this by using a model that *guarantees* delivery of the messages that consumers and providers use to communicate. Consumers and providers issue their requests in the form of application-defined messages that are stored in **message queues**. These queues are persistent – that is, their contents live on disk (unless you choose an 'express' queue, which only lives in memory, but is faster). Each operation in which a message is written (sent) or read (received) is guaranteed to succeed completely, or to fail. A 'send' commits the message to permanent storage until someone reads it, period. A 'retrieve' removes the message from permanent storage, period. If the retrieval operation is interrupted, the message stays in the queue.

In addition, send and receive operations can be part of larger transactions that are managed by the Microsoft Distributed Transaction Coordinator and/or Microsoft Transaction Server. If a send operation fails, any number of other operations on any number of other media (file, database, etc.) managed by the same transaction can be 'rolled back'.

Really then, messages are a communication mechanism between applications, just like RPC, sockets, and so forth, but they are more robust and more flexible in circumstances where guaranteed delivery is necessary without a guaranteed network connection. They are also highly versatile in the content they can hold: messages can contain any type of data, and can be any length up to 10MB in size; they can even contain objects. The difference between MSMQ and a system involving some type of mail messages is that the messages in MSMQ are completely general and multi-purpose.

Services and MSMQ

"What does this have to do with services?" I can hear you ask. Well, I could go on and on about MSMQ just because I think it's a really cool technology, but it turns out that services are actually a great place to implement the 'provider' side of a consumer-provider pair that uses messages as its communication method. In fact, MSMQ itself is implemented as an NT service called Microsoft Message Queue Service.

The reason that services are useful in an architecture that uses MSMQ is that MSMQ lacks the motif of a generic agent. In other words, it defines semantics for opening, closing, and creating queues, and for sending and receiving messages, but there is no explicit *housing* for applications that want to process messages.

> *Don't think that's a flaw, by the way: it* should *lack this housing – MSMQ is a communication protocol, not a provider of application-level services.*

In an architecture where clients send messages to a queue in anticipation that a server will act on those requests, how should the server be implemented? As another application that processes messages when it is launched? Perhaps, but who will launch it?

A service is a perfect place to implement a usage pattern known as the **Agent**. An Agent monitors a queue of requests posted by clients, performs the requested work, and then sends the result back to a results queue for the client to retrieve and use. In a sense, then, this pattern fills an architectural need for a 'drone' that can go out and perform work asynchronously, and send back the result. In short, it acts as the client's 'agent'. Examples of when a client might use an agent are a web search, a complicated algorithmic processing task, or for processing a complicated query to a data warehouse. Later on in this chapter, I'll demonstrate this pattern using MSMQ.

MSMQ Programming Concepts

This isn't intended to be a chapter about MSMQ, but in case you're unfamiliar with MSMQ's programming concepts and terminology, I'm going to spend a few pages explaining the concepts that I'll use in developing the Agent service. If you're happy with using and programming MSMQ, you can skip ahead to the next section.

Enterprises and Sites

When you install MSMQ, which you do from the NT Server version of the NT Option Pack, you'll be creating what's known as a **Primary Enterprise Controller (PEC)**. The PEC is the owner of the **enterprise configuration**, which is really just a logical concept that describes all of the machines that are connected by a network and might ever want to communicate with one another using MSMQ. All the computers in an organization that run MSMQ belong to the same enterprise, and access information from the same distributed database: the **MSMQ information store (MQIS)**. Typically, all of these computers are in the same NT domain. The MQIS contains information about all the public queues in the enterprise (as opposed to private queues, which can only be accessed by name).

A **Primary Site Controller (PSC)** is the main controller machine for a **site**. (The PEC is also the PSC for the site in which it resides.) A site is another logical concept; it describes a portion of the enterprise in which all the machines are likely to need access to the same queues. The distinguishing characteristic of machines in a site is usually that they share a high-bandwidth network for rapid communication between each other. The PSC has a replicated copy of the MQIS for the enterprise.

When they want to use MSMQ queuing capability, individual clients install either an **independent client** or a **dependent client**. An independent client can create and modify queues locally, and send and receive messages just as MSMQ servers can, but without synchronous access to an MSMQ server. However, MSMQ independent clients do not have the capability to hold a message for a period of time and then forward it on, and do not store information from the distributed MSMQ database. Dependent clients are similar to independent clients, but they cannot function without synchronous access to a PEC, PSC, or backup site controller, because they don't actually run the MSMQ service. MSMQ dependent clients rely on a supporting server to perform *all* MSMQ operations for them.

Queues

The first concept you need to understand is the queue itself. What exactly *is* an MSMQ queue, and how do we work with one? The answer is that a queue is simply a repository for messages. There are several types of queue in MSMQ, which all operate identically, but serve different purposes. Some queues are created and used by applications, while others are created and used by MSMQ itself.

There are six types of queue that differ in terms of what they do and who uses them:

- **Public** and **private message queues**. These are the ones defined by applications to send and receive messages. Public queues are registered and visible in the MSMQ Information Store, and their messages can be viewed using the administration tools (MSMQ Explorer). They are replicated across the enterprise by MQIS. Private queues are only registered on the local computer, and are unavailable to applications that don't have access to their pathname. Private queues are not replicated, and can be used when the MQIS is unreachable across the network.

- **Administration queues**. These are also created by the application, and they're used to store messages that indicate whether messages sent to the main message queue have reached the queue, or have been retrieved from the queue.
- **Response queues**. These don't differ in structure from 'normal' queues, but they're used in a special way. A response queue is the place where the recipient of a message can send messages to respond to the sender. The message sender sends the location of the desired response queue as a property of the main message. The receiver then reads this queue out and can send a response message to it.
- **Dead letter queues**. The dead letter queue is a queue maintained by the system. It stores messages that cannot be delivered. There are two dead letter queues: one for transactional messages (messages that are sent as part of a larger transaction that's managed, for instance, by Microsoft Transaction Server), and one for non-transactional messages (everything else).
- **Report queues**. These are system queues that are used to track the location and progress of messages as they move around the enterprise. Typically, applications are only allowed to *read* messages in the report queues.
- **Journal**. The system creates a journal queue for each message queue. The journal queue stores a copy of each message retrieved from the queue. 'Journaling' is not enabled by default on a queue, but can be turned on programmatically or through the MSMQ Explorer.

Queues and messages are viewable using the Message Queue Explorer, which is installed when you install MSMQ components. You can see a screenshot below:

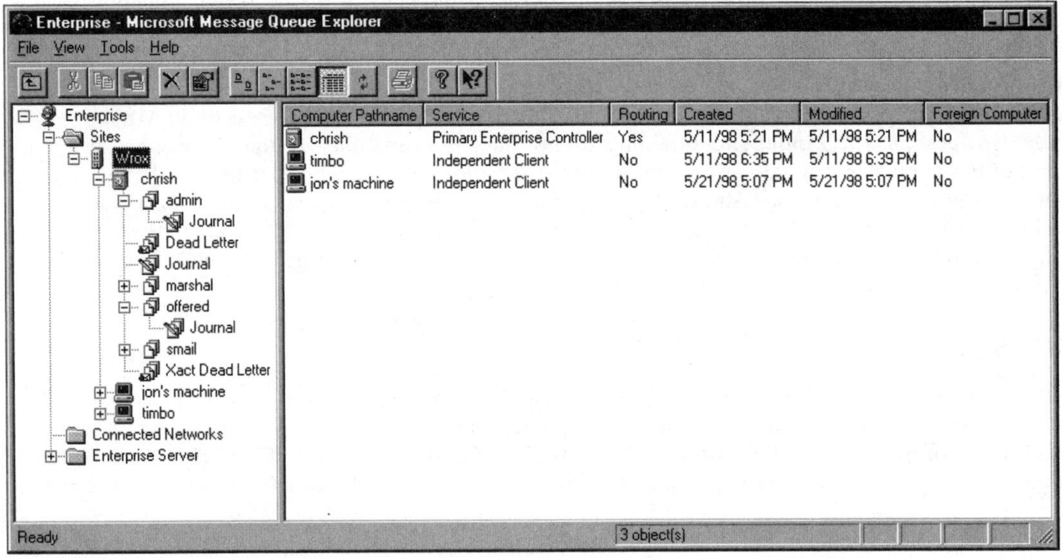

Identifying Queues

Queues can be referenced in a number of different ways, depending on the operations you're planning to perform on them.

Queue Pathname

When you first create a queue, you must give it a **queue pathname**. This is a simple string identifier that tells MSMQ on which machine the queue is to be created, what its name will be, and whether it is public or `private`. A queue pathname must be unique in the MSMQ enterprise; the format of a queue pathname is as follows:

Queue PathName	Meaning
`MachineName\QueueName`	Queue created on a machine
`.\QueueName`	Queue created on the local machine
`MachineName\PRIVATE$\QueueName`	Private queue on a machine
`.\PRIVATE$\QueueName`	Private queue on the local machine

Queue Label

Each queue also has a **queue label** that you specify when you create the queue. This label is used to identify the queue in the MSMQ Explorer. The label is stored as a property of the queue known as `PROPID_Q_LABEL`. Often, this label is just the `QueueName` portion of the pathname above, but not necessarily – it can be more descriptive.

Queue Properties

Every queue has a great deal of information about it that can be retrieved or changed using the `MQGetQueueProperties()` and `MQSetQueueProperties()` pair of functions. It is also necessary to specify certain information about a queue when you create it, such as its pathname and label information.

Throughout the remainder of this discussion, I'll be using versions of the MSMQ API functions that come from the January 1998 version of the Platform SDK. Earlier versions of the SDK have earlier versions of MSMQ and its headers that are incompatible with the code I'll develop here.

MSMQ Variant Properties

You specify queue properties using MSMQ's variant property structures. All types of object in MSMQ have a collection of properties that are stored as variant types (in structures of type `PROPVARIANT`). Like any variant, each `PROPVARIANT` instance has a data type, and a data value that's placed into the member of a union that matches the variant's type. For each MSMQ object, you can get or set multiple properties using a structure that describes a unique set of 1..*n* properties. This structure contains a `PROPVARIANT` array and a `QUEUEPROPID` array that maps a `PROPVARIANT` value to an enumerated tag value that starts with `PROPID_`. For queues, all property IDs start with `PROPID_Q_`.

MQQUEUEPROPS

The MQQUEUEPROPS structure is the container for queue properties described above. Each time you want to get or set the properties of a queue, you provide one of these structures formatted with the property IDs and PROPVARIANT structures that you want to set, or into which you want to receive the retrieved property information.

```
struct MQQUEUEPROPS
{
    DWORD         cProp;
    QUEUEPROPID aPropID[];
    PROPVARIANT aPropVar[];
    HRESULT       aStatus[];
};
```

To fill this structure, you create an array of PROPVARIANT structures and specify the data type and data value for each of them. Then, you create an array of QUEUEPROPIDs, specifying the PROPID_Q_XXX type of each property in the PROPVARIANT array, in the same order. You can also optionally specify a status array of HRESULTs that will contain an ordered HRESULT set – one for each property. (If you're not interested in a status array, you can just set this member to NULL.) After the function (get or set) in which you use the MQQUEUEPROPS structure is complete, this array will contain the return value for each get/set operation on each property in the array. Finally, you must specify the total count of all properties in the cProp member of the structure.

Available Queue Properties

There is a variety of queue properties available that I won't go into in detail, other than to list them. The key point to note is that each property ID has a VARIANT type that goes along with it. To find out the type you need to set your PROPVARIANT structure to for each property ID, consult the Platform SDK documentation for the particular property.

Queue Property	Meaning
PROPID_Q_AUTHENTICATE	Specifies if the queue accepts authenticated messages
PROPID_Q_BASEPRIORITY	The base priority for all messages routed to the queue. Used to determine routing cost.
PROPID_Q_CREATE_TIME	Queue creation time.
PROPID_Q_INSTANCE	Queue GUID.
PROPID_Q_JOURNAL	Specifies if journaling is turned on for the queue.
PROPID_Q_JOURNAL_QUOTA	Specifies the maximum journal size in KB.

Queue Property	Meaning
PROPID_Q_LABEL	The queue's friendly identifier.
PROPID_Q_MODIFY_TIME	The last time queue properties were modified.
PROPID_Q_PATHNAME	The queue's unique pathname.
PROPID_Q_PRIV_LEVEL	The level of privacy on the queue.
PROPID_Q_QUOTA	The maximum queue size in KB.
PROPID_Q_TRANSACTION	Specifies whether the queue is transactional or non-transactional.
PROPID_Q_TYPE	The queue's service type.

The best way to understand how to use these potentially confusing structures is to put them to work in a real function. Let's set some properties and create a queue.

Creating a Queue

To create a queue, you use the API call `MQCreateQueue()`:

```
HRESULT APIENTRY MQCreateQueue(PSECURITY_DESCRIPTOR pSecurityDescriptor,
                               MQQUEUEPROPS*          pQueueProps,
                               LPWSTR                 lpwcsFormatName,
                               LPDWORD                lpdwFormatNameLength);
```

Like so many objects in NT, the queue is securable, which means that it takes a security descriptor during creation. Passing `NULL` here results in the queue getting the default security descriptor. You can also arrange DACLs, enforce auditing and so on in the usual ways.

> *If you're not familiar with these terms, don't worry: we'll be looking at all aspects of NT security in the next chapter. Until then, just remember that queues are securable if you need them to be – it won't become an issue again in this discussion.*

The second parameter is that dangerous `MQQUEUEPROPS` structure we just talked about. Luckily, the only property information you *need* to give to the `MQCreateQueue()` function is the pathname for the new queue. Even the label is technically optional, though you really should supply one.

The third parameter is a pointer to a string buffer that MSMQ will use to return the queue's format name (see *Format Name*, below) when the creation function succeeds. Note that the format name is a *wide* character string, so `TCHAR`s are OK as long as your application is running under Unicode. The last parameter, the format name length, is used on input to tell MSMQ how long the buffer you supplied in parameter three was, and on output to tell you how long the format name was. Public queues require at least 44 characters, and private queues need at least 54.

MQCreateQueue() returns an HRESULT that indicates success, or the reason for failure. One of the most common reasons for failure is when the queue already exists, in which case the function returns MQ_ERROR_QUEUE_EXISTS. A sample of how to put all this together is shown below:

```
const DWORD cProps = 2;
MQQUEUEPROPS qp;
MQPROPVARIANT aVariant[cProps];
QUEUEPROPID aPropId[cProps];

DWORD cFN = 256;
TCHAR szFN[256];

// Set the PROPID_Q_PATHNAME property
aPropId[0] = PROPID_Q_PATHNAME;
aVariant[0].vt = VT_LPWSTR;
aVariant[0].pwszVal = _T(".\CoolQueue");

// Set the PROPID_Q_LABEL property
aPropId[1] = PROPID_Q_LABEL;
aVariant[1].vt = VT_LPWSTR;
aVariant[1].pwszVal = _T("CoolQueue");

// Set the MQQUEUEPROPS structure
qp.cProp = cProps;
qp.aPropID = aPropId;
qp.aPropVar = aVariant;
qp.aStatus = NULL;

HRESULT hr = MQCreateQueue(NULL, &qp, szFN, &cFN);

if(FAILED(hr))
    // Process errors
```

Format Name

After a queue has been successfully created, the creation function returns a **format name** that's subsequently used to identify the queue in other functions. The format name will be needed whenever you want to open the queue, delete the queue, or get and set its properties. This format name is not a property that stays with the queue permanently; rather, it's a unique identifier that's generated when it is asked for, and is never stored anywhere by MSMQ. In truth, the format name is just the string formulation of the queue's instance ID property (PROPID_Q_INSTANCE) or GUID.

Any time you want to open a particular queue after it has been created, you'll need to get hold of its format name. There are several ways to do this, depending on the information you have to hand. If you have the queue's path name, which is the most likely situation, you can use the MQPathNameToFormatName() function to return the format name:

```
HRESULT APIENTRY MQPathNameToFormatName(LPCWSTR lpwcsPathName,
                                       LPWSTR  lpwcsFormatName,
                                       LPDWORD lpdwCount);
```

If, on the other hand, you already have a handle to the queue, you can use `MQHandleToFormatName()` to return the format name, given the handle:

```
HRESULT APIENTRY MQHandleToFormatName(QUEUEHANDLE hQueue,
                                      LPWSTR      lpwcsFormatName,
                                      LPDWORD     lpdwCount);
```

Lastly, if you have the instance GUID (the information in `PROPID_Q_INSTANCE`), you can pass that to `MQInstanceToFormatName()`in order to retrieve the format name:

```
HRESULT APIENTRY MQInstanceToFormatName(GUID*   pGUID,
                                        LPWSTR  lpwcsFormatName,
                                        LPDWORD lpdwCount);
```

Opening a Queue

Once it has been created, opening a queue is pretty easy too: it's done with the `MQOpenQueue()` function. You simply pass it the format name of the queue you want to open. This can be tricky if you didn't just create the queue, so usually you'll have to make a quick call to `MQPathNametoFormatName()` to convert the queue's pathname into a format name. The prototype for `MQOpenQueue()` is below:

```
HRESULT APIENTRY MQOpenQueue(LPCWSTR       lpwcsFormatName,
                             DWORD         dwAccess,
                             DWORD         dwShareMode,
                             LPQUEUEHANDLE phQueue);
```

The second parameter is an access flag that specifies *how* you want to open the queue. These access flags are mutually exclusive; that is, they can't be ORed together. As usual, NT's security subsystems do an access check to make sure that the queue's DACL allows you the type of access you are requesting.

- `MQ_PEEK_ACCESS` means that messages can only be 'peeked at', and not retrieved (removed) from the queue
- `MQ_RECEIVE_ACCESS` means that messages can be retrieved or peeked at
- `MQ_SEND_ACCESS` means that messages can be sent to the queue.

The third parameter to `MQOpenQueue()` indicates the **sharing mode** for the open queue. It can be `MQ_DENY_NONE`, which means that the queue's access is not restricted (you must use this mode if you request 'send' access), or `MQ_DENY_RECEIVE_SHARE`, which means that only the current process can receive messages from the queue.

The final parameter is where you receive the `QUEUEHANDLE` that you'll use in subsequent 'send' and 'receive' message operations. The most common `HRESULT` value that gets returned from this function (other than `MQ_OK`, of course) is good old `MQ_ERROR_ACCESS_DENIED`, which indicates that you didn't have the access rights for the operation.

Closing a Queue

When you're finished using a queue, you should close it using the `MQCloseQueue()` API, shown below:

```
HRESULT APIENTRY MQCloseQueue(QUEUEHANDLE hQueue);
```

The only thing that can go wrong here is if the `hQueue` parameter is not valid, in which case you will receive an `MQ_ERROR_INVALID_HANDLE` return code.

Deleting a Queue

If you want to remove a queue permanently for all time from the MQ Information Store, you can delete it using `MQDeleteQueue()`. Remember: this actually *deletes* the queue for good; when you're simply closing your application, you should only *close* the queue. Queues should only be deleted when you are uninstalling the application and they will never be used again.

```
HRESULT APIENTRY MQDeleteQueue(LPCWSTR lpwcsFormatName);
```

Sending a Message

Once you have a handle to an open queue, you can start carrying out message 'send', 'receive', and 'peek' operations on the queue. To do that, though, you need to deal with yet another property structure, `MQMSGPROPS`, which is to messages what `MQQUEUEPROPS` is to queues. A message is really just a collection of message properties, which all have names beginning with `PROPID_M`. Sending a message really means sending a bunch of properties wrapped up in an `MQMSGPROPS` structure.

MQMSGPROPS and Message Properties

The layout of the `MQMSGPROPS` structure is identical to its queue counterpart:

```
struct MQMSGPROPS
{
   DWORD       cProp;
   MSGPROPID   aPropID[];
   PROPVARIANT aPropVar[];
   HRESULT     aStatus[];
};
```

However, message properties are much more numerous and rather more complex:

Message Property	Description
PROPID_M_ACKNOWLEDGE	Type of acknowledgment messages MSMQ should post.
PROPID_M_ADMIN_QUEUE	Format name of the administration queue where acknowledgment messages should be sent.
PROPID_M_ADMIN_QUEUE_LEN	Length of the administration queue's format name.
PROPID_M_APPSPECIFIC	A UINT that can specify an application-defined message type value.
PROPID_M_ARRIVEDTIME	Time the message arrived in the queue.
PROPID_M_AUTH_LEVEL	Whether the message needs to be authenticated.
PROPID_M_AUTHENTICATED	Whether the message was authenticated.
PROPID_M_BODY	The message body. This is where the application places the data or request information.
PROPID_M_BODY_SIZE	The actual size of the message body.
PROPID_M_BODY_TYPE	The data type of the information in the body.
PROPID_M_CLASS	The type of message. Can be 'normal', 'positive response', 'negative response', or 'report'.
PROPID_M_CONNECTOR_TYPE	Connector message properties.
PROPID_M_CORRELATIONID	Application-defined identifier that can be used to correlate send messages with response messages.
PROPID_M_DELIVERY	How the message will be delivered – express or recoverable. Express messages are quicker, but are not persisted to storage.
PROPID_M_DEST_QUEUE	Format name of the message's target queue.
PROPID_M_DEST_QUEUE_LEN	Length of the target queue's format name.
PROPID_M_DEST_SYMM_KEY	Encryption key for encrypting the message.
PROPID_M_DEST_SYMM_KEY_LEN	Length of encryption key.
PROPID_M_ENCRYPTION_ALG	Encryption algorithm type.
PROPID_M_EXTENSION	Application-defined, extended information that can be associated with the message.

Table Continued on Following Page

Message Property	Description
PROPID_M_EXTENSION_LEN	Length of extended data.
PROPID_M_HASH_ALG	Hashing algorithm used when authenticating messages.
PROPID_M_JOURNAL	Indicates whether the message should be journaled or sent to a dead-letter queue.
PROPID_M_LABEL	The message label. This is the visible identifier in MSMQ Explorer.
PROPID_M_LABEL_LEN	Length of the label.
PROPID_M_MSGID	The message's unique, 20-byte identifier.
PROPID_M_PRIORITY	Integer value of message priority, 0-7.
PROPID_M_PRIV_LEVEL	Message privacy level.
PROPID_M_PROV_NAME	Cryptographic encryption provider name.
PROPID_M_PROV_NAME_LEN	Cryptographic provider name length.
PROPID_M_PROV_TYPE	Cryptographic provider type.
PROPID_M_RESP_QUEUE	Format name of the queue to which response messages should be sent.
PROPID_M_RESP_QUEUE_LEN	Response queue name length.
PROPID_M_SECURITY_CONTEXT	Security authentication information.
PROPID_M_SENDER_CERT	Security certificate of the message sender.
PROPID_M_SENDER_CERT_LEN	Certificate length.
PROPID_M_SENDERID	Identifier of sender, used to authenticate the message.
PROPID_M_SENDERID_LEN	Sender ID length.
PROPID_M_SENDERID_TYPE	Type of the sender ID. Currently, either an NT SID or none.
PROPID_M_SENTTIME	Time the message was sent.
PROPID_M_SIGNATURE	Digital signature used to authenticate the message.
PROPID_M_SIGNATURE_LEN	Length of signature.
PROPID_M_SRC_MACHINE_ID	Computer where the message originated.

Message Property	Description
PROPID_M_TIME_TO_BE_RECEIVED	Time, in seconds, the message is allowed to live before being retrieved from the destination queue.
PROPID_M_TIME_TO_REACH_QUEUE	Time, in seconds, the message is allowed to get to the destination queue.
PROPID_M_TRACE	Specifies where the report messages will be sent.
PROPID_M_VERSION	Version of MSMQ used to send the message.
PROPID_M_XACT_STATUS_QUEUE	Format name of the transaction status queue on the source computer.
PROPID_M_XACT_STATUS_QUEUE_LEN	Length of transaction queue's format name.

You deal with MQMSGPROPS in exactly the same way as you deal with queue properties: set up an array of MSGPROPIDs and an array of PROPVARIANTs, and populate them with the information you want to send. Then, pass the structure to the MQSendMessage() API.

MQSendMessage

This API takes a queue handle, the MQMSGPROPS structure you just created, and an interface pointer to a transaction object (if you're enlisting the message send operation in a transaction). Below is the prototype:

```
HRESULT APIENTRY MQSendMessage(QUEUEHANDLE   hDestinationQueue,
                               MQMSGPROPS*   pMessageProps,
                               ITransaction* pTransaction);
```

Here's a function that uses MQSendMessage() to send a simple message, taken from the sample service that we'll begin building shortly. Manipulation of structures within structures is never the most transparent of operations, but this one is fairly clear – it just involves packaging a message label and body into an MQMSGPROPS structure, and then sending it.

```
bool SendMessage(LPTSTR szFNQueue, TCHAR* szLabel, TCHAR* szMsg)
{
   QUEUEHANDLE hQueue;
   HRESULT hr;

   hr = MQOpenQueue(szFNQueue, MQ_SEND_ACCESS, 0, &hQueue);
   if(FAILED(hr))
      return false;

   MQMSGPROPS msg;
   MQPROPVARIANT aVar[2];
   MSGPROPID aPropid[2];
```

```
    aPropid[0] = PROPID_M_LABEL;
    aVar[0].vt = VT_LPWSTR;
    aVar[0].pwszVal = szLabel;

    aPropid[1] = PROPID_M_BODY;
    aVar[1].vt = VT_VECTOR | VT_UI1;
    aVar[1].caub.pElems = (UCHAR*)szMsg;
    aVar[1].caub.cElems = (_tcslen(szMsg) + _tcslen(_T("\0"))) * sizeof TCHAR;

    msg.cProp = 2;
    msg.aPropID = aPropid;
    msg.aPropVar = aVar;
    msg.aStatus = 0;

    hr = MQSendMessage(hQueue, &msg, NULL);
    if(FAILED(hr))
    {
       MQCloseQueue(hQueue);
       return false;
    }

    MQCloseQueue(hQueue);
    return true;
}
```

Acknowledgment Messages

The sending application can request that MSMQ generate acknowledgment messages that tell the sender whether the message reached the queue for which it was destined and/or whether the message was retrieved within the expiration time. To use acknowledgments, the sender indicates the type of acknowledgment by setting the `PROPID_M_ACKNOWLEDGE` property value to flags that indicate positive receipt, negative receipt, or a combination of the two.

The sender also must set the `PROPID_M_ADMIN_QUEUE` property to the format name of the queue that is to receive the acknowledgment messages. The acknowledgment messages themselves are generated by MSMQ, not by the receiver.

Reading (or Peeking at) a Message

Receiving a message is pretty easy too, although it's a little more complex than sending one. There are two ways to get at the content in a message. You can *retrieve* the message, which gives you the message content and removes the message from the queue, or you can *peek* at the message, which allows you to view the content of its properties but does *not* remove it from the queue. The `MQReceiveMessage()` API allows you to specify either:

```
HRESULT APIENTRY MQReceiveMessage(QUEUEHANDLE        hSource,
                                  DWORD              dwTimeout,
                                  DWORD              dwAction,
                                  MQMSGPROPS         pMessageProps,
                                  LPOVERLAPPED       lpOverlapped,
                                  PMQRECEIVECALLBACK fnReceiveCallback,
                                  HANDLE             hCursor,
                                  Transaction*       pTransaction);
```

There are a few interesting parameters to this function. The second one, for example, is a timeout value that allows you to specify how long you want the function to block waiting for a message. This value is specified in milliseconds, or it can be `INFINITE`, which means that it should wait forever. A word of caution, though: `INFINITE` makes your application stop cold if there are no messages in the queue. If you use `INFINITE`, it is a good idea to move the `MQReceiveMessage()` call to a separate, worker thread.

The third parameter specifies what type of 'receive' operation you want: `MQ_ACTION_RECEIVE`, `MQ_ACTION_PEEK_CURRENT`, or `MQ_ACTION_PEEK_NEXT`. The first of these tells the function to take the message from the queue, while the other two instruct it to peek at the message using the current or the next cursor position respectively. (We'll discuss cursors shortly.)

The fourth parameter is the wonderful `MQMSGPROPS` structure that I just explained to you. Of course, it has to be set up and readied to receive all the properties that you want to obtain about the message.

The fifth and sixth parameters can be used to make the receive call asynchronous, and there are actually a couple of ways to do so. First, you can use an `OVERLAPPED` structure to specify the handle of a kernel event that gets signaled when a message comes in, or when the timeout value expires. You can then use `WaitForSingleObject()` to wait for the event to get signaled. The Agent usage pattern sample later on in this chapter will show an example of how to use the `OVERLAPPED` mechanism to monitor for new messages.

The second way to receive messages asynchronously is to specify a pointer to a specially formatted MSMQ callback function that gets called by the system when a message is received into the queue. You use these asynchronous mechanisms in an either/or fashion – if you use the callback mechanism, you must pass `NULL` to the fifth parameter, and vice versa.

More advanced operations involving receiving and peeking at messages can be accomplished with **cursors**, which allow you to peek into queues at specific entry points and look at particular messages. Cursors also allow you to iterate through a whole queue, peeking at each message and then moving on to the next one. Peeking with cursors can allow a retrieving application to go through all the messages in a queue looking for one with specific properties, to retrieve the one it wants, and to continue. The `MQReceiveMessage()` function allows you to specify a cursor handle (created with `MQCreateCursor()`) if you want to use one. Advanced operations with cursors are beyond the scope of this chapter.

Here's a simple example of a function for retrieving a message from a queue. It sets up an `MQMSGPROPS` structure that will be filled with the body of the message being received, and the name of a response queue to which a reply can be sent.

```
void GetMessage()
{
   // Get the message type - asynchronous
   MQMSGPROPS Msgp;
   MQPROPVARIANT aVar[3];
   MSGPROPID aPropid[3];

   const long BODY_LEN = 1024;                // Hardcoded
   aPropid[0] = PROPID_M_BODY;
   aVar[0].vt = VT_VECTOR | VT_UI1;
   aVar[0].caub.cElems = BODY_LEN;
   aVar[0].caub.pElems = new unsigned char[BODY_LEN];

   aPropid[1] = PROPID_M_RESP_QUEUE_LEN;
   aVar[1].vt = VT_UI4;
   aVar[1].ulVal = 256;

   aPropid[2] = PROPID_M_RESP_QUEUE;
   aVar[2].vt = VT_LPWSTR;
   aVar[2].pwszVal = new TCHAR[256];

   Msgp->cProp = 3;
   Msgp->aPropID = aPropid;
   Msgp->aPropVar = aVar;
   Msgp->aStatus = NULL;

   HRESULT hr = MQReceiveMessage(m_hQueue, 10000, MQ_ACTION_RECEIVE, &Msgp,
                                         NULL, NULL, NULL, NULL);

   if(SUCCEEDED(hr))
   {
      // Process the message
   }

   // Delete and clean up
}
```

The Agent Pattern

From my allusions to it so far, you'll already have a pretty good idea of the role the Agent pattern plays. It will monitor an MSMQ queue, and wait for messages to come into it. When one does so, the service will examine the message's `PROPID_M_APPSPECIFIC` tag and determine the type of the message. Then, it will go off and do some work based on the information in the body of the message. When it has completed the requested work, it will send a response message with the results of the request back to the queue designated in the original message.

The service itself will of course be implemented using the `CService` class I developed in Chapter 4. Derived from that class is `CQueueService`, which implements the specific functionality needed to monitor MSMQ queues for messages, and to send responses. I'll also present a Visual Basic application that acts as the client that sends request messages to the queue and retrieves the response messages from the server.

Service Code

In the best traditions of code reuse, you can begin this example by creating a new console application project and copying into it the files for the `CService`, `CServiceInstall` and `CEventLog` classes from earlier chapters; there is no need for me to reproduce that code here. Instead, I can get straight on with the new classes required for this sample.

CQueueService Fundamentals

Most interesting to our discussion is the implementation of `CQueueService`, the class derived from `CService`. First, let's take a look at its definition, which I placed in a file called `QService.h`:

```
#include "cservice.h"

const int MAX_QUEUE_PATH = 257;

class CQueueService : public CService
{
public:
   CQueueService(LPCTSTR szName, LPCTSTR szDisplay, DWORD dwType);
   virtual void Run();

DECLARE_SERVICE(CQueueService, MQAgent)

protected:
   virtual void OnStop();
   virtual void Init();
   virtual void DeInit();

   // Attributes
   bool m_bStop;

   // Implementation - work specific
   HRESULT CreateQueue();
   bool OpenQueue(LPWSTR wszName, LPWSTR wszLabel);

   bool SendMessage(LPTSTR szFNQueue, TCHAR* szLabel, TCHAR* szMsg);
   void RetrieveMessage();

   TCHAR m_wszQueueName[MAX_QUEUE_PATH];
   TCHAR m_wszFormatName[MAX_QUEUE_PATH];
   TCHAR m_wszQueueLabel[MAX_QUEUE_PATH];

   bool m_bOpen;

private:
   QUEUEHANDLE m_hQueue;
};
```

This is a pretty standard derivative of CService that implements the necessary overrides, and has its own set of implementation methods and data members. There's a function to create the queue that the service will monitor (if it has not already been created), one to open the queue, and functions for sending and retrieving messages. There are also member variables to store the queue handle for the opened queue, as well as its queue pathname, format name, and label.

You'll notice that the service has no pause or continue semantics. I suppose that I could have defined 'pause' in a way that stopped the service retrieving messages from the queue, but by choosing not to I was able to eliminate some of the complexity from the Run() loop that you might remember from the Monitor implementation in Chapter 4. Also, I didn't need to override the base class implementations of OnPause() and OnContinue().

Initialization

First of all, we have the standard construction motif that we use in any derivative of CService. To start, there's the IMPLEMENT_SERVICE macro. Then, a constructor to initialize derived-class-specific variables and call the base class constructor. Also, notice that I defined two application-specific message IDs, whose values I just picked at random. These will also need to be defined later, in the VB client application.

```
#include "precomp.h"
#include "qservice.h"

const int AGENT_REQUEST_1 = 239;
const int AGENT_REQUEST_2 = 240;

IMPLEMENT_SERVICE(CQueueService, MQAgent)

CQueueService::CQueueService(LPCTSTR szName, LPCTSTR szDisplay, DWORD dwType)
                                        : CService(szName, szDisplay, dwType)
{
   m_pThis = this;
   m_bOpen = false;
   m_bStop  = false;
   m_hQueue = NULL;
}
```

As part of the initialization of the service, Init() calls the local function OpenQueue() to open (or create if necessary) the queue that the Agent will be monitoring.

```
void CQueueService::Init()
{
   SetStatus(SERVICE_START_PENDING, m_dwCheckpoint++, 2000);

   // Initialize the Queue
   if(!OpenQueue(_T(".\\AgentMonitorQ"), _T("AgentMonitorQ")))
      ErrorHandler(_T("Open Queue"));

   return;
}
```

OpenQueue and CreateQueue

The first thing that `OpenQueue()` does is to set the values of the `m_wszQueueName` and `m_wszQueueLabel` members of the class. These will contain the label and pathname for the service's main queue.

```
bool CQueueService::OpenQueue(LPWSTR wszName, LPWSTR wszLabel)
{
   DWORD cFN = MAX_QUEUE_PATH;
   TCHAR szFN[MAX_QUEUE_PATH];
   HRESULT hr;

   _tcscpy(m_wszQueueName, wszName);
   _tcscpy(m_wszQueueLabel, wszLabel);
```

After that, the function calls `CreateQueue()`, which attempts to create the queue:

```
   hr = CreateQueue();
```

Changing horses for a moment and looking at `CreateQueue()`, we set the pathname and label queue properties from the member variables containing that information, and then call `MQCreateQueue()`. The `HRESULT` returned by that function is also the return value of `CreateQueue()`.

```
// Queue Specific Implementation
HRESULT CQueueService::CreateQueue()
{
   const DWORD cProps = 2;
   MQQUEUEPROPS qp;
   MQPROPVARIANT aVariant[cProps];
   QUEUEPROPID aPropId[cProps];

   DWORD cFN = MAX_QUEUE_PATH;
   TCHAR szFN[MAX_QUEUE_PATH];

   // Set the PROPID_Q_PATHNAME property
   aPropId[0] = PROPID_Q_PATHNAME;
   aVariant[0].vt = VT_LPWSTR;
   aVariant[0].pwszVal = m_wszQueueName;

   // Set the PROPID_Q_LABEL property
   aPropId[1] = PROPID_Q_LABEL;
   aVariant[1].vt = VT_LPWSTR;
   aVariant[1].pwszVal = m_wszQueueLabel;

   // Set the MQQUEUEPROPS structure
   qp.cProp = cProps;
   qp.aPropID = aPropId;
   qp.aPropVar = aVariant;
   qp.aStatus = NULL;

   HRESULT hr = MQCreateQueue(NULL, &qp, szFN, &cFN);
   return hr;
}
```

Picking up where we left off in `OpenQueue()`, you can see that if the return code from `CreateQueue()` represents a failure, and it's not an error indicating that the fail occurred because the queue already exists, then we know something bad happened (MSMQ is not functioning, for example). In that case, we return `false` to `Init()` so that an error can be logged.

```
      if(FAILED(hr) && hr != MQ_ERROR_QUEUE_EXISTS)
      {
         return false;
      }
      else
      {
         // Open the queue to get its handle
         hr = MQPathNameToFormatName(m_wszQueueName, szFN, &cFN);
         if(FAILED(hr))
            return false;

         hr = MQOpenQueue(szFN, MQ_RECEIVE_ACCESS, 0, &m_hQueue);
         if(FAILED(hr))
            return false;

         _tcscpy(m_wszFormatName, szFN);
         m_bOpen = true;
         return true;
      }
   }
```

If the creation succeeded, or it failed because the queue already existed, then we obtain the format name of the queue from the pathname, and then open the queue for 'receive' access. Finally, we set the format name member (`m_wszFormatName`) to the format name of the queue.

Run and OnStop

The main run loop and the stop handler for the service are very simple indeed. `Run()` delegates all its work to a local function called `RetrieveMessage()`, which we'll look at shortly. When `RetrieveMessage()` returns, work is finished, and the service stops.

```
   // The main processing logic belongs in this overridable
   // All start, running, and stop code here
   void CQueueService::Run()
   {
      SetStatus(SERVICE_RUNNING, 0, 0, SERVICE_ACCEPT_STOP);

      RetrieveMessage();                         // Loops until m_bStop is set

      // Stopped, so exit
      SetStatus(SERVICE_STOP_PENDING, 2, 5000);
   }
```

`OnStop()` uses the typical method of setting a Boolean value to `TRUE` to signal the run loop to stop.

```
void CQueueService::OnStop()
{
   SetStatus(SERVICE_STOP_PENDING, 1, 15000);

   // The ServiceMain thread could be reading this value!
   InterlockedExchange((LPLONG)&m_bStop, (LONG)TRUE);
}
```

Closing Down

When the service is ready to stop, it calls `DeInit()`, which simply closes the handle of the main queue that the service is monitoring.

```
void CQueueService::DeInit()
{
   if(m_hQueue)
      MQCloseQueue(m_hQueue);

   m_bOpen = false;
   CService::DeInit();
}
```

Retrieving Messages from the Queue

Having gone through the overall semantics of the service, we can now backtrack to talk about the main run loop. `RetrieveMessage()` is the main worker function for the service. It obtains three pieces of information from an incoming message: its type (which is application-specific), its message body, and the format name of the response queue to which that the reply message should be sent.

```
void CQueueService::RetrieveMessage()
{
   MQMSGPROPS* pMsgp;
   pMsgp = new MQMSGPROPS;

   MQPROPVARIANT* paVar;
   paVar = new MQPROPVARIANT[4];

   MSGPROPID* paPropid;
   paPropid = new MSGPROPID[4];

   paPropid[0] = PROPID_M_APPSPECIFIC;
   paVar[0].vt = VT_UI4;
   paVar[0].ulVal = 0;

   const long BODY_LEN = 1024;                    // Hardcoded
   paPropid[1] = PROPID_M_BODY;
   paVar[1].vt = VT_VECTOR | VT_UI1;
   paVar[1].caub.cElems = BODY_LEN;
   paVar[1].caub.pElems = new unsigned char[BODY_LEN];
```

```
paPropid[2] = PROPID_M_RESP_QUEUE_LEN;
paVar[2].vt = VT_UI4;
paVar[2].ulVal = MAX_QUEUE_PATH;

paPropid[3] = PROPID_M_RESP_QUEUE;
paVar[3].vt = VT_LPWSTR;
paVar[3].pwszVal = new TCHAR[MAX_QUEUE_PATH];

pMsgp->cProp = 4;
pMsgp->aPropID = paPropid;
pMsgp->aPropVar = paVar;
pMsgp->aStatus = NULL;
```

After setting up the properties to hold these bits of information, the function sets up an `OVERLAPPED` structure so that messages can be received asynchronously, using overlapped I/O. This allows the thread to wait for a message to come in without blocking on the receive call. When a message comes in and has been completely read from the queue, the kernel event object in the `OVERLAPPED` structure gets signaled. When that happens, the `WaitForSingleObject()` call that's waiting on the event breaks loose and the message properties begin to be processed.

```
OVERLAPPED* pov = new OVERLAPPED;
pov->hEvent = CreateEvent(0, TRUE, TRUE, 0);

while(m_bStop == false)
{
   HRESULT hr = MQReceiveMessage(m_hQueue, 10000, MQ_ACTION_RECEIVE,
                                           pMsgp, pov, NULL, NULL, NULL);

   if(SUCCEEDED(hr))
   {
      if(hr == MQ_INFORMATION_OPERATION_PENDING)
         WaitForSingleObject(pov->hEvent, INFINITE);

      if(paVar[0].ulVal == AGENT_REQUEST_1)
      {
         // Do work of type...
         TCHAR szMsg[25] = _T("Results of Request 1");
         SendMessage(paVar[3].pwszVal, _T("Type 1 Response"), szMsg);
         paVar[0].ulVal = 0;
      }
      else if(paVar[0].ulVal == AGENT_REQUEST_2)
      {
         TCHAR szMsg[25] = _T("Results of Request 2");
         SendMessage(paVar[3].pwszVal, _T("Type 2 Response"), szMsg);
         paVar[0].ulVal = 0;
      }
   }
   else
   {
      ErrorHandler(_T("MQReceiveMessage"));
      break;
   }
```

```
        }

        CloseHandle(pov->hEvent);
        delete pov;
        delete paVar[3].pwszVal;
        delete paVar[1].caub.pElems;
        delete [] paPropid;
        delete [] paVar;
        delete pMsgp;
    }
```

After determining what type of message it is (using the application-specific identifier property), the service calls `CQueueService::SendMessage()` with the format name of the response queue taken from the received message. `SendMessage()` then opens the response queue, formats the properties of the response, and sends it. Obviously, it is possible for the service to perform rather more work than this, but here we're just concerned with technicalities of sending and receiving. Exactly what your messages contain, and what you do with them, is entirely up to you and the needs of your application.

`RetrieveMessage()` makes use of a single Boolean flag, `m_bStop`, to indicate whether it should continue to run or not. When the service is supposed to stop, that flag is set to `true` (atomically) in the `OnStop()` function. `OnStop()` also sets the `SERVICE_STOP_PENDING` status for a reasonable period of time (15 seconds), knowing that the loop for waiting on new messages to come into the queue only breaks its cycle and checks the `m_bStop` flag every 10 seconds.

Queue Monitoring Using Asynchronous Receive

The `RetrieveMessage()` function waits in a loop for a message to come in. The time-out value for the asynchronous wait is 10 seconds, which means that it will wait for up to that length of time before breaking. The call to `MQReceiveMessage()` uses an `OVERLAPPED` structure to set an event object that gets signaled when a message has come in, or when the specified time-out (in the `dwTimeout` parameter) expires. In our little service, it's hardcoded for 10 seconds (10,000 ms).

The call to `MQReceiveMessage()` should execute immediately, returning an `HRESULT` with the value `MQ_INFORMATION_OPERATION_PENDING`, which is a success return code. If that occurs, then the `RetrieveMessage()` function waits on the event object that was specified. This wait can safely be `INFINITE`, because the expiration of the time-out value in the `MQReceiveMessage()` call will also signal the event.

Once the wait is broken, `RetrieveMessage()` checks the `PROPID_M_APPSPECIFIC` value of the incoming message to see what the type of the message was. If the event signaled because of a time-out, there is no type value and the loop goes back to the top, checking the value of `m_bStop` and repeating itself if necessary. What the service actually *does* here is unimportant; in this case, it just sends a response message. If the work was more complex or difficult, it might spawn a thread here to go off and do the work, post a thread message to a thread that was already waiting for work, or issue a request that gets serviced by threads on a completion port. Conceivably, you could have multiple threads waiting for incoming messages, but which each process the work on the same thread.

Using Response Queues

This sample makes use of response queues to send the results of work that has been done back to the calling application. The response queue is specified by the sending application when it sends its message using the PROPID_M_RESP_QUEUE property. In this case, the Visual Basic application will name the response queue as AgentMonitorRespQ. In other circumstances, a particular client application instance could create its own (per instance) private queue as a response queue and then send that queue name to the server. That way, each instance of the sending application would have its own individual queue, and would not have to cursor through others' messages to find responses to its messages.

SendMessage

This function, which you may remember from earlier in this chapter, is called from ReceiveMessage() whenever the service wants to send a message to the response queue identified in the incoming message. It begins by opening the response queue, then it sets up the values of the properties for the message it will send (the message label and body text). Finally, it sends the message and closes the queue.

```
bool CQueueService::SendMessage(LPTSTR szFNQueue, TCHAR* szLabel,
                                                          TCHAR* szMsg)
{
   QUEUEHANDLE hQueue;
   HRESULT hr;

   hr = MQOpenQueue(szFNQueue, MQ_SEND_ACCESS, 0, &hQueue);
   if(FAILED(hr))
      return false;

   MQMSGPROPS msg;
   MQPROPVARIANT aVar[2];
   MSGPROPID aPropid[2];

   aPropid[0] = PROPID_M_LABEL;
   aVar[0].vt = VT_LPWSTR;
   aVar[0].pwszVal = szLabel;

   aPropid[1] = PROPID_M_BODY;
   aVar[1].vt = VT_VECTOR | VT_UI1;
   aVar[1].caub.pElems = (UCHAR*)szMsg;
   aVar[1].caub.cElems = (_tcslen(szMsg) + _tcslen(_T("\0"))) * sizeof TCHAR;

   msg.cProp = 2;
   msg.aPropID = aPropid;
   msg.aPropVar = aVar;
   msg.aStatus = 0;

   hr = MQSendMessage(hQueue, &msg, NULL);
   if(FAILED(hr))
   {
      MQCloseQueue(hQueue);
      return false;
   }
   MQCloseQueue(hQueue);
   return true;
}
```

main

We're nearly there. Here's the code for `main()`, which ties together the all these classes. You won't be surprised to see that it's very similar indeed to the equivalent function at the end of the last chapter – it really only differs in the names of the objects it uses.

```
#include "precomp.h"
#include "eventlog.h"
#include "QService.h"
#include "CServiceInstall.h"

int main()
{
   LPTSTR szName = _T("MQAgent");
   LPTSTR szDisplay = _T("MQ Agent Service");

   // Process command line
   TCHAR* pszCmdLine = GetCommandLine();
   CharLowerBuff(pszCmdLine, lstrlen(pszCmdLine));
   if(_tcsstr(pszCmdLine, _T("-install")))
   {
      CServiceInstall si(szName, szDisplay);
      si.Install();

      CEventLog log(szName);
      log.RegisterLog(_T("D:\\Temp\\AgentMsg.dll"));

      return 0;
   }
   else if(_tcsstr(pszCmdLine, _T("-remove")))
   {
      CServiceInstall si(szName, szDisplay);
      si.Remove();
      return 0;
   }

   CQueueService Agent(szName, szDisplay, SERVICE_WIN32_OWN_PROCESS);

   // Set up an entry for the one service and go
   BEGIN_SERVICE_MAP
      SERVICE_MAP_ENTRY(CQueueService, MQAgent)
   END_SERVICE_MAP

   return 0;
}
```

That leaves just a couple more things to do. First, you should construct a very simple message DLL for the Agent service in the same way as we did for the Monitor in the last chapter, so that any entries it makes in the event log are properly formed. As you can see from the call to `RegisterLog()` in the above sample, the file should be called `AgentMsg.dll`, and it's created from the following message script:

```
MessageIdTypedef=DWORD

LanguageNames=(English=0x409:MSG00409)

MessageId=0x1
Severity=Error
SymbolicName=SERVICE_WIN32_ERROR
Language=English
%1
.
```

Finally, you need to add our usual precompiled header file with a couple of amendments from the last chapter – it needs to include the header file for this example's message IDs, and the `MQ.h` file that defines all the MSMQ functions. Then, add the message queue library `MQRT.lib` to the link libraries for the project, and compile it to produce the service executable. Before we can see how it works, though, we need to develop a quick client application.

Client Application Code

Our client, to be written in Visual Basic, will request that the service do some work on its behalf, using MSMQ as the communication protocol. In that sense, it's really no different from any other client asking any other server to do work on its behalf, using any other communication mechanism.

The code for the application that sends messages to the queue is implemented using MSMQ's ActiveX components. To use these, you need to add the Microsoft Message Queue Object Library to the project's references. The components don't have all the features available to the raw API, but they are very easy to use. Documentation for them is available on the MSDN Library, along with the documentation for the MSMQ API.

As usual, you can download the code for the project from the Wrox web site, but I'll run through it quickly here. First of all, here's the simple dialog I created. The text box is called `txtMsg`, the list box is `lstResponse`, the buttons are called `cmdType1` and `cmdType2`, and the checkbox's name is `chkAsync`.

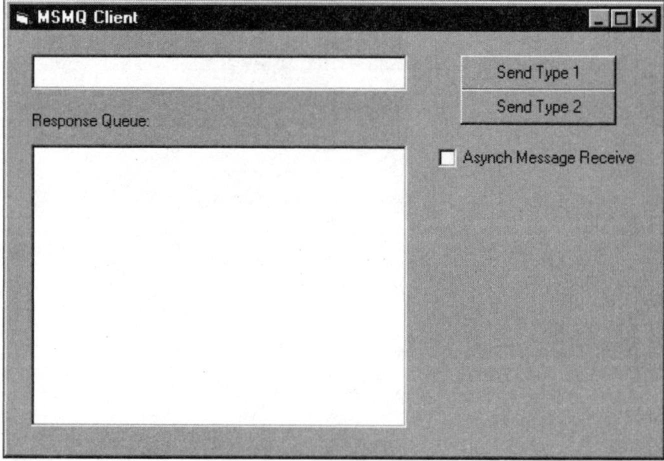

Here's the Visual Basic code that goes behind the dialog. Notice particularly the AGENT_REQUEST_1 and AGENT_REQUEST_2 constants that are set to the same values they had in the service project, as I explained they would need to be. The queue-handling functions at the top of the listing, which call methods of the ActiveX components, are used by the controls on the dialog to do their work.

```
Option Explicit
Dim WithEvents qEvent As MSMQEvent
Dim qrResp As MSMQQueue
Const cLabel = "AgentMonitorQ"
Const cPath = ".\AgentMonitorQ"
Const cRespLabel = "AgentMonitor Response Queue"
Const cRespPath = ".\AgentMonitorRespQ"
Const AGENT_REQUEST_1 = 239
Const AGENT_REQUEST_2 = 240

Function CreateQueue(ByVal label As String, ByVal path As String) _
                                                          As MSMQQueueInfo
   Dim qi As New MSMQQueueInfo
   qi.PathName = path
   qi.label = label
   qi.Create
   If Not qi Is Nothing Then
      Set CreateQueue = qi
   End If
End Function

Function CreateQueueInfo(ByVal label As String, ByVal path As String) _
                                                          As MSMQQueueInfo
   Dim qry As New MSMQQuery
   Dim qinfos As MSMQQueueInfos
   Dim qi As MSMQQueueInfo

   ' Find the queue or create it if it doesn't exist
   Set qinfos = qry.LookupQueue(label:=label)
   qinfos.Reset
   Set qi = qinfos.Next
   If qi Is Nothing Then
      Set qi = CreateQueue(label, path)
   End If

   If Not qi Is Nothing Then
      Set CreateQueueInfo = qi
   End If
End Function

Function OpenQueue(ByVal label As String, ByVal path As String, _
                                        ByVal qtype As Long) As MSMQQueue
   Dim qry As New MSMQQuery
   Dim qi As MSMQQueueInfo
   Dim qinfos As MSMQQueueInfos
```

```
    ' Find the queue or create it if it doesn't exist
    Set qinfos = qry.LookupQueue(label:=label)
    qinfos.Reset
    Set qi = qinfos.Next
    If qi Is Nothing Then
       Set qi = CreateQueue(label, path)
    End If

    ' Open the queue for send or receive
    Dim q As MSMQQueue
    Set q = qi.Open(qtype, MQ_DENY_NONE)
    If q.IsOpen = False Then
       Set OpenQueue = Nothing
    Else
       Set OpenQueue = q
    End If
End Function

Function SendMessage(ByVal msgtext As String, ByVal mtype As Long)
    Dim q As MSMQQueue
    Set q = OpenQueue(cLabel, cPath, MQ_SEND_ACCESS)

    Dim msg As New MSMQMessage

    ' Create the response queue information object
    Dim qiResp As MSMQQueueInfo
    Set qiResp = CreateQueueInfo(cRespLabel, cRespPath)

    Set msg.ResponseQueueInfo = qiResp
    msg.Body = msgtext
    msg.AppSpecific = mtype
    msg.label = "Agent Message"
    msg.Send q

    q.Close
End Function

Private Sub qEvent_Arrived(ByVal Queue As Object, ByVal Cursor As Long)
    Dim msg As MSMQMessage
    Set msg = Queue.Receive
    lstResponse.AddItem msg.label & "   " & msg.Body

    Queue.EnableNotification Event:=qEvent
End Sub

Private Sub chkAsync_Click()
    If chkAsync.Value = 1 Then
       Set qEvent = New MSMQEvent
       Set qrResp = OpenQueue(cRespLabel, cRespPath, MQ_RECEIVE_ACCESS)
       qrResp.EnableNotification Event:=qEvent, ReceiveTimeout:=1000
```

```
    Else
       qrResp.Close
       Set qEvent = Nothing
       Set qrResp = Nothing
    End If
End Sub

Private Sub cmdType1_Click()
    SendMessage txtMsg.Text, AGENT_REQUEST_1
End Sub

Private Sub cmdType2_Click()
    SendMessage txtMsg.Text, AGENT_REQUEST_2
End Sub
```

Running the Client

With service and client complete, we're about ready to go. Install the MQ Agent with the `-install` command-line option, and start it. You can then run the client, which is shown below. If you select **Send Type 1**, and click the **Asynch Message Receive** button, you'll get a **Type 1 Response** message. If you select the other button, you'll get the other type of message. It really is very simple indeed, but I hope you can see that the possibilities are vast. The messages you send, and the ones you receive, have hardly any restrictions on what they can be used for.

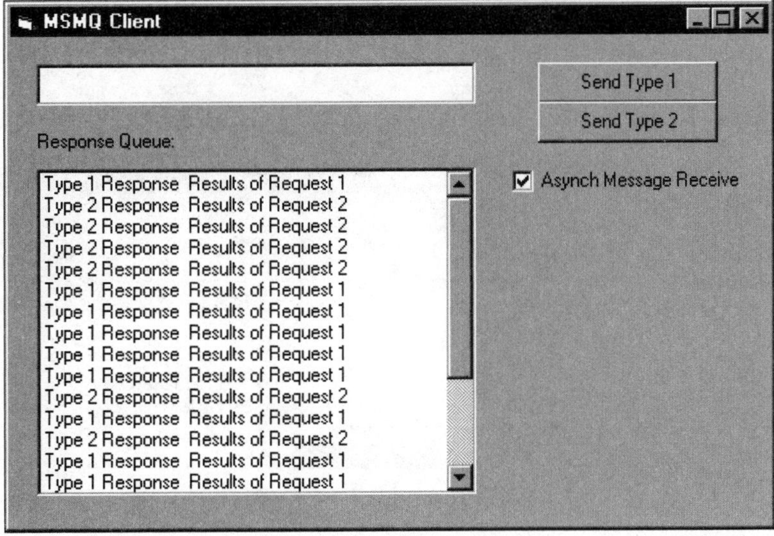

MSMQ Security and Services

To end this chapter, a word of warning about creating a queue from within a service: the default DACL gives everyone *send* access and the creator *all* access. The owner is always SYSTEM, which means that if you create the queue from a service running under LocalSystem with the default security descriptor, no interactive user will have the right to view the queue from MSMQ Explorer. The screenshots below show the two queues created in the sample; the first shows `AgentMonitorQ`, which was created by the service:

You can see from the output in the right pane that view access is denied.

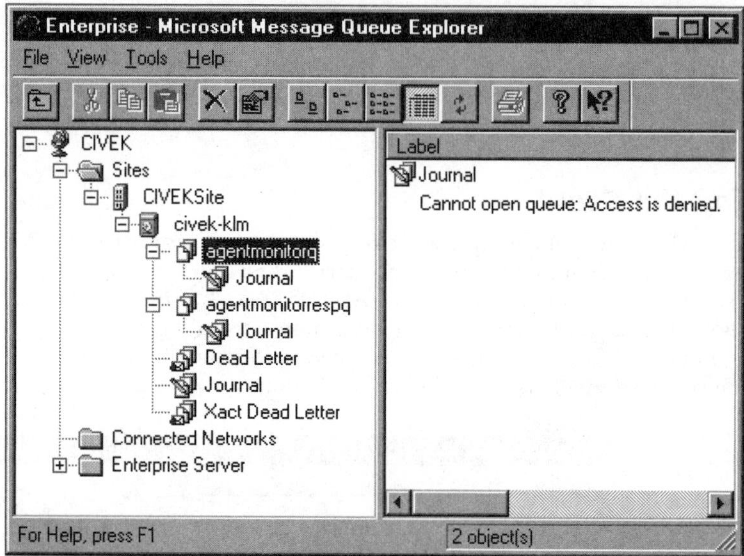

This screenshot to the right shows `AgentMonitorRespQ`, which was created by the VB client. It *is* possible to see the messages in this queue:

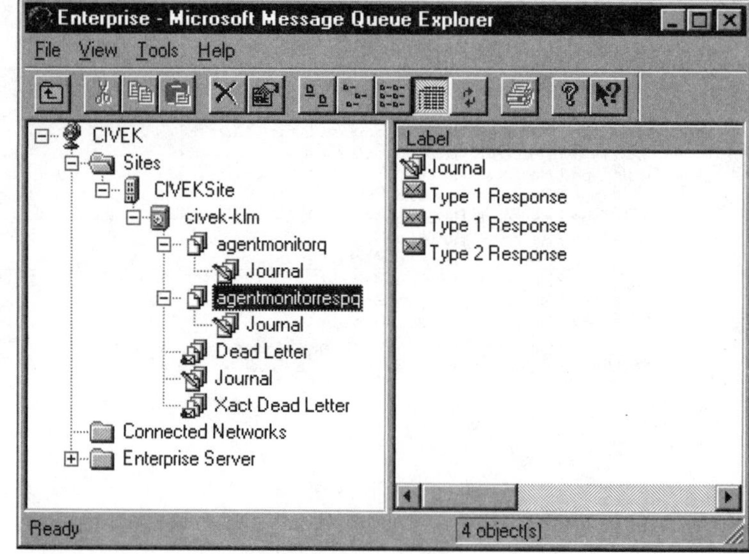

The next shot shows the permissions on the queue created by the service. The unfortunate thing about this scenario is that there is no way to change permissions to view the messages in the queue, without an Administrator taking ownership of the queue away from LocalSystem and assigning more permissions to interactive users.

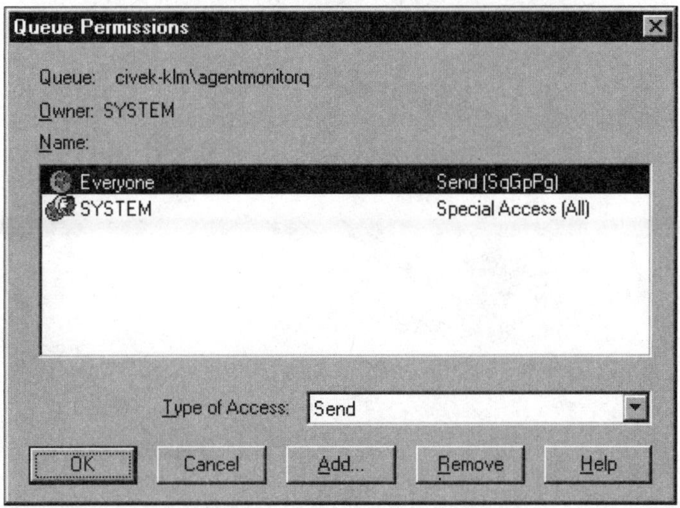

The gist of all this is that if you are going to create the queue from inside the service, you should make sure to specify the users you want to be able to view your queue at creation time, instead of using the default security descriptor. If you're wondering exactly how to do that, then never fear: NT security is our subject for the next chapter.

Summary

In this chapter, I've shown you some of the absolute basics about writing services that monitor MSMQ queues for messages containing work requests. The Agent usage pattern, which I've described in some detail, is a prime candidate to be implemented using this technology.

While my example here was simple, it's not hard to conceive how the service I've developed could be extended to perform (or delegate) considerable work on behalf of a client, or to prepare information in advance of clients connecting to it. Because of the versatility of MSMQ messages, all manner of things are possible.

7

Security

Security is a critical facet of server application development. Once you open up your development model to code being run on a different machine, you need to begin worrying about securing the interactions between the two (or more) machines. When a service receives a request from a client application, it has to know several things about the client in order to be confident that it should actually do the work requested of it. It needs to know that the client is who it says it is, and then, that it really can access the resources it's asking for. In a nutshell, this is the basic problem that must be solved by any security model.

Under Windows NT, you can secure access to *any* resource you make available to the client, whether it be a system object (see the list below) or a private data structure. The flexibility of NT security is such that objects can be secured on an individual basis, so that access to them is controlled. Among the kinds of object you can secure are:

- Files
- Services
- Printers
- Registry keys
- Network shares
- Kernel objects (Processes, threads, semaphores, events, mutexes, file mappings, timers, access tokens, pipes, etc.)
- Window station objects
- Arbitrary user objects

In addition to discussing the issues involved in manipulating the security settings of the objects listed above, this chapter will also examine the topic of **impersonation**. This is a process by which programs can take on the identity of their clients (or indeed of any user) in order to attempt to access secured resources that might otherwise be denied them, either on or off the machine on which they're executing.

Thirdly, we'll be looking in this chapter at the different options available when you want your service to interact with the logged-on user, and some of the problems this can cause. As we progress, we'll examine some of the strange behavior that can occur when services and security collide.

In this chapter, I'm going to assume that you're already familiar with the basic architecture of an NT network. If you're not, consider the NT Security Handbook *(ISBN 0078822408), by Tom Sheldon, to get you started.*

Security Basics

Before we get into the bits and bytes of security too deeply, we need to be clear on some basic terminology. A comprehensive architecture for security must grapple with four different issues:

- **Authentication**. The very first step is to determine whether the person requesting an action really is who they claim to be. In most security architectures, people prove their identities by entering a username and password when challenged to do so.
- **Authorization**. The security system must also deal with the problem of matching user identities with the different resources they can use. In other words, for each securable object on the system, the OS must map identities to possible actions the user can perform on that object.
- **Encryption**. Another issue, orthogonal to the first two, is that of securing the actual data packets that go over the network from prying eyes.
- **Auditing**. In a fully robust system, the activities of users and the objects they touch can be tracked and logged. We'll take a look at auditing in this chapter, but we'll only skim the surface.

C2 Level Security

From the very beginning, Windows NT was designed to meet the C2-level security criteria defined by the US Defense Department. While some other operating systems require special hardware to intercept server requests and enforce security, security policy enforcement on Windows NT is entirely software-based. In fact, in areas such as authentication, Windows NT meets the higher, B2-level security standards. Some of the criteria of C2 certification are:

- All users must identify themselves at the time of log-on
- System objects and private objects must be protected so they are not accessible to other processes on the same machine
- Access to objects must be controlled at both the individual and the group level
- Objects and resources must have owners who control what or who can access them
- All security related events must be audited, and only authorized users are able to access the audit data

The C2 requirements are responsible both for the rich features and the complexity present in the NT security architecture. Keep these requirements in mind as you consider the different aspects of programming NT security.

Overview of Security Topics

Thinking of NT security in very simple terms can help. Suppose that you need access to records kept in a secured building. When you enter the building, you check in with a security guard, to whom you must prove your identity. He then gives you your own personalized key, which provides access to some of the rooms and filing cabinets in the building. As you walk around the building, you try your key in various places; it works in some locks, but not in others. However, each time you use your key, the lock records your doing so.

Making the analogy with NT, the information you present to the guard is called your **credentials**, and the time you do it is called **logon**. What you get in return is an **access token**. The fact that your token works on some locks and not on others, in a predefined way, is called **access control**. The recording of the fact you've been there is called **auditing**.

> *As is usually the case with such analogies, this is an oversimplified explanation. Don't worry – we'll get into the specifics later on.*

The Mechanism of Logon and Authentication

The primary provider of authentication under Windows NT 4.0 is known as **NTLM**, or the **NT** **L**AN **M**anager authentication protocol. NTLM is a **security service provider** (**SSP**), which means that it's a system-level provider of security functionality. NT was designed so that SSPs could be plugged in or pulled out without disturbing the API functions needed to access their functionality. As you'll see later, NTLM will eventually be replaced by Kerberos as the default SSP for Windows NT.

When a user begins to try to use resources on an NT machine, the first thing they must do is present their credentials to the machine, in order to prove they are who they say they are. This initial act of getting the machine into a state where it can be used is known as the **interactive logon**, and it can be quite complex – especially when the logon is to a domain account and not merely a local machine account. The figure below represents the logon and authentication process, and while it introduces a few things with which you're not yet familiar, it might give you an idea of the layout, and it will certainly be something you can come back to as we continue with the story.

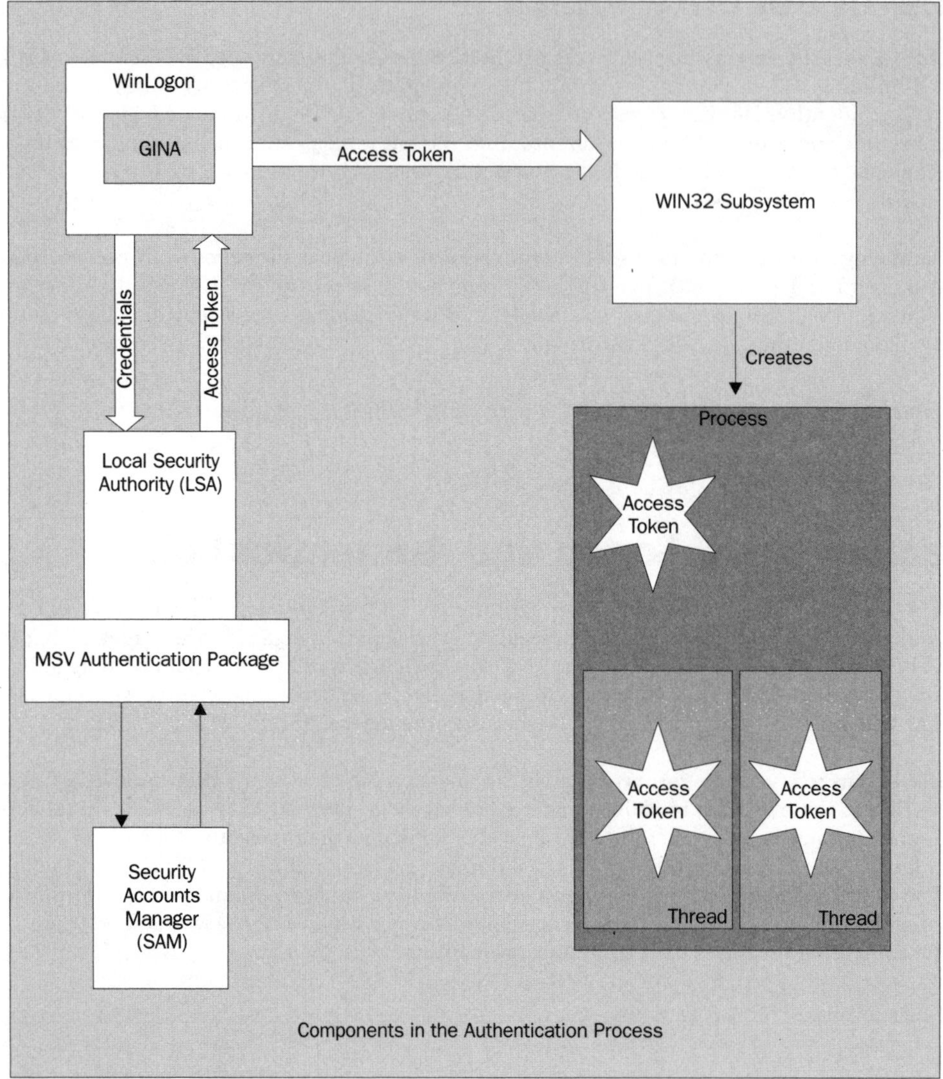

Components in the Authentication Process

The SAS and Winlogon

Authentication processes begin when the user presses *Ctrl+Alt+Delete* to get the system to bring up the user logon dialog box. This series of keystrokes is the **secure attention sequence**, or **SAS**, and it's there to ensure that the logon dialog you get isn't an impostor program trying to steal logon credentials. The SAS processes the hardware event telling the system that a user wants to log on; the actual hardware event could be the *Ctrl+Alt+Delete* key sequence, or the insertion of a smart card, or even turning on a retinal scanner.

A secure process known as `Winlogon.exe` – a task you've probably seen before in the task manager – manages logon itself. To provide the user interface for acquiring credentials, Winlogon utilizes a plug-in DLL component known as **GINA**, the **G**raphical **I**dentificatio**n** and **A**uthentication DLL. GINA is also responsible for activating the shell when the logon is successful.

The default GINA is `Msgina.dll`, but you can replace it with your own to provide a different authentication user interface for smart cards, fingerprint scanners, or whatever else you fancy. (Look at the resources in `Msgina.dll`, and you'll see the logon dialog you're familiar with.) To replace the default GINA with your own, you can follow the sample that comes with the Platform SDK, and then specify the name of the new DLL in the following registry key:

```
HKEY_LOCAL_MACHINE\Software\Microsoft\
                              Windows NT\CurrentVersion\Winlogon\GinaDLL=newgina.dll
```

Verifying Credentials

The plain text user ID and password that are typed into the logon dialog are first encrypted, and then routed to a component known as the **local security authority**, or **LSA**. On an NT Workstation machine, or an NT Server machine that isn't a primary domain controller, this component manages local user accounts. On a primary domain controller, the LSA actually manages *all* domain accounts.

The real job of the LSA is to convert the user's credentials (typed into the logon dialog) into an **access token**, which is required for an interactive user to launch a process. The LSA, which is packaged up in `Lsass.exe`, runs an **authentication package** to validate the user; the default package for NT is `Msv1_0.dll`. This package is replaceable, though, and other vendors can install different ones.

What the authentication package does next depends on whether the user is logging on using a local machine account, or a domain account. Let's look at the local account scenario first, since it's the simpler of the two.

Local Accounts

In this case, the encrypted password is sent to the *local* copy of the **security accounts manager** (**SAM**) for validation. The SAM's job is to compare the encrypted version of the typed-in password with the encrypted password stored in the user account database, which is also known as the SAM database. This is located in a secured, private area of the registry that's only accessible to the LocalSystem account. A member of the NT Administrators group has just enough access to know that he has no access by default. An Administrator has the ability to give himself access to these secure registry areas, though, and can give himself other rights if he wants.

However, getting access to the SAM database is no help when it comes to viewing passwords. The passwords are stored in doubly encrypted form – the first encryption uses a one-way function, and the result is then encrypted again for good measure. The one-way encryption means that even the SAM cannot decrypt the password; once a password is encrypted, it is never decrypted again. When the SAM compares the two passwords, it is comparing them in their *encrypted* form.

If the user is logging on with a local account, the *local* LSA and the *local* SAM handle the process of finding the appropriate user and comparing the two encrypted versions of the password. If the account is a domain account, the process is a bit more complex.

Domain Accounts

If a user logs on with a domain account, then the SAM database that contains the domain user information is located on one of the domain controllers (primary or secondary). This means that validation of credentials has to occur across the network. Isn't there a danger of a packet analyzer stealing the encrypted form of the password being sent from the client machine as it travels across the wire to the domain controller?

As it turns out, no. Thanks to the magic of NT's **challenge-response mechanism**, the actual password is *never* sent over the wire. Here's how it works:

- The credentials typed in by the user are encrypted using a one-way function.
- The encrypted credentials are sent to the LSA.
- The LSA calls the MSV1_0 authentication package. This package forwards the credentials (just the user ID, not the password) to the domain controller for the requested domain, via the Net Logon service.
- The domain controller issues a 16-byte challenge, or **nonce**, to the client machine.
- Using the one-way encrypted form of the user's password, the client machine encrypts the nonce. This is returned back to the domain controller as a response.
- In the meantime, the domain controller takes the nonce and gets the user's one-way encrypted password from its own SAM database. It encrypts the nonce using a process similar to the one in the previous step.
- The domain controller compares its calculated, encrypted nonce with the one sent back from the client machine. If they match, the credentials are considered authentic.

Logon Success

Once the credentials have been authenticated, on either the local machine or the domain controller, several things happen. The SAM (local or domain controller) returns **security identifiers** (**SIDs**) for the user and for each group of which the user is a member to the LSA. It also returns any account **privileges** that the user has. Last (and least), it returns information about things such as the home directory location and logon scripts. The LSA now has the special job of building an **access token** from the information returned from the SAM.

The authenticated credentials are also cached on the local machine, in case they are needed later for logging on to a remote resource.

The Access Token

The LSA takes the information returned to it by the SAM and assembles an access token for the interactive user. Essentially, the access token completely describes the identity of the user, and their rights (permissions to access an object) and privileges (system-wide 'abilities' to perform different types of actions), as they interact with secure objects during that interactive logon session. It contains several important pieces of information, including those listed below. Each of these pieces of information will be described in more detail in the sections to come, so don't worry if you see something you haven't heard of before.

- The security identifiers (SIDs) for the groups of which the user is a member
- A logon SID that identifies the current logon session
- A list of the privileges held by either the user or the groups to which the user belongs
- A SID for the owner
- The default discretionary access control list (also called a DACL) that the system uses when the user creates a securable object without specifying a security descriptor
- Whether the token is a primary or impersonation token
- The current level of impersonation, if any

Each time a process is launched on the system, some access token is attached to that process. That access token is called the **primary access token** for the process. Before we go on, though, it's important to realize that while there is *always* an access token for the interactive user, there can be many processes with many different access tokens running on the system at once. In a service, for example, the primary access token for a process is *not* the interactive user's access token. Furthermore, there may be many threads in a service process running with *different* access tokens, created to *impersonate* the user who logged on to a client machine and interacted with the service. So, while the token of the logged-on user is often the most interesting, it probably *won't* be the most interesting for you, the NT service developer.

There are several things that we can do to manipulate and use access tokens, and we'll take a look at some of them later on in the chapter.

Security IDs (SIDs)

I've mentioned SIDs a few times now, and you'll have got a fair idea of their use from the contexts in which they were discussed, but what exactly *are* they?

When a new user account or group is created, it is assigned a SID that's then placed in the SAM database. The SID is a variable-length identifier that's guaranteed to identify a user (or group) uniquely, because it gets generated from information about the domain, the user, the date, and the time. The security authority uses SIDs to build the access token that will later be duplicated to each process the user spawns.

Deleting a user account and then recreating it with the same name will result in a different SID. A typical user SID looks something like this:

```
S-1-5-21-53181065-1013871316-1714775081-1001
```

Each section of this hideous-looking string means something specific. Every SID begins with the same three sections, but there are then a variable number of extra sections after this initial triplet:

$$S\text{-}R\text{-}I\text{-}X_1\text{-}X_2\text{-}X_3\text{-}X_4\text{-}...\text{-}X_n$$

Label	Meaning	Value
S	Identifies this as a SID	S
R	The revision level	1
I	The authority identifier	5
X_1	Sub-authority IDs, also called RIDs (relative IDs). There can be a maximum of 15 of these.	21
X_2		53181065
X_3		1013871316
X_4		1714775081
X_n		1001

The S always stays the same, while the R section refers to the *version* of the SID, which (for the time being, at least) always contains a 1. However, that could change in future version revisions, where authentication packages may need to differentiate between SID versions.

The I section is the **authority identifier** for the top-level authority that created the SID The authority identifier value identifies the agency that issued the SID; the value of 5 given here is the one that's always used to denote standard user accounts. It represents the SECURITY_NT_AUTHORITY identifier. The complete range of identifiers is shown in the table below, as defined in Winnt.h:

Authority Identifier	Value	Description
SECURITY_NULL_SID_AUTHORITY	0	NULL authority
SECURITY_WORLD_SID_AUTHORITY	1	All users
SECURITY_LOCAL_SID_AUTHORITY	2	Local users
SECURITY_CREATOR_SID_AUTHORITY	3	Object creator
SECURITY_NON_UNIQUE_AUTHORITY	4	Non-unique IDs
SECURITY_NT_AUTHORITY	5	NT security authority

The final (variable-length) group of numbers consists of the **sub-authority identifiers**, sometimes known as **RIDs**. These also have a number of 'standard' values, listed below:

Relative Identifier	Value
SECURITY_NULL_RID	0
SECURITY_WORLD_RID	0
SECURITY_LOCAL_RID	0
SECURITY_CREATOR_OWNER_RID	0
SECURITY_CREATOR_GROUP_RID	1
SECURITY_CREATOR_OWNER_SERVER_RID	2
SECURITY_CREATOR_GROUP_SERVER_RID	3
SECURITY_DIALUP_RID	1
SECURITY_NETWORK_RID	2
SECURITY_BATCH_RID	3
SECURITY_INTERACTIVE_RID	4
SECURITY_SERVICE_RID	6
SECURITY_ANONYMOUS_LOGON_RID	7
SECURITY_PROXY_RID	8
SECURITY_SERVER_LOGON_RID	9
SECURITY_LOGON_IDS_RID	5
SECURITY_LOCAL_SYSTEM_RID	0x00000012L
SECURITY_NT_NON_UNIQUE	0x00000015L
SECURITY_BUILTIN_DOMAIN_RID	0x00000020L

As you can see, some of the standard authority identifiers and RIDs begin to coalesce into the SIDs for well-known entities, shown in the table below:

Name	SID value	Description
Null SID	S-1-0-0	No one
World	S-1-1-0	Everyone
Local	S-1-2-0	Local users
Creator Owner ID	S-1-3-0	Creator of the object.

Table Continued on Following Page

Name	SID value	Description
Creator Group ID	S-1-3-1	Primary group SID of object creator
Dialup	S-1-5-1	Dialup user
Network	S-1-5-2	User who logs on across the network
Batch	S-1-5-3	Batch user
Interactive	S-1-5-4	Interactive user logon
Service	S-1-5-6	Account for services
AnonymousLogon	S-1-5-7	Null logon session
ServerLogon	S-1-5-8	Domain controller account
Logon IDs	S-1-5-5-X-Y	Logon session
NT non-unique IDs	S-1-5-0x15-...	Starting point for building NT user accounts
Built-in domain	S-1-5-0x20	Built-in system domain

Hopefully, this discussion has given you a clear picture of what a SID is and how it is assembled.

Privileges

At a basic level, **privileges** are rights that give users the capability to perform certain types of activities that are *not* associated with particular securable objects. They differ from **permissions**, which are set on an object-by-object basis. Privileges are set not to give access to specific objects, but to give the user the right to perform more generic operations, such as backing up files or launching a debugger on a process. The system administrator usually assigns privileges to users or groups by using the User Manager tool (screenshot below). Privileges are *only* granted for the local machine, even though the grantees may be domain users or groups. They are *not* granted for domain entities or operations.

The capabilities that privileges allow supersede those given by individual permissions; that's why they are part of the access token. If, for instance, a user's access token has the Back up files privilege, they can read files regardless of whether they have specific permissions on a particular file. This is done so that one can avoid having to add a particular user to the permissions for each file object system-wide – a time consuming and space-wasting proposition.

The information returned from the SAM when a user is successfully authenticated includes a set of user privileges, which are identified by a 64-bit number called a **locally unique identifier**, or **LUID**. This is so called because while it is unique on the machine itself, it is not necessarily unique across machines – that is, the numeric LUID of a privilege on one machine is completely unrelated to that of the privilege of the same name on another machine. For this reason, privileges are usually identified by a string name.

The table below shows the privilege constants and names, and the descriptions associated with them in the User Manager application.

Privilege Constant	Name	Description
SE_CREATE_TOKEN_NAME	SeCreateTokenPrivilege	Create a token object
SE_ASSIGNPRIMARYTOKEN_NAME	SeAssignPrimaryTokenPrivilege	Replace a process-level token
SE_LOCK_MEMORY_NAME	SeLockMemoryPrivilege	Lock pages in memory
SECURITY_BATCH_RID	SeBatchSid	Log on as a batch job
SECURITY_SERVICE_RID	SeServiceSid	Log on as a service
SECURITY_NETWORK_RID	SeNetworkSid	Access this computer from network
SECURITY_LOCAL_RID	SeLocalSid	Log on locally
SE_INCREASE_QUOTA_NAME	SeIncreaseQuotaPrivilege	Increase quotas
SE_UNSOLICITED_INPUT_NAME	SeUnsolicitedInputPrivilege	Required to read unsolicited input from terminal device
SE_MACHINE_ACCOUNT_NAME	SeMachineAccountPrivilege	Add Workstations to Domain

Table Continued on Following Page

Privilege Constant	Name	Description
SE_TCB_NAME	SeTcbPrivilege	Act as part of the operating system
SE_SECURITY_NAME	SeSecurityPrivilege	Manage auditing and security log
SE_TAKE_OWNERSHIP_NAME	SeTakeOwnershipPrivilege	Take ownership of files or other objects
SE_LOAD_DRIVER_NAME	SeLoadDriverPrivilege	Load and unload device drivers
SE_SYSTEM_PROFILE_NAME	SeSystemProfilePrivilege	Profile system performance
SE_SYSTEMTIME_NAME	SeSystemtimePrivilege	Change the system time
SE_PROF_SINGLE_PROCESS_NAME	SeProfileSingleProcessPrivilege	Profile single process
SE_INC_BASE_PRIORITY_NAME	SeIncreaseBasePriorityPrivilege	Increase scheduling priority
SE_CREATE_PAGEFILE_NAME	SeCreatePagefilePrivilege	Create a pagefile
SE_CREATE_PERMANENT_NAME	SeCreatePermanentPrivilege	Create permanent shared objects
SE_BACKUP_NAME	SeBackupPrivilege	Back up files and directories
SE_RESTORE_NAME	SeRestorePrivilege	Restore files and directories
SE_SHUTDOWN_NAME	SeShutdownPrivilege	Shut down the system

Privilege Constant	Name	Description
SE_DEBUG_NAME	SeDebugPrivilege	Debug programs
SE_AUDIT_NAME	SeAuditPrivilege	Generate security audits
SE_SYSTEM_ENVIRONMENT_NAME	SeSystemEnvironmentPrivilege	Modify firmware environment values
SE_CHANGE_NOTIFY_NAME	SeChangeNotifyPrivilege	Bypass traverse checking
SE_REMOTE_SHUTDOWN_NAME	SeRemoteShutdownPrivilege	Force shutdown from a remote system

Privileges are unusual because not only do you have to have them, they also have to be *enabled* by a process in order for you to use them. In other words, a particular object has to *accept* the use of a privilege for it to be valid, in addition to you having it in your access token. Most privileges are disabled by default.

Later in this chapter, we will examine how to enable a privilege for a process access token. As we go along, I'll point out when a service needs a particular type of privilege to perform a particular action.

Launching the First Process

At last we have a valid access token, and we understand what all the parts of that token are. Having built it, the LSA now hands the token back to the Winlogon process; we say that it is now *attached* to that process. Next, Winlogon calls into the Win32 subsystem and creates a **security context** for this user, which means that every process created by this user in this logon session will also receive this access token. Furthermore, every thread created by any (interactively spawned) process *also* runs in this security context.

Changes to security settings that alter the properties of an access token (changing the user's group membership, or changing a privilege) do not take effect until the user has logged off and logged back on again.

This combination of an access token and a particular process instance is known as a **subject**, of which there are two types. **Simple subjects** only have the security context of the user that started them. For instance, the process/access token combination created when a user double-clicks Notepad is a simple subject. **Server subjects** are more complex, because they have both their own context *and* the security contexts of the clients that may be calling into them.

> **All non-trivial NT services can be considered server subjects, because they almost always have to deal with security on two levels: their own process security, and the security needed by the calling clients.**

Service Accounts

The account that a service runs under can be configured using the Services control panel applet. The account you choose becomes the security context for the service. Services can run under a particular NT account, or under the LocalSystem account. As I mentioned way back in Chapter 1, LocalSystem is a special account that's used by NT to perform all its intrinsic operating system duties. LocalSystem is also the account that an NT service is installed to run under, if you don't do anything special to change it. Take a look at the service configuration dialog below:

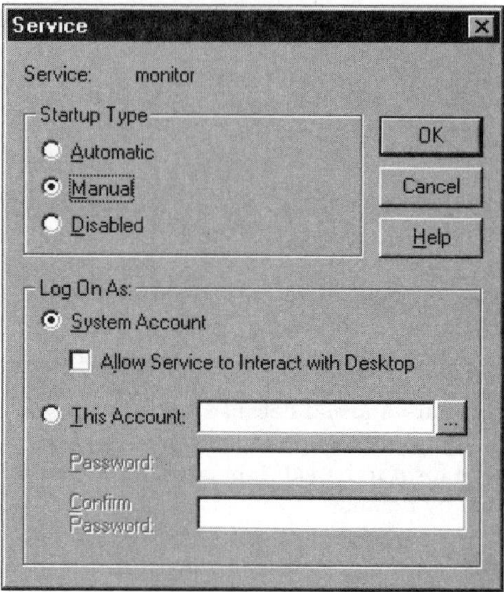

The LocalSystem account has some special properties that you'll learn more about later. Basically, though, it has *all* available privileges and access rights to all of the files on the local system, but *no* network capability – it has no power at all away from the local machine, because it has no network credentials.

Incidentally, a service that's installed as a shared service (`SERVICE_WIN32_SHARE_PROCESS`) doesn't allow you to log on as any account *except* LocalSystem. In such cases, the This Account option will be disabled.

If you change from LocalSystem, the account that you specify will need the "Log on as a service" privilege. If you're using the Services applet to make this change, it will automatically add that privilege to the user you enter. However, if you are changing the service programmatically, the raw API calls will *not* do that, so you will have to add that privilege to the user yourself.

A key point to remember here is that *all* services, whether they run under LocalSystem or "This Account", start with a different access token (and therefore a different security context) from that of the interactive user. When you think about it, this *must* be true in the case of auto-start services (because there is no interactive user when they start), but it's also true of services that are started after a user has logged on. This single issue is the reason why services seem to act oddly in many circumstances that appear to be fairly simple scenarios – they *look* like they're running as a process under the interactive user's security context, but they're not. We'll deal with several of these oddities in detail, later in the chapter.

Remote Logon Scenarios

Accessing a shared resource *after* you have logged on interactively is known as a **remote logon**. If an already logged-on, interactive user needs to access a resource (such as a file) on a remote server, that server must authenticate the user. This is where the credentials, that have been cached on the user's computer by the LSA, come into play. Here's what happens:

- The LSA calls the authentication package, which calls Net Logon. Net Logon on the client's machine then calls Net Logon on the other machine (the server with the resource). The Net Logon service supports pass-through authentication and domain logon on NT Workstation, and authenticates user logon and synchronizes security databases between the primary and backup domain controllers on NT Server.
- The LSA on the remote server asks its SAM to authenticate the user. It compares the credentials with information in the SAM database.
- If the information is valid, the LSA creates an access token and passes it to the Server service, which builds a user ID for the client.
- The user ID is returned to the client's machine, which will put the ID into any subsequent requests that it sends to the server for that interactive logon session.

This procedure happens once for each remote machine to which the user connects.

Service Issues

It's not hard to see how this is going to affect you as a service writer. If you're using LocalSystem as the security context for a service, then you have a slight problem. LocalSystem has no credentials; that is to say, it has **null credentials**. When the service running under the LocalSystem context tries to access a remote resource with null credentials, the remote machine views this as a **null session**. Access to the resource is only allowed if the machine allows null session access, which is configurable through the registry. You can specify that you want to allow null sessions on network shares at the following path:

```
HKEY_LOCAL_MACHINE\SYSTEM\CurrentControlSet\Services\
                                    LanmanServer\Parameters\NullSessionShares
```

This is a value of type `REG_MULTI_SZ`, so, on a new line in this value, add the share name, such as `MyShare`. The key for pipes is at:

```
HKEY_LOCAL_MACHINE\SYSTEM\CurrentControlSet\Services\
                                      LanmanServer\Parameters\NullSessionPipes
```

To enable null sessions on a pipe, just enter the pipe name. Alternatively, if you prefer massive security breaches and want anyone to be able to access your systems, add a `DWORD` value called `RestrictNullSessAccess` to the `Parameters` key, and set it to 0. I *don't* advise this; you're better off using **impersonation** when you need to access remote resources, as we'll see later on.

Authentication Programming Concepts

Now that you understand how the mechanisms of authentication occur, you probably want to learn something about programming them. You'll remember that authentication portion of the security equation relates to the things that verify users' identities, or the things that they have the intrinsic capability to do. There are a few basic concepts we talked about in that area: SIDs, access tokens, and privileges.

Programming Security Identifiers

Although you would never manipulate one directly, there are a variety of things you can do with a security identifier, and of course there are some API functions to support you in your endeavors. The functions I shall describe below can be invaluable when you're working with NT services.

Finding a SID or an Account Name

Unless you're an Administrator (in which case you can call `NetUserEnum()`), Windows NT won't allow you to get a list of all the valid account names on a machine for security reasons. Instead, you have to ask for each individual user by name or by SID. If you don't have a SID, or if you have a SID and need an account name, you can use one of this pair of functions:

Function	Description
`LookupAccountSid()`	Given a SID, this function returns a user or group name, and the domain of which the account is a member
`LookupAccountName()`	Given an account name, this function returns a user or group SID, and the domain of which the account is a member

The prototype of the first of these functions, `LookupAccountSid()`, is:

```
BOOL LookupAccountSid(
      LPCTSTR lpSystemName,                   // String for system name (in)
      PSID    Sid,                            // Security identifier (in)
      LPTSTR  Name,                           // String for account name (out)
      LPDWORD cbName,                         // Size of account string (in/out)
      LPTSTR  ReferencedDomainName,           // String for referenced domain (out)
      LPDWORD cbReferencedDomainName,         // Size of domain string (in/out)
      PSID_NAME_USE peUse                     // SID type enumeration (out)
);
```

The system looks for the SID in question by searching according to a predefined method. First, it checks well-known SIDs (from the table of well-known SIDs in the *Security Identifiers* section above), then built-in and local accounts, then primary domain accounts, then trusted domain accounts. In addition, the function returns an account type defined in the `SID_NAME_USE` enumeration, listed below:

Enumeration value	Description
SidTypeUser	User SID
SidTypeGroup	Group SID
SidTypeDomain	Domain SID
SidTypeAlias	Alias
SidTypeWellKnownGroup	Well-known group SID
SidTypeDeletedAccount	An account that was deleted
SidTypeInvalid	The SID was invalid
SidTypeUnknown	Obvious

We'll have an example of using `LookupAccountSid()` a little later on, in the section called *Getting Token Information.* In the meantime, here's the prototype for the very similar `LookupAccountName()`:

```
BOOL LookupAccountName(
    LPCTSTR lpSystemName,           // Address of string for system name
    LPCTSTR lpAccountName,          // Address of string for account name
    PSID    Sid,                    // Address of security identifier
    LPDWORD cbSid,                  // Address of size of security identifier
    LPTSTR  ReferencedDomainName,   // Address of string for referenced domain
    LPDWORD cbReferencedDomainName, // Address of size of domain string
    PSID_NAME_USE peUse             // Address of SID-type indicator
);
```

Other SID Functions

In addition to the lookups, there are several other SID-manipulation functions that are less frequently needed; I list them here for completeness' sake. The table below lists the ones aimed at creating, copying, and comparing SIDs.

Function	Description
AllocateAndInitializeSid()	Allocates a SID based on information passed in
CopySid()	Copies a SID to a buffer
EqualPrefixSid()	Checks two SIDs for equality except for the last sub-authority, X_n
EqualSid()	Checks two SIDs for equality

Table Continued on Following Page

Function	Description
`InitializeSid()`	Initializes a SID with the authority, but not the sub-authorities
`GetSidLengthRequired()`	Returns the length of buffer needed to hold a SID with the passed in number of sub-authorities
`FreeSid()`	Frees a SID allocated by `AllocateAndInitializeSid()`

Once you have a SID, you can get information out of it by using the functions below:

Function	Description
`IsValidSid()`	Checks whether the SID has a valid format
`GetLengthSid()`	Gets the SID length
`GetSidIdentifierAuthority()`	Gets the authority for the SID
`GetSidSubAuthority()`	Gets a specified sub-authority
`GetSidSubAuthorityCount()`	Returns the number of sub-authorities in the SID

Access Tokens

The next major authentication entity is the access token. So far, we've discussed access tokens in quite a bit of detail, but we haven't talked about programming aspects. In truth, these aspects are most interesting in the context of *Impersonation*, which is slated for a later section, but we can cover the basics here.

Obtaining the Process Token

Getting hold of the access token for a process is quite easy – just call the `OpenProcessToken()` function, shown below:

```
BOOL OpenProcessToken(
     HANDLE  ProcessHandle, // Handle to process
     DWORD   DesiredAccess, // The access rights you desire for the process
     PHANDLE TokenHandle    // Pointer to handle of open access token
);
```

You can just pass in the handle to your process (obtained using `GetCurrentProcess()`) and you'll be ready to go.

Tokens, just like other securable NT objects, have an **access control list** (ACL). I'll have a lot more to say about these when we come to discuss authorization in a few pages' time, but at the moment you just need to know that they contain a list of the permissions that a particular user or group has, to do things to an object. In this case, when you open a token, you have to specify the permissions you want in the `DesiredAccess` parameter. The values you can pass are listed below:

Value	Description
TOKEN_ADJUST_DEFAULT	Required for changing the default ACL, primary group, or owner of an access token
TOKEN_ADJUST_GROUPS	Required for changing the groups specified in an access token
TOKEN_ADJUST_PRIVILEGES	Required for changing the privileges specified in an access token
TOKEN_ALL_ACCESS	Combines the STANDARD_RIGHTS_REQUIRED standard access rights and all individual access rights for tokens
TOKEN_ASSIGN_PRIMARY	Required for attaching a primary token to a process, in addition to the SE_CREATE_TOKEN_NAME privilege
TOKEN_DUPLICATE	Required for duplicating an access token
TOKEN_EXECUTE	Combines the STANDARD_RIGHTS_EXECUTE standard access rights and the TOKEN_IMPERSONATE access right
TOKEN_IMPERSONATE	Required for attaching an impersonation access token to a process
TOKEN_QUERY	Required for querying the contents of an access token
TOKEN_QUERY_SOURCE	Required for querying the source of an access token
TOKEN_READ	Combines the STANDARD_RIGHTS_READ standard access rights and the TOKEN_QUERY access right
TOKEN_WRITE	Combines the STANDARD_RIGHTS_WRITE standard access rights and the TOKEN_ADJUST_PRIVILEGES, TOKEN_ADJUST_GROUPS, and TOKEN_ADJUST_DEFAULT access rights

Another function called OpenThreadToken() is available to you if you need the token for a thread. This will be useful in later scenarios dealing with impersonation.

```
BOOL OpenThreadToken(
   HANDLE  ThreadHandle,        // Handle to thread
   DWORD   DesiredAccess,       // The access rights you desire
   BOOL    OpenAsSelf,          // Flag for process or thread security
   PHANDLE TokenHandle          // Pointer to handle of open access token
);
```

The interesting thing about this function is the extra parameter, OpenAsSelf, which allows you to specify whether the access check is made against the security context of the calling process (TRUE) or against the context of the current thread (FALSE).

Getting Token Information

Knowing how to get hold of an access token means you can also get to the information inside it. To obtain the wealth of information that access tokens contain, call `GetTokenInformation()`, shown below:

```
BOOL GetTokenInformation(
    HANDLE TokenHandle,                            // Handle of access token
    TOKEN_INFORMATION_CLASS TokenInformationClass, // Type to retrieve
    LPVOID TokenInformation,                 // Address of retrieved information
    DWORD  TokenInformationLength,           // Size of information buffer
    PDWORD ReturnLength                      // Address of required buffer size
);
```

In the second parameter, you pass the function a value of an enumerated type (listed below) to specify the type of information you want. `GetTokenInformation()` then returns one of the structures in the chart:

Enumeration Value	Type Returned	Description
`TokenUser`	`TOKEN_USER`	The SID of the user associated with the token
`TokenGroups`	`TOKEN_GROUPS`	The SIDs of the groups in the token and whether any privileges are enabled on those groups
`TokenPrivileges`	`TOKEN_PRIVILEGES`	Privileges of the token and whether they are enabled
`TokenOwner`	`TOKEN_OWNER`	Default owner SID that will be applied to newly created objects
`TokenPrimaryGroup`	`TOKEN_PRIMARY_GROUP`	The SID of the token's primary group. This is used for POSIX support
`TokenDefaultDacl`	`TOKEN_DEFAULT_DACL`	The default DACL that the system uses in the security descriptors of new objects created by a thread using this access token
`TokenSource`	`TOKEN_SOURCE`	Contains information about who created the token

Enumeration Value	Type Returned	Description
TokenType	TOKEN_TYPE	An enumeration set to either TokenPrimary or TokenImpersonation. Indicates the type of the token
TokenStatistics	TOKEN_STATISTICS	Contains information about the token, such as the token ID, token type, the number of groups, the number of privileges, and a modified LUID that can be used to see if the token has changed

This is another one of those API functions that returns a variable amount of information. If you pass NULL as the third argument to GetTokenInformation(), and 0 as the fourth, the API will return the size of the buffer you need. You can then call it again with the right size. Of course, you need to have opened the token with the proper access rights to make the call in the first place (TOKEN_QUERY).

Sample: Token Information

Let's take a look at a short sample that uses GetTokenInformation() to retrieve the TokenUser information for the current process, and then looks up the name and domain name by SID using LookupAccountSid(). Then, it prints that user name out to the console window.

```
#include <windows.h>
#include <TCHAR.h>
#include <iostream>
using namespace std;

int main()
{
   HANDLE hToken;
   if(OpenProcessToken(GetCurrentProcess(), TOKEN_QUERY, &hToken))
   {
      // Determine buffer space needed
      DWORD cbInfo = 0;
      if(!GetTokenInformation(hToken, TokenUser, 0, 0, &cbInfo) &&
                                 ERROR_INSUFFICIENT_BUFFER == GetLastError())
      {
         TOKEN_USER* pTUser = reinterpret_cast<TOKEN_USER*>
                                                     (new BYTE[cbInfo]);
         GetTokenInformation(hToken, TokenUser, pTUser, cbInfo, &cbInfo);

         PSID pSID = pTUser->User.Sid;
```

```
            DWORD cbName = 255;
            TCHAR lpName[255] = {0};
            DWORD cbDomName = 1024;
            TCHAR lpDom[1024] = {0};
            SID_NAME_USE Use;

            if(LookupAccountSid(0, pSID, lpName, &cbName, lpDom,
                                                   &cbDomName, &Use))
            {
                cout << "Account Name: " << lpDom << "\\" << lpName << endl;
            }
            delete pTUser;
        }
    }
    return 0;
}
```

Other Functions

There are a number of other functions available to manipulate tokens, although most of them won't interest us until we talk about impersonation a little later on.

Function	Description
`AdjustTokenGroups()`	Change the groups in an access token
`AdjustTokenPrivileges()`	Enable/disable the privileges that are in a token
`DuplicateToken()`	Copy an existing token for impersonation
`DuplicateTokenEx()`	Copy an existing token, creating a primary or an impersonation token
`SetTokenInformation()`	Sets the information in a token. Counterpart to `GetTokenInformation()`
`SetThreadToken()`	Sets an impersonation token on a thread

Privileges

Earlier, we talked about what the different privileges are and what they do. When you work with privileges, most of the time you will be concerned with enabling or disabling individual privileges in the access token, so that the security context is capable of performing certain types of standard NT operations.

Enabling or Disabling Privileges

The workhorse of privilege manipulation is the `AdjustTokenPrivileges()` function. It enables or disables privileges in the access token whose handle you pass in, which must have been opened with `TOKEN_ADJUST_PRIVILEGES` access. Here's the prototype:

```
BOOL AdjustTokenPrivileges(
     HANDLE TokenHandle,         // Handle to token that contains privileges
     BOOL DisableAllPrivileges,  // Flag for disabling all privileges
     PTOKEN_PRIVILEGES NewState, // Pointer to new privilege information
     DWORD BufferLength,         // Size, in bytes, of PreviousState buffer

     // Receives original state of changed privileges
     PTOKEN_PRIVILEGES PreviousState,

     // Receives required size of the PreviousState buffer
     PDWORD ReturnLength
);
```

You'll remember from earlier in the chapter that privileges are assigned *locally* to each machine. Therefore, each privilege will have a different LUID value on every machine, and so must be looked up individually. There are three functions that support such operations on privileges.

Function	Description
`LookupPrivilegeValue()`	Returns the LUID for the named privilege
`LookupPrivilegeName()`	Returns the name of the privilege specified in the LUID
`LookupPrivilegeDisplayName()`	Returns a description for the privilege passed in by name

Sample: Enabling a Privilege on a Process

This sample will demonstrate a technique by which you can kill a service from the task manager. Usually, if you try to kill a service this way, you'll get an Access is denied message box. This is because even if you're an Administrator, you don't have permission to open a process that has been created in the security context of another user (in this case, LocalSystem). Now, NT will override that permission in cases where you have the privilege `SeDebugPrivilege` (debug a process) enabled in your access token. If you *are* an Administrator, then you already have this privilege. If not, you'll have to add it through the User Rights dialog.

If you *do* have this privilege, then why doesn't the task manager allow you to kill the process? The problem is that, by default, this privilege is not *enabled* by the task manager. The sample below will show you how to enable the privilege by creating a process that enables it, and then launch the task manager using *that* process token. It might come in handy in your service debugging...

```
#include <windows.h>

int main()
{
   TCHAR* pszCmdLine = __TEXT("TaskMgr.exe");
```

```
    HANDLE hToken;
    TOKEN_PRIVILEGES tokpriv;
    tokpriv.PrivilegeCount = 1;
    LookupPrivilegeValue(NULL, SE_DEBUG_NAME, &tokpriv.Privileges[0].Luid);
    tokpriv.Privileges[0].Attributes = SE_PRIVILEGE_ENABLED;

    if(OpenProcessToken(GetCurrentProcess(), TOKEN_ADJUST_PRIVILEGES,
                                                                  &hToken))
    {
       if(AdjustTokenPrivileges(hToken, FALSE, &tokpriv,
                                              sizeof(tokpriv), NULL, NULL))
       {
          ShellExecute(NULL, NULL, pszCmdLine, NULL, NULL, SW_SHOWNORMAL);
       }
    }
    CloseHandle(hToken);
    return 0;
}
```

Checking Privileges Manually

If you need to check the privileges on an access token manually, and then grant access to some operation within your service based on the token having those privileges, you can do so by calling `PrivilegeCheck()`, shown below:

```
BOOL PrivilegeCheck(
    HANDLE          ClientToken,                    // Handle of access token
    PPRIVILEGE_SET  RequiredPrivileges,             // Address of privileges
    LPBOOL          pfResult                        // Address of flag for result
);
```

This function accepts a handle to an access token and a structure that contains the privileges that you want to check are enabled. It returns an out parameter to a `BOOL` that tells you if the privileges *were* enabled.

The Mechanism of Authorization

OK, so you've got an access token. I would imagine that the question burning in your mind now is, "How does NT use an access token to know what I can or can't do on the system?" Well, that's what authorization is all about. Authorization, you will recall, is the process of giving an (authenticated) user permission to access certain resources, and denying them permission to access other resources.

Each securable object in NT has a list that contains users and groups who can explicitly access it, and who are explicitly *denied* access to it. All the deep security grunge we're about to discuss boils down to controlling that list of users and groups. Keep that in mind, and you won't miss the forest for the trees.

Access Control Structures

In brief, authorization works like this: when you create one of the securable objects in NT, you pass that object a structure called a **security descriptor** that specifies several things about how you want security to be enforced on that object. The most important thing in the security descriptor is a list (called a **discretionary access control list**, or **DACL**) of user SIDs and the permissions that you are allowing (or denying) to those SIDs for the object. We just said that when a user logs on, they receive an access token. When the system checks security on an NT object, it compares the SID and the groups in the access token against the entries in the DACL associated with the object, to determine whether the user is allowed to access the object. The core of that authorization operation is the `AccessCheck()` function, which lurks deep down in the guts of the NT kernel.

Security Descriptors

The **security descriptor** (SD) is the key item that NT uses to describe the security settings of each securable object. All the information about the object's security is contained in this descriptor, which is attached to the object at creation time. It can also be modified at any point during the object's lifetime. The security descriptor describes three simple things about the object:

- The **permissions** that various users and groups have to perform various types of actions on the object
- The activities of various users and groups that should be **audited**
- The **owner** of the object

Let's take a look at the structure of a security descriptor (`SECURITY_DESCRIPTOR`), as it is defined in `Winnt.h`:

```
typedef struct _SECURITY_DESCRIPTOR
{
   BYTE Revision;
   BYTE Sbz1;
   SECURITY_DESCRIPTOR_CONTROL Control;
   PSID Owner;
   PSID Group;
   PACL Sacl;
   PACL Dacl;
}  SECURITY_DESCRIPTOR, *PISECURITY_DESCRIPTOR;
```

As you might expect, the security descriptor identifies users and groups in this structure by their SIDs. The actual memory layout of the structure is defined like so:

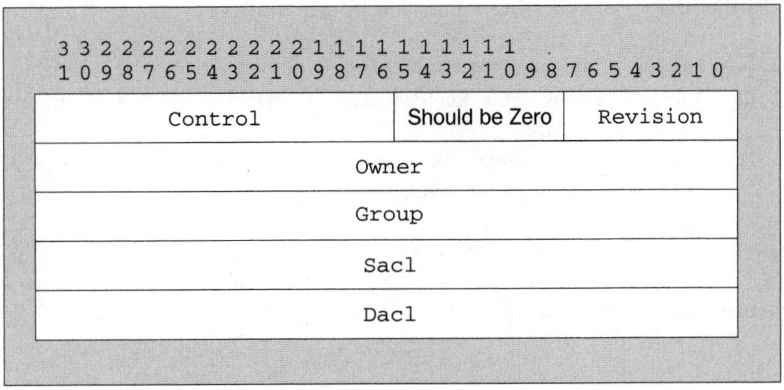

<table>
<tr><td colspan="3">3 3 2 2 2 2 2 2 2 2 2 2 1 1 1 1 1 1 1 1 1 1
1 0 9 8 7 6 5 4 3 2 1 0 9 8 7 6 5 4 3 2 1 0 9 8 7 6 5 4 3 2 1 0</td></tr>
<tr><td>Control</td><td>Should be Zero</td><td>Revision</td></tr>
<tr><td colspan="3">Owner</td></tr>
<tr><td colspan="3">Group</td></tr>
<tr><td colspan="3">Sacl</td></tr>
<tr><td colspan="3">Dacl</td></tr>
</table>

The first 32 bits contain structural information that you really don't need to be concerned about. The rest of the structure contains pointers to other pieces of data: the owner's SID, the primary group SID (not used in NT; only for POSIX or Macintosh integration), an access control list for auditing (known as a SACL) and an access control list for permissions.

> **The structure should be treated as though you don't know what's inside it, so don't manipulate the contents directly in memory. Always use the Win32 API functions to do so instead.**

Absolute and Self-relative Descriptors

Technically, there are two types of security descriptors that share the same structure but work slightly differently: **absolute** and **self-relative**. An absolute descriptor works in the way I just described – it has a header and pointers to other memory structures that are allocated elsewhere. A self-relative security descriptor always begins with the `SECURITY_DESCRIPTOR` structure, but the parts being pointed to follow the structure immediately in memory, in any order. The pointers in the structure itself contain offsets to the beginnings of the various structure blocks.

A security descriptor in absolute format is useful when you have access to the actual typed memory structures for owner, group, SACL, and DACL. The self-relative format is needed when the security descriptor must be stored in contiguous state somewhere, copied, or transmitted. Win32 API functions that return security descriptors always do so using the self-relative format.

Access Control Lists (ACLs)

Since we already know all about SIDs, let's move on to the DACL portion of the security descriptor. What are those ACLs, and how do we use them?

An ACL is really very simple. For a DACL (discretionary access control list), it's just a list of **access control entries** (**ACEs**), each of which describes the permissions that are allowed or denied for a particular user or group. A **SACL** (**system access control list**) is also a list of ACEs, but this time each describes the activities that should be audited for a particular user or group.

Access Control Entries (ACEs)

ACEs themselves contain three pieces of information:

- The SID of the user or group to which it applies
- A mask of access rights. Each access right gives a specific capability in the context of the object that is being secured
- A flag to indicate whether the access mask is allowed (access-allowed ACE), denied (access-denied ACE), or audited (system-audit ACE)

Accordingly, there are three different types of ACE (actually there are four – the last is the system alarm ACE, but I won't go into that here), although in fact they each have an identical physical structure. The structure of an ACE, from `Winnt.h`, looks like this:

```
typedef struct _ACCESS_ALLOWED_ACE
{
   ACE_HEADER Header;
   ACCESS_MASK Mask;
   DWORD SidStart;
} ACCESS_ALLOWED_ACE;
typedef struct _ACCESS_DENIED_ACE
{
   ACE_HEADER Header;
   ACCESS_MASK Mask;
   DWORD SidStart;
} ACCESS_DENIED_ACE;
typedef struct _SYSTEM_AUDIT_ACE
{
   ACE_HEADER Header;
   ACCESS_MASK Mask;
   DWORD SidStart;
} SYSTEM_AUDIT_ACE;
```

Here's what the memory layout looks like. The type of the ACE is actually determined by the `AceType` member of the `ACE_HEADER` structure that comes at the top:

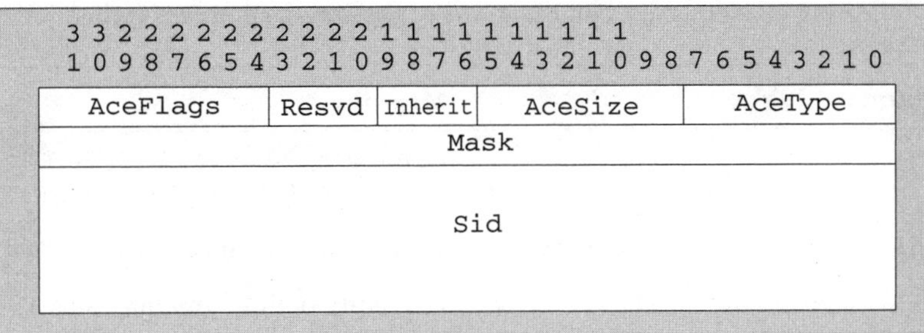

Access Rights

We've already encountered access rights, to some degree, in several of the Win32 API service functions. If you recall, a service can only be started, stopped, paused, queried for configuration information, etc., if the user requesting the action has a specific set of rights.

In fact, there are three types of rights: **generic**, **standard**, and **specific**. Generic rights are – you guessed it – completely generic. In fact, they are *so* generic that it's up to the individual object to define what those rights mean to it. Objects do that using a by calling an API function called `MapGenericMask()` to define how NT's generic rights specifiers map to their own standard and specific rights. Typically, the object then lists (in its documentation) what specific/standard rights each of the generic rights map to. The table below shows the generic rights that are defined by NT:

Generic Right	Meaning
`GENERIC_READ`	Read access
`GENERIC_WRITE`	Write access
`GENERIC_EXECUTE`	Execute access
`GENERIC_ALL`	All of the above

Standard rights, shown in the table below, are more clearly defined. Many of these affect a user's access to the object's security descriptor.

Standard Right	Meaning
DELETE	The right to delete the object
READ_CONTROL	The right to read the information in the object's security descriptor, not including the information in the SACL
SYNCHRONIZE	The right to use the object for synchronization. This enables a thread to wait until the object is in the signaled state. Only objects that can be waited on using WaitFor…Objects() (such as events, threads, and mutexes) can have this right
WRITE_DAC	The right to modify the DACL in the object's security descriptor
WRITE_OWNER	The right to change the owner in the object's security descriptor

The following constants are combinations of the standard access rights.

Standard Right	Meaning
STANDARD_RIGHTS_ALL	Combines DELETE, READ_CONTROL, WRITE_DAC, WRITE_OWNER, and SYNCHRONIZE access
STANDARD_RIGHTS_EXECUTE	Currently defined to equal READ_CONTROL
STANDARD_RIGHTS_READ	Currently defined to equal READ_CONTROL
STANDARD_RIGHTS_REQUIRED	Combines DELETE, READ_CONTROL, WRITE_DAC, and WRITE_OWNER access
STANDARD_RIGHTS_WRITE	Currently defined to equal READ_CONTROL

Finally, specific rights are those that denote particular types of custom access. For instance, we saw that the OpenService() call requires the requester to request a particular type of access, depending on what they are doing. To enumerate dependencies, the requester must ask for (at least) the specific right SERVICE_ENUMERATE_DEPENDENTS. The DACL is then checked to see if that user has that specific right allowed.

Often, those specific rights are then mapped to generic rights, as described above. In the case of the service example, one could also ask for the GENERIC_READ right in the OpenService() call and be able to enumerate dependencies.

Be aware that since the system validates each request for access against the access token, requests for very broad access, such as STANDARD_RIGHTS_ALL, can require significant time to authorize. Generally, it is better to request only the specific rights you will need to perform a task.

System Access Control Lists (SACLs)

To use auditing, an Administrator must first enable the auditing of various event types from the User Manager (see the screenshot on the right). This is so that auditing (a fairly expensive process) is not done willy-nilly, without the knowledge of the Administrator. Once that's done, the system will log audit information for accesses to the rights specified by the SID in the ACE.

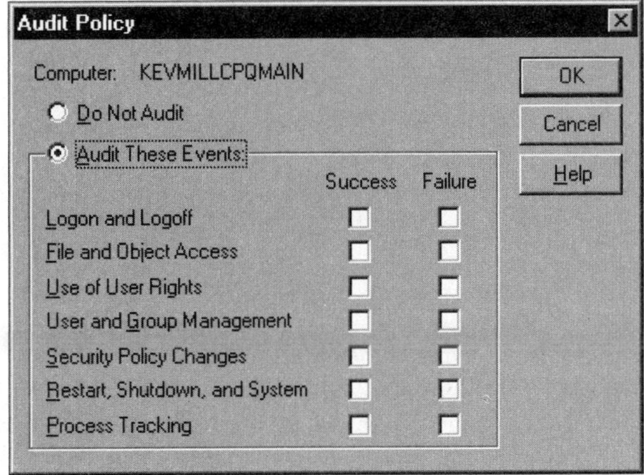

Access Check

The final piece of the authorization puzzle comes together when a requester attempts an actual operation on the secured object. This step is known as the **access check**, and it's when NT compares the security information in the requester's access token with the information in the security descriptor of the object in question. The actual comparison of access token with security descriptor happens down in the kernel itself, in a component known as the **security reference monitor**, or SRM.

Depending on the operation you are attempting, a 'desired access' mask is created for the object in question. For well-known secured objects, such as files, NT knows what mask is required by the operation you are attempting. Opening a file programmatically means you need, for instance, something like `GENERIC_READ` access. For other types of secured objects, the operation you are carrying out in the application may determine the mask needed (according to what the application specifies), or you may be asked to specify the mask, as in the case of `OpenService()`.

The access check process happens as a result of a call to `AccessCheck()`. Based on the operation you are attempting, this call may be made implicitly by the system, or else (in the case of private objects you may be securing) you will call it explicitly from your code. `AccessCheck()` takes a variety of parameters, including the security descriptor, the client access token, the mask of requested access rights, and the mask for mapping generic to specific rights. It returns the privileges required for the access, a mask of the rights that were granted, and, of course, whether the access was granted at all. Below is the function prototype for `AccessCheck()`:

```
BOOL AccessCheck(
   PSECURITY_DESCRIPTOR pSecurityDescriptor,     // Security descriptor
   HANDLE ClientToken,                        // Handle to client access token
   DWORD DesiredAccess,                       // Requested access rights
   PGENERIC_MAPPING GenericMapping,           // Map generic to specific rights
   PPRIVILEGE_SET PrivilegeSet,               // Receives privileges used
   LPDWORD PrivilegeSetLength,                // Size of privilege-set buffer
   LPDWORD GrantedAccess,                     // Retrieves mask of granted rights
   LPBOOL AccessStatus                        // Retrieves results of access check
);
```

The AccessCheck Algorithm

The `AccessCheck()` function uses a well-defined algorithm to determine whether to grant or deny access with the rights requested in the mask. Essentially, it enumerates through each ACE in the DACL, from beginning to end, as follows:

- The security ID in the ACE is compared with all the security IDs in the user's access token. If a match is not found, the ACE is skipped.
- If a match *is* found, what happens next depends on the type of ACE. By convention, 'access denied' ACEs are ordered before 'access allowed' ACEs, and the former are therefore processed first.
- If a SID matches an 'access denied' ACE, the system checks whether the original desired access mask contained only `READ_CONTROL` and `WRITE_DAC`. If so, the system checks whether the requester is the owner of the object. If that's the case, then access is granted. The owner of an object is always allowed access for `READ_CONTROL` and `WRITE_DAC`.
- For an 'access denied' ACE, the actions in the ACE access mask are compared with those in the desired access mask. If any access is found in both masks, all access is denied. Otherwise, processing continues with the next ACE.
- For an 'access allowed' ACE, the actions in the ACE are compared with those listed in the desired access mask. If all accesses in the desired access mask are matched in the ACE, no further processing is necessary, and access is granted. Otherwise, processing continues with the next ACE.
- If, at the end of processing all the ACEs with matching SIDs, the contents of the desired access mask are still not completely matched, access is implicitly denied.

If access is granted, the `AccessStatus` parameter to `AccessCheck()` returns `TRUE` and the `GrantedAccess` mask contains the `DesiredAccess` mask that was requested. If access fails, `AccessStatus` contains `FALSE` and `GrantedAccess` is 0.

An interesting side note to the access check mechanism is that a null DACL is *not* the same as an empty DACL. A null DACL implicitly allows *everyone* to access the object – in effect, it's saying that no security checks should be made. At the opposite extreme, an **empty DACL** explicitly denies access to everyone. This is why it's important that the owner always be able to change permissions using `READ_CONTROL` and `WRITE_DAC`.

Programming Authorization

You'll have noticed that during my description of authentication and authorization, I've avoided doing too many code samples. I didn't want to interrupt the flow of what's really quite a simple story with details of *how* to insert ACEs into ACLs, and so forth. That's what most descriptions of security do and frankly, that's why NT security can seem more confusing than it is. Now, however, we are ready to move on to programming issues.

Programming authorization isn't as difficult as it might sound, especially since the introduction of some easier ACL programming functions in NT 4.0. In the future, NT 5.0 promises to make programming authorization easier still, and we'll look at some of the proposed NT 5.0 functions in this section as well.

First of all, I'll summarize what you have to do by recapping the last section, and I must begin by confessing to a little white lie. When I talked about passing a pointer to a SECURITY_DESCRIPTOR structure to a securable object, I didn't tell you that what you *actually* pass is a pointer to a SECURITY_ATTRIBUTES structure, which in turn points to the SECURITY_DESCRIPTOR. However, the descriptor is the more important of the two structures; SECURITY_ATTRIBUTES is just a simple wrapper around it.

The security descriptor contains the SID of the object's owner and two ACLs, or access control lists. The first ACL, called a discretionary ACL or DACL, contains a list of entries that specifies the SID of each user or group allowed or denied access to the object. Each entry in this list is called is an access control entry, or ACE. The second ACL in the security descriptor is called a SACL, or system ACL. The system ACL is a list of ACEs specifying which users and groups the system will audit when they access the object. As you know, audit information gets reported to the audit section of the event log.

As we look at how to program these structures, we'll look at building ACLs first, and then at manipulating the security descriptors they go into.

Programming ACLs

Prior to NT 4, when you wanted to program access control lists, you were forced to handle the ACEs directly. You also had to make sure that when you changed or added ACEs in the ACL, you kept the ACEs in order – that is, with 'access denied' ACEs first. Needless to say, this was very error-prone and time consuming. Starting with NT 4, some new programming structures and APIs came along to make direct ACL manipulation mostly unnecessary. To use these new features, though, you must put the following line in your source code:

```
#include <aclapi.h>
```

Two new structures are the key to this greater ease of use: TRUSTEE and EXPLICIT_ACCESS. Let's look at each in some detail.

Trustees

A **trustee** represents a user or group by name *or* by SID. This in itself is very handy, because it allows you to represent a user/group using whatever information you have, rather than having to trace user names back to SIDs or vice versa. The trustee is then used in security API calls to denote to whom an ACE applies. Let's take a look at the structure:

```
struct TRUSTEE
{
   PTRUSTEE                    pMultipleTrustee;
   MULTIPLE_TRUSTEE_OPERATION MultipleTrusteeOperation;
   TRUSTEE_FORM                TrusteeForm;
   TRUSTEE_TYPE                TrusteeType;
   LPTSTR                      ptstrName;
};
```

For now, the first member of the structure must be NULL, and the second must be set to NO_MULTIPLE_TRUSTEE. In NT 5, these members will be used to support a more comprehensive impersonation model than is available in NT 4.

TrusteeForm must be either TRUSTEE_IS_SID or TRUSTEE_IS_NAME, while TrusteeType is one of TRUSTEE_IS_USER, TRUSTEE_IS_GROUP or TRUSTEE_IS_UNKNOWN. Depending on the form, the final member contains either the name or the SID of the trustee. If ptstrName is a SID, it can be any user or group SID, or any of the well-known SIDs. If it is a user or a group name, it can be:

- A fully qualified name
- A domain account name
- One of the predefined group names
- One of the special names CURRENT_USER, CREATOR OWNER, or CREATOR GROUP

Easier Trustees

There are a couple of handy functions that you can use to build the trustee structure. BuildTrusteeWithName() builds a TRUSTEE given only a user or group string name; BuildTrusteeWithSid() builds one given a SID. The prototypes are below:

```
VOID BuildTrusteeWithName(
   PTRUSTEE pTrustee,       // Pointer to the structure to initialize
   LPTSTR   pName           // Name of the trustee to put in the structure
);
```

```
VOID BuildTrusteeWithSid(
   PTRUSTEE pTrustee,       // Pointer to the structure to initialize
   PSID     pSid            // SID of the trustee to put in the structure
);
```

Explicit Access

The TRUSTEE structure takes on the role of, "To whom does this apply?" in an ACE. The EXPLICIT_ACCESS structure takes a trustee and specifies access control information for it – it's really a substitution structure for the whole ACE that you can use to modify or replace an existing ACE.

```
struct EXPLICIT_ACCESS
{
   DWORD       grfAccessPermissions;
   ACCESS_MODE grfAccessMode;
   DWORD       grfInheritance;
   TRUSTEE     Trustee;
};
```

As you might have guessed, grfAccessPermissions is the ORed-together access mask this trustee is allowed. The second member of the structure, the access mode, can be set to any of the values listed below:

Access Mode	Meaning
GRANT_ACCESS	Creates a new 'access allowed' ACE that contains the rights specified in the structure *and* any existing rights of the trustee. The new ACE replaces any existing 'access allowed' ACE for the trustee. The function also modifies or deletes any existing 'access denied' ACE for the trustee that denies the specified rights.
SET_ACCESS	Like GRANT_ACCESS, except that the new 'access allowed' ACE allows *only* the specified rights, discarding any existing rights. It also removes any existing 'access denied' ACE for the trustee.
DENY_ACCESS	Creates a new 'access denied' ACE that replaces any existing 'access denied' ACE. The new ACE denies the specified rights in addition to any currently denied rights of the trustee. The function also modifies or deletes any existing 'access allowed' ACE for the trustee that allows the specified rights.
REVOKE_ACCESS	Removes *any* existing ACEs for the specified trustee. Ignores the rights specified in the grfAccessPermissions member.
SET_AUDIT_SUCCESS	Creates a new 'success audit' ACE that replaces any existing audit ACE for the trustee. The new ACE combines the specified rights with any existing audited access rights for the trustee.
SET_AUDIT_FAILURE	Creates a new 'failure audit' ACE that replaces any existing audit ACE for the trustee.

Certain types of objects, such as directories, allow sub-objects to *inherit* their permissions. Returning to the EXPLICIT_ACCESS structure, the grfInheritance member indicates whether and how other objects can inherit ACL information from this object. Finally, the Trustee member is a trustee structure, as described above.

EXPLICIT_ACCESS Quickly

There is a nice shortcut function that you can use to skip having to build a separate trustee at all. BuildExplicitAccessWithName() will build an EXPLICIT_ACCESS structure with the rights you choose, given only a user or group name in the format shown in the TRUSTEE structure above. The function is shown here:

```
VOID BuildExplicitAccessWithName(
   PEXPLICIT_ACCESS pExplicitAccess, // Pointer to structure to initialize
   LPTSTR pTrusteeName,              // Name of trustee to put in the structure
   DWORD AccessPermissions,          // Access mask to put in the structure
   ACCESS_MODE AccessMode,           // Access mode to put in the structure
   DWORD Inheritance                 // Inheritance type to put in the structure
);
```

Working with ACLs

These days, building, changing, and viewing ACLs is a heck of a lot easier than it was under NT 3.*x*. There's a set of ACL programming functions that hails from those times that I won't even mention. However, if you *enjoy* detailed manipulation of structures full of structures full of structures, those functions are in the API documentation.

Getting Entries in an ACL

You can retrieve an array of EXPLICIT_ACCESS entries for a specified ACL by calling GetExplicitEntriesFromAcl(), shown below:

```
DWORD GetExplicitEntriesFromAcl(
   PACL pacl,       // Pointer to the ACL from which to get entries

   // Receives number of entries in the list
   PULONG pcCountOfExplicitEntries,

   // Receives pointer to list of entries
   PEXPLICIT_ACCESS* pListOfExplicitEntries
);
```

This function takes a pointer to the ACL, and returns a pointer to the array of entries and a count. You must be sure to call LocalFree() on the EXPLICIT_ACCESS pointer when you're done.

Building or Changing an ACL

You can build a new ACL using the SetEntriesInAcl() function, and you can use the same function to merge new permissions into an existing ACL. This is handy when you need to add or change an explicit entry in the ACL for an object without changing any other ACL information in the object:

```
DWORD SetEntriesInAcl(
   ULONG cCountOfExplicitEntries,        // Number of entries in the list
   PEXPLICIT_ACCESS pListOfExplicitEntries,       // Pointer to new list
   PACL  OldAcl,                         // Pointer to the original ACL
   PACL* NewAcl                          // Receives a pointer to the new ACL
);
```

The first parameter is the count of the number of EXPLICIT_ACCESS entries in the array in the second parameter, OldAcl is a pointer to the old ACL you want to merge these new entries with, and NewAcl is the pointer you receive back from the function on return. You must remember to call LocalFree() on this pointer when you are finished with the ACL.

If you're not quite sure how these functions fit into the scheme of things, don't worry: we'll have some examples of these functions in code in the next section.

Programming Security Descriptors

You'll remember that security descriptors are the structures that contain all the security information about a particular secured object, including the DACL. In order to apply what we know about building and changing DACLs, we now need access to the security descriptors of objects to make those changes.

Security Attributes

As I explained at the beginning of this section, the security descriptor is not *directly* a part of the object. A pointer to it is maintained in the `SECURITY_ATTRIBUTES` structure that's passed to the creation function of all the secured objects in NT. Take, for example, `CreateMutex()`:

```
HANDLE CreateMutex(
   LPSECURITY_ATTRIBUTES lpMutexAttributes, // Pointer to security attributes
   BOOL bInitialOwner,                      // Flag for initial ownership
   LPCTSTR lpName                           // Pointer to mutex object name
);
```

It takes a pointer to a `SECURITY_ATTRIBUTES` structure, shown below:

```
struct SECURITY_ATTRIBUTES
{
    DWORD nLength;
    LPVOID lpSecurityDescriptor;
    BOOL bInheritHandle;
};
```

If you usually do what most programmers do, you don't really care about security and you pass `NULL` as the pointer to this parameter. This means, "Take the default security descriptor." What this *actually* means depends on the type of secure object, and whether there is a container/inheritance hierarchy in play.

Since we're talking about services in a client-server environment, though, we very probably *do* care about security, and therefore we might need to modify the security descriptors on either our own service object, or on the objects we're sharing.

Building the Security Descriptor

When building a security descriptor, you have two options. First, you can build a descriptor *before* creating the object, then add the pointer to the descriptor into the `SECURITY_ATTRIBUTES` structure, and then pass that into the object's creation function. Alternatively, you can set the object's security descriptor *after* creating it, which involves a slightly different method. In the security API, there are several different functions that do the same or similar things, and building and using security descriptors is no exception. Choose the best method for you depending on what bits of information you have in hand at the time.

Before Creating the Object

In this scenario, the first thing you need to do is to build a DACL for the object, using the functions described in the section above. Once that's done, there are a couple of different options open to you.

First, you can call `InitializeSecurityDescriptor()` to create a raw security descriptor that is initialized with no owner, no group, and all flags unset. This means that before using it, you'll have to go in and use the `SetSecurityDescriptorGroup()`, `SetSecurityDescriptorOwner()`, `SetSecurityDescriptorSacl()`, and `SetSecurityDescriptorDacl()` functions to set the individual parts of the security descriptor. The prototype of `InitializeSecurityDescriptor()` is:

```
BOOL InitializeSecurityDescriptor(
   PSECURITY_DESCRIPTOR pSecurityDescriptor,  // Addr of security descriptor
   DWORD dwRevision                           // Must be SECURITY_DESCRIPTOR_REVISION
);
```

Once you've done this, you can use `SetSecurityDescriptorDacl()` to set the DACL in the security descriptor:

```
BOOL SetSecurityDescriptorDacl(
   PSECURITY_DESCRIPTOR pSecurityDescriptor,  // Addr of security descriptor
   BOOL bDaclPresent,                        // Flag for presence of discretionary ACL
   PACL pDacl,                               // Address of discretionary ACL
   BOOL bDaclDefaulted                       // Flag for default discretionary ACL
);
```

There are three ways to vary the use of this function, each of which achieves very different results:

- To assign a DACL with explicit access, such as the one you just created:

```
SetSecurityDescriptorDacl(pSD, TRUE, pDacl, FALSE);
```

- To assign a DACL that allows access to everyone (an unsecured, null DACL):

```
SetSecurityDescriptorDacl(pSD, TRUE, 0, FALSE);
```

- To assign the default DACL for the object:

```
SetSecurityDescriptorDacl(pSD, FALSE, 0, TRUE);
```

The other option, instead of using `InitializeSecurityDescriptor()` and `SetSecurityDescriptorDacl()`, is to use `BuildSecurityDescriptor()` to build everything in one shot. As you might imagine, this function is big because of all the information it needs at once to build the security descriptor:

```
DWORD BuildSecurityDescriptor(
    PTRUSTEE pOwner,              // Identifies owner for new security dscrptr
    PTRUSTEE pGroup,              // Identifies group for new security dscrptr
    ULONG cCountOfAccessEntries,  // No. of access-control entries in the list
    PEXPLICIT_ACCESS pListOfAccessEntries,  // Ptr to list of entries for DACL
    ULONG cCountOfAuditEntries,   // No. of audit-control entries in the list
    PEXPLICIT_ACCESS pListOfAuditEntries,   // Ptr to list of entries for SACL
    PSECURITY_DESCRIPTOR pOldSD,  // Ptr to an existing security descriptor
    PULONG pSizeNewSD,            // Ptr to size of the new security dscrptr
    PSECURITY_DESCRIPTOR* pNewSD  // Ptr that receives new security dscrptr
);
```

This function is handy because it's very flexible. It allows you to send an owner, group, DACL, and SACL, or any combination of those at once. It will also take a pointer to an existing security descriptor and use it as the starting point for the new one. If any of `pOwner`, `pGroup`, `pListofAccessEntries`, or `pListofAuditEntries` is `NULL`, then if the function has a non-null `pOldSD`, it will use the old security descriptor's values for those entries in creating the new security descriptor. If `pOldSD` is also `NULL`, then the new security descriptor will have `NULL` entries for those members.

Whichever way you choose to build the security descriptor, you can now use it to create a `SECURITY_ATTRIBUTES` object, and then pass that into the creation function. The whole procedure is shown below in code:

```
#include <windows.h>
#include <aclapi.h>
int main()
{
    SECURITY_DESCRIPTOR sd;
    InitializeSecurityDescriptor(&sd, SECURITY_DESCRIPTOR_REVISION);

    EXPLICIT_ACCESS ea[2];
    BuildExplicitAccessWithName(&ea[0], _T("Guests"), MUTEX_ALL_ACCESS,
                                GRANT_ACCESS, NO_INHERITANCE);

    BuildExplicitAccessWithName(&ea[1], _T("kxm"), MUTEX_ALL_ACCESS,
                                GRANT_ACCESS, NO_INHERITANCE);

    ACL* pdacl = 0;
    SetEntriesInAcl(2, &ea[0], 0, &pdacl);

    SetSecurityDescriptorDacl(&sd, TRUE, pdacl, FALSE);
    SECURITY_ATTRIBUTES sa = {sizeof sa, &sd, FALSE};
    HANDLE hMutex = CreateMutex(&sa, FALSE, __TEXT("MyMutex"));

    LocalFree(pdacl);

    // Do work
    // ...
    CloseHandle(hMutex);
    return 0;
}
```

After Creating the Object

If you choose to set the security after you've created the object, or to change the security of an existing object, the process is a bit different. You have to obtain the security descriptor (or other information), make changes, and then reassign the changed structures back to the object.

The way to obtain security information from an existing object is to use a special pair of functions, `GetSecurityInfo()` and `GetNamedSecurityInfo()`, which work very similarly to one another. The first gets security information about an object to which you have a handle, while the second gets the same information about an object using its 'name'. You could use the latter to get information about a mutex that you only have the name of, for instance. The prototypes for both functions are below:

```
DWORD GetSecurityInfo(
   HANDLE handle,                        // Handle to the object
   SE_OBJECT_TYPE ObjectType,            // Type of object
   SECURITY_INFORMATION SecurityInfo,  // Type of security info to retrieve
   PSID* ppsidOwner,                     // Receives pointer to the owner SID
   PSID* ppsidGroup,                     // Receives ptr to primary group SID
   ACL* ppDacl,                          // Receives pointer to the DACL
   ACL* ppSacl,                          // Receives pointer to the SACL
   // Receives a pointer to the security descriptor
   PSECURITY_DESCRIPTOR* ppSecurityDescriptor
);
```

```
DWORD GetNamedSecurityInfo(
   LPTSTR pObjectName,                   // Name of the object
   SE_OBJECT_TYPE ObjectType,            // Type of object
   SECURITY_INFORMATION SecurityInfo,  // Type of security info to retrieve
   PSID* ppsidOwner,                     // Receives pointer to the owner SID
   PSID* ppsidGroup,                     // Receives ptr to primary group SID
   PACL* ppDacl,                         // Receives pointer to the DACL
   PACL* ppSacl,                         // Receives pointer to the SACL
   // Receives a pointer to the security descriptor
   PSECURITY_DESCRIPTOR* ppSecurityDescriptor
);
```

In the third parameter, both of these functions take a set of type flags that indicate which of the structures pointed to in the following parameters to fill – one or more can be filled. The possible values are `OWNER_SECURITY_INFORMATION`, `GROUP_SECURITY_INFORMATION`, `DACL_SECURITY_INFORMATION`, and `SACL_SECURITY_INFORMATION`. You also have to specify the object's type in the second parameter, using one of the enumerated types in `SE_OBJECT_TYPE`:

```
typedef enum _SE_OBJECT_TYPE
{
   SE_UNKNOWN_OBJECT_TYPE = 0,
   SE_FILE_OBJECT,
   SE_SERVICE,
   SE_PRINTER,
   SE_REGISTRY_KEY,
   SE_LMSHARE,
   SE_KERNEL_OBJECT,
   SE_WINDOW_OBJECT
} SE_OBJECT_TYPE;
```

> **A word to the wise: to get the owner, group, or DACL from the object's security descriptor, the process must have requested `READ_CONTROL` access when it initially opened the object.**

Now that you have security information for the object in hand, you can make changes to it. Doing so is simple: just set up a bunch of `EXPLICIT_ACCESS` structures (by building trustees or by calling `BuildExplicitAccessWithName()`) containing the accounts and the rights you want them to have. Then, call `SetEntriesInAcl()`, specifying the object's existing DACL to merge the old and the new, or not specifying it if you want to wipe out the object's existing DACL completely.

You can now use the twin functions `SetSecurityInfo()` and `SetNamedSecurityInfo()` to enact the changes on the object. The stubs are below:

```
DWORD SetSecurityInfo(
   HANDLE handle,                        // Handle to the object
   SE_OBJECT_TYPE ObjectType,            // Type of object
   SECURITY_INFORMATION SecurityInfo,    // Type of security information to set
   PSID psidOwner,                       // Pointer to the new owner SID
   PSID psidGroup,                       // Pointer to the new primary group SID
   PACL pDacl,                           // Pointer to the new DACL
   PACL pSacl                            // Pointer to the new SACL
);
```

```
DWORD SetNamedSecurityInfo(
   LPTSTR pObjectName,                   // Name of the object
   SE_OBJECT_TYPE ObjectType,            // Type of object
   SECURITY_INFORMATION SecurityInfo,    // Type of security information to set
   PSID psidOwner,                       // Pointer to the new owner SID
   PSID psidGroup,                       // Pointer to the new primary group SID
   PACL pDacl,                           // Pointer to the new DACL
   PACL pSacl                            // Pointer to the new SACL
);
```

It goes almost without saying that everything I've just described also works on the SACL.

> **Be aware that objects created in the security context of LocalSystem using the default DACL get empty DACLs, so by default no one has access to them. That means that in order to share any object that it creates (such as a mutex), a service running as LocalSystem must explicitly assign a DACL to the object that gives the appropriate permissions.**

Sample: Changing an ACL

```
void ChangeMutexDacl()
{
   ACL* pOlddacl = 0;
   ACL* pNewdacl = 0;
   EXPLICIT_ACCESS ea;

   BuildExplicitAccessWithName(&ea, _T("Guests"), MUTEX_ALL_ACCESS,
                                                GRANT_ACCESS, NO_INHERITANCE);

   HANDLE hMutex = OpenMutex( MUTEX_ALL_ACCESS, FALSE, __TEXT("MyMutex"));

   GetSecurityInfo(hMutex, SE_KERNEL_OBJECT, DACL_SECURITY_INFORMATION,
                                          NULL, NULL, &pOlddacl, NULL, NULL);

   SetEntriesInAcl(1, &ea, pOlddacl, &pNewdacl);

   SetSecurityInfo(hMutex, SE_KERNEL_OBJECT, DACL_SECURITY_INFORMATION,
                                                  NULL, NULL, pNewdacl, NULL);

   LocalFree(pNewdacl);
   LocalFree(pOlddacl);
   CloseHandle(hMutex);
}
```

Private Object Security

It is also possible to employ NT's security infrastructure for your own secret and nefarious purposes. You can create your own data structures, classes, etc., define their access rights, then assign them security descriptors, DACLs, SACLs, owners, and so on. The benefit of using this mechanism is that you can avoid reinventing a security system, maintaining your own groups and users, and creating your own administration tools. In addition, you get a single, integrated security model for your applications and NT. And, as NT's security model gets enhanced, so does yours.

Setting Object Security

To implement security for your objects, you use a function called `CreatePrivateObjectSecurity()` to create a self-relative security descriptor that can then be handed to your object's creation function:

```
BOOL CreatePrivateObjectSecurity(
    PSECURITY_DESCRIPTOR ParentDescriptor,   // Pointer to parent directory SD
    PSECURITY_DESCRIPTOR CreatorDescriptor,  // Pointer to creator SD
    PSECURITY_DESCRIPTOR* NewDescriptor,     // Pointer to pointer to new SD
    BOOL IsDirectoryObject,                  // Container flag for new SD
    HANDLE Token,                           // Handle to client's access token
    PGENERIC_MAPPING GenericMapping         // Pointer to access-rights struct
);
```

This function takes several interesting parameters. The first is a pointer to a parent security descriptor, so that SDs can be inherited from higher-level object containers (such as in a hierarchy of private objects). The second is a pointer to the creator's SD, which is used to pass security descriptor information from the creator to the new object. Both of these parameters can be `NULL`.

The third parameter holds a pointer to where the new security descriptor will be stored, while the fourth specifies `TRUE` if this object is to be a container. The fifth parameter is the access token of the client who is asking for this object to be created; it's used to get default security information, such as the owner and the DACL.

The last parameter is a pointer to a `GENERIC_MAPPING` structure, which maps object specific and standard rights to generic rights. The layout of the structure is shown below:

```
struct GENERIC_MAPPING
{
   ACCESS_MASK GenericRead,
   ACCESS_MASK GenericWrite,
   ACCESS_MASK GenericExecute,
   ACCESS_MASK GenericAll
};
```

When you've finished with the private object, you should call `DestroyPrivateObjectSecurity()` to free up the security descriptor. If you need specific information about a private object's security descriptor, you can call `GetPrivateObjectSecurity()`. It's a bit different structurally, but this function accomplishes the same thing as `GetSecurityInfo()` does for system objects.

Pseudo-code for Creating a Private Object with Security

Here's some simple pseudo-code for doing what I just described:

```
static const GENERIC_MAPPING g_gmMyObject =
{
   READ_CONTROL | MYOBJ_READ,
   READ_CONTROL | WRITE_DAC | WRITE_CONTROL | MYOBJ_WRITE,
   STANDARD_RIGHTS_EXECUTE | MYOBJ_EXECUTE,
   STANDARD_RIGHTS_REQUIRED | MYOBJ_ALL
};

void CreatePrivateObjectWithSecurity()
{
   HANDLE hToken = GetToken();

   CreatePrivateObjectSecurity(NULL, pSDCreator, &pSD,
                                          FALSE, hToken, &g_gmMyObject);

   CloseHandle(hToken);

   CreateMyPrivateObject(pSD);

   // Delete when you are done
   DestroyPrivateObjectSecurity(&pSD);
}
```

Checking Access to Private Objects

Now, to enforce the security policy you've just created, you have to check a client's access rights against the object. To do this, you have to use the `AccessCheck()` function, which we took a look at earlier. It's the 'manual' way to perform security authorization, by passing an access token, a descriptor, and a set of requested rights, and letting the SRM make sure the caller's access token has them.

Pseudo-code for Access Checking

```
BOOL CheckAccessToMyObject(DWORD dwAccess, MYOBJECT* myobject)
{
    // Get the SD from the private object
    void* pSD = GetSDFromMyObject(myobject);

    HANDLE hToken = GetToken();

    PRIVILEGE_SET ps;
    DWORD dwPrivBuf;
    DWORD dwGrantedAccess;
    BOOL bGranted
    AccessCheck(pSD, hToken, dwAccess, &g_gmMyObject,
                                 &ps, &dwPrivBuf, &dwGranted, &bGranted);

    CloseHandle(hToken);

    return bGranted;
}
```

As you can see, private object security can be quite easy to use, and quite useful too.

Changes in NT 5.0

Beta 1 of Windows NT 5.0, which is of course subject to change, revealed a number of new API functions and structures will change the ACL programming landscape once again. NT 5.0 will introduce functions that support object-specific ACEs, directory service (DS) objects, securable objects on systems other than Windows NT, and the issues surrounding delegated impersonation. The new APIs are aimed at provider independence in authorization. Many of the common access rights will be mapped to provider-independent names.

`GetSecurityInfoEx()` and `GetNamedSecurityInfoEx()` will replace the earlier functions of NT 4.0, while a new structure called `ACTRL_ACCESS_ENTRY` will take the place of `EXPLICIT_ACCESS` in these new APIs, as well as in others. Similarly, `SetEntriesInAccessList()` will replace `SetEntriesInACL()`, using a new structure called `ACTRL_ACCESS` that supersedes `ACL`.

Thankfully, the `SECURITY_DESCRIPTOR`, `SECURITY_ATTRIBUTES`, and `TRUSTEE` structures seem to be staying the same. However, there are plans for many new functions that are aimed at supporting new functionality in security descriptors, and at converting old security structures to new ones. One such function, `ConvertSecurityDescriptorToAccess()`, is to be used to convert the SIDs and ACLs in an existing security descriptor to the new access control structures. The structures and functions that deal with privileges and tokens also appear to be intact, as do the SID structures and functions.

Impersonation

If your service contains resources that you want to be secured, or accesses some other resource on the local machine or across the network, you're in a weird kind of a predicament. The scenario is this: your service executable is running under the service account that you gave it when you installed the service (or under the one you didn't give it, which would be LocalSystem). So, the process's access token is the token of, for the sake of argument, LocalSystem. If you are hitting resources that might be secured, you probably want to make sure that the client who is calling into your service is actually authorized to use those resources.

Now, you can do this the easy way or the hard way. The hard way would be to run *everything* under LocalSystem, and then have each client process pass in some sort of credentials to identify the user. Your service would then check those credentials against its own internal storage and authorize or deny access to the requested resource, based on some internal list of which users can do what. In short, you could roll your own authentication and authorization mechanism. Yuck.

The easy way is to have the service *pretend* to be the NT user who called in, and then attempt to access the secured resource. NT's mechanisms will kick in to compare the token of the *client* your service is pretending to be with the security descriptor on the secured object, using the normal access checking mechanisms you just learned about. In this case, you're simply making use of NT's authentication and authorization infrastructure and not reinventing the wheel. This act of having your service pretend to be the client while it accesses secure objects is known as **impersonation**.

> *Technically, impersonation is how a thread can execute in a security context different from the one possessed by the process that owns it. In essence, it steals the access token of a different user and uses that token to attempt access to secure objects.*

In general, a service is likely to be serving many clients at the same time, and this is probably why there is no API for changing the process token. If you were to change it with each calling client, the service would have to serialize on the call to the hypothetical `ChangeProcessToken()` function. The process could only have one access token at a time, and so it could only service one client at a time – this is far from ideal. Instead, you impersonate your clients, and change the *thread*'s access token to that of the impersonated client. That way, you can have as many impersonations going on concurrently as you have different threads servicing client requests.

Ways to Implement Impersonation

There are many different ways to implement impersonation in a service, and some are better than others. All of them are useful, though, depending on what you're dealing with and precisely what you need to do. Here's a list of possible scenarios:

- The network communications package or subsystem will allow you to perform the impersonation by calling its special impersonation function. It's necessary for each networking package to have its own special function in order to hide the details of the authentication process:

    - An RPC server can call `RpcImpersonateClient()`
    - A COM server can call `CoImpersonateClient()`

  - A named-pipe server can call `ImpersonateNamedPipeClient()`
  - A DDE server can call `DdeImpersonateClient()`
  - `ImpersonateSecurityContext()` can be called at the raw security service
  - provider level

- Use `CreateProcessAsUser()` to create a new process based on a token you've got from one of the networking impersonation functions and then converted to a primary token using `DuplicateTokenEx()`.
- The `ImpersonateSelf()` function allows a thread to generate a copy of its own access token.
- Use `LogonUser()` to log on as a particular user. A successful logon generates a primary access token for the specified user. You can then use this token in a call to `ImpersonateLoggedOnUser()` to impersonate the user and use the resource.

Primary and Impersonation Tokens

Before you can start impersonating, you need to understand a few more things about access tokens. For a start, there are really two kinds: **primary tokens** and **impersonation tokens**. *Processes* always have an access token that determines their security context (a primary token). *Threads*, on the other hand, do not have an access token by default – they assume the token of the process that created them. However, they *can* have a different token if desired (an impersonation token).

To reiterate, processes must always have a primary token, but threads are less finicky and only need impersonation tokens. The difference between the two is deep down inside the access token itself, so let's take a closer look at a couple of areas in the token structure:

```
typedef enum _TOKEN_TYPE
{
   TokenPrimary = 1,
   TokenImpersonation
} TOKEN_TYPE;

typedef enum _SECURITY_IMPERSONATION_LEVEL
{
   SecurityAnonymous,
   SecurityIdentification,
   SecurityImpersonation,
   SecurityDelegation
} SECURITY_IMPERSONATION_LEVEL, *PSECURITY_IMPERSONATION_LEVEL;
```

The `TOKEN_TYPE` enumeration specifies what type of token it is, primary or impersonation. If the token is impersonated, a later bit specifies the levels of impersonation, of which there are four:

Impersonation Level	Description
`SecurityAnonymous`	Indicates that the server cannot obtain information about the client and therefore cannot impersonate it.
`SecurityIdentification`	Allows the server to obtain information about the client, such as SIDs and privileges, without actually being able to impersonate it. This method can be useful when the server needs to use NT authentication (to prove the client's identity), but still has to roll its own authorization mechanism for private objects.
`SecurityImpersonation`	The server can discover information about the client (as above), and impersonation is allowed for local resources, but not for network resources. In other words, RPC callouts cannot be made from a server that's impersonating a client.
`SecurityDelegation`	Impersonation is allowed for local and remote resources from an impersonation (non-primary) token. Off host calls are made with the impersonated security context. Not available until Windows NT 5.0.

Using Impersonation

Let's take a look at a few examples that illustrate the different impersonation models I described above. This will introduce you to the API semantics and get things rolling.

Impersonating a Network Caller

Impersonating a client that's calling in using one of the client-server access mechanisms (RPC, DDE, etc.) is probably the most frequent situation, especially for services. To impersonate the calling client, you use:

```
RPC_STATUS RPC_ENTRY RpcImpersonateClient(RPC_BINDING_HANDLE CallHandle);
```

To return the thread to the security context of the process, you call `RpcRevertToSelf()` or `RpcRevertToSelfEx()` when you're done. The '`Ex`' version allows you to specify a different thread (such as a worker thread) to revert:

```
RPC_STATUS RPC_ENTRY RpcRevertToSelf(VOID);
```

```
RPC_STATUS RPC_ENTRY RpcRevertToSelfEx(RPC_BINDING_HANDLE CallHandle);
```

We haven't looked at RPC and its uses, but the semantics of a simple function that demonstrates using impersonation with RPC aren't too difficult to grasp. The function below impersonates a client and then attempts to open a file under the guise of the impersonation token for that client. The point is to make sure that the calling client really has access to work on or view the file.

```
// RPC Impersonation
void RemoteFunction(const char* pszFile)
{
   // Impersonate the client's identity
   RpcImpersonateClient(0);                          // 0 means the current thread

   // Do work
   HANDLE h = CreateFile(pszFile, GENERIC_READ, 0, 0, OPEN_EXISTING, 0, 0);

   if((h == INVALID_HANDLE_VALUE ) && (GetLastError() == ACCESS_DENIED))
      cout << "Access Denied";
   else
      // Do work

   RpcRevertToSelf();
}
```

Creating a Process as Another User

Less common for a service, but sometimes useful, is the ability to create a process on behalf of an impersonated user. In order to do that, you *can't* simply use one of the `XXXImpersonateClient()` functions and then call `CreateProcess()`. This function always uses the primary token for the *process*, not the thread, to inherit from when creating the new process. To create a process as another user, you need to use `CreateProcessAsUser()`, shown below.

```
BOOL CreateProcessAsUser(
   HANDLE hToken,        // Handle to a token that represents a logged-on user
   LPCTSTR lpApplicationName,        // Pointer to name of executable module
   LPTSTR lpCommandLine,             // Pointer to command line string
   LPSECURITY_ATTRIBUTES lpProcessAttributes, // Ptr to process attributes
   LPSECURITY_ATTRIBUTES lpThreadAttributes,  // Pointer to thread attributes
   BOOL bInheritHandles,             // New process inherits handles
   DWORD dwCreationFlags,            // Creation flags
   LPVOID lpEnvironment,             // Pointer to new environment block
   LPCTSTR lpCurrentDirectory,       // Pointer to current directory name
   LPSTARTUPINFO lpStartupInfo,      // Pointer to STARTUPINFO
   LPPROCESS_INFORMATION lpProcessInformation // Ptr to PROCESS_INFORMATION
);
```

Most of this is just the same information you're used to using when you create a new process with `CreateProcess()`, the one difference being the first parameter, `hToken`. This parameter is a handle to a primary access token that represents a user. Of course, the user represented by the token must have read and execute access to the application specified by the `lpApplicationName` or the `lpCommandLine` parameter.

The thing is, you can't just pass in the access token of the thread on which you're impersonating the client. That's because that thread token is an *impersonation* token, and you can't create a process with an impersonation token, only with a primary token. To create the process, you'll need to use the impersonation token to get hold of a primary token. Moreover, you need TOKEN_QUERY, TOKEN_DUPLICATE, and TOKEN_ASSIGN_PRIMARY access rights to the new token, so be sure to specify those.

DuplicateToken and DuplicateTokenEx

Fortunately, there's an easy way to get hold of a primary access token. The DuplicateToken() function creates an impersonation token when given either a primary or an impersonation token, but the function we'll need, DuplicateTokenEx(), can create either an impersonation *or* a primary token. Here is the syntax of both functions:

```
BOOL DuplicateToken(
   HANDLE ExistingTokenHandle,                          // Handle to token to duplicate
   SECURITY_IMPERSONATION_LEVEL ImpersonationLevel,    // Impersonation level
   PHANDLE DuplicateTokenHandle                         // Handle to duplicated token
);
```

```
BOOL DuplicateTokenEx(
   HANDLE hExistingToken,                               // Handle to token to duplicate
   DWORD dwDesiredAccess,                               // Access rights of new token
   LPSECURITY_ATTRIBUTES lpTokenAttributes,            // Attributes of the new token
   SECURITY_IMPERSONATION_LEVEL ImpersonationLevel,    // Impersonation level
   TOKEN_TYPE TokenType,                               // Primary or impersonation token
   PHANDLE phNewToken                                  // Handle to duplicated token
);
```

ImpersonateSelf

There is also a shortcut function called ImpersonateSelf() that allows you to grab an impersonation token for the security context of the calling process and assign it to the calling thread. Here's the stub:

```
BOOL ImpersonateSelf(
   SECURITY_IMPERSONATION_LEVEL ImpersonationLevel      // Impersonation level
);
```

The ImpersonateSelf() function is handy for such things as enabling a privilege for a single thread rather than for the entire process, or for changing the default discretionary access-control list for a single thread. The way this works is that when the thread calls the function, it gets assigned an access token that's identical to the one for the calling process. The thread can then modify its token without modifying the process's token. When the impersonation is complete, the thread can call RevertToSelf().

Limitations of Impersonation

Before we move on to the last possibility for impersonation, you need to understand that there are several limitations to the impersonation architecture as it is implemented in NT 4.0.

First, and biggest, is that impersonated tokens hold *no* network credentials. Remember that in an interactive logon scenario, the client credentials are cached and transparently re-issued when the client needs to access a remote resource. This simply isn't possible under impersonation, because the client credentials are not passed over the network with the token.

Of course, this is actually a good thing, because passing client credentials over the network would break the challenge-response model. The upshot, though, is that a server cannot access a remote resource on behalf of a client it is impersonating – there are no cached credentials to reissue. `ACCESS_DENIED`!

So, we have a mechanism that's consistent with NT's security model, but which can be limiting and painful. When **delegation** is introduced in NT 5.0, you'll be able to access network resources in a secure and seamless manner, but until then we need to find a way of working around the limitations to create a substitute for delegation.

Faking Delegation

To get a token that has valid credentials for using on the network, you need to obtain... valid credentials. The only way to do that is actually to log the client on to the server programmatically. The `LogonUser()` API call is what you need to do this. Once you have logged on as a particular user, you can then impersonate the *user* by using `ImpersonateLoggedOnUser()`, and access the remote resources needed. The function stub for `LogonUser()` is:

```
BOOL LogonUser(
   LPTSTR  lpszUsername,        // String that specifies the user name
   LPTSTR  lpszDomain,          // String that specifies the domain or server
   LPTSTR  lpszPassword,        // String that specifies the password
   DWORD   dwLogonType,         // Specifies the type of logon operation
   DWORD   dwLogonProvider,     // Should be LOGON32_PROVIDER_DEFAULT for
                                // maximum forward compatibility
   PHANDLE phToken              // Pointer to variable to receive token handle
);
```

The `dwLogonType` parameter indicates how the logon is to be performed. It can be one of four types, shown in the table below. The one you'll find most useful for the types of scenarios that services handle will be `LOGON32_LOGON_BATCH`, because credentials aren't cached for this type. You don't want to use `LOGON32_LOGON_SERVICE` (even though that might seem the most logical choice) because if you're *inside* the service, you're logging on as a *client* in order to impersonate him, not as a service.

dwLogonType Parameter	Meaning
LOGON32_LOGON_BATCH	For 'batch servers', or situations where a process is executing on behalf of a user without their intervention. This is for high-performance servers, because credentials aren't cached for this type
LOGON32_LOGON_INTERACTIVE	For users who will use the machine interactively. Client credentials *are* cached for this type, which is more expensive. Not for high-performance server applications
LOGON32_LOGON_SERVICE	A service logon. Account must have the Log on as a service privilege enabled
LOGON32_LOGON_NETWORK	For high-performance server authentication. Credentials are not cached. This is the fastest logon type, but is limited in that it only returns an impersonation access token

Be aware that to call `LogonUser()`, you need the `SE_TCB_NAME`, or Act as part of the operating system privilege as part of the primary token for the *service process* (not as part of the token of the user you're logging on). It doesn't need to be explicitly *enabled* by you, though, because the `LogonUser()` API itself will enable the privilege.

The `ImpersonateLoggedOnUser()` function lets a thread that calls it impersonate the security context of a logged-on user by passing it the token handle of the user that was generated in the call to `LogonUser()`. The token must have `TOKEN_QUERY` access if it is an impersonation token, or `TOKEN_QUERY` and `TOKEN_DUPLICATE` if it's a primary token. You'll only receive an impersonation token from `LogonUser()` if you called the function with `LOGON32_LOGON_NETWORK`.

```
BOOL ImpersonateLoggedOnUser(
    HANDLE hToken         // Handle to a token that represents a logged-on user
);
```

Here's how you might access a remote resource using this 'simulated' delegation method. Essentially, this function does the same work as the RPC impersonation sample above, but uses `LogonUser()` with a name and password to obtain a primary token first. With the primary token, the `CreateFile()` call could be made on a network share.

```
// Logon User and Impersonate
void FakeDelegation(LPTSTR pszFile, LPTSTR pszPassword,
                                            LPTSTR pszUser, LPTSTR pszDomain)
{
    HTOKEN hToken = 0;
    LogonUser(pszUser, pszDomain, pszPassword, LOGON32_LOGON_BATCH,
                                          LOGON32_PROVIDER_DEFAULT, &hToken);
    ImpersonateLoggedOnUser(hToken);
```

```
    // Do work
    HANDLE h = CreateFile(pszFile, GENERIC_READ, 0, 0, OPEN_EXISTING, 0, 0);

    if((h == INVALID_HANDLE_VALUE) && (GetLastError() == ACCESS_DENIED))
       cout << "Access Denied";
    else
    {
       // Do work
    }

    // Clean up
    CloseHandle(hToken);
    RevertToSelf();
}
```

The Catch

You've probably noticed the problem here already. `LogonUser()` requires you to have the username, password, and domain name of the user you're logging on! That means one of two things: either the client has to pass in its credentials at some point during its connection session, or else they have to be given to the server in advance and stored. In turn, this means that either the client and server must invent some secure way to transmit the credentials between themselves (as opposed to clear text over the wire), or the server needs a secure way to store the credentials locally.

To accomplish the first method, you can set up a secure channel (or use an existing one) that's part of your network connection between the client and server, such as authenticated RPC or COM with privacy. This will encrypt packet traffic between the client and server.

To use the second method, you need to store the password in some secret place on the server. In fact, this is the method the SCM uses when you assign a logon account to a service – it uses the LSA to store the password in a secure way. If you're interested in this method, look into the LSA API and the 'Lsasamp' SDK sample. The difficulty this time (although it's not a significant one) is that to have access to the Local Security Policy, the service's security context needs to be either LocalSystem or a local administrator. You'll need to run your service under a user with enough power if you're not going to use LocalSystem. Alternatively, you could roll your own encryption and storage method, using the Crypto API to encrypt the credentials and the registry to store them.

So, with a little bit of extra work, `LogonUser()` can be a reasonable substitute for delegation. However, it can be slow, especially if the authentication process requires trips to the domain controller for authentication. Also, remember that this method requires that the client have a fair degree of trust in the server – whichever technique you use, the only way to get the password is for the client to give it to the server. At that point, the server can do anything it wants, and there is no way to distinguish the impersonator from the real client.

Service Object Security

Now that you know something about the mechanisms of security, it makes sense to talk about security that's specifically related to service objects themselves. As you are probably aware from the beginning of the chapter, services are securable objects just like threads, mutexes, files, and so forth. For that reason, there is a set of functions for viewing and changing the different components of a service's security descriptor.

Getting Service Security

Whenever you want to make changes to who can perform various operations on a service, such as starting it, stopping it, and deleting it, you will need to use this set of functions. For a start, in order to obtain information about the security settings on a service, you use the `QueryServiceObjectSecurity()` function, shown below.

```
BOOL QueryServiceObjectSecurity(SC_HANDLE            hService,
                                SECURITY_INFORMATION dwSecurityInformation,
                                PSECURITY_DESCRIPTOR lpSecurityDescriptor,
                                DWORD                cbBufSize,
                                LPDWORD              pcbBytesNeeded);
```

This function takes a handle to a service that was opened with `OpenService()`, a pointer to a security descriptor (which is filled by the function and returned in self-relative format), the size in bytes of the buffer that was sent in `lpSecurityDescriptor`, and a `DWORD` pointer that is filled if additional bytes are needed in the buffer to get the information.

The second parameter, which you'll have noticed was missing from the above descriptions, is a set of `DWORD` flags that can be passed to specify which security information you want to obtain.

`SECURITY_INFORMATION` **Flag**	**Description**
`OWNER_SECURITY_INFORMATION`	The service's owner's security identifier (SID)
`GROUP_SECURITY_INFORMATION`	The service's primary group SID
`DACL_SECURITY_INFORMATION`	The service's DACL
`SACL_SECURITY_INFORMATION`	The service's SACL. In order to get SACL information, the calling process must have the `SE_SECURITY_NAME` privilege

To read the owner, group, or DACL, the caller must have opened the service requesting (and have been granted, of course) `READ_CONTROL` access.

Setting Service Security

Setting security on a service is just as easy; the `SetServiceObjectSecurity()` function handles those details:

```
BOOL SetServiceObjectSecurity(SC_HANDLE            hService,
                              SECURITY_INFORMATION dwSecurityInformation,
                              PSECURITY_DESCRIPTOR lpSecurityDescriptor);
```

Once again, to use this function, you need a handle you've previously opened with `OpenService()`. Depending on what flag values you send in `dwSecurityInformation`, you may need to have opened the service with different levels of access. If you want to change the owner or group information, you must have opened the handle with `WRITE_OWNER` access; if you want to change the DACL, you need `WRITE_DAC` access.

Example of Changing the DACL of a Service

The following little program shows you how to put some of the calls we've looked at in this chapter together to *deny* access to me (my domain and user ID are hard-coded) to start the MQAgent service from the last chapter. It is commented so that you can see what's going on.

```
#define UNICODE
#define _UNICODE

#include <windows.h>
#include <aclapi.h>
#include <TCHAR.h>
#include <stdio.h>

int main()
{
   ACL* pNewdacl = 0;
   ACL* pOlddacl = 0;

   SECURITY_DESCRIPTOR sd;
   PSECURITY_DESCRIPTOR psd = 0;
   DWORD dwNeeded = 0;

   EXPLICIT_ACCESS ea;
   SC_HANDLE hSCM = NULL;
   SC_HANDLE hService = NULL;
   BOOL bDaclHere = FALSE;
   BOOL bDaclDefault = FALSE;

   // Set up the ACE that I want to put into the DACL
   BuildExplicitAccessWithName(&ea, _T("NORTHAMERICA\\kevmill"),
                              SERVICE_START, DENY_ACCESS, NO_INHERITANCE);

   // Open SCM and service, requesting proper access (WRITE_DAC|READ_CONTROL)
   hSCM = OpenSCManager(NULL, NULL, SC_MANAGER_CONNECT);
   hService = OpenService(hSCM, _T("MQAgent"), WRITE_DAC | READ_CONTROL);

   // Query the service for its existing DACL
   // Don't know how big a buffer to allocate, so ask first
   BOOL bret = QueryServiceObjectSecurity(hService,
                              DACL_SECURITY_INFORMATION, psd, 0, &dwNeeded);
   if(!bret)
   {
      // Allocate a buffer of the size the Query call said it needed
      psd = (PSECURITY_DESCRIPTOR)LocalAlloc(LHND, dwNeeded);

      // Call again with the right size buffer
      bret = QueryServiceObjectSecurity(hService,
                        DACL_SECURITY_INFORMATION, psd, dwNeeded, &dwNeeded);
   }
```

```
    if(bret)
    {
       // Get the DACL out of the SD we just obtained
       GetSecurityDescriptorDacl(psd, &bDaclHere, &pOlddacl, &bDaclDefault);

       // Merge the new ACE with the old DACL.
       SetEntriesInAcl(1, &ea, pOlddacl, &pNewdacl);

       // Initialize a new SD to hold the new DACL
       InitializeSecurityDescriptor(&sd, SECURITY_DESCRIPTOR_REVISION);

       // Add the new DACL to the new SD
       SetSecurityDescriptorDacl(&sd, TRUE, pNewdacl, FALSE);

       // Replace the existing SD on the service with the new SD
       bret = SetServiceObjectSecurity(hService,
                                      DACL_SECURITY_INFORMATION, &sd);

       if(bret)
          _tprintf(_T("SetObjectSecurity Succeeded!"));
       else
          _tprintf(_T("SetObjectSecurity Failed!"));
    }

    if(hService) CloseServiceHandle(hService);
    if(hSCM) CloseServiceHandle(hSCM);
    LocalFree(pNewdacl);
    LocalFree(psd);
    return 0;
}
```

After running the program, when I go to the Services applet and try to start the service, I receive the following error message:

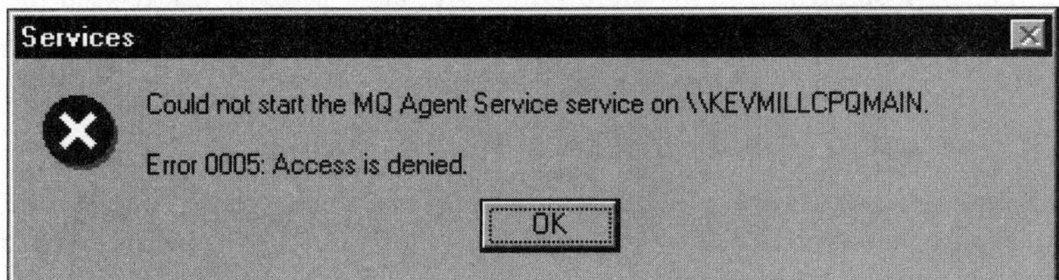

You can add this type of code to your own service configuration or installation programs to give access to the people and groups you want to be able to administer or otherwise use your service.

Window Stations and Desktops

Window stations are one of the most arcane topics in all of NT programming, and when you're writing Win32 applications that have a user interface, you need to know very little about them. To write NT services, however, you need to know a little bit more because some very subtle problems can occur if you are not clear on the issues. At least, these subtle problems can occur if you are set on having your service interact with a user directly, or on having the service interact with an application that has a user interface.

> *Before I embarked on this section, I thought long and hard to try to come up with an example of a reasonable interactive service, but I came up blank: there was always a better way. While window stations and desktops are a very interesting topic, you* can *avoid having to know about them completely if you take my advice and don't write your services to interact with the user. You have been warned.*

To understand what window stations are, you'll need a bit of background. Before NT 3.5, it was not possible for non-interactive logon sessions (such as those needed by NT services) to call USER or GDI functions (API calls in `User32.dll` or `GDI32.dll`). For this reason, existing GUI applications could not be launched in a non-interactive service logon. Beginning with NT 3.5, the concept of the window station was introduced to make it possible for Win32 services to make USER and GDI calls, while still allowing applications running in the interactive user context to remain secure.

What is a Window Station?

A window station is a secure kernel object, like many of the secure objects you are familiar with. A window station (commonly referred to as a **winstation**) contains its own clipboard and its own group of **desktops**, which we'll talk about soon. In short, it has its own user environment. A machine can have many winstations running simultaneously; each process is attached to (or runs under) a winstation. In most cases, this is the interactive winstation, but you can create your own by calling the `CreateWindowStation()` function.

Interactive and Non-Interactive Winstations

The **interactive winstation** is assigned to the interactively logged-on user, and it has access to the keyboard, mouse, and display. All the other winstations besides the interactive one (which is called `winsta0`) are non-interactive, and cannot be seen by or receive input from the user. These non-interactive winstations are where Win32 services typically run.

Even though these winstations have interfaces that can never be seen, they still happily accept USER and GDI calls. A message box or modal dialog popping up in a non-interactive winstation is hung for good, because that winstation cannot accept mouse or keyboard input. This is why, early on, I told you it was generally a bad idea to write services with a user interface. If you do, you need to qualify their type with the `SERVICE_INTERACTIVE_PROCESS` flag.

Desktops

A **desktop** is a secure user object that's contained within a winstation. A desktop has a display surface, and is the container for windows, menus, and hooks. Each winstation can have many desktops. Any desktops on the interactive winstation have the capability to become active. On the interactive winstation, the one active desktop is known as the **input desktop**.

Under a standard NT interactive user session, there are three desktops:

- Default, the one you see with the shell
- Winlogon, the one you see when you log on, and when you hit *Ctrl+Alt+Del* to view the NT task manager
- The desktop with the screensaver

Just as each process is contained in a window station, each thread is attached to a single desktop. You can call `CreateDesktop()` from within the calling process's winstation to create a new desktop.

Creation of Winstations and Desktops

The interactive window station is created automatically by WinLogon the first time an interactive user logs on. It then associates the interactive winstation with the user's logon session. Non-interactive processes such as Win32 services cause the system to create a winstation and desktop for that logon session.

When a process is created, the winstation it gets is determined by the contents of the `lpDesktop` member of the `STARTUPINFO` structure that is passed to `CreateProcess()`. If a winstation name was specified in the member, then that window station is used. If this member is `NULL`, the new process inherits the winstation and desktop from the parent. If the member is an empty string, the process does not inherit, and the system either connects the process to the interactive winstation (if the process is running in the logon session of the interactive user), or forms the winstation name based on the LUID of the logon session. If that winstation exists, then the process is connected to it; otherwise, the system creates the winstation and a default desktop.

You can change the window station associated with a process at any time, by calling `SetProcessWindowStation()`.

Window Station Security

Since winstations are secure NT objects, you need various rights to carry out different activities on them. Like any NT object, these rights have to be given in the object's DACL and then requested in functions like `OpenWindowStation()` when you obtain a handle to the winstation.

Winstation Specific Rights	Description
`WINSTA_ENUMDESKTOPS`	Enumerate the desktops
`WINSTA_READATTRIBUTES`	Required to read the winstation's attributes
`WINSTA_ACCESSCLIPBOARD`	Required to cut and paste from the clipboard
`WINSTA_CREATEDESKTOP`	Required to create a desktop on the winstation
`WINSTA_WRITEATTRIBUTES`	Required to modify the winstation's attributes

Table Continued on Following Page

Winstation Specific Rights	Description
WINSTA_ACCESSGLOBALATOMS	Required to get at the atoms
WINSTA_EXITWINDOWS	Required to call ExitWindows(Ex)() from this window station
WINSTA_ENUMERATE	Enumerate the window stations
WINSTA_READSCREEN	Required to read screen objects

Services, Winstations, and Desktops

Depending on the 'log on as' configuration of a service, different winstation\desktop configurations get created. All LocalSystem services run under the same winstation, but each service that runs under a different account – that of a domain user, for example, runs under a different window station. In fact, even services that are running under the *same* account name do so under different winstations (with the exception of LocalSystem, which is special – it runs under `Service-0x0-3e7$\default`). This is because the window station name is based on the LUID of the logon, and separate instances of the same logon generate different LUIDs. Here's a summary:

- A non-interactive service running as LocalSystem uses the `Service-0x0-3e7$\default` winstation and desktop
- An interactive service (with the interactive bit set) running as LocalSystem uses the interactive winstation and desktop, or `Winsta0\default`.
- A service running under a 'log on as' account of a user will receive its own unique, non-interactive winstation and desktop, which will be uniquely identified by its logon SID (a LUID).

Interacting with the User

If you follow my advice, touching the winstation\desktop of the interactive user is something you'll rarely, if ever, need to do when you're writing NT services. Still, *if* you do...

Creating a Process on the User Desktop

If you need to create a process that can be seen and be used by the interactive user, you can create the process on the desktop of the user like this. Remember, though, that you'll need some sort of winstation-independent mechanism for the process to communicate with your service, such as named pipes or RPC – Windows messages don't work between winstations. Here's some sample code that would allow you to create a process in the interactive user's desktop; you might use such a mechanism to launch an application that allows the user to interface with the service in some way. The `SERVICE_INTERACTIVE_PROCESS` bit does *not* need to be set to use such a method.

```
// Creating a process on the interactive user's desktop
STARTUPINFO si;
PROCESS_INFORMATION pi;

si.cb = sizeof(STARTUPINFO);
si.lpReserved = NULL;
si.lpTitle = NULL;
si.lpDesktop = "WinSta0\\Default";
si.dwX = si.dwY = si.dwXSize = si.dwYSize = 0L;
si.dwFlags = 0;
si.wShowWindow = SW_SHOW;
si.lpReserved2 = NULL;
si.cbReserved2 = 0;

if(CreateProcess(NULL, lpszCmdLine, NULL, NULL, FALSE, 0,
                                                   NULL, NULL, &si, &pi))
{
   // Don't need these handles
   CloseHandle(pi.hProcess);
   CloseHandle(pi.hThread);
}
```

Note particularly the `lpDesktop` member – it's the key to the whole operation. The rest of the members of the `STARTUPINFO` structure are merely standard settings for use in a call to `CreateProcess()`.

Interacting from a Non-interactive Winstation

On the other hand, you may want your service to interact directly with the user in some way, such as by displaying a dialog box. Typically only LocalSystem (and the user themselves) has access to the interactive winstation and desktop. So, for a service running as a different account, one of two things must happen:

- The server must impersonate the user before opening and using their winstation.
- The client must change the DACL on the interactive winstation to grant the service account access to the winstation. This can be done with the `SetUserObjectSecurity()` function.

Service MessageBox

A much easier way to notify a user that something has happened in your service (if the event log isn't good enough for you) is to use the `MessageBox()` function with the `MB_SERVICE_NOTIFICATION` flag, like so:

```
// MessageBox from service
int i = MessageBox(NULL, _T("An error occurred"),
                             _T("MyService"), MB_SERVICE_NOTIFICATION);
```

This will cause the message to be displayed even if there is no user currently logged on. Be careful, though, if you want to write a service that runs on older versions of NT (3.5) *and* NT 4.0: the constant value of `MB_SERVICE_NOTIFICATION` has changed.

Final Comments on Winstations

Here's a hotchpotch of other miscellaneous issues resulting from the unique characteristics of winstations.

LocalSystem and the Winstation Heap

If at all possible, you should try to run your services under the LocalSystem account. Of course, when you use LocalSystem, you're cut off from accessing remote network resources, but you can always use one of the impersonation techniques I've talked about. On the flip side, the good reasons to use LocalSystem are many. Not only is this account already set up with all the rights and privileges you're likely to need, it's more efficient for the system in terms of its allocation of resources to winstations.

Here's why. Every desktop requires a USER heap, which requires a contiguous, linear address space. The thing is, there's an upper limit on linear user heap space of about 48Mb, and since each USER heap typically consumes 3Mb of memory, you can do the math yourself: only about 16 winstations can be created. Now, remember that each service that's set up with a 'log on as' principal gets *its own* window station (even those with the *same* 'log on as' principal). You can quickly see that too many such services will use a lot of precious resources. If you run out, you'll quickly be rewarded with the "User32.dll initialization failure" message, which is informing you that there wasn't enough heap space for USER to do its work.

Now, if you absolutely need to, you can increase the number of winstations that you can create by changing a registry key:

```
HKEY_LOCAL_MACINE/System/CurrentControlSet/Control/
                                     Session Manager/Subsystems/Windows
```

Inside the string value at this path is an embedded `SharedSection` string. Normally, this reads

```
SharedSection=1024, 3072
```

If you change it to

```
SharedSection=1024, 3072, 512
```

Then you will effectively limit heap space for interactive logons to 512Mb, giving you more room overall. If you have previously installed Microsoft Transaction Server (MTS) on your machine, this change will have already been made for you.

Winstation Security

Another way to get to see the "User32.dll initialization failure" (or even "Kernel32.dll initialization failure") message is for the user security context not to have proper access rights to do what it is requesting on the winstation or desktop objects. For instance, if a user does not request `DESKTOP_CREATEWINDOW` rights on the desktop when they create or open a desktop, then they will receive this message when they attempt to create a window in a thread using that desktop. (GUI applications return the "User32..." failure message; console applications the "Kernel32..." message.)

Last of All...

A further interesting property of winstations is that because they have their own user environments, `HWND`s (and thus window messages and window hooks) have no meaning across winstation boundaries. You cannot use those normal mechanisms for interprocess communication.

Furthermore, interactive services are not secure from being terminated by interactive users. While you can't (by default) use the Task Manager to kill a service (the privilege is not enabled), if the service has an unhidden top-level window (as presumably an interactive service would), it can be killed from the Applications tab on the task manager.

Next, you should be careful about creating auto-start interactive services. The default desktop for the interactive winstation is not created until the first interactive user logs on, so a service that tries to use that desktop before that will have problems such as, "User32.dll initialization failure," as noted above.

Finally, I strongly, strongly encourage you to use non-interactive services whenever you can. And, if you don't think you can, think about it one more time before you go ahead and give your service direct user interface features.

LocalSystem and the Registry

LocalSystem may be the default account under which to run a service, but there are some additional eccentricities in using LocalSystem for services, which you may become aware of when you try to access the `HKEY_CURRENT_USER` key of the registry. In this section, I'll try to identify some of the issues you may run across when working with the registry from a service running under LocalSystem.

`HKEY_CURRENT_USER` is really a mapping that the system makes to `HKEY_USERS\`*`UserSID`*. The system maps the user's SID, derived from the security context, when an application refers to `HKEY_CURRENT_USER` by making an explicit or implicit registry request. When the user's hive is not loaded, the system maps `HKEY_CURRENT_USER` to `.DEFAULT` instead. The hive is loaded when the service is set to run under an account other than LocalSystem.

Since LocalSystem does not have its own user hive, it uses `.DEFAULT`. Now, if all the service running under LocalSystem is ever going to do is write and read some entries to `HKEY_CURRENT_USER`, then you're fine – those will always be stored under `.DEFAULT`. However, if you need to access the `HKEY_USERS` hive of the registry for a particular user, including the interactive user, doing so is going to be difficult. Here's what you can do:

- Use `LogonUser()` to do a primary token impersonation (not thread impersonation) of the calling user or of the user whose registry you need. Simple impersonation of the client does not solve the problem, because impersonated clients (those not using a primary token) are also mapped to `.DEFAULT`.
- After impersonating, grab the user's SID and go directly to the `HKEY_USERS\`*`UserSID`* path in the registry.

The best source of information on how to perform this task is Microsoft Knowledge Base article Q168877.

Lastly, don't try accessing *user* environment variables from a LocalSystem service; there aren't any, because they go along with HKEY_CURRENT_USER. If you need environment variables, you'll have to use *system* ones instead.

These oddities are another good reason to avoid writing services that interact directly with a user or his configuration. In order even to have a registry hive to use, the user would have had to log on interactively at least once on the machine where the service is running.

Encryption

The topic of encryption is usually about encrypting the actual data that's flowing across the network, over the wire. Once you've dealt with authentication and authorization, encryption is the third leg of the security stool. In NT 4.0, encryption is *not* supported as part of the base security API; instead, it's implemented at the **Security Service Provider** (**SSP**) protocol level. The SSPI, or Security Service Provider Interface, is the common interface to those lower level protocols. NTLM and Secure Sockets Layer (SSL) are two of the commonest; when NT 5.0 comes along, the Kerberos SSP will also be provided.

NT 5.0 Kerberos Model

In NT 5.0, an additional Security Service Provider protocol will be added to the existing mix. This new model will be based on the implementation of the Kerberos security protocol, which will replace NTLM as the primary authentication model in NT.

Kerberos is a standard (RFC 1510) based on work done by MIT in the 1980s. It is a shared-secret, key-based method of authentication, consisting of three main concepts:

- An authentication service. This is referred to as the Key Distribution Center (KDC) under NT, and runs as an NT service on each domain controller. It uses the NT directory service as the database for account information. All accounts' identities and master keys are stored here, encrypted by the server's own private master key. This service is also known as the Ticket Granting Server (TGS).
- The **principal** is the user whose identity needs to be verified. This is the interactive user either logging on, or needing access to a remote resource. Also known as the client.
- The **verifier** is the server resource that needs to be sure of the client's identity.

The NT implementation of Kerberos was designed with three things in mind. First, to eliminate the need for a client to send passwords across the wire for authentication purposes. Second, to improve the scalability and performance of user authentication in many-user environments by keeping traffic against the authentication server to a minimum. Third, to provide some degree of interoperability in a heterogeneous network by supporting a common protocol. Clients on non-NT systems won't have SIDs to present, but NT will create an access token from the SID of some designated account to hand to non-NT based requesters.

Keep in mind that this is a new *authentication* model for NT, not a new *authorization* model. SIDs, DACLs, and so forth are still in place on the authorization side; they've simply changed a little bit to support the heterogeneous authentication that Kerberos provides.

Summary

In this chapter, we've discussed how NT's security architecture is implemented at the system and the programming level. NT has all the features of a robust security model, including authentication, authorization, and auditing. We've also discussed how a service can take on the security context of a calling client by using impersonation, which allows the service to check the client's rights to access certain resources before performing secured operations.

We've seen how the NT 4.0 model for impersonation is incomplete, and that NT 5.0's delegation features will remedy some of the limitations. Lastly, we talked about several odd effects that can occur when you try to have a service interact with a user, and how to work around some of those issues.

Final thoughts: The general model that I would suggest you use is to create non-interactive services that run under the LocalSystem account. You can then use impersonation to authorize access to private and system resources on the same machine or across the network. My suggestion is to always begin with this presumption in mind, and only depart from it when you have very good reason to do so.

8

Pooling Resources

One of the usage patterns for services I identified at the beginning of the book was the **Quartermaster**. Depending on the circumstances, the exact meaning of this term can vary a little, but in general the challenge is somehow to reconcile the requests of a large number of consumer-clients with a much smaller number of resources. The resources themselves can be anything at all – database connections, file handles, ports in a modem pool; you name it.

For most of the time, a consumer holding a resource is not actively *using* it. In fact, the consumer isn't usually using the resource for a very large percentage of the time of the time at all – it's just holding on to the resource because it was rather expensive to acquire in the first place.

Allowing consumers to hold onto scarce resources for long periods of time is one of the easiest ways to *reduce* scalability in your software system. In situations like this, the provider has to maintain resources for lots of clients doing very little work. The same amount of work has to be done, to be sure, but the provider has to expend more resources than necessary hanging on to information about connected consumers.

Of course, it is easy to understand why consumers do this – acquiring and releasing resources is expensive for them, too. If a connection to a database, for example, takes 1 second to acquire and 0.25 seconds to release, is a consumer likely to want to release after each call and reconnect in order to make the next one? By the same token, consider a typical web scenario. Each web page hit connects to a database, runs a query, and releases the connection. This incessant connecting and disconnecting is lots of extra work for the data provider.

If connecting and disconnecting is expensive for both the consumer and the provider, and a consumer that holds on to resources that it doesn't fully utilize is expensive for the provider, what's the middle ground? The solution must be to remove the impetus for clients to hold on to resources by making acquisition fast and easy. If a client grabs an initialized resource, does its work, and then releases the resource immediately to make it available to other consumers, this ensures that the resource is being fully utilized all the time (unless it is latent, which is fine). Overall, this reduces the number of connection resources the provider needs to hold on to, and frees it from the extra overhead of incessantly connecting and disconnecting consumers from those resources.

Furthermore, there's usually a performance advantage to handing a consumer-client a resource that's already initialized and ready to perform work. This tends to be much more efficient than asking the resource provider to establish a new resource each time a consumer asks for work to be done, to do the work, and then to destroy the resource. In the improved scenario, you cast off the time required for creation and destruction (allocating that work to the service initialization and de-initialization processes), and just hand out a waiting resource when a consumer wants one. This frees the resource provider to do the task at hand, rather than creating and destroying resource buffers and the like.

A Quartermaster, then, is usually an intermediate-tier component that sits somewhere between the consumer and the resource provider, and handles the work of optimizing the use of provider resources for large numbers of consumer-clients. As you can imagine, an NT service is a *perfect* place to implement a Quartermaster. An NT service can be started automatically, so that resources are ready and initialized before consumers start trying to connect. And, it's always alive and waiting.

ODBC

One of the more common scenarios you will encounter when developing services is the need to access databases from a service. Typically, this will take the form of a client calling in and asking for a query to be run on its behalf, and for the results to be returned to it. In response, the service will select a pre-allocated database handle (as in the Quartermaster description above), do the work using the handle, and return the handle to the client.

In this chapter, I'm going to start by talking about **connection pooling**, which is ODBC's very own resource pooling mechanism. As I do so, I'll explain what benefits it brings, but I'll also point of a couple of its failings. After that, we'll go through my generic implementation of the Quartermaster usage pattern, which attempts to address some of these problems. Finally, in preparation for the next chapter where we'll put the Quartermaster to more practical use, I'll return to the theme of ODBC and examine some issues regarding its use in a service.

In these discussions, I won't be going into great detail about ODBC calls; there is already plenty of documentation on those in other books, and in the Platform SDK.

Connection Pooling in ODBC 3.*x*

With the advent of ODBC 3.0, a new feature known as **connection pooling** was introduced. In essence, connection pooling is the Quartermaster usage pattern implemented specifically for database connections: it enables an ODBC application to reuse a connection from a pool of connections. As you know from our discussion of the Quartermaster, an application that connects and disconnects frequently (such as a web application with database code on each page) can gain a significant performance advantage from pooled database connections.

The database driver manager (`odbc32.dll`) implements the pooling. Once a connection has been created, an ODBC application can reuse connections within the context of the *same* driver and the *same* environment. Connections to the same server cannot be reused between different drivers, between different environments, or between different logon credentials (passed in **`SQLConnect()`**). In short, to be reused from the pool, the connection needed has to be identical (by DSN) to one running under the same environment handle in the same process.

While it looks to the application code as if each connection is a 'full' call, reusing a connection is really only a matter of the driver manager checking to see if it is holding a connection in the pool with `SQLConnect()` attributes that match the ones being requested. If a match is found, the connection is handed over without incurring any connection penalty on the data server. Disconnecting also looks the same as usual to the application, but to the driver manager a `SQLDisconnect()` call just returns the connection to its pool.

Connection pooling can be used by an ODBC application using ODBC 2.*x* (including 2.*x* database drivers), as long as the application can call `SQLSetEnvAttr()`. When using pooling, the application should not execute SQL statements that change the database or the database context. You can see why this would be a bad idea: the connection will be tagged with a particular set of attributes, but will really be using a different database from the one it originally logged on to.

Connection Pool Timeouts

How long a connection remains in the pool depends on the `CPTimeout` property of the individual ODBC driver, which is shown in the screenshot below. Once that timeout expires, the connection is closed and removed from the pool.

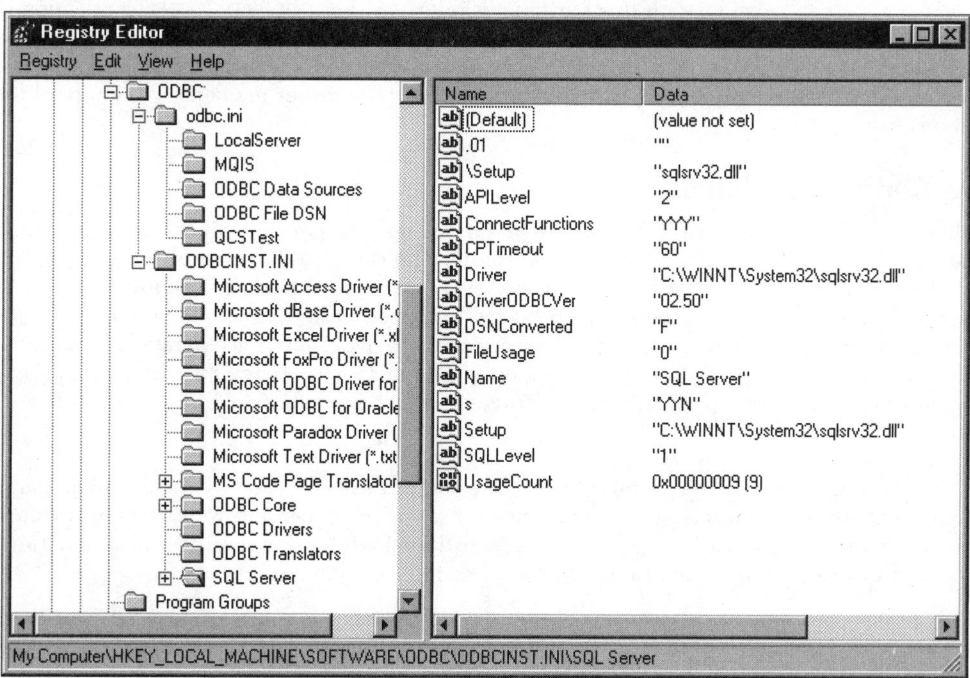

The timeout value you're looking at is located in the registry at:

```
HKEY_LOCAL_MACHINE\SOFTWARE\ODBC\ODBCINST.INI\driver-name\CPTimeout
```

Notice that the timeout is *per driver*. This means that changing `CPTimeout` for the driver changes it for all applications that use it, affecting every other user of that driver. Consider carefully what might happen to other applications running on the machine before you change this value.

Tuning the Connection Pool

There is currently no way to 'tune' pooling, or to cap the maximum number of connections a process can use. No registry setting allows you to tell ODBC how many connections it can have pooled at once. This may be an important feature of a very high utilization application, such as a 'weblication', which could conceivably have more concurrent users all actively using connections than it's possible for the database server to support efficiently. If you really need the ability to tune your connections to this degree, I'll show you in my implementation of the Quartermaster pattern how to implement a maximum cap on connections, and how to make a client wait for a connection when one is not available.

Dead Connections

A problem that plagued the connection pooling mechanism in v3.0 of ODBC was that if a connection was dead, the driver manager had no way to know, and would continue to hand the dead connection back out.

In ODBC 3.5, a new connection attribute called `SQL_ATTR_CONNECTION_DEAD` was introduced. When `SQLConnect()` is called with this attribute, it returns either `SQL_CD_TRUE` (connection is lost) or `SQL_CD_FALSE` (connection is alive). To support this mechanism efficiently (which, as yet, no drivers that I know of do), drivers return the last known state of the connection. As soon as a call to the server fails, the last state becomes `SQL_CD_TRUE`, and the driver manager will not pool the connection.

Enabling Connection Pooling

To enable connection pooling within a process, an ODBC application can call `SQLSetEnvAttr()` with the `SQL_ATTR_CONNECTION_POOLING` attribute. The call to set up connection pooling lets you specify whether pooling should occur at the driver level or at the environment handle level. However, this does not mean that pools can be *shared* across environments (as the ODBC 3.0 documentation mistakenly states), only that the driver manager can build a separate comparison stack for each environment or each driver, depending on what you specify. Using environment comparisons can mean better performance for processes that have many environments but few drivers.

Here's a piece of sample code that demonstrates how you can use this call to enable connection pooling in your process. Run this program as a project in the debugger and watch (count to yourself) how much faster the second call to `SQLConnect()` is than the first. (Obviously, you'll have to modify the call to connect to a data source that's registered on your system.)

```
#include <windows.h>
#include <stdio.h>
#include <sql.h>
#include <sqlext.h>

int main()
{
   SQLHENV henv;
   SQLHDBC hdbc;

   SQLSetEnvAttr(NULL, SQL_ATTR_CONNECTION_POOLING,
                       (SQLPOINTER)SQL_CP_ONE_PER_DRIVER, SQL_IS_INTEGER);

   SQLAllocHandle(SQL_HANDLE_ENV, NULL, &henv);

   // Set the ODBC behavior version
   // ODBCv2 driver working with driver manager v3
   SQLSetEnvAttr(henv, SQL_ATTR_ODBC_VERSION,
                             (SQLPOINTER)SQL_OV_ODBC2, SQL_IS_INTEGER);

   // Set the matching condition - in this case relaxed, not strict
   SQLSetEnvAttr(henv, SQL_ATTR_CP_MATCH,
                        (SQLPOINTER)SQL_CP_RELAXED_MATCH, SQL_IS_INTEGER);

   // Sample of usage
   // First connection is pooled; subsequent connections are reused
   // without a real reconnect
   for(int i = 0 ; i < 10 ; i++)
   {
      SQLAllocHandle(SQL_HANDLE_DBC, henv, &hdbc);
      SQLConnect(hdbc, (unsigned char*)"myserver\0", SQL_NTS,
                       (unsigned char*)"sa\0", SQL_NTS,
                       (unsigned char*)"\0", SQL_NTS);

      SQLDisconnect(hdbc);
      SQLFreeHandle(SQL_HANDLE_DBC, hdbc);
   }

   SQLFreeHandle(SQL_HANDLE_ENV, henv);
   return 0;
}
```

Pooling in Internet Information Server (IIS)

As I've said already, 'weblications' that rapidly establish and terminate database connections on each page hit can drastically reduce database server performance. In IIS 3.0, using Active Server Pages, you can implement connection pooling in your 'weblication' by changing the following registry setting, although you'll have to stop and restart the web server service for the change to take effect:

```
HKEY_LOCAL_MACHINE\System\CurrentControlSet\Services\W3SVC\ASP\Parameters\
StartConnectionPool=1
```

In IIS 4.0, pooling is enabled automatically, by virtue of the fact that processes run within the context of Microsoft Transaction Server (MTS). MTS automatically enables connection pooling on all packages (which are essentially processes). As you may know, IIS 4.0 is capable of running each individual web application in a separate process space. Each of these process spaces is really an MTS package in its own right, and so each application gets to pool ODBC connections, by default.

If you really need to turn connection pooling *off* in IIS 4.0, you can do so only by changing the `CPTimeout` registry value for the driver you want to disable. The consequence of this, of course, is that you will disable pooling for all other users of the driver on that machine as well. (By the way, the IIS metabase property `PoolIDCTimeout` applies only to database connections made from legacy `.idc` files.)

The Quartermaster Usage Pattern

Let's leave OBDC to one side for now and turn our attention back to the Quartermaster usage pattern. In implementing it, I took a generic approach in order to illustrate the concepts. That is, I didn't choose a specific 'resource' to pool – I simply implemented a mechanism whereby handles to some theoretical resource could be allocated efficiently.

The structures in the pattern's implementation manage *handles* to resources, not the resources themselves, which presumably are provided by some other technology such as a DBMS. This means that I can demonstrate the pattern without getting bogged down in the implementation of a specific technology, but you'll see that you can plug in ODBC connection handles (or other types of handles to resources) relatively easily. You'll see an example of this in the next chapter, when I'll demonstrate using the Quartermaster pattern as part of a COM service.

Hopefully, some of the design and implementation decisions I made will give you an idea of the rich complexity of this pattern, and a starting point should you need it in your own work. As we go through, I'll also take the opportunity to point out any interesting synchronization and multithreading issues.

Design Principles

When I designed the Quartermaster, I had several principles in mind right from the start, and these eventually drove the implementation. Here are the major design guidelines I used:

- **A resource can only be allocated to one user at a time.** This first principle is pretty obvious: two consumers cannot both be using the same resource at the same time. However, it drives other design issues because it means that the state of each resource handle must be tracked so that it is not handed out to more than one consumer at a time.
- **Consumers must be able to 'check out' a resource to be used for multiple calls.** In other words, a pool of 'unnamed' worker handles is not good enough, because a client must be able to keep a single handle through several operations on the resource. The check out operation itself must be quick and easy for the client to use.

- **Finding a free resource in the pool must be fast.** It is important for a high performance system that the resource allocator should not spend a lot of time looking for a free resource. It must be able to choose a known free resource without having to search for one.
- **The resources should be used in a 'round-robin' fashion.** This is to ensure that resources get used evenly over the life of the system, and that they don't go inactive or time out due to infrequency of use. This principle is more important for some types of resources than for others, but in general it is reasonably important for all types.
- **It must be possible to allocate more resources on the fly when they are needed.** There should be a mechanism whereby the system can do its own tuning, so that heavily utilized systems can dynamically adjust the number of pooled resources they have available. If clients start having to wait an excessive amount of time for resources, then the allocator should scale them up on the fly.
- **Clients should be able to wait for resources.** If there are no resources remaining, a client should be able to wait a configurable amount of time for one to become available, rather than immediately returning a "no resources available" error code. The mechanism that implements ODBC connection pooling does not have this feature, but I wanted to have it in the Quartermaster because it makes sense to keep the number of resources from being ramped up unnecessarily if they can be obtained in a reasonable amount of time.
- **It must be possible to recover resources that have not been returned by ill-behaved clients.** After a certain amount of time, it is reasonable to assume that resources that have been checked out but not returned to the pool have not been freed properly by the client. There should be a way to check this periodically and recover these overdue resources for the pool.

Implementation

Using the above principles as a guideline, I decided on the following overall design for my implementation:

- Use an array to store information about each resource in the pool. Each element in the array will store a pointer to a 'header' structure that contains a pointer to a resource handle structure, a 'time-stamp' to show when the resource was last checked out, and a flag indicating whether it is currently free or busy. The resource handle structure also contains the position of its pointer in the array, so that when a client frees a resource, it can quickly be found again by array position, rather than by searching the array.
- A FIFO linked list will be used to find a free resource quickly. This list stores pointers to the resource handle structures that are not being used – these are the same structures that are pointed to by the master array. To obtain a new resource, the allocator simply pops the next available resource off the top of the list and hands it back to the client. To release a resource, the allocator returns the resource to the *bottom* of the list. In this way, the resources are utilized in a round-robin fashion. I specifically used the FIFO method to handle the case of resource providers that *don't* do their own resource caching. If they did, a LIFO method would probably perform better. I also used the FIFO method so that any resources that might have built-in timeouts associated with them would not be as likely to be freed by the resource provider.

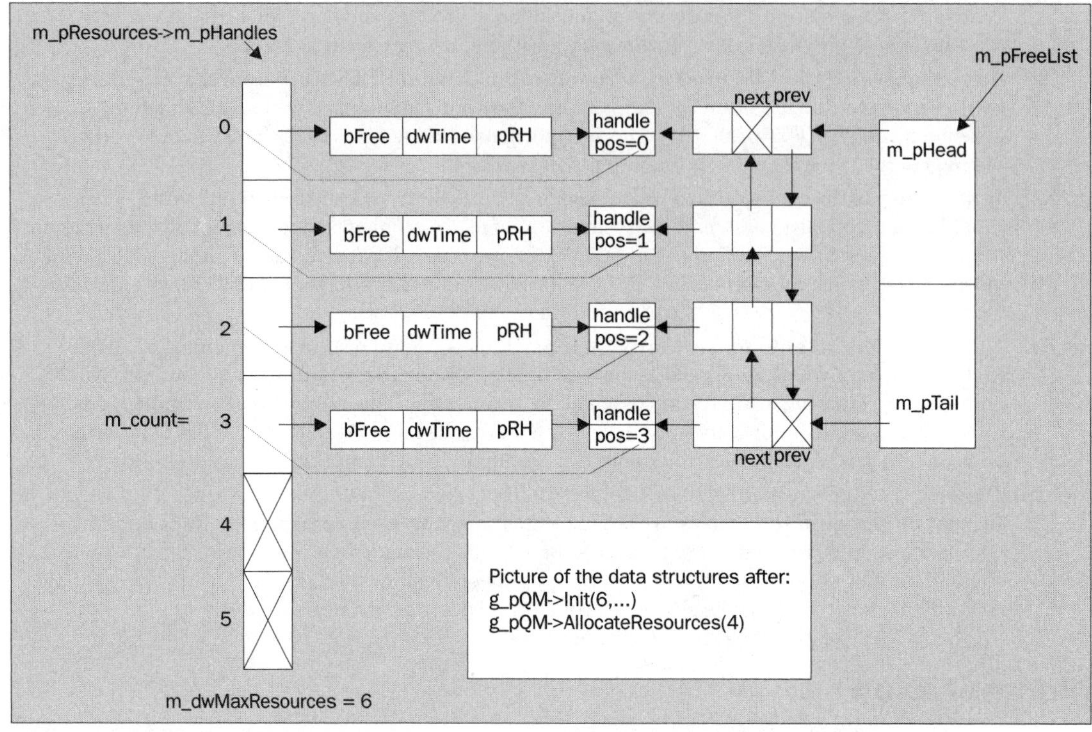

- To allocate additional handles when needed, a separate thread will watch the number of free resources available. When the thread sees that the allocator is down to a registry-configurable minimum, it will allocate more in configurable block sizes. This keeps upsizing of the pool from occurring on more than one thread, and keeps individual clients from blocking while the allocator adds more resources.
- On a configurable time schedule, an additional thread will walk the handle array to find dead handles that have been checked out for too long.
- Most wait times, resource allocation measurements, and so on will be configurable.
- Whenever there are no more free sessions, the allocator can wait on a semaphore for a configurable amount of time before returning an error condition to the client. This keeps the client from receiving an instantaneous "no more resources" message if the allocator is heavily loaded, when all it really needs to do is wait a fraction of a second for one to become available.

Quartermaster Code

Let's take a look at the code for the Quartermaster project. Since its job is simply to allocate generic resource handles, this sample *won't* show the Quartermaster implemented inside a service – I'll do that in the next chapter, where you'll see how to use it to allocate ODBC connections to COM objects resident inside a service. For now, we'll just look at it in the abstract, and run it inside a test client executable.

The Quartermaster consists of three main classes:

- `CResourceArray` implements the functionality needed for maintaining the array of resources, and for adding a new resource to the array.
- `CFreeList` implements a thread-safe, linked-list based FIFO queue containing the free connections.
- `CQuartermaster` is the main implementation class that gets instantiated to make the whole thing work. It owns the resource array and the free list. It also handles allocating and releasing resources, as well as dead resource cleanup and re-allocations.

The structures `RHANDLE` and `RHANDLEHEADER` contain information about the resources themselves. The former is the one that holds the theoretical resource handle and its index in the `CResourceArray` object. This is so that the list of handles can be used as rapidly as possible. When a client thread asks for a handle, it receives a pointer to an `RHANDLE` object. When it wants to release the session, it returns that pointer to the allocator. Since the index in the resource array is embedded in the structure, the resource release code can quickly mark the session as freed, without having to walk the array looking for it.

```
struct RHANDLE
{
   long handle;
   long pos;
};
```

The second structure, `RHANDLEHEADER`, is used by `CResourceArray` to keep track of `RHANDLE`s. It holds a pointer to the original `RHANDLE`, a marker to indicate whether it is free or busy, and a time-stamp value that's used to indicate when the handle was last given out. This way, it can be freed after a certain amount of time if the client thread does not return it properly.

```
struct RHANDLEHEADER
{
   const RHANDLE* pRH;
   bool bFree;
   DWORD dwTime;
};
```

CQuartermaster

Enough talk! Let's take a look at the code for `CQuartermaster`, which is the main class that clients will use to interface with the resource pooling mechanism:

```
class CQuartermaster
{
public:
   static CQuartermaster* m_pThis;

   // Constructors / destructors
   CQuartermaster();
   ~CQuartermaster();
```

```
    // Public methods
    void Init(DWORD dwMaxResources,       DWORD dwStartResources,
              DWORD dwWaitForHandleTime, DWORD dwHandleLifeTime,
              DWORD dwAllocationPoll,     DWORD dwMinPoolSize,
              DWORD dwResourceAllocSize, DWORD dwDeadResourcePoll);

    DWORD AllocateResources(DWORD dwNumAdd);
    void DeallocateResources();

    DWORD GetFreeResource(const RHANDLE** poutHandle);
    void ReleaseResource(const RHANDLE* pResource);
    void ReleaseDeadResources();

    DWORD FreeResourcesLeft()
    {
       DWORD dwCount;
       dwCount = m_pFreeList->GetCount();
       return dwCount;
    }

    DWORD GetNumResources()
    {
       DWORD dwCount;
       EnterCriticalSection(&m_cs);
       dwCount = m_dwNumCurrentResources;
       LeaveCriticalSection(&m_cs);
       return dwCount;
    }

    void SetStop()
    {
       SetEvent(m_hStopEvent);
       WaitForSingleObject(m_hAllocThread, INFINITE);
       WaitForSingleObject(m_hRefreshThread, INFINITE);
    }

    static DWORD WINAPI AllocateMoreResourcesThread(LPVOID lpParameter);
    static DWORD WINAPI RefreshDeadResourcesThread(LPVOID lpParameter);

 private:
    // Private attributes
    CFreeList* m_pFreeList;
    CResourceArray* m_pResources;

    DWORD m_dwNumCurrentResources;

    // Registry defaults
    DWORD m_dwStartResources;
    DWORD m_dwMaxResources;
    DWORD m_dwWaitForHandleTime;
    DWORD m_dwHandleLifeTime;
    DWORD m_dwAllocationPoll;
    DWORD m_dwMinPoolSize;
    DWORD m_dwResourceAllocSize;
    DWORD m_dwDeadResourcePoll;
```

```
    HANDLE m_hSem;                                    // Semaphore
    CRITICAL_SECTION m_cs;
    HANDLE m_hStopEvent;
    bool m_bStartAllocator;

    // Static threads
    HANDLE m_hAllocThread;
    HANDLE m_hRefreshThread;
};
```

Of the three inline functions in this class, `GetNumResources()` is the most noteworthy at this point. The function simply returns the number of resources being managed, but it has to be protected by a critical section because multiple threads can be reading and writing this member simultaneously.

Construction

Most of the initialization is performed when the user of a `CQuartermaster` object calls `Init()`, which I'll show you in a moment, so there isn't a great deal left for the constructor to do:

```
CQuartermaster* CQuartermaster::m_pThis = 0;

CQuartermaster::CQuartermaster() : m_dwNumCurrentResources(0),
                                   m_bStartAllocator(false)
{
   m_pThis = this;
   InitializeCriticalSectionAndSpinCount(&m_cs, SPINX);
}
```

Beyond the pair of member variables that are set to appropriate values, the static pointer `m_pThis` is set to `this` so that the thread functions can use it to access the class members, and a class critical section is initialized.

Spin Lock Critical Sections

This special type of critical section was added in NT 4.0 Service Pack 3. To use them, you'll need the January 1998 version of the Platform SDK installed, and your Visual C++ headers mapped to the SDK `lib` and `include` directories.

Under certain circumstances, the `InitializeCriticalSectionAndSpinCount()` function can make a dramatic difference to an application's performance. You may not have been aware that whenever a normal critical section blocks, NT's internals convert it to a mutex that gets waited on internally with `WaitForSingleObject()`. That means that in a server, where heavily-used functions are constantly blocking because lots of threads are pounding them at the same time, the OS is always making expensive wait calls. The result is that the performance of a frequently used critical section might be no better than it would be were it a mutex. A critical section initialized with the new spin count function will cause an internal loop to spin the requested number of times before rolling over to the wait call. Often, if this spin count is set reasonably, the critical section will release while the OS is waiting in the spin and before it calls the wait function. Note that the spin count is *not* a time in milliseconds; it is an empty loop spin time.

```
BOOL InitializeCriticalSectionAndSpinCount(
        LPCRITICAL_SECTION lpCriticalSection, // Pointer to critical section
        DWORD               dwSpinCount       // Spin count for critical section
);
```

If you cannot obtain newest Platform SDK, then you can remove the call to the `InitializeCriticalSectionAndSpinCount()` function and replace it with a standard `InitializeCriticalSection()` call.

Init

The `Init()` function works much like a constructor, accepting a number of parameters that it uses to set class member variables. After a `CQuartermaster` object has been created, a user of the class should call `Init()` to set up remaining variables, events, and threads.

```
void CQuartermaster::Init(DWORD dwMaxResources,       DWORD dwStartResources,
                          DWORD dwWaitForHandleTime, DWORD dwHandleLifeTime,
                          DWORD dwAllocationPoll,    DWORD dwMinPoolSize,
                          DWORD dwResourceAllocSize, DWORD dwDeadResourcePoll)
{
    // Event to signal workers to stop
    m_hStopEvent = CreateEvent(NULL, TRUE, FALSE, NULL);

    m_dwStartResources = dwStartResources;
    m_dwMaxResources = dwMaxResources;
    m_dwWaitForHandleTime = dwWaitForHandleTime;
    m_dwHandleLifeTime = dwHandleLifeTime;
    m_dwAllocationPoll = dwAllocationPoll;
    m_dwMinPoolSize = dwMinPoolSize;
    m_dwResourceAllocSize = dwResourceAllocSize;
    m_dwDeadResourcePoll =dwDeadResourcePoll;

    m_pResources = new CResourceArray(dwMaxResources);
    m_pFreeList = new CFreeList;

    // Initialize the Semaphore with max possible no. of resources
    m_hSem = CreateSemaphore(NULL, 0, dwMaxResources, NULL);

    DWORD dwAid;
    DWORD dwPid;
    m_hAllocThread = (HANDLE)_beginthreadex(NULL, 0,
            (PBEGINTHREADEX_TFUNC)CQuartermaster::AllocateMoreResourcesThread,
             0, 0, (PBEGINTHREADEX_TID)&dwAid);
    m_hRefreshThread = (HANDLE)_beginthreadex(NULL, 0,
             (PBEGINTHREADEX_TFUNC)CQuartermaster::RefreshDeadResourcesThread,
             0, 0, (PBEGINTHREADEX_TID)&dwPid );
}
```

After initializing some member data that configures the operational parameters of the Quartermaster (you'll see how these work when I create a simple 'user' of the object), the `Init()` function initializes two other objects: `m_pResources` and `m_pFreeList`. The first of these points to a `CResourceArray` object that manages the array of resources, as we will see shortly. The second is the list that manages the FIFO queue of unused resources. Next, the class semaphore is created that will allow clients to wait a short time for a resource to become free – I'll have more to say about this when we discuss the `GetFreeResource()` member. Finally, the function starts the 'allocate more resources' thread and the 'refresh dead resources' thread, which will run periodically to add resources to the pool if necessary, or return improperly-freed resources to the pool.

Destruction

Inevitably, the class destructor has to clean up after both the constructor and `Init()`, and so it looks something like this:

```
CQuartermaster::~CQuartermaster()
{
   if(m_hAllocThread)
      CloseHandle(m_hAllocThread);
   if(m_hRefreshThread)
      CloseHandle(m_hRefreshThread);

   CloseHandle(m_hSem);

   delete m_pResources;
   m_pResources = NULL;

   delete m_pFreeList;
   m_pFreeList = NULL;

   DeleteCriticalSection(&m_cs);
}
```

AllocateResources

After `Init()`, the first function that a user of the Quartermaster will typically call is `AllocateResources()`. This function creates the number of resources requested in its parameter, adds them to the array, and then adds them to the free list as well, so they can be used immediately.

```
DWORD CQuartermaster::AllocateResources(DWORD dwNumAdd)
{
   DWORD count = 0;
   const RHANDLE* pRH = 0;
   DWORD newRes = 0;

   DWORD dwNumRes = GetNumResources();

   if(dwNumAdd + dwNumRes > m_dwMaxResources)
      newRes = m_dwMaxResources - dwNumRes;
   else
      newRes = dwNumAdd;
```

```
    // Connect the sessions
    for(DWORD i = 0 ; i < newRes ; i++)
    {
       pRH = m_pResources->Add();
       if(pRH)
       {
          m_pFreeList->AddTail(pRH);
          count++;
       }
    }

    InterlockedExchangeAdd((long*)&m_dwNumCurrentResources, count);

    // Release Semaphore 'count' number of times
    if(count > 0)
    {
       long dwPrev;
       ReleaseSemaphore(m_hSem, (long)count, &dwPrev);
    }

    // Write to event log that x new handles were allocated
    // Also write if maximum session limit was reached

#ifdef _DEBUG
    CHAR sz[100] = {0};
    wsprintf(sz, "Allocations were increased----->%lu\n",
          m_dwNumCurrentResources);
    OutputDebugString(sz);
#endif

    // Allow the allocator thread to start, if it hasn't before
    if(!m_bStartAllocator)
       InterlockedExchange((long*)&m_bStartAllocator, true);

    return count;
}
```

The first thing this function does is to obtain a count of the current number of resources, and then make sure that the number of resources to add does not exceed the maximum cap on resources (`m_dwMaxResources`) that was passed into `Init()`. If so, it adjusts the requested allocation to equal the maximum cap. Then, it calls the `CResourceArray::Add()` function (which we'll see shortly) to create new resources and add them to the array; it also adds them to the free queue so that they can be used. After that, it increases the stored number of current resources (atomically, since another thread might be reading this value).

That done, `AllocateResources()` calls `ReleaseSemaphore()` on the class's resource semaphore in order to bump up the number of available resources by whatever number was added. Finally, it sets a Boolean flag that signals to `AllocateMoreResourcesThread()` that it can begin doing work. This is so that the allocator thread, which will start before the first call to `AllocateResources()`, doesn't jump the gun and start trying to add resources before the initial allocation can be accomplished.

InterlockedExchangeAdd

A function you may not have seen before is `InterlockedExchangeAdd()` – it's one of those functions that makes certain operations that are usually non-atomic for the processor, into atomic operations. `InterlockedExchangeAdd()` will increment a `LONG` value by the requested amount in a single, atomic operation, assuring that its state remains consistent.

```
LONG InterlockedExchangeAdd(PLONG Addend,            // Pointer to the addend
                            LONG  Increment          // Increment value);
```

About Semaphores

Semaphores are not new, but you may not have used them before. They behave rather like mutexes (in fact, mutexes are sometimes called "binary semaphores"), except that instead of only being able to manage whether *one* object is being used or not, they are used to manage usage counts on pools of objects. Most importantly, threads can wait on a semaphore for *one* of the objects it's protecting to become available.

For example, if there were five people at dinner but only four forks on the table, then instead of asking the waiter for another fork (much too easy!), you could implement a semaphore on the four available forks. As each person took a bite and then laid their fork down, the person waiting for a fork at that time could pick it up and take a mouthful of their meal.

With that rather unhygienic analogy out of the way, let's move on to see how semaphores work in code. To create one, you use the `CreateSemaphore()` API function, as I did in the `Init()` function.

```
HANDLE CreateSemaphore(
      LPSECURITY_ATTRIBUTES lpSemaphoreAttributes,
      LONG                  lInitialCount, // Initial count
      LONG                  lMaximumCount, // Maximum count
      LPCTSTR               lpName        // Pointer to semaphore object name
);
```

For our purposes, the interesting parts of this function are the initial and the maximum count. Now, a semaphore actually keeps a *reverse* usage count, which means that it *decrements* its count when a resource is used, and *increments* it when the object is released. The initial count, then, is the number of resources the semaphore starts with. Often, you'll want to create a semaphore with a initial count of zero and then call `ReleaseSemaphore()` (described below) as you are initializing resources, in order to increment the count. The maximum count is largest number of resources that the semaphore can ever have.

To use a semaphore, you simply wait on the handle returned by `CreateSemaphore()` using one of the 'wait' functions: `WaitForSingleObject()` or `WaitForMultipleObjects()`. If the semaphore becomes available before the timeout on the wait function expires, the semaphore count is decremented.

Once you've finished using the object that was being protected, you should release the semaphore by calling ReleaseSemaphore():

```
BOOL ReleaseSemaphore(HANDLE hSemaphore,    // Handle of the semaphore object
                      LONG   lReleaseCount, // Amount to add to current count
                      LPLONG lpPreviousCount   // Address of previous count);
```

This function actually allows you to add up to lReleaseCount to the semaphore count; you're not limited to adding just 1 each time you call it.

In my implementation, I use a semaphore to keep track of the number of free resources. If there aren't any available at the instant I ask for one, I can wait for a short time to see if one becomes free. This helps to minimize the number of client calls to GetFreeResource() that return "no resources available" when resources are running out and the allocator has not had time to allocate more.

The semaphore is created with a maximum count equal to the maximum possible handles, and an initial count of zero. Each time I call AllocateResources(), I release the semaphore (and so increase the count) by however many new sessions I allocate. Each client call to GetFreeResource() waits on the semaphore for some maximum acceptable time. If it gets a handle, then great – the semaphore is decremented. Otherwise, the wait timeout expires and the function returns E_NORESOURCESAVAILABLE. When the handle is finished with, the ReleaseResource() function releases the semaphore once to increment the count.

GetFreeResource

I've mentioned this function a couple of times already. The requesting client calls it any time that it wants a resource. As you can see from the comment, GetFreeResource() does no checking to assure that the resource it hands out is valid or otherwise usable – that is up to the client to do. It merely hands back the RHANDLE pointer that contains the handle to the resource that the client will use.

```
DWORD CQuartermaster::GetFreeResource(const RHANDLE** poutHandle)
{
   // Function does *not* find a handle *known* to be valid. It is up to the
   // client to check handle validity and retry if necessary.
   const RHANDLE* pHandle = 0;

   // Wait on the semaphore. I can block for a short time if no handles left.
   if(WaitForSingleObject(m_hSem, m_dwWaitForHandleTime) == WAIT_OBJECT_0)
   {
      // Get the handle and give it out
      pHandle = m_pFreeList->Pop();
```

```
        if(pHandle)
        {
            // Mark time and busy
            m_pResources->SetBusy(pHandle->pos);
            *poutHandle = pHandle;
            return 0;
        }
    }

    *poutHandle = NULL;
    return E_NORESOURCESAVAILABLE;
}
```

The first thing that this function does is to wait on the semaphore for a resource to become available. It will wait up to the time specified in `m_dwWaitForHandleTime`, after which it will return `E_NORESOURCESAVAILABLE` to the requesting client.

If the wait succeeds, a resource handle structure is popped off the top of the free handle queue. Then, the handle is marked as busy (the `bFree` member of its associated `RHANDLEHEADER` structure, stored in the resource array, is marked `false`) and its time count is marked. Finally, the `RHANDLE` is handed back to the client.

ReleaseResource

When the client has completed its work with the handle, it passes back the `RHANDLE` pointer to `ReleaseResource()`, which undoes the work that was performed by `GetFreeResource()`:

```
void CQuartermaster::ReleaseResource(const RHANDLE* handle)
{
    // Make sure handle hasn't been released twice by client accidentally
    if(handle)
    {
        if(m_pResources->IsFree(handle->pos) == false)
        {
            long lPrev;
            m_pResources->SetFree(handle->pos);
            m_pFreeList->AddTail(handle);
            ReleaseSemaphore(m_hSem, 1, &lPrev);
        }
    }
}
```

After checking to make sure that the resource hasn't already been released (a client could inadvertently call `ReleaseResource()` twice with the same `RHANDLE`) by examining the `bFree` member in its associated `RHANDLEHEADER` structure, the resource is marked as free and added back to the bottom of the free queue. Finally, the semaphore is released once to 'recover' a resource.

AllocateMoreResourcesThread

One of the processes in the class that runs on its own thread is the one that allocates additional resources if it sees that the free queue is running dry. Remember that this thread was started in `Init()`.

```
DWORD WINAPI CQuartermaster::AllocateMoreResourcesThread(LPVOID lpParameter)
{
   while(WaitForSingleObject(m_pThis->m_hStopEvent,
                             m_pThis->m_dwAllocationPoll) == WAIT_TIMEOUT)
   {
      if(m_pThis->FreeResourcesLeft() <= m_pThis->m_dwMinPoolSize &&
                                        m_pThis->m_bStartAllocator)
      {
         m_pThis->AllocateResources(m_pThis->m_dwResourceAllocSize);
         Sleep(HANDLEALLOCCOST);  // *Simulation* of amount of time it takes
      }
   }
   return 0;
}
```

Despite appearances, this has a simple motif, just waiting for one of two things. It either wants the `m_hStopEvent` to get set, which is used to signal the thread that the Quartermaster is terminating, or a timeout to expire – this is set at the time between 'polls' to check whether more resources are needed.

If the event gets set (by a call to `SetStop()` made from the `DeallocateResources()` function), the thread function terminates. If the timeout expires, then the function checks to see whether the number of resources remaining is fewer than the lowest number of resources to which the user of the Quartermaster wanted to be reduced. You should note the `m_bStartAllocator` variable here; it was initialized to `false` in the constructor, and, while the thread was created in `Init()`, it doesn't actually begin doing work until this Boolean value is set to `true` by the user's first call to `AllocateResources()`.

If the timeout did indeed expire, the function calls `AllocateResources()` to add some more resources to the pool (the number added is equal to the `dwResourceAllocSize` value you passed into `Init()` earlier). There is also a built-in 'sleep' here that should be removed when you use this in a real scenario. The sleep call merely *simulates* how long it would take to allocate another resource, and it's helpful for modeling the load on the Quartermaster.

RefreshDeadResourcesThread

Another thread in the class runs at intervals you specify to clean up any resources that have been checked out for an excessive amount of time. Presumably, such resources are actually free, and were just not released properly by the clients that obtained them.

```
DWORD WINAPI CQuartermaster::RefreshDeadResourcesThread(LPVOID lpParameter)
{
   while(WaitForSingleObject(m_pThis->m_hStopEvent,
                             m_pThis->m_dwDeadResourcePoll) == WAIT_TIMEOUT)
   {
      m_pThis->ReleaseDeadResources();
   }
   return 0;
}
```

The function has a similar *modus operandi* to `AllocateMoreResourcesThread()`, above. In this case, most of the work is done by a helper function called `ReleaseDeadResources()`, which is shown next. The function that it calls is fairly resource intensive, so the timeout in `m_dwDeadResourcePoll` should be set to run relatively infrequently – every 10 minutes, perhaps.

ReleaseDeadResources

When called, `ReleaseDeadResources()` walks the array of `RHANDLEHEADER` structures that's stored in the `CResourceArray` object `m_pResources`, and checks each one to see if it is busy. If it is, the function checks to see whether the timestamp noting when the resource was checked out (minus the timestamp for right now) exceeds the maximum checkout lifetime for resources. If it does, then it sets the resource as 'free' and adds it back to the bottom of the free queue.

```
// Will be called on a schedule by another thread
void CQuartermaster::ReleaseDeadResources()
{
   // Walk the list and see if any bFrees are false with
   // (now - timestamp) > m_dwHandleLifetime
   // If so, bFree = true and add back to free list
   CRITICAL_SECTION cs;
   InitializeCriticalSection(&cs);

   DWORD now = GetTickCount();
   RHANDLEHEADER* pTemp = 0;
   DWORD stamp = 0;

   long count = m_pResources->GetCount();
   for(long i = 0 ; i < count ; i++)
   {
      pTemp = m_pResources->m_pHandles[i];
      if(pTemp)
      {
         EnterCriticalSection(&cs);
         if(m_pResources->IsFree(i) == false)
         {
            stamp = pTemp->dwTime;
            if(now - stamp > m_dwHandleLifeTime)
            {
```

```
                    if(pTemp->pRH)
                    {
                        m_pResources->SetFree(i);
                        m_pFreeList->AddTail(pTemp->pRH);
                    }
                }
            }
            LeaveCriticalSection(&cs);
        }
    }
    DeleteCriticalSection(&cs);
}
```

One interesting thing to notice here is that it's possible that other threads could be manipulating the values of the various entries in the resource array (changing their free/busy state and so forth). To guard against any problems this might cause, the function protects all the work that it might do to a single array item with a critical section.

DeallocateResources

When the user of the `CQuartermaster` class has finished using it, the former calls `DeallocateResources()`, which does the work of stopping the two additional threads by calling the inline `SetStop()` function. It then removes all the objects stored in the queue and the array by calling those objects' `RemoveAll()` functions.

```
void CQuartermaster::DeallocateResources()
{
    EnterCriticalSection(&m_cs);

    // Stop the allocator/deadresource threads
    SetStop();

    m_dwNumCurrentResources = 0;
    m_pResources->RemoveAll();
    m_pFreeList->RemoveAll();

    LeaveCriticalSection(&m_cs);
}
```

CResourceArray

The `CResourceArray` class manages the `RHANDLEHEADER` data structures that keep track of all the resources that have been created (both used and unused).

```
// CResourceArray Class manages data structures for handle information
class CResourceArray
{
public:
    CResourceArray(long dwSize);
    ~CResourceArray();

    RHANDLEHEADER** m_pHandles;
    long m_size;
    const RHANDLE* Add();
    void RemoveAll();
```

The three functions for setting and checking the 'busy' state are made inline for speed. They simply set the state of the RHANDLEHEADER's bFree and dwTime members.

```
      void SetBusy(const long position)
      {
         m_pHandles[position]->bFree = false;
         m_pHandles[position]->dwTime = GetTickCount();
      }

      void SetFree(const long position)
      {
         m_pHandles[position]->bFree = true;
         m_pHandles[position]->dwTime = 0;
      }

      bool IsFree(const long position)
      {
         return m_pHandles[position]->bFree;
      }
```

The remainder of the class declaration follows.

```
      long GetCount()
      {
         long lRet;
         EnterCriticalSection(&m_cs);
         lRet = m_count;
         LeaveCriticalSection(&m_cs);
         return lRet;
      }

      long GetResourceHandle();
      void ReleaseResourceHandle(long hResHandle);

   private:
      CRITICAL_SECTION m_cs;
      long m_count;
   };
```

Construction

The constructor for the class sets the stage by initializing the class critical section and setting up the m_pHandles array with dwSize slots for RHANDLEHEADER structures. dwSize will be equal to whatever m_dwMaxResources was equal to when it was originally passed to CQuartermaster::Init(). The number of resources managed can never exceed this size.

```
   CResourceArray::CResourceArray(long dwSize) : m_size(dwSize), m_count(0)
   {
      InitializeCriticalSectionAndSpinCount(&m_cs, SPINX);

      m_pHandles = new RHANDLEHEADER* [dwSize];
      memset(m_pHandles, 0, sizeof(RHANDLEHEADER*) * dwSize);
   }
```

Add

The `Add()` function is the main workhorse of this class. It calls `GetResourceHandle()` to obtain a new resource handle from the underlying resource manager, and then creates `RHANDLEHEADER` and `RHANDLE` structures to manage the context information (array position, free/busy state, timeout) that surrounds the resource. It then passes back the `RHANDLE` structure's pointer to the caller (`CQuartermaster::AllocateResources()`) so that the pointer can be added to the free queue.

```
const RHANDLE* CResourceArray::Add()
{
   long hSession = 0;
   RHANDLE* chd = 0;

   EnterCriticalSection(&m_cs);
   if(m_count < m_size)
   {
      hSession = GetResourceHandle();
      if(hSession != 0)
      {
         RHANDLEHEADER* pSH = new RHANDLEHEADER;
         chd = new RHANDLE;
         chd->handle = hSession;
         chd->pos = m_count;

         pSH->pRH = chd;
         pSH->bFree = true;
         pSH->dwTime = 0;

         m_pHandles[m_count] = pSH;
         m_count++;
      }
      else
      {
         // Event Log call
         OutputDebugString(__TEXT("Handle could not be allocated\n"));
      }
   }
   LeaveCriticalSection( &m_cs );

   return chd;
}
```

GetResourceHandle and ReleaseResourceHandle

In this implementation, these functions are merely stubs that do very little:

```
long CResourceArray::GetResourceHandle()
{
   // Call connection function (fake allocator below)
   long handle = 10000 + m_count;
   return handle;
}
```

```
void CResourceArray::ReleaseResourceHandle(long hResHandle)
{
#ifdef _DEBUG
   CHAR sz[100] = {0};
   wsprintf(sz, "Handle Dellocated-------------->%Handle: %d\n", hResHandle);
   OutputDebugString(sz);
#endif
}
```

Of course, they're trivial because they are not managing any real resources. In a real implementation of the Quartermaster, you would provide your own implementations for these functions that allocated and deallocated whatever underlying resource you were trying to manage (such as ODBC connection handles, or some proprietary resource).

RemoveAll

The `RemoveAll()` function merely loops through the array, obtaining the resource handle that's buried inside the `RHANDLE` structure, which is in turn buried inside the `RHANDLEHEADER` structure, calling `ReleaseResourceHandle()` on it to deallocate it with its resource manager. Then, it deletes the memory associated with each heap object (the `RHANDLE` and the `RHANDLEHEADER`) that was being managed.

```
void CResourceArray::RemoveAll()
{
   RHANDLEHEADER* pTemp = 0;

   EnterCriticalSection(&m_cs);
   for(int i = 0 ; i < m_count ; i++)
   {
      pTemp = m_pHandles[i];
      if(pTemp)
      {
         const RHANDLE* pRHTemp = pTemp->pRH;
         if(pRHTemp)
         {
            ReleaseResourceHandle(pRHTemp->handle);
            delete (RHANDLE*)pRHTemp;
         }
         delete pTemp;
      }
      m_pHandles[i] = NULL;
   }
   m_count = 0;
   LeaveCriticalSection(&m_cs);
}
```

Typically, this function is called by `CQuartermaster::DeallocateResources()`, but it can also be called by the object's destructor:

```
CResourceArray::~CResourceArray()
{
   RemoveAll();                                    // Just in case
   delete [] m_pHandles;
   m_size = 0;
   m_pHandles = NULL;
   DeleteCriticalSection(&m_cs);
}
```

CFreeList

Finally, let's look at `CFreeList`, which implements the FIFO queue for managing all the pointers to `RHANDLE`s that are not being used. The implementation of this class is nothing special – it's just a linked list with 'queue' behavior: a 'pop' mechanism and an 'add-to-tail' mechanism. A simple structure manages the nodes in the linked list:

```
struct NODE
{
   const RHANDLE* pRH;
   NODE* prev;
   NODE* next;
};
```

The class itself just contains a head pointer, a tail pointer, and a count of the number of nodes in the list:

```
// List class is linked list of RHANDLEs
class CFreeList
{
public:
   CFreeList();
   ~CFreeList();

   const RHANDLE* Pop();
   void AddTail(const RHANDLE* newHandle);
   void RemoveAll();

   DWORD GetCount()
   {
      DWORD dwCount;
      EnterCriticalSection(&m_cs);
      dwCount = m_Count;
      LeaveCriticalSection(&m_cs);
      return dwCount;
   }

private:
   DWORD m_Count;
   NODE* m_pHead;
   NODE* m_pTail;
   CRITICAL_SECTION m_cs;
};
```

Construction

Construction of the object simply initializes the class critical section `m_cs`.

```
CFreeList::CFreeList() : m_pHead(NULL), m_pTail(NULL), m_Count(0)
{
   InitializeCriticalSectionAndSpinCount(&m_cs, SPINX);
}
```

AddTail

The `AddTail()` function allocates a new `NODE` object, initializing it with the pointer to the `RHANDLE` that you're adding to the tail of the list. Then, it reassigns the tail pointer to point to the new object. Since the operations in this function are class-wide, they are protected by a critical section.

```
void CFreeList::AddTail(const RHANDLE* newHandle)
{
   NODE* pNew = new NODE;
   pNew->pRH = newHandle;
   pNew->prev = NULL;
   pNew->next = NULL;

   EnterCriticalSection(&m_cs);

   if(m_pTail == NULL)                              // List is empty
      m_pHead = pNew;
   else
   {
      pNew->prev = m_pTail;
      m_pTail->next = pNew;
   }

   m_pTail = pNew;
   m_Count++;

   LeaveCriticalSection(&m_cs);
}
```

Pop

`Pop()` does the work of grabbing the head node in the list, getting the `RHANDLE` pointer out of the node, then removing the node from the list and reshuffling the pointers. It then deletes the `NODE` object and passes back the `RHANDLE` to the calling function, which is `CQuartermaster::GetFreeResource()`. Once again, a critical section protects the function in order to isolate the class members:

```
const RHANDLE* CFreeList::Pop()
{
   const RHANDLE* rh = 0;
   EnterCriticalSection(&m_cs);
```

```
    NODE* p = m_pHead;
    if(p != NULL)
    {
       // Obtain RHANDLE
       rh = p->pRH;

       if(p->next)
       {
          p->next->prev = NULL;
          m_pHead = p->next;
       }
       else
          m_pHead = m_pTail = NULL;

       delete p;
       m_Count--;
    }

    LeaveCriticalSection(&m_cs);
    return rh;
 }
```

Destruction

Predictably, the class destructor has to tidy up after all that has gone before, which in this case means the work done by the constructor, and whatever has been left behind by the `AddTail()` and `Pop()` functions:

```
CFreeList::~CFreeList()
{
   RemoveAll();
   DeleteCriticalSection(&m_cs);
}
```

As you can see, the destructor defers the majority of its work to `RemoveAll()`, which is also called by `CQuartermaster::DeallocateResources()`:

```
void CFreeList::RemoveAll()
{
   NODE* pNext = 0;

   EnterCriticalSection(&m_cs);

   NODE* p = m_pHead;
   while(p != NULL)
   {
      pNext = p->next;
      delete p;
      p = pNext;
   }
   m_pHead = m_pTail = NULL;
   m_Count = 0;

   LeaveCriticalSection(&m_cs);
}
```

Constructing the Project

If you don't have access to the source code that's available for download from the Wrox web site, you can put together the Quartermaster sample from the code I've presented so far. You've seen the definitions of three structures and three classes, and I placed those all together in a file called `Quartermaster.h`. Similarly, all the function implementations go in `Quartermaster.cpp`, which should be prefixed by these four lines:

```
#include "precomp.h"
#include "Quartermaster.h"

const int HANDLEALLOCCOST = 1000;  // Simulated time for allocation
const int SPINX = 5000;            // Spin count for critical sections
```

Finally, the file for precompiled headers, `precomp.h`, looks like this:

```
#define _WIN32_WINNT 0x500    // For InitializeCriticalSectionAndSpinCount()
#define E_NORESOURCESAVAILABLE 0x80002838

#include <windows.h>
```

Running the Quartermaster

Here's a little sample program that allows you to see the Quartermaster in action. The program lets you configure the initial number of resources in the pool, the number of simultaneous clients (threads), and the number of calls each client will make. You can also set the average time each client will hold on to a resource, and the time it takes to allocate another resource on the fly. By tuning the values to model your scenario, it's possible to get more information on how many resources it would take to service a prospective client load.

```
#include "precomp.h"
#include "Quartermaster.h"

DWORD WINAPI ThreadFunc(LPVOID lpParameter);
CQuartermaster* g_pQM = new CQuartermaster;

const int NUMCLIENTS = 64;
const int SLEEP = 0;                   // 'Work time' for each thread - i.e. how
                                        // long it will hold the resource
const int NUMALLOC = 1000;              // Number of times each thread will run
const int NUMSTARTRESOURCES = 5;        // Number of handles to start with
const int MAXPOSSIBLE = 100;            // Maximum number of handles that can be
                                        // allocated
const int WAITFORHANDLE = 2000;         // Time a client will wait for a handle
const int HANDLEEXPIRES = 600000;       // 10 minutes-time each resource can
                                        // live before being considered 'dead'
const int DEADRESOURCEPOLL = 600000;    // 10 minutes-time between each garbage
                                        // collection
const int ALLOCATIONPOLL = 2000;        // ms between each check for whether to
                                        // allocate more
```

```
const int RESOURCEALLOCSIZE = 1;      // Number of resources to add at a time
const int MINPOOLSIZE = 0;            // Least amount of resources before
                                      // adding more

int main()
{
   g_pQM->Init(MAXPOSSIBLE, NUMSTARTRESOURCES, WAITFORHANDLE, HANDLEEXPIRES,
         ALLOCATIONPOLL, MINPOOLSIZE, RESOURCEALLOCSIZE, DEADRESOURCEPOLL);

   // Do a bunch of allocations
   g_pQM->AllocateResources(NUMSTARTRESOURCES);

   // Main line client calls
   DWORD sTime = GetTickCount();
   CHAR sz[100];

   HANDLE hThread[NUMCLIENTS] = {0};
   DWORD dwID[NUMCLIENTS] = {0};
   for(int s = 0 ; s < NUMCLIENTS ; s++)
   {
      hThread[s] = CreateThread(0, 0, &ThreadFunc, 0, 0, &dwID[s]);
      wsprintf(sz, "Thread %d created with id: %lu\n", s, dwID[s]);
      OutputDebugString(sz);
   }

   // Wait for threads to complete. Can only wait for 64!
   WaitForMultipleObjects(NUMCLIENTS, &hThread[0], TRUE, INFINITE);

   // Timing output
   sTime = (GetTickCount() - sTime);
   wsprintf(sz, "Total Time was: %lu\n", sTime);
   OutputDebugString(sz);

   // FYI
   wsprintf(sz, "Final Allocated Resources were: %lu\n",
                                         g_pQM->GetNumResources());
   OutputDebugString(sz);

   // Deallocate
   g_pQM->DeallocateResources();

   for(int t = 0 ; t < NUMCLIENTS ; t++)
      CloseHandle(hThread[t]);

   delete g_pQM;
   return 0;
}
```

```
DWORD WINAPI ThreadFunc(LPVOID lpParameter)
{
   DWORD dwID = GetCurrentThreadId();
   CHAR sz[100];
   long h;
   const RHANDLE* pHandle = 0;
   for(int x = 0 ; x < NUMALLOC ; x++)
   {
      h = 0;
      DWORD ret = g_pQM->GetFreeResource(&pHandle);
      if(ret == 0)
      {
         h = pHandle->handle;

#ifdef _DEBUG
         wsprintf(sz, "Thread: %lu -- Count: %d -- HandleVal: %li \n",
                                                               dwID, x, h);
         OutputDebugString(sz);
#endif

         Sleep(SLEEP);
         g_pQM->ReleaseResource(pHandle);
      }
      else
      {
         wsprintf(sz, "Could not get handle---->
               Thread: %lu -- Count: %d -- HandleVal: %li \n", dwID, x, h);
         OutputDebugString(sz);
      }
   }
   return 0;
}
```

The sample just creates some resources, then sets up some number of client threads to pound against the data structures, getting resources, sleeping for a configurable amount of time, then releasing those resources. All of the parameters to `Init()` are just pre-configured constants; in real life, they would be read in from the registry and then passed to `Init()`.

You'll notice that throughout the code, `OutputDebugString()` is used to send data about the operation of the system to the debug window, so that you can get a visual idea of what's going on. If you start the DbMon application, available in the platform SDK, and run the debug version of the executable, you'll see the results in the DbMon window:

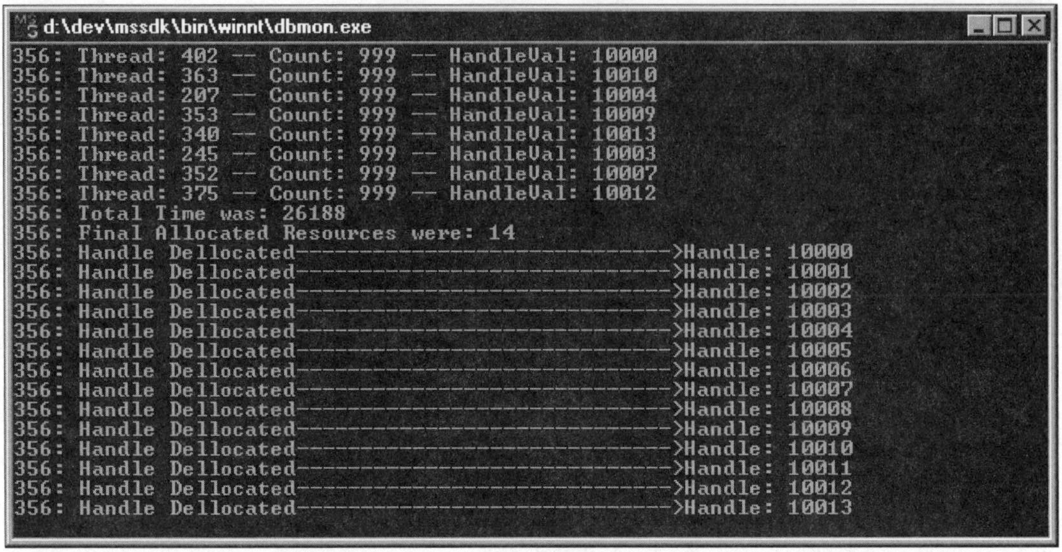

```
d:\dev\mssdk\bin\winnt\dbmon.exe
356: Thread: 402 -- Count: 999 -- HandleVal: 10000
356: Thread: 363 -- Count: 999 -- HandleVal: 10010
356: Thread: 207 -- Count: 999 -- HandleVal: 10004
356: Thread: 353 -- Count: 999 -- HandleVal: 10009
356: Thread: 340 -- Count: 999 -- HandleVal: 10013
356: Thread: 245 -- Count: 999 -- HandleVal: 10003
356: Thread: 352 -- Count: 999 -- HandleVal: 10007
356: Thread: 375 -- Count: 999 -- HandleVal: 10012
356: Total Time was: 26188
356: Final Allocated Resources were: 14
356: Handle Dellocated------------------------------>Handle: 10000
356: Handle Dellocated------------------------------>Handle: 10001
356: Handle Dellocated------------------------------>Handle: 10002
356: Handle Dellocated------------------------------>Handle: 10003
356: Handle Dellocated------------------------------>Handle: 10004
356: Handle Dellocated------------------------------>Handle: 10005
356: Handle Dellocated------------------------------>Handle: 10006
356: Handle Dellocated------------------------------>Handle: 10007
356: Handle Dellocated------------------------------>Handle: 10008
356: Handle Dellocated------------------------------>Handle: 10009
356: Handle Dellocated------------------------------>Handle: 10010
356: Handle Dellocated------------------------------>Handle: 10011
356: Handle Dellocated------------------------------>Handle: 10012
356: Handle Dellocated------------------------------>Handle: 10013
```

The profile of the run shown here had the following configuration: 64 threads, each running a Get/Release call 1000 times. Note that it took 14 handles and approximately 26 seconds to run. However, most of this was due to running it in debug mode and getting all of those debug output strings. I ran it in release mode, and it only took 2.7 seconds and 6 resources:

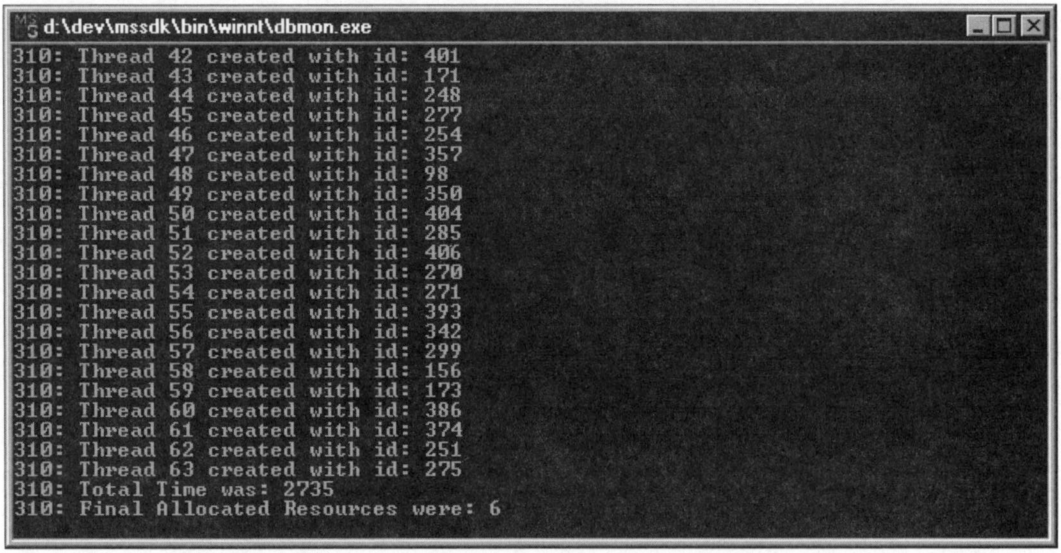

```
d:\dev\mssdk\bin\winnt\dbmon.exe
310: Thread 42 created with id: 401
310: Thread 43 created with id: 171
310: Thread 44 created with id: 248
310: Thread 45 created with id: 277
310: Thread 46 created with id: 254
310: Thread 47 created with id: 357
310: Thread 48 created with id: 98
310: Thread 49 created with id: 350
310: Thread 50 created with id: 404
310: Thread 51 created with id: 285
310: Thread 52 created with id: 406
310: Thread 53 created with id: 270
310: Thread 54 created with id: 271
310: Thread 55 created with id: 393
310: Thread 56 created with id: 342
310: Thread 57 created with id: 299
310: Thread 58 created with id: 156
310: Thread 59 created with id: 173
310: Thread 60 created with id: 386
310: Thread 61 created with id: 374
310: Thread 62 created with id: 251
310: Thread 63 created with id: 275
310: Total Time was: 2735
310: Final Allocated Resources were: 6
```

Multithreading Features

You may be wondering about the way I serialized access to the free list (`CFreeList`) to prevent the multiple threads that come in and out of it from walking all over the data structure. In fact, there were a couple of options: one choice I could have made would have been simply to place a critical section around the `GetFreeResource()` and `ReleaseResource()` methods of `CQuartermaster`. However, you can probably see that this would have had the unfortunate effect of serializing access to the allocation mechanism. Not only would it be impossible for more than one `GetFreeResource()` operation to go on at a time, you wouldn't even be able to have one client getting and another client releasing at the same time – only one client at a time could own the class critical section!

Instead, I pushed the locking mechanisms back to the level of the data structures themselves. The free list is a FIFO queue, so things are constantly popping off the top and being added back to the bottom. There are no real 'readers' of the data structure, only write operations. That means that the `Pop()`, `AddTail()`, and `GetCount()` functions must be serialized. I chose to protect the class data with a single critical section at the class level. In the final analysis, *all* updates to `CFreeList` have to be serialized, but it doesn't make sense to block at the higher level (only allowing `GetFreeResource()` *or* `ReleaseResource()` to be called by one client at a time). Pushing the locking to a lower level allows me to reduce the number of instructions that are protected, and therefore reduce contention.

The `CResourceArray` class is a bit different. It requires thread protection mechanisms whenever it adds new sessions into the array. However, we know that the data structure is managed in such a way that only one thread should be doing an operation on any `RHANDLEHEADER` at any time (we guarantee that because of the way the `GetFreeSession()` mechanism works). This means that we can actually safely get away without protecting access to the members of `RHANDLEHEADER`. Each call from a thread is accessing unrelated data members, so there is no reason for one thread to block on another.

Using ODBC in a Service

With the generic implementation out of the way, and in preparation for the next chapter, we can turn our attention once again to the subject of ODBC. Using ODBC in a service for database connectivity is fairly straightforward as long as you keep a few things in mind. In the remainder of this chapter, I'll explain what those things are, and why they're so important.

Use a Thread-aware Database Driver

There are two criteria that a database driver must meet in order for it to be used effectively in a service:

- The driver must not have **thread affinity**. That means that its objects must be safely accessible from threads other than the one that created them. In a service, a connection might be created on one thread, used from one or more other threads, and disconnected from still another thread.
- The driver must be thread-safe. That means that (on some level) it must be able to handle concurrent calls from any thread at any time.

How these design criteria end up being achieved depends upon the driver itself. Different drivers are safe at different levels – some are safe only at the driver level, some at the connection handle level, and others are safe all the way to the statement handle level. The level to which a driver is 'safe' depends on where it blocks to serialize calls. Proper serialization is not necessarily the same as a high-performance threading model!

For instance, the Microsoft Oracle ODBC driver v2.573 (`msorcl32.dll`) is completely thread-safe, but blocks at the *connection* level, meaning that only one thread per connection can be in the driver at a time. This means that multiple threads holding the same connection handle are effectively serialized. A previous version of the Oracle driver, v2.0 (`msorcl10.dll`), was also thread-safe, but was serialized at the *driver* level, meaning that only one thread was allowed in the driver at any one time.

If you plan to implement a pooling mechanism for database connections in a service, then at the very least you'll need a driver that's thread-safe and that only blocks at the connection level in order to reap any real performance benefits. You'll get nowhere if you have fifty clients using thirty connections, but calls can only operate one by one because they are all serialized at the driver level. Check out the documentation for the driver before you use it, but a good rule of thumb is that drivers based on Jet are not suitable because of theses threading issues. Drivers for high-performance DBMSs (such as Microsoft SQL Server, and Oracle), on the other hand, *are* usually thread-safe.

Protect the Handle State

Even if the driver is thread-safe, you may still need to ensure that the state of various handles that it uses stays consistent. This means that you have to make sure that a given handle to any object is only used by one thread at a time. Consider, for example, what would happen if Thread A had just used a connection handle to run a query, and was currently in the act of processing the results of that query. Then, Thread B comes along and tries to use the *very same* connection handle to run another query. In the best case, you'd get an error message. In the worst case, you'd get a corrupted or incomplete dataset in Thread A.

The best way to protect the state of a handle is to make sure that more than one thread doesn't get hold of the same handle at the same time! Of course, this can be challenging when you also want the handle to be used for doing work for a high percentage of the time, which is the whole point of connection pooling to begin with. The allocation mechanism I implemented for my Quartermaster example fulfills both of these criteria.

Use a System DSN

Up until ODBC v2.5, it could be a problem to use a DSN (data source name) within a service. That was because until then, DSNs were stored *per user*, in `HKEY_CURRENT_USER` – whichever user set up the DSN stored it in their user area in the registry. As you saw in the last chapter, a service running under the LocalSystem account doesn't have access to `HKEY_CURRENT_USER` in the way that you'd expect. To use a DSN, you'd have to make some different arrangements for the service, such as running it under a real user account.

With ODBC v2.5, though, came the concept of the **system DSN**, which is a type of DSN that *all* users have access to. The `HKEY_LOCAL_MACHINE\SOFTWARE\ODBC\odbc.ini` area of the registry stores the information for system DSNs, but as it stands now, an administrator actually has to go to each machine and set up a system DSN using the ODBC control panel tool.

A further possibility is to use a **file DSN**. This stores its ODBC configuration information in a special file that can be moved around from machine to machine, the goal being to make administration and configuration of DSNs easier across many (possibly remote) machines. A file DSN can just be copied to the file DSN directory (the default is `C:\Program Files\Common Files\ODBC\DataSources`) during a normal batch installation process. However, file DSNs are considerably (up to 3×) slower to access than system DSNs, at least up until ODBC v3.5. My advice is to use system DSNs and suffer with the administration problems. If you need to, you can write an installation program that hacks the configuration information manually into the registry for the pool of machines that will run your service.

Impersonate a Valid User

If your SQL Server uses NT integrated authentication (when SQL Server uses the token from the calling client to validate access to its databases), you may need to impersonate a valid user in order to gain access to it. In such cases, you may find accessing a SQL Server that's on a different machine from the service to be difficult, particularly when you run under the LocalSystem account. The LocalSystem account has no network credentials, so unless you impersonate a valid domain user (using a primary token obtained from `LogonUser()`) before making the call, run the service under a valid account name, enable the guest account, or enable null sessions, you won't be able to gain access.

Summary

In this chapter, we've interleaved discussion of two different topics that we'll shortly be using in tandem. We began by examining the rationale and motivation for wanting to implement resource-pooling mechanisms, and then looked at the way one such mechanism – the one used by current ODBC technology – works.

Having done that, we explored the general principles involved in the design of the Quartermaster usage pattern, and looked in depth at an implementation that took these into account, improving in some areas on the ODBC mechanism. Finally, in preparation for the next chapter, we also covered some of the issues that are important when you use ODBC inside a service.

9

COM and Services

Basically, there are two ways to slice the question of COM and services. First, you can consider what it means for a service to *use* COM to perform internal operations or other work. This means that the service either instantiates custom COM components, or uses COM-based operating system interfaces to get work done. The other way to think about services is as COM object *providers* – in other words, the service exposes COM objects for use by clients. In this scenario, COM objects get instantiated inside the service process space when a client calls in. The service then uses DCOM (and RPC) as the communication mechanism between client and server, rather than one of the other methods – sockets, pipes, MSMQ messages, etc. In certain situations (such as the Business Object usage pattern we'll investigate later in the chapter), COM is the perfect choice for communicating between client and server.

In this chapter, we will look at both of these scenarios, considering the issues both of using COM in a service, and of providing COM objects for clients to use. However, I'm *not* going to attempt to explain COM in detail – there are plenty of great books on the topic of COM, and there is no way of encapsulating all that information here. If you don't know anything about COM at all, I would suggest picking up a book on COM (and particularly ATL) to support your effort. If you're just starting in COM and know the basics, it is probably safe to proceed; I'm not going to be using advanced COM techniques in this chapter. My goal is purely to explain certain COM issues when they are relevant to the way an NT service provides or consumes COM objects. I'll also discuss COM security, which is already pretty hairy, but can get hairier still when services are involved. My big challenge in this chapter is not to spoil the fun by diverting too far from the topic of services; I hope you'll agree that I've succeeded.

> *For a tutorial along the lines suggested above, you might like to try* Beginning ATL COM Programming *by Grimes et al., also published by Wrox Press (ISBN 1-861000-11-1).*

General Architecture of COM and Services

Starting with Windows NT version 4.0 and ATL 2.1, it became much easier to do COM work inside a service. In this section, we will briefly examine some of the issues surrounding using services to expose COM objects. Then, after breaking to consider the topics of COM threading and COM security in the context of NT services, we'll return to look at this subject in more detail in a later section.

The COM SCM

Back in Chapter 1, I mentioned that NT really has *two* service control managers. The first is the NT SCM, housed in `Services.exe`, which we have been using all along in this book. The second, however, is the **COM SCM**, which is housed in `RPCSS.exe`. The COM SCM is itself an NT service that gets auto-started by the NT SCM (how circular!); in the Services control panel applet, it is displayed as the Remote Procedure Call (RPC) Service.

The role of the COM SCM is to act as the central routing point for all requests for object activation on the system. Every time that a COM client wants to create an instance of an object, it contacts the COM SCM by calling some API functions that we'll discuss in a moment. If it's an out-of-process component, the COM SCM handles the job of finding it in the registry and loading the EXE that houses it. If it's an in-process component, the SCM takes care of loading the DLL that owns it into the process space of the caller. If there is a choice to be made as to where the component should come from (that is, if there are in-process, out-of-process, and even remote implementations), and if the client does not indicate a preference, the COM SCM decides which will be most efficient.

The COM SCM's functionality is made available through the COM API functions, whose names typically begin with the letters `Co` (such as `CoCreateIntance()` or `CoGetClassObject()`). These functions are implemented in `OLE32.dll`, so when you make a call to `CoCreateInstance()`, you're really talking through `OLE32.dll` to the COM SCM, which is doing the work of finding out how to activate the object you have requested. The diagram below shows the position of the COM SCM in the COM architecture.

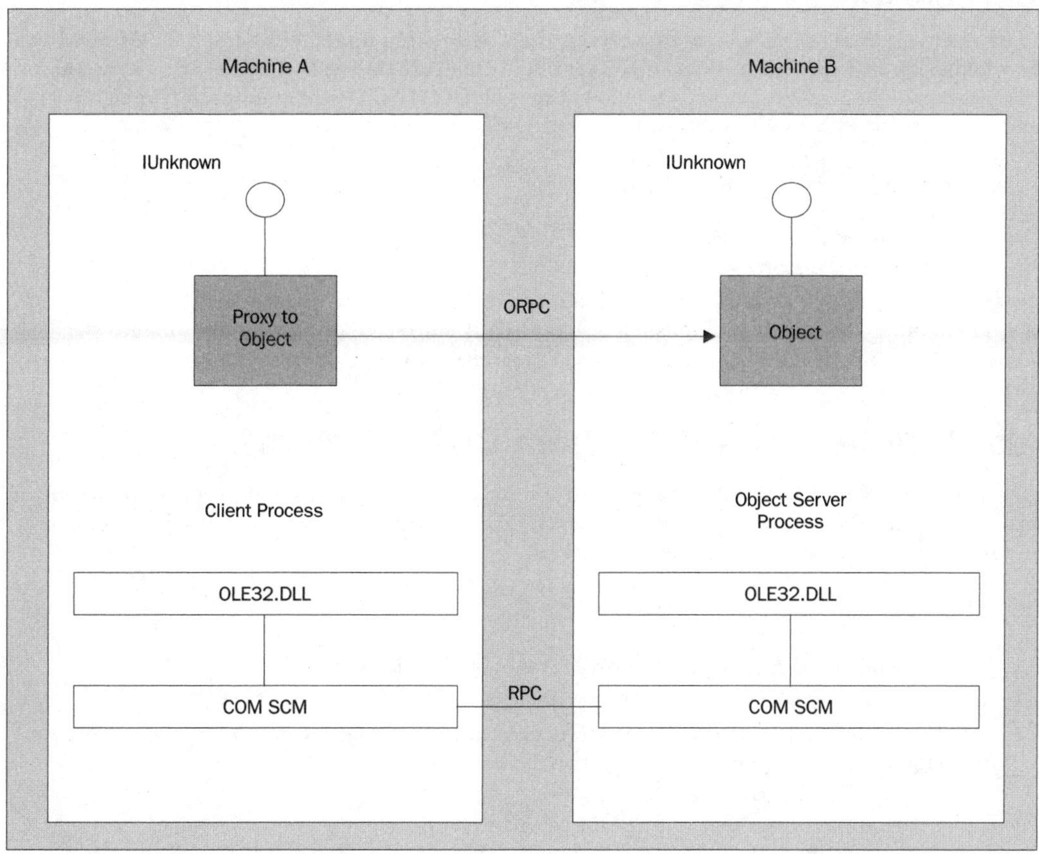

If the COM component is in-process, then once it has been activated, the COM SCM pretty much steps out of the way and the client and object communicate with one another directly.

If the object is housed out-of-process, then the COM SCM takes care of finding and loading the proxy-stub DLL (unless the proxy-stub is inside the executable itself) so that method requests and results can be marshaled back and forth between the client and server. Then, the proxy and the stub communicate through COM Object RPC (ORPC), a lightweight protocol that runs on top of Microsoft RPC. When the component is on the same machine as the caller, COM uses an efficient, local transport for communication.

If the component is on a remote machine, the COM SCM on machine A (the client) contacts the COM SCM on machine B (the server) for help in instantiating the object remotely. In this case, A's SCM asks B's SCM to find or launch the server in which the object is housed, create the object, and then return the interface pointer. A's SCM then returns the interface pointer to the requesting client. After that, they talk directly. For off-host requests, COM prefers UDP (the datagram IP protocol) because it is connectionless and efficient. However, other common protocols (such as TCP, which is the choice on the Windows 95 version of DCOM) are also supported.

The COM SCM with Services

If a component is housed in an executable server, then by looking up its APPID, the COM SCM can decide whether to attempt to start it as an NT service. If the APPID has the `LocalService` and `ServiceParameters` entries, as shown below, then the COM SCM will attempt to launch a demand-start service with a call to the API `StartService()` function.

```
[HKEY_CLASSES_ROOT\AppID\{My AppID GUID}]
LocalService= "Myservice"
ServiceParameters= "-service"
```

Of course, the service has to have been installed using the `CreateService()` API. If the service is *already* started, either because a previous client has already started it, or because it's an auto-start service, then the process's class objects are already registered and the COM SCM knows where to find them.

How do COM Services differ from COM Servers?

A COM service *is* a COM server that happens to run as a service, and so the differences between COM services and COM servers are pretty much the same as those between *any* service and *any* executable server. Some of these are outlined below.

Both COM services and COM servers can:

- Be started on demand, based on COM's activation mechanisms
- Run under a different security context than the client
- Remain running indefinitely. A COM server can choose to do this by not closing the process when the last interface pointer is released on the last object

However, there are some things that only COM services can do:

- Auto-start at boot time
- Cause dependent, non-COM NT services to auto-start
- Run under the LocalSystem account
- Be started and stopped from remote machines

Conversely, some of the advantages of COM servers are:

- They can run under the security context of the interactive user or the activator of the object with a simple DCOM setting. However, you rarely, if ever, want to run as either of these
- They are much easier to debug

Why Choose One or the Other?

The reasons why you would choose a to use a COM service rather than a COM server should be pretty clear, because they're just the ones we've talked about all along. You may want to host your COM object in a service if:

- You need to be running even when no user is logged on
- Your server has costly initialization processes
- You need to run 'agent-style' background processes that support the work the COM objects are doing, such as gathering data from a data feed
- You need to keep process state independently of the hosted objects. For instance, you might need to keep a global data buffer across all objects whose existence you want to preserve even when there are no objects
- You need to auto-start, or run under the security context of LocalSystem

This list is certainly not exhaustive; the reasons to do one or the other are as different as the projects you might have to decide about. However, if you at least understand the issues, you can make an informed decision.

COM Threading Models

Before we go on, it's worth spending a little time on COM's threading models, and on the implications of choosing a particular model. If you're an 'old hand' at COM, you may want simply to skim this section. However, if you're newer to COM, and have perhaps avoided threading issues so far, I'd recommend that you read on in order to clarify the context of later discussions.

A Brief History of COM Threading

The very first implementations of COM did not support multithreading. Around the time of Windows NT 3.51, multithreaded support was added to COM, but Microsoft still had to support legacy, thread-oblivious implementations in a way that would allow them to inter-operate with newer designs. In order to do that, several **threading models** were outlined that allowed older designs to carry on in isolation and safety, while allowing newer designs to take advantage of the new threading concepts.

The different threading models provide different degrees of thread safety to COM components by creating a unit of isolation known as an **apartment**. There are two types of apartments in COM: the **single-threaded apartment** (**STA**), and the **multithreaded apartment** (**MTA**). Again, the goal of having these different levels was so that old components could carry on in their ignorance while others, at the cost of greater complexity, could reap the performance benefits of allowing multiple threads to access them at one time.

Single-Threaded Apartment Model

In order to ensure thread safety in the single-threaded apartment model, COM relies on message queues to serialize method calls. When an object gets an incoming method call, COM posts a message to the message queue for the apartment. Therefore, any component using the STA model must contain a message loop, like you're used to writing for any standard Win32 application with a user interface. However, this does *not* mean that the component has to create a window or have a user interface; COM takes care of most of the dirty work itself when you initialize it and specify the apartment model (with a call to `CoInitializeEx()`).

For every STA, COM creates a message queue that is then used to receive the messages – you just have to make sure that the thread has a message loop to dispatch them. COM itself implements the window procedure that then takes care of calling the requested method. Only one message (method call) gets dispatched at a time. This model ensures that only one method call will execute on the object at any given time, and that the object does not need to provide synchronization or class member variable protection inside its methods.

The defining characteristic of the STA model, then, is that all calls to an object are executed on the thread that created it. Only one thread will *ever* execute the object's methods. Legacy (thread-oblivious) components are termed **single-threaded**, meaning that COM objects can only be instantiated on a single thread in the process they run in. In other words, there is only *one* STA in the process, and for legacy components, this STA must live on the process's main thread. This STA is called the **main STA**. You can think of a single-threaded COM process as having one and only one STA.

When COM became more refined, a single process was allowed to contain more than one STA. This has improved performance considerably, because it's now possible for more than one thread to instantiate and make method calls on COM objects at a time.

It is important to clarify that more than one object can live in a single apartment. The restriction is that the *same* object cannot be owned by more than one apartment. No other threads can enter an STA or use its objects without taking special steps. Another important thing to note is that if an object has thread affinity (if, for example, it uses thread-local storage), it should use the STA model. This ensures that all calls to the object are made on the same thread.

Declaring the Threading Model

To declare the type of apartment you want to use, you specify it in the call to `CoInitializeEx()`, shown below. You must make a call to `CoInitializeEx()` on each thread that uses COM.

```
HRESULT CoInitializeEx(void* pvReserved, DWORD dwCoInit);
```

The first argument in calls to this function is always `NULL`; to specify that the thread should use the STA model, use the flag `COINIT_APARTMENTTHREADED` as the second argument. This is also the default model if you use the older `CoInitialize(NULL)` method of initializing COM. To declare that the thread should support the MTA model, use the flag `COINIT_MULTITHREADED`.

> **Note that a thread cannot change its threading model until it calls `CoUninitialize()` once for each time it has called `CoInitialize(Ex)()`.**

Multithreaded Apartment Model

The MTA model is significantly different from the STA model. First of all, there is only one MTA per process, unlike the STA model, in which there's a separate apartment for each thread that uses COM. So, when the first thread calls `CoInitializeEx()` with the `COINIT_MULTITHREADED` flag, COM creates the MTA. Any subsequent calls to `CoInitializeEx()` (with the `COINIT_MULTITHREADED` flag) by other threads will simply cause them to join the existing MTA.

COM does not use messages to serialize method calls on objects in the MTA, because it just isn't interested – by choosing an MTA, you have implicitly agreed to deal with serialization yourself. Calls are made directly through the vtable (or via the proxy), not through the posting of window messages. By using the MTA model, you are guaranteeing that you will handle synchronization of class member data. You are also guaranteeing that the objects inside do not have thread affinity.

All calls to objects running in an MTA run on a pool of RPC threads allocated by COM and owned by the process that contains the MTA. COM manages the lifetimes of these threads – they are created, pooled, reused, and destroyed at the whim of COM during the life of the process. A call to any object created in the MTA can come in on *any* random RPC thread. Multiple clients can simultaneously execute methods on an object (indeed, on multiple objects) from different threads, and those threads are not guaranteed to be the ones the object was created on.

The upside of all this is that the MTA model usually has better performance than the STA model. Calls are not serialized through a message queue, so more than one method call at a time can be handled by objects running in the apartment. The downside is that it is up to you, the developer of the object, to ensure proper serialization by using critical sections, mutexes, events, or whatever, to protect class member data or any other shared memory from simultaneous access. It is also incumbent on you that your objects do not have thread affinity.

In-process Components

So far, I've been talking about an executable's ability to define what threading model it uses, but what happens when an executable wants to use an in-process COM component? An in-process component is loaded into the process space of its caller, and therefore doesn't call `CoInitializeEx()` directly – it relies on the caller to do so. Presumably, though, an in-process component is built to support a particular model – that is, it either protects its member data and has no behavior that demands thread affinity (MTA), or else it relies on COM to serialize access to it (STA).

To solve this apparent problem, an in-process component class nominates which model it supports by setting the `ThreadingModel` value in the `HKEY_CLASSES_ROOT\CLSID\{GUID}\InprocServer32` path in the registry. There are four possible settings for this value, listed in the table below:

ThreadingModel Setting	Meaning
`Apartment`	Use me in an STA
`Free`	Use me in an MTA
`Both`	I support either STAs or MTAs
No setting (or `Single`)	I am thread-oblivious. Use me only in the process's main STA

Notice here that the value to be set uses older, less accurate descriptions for STA and MTA, known as **apartment threading** and **free threading** respectively. Incidentally, different COM classes in the same component (DLL) can support different threading models. The threading model has nothing to do with how the DLL is loaded into memory, only with how it is handled by COM.

Inter-apartment Communication

Up until now, I've been talking as if threading models are 'pure' – as if a process only has one model or the other at any time. As so often, though, it is less simple than that: COM clients and servers can have both types of apartment at the same time. In situations where both models are present, it is important to understand the ramifications.

For a particular object, what are the consequences of being 'in an apartment'? If an instance of a COM object is created inside an apartment, then the object cannot be used *outside* that apartment without special steps. An object (or, more accurately, its interface pointer) is locked into the apartment in which it was created. This is because COM needs to ensure serialization of access to STA apartments; if COM allowed raw interface pointers to be used by other threads, that serialization mechanism would be broken. When using STAs, if you try to use a raw interface pointer on a different thread from the one on which it was created, you'll probably receive an `HRESULT` return value of `RPC_E_WRONG_THREAD` from the method call.

Any time you want to use an interface pointer to an object that was created in one apartment from another apartment, the interface pointer must be marshaled. The COM way to do this is for the 'owning' apartment to call `CoMarshalInterthreadInterfaceInStream()` to marshal up the interface pointer into a stream object. The `IStream` pointer is then passed (in a variable or a function parameter) to the apartment that wants to use the object. The 'using' apartment then calls `CoGetInterfaceAndReleaseStream()` to unmarshal the interface pointer from the stream, and obtain the apartment-relative pointer. Stubs for these two functions are shown below:

```
HRESULT CoMarshalInterThreadInterfaceInStream(
                REFIID    riid, // IID of interface to be marshaled
                LPUNKNOWN pUnk, // Pointer to interface to be marshaled
                LPSTREAM* ppStm // Receives the stream pointer
);
```

```
HRESULT CoGetInterfaceAndReleaseStream(
 LPSTREAM pStm, // Pointer to stream from which object is to be marshaled
 REFIID   riid, // Reference to the identifier of the interface
 LPVOID*  ppv   // Address of output variable that receives interface pointer
);
```

The following code snippet demonstrates possible usage of these functions:

```
// Marshaling an interface pointer across apartments
void CreateObjectAndCreateStream()
{
   // ...

   IAnyInterface* pAnyI;
   CoCreateInstance(CLSID_AnyClass, NULL, CLSCTX_LOCAL_SERVER,
                                   IID_IAnyInterface, (void**)&pAnyI);
```

```
    IStream* pStm;
    CoMarshalInterThreadInterfaceInStream(IID_IAnyInterface, pAnyI, &pStm);

    // Create thread with another apartment
    DWORD tid;
    HANDLE hThread = CreateThread(NULL, 0, TFunc, pStm, 0, &tid);

    // Do work
    // ...

    WaitForSingleObject(hThread, INFINITE);
    CloseHandle(hThread);

    pAnyI->Release();
}

// Second STA
DWORD TFunc(LPVOID lpParameter)
{
    CoInitializeEx(NULL, COINIT_APARTMENTTHREADED);

    // Get stream pointer from lpParameter and do other work
    IAnyInterface* pAnyI;

    // Stream pointer is released here
    CoGetInterfaceAndReleaseStream(pStm, IID_IAnyInterface, (void**)&pAnyI);

    // Use the object
    // ...

    pAnyI->Release();
    CoUninitialize();

    return 0;
}
```

If you're an old hand at COM, you'll know that marshaling means using a proxy and stub. Yes, it's true: a proxy and stub will be needed even if you're just going to pass interface pointers around between apartments. This is why it's important to build a proxy and stub even for in-process components. However, because inter-apartment marshaling is much slower than direct access, you'll want to try to minimize it in your design as much as possible.

MTAs are a little different. You know that there is only one MTA per process, and that within that apartment, any thread can access any object. Since objects in an MTA are inherently thread-safe, any thread that lives in the MTA can use the interface pointer of an object in the MTA without marshaling. Direct (vtable) access to any object is available to any thread that joins the MTA.

Again, just to emphasize the point, directly accessing an object that was created in an STA from an MTA thread is *not* legal, and nor is directly accessing an MTA object from an STA. The following table summarizes the rules the govern marshaling between apartments; any time the pointer has to cross an apartment boundary, marshaling will be necessary:

Apartment Type	Access
MTA to other threads in the same MTA	Direct
MTA to STA	Marshaled
STA to another STA	Marshaled
STA to MTA	Marshaled

Supporting STAs and MTAs

It's clear from the above discussion that components that must perform inter-apartment marshaling incur considerable additional overhead. Consider, for example, the following scenario: an STA client apartment wants to instantiate an in-process class that's marked as `Free` (MTA). At first glance, it might seem that everything is OK – an STA can just treat the MTA class as though it were STA and create the instance in 'its' apartment, thus eliminating the overhead of inter-apartment marshaling, right? Even though the client may not take advantage of the class's fancy multithreading features, it can at least use it as if it were STA.

Unfortunately, that's not right. The component class may be thread-safe, but COM needs to protect the *client* from errant multithreaded behavior. Specifically, COM needs to make sure that, in callback situations, the object does not call back to the client on a random, unknown thread. The only way to arrange this is for COM to instantiate the object into an MTA that talks to the client STA via a proxy. COM does this behind the scenes by taking the liberty of spawning a new thread, calling `CoInitializeEx()` to create an MTA (or join an existing one), and then instantiating the object into the MTA. There you go: marshaling again!

However, there is a way around this problem. You can write your component to support both the STA *and* MTA models. The way to do this is:

- Guarantee that it is thread-safe by making it suitable to be used in an MTA: protect members, don't require thread affinity, etc.
- Guarantee that you will *only* call the client back on the thread from which you were originally handed the interface pointer to the callback object.

Such an in-process component is able to declare `ThreadingModel=Both` in the registry. This means that a client that calls the component from an STA instantiates it into the STA, while a client that calls it from an MTA instantiates it into an MTA. Marshaling is thereby avoided.

The Free-threaded Marshaler

Creating a component that supports both threading models still doesn't prevent the client from having to marshal between two *different* apartments in the same process, as I described earlier. However, an object that uses the **free-threaded marshaler** (**FTM**) allows threads in different apartments (but in the same process) to access it without using a proxy.

The FTM is implemented by the COM library, and can be accessed via a call to `CoCreateFreeThreadedMarshaler()`. However, the FTM is not a 'stand-alone' entity; the intention is for it to be aggregated with an object. The FTM works by providing a custom implementation of `IMarshal` that's able to tell when interface pointers are being marshaled between apartments in the same process. When that happens, it simply forwards the *actual* interface pointer on in the marshaling stream, instead of using a proxy.

> *For more information about the free-threaded marshaler, have a look at* Professional ATL COM Programming *by Dr Richard Grimes (Wrox Press, ISBN 1-861001-40-1).*

Mixing the Models

At this juncture, it is probably appropriate to recap the implications of mixing different component apartment types with different client apartment models. First, let's look at an *in-process* component, since it entails the greater complexity. The matrix below summarizes the implications of combining the different models; the apartment models are across the top, while the component types are down the side:

	Main STA	**Other STA**	**MTA**
Apartment	Direct. Created in main STA.	Direct. Created in calling STA.	Proxy. Object will be instantiated in a COM-created STA.
Free	Proxy. Object created in the MTA, created by COM if necessary.	Proxy. Object created in the MTA, created by COM if necessary.	Direct. Created in MTA.
Both	Direct. Created in main STA.	Direct. Created in calling STA.	Direct. Created in MTA.
None	Direct. Created in main STA.	Proxy. Object will be instantiated in the main STA.	Proxy. Object will be instantiated in the main STA, created by COM if necessary.

The point hardly needs laboring; the basic gist here is that when possible, you should avoid mixing models where access is by proxy rather than direct.

Out-of-process (Local and Remote) Servers

Out-of-process components are rather different conceptually, and in some ways they are easier to understand because there isn't the same complexity of interactions that in-process components can have.

In situations where the component is out-of-process, both the client and the server have a threading model that is declared independently of the other's. The client calls `CoInitializeEx()` on the thread that's calling the component, while the server (EXE) calls `CoInitializeEx()` on the thread where the object it is exposing is instantiated. The communication between them takes place using DCOM and standard RPC marshaling with a proxy-stub. Since the component is out of process anyway, marshaling is mandatory. There is no extra penalty for mixing your apartment models.

The first client that requests the creation of a component in the out-of-process server causes the COM SCM to load the EXE server in which the component is housed. The server creates and registers the class objects for all of the classes it exposes, and the client can then get the object it requires. Any future requests for the object from other clients cause COM to return the already-running server and use the class objects that it has already registered. In the case of STA servers, calls to methods in objects created by the class object will be made on the same thread that originally caused the objects to be created. In the case of MTA servers, those method calls could be on any of COM's RPC worker threads.

STA Out-of-process Servers

If multiple clients call an object running in an STA, COM synchronizes access to the object in the way that you'd expect: by posting messages to the thread's message queue. Messages from the queue are then picked up by the stub and handed off to the object. The diagram below shows an STA client calling into an object in an STA on the server:

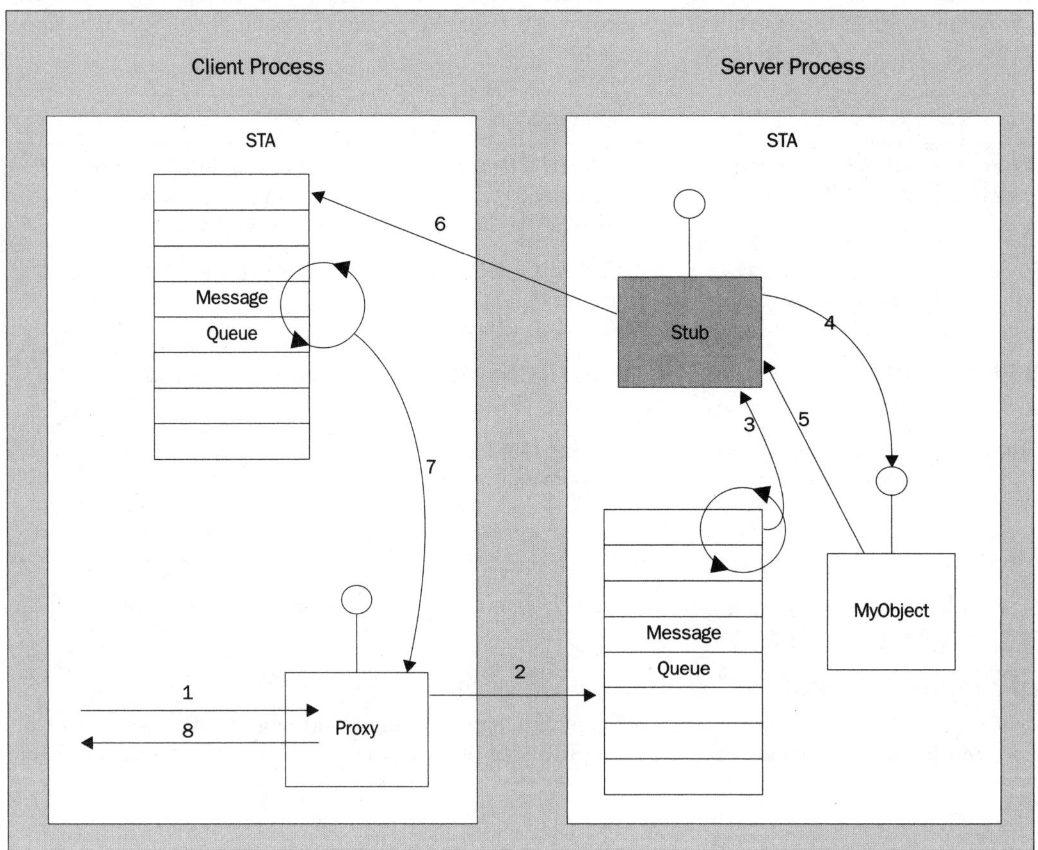

MTA Out-of-process Servers

If, on the other hand, the object is running in an MTA, then COM allows direct access to the stub and no message queue is used for synchronization. When an object hosted in an MTA receives simultaneous calls from multiple clients, a listener thread in COM picks up those calls and delegates the work of calling the stub to a random thread from a pool of RPC threads created by COM. The call can therefore come into the object on any thread; the stub simply unmarshals the request packet and calls the method on the real object. This allows COM to make much more efficient use of threads than it can in the STA mode, since access to method calls does not have to be serialized. The drawback, of course, is that both the object and its class object must implement synchronization mechanisms.

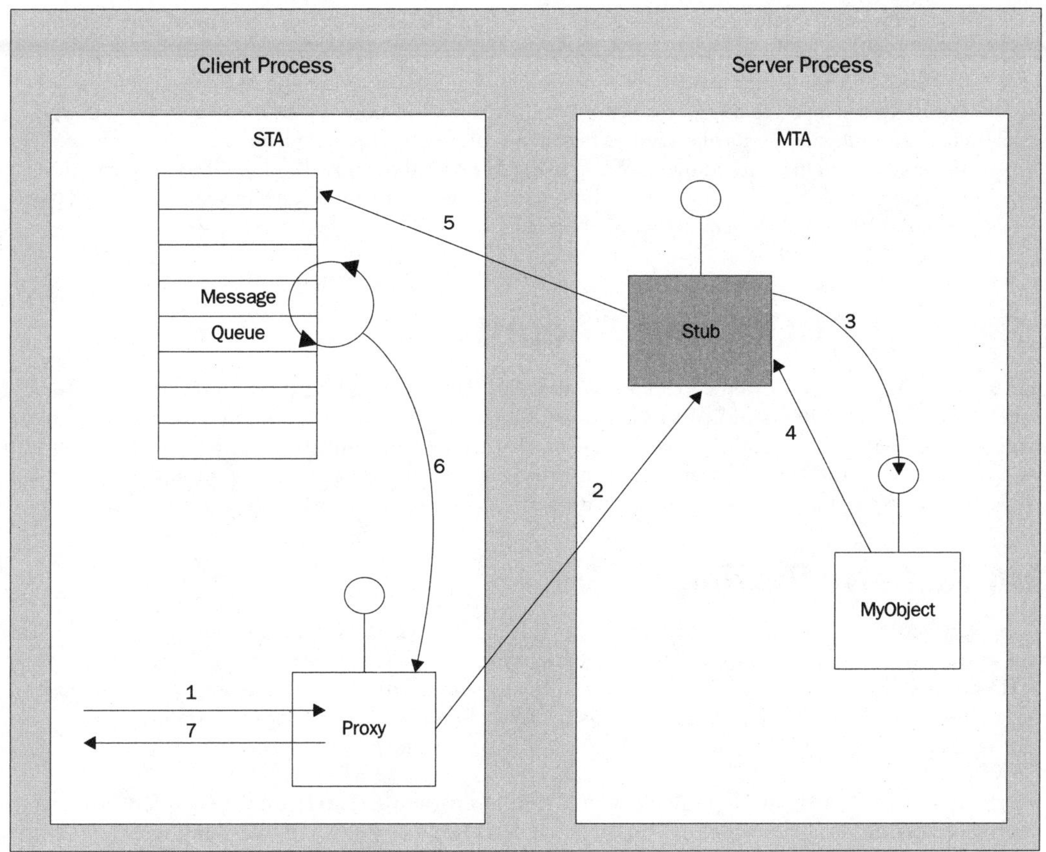

This figure does not show the RPC runtime, which sits between the two processes and dishes out threads from its own thread pool.

Implications of Threading Model on Service Design

We'll be looking at the how the differences between these models impact service design and implementation issues as we go along, but we can say a few things even at this early stage:

- The only way to have concurrent server processes using STAs is to have multiple apartments. Of course, this means that multiple threads are needed in the process, and depending on the number needed, the overhead for thread switching can be a penalty in itself. In any case, the degree of multithreading can't exceed the number of objects. We'll discuss this in greater detail later, but a general rule is to use MTA whenever possible.
- As for *using* COM objects inside a service, if you're going to use in-process components on many service threads, use the `Free` model, or choose `Both` and employ the free-threaded marshaler. Try to avoid using the `Apartment` model.
- Use the MTA model for maximum concurrency, but beware of unexpected consequences, especially when you're using one of the Win32 synchronization objects that has thread affinity, such as a mutex or a critical section. These types of objects expect to have their locks released on the same thread that locked them. When using MTAs, different method invocations come in on different threads, so it is dangerous to hold a lock between method calls. In the STA model, there is no problem holding locks across method calls.

Configuring DCOM and Security

When services expose COM objects, it's inevitable that DCOM is going to be involved – to the consumers of their objects, COM services are just COM servers. Since we know that clients of our service will be dealing with out-of-process objects that they communicate with through DCOM, let's have a quick look at the DCOM configuration settings that will be necessary to set up a service as a DCOM server. We'll also discuss some security settings and examine what they mean.

DCOM Registry Settings

The registry settings for configuring an object to run inside a COM service are pretty straightforward if you know where to look. As usual in COM, the name of the class you are exposing is shown as a ProgID in the `HKEY_CLASSES_ROOT` section of the registry. To serve as an example, I created a quick COM service called `EmptyService` using ATL, and exposed an object from it called `DoSomething`. The ProgID is therefore `EmptyService.DoSomething`.

If you look up this ProgID in the registry, you'll find almost immediately that it is a placeholder for the 'current version' ProgID, which is `EmptyService.DoSomething.1`. Looking under *that* key, you find that it points to a CLSID for the object, which is {99590E9E-FF93-11D1-9309-00104B4C822A} on my computer. Looking up the CLSID, we find a key like the one in the screenshot below:

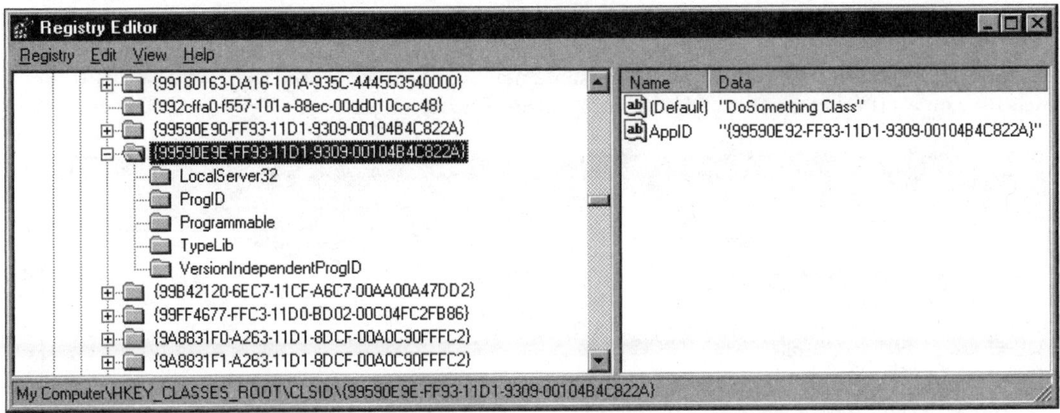

The most interesting thing here is actually the APPID (Application ID) value, which points to yet another GUID in another area of the registry. We'll return to the subject of APPIDs in just a few moments, after we've taken a quick look at the keys beneath the CLSID.

The first of these is the LocalServer32 value, which tells COM that the object being described is exposed from a local server (rather than an in-process DLL), and provides it with the path to the executable that exposes the object. However, this entry is basically ignored for objects exposed from services, since the SCM defers to the APPID key to find the service name. The other keys are simply standard settings that will be familiar to you if you've done much COM development work.

Application IDs

Now let's move on to the APPID, which is stored under the `AppID` subtree in `HKEY_CLASSES_ROOT`. Each APPID is a GUID that contains important information about the behavior of the *executable* that COM objects run in. You can think of CLSID entries as being particular to an *object*, while APPID entries are particular to an *executable process* that can house one or more objects. The APPID is where all the entries are located that are to do with the process itself, rather than its individual objects. The screenshot below depicts the APPID for the executable that houses the object we've been working with:

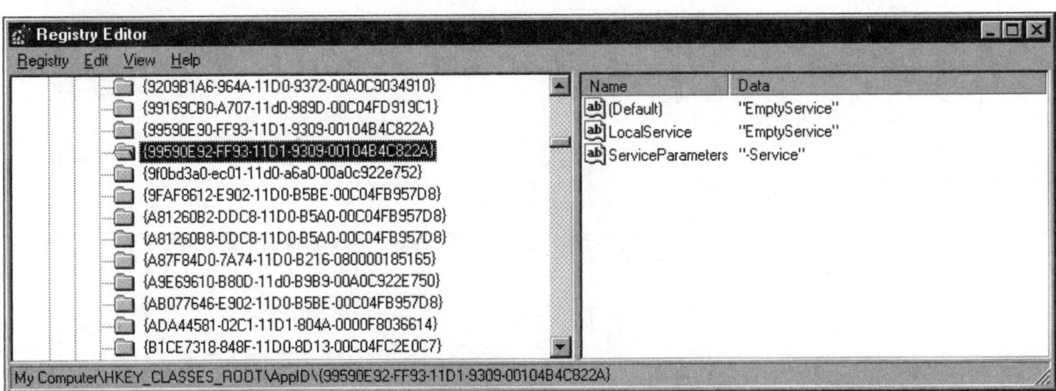

The most interesting value here is `LocalService`, which shows the name of the service that owns the code for this process. It is also the service that the COM SCM (`RPCSS.exe`) should start when a client requests an object that's housed in a stopped, demand-start service. Note that this service is a 'local service', which means that it runs on the same machine as the registry we're looking at. If the service runs on a different machine, the registry entries change slightly:

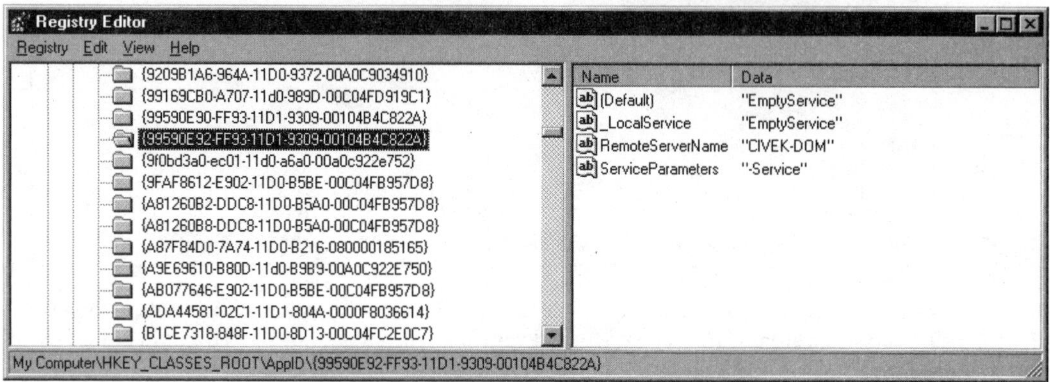

The `LocalService` entry is prefixed with an underscore so that it is no longer used (but still contains the service name), and an entry called `RemoteServerName` is inserted that contains the name of the machine on which the service is to be run. The final value in this key, `ServiceParameters`, lists any parameters that might be passed to the service in the `StartService()` call.

The DCOM Configuration Tool

Let's take a brief look at the DCOM configuration tool settings, which we can use as a departure point for discussing other security-related issues. When you first bring up the `DCOMCnfg` dialog, you are presented with a list of the available classes that are housed in executable servers. This means *any* local or remote server, or any in-process object housed in a surrogate. For practical purposes, we're talking about all classes that reference an APPID. If the object doesn't reference an APPID, it won't be in this list.

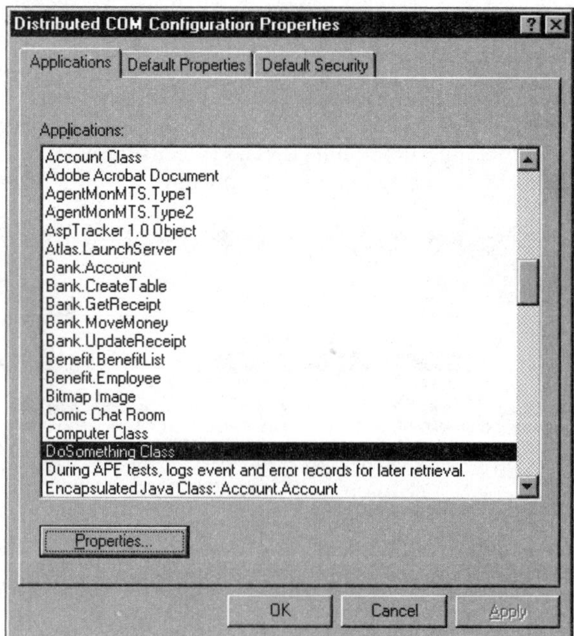

After you've selected the class you want to configure, select the Properties... button to bring up the tabbed configuration dialog for the class and its related APPID, shown below:

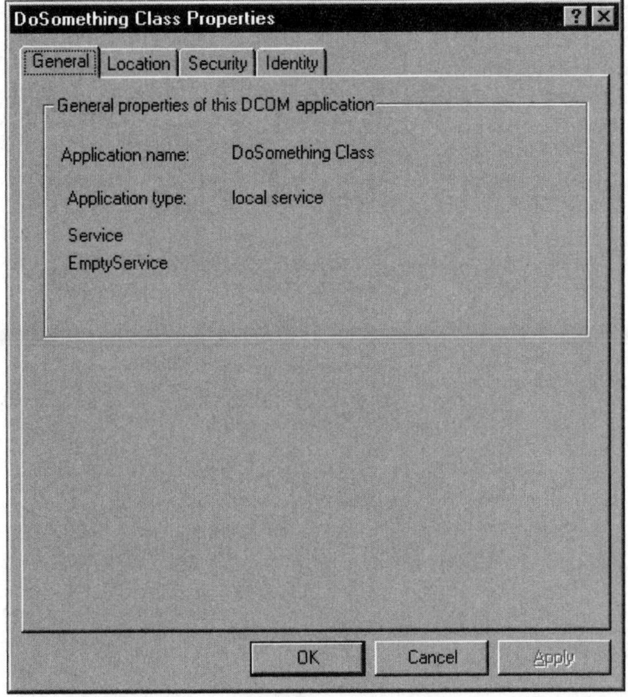

Be aware that the DCOM configuration tool will change the *display name* of your service to the name of the class you're configuring at the time you make the change to the APPID. For instance, if you make changes to the DoSomething Class **above, the display name (which was** EmptyService**) will be changed to** DoSomething Class**. This is probably not the desired effect, so be careful.**

Server Location

We discussed the location of the server executable briefly when we talked about the registry entries stored beneath the APPID, above. The Location tab on this dialog allows us to manipulate those entries.

The first checkbox, labeled Run application on the computer where the data is located, is not really relevant to services; it allows non-DCOM aware COM server applications to be activated remotely. For instance, if a client binds to an object on a remote machine using a file moniker, the actual server application that reads the file would typically get launched on the client machine. With this box checked, the server would be run on the remote machine.

The second checkbox specifies that the service should be run on the current machine, while the third box allows the service to be run on a remote machine; you can then enter the name of that remote machine in the text box below. You can set one or both of these two checkboxes – choosing them both has the useful effect of making the COM SCM look for the server on the local machine first, or launching it on the remote machine if it is unable to find it locally.

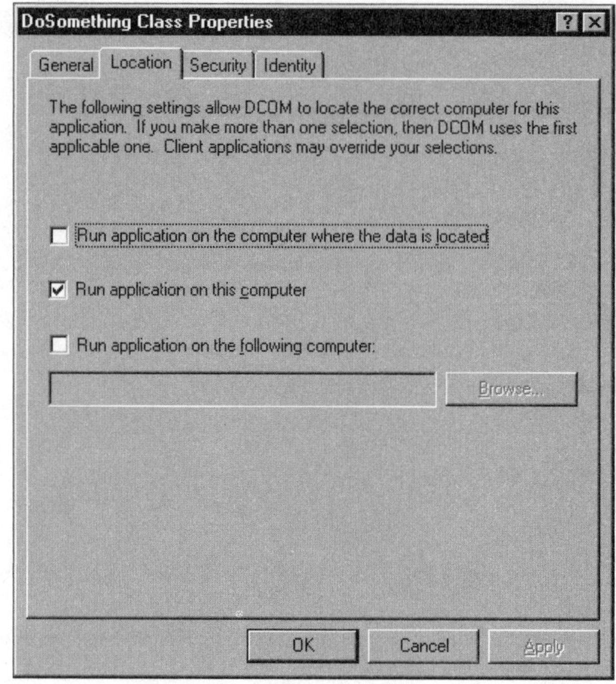

Server Identity

The Identity tab, shown below, allows you to specify the `RunAs` user name under which the DCOM server will run. For services, you can run the service either as LocalSystem, or as a particular user. Ordinary local servers are not allowed to select LocalSystem as a `RunAs` context.

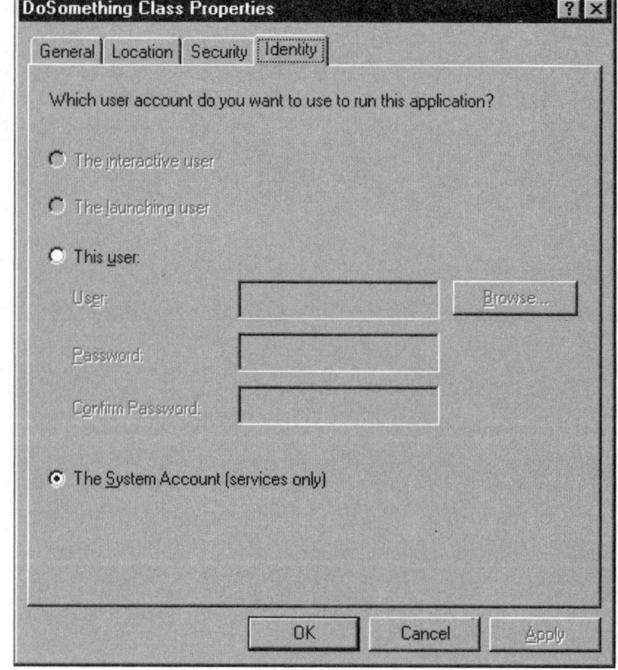

The other two options – The interactive user and The launching user – are unavailable to COM servers running as services, simply because services can't run in these modes, as we discussed in Chapter 7. As you know, services run in a different security context from regular applications. Furthermore, even though services *can* touch the interactive user's window station and desktop if they have the Allow Service to Interact with Desktop box checked, they do *not* run in the interactive user's security context. Having a service run in the context of a 'launching user' is similarly nonsensical – clearly, a service cannot rely on the security context of whoever started it first in order to do its work!

If you choose to run as a particular user instead of LocalSystem, `DCOMCnfg` places the `RunAs` key value in the registry, as shown below. The `RunAs` account password is stored in a secure area of the registry.

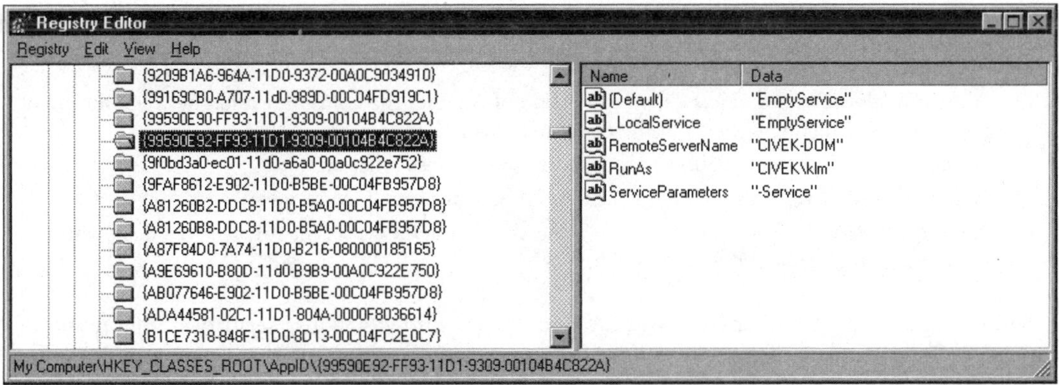

Be aware that if you set up the identity as a particular user in this dialog box, you must *also* configure the service to have that same identity. The reason for this is that, usually, DCOM has complete control over the account under which an object server will run. However, when that server is a service, there is the additional complication that a service *also* has control over the account that *it* logs on as; if the two don't match, all manner of confusion could ensue. In fact, failure to sort this out properly will result in your call to `CoRegisterClassObject()` returning `CO_E_WRONG_SERVER_IDENTITY` when you start the service. Since `CoRegisterClassObject()` is not a secure operation, COM can only trust the registry entries.

> **This is important: a service's 'log on as' name and DCOM identity *must* be the same account!**

Also remember that if a service exposes two objects, and you edit the Location or Identity information for one of them, you will be changing it for the other one as well. This, of course, is because these settings actually refer to the underlying *APPID*, not just the CLSID.

COM Security Settings

Before I discuss the remaining tab in the DCOM configuration tool (Security), I need to set up the proper framework for the discussion, so that the actions you'll take actually have meaning. We covered NT security in some detail in Chapter 7, but now that we're dealing with exposing and using COM objects, we have to take COM security into consideration as well. When things seem like they should work, but don't, and you can't understand why, security is often at the root of the problem. COM is no exception.

Security Concepts

First, let's get the terminology under our belts. When people talk about COM security, they mean one of two (or three) things: **activation security** and **call security**, the latter of which can be further broken down into **authentication** and **authorization**.

- **Authentication.** Poses and answers the question of whether the communication between the client and server is authentic – that is, is the client really who it says it is?
- **Authorization.** Is the client allowed to perform the requested action?
- **Activation security.** Deals with the question, "Who can start COM servers?"
- **Launch Identity.** Answers the question, "Who should the COM server run as?" We dealt with this topic when we discussed the Identity tab.

You will recognize these from Chapter 7 as the same issues with which any security system must grapple, with the exception of activation. This is a fundamentally different idea that's important to DCOM because, when code is allowed to run on remote machines, someone has to launch it, and exactly who can do that is an important security consideration. Authentication is layered on top of secure RPC, while authorization is handled by assigning a DACL to the object and doing an access check using a mechanism very similar to the way that NT would check access on any secure system object.

Authentication, Authorization, and Activation

First of all, let's look at security configurations from a simple perspective by examining what can be done from the registry, and from the DCOM configuration tool.

Activation Security

Activation security, which controls who is able to start a COM server, can be configured most easily from the Security tab in the DCOM configuration tool, as shown in the screenshot below. Under the topic of **launch permissions**, the dialog allows you either to select the system-wide, default values or to configure custom activation security for each APPID. If you choose the system-wide defaults, you get the values stored in the registry key `HKEY_LOCAL_MACHINE\SOFTWARE\Microsoft\Ole\DefaultLaunchPermission`.

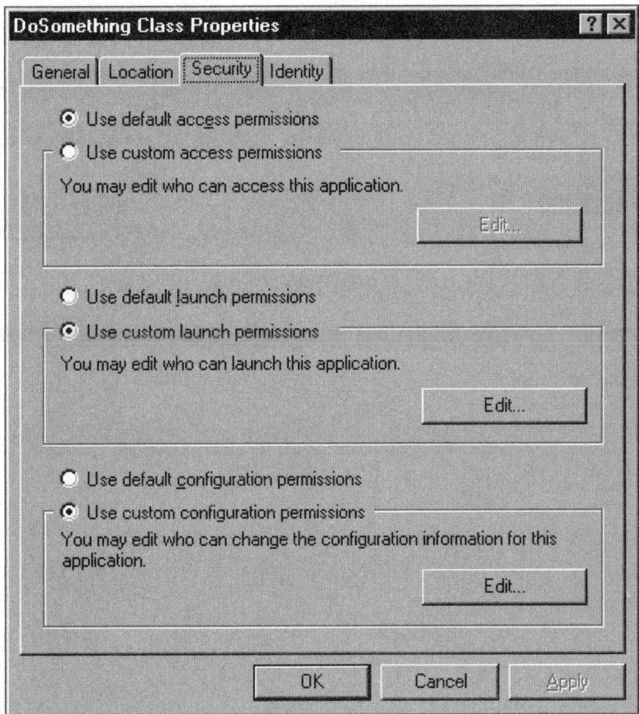

If you choose to Use custom launch permissions, you can click on the Edit... button to bring up the following dialog, which is much like any dialog that allows you to edit access control lists. It allows you to add or remove accounts from the DACL, and to allow or deny launch permissions for each user or group in the list. Notice that there are a couple of 'special' accounts in the list to allow web clients to launch the server; we'll discuss these in more detail later in the chapter.

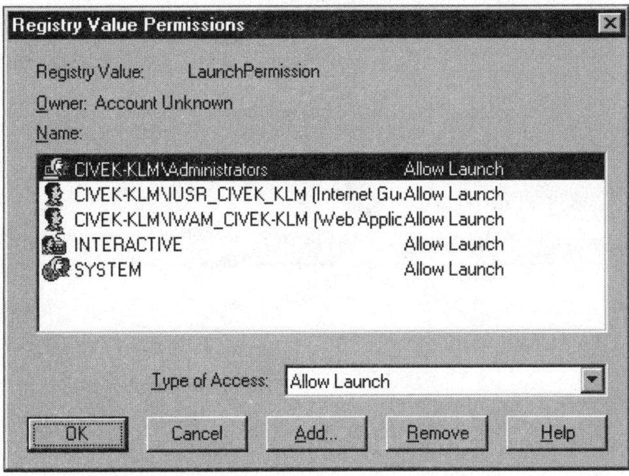

If you elect to go with custom settings, then the security information is serialized to the registry value `LaunchPermission` underneath the `AppID` key, as shown:

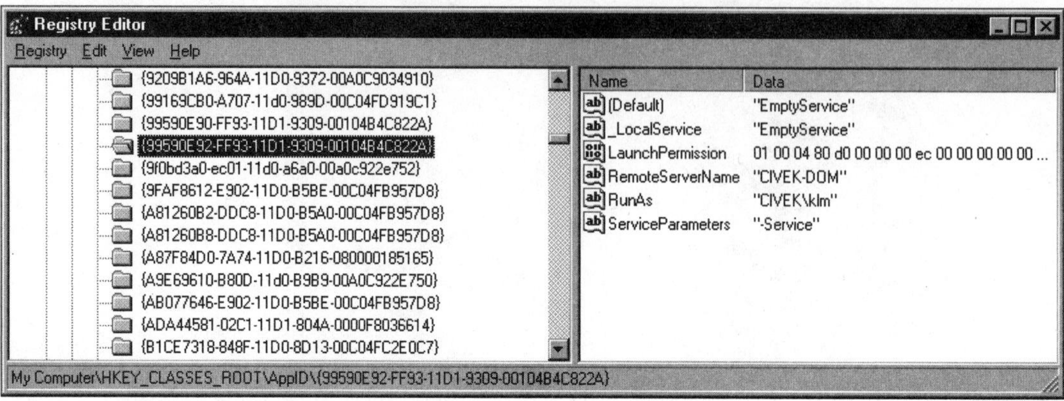

Authorization Security

Under the topic of **access permissions**, the Security tab also allows you to specify who is able to use objects in the server once it has been launched. They work just like the launch permissions, and are once again based on an ACL motif. If the objects do not have more specific permissions, the system uses default values located in
`HKEY_LOCAL_MACHINE\SOFTWARE\Microsoft\Ole\DefaultAccessPermission`.

Any custom access permissions are stored in the registry, under `AppID`, in the `AccessPermission` value that's shown below:

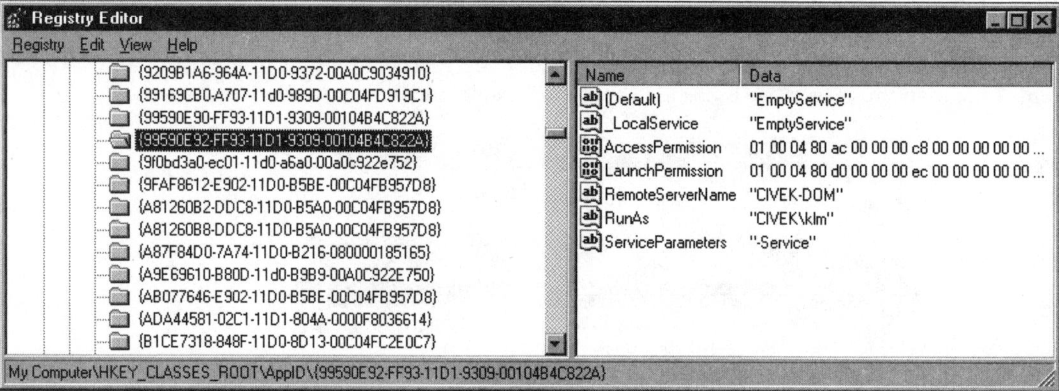

It's a good idea always to have launch permissions that are more restrictive than (or at least equally as restrictive as) access permissions. To have an account that was allowed to launch a server, but not to access it, would be more than a little strange. It is also wasteful of server resources to have a situation where the server has to launch a process only to have to close it because the caller doesn't have rights to create an object. Furthermore, security problems of this kind are difficult to debug.

Authentication Security

Authentication security deals with how servers and clients negotiate so that each party knows the other is who they say they are, and COM relies on RPC's underlying security provider to handle this negotiation. Authentication security configuration takes place on a different tab in the DCOM configuration tool: Default Properties. This is mainly because it is not possible to configure authentication security on a per-CLSID or per-APPID basis, except programmatically (as you'll soon see).

Authentication Level

There are two settings you can change here, the first of which is the Default Authentication Level. Again, this all uses RPC, so the possible values are based on RPC's security provider. The table below lists and describes the different options.

Level	Symbol	Meaning
Default	`RPC_C_AUTHN_LEVEL_DEFAULT`	Queries the authentication service (security provider) for its default authentication level.
None	`RPC_C_AUTHN_LEVEL_NONE`	No authentication
Connect	`RPC_C_AUTHN_LEVEL_CONNECT`	Authentication happens when a connection is made.
Call	`RPC_C_AUTHN_LEVEL_CALL`	Authentication occurs when the server receives a call.
Packet	`RPC_C_AUTHN_LEVEL_PKT`	Authentication occurs on a packet-by-packet basis. This is the lowest form of authentication that a connectionless protocol (such as UDP) can use.

Table Continued on Following Page

Level	Symbol	Meaning
Packet Integrity	RPC_C_AUTHN_LEVEL_PKT_INTEGRITY	Authenticates just like _PKT, but also checks that the data has not been tampered with by using a checksum.
Packet Privacy	RPC_C_AUTHN_LEVEL_PKT_PRIVACY	Authenticates and checks just like _INTEGRITY, but also encrypts the packet.

Connect level security is the legacy default; it is the highest level of authentication that *all* DCOM clients (including, and because of, DCOM for Windows 95) can use. In fact, Windows 95 can make outbound calls at any level, but it can only accept calls using the Connect level at most.

Impersonation Level

The second configurable setting is the Default Impersonation Level, which specifies how far the server is capable of going to impersonate the client. The following chart shows you the alternatives:

Level	Symbol	Meaning
Anonymous	RPC_C_IMP_LEVEL_ANONYMOUS	Clients can be anonymous. Not currently supported in DCOM.
Identify	RPC_C_IMP_LEVEL_IDENTIFY	Server can impersonate the client to check permissions, but not to access secure system objects.
Impersonate	RPC_C_IMP_LEVEL_IMPERSONATE	Server can impersonate clients and access system objects on clients' behalf.
Delegate	RPC_C_IMP_LEVEL_DELEGATE	Like impersonation, but works across remote servers as well. Not supported in NT 4.0.

You'll recall from Chapter 7 that even when the client allows the server to perform Impersonate level impersonation, the server still can't access *network* resources while impersonating that client. Delegate level impersonation would allow this, but it's not supported in NT 4.0. In the meantime, the only option for accessing remote resources under the client's principal (security context) is to have the client pass a user ID and password through to the server, and call `LogonUser()` from within the service to obtain a fully-empowered process token. (I suppose that you could also allow null sessions on the remote server, but I'd never recommend that!)

Changing settings in the dialog shown below alters the defaults for *all* the COM servers on the machine; this tool actually manipulates the `LegacyAuthenticationLevel` and `LegacyImpersonationLevel` values beneath the `HKEY_LOCAL_MACHINE\SOFTWARE\Microsoft\Ole` key. If a server or a client fails to call `CoInitializeSecurity()` explicitly, then COM intercedes and makes the call for them implicitly, using the legacy values as defaults.

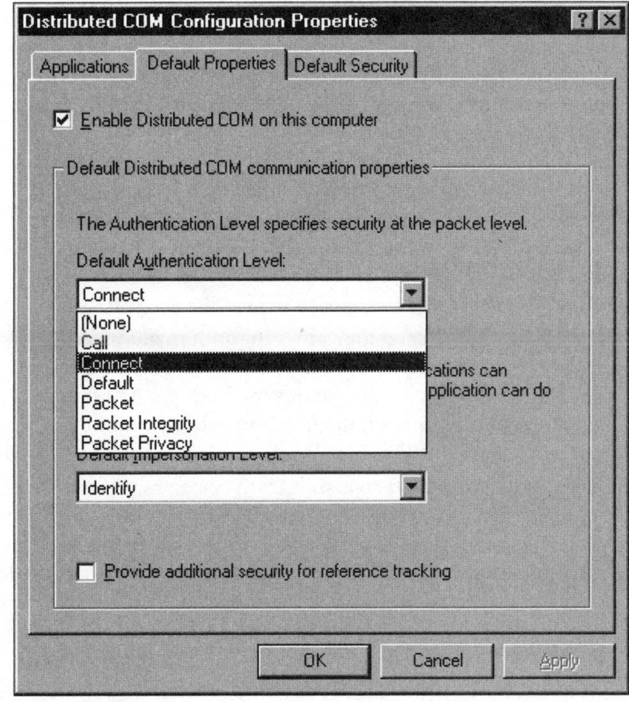

Programming COM Security

It is important to be aware that all of the settings you can configure using `DCOMCnfg` can also be made by the client and server components in code, at runtime.

CoInitializeSecurity

Without a shadow of a doubt, the real workhorse of COM security is `CoInitializeSecurity()`. This function handles the work of setting *all* the security for the process:

```
HRESULT CoInitializeSecurity(
   PSECURITY_DESCRIPTOR          pVoid,       // Points to security descriptor
   DWORD                         cAuthSvc,    // Count of entries in asAuthSvc
   SOLE_AUTHENTICATION_SERVICE* asAuthSvc,     // Array of names to register
   void*                         pReserved1,    // Reserved for future use
   DWORD dwAuthnLevel,     // The default authentication level for proxies
   DWORD dwImpLevel,       // The default impersonation level for proxies
   RPC_AUTH_IDENTITY_HANDLE      pAuthInfo,   // Reserved; must be set to NULL
   DWORD dwCapabilities, // Additional client and/or server-side capabilities
   void*                         pvReserved2    // Reserved for future use
);
```

`CoInitializeSecurity()` should be called early in the life of the process (right after calling `CoInitializeEx()`) – before *marshaling* the first interface pointer in the case of the server, and before *receiving* the first marshaled pointer in the case of the client. If the function is not called explicitly from code, COM will call it under the covers on the first occasion that an interface pointer is marshaled, using the 'legacy' settings configured using `DCOMCnfg`.

The function itself is marvelously flexible. For example, the first parameter allows you to do any of three things for configuring authorization:

- Pass a properly formatted security descriptor with the DACLs, owner, etc. already set up. If you do this, the `dwCapabilities` flag should be set to `EOAC_NONE`. If you use this method, be sure to set up the owner and group SIDs in the security descriptor properly.
- Instruct COM to read the values for authorization from the registry (the `AccessPermission` value) by providing the APPID for the server. In this case, `dwCapabilities` should be set to `EOAC_APPID`. If you choose this method, *all* the other parameters (besides `dwCapabilities`) will be ignored. Instead, the function will look under the `AppID` key for values for these parameters, and will use the 'legacy' values if they are not found.
- Implement your own custom `IAccessControl` interface by passing an `IAccessControl` pointer. The `dwCapabilities` flag should be set to `EOAC_ACCESS_CONTROL`. Creating your own version of this interface allows you to do absolutely anything you want to check access security on the object, like checking against your own user ID/password table in a database. You can also create an instance of the standard `IAccessControl` implementation by calling `CoCreateInstance()` on `CLSID_DCOMAccessControl` and passing in the interface pointer.

To reiterate, `CoInitializeSecurity()` sets the low-water mark for both the client and the server, and the net effect is that the higher security level 'wins'. Typically, you'll want to use **Connect** level authentication, and then beef up the security for individual proxies, as we'll discuss shortly. A call to the function might look like the sample below, which sets process security to be packet level, with impersonation, and with whatever rights are set up in the security descriptor.

```
// Using CoInitializeSecurity()
void Foo()
{
   // Build a security descriptor
   // ...

   HRESULT hr = CoInitializeSecurity(&sd,
                                     -1,
                                     NULL,
                                     NULL,
                                     RPC_C_AUTHN_LEVEL_PKT,
                                     RPC_C_IMP_LEVEL_IMPERSONATE,
                                     NULL,
                                     EOAC_NONE,
                                     NULL);

   // ...
}
```

Per-interface Security

When setting security information for the whole process isn't quite fine-grained enough, you can consider using **per-interface security**. In this regime, the proxy for each interface actually maintains its own security information for use on each call. When `CoInitializeSecurity()` is used to set process-wide security, that simply sets the *default* security for each proxy. Each interface is free to be configured with different security settings.

Client-side

On the client side, the proxy implements the `IClientSecurity` interface. There is typically no need for you to deal with this interface yourself, since all MIDL-generated proxies have it built in. The interface has three methods – `QueryBlanket()`, `SetBlanket()`, and `CopyProxy()` – that can be used respectively to view, modify, or copy security settings for an individual interface pointer to an out-of-process object. You can get a pointer to the `IClientSecurity` interface for an object simply by calling `QueryInterface()` and asking for one.

A common reason for needing to adjust security on an interface is to increase it to a level that is higher than that set for the process as a whole (in fact, you can only ever *increase* security, never decrease it). For example, you might want to increase the security on an interface with a method that accepts credit card information over the wire to `RPC_C_AUTHN_LEVEL_PKT_PRIVACY`, so that it is encrypted. You can do so using `IClientSecurity`.

Among other things, the `SetBlanket()` method takes a pointer to a `COAUTHINFO` structure, which basically allows you to specify the common security settings you already know about, including the authentication and impersonation levels for the interface.

There are three COM API functions that wrap calls to the methods of `IClientSecurity`, making them a little bit easier to use:

- `CoQueryProxyBlanket()` – equivalent of obtaining the interface, calling `QueryBlanket()`, and releasing
- `CoSetProxyBlanket()` – equivalent of obtaining the interface, calling `SetBlanket()`, and releasing
- `CoCopyProxy()` – equivalent of obtaining the interface, calling `CopyProxy()`, and releasing

To take customization even further, you can write your own custom marshaler and your own implementation of `IClientSecurity` to do whatever you like.

Server-side

The server-side counterpart of `IClientSecurity` is named `IServerSecurity`. The stub on the server side of the RPC connection implements this interface. In addition to (or instead of) manipulating interface security on the proxy side, you can also gather information about the incoming call's security settings and take special actions. For instance, if a client calls the `IBuy::SendCreditCardNo()` method, first boosting the authentication level to the maximum, then the server can read the incoming security level, check it, and allow the incoming call.

The `IServerSecurity` interface has several methods:

Function	Description
`QueryBlanket()`	Obtains the authentication information about the incoming client call
`ImpersonateClient()`	Impersonates the credentials of the incoming client
`RevertToSelf()`	Returns the server to its normal security context
`IsImpersonating()`	Returns whether the server is currently impersonating a client

The server can obtain a pointer to the `IServerSecurity` interface by calling the COM API function `CoGetCallContext()` *while inside a method invoked by a client.* Outside this context, the call has no meaning. Once it has a pointer, the server can then party on one of the methods listed above. Alternatively (and again, while inside a method invoked by a client), the server can call `CoQueryClientBlanket()`, `CoImpersonateClient()`, or `CoRevertToSelf()`, which are wrapper functions that get the interface pointer, call the method, and release the pointer all at once.

Impersonation

You should be pretty familiar with the idea of impersonation from the material in Chapter 7, but there are a few things that bear repeating. First, the server can only impersonate to the degree that the client allows it. If the client only permits `RPC_C_IMP_LEVEL_IDENTIFY` impersonation, the server can only impersonate for the purpose of checking permissions, using an API function such as `AccessCheck()`. If the client allows `IMPERSONATE` rights, then the server can access system objects and local resources, but nothing from the network. In NT 5.0, when `DELEGATE` level impersonation is supported, a server will (if allowed) be able impersonate a client's credentials even when making calls off the local machine.

By the way, in the apartment model, impersonation is *nested.* This means that if a thread is impersonating and then gets interrupted by another method call, the new call begins with no impersonation token. When it is complete, COM reverts to the previous call's impersonation token.

Activation Security

We've talked about authorization and authentication security in the last couple of sections, so now we need to talk about the final piece of the puzzle. Activation security can also be handled programmatically, at least in the sense that, when a client instantiates an object, the client can specify who it wants to be known as for the purposes of activation. This way, a client can use a different security context to call the server than the one the client itself is in. It works almost like a built-in `LogonUser()` call before calling out to the server. Of course, activation security for the object implementer (server) cannot be set programmatically, because its security settings have to be examined by the COM SCM before it is even loaded – that information is stored in the registry settings for the server.

The *way* that a client can specify which user it wants to launch the server as, is to populate the `COSERVERINFO` structure that gets passed to the COM instantiation functions: `CoCreateInstanceEx()`, `CoGetClassObject()`, `CoGetInstanceFromFile()`, and `CoGetInstanceFromIStorage()`. The place to specify the 'launch as' identity is buried three levels deep: in addition to allowing you to specify the name of the remote server on which you wish to instantiate the object, `COSERVERINFO` contains a pointer to a `COAUTHINFO` structure. That structure contains a pointer to a `COAUTHIDENTITY` structure, and by changing the information in this structure, you can specify which user you want to run the server as.

```
typedef struct _COAUTHIDENTITY
{
   USHORT __RPC_FAR* User;
   ULONG             UserLength;
   USHORT __RPC_FAR* Domain;
   ULONG             DomainLength;
   USHORT __RPC_FAR* Password;
   ULONG             PasswordLength;
   ULONG             Flags;
} COAUTHIDENTITY;
```

Now that you have a better understanding of some of the subtleties of COM security, let's move on to talk about how to use a service to house COM objects.

Exposing COM Objects from a Service

When you write a COM service, you're really only writing a server process that hosts COM objects, just like any standard EXE server would; the difference is that the EXE has special needs in the area of lifetime management and security. By now, you should have a fairly good handle on what those security requirements are. In this section, I'll discuss how to create and use executable COM components, particularly focusing on the needs that services have. After that, we'll look at the special needs of certain *consumers* of COM objects running in a service.

The COM EXE Server

Creating an executable server is a little bit different from creating a COM DLL, because a COM EXE has to deal with its own lifetime management. It also needs to make sure that it exposes a proxy-stub, as well as doing a few other things. Typically, a COM server that resides in an executable file works like this:

- The executable starts up in a `main()` function
- The apartment is initialized
- The class object(s) are created
- The class object(s) are registered
- Some mechanism is implemented whereby the process stays alive while waiting for the object to finish its work – a kernel event or message loop, for example
- The class object(s) are revoked and `Release()` is called on them
- The apartment is uninitialized
- Exit

Now let's take a look at what this might look like in the barest minimum of code samples:

```
// Building an EXE server - STA
int main()
{
   CoInitializeEx(NULL, COINIT_APARTMENTTHREADED);

   // Register class factory
   IClassFactory* pCF = new CCFactory;

   DWORD dwReg;
   CoRegisterClassObject(CLSID_MyCOM,
                         pCF,
                         CLSCTX_LOCAL_SERVER,
                         REGCLS_MULTIPLEUSE,
                         &dwReg);

   // Wait for quit message
   MSG msg;
   while(GetMessage(&msg, 0, 0, 0) > 0)
      DispatchMessage(&msg);

   CoRevokeClassObject(dwReg);
   pCF->Release();

   CoUninitialize();
   return 0;
}
```

The code example above demonstrates how an *apartment-threaded* server might handle lifetime management. Typically, an apartment-threaded server will use the message loop (which it needs anyway) to process the signal that it is time for it to quit. Servers usually call `PostQuitMessage()` from the server lock-counting function to send their own message loops a quit message, which of course causes the `GetMessage()` loop to end.

The following code sample, on the other hand, shows how a naïve implementation of lifetime management in an MTA server might look. Notice that since there doesn't need to be a message loop in an MTA local server, other mechanisms should be used for synchronization. A handy one to use is a kernel event; when the event gets set, `main()` falls through and terminates.

```
// Building an EXE server - MTA
int main()
{
   CoInitializeEx(NULL, COINIT_MULTITHREADED);

   // Register class factory
   IClassFactory* pCF = new CCFactory;
```

```
    DWORD dwReg;
    CoRegisterClassObject(CLSID_MyCOM,
                          pCF,
                          CLSCTX_LOCAL_SERVER,
                          REGCLS_MULTIPLEUSE,
                          &dwReg);

    // Wait for a signal to quit
    g_hEvent = CreateEvent(NULL, TRUE, FALSE, NULL);

    //Thread waits here for objects to die
    WaitForSingleObject(g_hEvent, INFINITE);

    CoRevokeClassObject(dwReg);
    pCF->Release();

    CoUninitialize();
    return 0;
}
```

At this point, you may be asking, "Where do I set the event or send the message from to tell the main thread that I am ready to shut down?" Usually, you maintain a module locking/unlocking mechanism that gets operated when objects call `AddRef()` and `Release()`, but the precise details of how this should be done are the subject of some discussion and debate in the COM community. We're going to discuss it in a bit more detail very shortly, in the section entitled *Race Conditions in Server Lifetime.*

CoRegisterClassObject

First, though, let's take a look at `CoRegisterClassObject()`. This function takes on the burden of registering the server's class object with the COM SCM, so clients who want to create the objects that the class object produces can do so. The stub for this function is shown below:

```
STDAPI CoRegisterClassObject(
          REFCLSID  rclsid,      // Class identifier (CLSID) to be registered
          IUnknown* pUnk,          // Pointer to the class object
          DWORD     dwClsContext, // Context for running executable code
          DWORD     flags,         // How to connect to the class object
          LPDWORD   lpdwRegister  // Pointer to the value returned
);
```

Each call to `CoRegisterClassObject()` registers a single class object, identified by the CLSID that's passed in the first parameter. The second parameter takes a pointer to the class object for that CLSID. The last parameter gets filled with a registration identifier to be passed to a later call to `CoRevokeClassObject()` when the server wants to revoke registration.

Class Context

The third and fourth parameters are the most interesting for our discussion. dwClsContext specifies from where the class object will be visible to the client. It has several possible values, defined by the following enumeration:

```
typedef enum tagCLSCTX
{
   CLSCTX_INPROC_SERVER  =  1,
   CLSCTX_INPROC_HANDLER =  2,
   CLSCTX_LOCAL_SERVER   =  4,
   CLSCTX_REMOTE_SERVER  = 16
} CLSCTX;
```

Class Context Flag	Meaning
CLSCTX_INPROC_SERVER	The class object is run in-process with the client.
CLSCTX_INPROC_HANDLER	The class object is an in-process handler, which is a DLL that runs in the client process and implements structures of the registered class when instances of it are accessed remotely.
CLSCTX_LOCAL_SERVER	The class object is run out-of-process on the same machine.
CLSCTX_REMOTE_SERVER	The class object is run out-of-process on a remote machine.

These values can be combined in a bitmask. For a local server (or service) that's exposing objects, the first flag doesn't make much sense *except* in cases where a server is actually creating instances of its own exported object classes; this flag is used for in-process components only. The important flags are CLSCTX_LOCAL_SERVER and CLSCTX_REMOTE_SERVER. By combining them, you can make sure that the object can be created either from a server running on the current machine, or from one on a different machine.

Connection Method

The fourth parameter specifies the way in which clients are allowed to connect to the class object. This parameter accepts values from the REGCLS enumeration, the possible values of which are:

Connection Method Flag	Meaning
REGCLS_SINGLEUSE	A legacy setting that allows only one client at a time to access the class object. Additional requests will cause COM to load a new instance of the server.
REGCLS_MULTIPLEUSE	Enables multiple clients to connect to a single instance of the class object. Also allows servers to access their own class objects from inside the process.

Connection Method Flag	Meaning
REGCLS_MULTI_SEPARATE	Allows the object to register different class objects for in-process clients and out-of-process clients.
REGCLS_SUSPENDED	Allows the object to be registered in a suspended state, to be awakened later by a call to `CoResumeClassObjects()`. Any of the first three parameters can be ORed with the `SUSPENDED` flag to suspend registration.
REGCLS_SURROGATE	The class object is a surrogate process used to run DLL servers out of process.

Interactions between the connection method and the class context can be complex; the following chart, borrowed from the Win32 API documentation, shows the combinations that we're interested in.

	REGCLS_SINGLEUSE	REGCLS_MULTIPLEUSE	REGCLS_MULTI_SEPARATE
CLSCTX_INPROC_SERVER	Error	In-process	In-process
CLSCTX_LOCAL_SERVER	Local	In-process/Local	Local
Both of the above	Error	In-process/Local	In-process/Local

`REGCLS_MULTIPLEUSE` (or `REGCLS_MULTI_SEPARATE`) is really your only choice for services. If you choose `REGCLS_SINGLEUSE`, only one client can access the class object at a time, and additional requests will cause COM to load another instance of the executable server. That just isn't possible for a service, and things will start to go wrong very quickly.

Race Conditions in Registering Class Objects

Everything sounds OK so far, but in fact there's a problem. In an MTA server, the first call to `CoRegisterClassObject()` enables incoming activation requests to start immediately. So, in situations where there is more than one class object to register, it is possible for the server to register a class object, take a request, and begin shutting down *before* the final class object is registered.

To handle such conditions, you should create your class objects with the `REGCLS_SUSPENDED` flag so that they are created *without* telling the COM SCM. Once all the class objects have been registered, you can then call `CoResumeClassObjects()` to enable all the class objects to be used. This function is atomic. The following snippet shows the process:

```
// Proper way to register more than one class object - MTA
int main()
{
   CoInitializeEx(NULL, COINIT_MULTITHREADED);

   // Register class factory
   IClassFactory* pCF1 = new CCFactory1;
   IClassFactory* pCF2 = new CCFactory2;

   DWORD dwReg[2];
   CoRegisterClassObject(CLSID_MyCOM_One, pCF1, CLSCTX_LOCAL_SERVER,
                              REGCLS_MULTIPLEUSE | REGCLS_SUSPENDED, &dwReg[0]);
   CoRegisterClassObject(CLSID_MyCOM_Two, pCF2, CLSCTX_LOCAL_SERVER,
                              REGCLS_MULTIPLEUSE | REGCLS_SUSPENDED, &dwReg[1]);

   // Notify the SCM that objects can be used
   CoResumeClassObjects();

   g_hEvent = CreateEvent(NULL, TRUE, FALSE, NULL);
   WaitForSingleObject(g_hEvent, INFINITE);

   for(int i = 0 ; i < 2 ; i++)
      CoRevokeClassObject(dwReg[i]);

   pCF1->Release();
   pCF2->Release();

   CoUninitialize();
   return 0;
}
```

Using the handy `CoResumeClassObjects()` function assures that the server has the time it needs to set up all of its class objects properly before having to deal with activation and shutdown requests.

Race Conditions in Server Lifetime

You may already be aware of some of the race conditions that can occur in COM servers. If a COM server has just discovered that it can shut down (because the last interface pointer on the last object has just been released), it may post a `WM_QUIT` message to the STA's message loop, or signal a kernel event that the MTA thread is waiting on. If a new activation request comes in between the time that the apartment handles the call and the time it gets round to revoking the class objects, the server will be revoking objects right under the nose of a new client.

When NT 4.0 came along, COM got a couple of new functions to help eliminate this race condition: `CoAddRefServerProcess()` and `CoReleaseServerProcess()`. These new functions were added to help out-of-process servers manage their lifetimes more effectively by implementing a module-wide lock count for the server that calls them. The functions do their magic by blocking access to the COM server so that no new activation requests can be serviced by the SCM until the lock count is adjusted. These functions take the place of the module lock-counting mechanism you may be used to rolling yourself with global variables. It is intended that they be used in the module's lock functions:

```
void CModule::LockModule()
{
   CoAddRefServerProcess();
}

void CModule::UnlockModule()
{
   if(CoReleaseServerProcess() == 0)
      SetEvent(g_hEvent);
}
```

The nicest thing about the call to `CoReleaseServerProcess()` is that internally, the SCM will make an implicit call to `CoSuspendClassObjects()` (which I'll describe in a moment) when it detects that the module lock count is zero. This keeps new activation requests from causing problems during shutdown; the SCM will simply launch a brand new instance of the server process.

`CoSuspendClassObjects()` complements `CoResumeClassObjects()`, and immediately (atomically) suspends activation of all registered class objects in the process. Ordinarily, during shutdown, another activation request might occur between calls to `CoRevokeClassObject()`. Using this function before revoking each object assures that no new activation request occurs between calls.

Having said all that, these race conditions are usually less critical for COM services, because the service shuts down in response to a control message from the SCM, and not because its objects have stopped being used. Indeed, that is the very purpose of a service – to keep running! However, when the service *is* ready to shut down, it's often useful to suspend class objects so that activations stop while it does so.

The Proxy-stub DLL

It should go without saying that if an object is in a local or remote server (or a service), the client will need to talk to it through a proxy-stub DLL. If it didn't go without saying, I've said it now. As far as the proxy-stub itself goes, you have quite a few options:

- Standard marshaling
- Type library marshaling
- Custom marshaling, which allows you to replace (and presumably improve) COM's built-in marshaling mechanisms
- Handler marshaling

I'm only going to discuss the first two here, since they're what the vast majority of COM components need. If you build your object's interfaces with IDL and the MIDL compiler, then standard marshaling is what you get when building the DLL from the `<component>_i.c` and `<component>_p.c` files generated by MIDL.

If you're exposing the objects in your service primarily for consumption by scripting languages such as VBScript and JScript, type-library marshaling might be for you. This type of marshaling is possible only if the data types your component accepts and returns are Automation-compatible, and you register a type library. If you mark your interfaces with the `[oleautomation]` tag, the MIDL compiler will force you to use only these special types, and your interfaces will be able to be marshaled by type library.

The advantage of using type-library marshaling is that it's handled by a standard proxy-stub DLL called the **universal marshaler**, `OLEAut32.dll`. This means that you're not required to build and register a custom proxy-stub DLL on each machine that uses your component. The drawback to this method is that the generic marshaler is slightly slower than a standard marshaling proxy-stub would be, because of the time needed for the type library lookup.

Singletons

Certain objects that are implemented in services are perfect candidates for **singletons**. A singleton is typically used for an object that has no **per-instance state** – that is, it doesn't store any per-instance information about its clients. If an object does not store any state, then why consume the resources to create multiple instances of the object for each client? Instead, you could share the same instance among all the clients. Under most circumstances, this model is more scalable for large numbers of clients than is the typical multi-instance model.

Singletons fit well inside a service, because the service is already alive and will stay running until it is told to stop. The singleton object typically stays alive and running as well – the final call to `Release()` should not delete the object. A reasonable way to implement a singleton is simply always to return the same object instance from `IClassFactory::CreateInstance()` when it is called, like so:

```
HRESULT CCFactory::CreateInstance(IUnknown* pUnkOuter, REFIID riid,
                                                       void** ppv)
{
   if(pUnkOuter != NULL)
      return CLASS_E_NOAGGREGATION;

   static CSurfer singleSurfer;
   return singleSurfer.QueryInterface(riid, ppv);
}
```

Also, since there is no real reference counting going on, you could just return dummy values from `AddRef()` and `Release()`:

```
ULONG CSurfer::AddRef()
{
   return 2;
}

ULONG CSurfer::Release()
{
   return 1;
}
```

Certain usage patterns for services, such as the Agent pattern, are perfect opportunities to use singletons. Take, for example, an Agent service that was designed to gather a list of web sites on certain topics. It would constantly 'crawl' the Web to build a static table of these sites. The service would expose an object that, when requested, would deliver a list of hyperlinks to the client. Such an object would have no per-instance state, and be an ideal candidate for a singleton.

Recap of COM Service Design Issues

Let's quickly recap some of the issues we've talked about that are particularly important to services:

- Clients are usually remote (not local) in a real *n*-tier architecture that requires services. This means that marshaling is always relatively costly. Understand this and try to make your interfaces as efficient as possible in terms of round trips.
- Register class objects with the `CLSCTX_REMOTE_SERVER` and `CLSCTX_LOCAL_SERVER` flags, and with the `REGCLS_MULTIPLEUSE` connection type. This ensures that the service can be started locally or remotely, and that multiple clients can use it.
- Consider using the MTA model to host your objects. It's usually more work for you, but COM (and, ultimately, the clients of the object) can be much more efficient at managing resources under MTA.
- When registering multiple class objects from the service, do so with the `REGCLS_SUSPENDED` flag and then start them all off at once with a call to `CoResumeClassObjects()`. This ensures you won't have to worry about activation race conditions.
- When stopping the service, make a call to `CoSuspendClassObjects()` before calling `CoRevokeClassObject()`. This ensures that you won't get any new activations on one object after another has been revoked.
- Be sure to create and properly install a proxy-stub DLL on the client machine, unless you're using type-library marshaling.

ATL

I've said quite a lot about COM services now, and it's about time we got down to the dirty work of actually *writing* them. And, when writing COM of any type, it is hard to find a better tool than the Active Template Library (ATL). In this section, I'm not going to talk about ATL as a whole – that would take more time and real estate than I have. Instead, I want to discuss ATL's implementation of the supporting infrastructure for building COM services; this has several niceties, as well as a number of areas where it could do with improvement. After we discuss the ATL supporting classes, I'll show you how to beef up ATL in the couple of the areas where it falls short.

Building an ATL Service

Using ATL to create a COM service is remarkably simple, and I'll walk you through the steps. First of all, create a new project in Visual C++ using the ATL COM AppWizard. Once you're past the formalities of giving it a name and a location, you'll see this dialog:

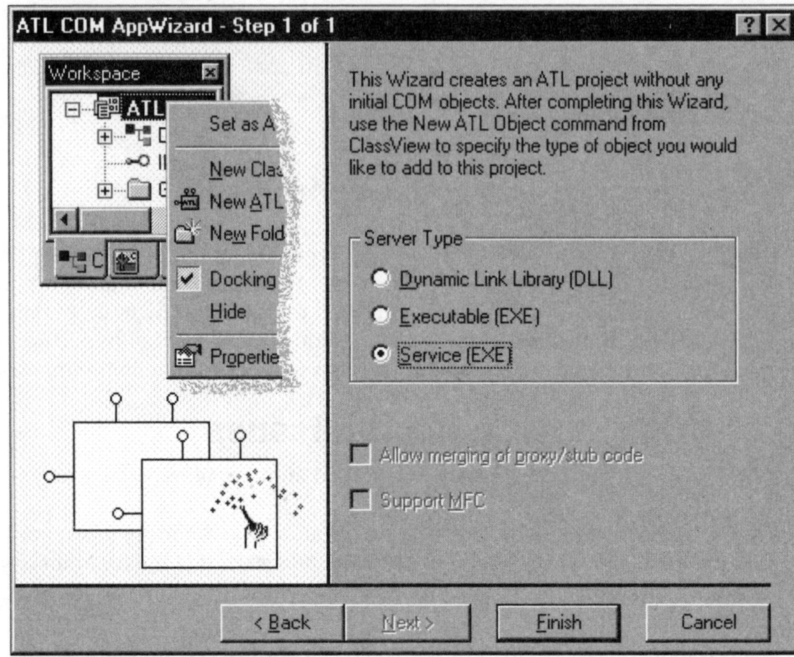

Select Service (EXE) and click Finish; that's all you have to do. Congratulations! You now have an ATL service project that contains the following files (which will of course be named differently depending on the name of the project):

File	Purpose
`EmptyService.cpp`	The main implementation file. It contains the definitions of all the `CServiceModule` functions, as well as `_tWinMain()` and all the globals.
`EmptyService.idl`	Contains the IDL for each of the objects in the server.
`EmptyService.rc`	Resource script.
`Stdafx.cpp`	Precompiled header source file.
`Resource.h`	Resource header.
`Stdafx.h`	Contains the declaration for `CServiceModule` and any other global includes. Also the precompiled header for the project.
`EmptyService.rgs`	The registry script for setting up the executable's APPID. When compiled, the script in this file will define a registry resource.

Adding Objects

Each time you add a COM object to the service, the Wizard will do the following:

- Add `.h` and `.cpp` files that define the object's implementation class
- Add a `.rgs` script that outlines the CLSID entries for the new object
- Add the object and its interfaces to the `.idl` file
- Add the object's class ID to the global object map in `EmptyService.cpp`
- Add a `#include` for the object's `.h` file to the `EmptyService.cpp` file

ATL 2.1 Implementation

The real meat of ATL's service implementation is in the Wizard-generated derivative of `CComModule` called `CServiceModule`, the declaration of which is reproduced below. This code is actually inserted directly into the project's `StdAfx.h` file, apparently so that each of the supporting files in the project will be able properly to resolve references to the declaration. You'll notice that some parts of it have similarities to the `CService` class that we built in Chapter 4.

```
class CServiceModule : public CComModule
{
public:
    HRESULT RegisterServer(BOOL bRegTypeLib, BOOL bService);
    HRESULT UnregisterServer();
    void Init(_ATL_OBJMAP_ENTRY* p, HINSTANCE h, UINT nServiceNameID);
    void Start();
    void ServiceMain(DWORD dwArgc, LPTSTR* lpszArgv);
    void Handler(DWORD dwOpcode);
    void Run();
    BOOL IsInstalled();
    BOOL Install();
    BOOL Uninstall();
    LONG Unlock();
    void LogEvent(LPCTSTR pszFormat, ...);
    void SetServiceStatus(DWORD dwState);
    void SetupAsLocalServer();

// Implementation
private:
    static void WINAPI _ServiceMain(DWORD dwArgc, LPTSTR* lpszArgv);
    static void WINAPI _Handler(DWORD dwOpcode);

// Data members
public:
    TCHAR m_szServiceName[256];
    SERVICE_STATUS_HANDLE m_hServiceStatus;
    SERVICE_STATUS m_status;
    DWORD dwThreadID;
    BOOL m_bService;
};
```

A global instance of this class is declared right off in the project's main source code file, a short section of which is shown below. The `_Module` object is the main workhorse, from which just about every other activity originates.

```
#include "stdafx.h"
#include "resource.h"
#include "initguid.h"
#include "EmptyService.h"

#include "EmptyService_i.c"


#include <stdio.h>

CServiceModule _Module;
```

In order better to understand how ATL implements its service functionality, I'm going to divide the member functions into two categories: utilities and execution. To warm up, let's go through the utility functions first.

Utility Functions

Under the general heading of 'utilities', I group all of the following members:

```
HRESULT RegisterServer(BOOL bRegTypeLib, BOOL bService);
HRESULT UnregisterServer();
BOOL Install();
BOOL Uninstall();
BOOL IsInstalled();
void LogEvent(LPCTSTR pszFormat, ...);
void SetupAsLocalServer();
```

We will discuss each of these functions in turn, with the exception of `SetupAsLocalServer()`, which appears to be a function stub that slipped through the cracks – there is no implementation for it anywhere I can find, and nor does it appear to be called from any of ATL's internals.

RegisterServer

It's the job of `RegisterServer()` to handle the registration of the component's classes in the registry; it is called in response to the executable being launched with the `-regserver` (or `/regserver`) command line parameter. It is also called in a custom build step for all ATL projects. The code for `RegisterServer()` is shown below:

```
inline HRESULT CServiceModule::RegisterServer(BOOL bRegTypeLib,
                                              BOOL bService)
{
   HRESULT hr = CoInitialize(NULL);
   if(FAILED(hr))
      return hr;

   // Remove any previous service since it may point to the incorrect file
   Uninstall();
```

```
        // Add service entries
        UpdateRegistryFromResource(IDR_EmptyService, TRUE);

        // Adjust the AppID for Local Server or Service
        CRegKey keyAppID;
        LONG lRes = keyAppID.Open(HKEY_CLASSES_ROOT, _T("AppID"));
        if(lRes != ERROR_SUCCESS)
           return lRes;

        CRegKey key;
        lRes = key.Open(keyAppID, _T("{E6262F24-ED81-11D1-8465-0020AF05ED45}"));
        if(lRes != ERROR_SUCCESS)
           return lRes;
        key.DeleteValue(_T("LocalService"));

        if(bService)
        {
           key.SetValue(_T("EmptyService"), _T("LocalService"));
           key.SetValue(_T("-Service"), _T("ServiceParameters"));

           // Create service
           Install();
        }

        // Add object entries
        hr = CComModule::RegisterServer(bRegTypeLib);

        CoUninitialize();
        return hr;
    }
```

This function is relatively straightforward, and the first thing it does is to initialize an STA COM apartment. You may wonder why it needs to do this, but the answer lies in the `UpdateRegistryFromResource()` function call a few lines down. After jumping through a couple of intermediary functions, this call ends up in a function called `AtlModuleUpdateRegistryFromResourceD()`, which uses a registry resource that was compiled from a `.rgs` script to make entries into the registry. The function uses a COM component known as the registrar to make these entries, and that's why a COM apartment is needed. This function accepts the ID of the resource containing the information the registrar needs, and a Boolean value indicating whether the registry entries should be inserted or removed.

The next part of the function makes some changes to the server's APPID using the handy ATL registry wrapper class, `CRegKey`, which is there to make raw registry manipulation just a little bit easier. ATL's service code actually allows you to install the executable *either* as a service *or* as a local server by setting the `bService` parameter to `RegisterServer()` equal to `TRUE` or `FALSE`. If it's being installed as a service, the code sets the `LocalService` entry in the `AppID` key, and sets up the `ServiceParameters` value as well. Finally, it makes a call to `Install()`, which creates the service with the SCM.

In either case, the function now defers to CComModule::RegisterServer() to register the classes that appear in the component's object map; this function actually calls AtlModuleRegisterServer() to do the work. The object map is simply a map of all the COM objects that are housed in the server, and it's located at the very top of the primary source file, called <myservicename>.cpp. Here's what the object map looks like for the little test service I built in the earlier portion of the chapter:

```
BEGIN_OBJECT_MAP(ObjectMap)
   OBJECT_ENTRY(CLSID_DoNothing, CDoNothing)
   OBJECT_ENTRY(CLSID_DoSomething, CDoSomething)
END_OBJECT_MAP()
```

UnregisterServer

The UnregisterServer() function, shown below, takes on the simple task of undoing the work done by RegisterServer():

```
inline HRESULT CServiceModule::UnregisterServer()
{
   HRESULT hr = CoInitialize(NULL);
   if(FAILED(hr))
      return hr;

   // Remove service entries
   UpdateRegistryFromResource(IDR_EmptyService, FALSE);

   // Remove service
   Uninstall();

   // Remove object entries
   CComModule::UnregisterServer();

   CoUninitialize();
   return S_OK;
}
```

First, it removes the registry entries delineated in the resource, then it calls the Uninstall() function, and finally it unregisters the entries for the objects in the object map.

Install

The Install() function handles the installation of the service using the CreateService() API function – now there's some code you ought to be familiar with!

```
inline BOOL CServiceModule::Install()
{
   if(IsInstalled())
      return TRUE;
```

```
    SC_HANDLE hSCM = ::OpenSCManager(NULL, NULL, SC_MANAGER_ALL_ACCESS);
    if(hSCM == NULL)
    {
       MessageBox(NULL, _T("Couldn't open service manager"),
                                                   m_szServiceName, MB_OK);
       return FALSE;
    }

    // Get the executable file path
    TCHAR szFilePath[_MAX_PATH];
    ::GetModuleFileName(NULL, szFilePath, _MAX_PATH);

    SC_HANDLE hService = ::CreateService(
                            hSCM, m_szServiceName, m_szServiceName,
                            SERVICE_ALL_ACCESS, SERVICE_WIN32_OWN_PROCESS,
                            SERVICE_DEMAND_START, SERVICE_ERROR_NORMAL,
                            szFilePath, NULL, NULL, _T("RPCSS\0"),
                                                    NULL, NULL);

    if(hService == NULL)
    {
       ::CloseServiceHandle(hSCM);
       MessageBox(NULL, _T("Couldn't create service"),
                              m_szServiceName, MB_OK);
       return FALSE;
    }

    ::CloseServiceHandle(hService);
    ::CloseServiceHandle(hSCM);
    return TRUE;
 }
```

First of all, the function opens the SCM, and then it determines the full path of the executable so that it can be used when installing the service in the SCM database. The real work of the function is done in the call to `CreateService()`, which creates the service as a single service process, which is demand started and has a simple dependency on the COM SCM, `RPCSS.exe`. This is handy because the COM SCM will be needed for the service to expose its objects, but all-in-all you're looking at a pretty simple function.

Uninstall

The `Uninstall()` function first stops the service, and then deletes it from the services database. Here's the implementation:

```
 inline BOOL CServiceModule::Uninstall()
 {
    if(!IsInstalled())
       return TRUE;
```

```
    SC_HANDLE hSCM = ::OpenSCManager(NULL, NULL, SC_MANAGER_ALL_ACCESS);
    if(hSCM == NULL)
    {
       MessageBox(NULL, _T("Couldn't open service manager"),
                                                   m_szServiceName, MB_OK);
       return FALSE;
    }

    SC_HANDLE hService = ::OpenService(hSCM, m_szServiceName,
                                                   SERVICE_STOP | DELETE);
    if(hService == NULL)
    {
       ::CloseServiceHandle(hSCM);
       MessageBox(NULL, _T("Couldn't open service"), m_szServiceName, MB_OK);
       return FALSE;
    }

    SERVICE_STATUS status;
    ::ControlService(hService, SERVICE_CONTROL_STOP, &status);

    BOOL bDelete = ::DeleteService(hService);
    ::CloseServiceHandle(hService);
    ::CloseServiceHandle(hSCM);

    if(bDelete)
       return TRUE;

    MessageBox(NULL, _T("Service could not be deleted"),
                                                   m_szServiceName, MB_OK);
    return FALSE;
}
```

This is simple and straightforward, although the choice to first stop the service and then delete it is questionable. Under some circumstances, it might be preferable simply to call `DeleteService()` *without* stopping it first. This would delete the service if it were not running, and mark the service for deletion next time it stops if it were. However, given the way that `UnregisterServer()` is arranged to remove class registry entries right after calling `Uninstall()`, it is probably the only acceptable thing to do. On the other hand, the call to stop the service is asynchronous, and the code as it stands does not wait for it to complete, so the call to `DeleteService()` is not going to have the instantaneous effect that was presumably desired, anyway.

IsInstalled

This handy function, listed below, does a quick check with the SCM to try to open the service. If the SCM returns a non-null service handle, then the service is installed.

```
BOOL CServiceModule::IsInstalled()
{
    BOOL bResult = FALSE;
```

```
    SC_HANDLE hSCM = ::OpenSCManager(NULL, NULL, SC_MANAGER_ALL_ACCESS);
    if(hSCM != NULL)
    {
        SC_HANDLE hService = ::OpenService(hSCM, m_szServiceName,
                                                        SERVICE_QUERY_CONFIG);
        if(hService != NULL)
        {
            bResult = TRUE;
            ::CloseServiceHandle(hService);
        }
        ::CloseServiceHandle(hSCM);
    }
    return bResult;
}
```

LogEvent

This function implements the bare-bones necessities for writing a string to the NT event log. It is shown below:

```
void CServiceModule::LogEvent(LPCTSTR pFormat, ...)
{
    TCHAR chMsg[256];
    HANDLE hEventSource;
    LPTSTR lpszStrings[1];
    va_list pArg;

    va_start(pArg, pFormat);
    _vstprintf(chMsg, pFormat, pArg);
    va_end(pArg);

    lpszStrings[0] = chMsg;

    if(m_bService)
    {
        /* Get a handle to use with ReportEvent(). */
        hEventSource = RegisterEventSource(NULL, m_szServiceName);
        if (hEventSource != NULL)
        {
            /* Write to event log. */
            ReportEvent(hEventSource, EVENTLOG_INFORMATION_TYPE,
                         0, 0, NULL, 1, 0, (LPCTSTR*) &lpszStrings[0], NULL);
            DeregisterEventSource(hEventSource);
        }
    }
    else
    {
        // As we're not running as a service, just write error to the console.
        _putts(chMsg);
    }
}
```

To do its job, the function accepts a variable list of strings, opens the event source, blasts the strings out to the event log, and closes the source. If the server is not running as a service (denoted by the value of the m_bService Boolean), it instead sends the error string to the console window. This ATL version of an event-logging function is a reasonable beginning, but lacks any real robustness; I'll show you how to make event-logging work a little better in a later section.

Execution Functions

That's it for the utility functions; let's move on to the interesting stuff. In this section, we'll consider everything remaining in the CComModule-derived class, including several important member variables:

```
void Init(_ATL_OBJMAP_ENTRY* p, HINSTANCE h, UINT nServiceNameID);
void Start();
void ServiceMain(DWORD dwArgc, LPTSTR* lpszArgv);
static void WINAPI _ServiceMain(DWORD dwArgc, LPTSTR* lpszArgv);
void Run();
void Handler(DWORD dwOpcode);
static void WINAPI _Handler(DWORD dwOpcode);
LONG Unlock();
void SetServiceStatus(DWORD dwState);

TCHAR m_szServiceName[256];
SERVICE_STATUS_HANDLE m_hServiceStatus;
SERVICE_STATUS m_status;
DWORD dwThreadID;
BOOL m_bService;
```

_tWinMain

First though, let's look at the 'main' function for the service, which is located in the file that contains the implementations of CServiceModule's functions. Like any 'main' function, it exists at global scope.

```
extern "C" int WINAPI _tWinMain(HINSTANCE hInstance,
            HINSTANCE /*hPrevInstance*/, LPTSTR lpCmdLine, int /*nShowCmd*/)
{
   lpCmdLine = GetCommandLine(); // This line necessary for _ATL_MIN_CRT
   _Module.Init(ObjectMap, hInstance, IDS_SERVICENAME);
   _Module.m_bService = TRUE;

   TCHAR szTokens[] = _T("-/");

   LPCTSTR lpszToken = FindOneOf(lpCmdLine, szTokens);
   while(lpszToken != NULL)
   {
      if(lstrcmpi(lpszToken, _T("UnregServer")) == 0)
         return _Module.UnregisterServer();

      // Register as Local Server
      if(lstrcmpi(lpszToken, _T("RegServer")) == 0)
         return _Module.RegisterServer(TRUE, FALSE);
```

```
        // Register as Service
        if (lstrcmpi(lpszToken, _T("Service")) == 0)
            return _Module.RegisterServer(TRUE, TRUE);

        lpszToken = FindOneOf(lpszToken, szTokens);
    }

    // Are we Service or Local Server
    CRegKey keyAppID;
    LONG lRes = keyAppID.Open(HKEY_CLASSES_ROOT, _T("AppID"));
    if(lRes != ERROR_SUCCESS)
        return lRes;

    CRegKey key;
    lRes = key.Open(keyAppID, _T("{E6262F24-ED81-11D1-8465-0020AF05ED45}"));
    if(lRes != ERROR_SUCCESS)
        return lRes;

    TCHAR szValue[_MAX_PATH];
    DWORD dwLen = _MAX_PATH;
    lRes = key.QueryValue(szValue, _T("LocalService"), &dwLen);

    _Module.m_bService = FALSE;
    if(lRes == ERROR_SUCCESS)
        _Module.m_bService = TRUE;

    _Module.Start();

    // When we get here, the service has been stopped
    return _Module.m_status.dwWin32ExitCode;
}
```

To begin, it calls the `Init()` function on the global `_Module` object declared earlier in the file. Next, it tests the command line to see how the executable is starting – in registration mode, unregistration mode, or service registration mode.

If the executable is not being run with a command-line parameter, the function tests to see if the service is running as a local server or as a service by checking the `LocalService` value under the APPID for the executable. If the value is there, it is presumed that the process is running as a service. The function then calls `Start()`, which you'll see shortly.

Init

This function simply initializes a number of member variables and other data structures for the class. As described above, it is the first function called in the processing of `_tWinMain()`.

```
inline void CServiceModule::Init(_ATL_OBJMAP_ENTRY* p, HINSTANCE h,
                                                    UINT nServiceNameID)
{
    CComModule::Init(p, h);

    m_bService = TRUE;
```

```
    LoadString(h, nServiceNameID, m_szServiceName,
                                  sizeof(m_szServiceName) / sizeof(TCHAR));

    // Set up the initial service status
    m_hServiceStatus = NULL;
    m_status.dwServiceType = SERVICE_WIN32_OWN_PROCESS;
    m_status.dwCurrentState = SERVICE_STOPPED;
    m_status.dwControlsAccepted = SERVICE_ACCEPT_STOP;
    m_status.dwWin32ExitCode = 0;
    m_status.dwServiceSpecificExitCode = 0;
    m_status.dwCheckPoint = 0;
    m_status.dwWaitHint = 0;
}
```

`Init()` accepts a pointer to the global object map as its first parameter, then the instance handle of the module, and finally a resource ID identifying the string resource that contains the name of the service. The function immediately passes on the object map pointer and the instance handle to the base class method, `CComModule::Init()`. This function in turn defers to `AtlModuleInit()`, which initializes several structures and a couple of critical sections used for other data structures.

After that, `Init()` loads from the string resource the value that will be the service name. Then, it initializes a clean set of values for the `SERVICE_STATUS` structure, `m_status`.

Start

`Start()` has the task of setting up the service control dispatcher structures so that the SCM can do its work. You're no doubt starting to get rather used to this drill by now...

```
inline void CServiceModule::Start()
{
    SERVICE_TABLE_ENTRY st[] =
    {
        { m_szServiceName, _ServiceMain },
        { NULL, NULL }
    };

    if (m_bService && !::StartServiceCtrlDispatcher(st))
    {
        m_bService = FALSE;
    }
    if(m_bService == FALSE)
        Run();
}
```

If the service control dispatcher cannot be properly started, or if the executable is running, not as a service, but as a local server (`m_bService = FALSE`), then the `Run()` function, which is where the run loop for the service is located, is called directly. Notice that the service table entry for the service is given a function pointer to the `_ServiceMain()` function, a static class member. That static member function will, in turn, end up calling the real member function `ServiceMain()`, where all the work for the service thread begins. It is a very similar model to the one you are familiar with from our own `CService` class.

ServiceMain

`ServiceMain()` is where the real fun begins. Take a look:

```
inline void CServiceModule::ServiceMain(DWORD /* dwArgc */,
                                        LPTSTR* /* lpszArgv */)
{
   // Register the control request handler
   m_status.dwCurrentState = SERVICE_START_PENDING;
   m_hServiceStatus = RegisterServiceCtrlHandler(m_szServiceName, _Handler);
   if(m_hServiceStatus == NULL)
   {
      LogEvent(_T("Handler not installed"));
      return;
   }
   SetServiceStatus(SERVICE_START_PENDING);

   m_status.dwWin32ExitCode = S_OK;
   m_status.dwCheckPoint = 0;
   m_status.dwWaitHint = 0;

   // When the Run function returns, the service has stopped.
   Run();

   SetServiceStatus(SERVICE_STOPPED);
   LogEvent(_T("Service stopped"));
}
```

The first thing this `ServiceMain()` function does is to set the state of the internal service status structure, though it's not very clear why. The actual status cannot be updated until after the call to `RegisterServiceCtrlHandler()`, which returns a `SERVICE_STATUS_HANDLE`. I think that the state-setting call being made here is probably just a mistake someone forgot to remove. In any case, its status is reset after the control handler is registered in the next call.

Next, a few more fields of the class's `SERVICE_STATUS` structure are set, and `ServiceMain()` then pops out to the `Run()` function to loop until told otherwise. When `Run()` returns, the service is essentially stopped, so the final `SERVICE_STOPPED` service status call is made.

Run

The `Run()` function is where the service lives for most of the time:

```
void CServiceModule::Run()
{
   HRESULT hr;

   _Module.dwThreadID = GetCurrentThreadId();

   HRESULT hRes = CoInitialize(NULL);
// If you are running on NT 4.0 or higher you can use the following call
// instead to make the EXE free threaded.
// This means that calls come in on a random RPC thread
//   HRESULT hRes = CoInitializeEx(NULL, COINIT_MULTITHREADED);

   _ASSERTE(SUCCEEDED(hr));
```

```
    // This provides a NULL DACL which will allow access to everyone.
    CSecurityDescriptor sd;
    sd.InitializeFromThreadToken();
    hr = CoInitializeSecurity(sd, -1, NULL, NULL, RPC_C_AUTHN_LEVEL_PKT,
                         RPC_C_IMP_LEVEL_IMPERSONATE, NULL, EOAC_NONE, NULL);
    _ASSERTE(SUCCEEDED(hr));

    hr = _Module.RegisterClassObjects(CLSCTX_LOCAL_SERVER |
                                   CLSCTX_REMOTE_SERVER, REGCLS_MULTIPLEUSE);
    _ASSERTE(SUCCEEDED(hr));

    LogEvent(_T("Service started"));
    SetServiceStatus(SERVICE_RUNNING);

    MSG msg;
    while(GetMessage(&msg, 0, 0, 0))
       DispatchMessage(&msg);

    _Module.RevokeClassObjects();

    CoUninitialize();
}
```

The first thing that `Run()` does is to initialize the apartment that the objects will run in as `COINIT_APARTMENTTHREADED` (this is implied by the old fashioned `CoInitialize()` call). It also gives you a quick note saying that you can make the apartment MTA just by commenting out the `CoInitialize()` call and uncommenting the call to `CoInitializeEx()`. I would argue that making this capable of being a real MTA has a bit more to it than that, but we'll talk about that in the next section.

The next thing `Run()` does is to set up security for the process using the security descriptor method. To do that, it creates a `CSecurityDescriptor` object (which is just an ATL wrapper class for handling SDs) and calls `InitializeFromThreadToken()` on it. This function grabs the thread's owner and group SIDs, sets the security descriptor's owner and group SIDs to these values, and then sets a null DACL and SACL. Be aware that as long as this call is present, it really doesn't matter what access rights you set up in `DCOMCnfg`. *Everyone* is going to have access, because this call resets the DACL to `NULL`.

> *Notice also that the connection and impersonation levels are beefed up from their default values. The connection level is set to* `RPC_C_AUTHN_LEVEL_PKT` *and the impersonation level to* `RPC_C_IMP_IMPERSONATE`*, one level higher than the default legacy values.*

Next, `Run()` calls the class's implementation of `RegisterClassObjects()`, passing the 'local server', 'remote server', and 'multiple use' flags. All this does is call `AtlModuleRegisterClassObjects()` (below), which loops through the global object map and calls `RegisterClassObject()` on each object map entry.

```
ATLAPI AtlModuleRegisterClassObjects(_ATL_MODULE* pM, DWORD dwClsContext,
                                                            DWORD dwFlags)
{
   _ASSERTE(pM != NULL);
   if(pM == NULL)
      return E_INVALIDARG;

   _ASSERTE(pM->m_pObjMap != NULL);
   _ATL_OBJMAP_ENTRY* pEntry = pM->m_pObjMap;
   HRESULT hRes = S_OK;

   while(pEntry->pclsid != NULL && hRes == S_OK)
   {
      hRes = pEntry->RegisterClassObject(dwClsContext, dwFlags);
      pEntry++;
   }
   return hRes;
}
```

The object map entry is an interesting enough structure in itself, but the `RegisterClassObject()` function is what we're particularly concerned with here. What it does (more or less) is to create an instance of the class object for the object in question, and then register that class object via the usual call to `CoRegisterClassObject()`:

```
struct _ATL_OBJMAP_ENTRY
{
   const CLSID* pclsid;
   HRESULT (WINAPI *pfnUpdateRegistry)(BOOL bRegister);
   _ATL_CREATORFUNC* pfnGetClassObject;
   _ATL_CREATORFUNC* pfnCreateInstance;
   IUnknown* pCF;
   DWORD dwRegister;
   _ATL_DESCRIPTIONFUNC* pfnGetObjectDescription;

   HRESULT WINAPI RevokeClassObject()
   {
      return CoRevokeClassObject(dwRegister);
   }

   HRESULT WINAPI RegisterClassObject(DWORD dwClsContext, DWORD dwFlags)
   {
      IUnknown* p = NULL;
      HRESULT hRes = pfnGetClassObject(pfnCreateInstance, IID_IUnknown,
                                                            (LPVOID*)&p);
      if(SUCCEEDED(hRes))
         hRes = CoRegisterClassObject(*pclsid, p, dwClsContext,
                                                   dwFlags, &dwRegister);
      if(p != NULL)
         p->Release();
      return hRes;
   }
};
```

Having registered the class objects, Run() logs the fact that it has been started in the event log, and then notifies the SCM that it has started with a SERVICE_RUNNING status update. After that it launches into the message loop, dispatching method request messages to each of the objects, and waiting to be told to quit when it receives a WM_QUIT message. This method of notifying the service to stop works nicely, since it already uses a message loop to handle STA message processing. It also works well if the service is running in 'server' mode, in case someone clicks the 'close' button on the console window.

Once the message loop is broken, the class objects are revoked through a set of calls that is the mirror image of the class object registration, eventually calling CoRevokeClassObject() for each object in the object map. After that, the apartment is uninitialized and the function returns to ServiceMain(), which sends a STOPPED notification to the SCM.

Handler

But how does the run loop get a notification to stop? Well, back in ServiceMain(), the service control handler was set up. Let's look at the implementation of that:

```
inline void CServiceModule::Handler(DWORD dwOpcode)
{
   switch(dwOpcode)
   {
   case SERVICE_CONTROL_STOP:
      SetServiceStatus(SERVICE_STOP_PENDING);
      PostThreadMessage(dwThreadID, WM_QUIT, 0, 0);
      break;
   case SERVICE_CONTROL_PAUSE:
      break;
   case SERVICE_CONTROL_CONTINUE:
      break;
   case SERVICE_CONTROL_INTERROGATE:
      break;
   case SERVICE_CONTROL_SHUTDOWN:
      break;
   default:
      LogEvent(_T("Bad service request"));
   }
}
```

This is not difficult to follow – it simply switches on the control message received, although the only one processed by ATL's default implementation is a STOP request. The function sets the service status to SERVICE_STOP_PENDING, and then posts a WM_QUIT message to the thread saved in the class member dwThreadID (the ServiceMain() thread). Interestingly, it sets the pending status with no checkpoint or wait hint to the SCM. I hope those objects finish up and revoke quickly!

SetServiceStatus

There's really not much to say about this, except that the implementation is about as thin as it could possibly be:

```
void CServiceModule::SetServiceStatus(DWORD dwState)
{
   m_status.dwCurrentState = dwState;
   ::SetServiceStatus(m_hServiceStatus, &m_status);
}
```

Later, I'll suggest that we pull this out and make it a little more robust.

Unlock

The last function I'll talk about is `Unlock()`, which basically takes on the responsibility for handling the closing down of the executable when it is running in server mode. It's actually called in the internals of ATL.

```
LONG CServiceModule::Unlock()
{
   LONG l = CComModule::Unlock();
   if(l == 0 && !m_bService)
      PostThreadMessage(dwThreadID, WM_QUIT, 0, 0);
   return l;
}
```

The function first calls the base class `Unlock()`, then tests to see if the executable is running in service mode. If it isn't, and the lock count is zero (no outstanding objects), then it posts a `WM_QUIT` message to the thread so that `Run()`'s message loop breaks out and the executable shuts down.

ATL Service Limitations

As it comes out of the box, the ATL service implementation has a few problems. Most of these are minor, but there are a couple that I consider quite important. Here's a laundry list of what I consider those limitations to be:

- **Only one service per executable.** We can live with this, and I won't try to fix it. Just be aware of this potential limitation.
- **Service display name is the same as the service name.** Often, you'll want these to be different.
- **Weak event logging.** The event logging is fine for a demonstration or a toy service, but not for one that you want to ship. With this implementation, you'll get the message in the event viewer that we talked about back in Chapter 3: The description for Event ID (0) in Source (My Service) could not be found. It contains the following insertion string(s):
- **You need to provide a mechanism for having custom registry parameters for the service.** I will show you how to roll this yourself, using `.rgs` scripts.
- **Weak implementation of `SetServiceStatus()`.** This function needs to provide more intuitive facilities for checkpoints and wait hints.
- **Handler.** The control handler needs a few changes, along the lines of what you saw in Chapter 2.
- **Poor threading performance.** Basically, the default STA implementation locks down all access to all objects to a single thread. It also serializes access to all objects through that one thread. This clearly isn't what you would want for a high-performance service.

- **Unsuitability for the MTA model.** Even if you change the server apartment to MTA, there are still potential problems, particularly with the registration of class objects and with the use of a message loop to handle stop messages. It also needs to be built with the multithreaded version of the C runtime library.
- **Non-debug settings don't work out of the box.** This is a common problem that's addressed in the ATL FAQ, but it is worth mentioning the fix. This is discussed in the *Miscellaneous* section, below.

Tuning ATL's Service Implementation

Let's begin making changes to the default ATL implementation in order to make it work a little better. I'll deal with the easier, less important stuff first, and then work my way up. Like the rest of the code in the book, a project that contains the changes I make here is available for download from the Wrox web site – the project is called `ModifiedATL`.

Service Display Name

As is quite clear from the code, the default ATL implementation uses the same string for both the display name and the service name. Some folks (like me) prefer the display name to be a little more descriptive, so here's how you can do it better.

First of all, go into the project's string resource and add a new string called `IDS_DISPLAYNAME`, giving it whatever caption you want. Then, add a new `TCHAR` member to the `CServiceModule` class, like so:

```
TCHAR m_szServiceName[256];
TCHAR m_szDisplayName[256];
SERVICE_STATUS_HANDLE m_hServiceStatus;
```

Next, go into the main `.cpp` file and make the following change to the `Init()` function:

```
m_bService = TRUE;

LoadString(h, nServiceNameID, m_szServiceName,
                              sizeof(m_szServiceName) / sizeof(TCHAR));
LoadString(h, IDS_DISPLAYNAME, m_szDisplayName,
                              sizeof(m_szDisplayName) / sizeof(TCHAR));

// Set up the initial service status
m_hServiceStatus = NULL;
```

Finally, modify the `Install()` function like so:

```
SC_HANDLE hService = ::CreateService(
                        hSCM, m_szServiceName, m_szDisplayName,
                        SERVICE_ALL_ACCESS, SERVICE_WIN32_OWN_PROCESS,
                        SERVICE_DEMAND_START, SERVICE_ERROR_NORMAL,
                        szFilePath, NULL, NULL, _T("RPCSS\0"),
                                                   NULL, NULL);
```

The changes you've just made create an additional string resource string that contains the display name, so that the call to CreateService() can use different strings.

Event Logging

The event logging facilities of the standard ATL implementation are weak, and I would suggest several steps to make them more effective. For a start, you should build a real message DLL for your service using the MC compiler, as I described in detail in Chapter 5. Then, you can add the EventLog.cpp source file to the project, and #include the EventLog.h file in StdAfx.h file. This will allow you to create an error-logging object anywhere.

Now you can remove the CServiceModule::LogEvent() function, and pull out the references to it in the implementation source code. Then, you can add a member variable of type CEventLog* to the class and initialize it in the Init() function, like so:

```
LoadString(h, nServiceNameID, m_szServiceName,
                              sizeof(m_szServiceName) / sizeof(TCHAR));
LoadString(h, IDS_DISPLAYNAME, m_szDisplayName,
                              sizeof(m_szDisplayName) / sizeof(TCHAR));
// set up the initial service status
m_hServiceStatus = NULL;
m_pEl = new CEventLog(m_szServiceName);
```

With this change, instead of things like:

```
LogEvent(_T("Service started"));
```

You can use code like this to generate messages in the event log:

```
m_pEl->LogEvent(MODATL_STARTED, EVENTLOG_INFORMATION_TYPE);
```

Here, MODATL_STARTED is one of the messages you defined in your message script. Using CEventLog may be a little more trouble, but what you lose in simplicity you'll more than make up for in flexibility and professionalism.

Another thing you should remember from Chapter 5 is that you'll need somehow to make the registry entries that set up the message DLL beneath the EventLog *key, so that the log viewer will know where to find the DLL. You can do that either as part of a setup program, or in the* -RegServer *command-line processing for the project executable. If you choose the latter option, you can use a* .rgs *script, as I'll describe in the next section.*

You'll also need a simple destructor to remove the CEventLog object when the service closes:

```
~CServiceModule()
{
   // Delete the event log object in CServiceModule
   delete m_pEl;
}
```

Custom Service Parameters

Just about any service worth its salt will have some extra parameters that need to be configured from the registry in order to set defaults, timeouts, or whatever. The place that custom service parameters typically go is the `Parameters` subkey beneath the service key – in other words, `HKEY_LOCAL_MACHINE\SYSTEM\CurrentControlSet\Services\ModifiedATL\Parameters`. Some folks debate about whether service parameters should go here or under `HKEY_LOCAL_MACHINE\Software\Vendor\Product`, but I think '`Parameters`' is the better choice unless there is a good reason to put them elsewhere. Some products even use both places. My advice would be to choose one, and not worry too much about it.

It would be nice if we didn't have to write all that grungy registry code to put defaults for the parameters into the registry when the service is registered and installed – and that's just what the registrar and `.rgs` scripts are for, so let's make use of them!

First, create a `.rgs` script with the entries you want to add – I'll trust that you can read the ATL documentation to learn about the `.rgs` script notation. I created a script called `serviceparams.rgs` and put two dummy registry values into it. The script looks like this:

```
HKLM
{
   NoRemove SYSTEM
   {
      NoRemove CurrentControlSet
      {
         NoRemove Services
         {
            NoRemove ModifiedATL
            {
               ForceRemove Parameters
               {
                  val MaxTimeout = d '10'
                  val Server = s 'CIVEK-DOM'
               }
            }
         }
      }
   }
}
```

Next, add a new resource of type "REGISTRY" to the project. Bring up the properties for the new, empty resource (below); complete the `IDR_` identifier name in any way you want, and type the name of the `.rgs` script you just created into the File name box. Next time you link the project, you'll be set up with the new resource.

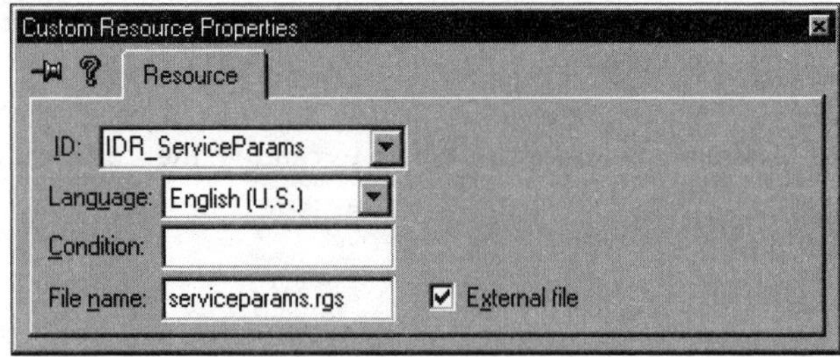

To make use of the script, you have to make the call to invoke the registrar. You'll want to do that inside the `RegisterServer()` function, right after the call to `Install()` in the service block. The location of this call is important, because the service needs to be installed (its entries must be in the registry) before you can add a `Parameters` key.

```
if(bService)
{
   key.SetValue(_T("ModifiedATL"), _T("LocalService"));
   key.SetValue(_T("-Service"), _T("ServiceParameters"));

   // Create service
   Install();
   UpdateRegistryFromResource(IDR_ServiceParams, TRUE);
}
```

For the sake of completeness, you could add a similar call in `UnregisterServer()` to reverse the damage, but in truth the `Uninstall()` call will delete the service and every one of its subkeys anyway.

Unfortunately, you still have to write code to *read* the service parameters from the registry when the service starts. You may want to add a new function to `CServiceModule` (let's call it `ReadParameters()`) that contains the registry-reading code. Then, call that function from some convenient place (probably `_tWinMain()`) to grab the values. Here's my version of the function, which requires a couple of new data members: a `DWORD` called `m_dwMaxTimeout`, and a `TCHAR[25]` named `m_szServer`.

```
inline long CServiceModule::ReadParameters()
{
 // Assemble key name
 TCHAR szKey[100] = {0};
 DWORD slen = 25;  // Arbitrary length of a server name for this application
 TCHAR psz[100] = {0};

   wsprintf(szKey,
            _T("SYSTEM\\CurrentControlSet\\Services\\%s\\Parameters\0"),
            _Module.m_szServiceName);

   CRegKey keyAppID;
   LONG lres = keyAppID.Open(HKEY_LOCAL_MACHINE, szKey);
   if(lres != ERROR_SUCCESS)
      goto RegistryError;

   _tcscpy(psz, _T("Server"));
   lres = keyAppID.QueryValue(m_szServer, psz, &slen);
   if(lres != ERROR_SUCCESS)
      goto RegistryError;

   _tcscpy(psz, _T("MaxTimeout"));
   lres = keyAppID.QueryValue(m_dwMaxTimeout, psz);
   if(lres != ERROR_SUCCESS)
      goto RegistryError;
```

```
    // Close key
    lres = keyAppID.Close();
    return ERROR_SUCCESS;

RegistryError:
    m_pEl->LogEvent(MODATL_CONFIGURATION_DATA_MISSING, psz);
    return lres;
}
```

A possible side effect of placing these registry values beneath the `Parameters` subkey is that you break ATL's nice model allowing you to run the service executable as a local server. If the executable is not installed to run as a service, these keys won't be present below the `Services` key! If breaking that model is a problem in your application, you could temporarily locate the keys somewhere else (such as beneath the executable's APPID) until you're ready to ship as a service. Then, you can make changes to the script and to the registry-reading code. Alternatively, you take the other option I gave you above and store the settings under `HKEY_LOCAL_MACHINE\Software\Vendor\Product`. It's your call!

Setting Service Status

Next on my list is making setting the service status a little bit easier. I propose replacing the ATL Wizard-provided `SetServiceStatus()` function with one of my own that will take many of the structure members, such as the wait hint and the checkpoint, as parameters. This will keep us from having to manipulate each of the members in `m_status` before sending off a status update to the SCM. As you saw, the ATL implementation is rather lackadaisical about updating status, particularly `PENDING` statuses.

To make the new function work, replace the existing `SetServiceStatus()` declaration with the following:

```
void SetServiceStatus(DWORD dwNewState,
                      DWORD dwNewCheckpoint  = STATE_NO_CHANGE,
                      DWORD dwNewHint        = STATE_NO_CHANGE,
                      DWORD dwNewControls    = STATE_NO_CHANGE,
                      DWORD dwExitCode       = S_OK,
                      DWORD dwSpecificExit   = 0);
```

Of course, you'll also need to replace the implementation, like so:

```
void CServiceModule::SetServiceStatus(DWORD dwNewState,
                                      DWORD dwNewCheckpoint,
                                      DWORD dwNewHint,  DWORD dwNewControls,
                                      DWORD dwExitCode, DWORD dwSpecificExit)
{
    // The only state that can set Exit Codes is STOPPED
    if(dwNewState != SERVICE_STOPPED)
    {
        dwExitCode = S_OK;
        dwSpecificExit = 0;
    }
```

```
    // Only pending states can set checkpoints or wait hints
    // and pending states *must* set wait hints
    if(dwNewState == SERVICE_STOPPED ||
            dwNewState == SERVICE_PAUSED || dwNewState == SERVICE_RUNNING)
    {
       // Requires hint and checkpoint == 0
       // Fix it so that NO_CHANGE from previous state doesn't cause nonzero
       dwNewHint = 0;
       dwNewCheckpoint = 0;
    }
    else
    {
       // Requires hint and checkpoint != 0
       if(dwNewHint == 0 || dwNewCheckpoint ==0)
       {
          m_pEl->LogEvent(MODATL_GENERIC_ERROR,
                       _T("SetServiceStatus: Pending statuses require
                                                  a hint and checkpoint"));
       }
    }

    m_cs.Lock();

    m_status.dwCurrentState = dwNewState;

    if(dwNewCheckpoint != STATE_NO_CHANGE)
       m_status.dwCheckPoint = dwNewCheckpoint;

    if(dwNewHint != STATE_NO_CHANGE)
       m_status.dwWaitHint = dwNewHint;

    if(dwNewControls != STATE_NO_CHANGE)
       m_status.dwControlsAccepted = dwNewControls;

    m_status.dwWin32ExitCode = dwExitCode;
    m_status.dwServiceSpecificExitCode = dwSpecificExit;

    m_cs.Unlock();

    if(!::SetServiceStatus(m_hServiceStatus, &m_status))
       m_pEl->LogWin32Error(MODATL_WIN32_ERROR, _T("SetServiceStatus"));
}
```

You should be mostly familiar with the way this function works – it's very similar to the `SetStatus()` function of our `CService` class from Chapter 4, and as you did there, you'll need to define the symbol `STATE_NO_CHANGE` as some arbitrary value. A slight difference is that it directly manipulates members of a class member that's a `SERVICE_STATUS` type, rather than storing the individual members of that structure as separate members, as the Chapter 4 implementation does.

The one *real* difference between this and the older function is that I've added a private critical section member (called m_cs) of type CComMultiThreadModel::AutoCriticalSection to the class, which allows me to update the m_status member atomically. It has handy Lock() and Unlock() members to handle entering and leaving. This is important now, because the Handler() function updates service status, and it's on a different thread from ServiceMain().

Naturally, using the new function to its full potential requires calling it a little differently from the way it's done in the default ATL implementation (although, of course, the old calls will still work). For instance, to send a 'stop pending' request, you would use something like

```
SetServiceStatus(SERVICE_STOP_PENDING, 1, 5000);
```

Handler

There really isn't too much to worry about in the Handler() function, because it does so little to begin with! At this point, the only thing that's really worth adding is a check to make sure that an additional control request doesn't come in when the service is already handling one of the same type. To do that, I added a private member variable to CServiceModule called m_dwRequestedControl, and made sure that it gets updated each time Handler() handles a request.

```
if(m_dwRequestedControl == dwOpcode)
   return;

switch(dwOpcode)
{
   // Omitted for brevity
}

m_dwRequestedControl = dwOpcode;
```

There are some other changes to be made to Handler(), but I'll describe those in the next section.

Threading and MTA Issues

To get the service ready for high-performance, multithreaded prime time, we need to make several changes, all of which revolve around setting up a proper MTA for the COM objects to live in. Let's try to make them in an orderly fashion.

1. Change the apartment type. To do that, remove the call to CoInitialize() at the top of the Run() function, and replace it with CoInitializeEx(NULL, COINIT_MULTITHREADED), as directed by the comments.

2. Go to the StdAfx.h file and change the #define from _ATL_APARTMENT_THREADED to _ATL_FREE_THREADED.

3. In the Code Generation category on the C/C++ tab of the Project Settings dialog, change the project to use a multithreaded C runtime library.

4. Back in the `Run()` function, add the `REGCLS_SUSPENDED` flag to the call to `_Module.RegisterClassObjects()`. Every object will now be created in the suspended state; this is important for MTA objects for the reasons we talked about earlier in the chapter.

5. Once that's done, we must immediately call `CoResumeClassObjects()` to notify the SCM about all registered objects atomically. The previous two changes look like this:

```
hr = _Module.RegisterClassObjects(CLSCTX_LOCAL_SERVER |
            CLSCTX_REMOTE_SERVER, REGCLS_MULTIPLEUSE | REGCLS_SUSPENDED);
_ASSERTE(SUCCEEDED(hr));

hr = CoResumeClassObjects();
_ASSERTE(SUCCEEDED(hr));
```

6. We need to pull the message loop out of `Run()` and replace it with a call to wait for an event notification. To do this, add a `HANDLE` member called `m_hStopEvent` to the `CServiceModule` class, and create the event in the `Run()` function fairly early, before anything else happens. You don't want to put this in `ServiceMain()`, because you want to keep open the option of running as a regular EXE server – and `ServiceMain()` won't be called if the EXE is not being run as a service.

```
HRESULT hr;
_Module.dwThreadID = GetCurrentThreadId();

// Initialize Event
m_hStopEvent = CreateEvent(NULL, TRUE, FALSE, NULL);
```

7. Close the event handle at the last possible point, like right after the call to `CoUninitialize()`:

```
CoUninitialize();
CloseHandle(m_hStopEvent);
```

8. Now you're ready to remove the message loop. Delete it and replace it with the following call to wait for the stop event handle to signal. Of course, you could have more complicated wait conditions if you were waiting for pause or continue requests as well:

```
// Waits here till STOP request
WaitForSingleObject(m_hStopEvent, INFINITE);
```

9. You need to make sure that the proper type of signal gets sent when the service is being stopped. In the control handler for the 'stop' request, change the `PostThreadMessage()` call to a `SetEvent()` call, like so:

```
case SERVICE_CONTROL_STOP:
   SetServiceStatus(SERVICE_STOP_PENDING, 1, 5000);
   SetEvent(m_hStopEvent);
   break;
```

10. Also, to keep open the option of running the service as a server, change the `Unlock()` function to set the stop event, rather than posting a quit message:

```
LONG CServiceModule::Unlock()
{
   LONG l = CComModule::Unlock();
   if(l == 0 && !m_bService)
      SetEvent(m_hStopEvent);
   return l;
}
```

11. Finally, place a call to `CoSuspendClassObjects()` just after the `WaitForSingleObject()` call in the `Run()` function. This keeps any new activation from having problems while your class objects are being revoked. For your perusal, here is the whole, modified `Run()` function once again:

```
void CServiceModule::Run()
{
   HRESULT hr;
   _Module.dwThreadID = GetCurrentThreadId();

   // Initialize Event
   m_hStopEvent = CreateEvent(NULL, TRUE, FALSE, NULL);

   HRESULT hRes = CoInitializeEx(NULL, COINIT_MULTITHREADED);

   _ASSERTE(SUCCEEDED(hr));

   // This provides a NULL DACL which will allow access to everyone.
   CSecurityDescriptor sd;
   sd.InitializeFromThreadToken();
   hr = CoInitializeSecurity(sd, -1, NULL, NULL, RPC_C_AUTHN_LEVEL_PKT,
                        RPC_C_IMP_LEVEL_IMPERSONATE, NULL, EOAC_NONE,NULL);
   _ASSERTE(SUCCEEDED(hr));

   hr = _Module.RegisterClassObjects(CLSCTX_LOCAL_SERVER |
                                     CLSCTX_REMOTE_SERVER,
                                     REGCLS_MULTIPLEUSE | REGCLS_SUSPENDED);
   _ASSERTE(SUCCEEDED(hr));

   hr = CoResumeClassObjects();
   _ASSERTE(SUCCEEDED(hr));

   m_pEl->LogEvent(MODATL_STARTED, EVENTLOG_INFORMATION_TYPE);
   SetServiceStatus(SERVICE_RUNNING);

   // Waits here till STOP request
   WaitForSingleObject(m_hStopEvent, INFINITE);

   CoSuspendClassObjects();

   _Module.RevokeClassObjects();
   CoUninitialize();
   CloseHandle(m_hStopEvent);
}
```

Miscellaneous

A few miscellaneous changes remain. First, there are problems when building in any of the release modes. This problem is well documented in the ATL FAQ, and is related to entry point conflicts when building with the `_ATL_MIN_CRT` preprocessor directive. Remove this directive and your project will build. See the FAQ for more details and options – it's Microsoft Knowledge Base article Q166480.

Second, once I get to the point where I want to debug the executable while it's running as a *service* (not just as a server), I like the MIDL build step to register my executable using the `/service` command line option, so that service installation is done properly. To do that, I make modifications to the MIDL build step, as shown below.

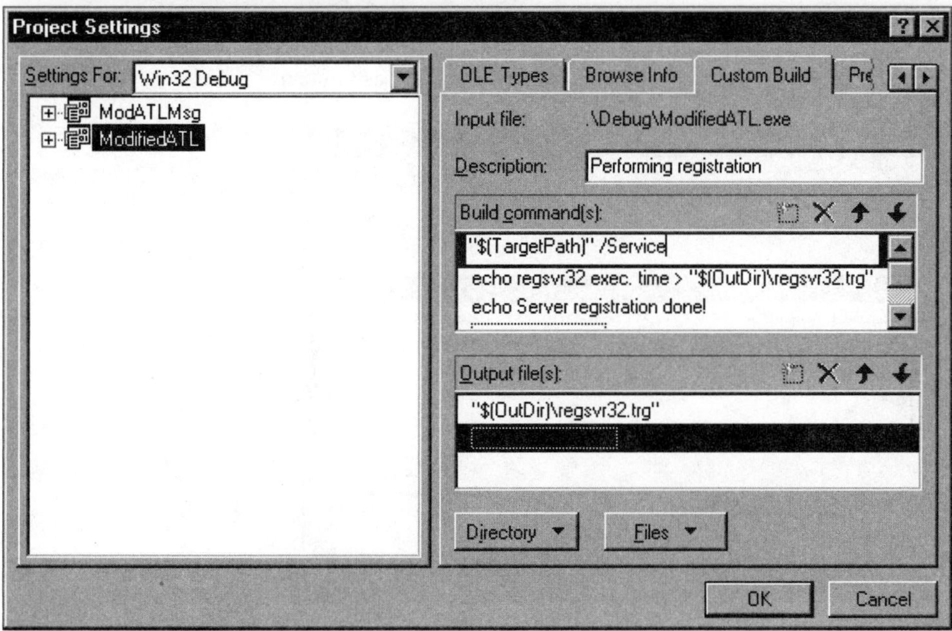

Lastly, don't forget that if you want more (or different) security on your service, you'll have to make changes to the `CoInitializeSecurity()` call in `Run()`.

Clients of COM Objects in a Service

From the client's perspective, using COM objects that are resident in a service is pretty much the same as for any executable server. As long as the registry is properly configured, things just work. However, there are a few special considerations for clients that use a COM service from web pages; these are really just security issues.

ASP Security Context

If you've ever done web programming, you might already know the security context under which ASP web applications run. If you don't, these are the rules:

- If a script is part of an in-process ASP application, and authentication (challenge-response or basic) is not exclusively enabled, the scripts run as `IUSR_`*`MACHINENAME`* (or whatever you've configured as the account for anonymous users).
- For out-of-process ASP applications, scripts run under `IWAM_`*`MACHINENAME`* if authentication is not enabled.
- If authentication *is* enabled, the scripts always run under the client's credentials.

The consequence of this is that the two accounts mentioned above must have explicit activation and access permissions to run the service's exposed COM objects. A new installation of IIS 4.0/MTS will automatically add the correct permissions to the DCOM defaults, as you can see below:

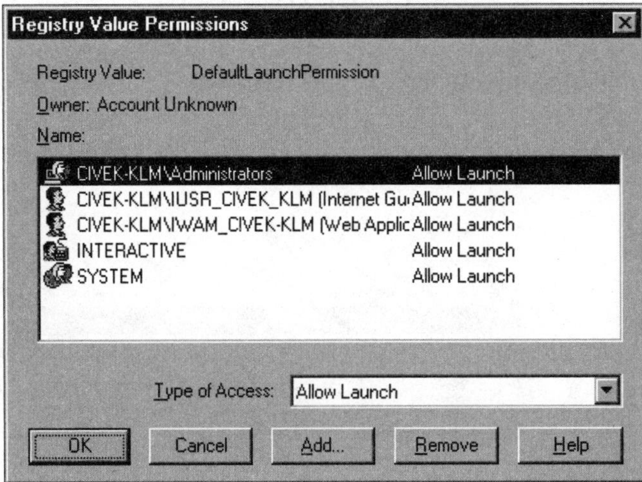

However, if the service is on a different machine from the web server, which is often the case in larger, truly multi-tiered installations, security *won't* be set up correctly. In such cases, it will probably be necessary to set up a domain account as the security context for anonymous users, and give that account access permissions and activation permissions, either through the registry or through explicit calls to `CoInitializeSecurity()`.

Firewalls

Again, if the service is in a true production environment with multiple tiers, the web machines may be separated from the rest of the machines (data servers and application servers) by a firewall. There are a number of issues relating to running DCOM in installations with firewalls, and these are well outlined in an article posted on the Web at http://www.wam.umd.edu/~mikenel/dcom/dcomfw.htm

DNS Names

For the `RemoteServer` value in an object's APPID in the registry, a UNC name, an IP address, or a DNS name can be specified. This means that it is possible to set up multiple machines with the same DNS name, and do DNS round robin. This is a good option in a very busy installation, because several machines can be installed with the same NT service, and the exposed objects on each client machine (a web server, for instance) can be configured to point to a remote machine named with a DNS name. This will do a better job of balancing usage across the servers than a static load-balancing mechanism would do. It also provides for better fault tolerance, because if one server goes down, it is implicitly removed from the round robin.

The Business Object Usage Pattern

Any component that encapsulates nuggets of complex business logic/processing is commonly known as a **Business Object**. These types of objects can take many forms – they can wrap up complex database queries, combine queries with calculations, or handle the dirty details of sets of complex operations, all the while presenting an easy-to-use, intuitive interface to the programmer who is using them. For instance, a Business Object exposing the `IBank` interface (yes, I know it's hackneyed) might present simple methods such as `Deposit()`, `Withdraw()`, and `Transfer()` to the programmer who is designing a web site. To him, the programming is simple and task-based: take the values out of certain HTML controls and pass them as parameters to simple methods. Underneath the covers, though, what might be going on is much more complex – transactions, integration with host systems, security verification, currency exchange rate calculations, and on and on. In fact, most of the COM objects written today could be considered Business Objects.

Most business objects are implemented as DLLs that run in the process space of the caller, so why choose to locate them in a service instead? Well, there are several reasons:

- **Security.** The called object can run in its own, isolated security context that's different from that of the caller. Activation and access control can be secured.
- **Performance.** It may seem strange to talk about performance as a benefit of an out-of-process component, but it really can be improved if the resources that are being used to do the work are expensive to acquire. We talked about this in some detail in Chapter 8, when we discussed resource pooling.
- **Reliance on state.** The object may need to keep some state independent of who is calling it, and global data structures in an ever-living process are often a good place to do so.
- **Reliance on cached or hard-to-calculate information.** Perhaps the object relies on information that is hard to calculate, but relatively static? Or maybe it requires the information gathered by a constantly running background task?
- **Distributed computation.** The object may need to be run on a machine with more horsepower than the client machine can provide, or the centralized machine could provide better economies of scale (cost per transaction).

The Business Object Service

To illustrate one possible implementation of the pattern, I've developed a Business Object service, which is an NT service based on the modified ATL code I discussed at length earlier in the chapter. In operation, the service is similar to the Quartermaster from Chapter 8, although it has been customized slightly to act as an allocation manager for ODBC connection handles. As usual, you can save yourself a lot of typing by downloading the source code for the project from the Wrox web site.

This service uses the Quartermaster to dole out ODBC connections to a Business Object that runs a simple query on the `Authors` table in the SQL Server `pubs` database, which comes as a sample with Visual C++. The idea is that this might simulate an object exposed to a web client through ASP. When a client connects and calls the object's single method, it receives back a variant array containing a number of rows.

The Business Object that the service exposes will be called `BusObject.Author`. The `IAuthor` interface will have only one method, `GetAuthorList()`, which will accept an input parameter from the caller to specify whether authors with contracts or without contracts are required. The method will then grab a connection handle from the pool, run a query against the SQL Server `pubs` database, and then put the return data into a `VARIANT` array that is suitable for both VB and VBScript (Active Server Pages) clients to read. To give you an idea of the semantics for interfacing with the `Author` object, here's the IDL for the `GetAuthorList()` method.

```
HRESULT GetAuthorList([in] long nContract,
                      [out, retval] VARIANT* pDataArray);
```

So that I could demonstrate the use of the Quartermaster in a Business Object pattern, I intentionally *didn't* turn on ODBC 3.0 connection pooling.

Administrative Details

Before you can start adding code to build the sample, there's plenty of administrivia. Follow the instructions below, though, and you'll be able to get up and running quickly.

- This example uses a spin count critical section, and therefore requires (at least) the January 1998 edition of the Platform SDK. Be sure to move the SDK's `Lib` and `Include` directories to the tops of their respective lists in the **Directories** tab of Visual C++ 5.0's **Tools | Options...** dialog.
- I used the ODBC 3.5 SDK for the ODBC work in this application, but you can get by with the 3.0 libraries – I didn't use any 3.5-specific functions.
- You need access to a SQL Server database with `pubs` installed.
- Create a system DSN called `BusObject` that defaults to the SQL Server `pubs` database.
- To get the example started, begin with the `ModifiedATL` project and add to it your `CEventLog` and `CQuartermaster` files. It's probably easiest if you add `#include` directives for the header files directly to `StdAfx.h`, and you can add one for `SQLExt.h` while you're there.
- Use the ATL Object Wizard to add a simple ATL object that implements the `IAuthor` interface to the project. It should be a dual interface, and you can add the `GetAuthorList()` method (prototyped above) to it.

- The service will register its objects and install itself when you build it, so don't worry. The only thing you might have to configure is the login ID and password for your SQL Server database; these will be set in the `serviceparams.rgs` script, which will expand considerably from its incarnation in the `ModifiedATL` sample.

Code Time

At this point, we're ready to start adding some new code of our own, so let's begin by looking at some changes that were necessary for the Quartermaster code.

Quartermaster Code

In fact, I only had to make a few modifications to this code, all of which were to support the fact that the Quartermaster is now managing real ODBC connections, rather than the hypothetical resources of Chapter 8. For a start, the `RHANDLE` structure must now manage `SQLHDBC` handles instead of just `longs`, which means you'll have to make a corresponding change to the first line of the `Add()` function as well:

```
struct RHANDLE
{
   SQLHDBC handle;
   long pos;
};
```

I also put some real code into the `CResourceArray::GetResourceHandle()` method, and changed it to return an `SQLHDBC`:

```
SQLHDBC CResourceArray::GetResourceHandle()
{
   if(!m_hEnv)
      AllocateEnvironment();

   if(!m_hEnv)
      goto ErrorH;

   SQLHDBC hdbc;
   SQLRETURN rc;

   // Open connection
   rc = SQLAllocHandle(SQL_HANDLE_DBC, m_hEnv, &hdbc);
   if(rc != SQL_SUCCESS && rc != SQL_SUCCESS_WITH_INFO)
      goto ErrorH;

   // Set login timeout to 5 seconds
   SQLSetConnectAttr(hdbc, SQL_ATTR_LOGIN_TIMEOUT, (SQLPOINTER)5, 0);

   // Connect to data source
   rc = SQLConnect(hdbc,(SQLCHAR*)m_szServer, SQL_NTS,
                        (SQLCHAR*)m_szLogin, SQL_NTS,
                        (SQLCHAR*)m_szPassword, SQL_NTS);

   if(rc != SQL_SUCCESS && rc != SQL_SUCCESS_WITH_INFO)
      goto ErrorH;
   return hdbc;
```

```
ErrorH:
    CEventLog el(_Module.m_szServiceName);
    el.LogEvent(BUSOBJ_HANDLE_CONNECTION_FAILED, EVENTLOG_ERROR_TYPE);
    return NULL;
}
```

First of all, I check to see whether an environment handle has been allocated, and call a new helper function called `AllocateEnvironment()` to allocate one if necessary. This operation makes use of a new `HANDLE` member variable called `m_hEnv`, which is initialized to `NULL` in the `CResourceArray` constructor.

```
void CResourceArray::AllocateEnvironment()
{
    SQLRETURN rc;
    rc = SQLAllocHandle(SQL_HANDLE_ENV, SQL_NULL_HANDLE, &m_hEnv);
    rc = SQLSetEnvAttr(m_hEnv, SQL_ATTR_ODBC_VERSION, (void*)SQL_OV_ODBC3, 0);
    return;
}
```

The rest of the function is typical ODBC code for connecting; the call to `SQLConnect()` uses three new member variables that are filled in another new helper called `CResourceArray::Init()`.

```
void CResourceArray::Init(LPTSTR szServer, LPTSTR szLogin, LPTSTR szPassword)
{
    _tcscpy(m_szServer, szServer);
    _tcscpy(m_szLogin, szLogin);
    _tcscpy(m_szPassword, szPassword);
}
```

This function is called from `CQuartermaster::Init()`, which passes it three new parameters that are filled from registry settings. If there is an error allocating a handle, I write a message string to the event log saying that the connection could not be made.

When it's ready to close down a connection, the Quartermaster calls `ReleaseResourceHandle()`, shown below. In typical fashion, this function closes the connection handle:

```
void CResourceArray::ReleaseResourceHandle(SQLHDBC hResHandle)
{
    if(hResHandle)
    {
        SQLDisconnect(hResHandle);
        SQLFreeHandle(SQL_HANDLE_DBC, hResHandle);
    }
}
```

While I'm describing changes, I also modified the `AllocateResources()` method so that it outputs new allocations as an event log message:

```
DWORD CQuartermaster::AllocateResources(DWORD dwNumAdd)
{

   // Rest of code as before; omitted for brevity
   // ...

   InterlockedExchangeAdd((long*)&m_dwNumCurrentResources, count);

   // Release Semaphore 'count' number of times
   if(count > 0)
   {
      long dwPrev;
      ReleaseSemaphore(m_hSem, (long)count, &dwPrev);
   }

   // Write to event log that x new handles were allocated
   TCHAR sz1[5], sz2[5];
   wsprintf(sz1, _T("%lu"), count);
   wsprintf(sz2, _T("%lu"), dwNumRes);
   const TCHAR* rgsz[2] = { sz1, sz2 };

   CEventLog el(_Module.m_szServiceName);
   el.LogEvent(BUSOBJ_MORESESSIONS_ALLOCATED, rgsz,
                          2, EVENTLOG_INFORMATION_TYPE);

   // Also write if maximum session limit was reached
   if(GetNumResources() >= m_dwMaxResources)
   {
      el.LogEvent(BUSOBJ_MAXIMUM_SESSIONS_ALLOCATED,
                          EVENTLOG_INFORMATION_TYPE);
   }

   // Allow the allocator thread to start, if it hasn't before
   if(!m_bStartAllocator)
      InterlockedExchange((long*)&m_bStartAllocator, true);

   // Return
   return count;
}
```

I'm not going to present the `.mc` *file containing details of all the* `BUSOBJ_` *error constants here; it's built in exactly the same way you've seen before, and I'm sure you can come up with suitable error strings if you need to. Just don't forget to arrange for your registry entries to point to the message DLL so that the Event Viewer can use it!*

Run

TheTurning now to the `CServiceModule` class, the `Run()` function contains a number of new things – in fact, most of the interesting aspects of the service implementation go on here:

```
void CServiceModule::Run()
{
   HRESULT hr;
   _Module.dwThreadID = GetCurrentThreadId();

   // Initialize Event
   m_hStopEvent = CreateEvent(NULL, TRUE, FALSE, NULL);

   // Allocate the handles
   SetServiceStatus(SERVICE_START_PENDING, 1, 5000);
   m_pQM = new CQuartermaster;

   // Transfer registry settings
   m_pQM->Init(m_dwMaxResources,          m_dwStartResources,
               m_dwMaxWaitForHandleTime, m_dwHandleLifeTime,
               m_dwAllocationPoll,        m_dwMinPoolSize,
               m_dwResourceAllocSize,     m_dwDeadResourcePoll,
               m_szServer,   m_szUser,    m_szPassword);

   SetServiceStatus(SERVICE_START_PENDING, 2,
                    1000*m_dwStartResources + 5000);
   m_pQM->AllocateResources(m_dwStartResources);

   // Some kind of *big* database problem. Exit.
   if(m_pQM->GetNumResources() == 0)              // No sessions connected
   {
      SetServiceStatus(SERVICE_STOP_PENDING, m_status.dwCheckPoint++, 5000);
      delete m_pQM;
      return;
   }

   // Initialize MTA and Security
   HRESULT hRes = CoInitializeEx(NULL, COINIT_MULTITHREADED);
   _ASSERTE(SUCCEEDED(hr));

   CSecurityDescriptor sd;
   sd.InitializeFromThreadToken();
   hr = CoInitializeSecurity(sd, -1, NULL, NULL, RPC_C_AUTHN_LEVEL_PKT,
                     RPC_C_IMP_LEVEL_IMPERSONATE, NULL, EOAC_NONE, NULL);
   _ASSERTE(SUCCEEDED(hr));

   // Register class objects suspended
   hr = _Module.RegisterClassObjects(CLSCTX_LOCAL_SERVER |
            CLSCTX_REMOTE_SERVER, REGCLS_MULTIPLEUSE | REGCLS_SUSPENDED);
   _ASSERTE(SUCCEEDED(hr));

   hr = CoResumeClassObjects();
   _ASSERTE(SUCCEEDED(hr));
```

```
    // The service is running!
    m_pEl->LogEvent(BUSOBJ_STARTED, EVENTLOG_INFORMATION_TYPE);

    SetServiceStatus(SERVICE_RUNNING, STATE_NO_CHANGE, STATE_NO_CHANGE,
                     SERVICE_ACCEPT_STOP | SERVICE_ACCEPT_PAUSE_CONTINUE);

    // Waits here till STOP request
    DWORD why = WaitForSingleObject(m_hStopEvent, INFINITE);
    if(why == WAIT_OBJECT_0)
    {
       // Immediately suspend so no new activations happen
       CoSuspendClassObjects();
       InterlockedExchange((long*)&m_Stopped, (long)TRUE);

       DWORD dwCP = 2;
       SetServiceStatus(SERVICE_STOP_PENDING, dwCP, 30000,
                                          SERVICE_ACCEPT_STOP);

       // Wait for all handles to be finished with active, in-method work
       // This allows clients to clean up
       // Only wait configured seconds then cut everyone off
       while(m_pQM->FreeResourcesLeft() < m_pQM->GetNumResources() &&
                       dwCP < m_dwWaitForClientsBeforeClosing)
       {
          SetServiceStatus(SERVICE_STOP_PENDING, dwCP++, 2000);
          Sleep(1000);
       }
    }

    // Revoke all class objects
    _Module.RevokeClassObjects();

    // Another status update
    SetServiceStatus(SERVICE_STOP_PENDING, m_status.dwCheckPoint++, 5000);

    // Close all resource handles
    m_pQM->DeallocateResources();

    CoUninitialize();
    CloseHandle(m_hStopEvent);
    delete m_pQM;
}
```

First of all, I create an instance of the `CQuartermaster` class that will handle all the pooling needs, and assign it to the `CServiceModule` class member `m_pQM`. I then initialize the Quartermaster and send it the default registry entries that `CServiceModule` has been saving in member data since it read them from the registry in its `ReadParameters()` function. After that, I call `AllocateResources()` to begin the process of making the actual connections to the database. If no sessions were allocated, I know that there is some problem with the database and stop the service without further ado.

Backtracking for a moment to `ReadParameters()`, this function has the same form as it had earlier in the chapter, although as you can see, there are now rather more parameters to deal with; *this* project's `serviceparams.rgs` file looks like this:

```
HKLM
{
   NoRemove SOFTWARE
   {
      NoRemove WroxBook
      {
         NoRemove BusObject
         {
            ForceRemove Parameters
            {
               val ResourceStartPool = d '10'
               val ResourceMaxPool = d '50'
               val ResourceAllocationSize = d '2'
               val DeadResourcePollTime = d '300000'
               val AllocPollTime = d '1000'
               val MaxWaitForResourceTime = d '2000'
               val HandleLifeTime = d '600000'
               val MinPoolSize = d '0'
               val WaitForClientsBeforeClosing = d '20'
               val Server = s 'BusObject'
               val User = s 'sa'
               val Password = s 'pw'
            }
         }
      }
   }
}
```

In the other block of changes to the `Run()` method, I mark the service as running and then sit and wait for the stop event to signal that it is time to stop. In the background, and presumably for days at a time, the service is dishing up instances of the `Author` object and doing work on behalf of thousands of clients.

When it does eventually become time to stop, I immediately suspend the class objects and set a Boolean member called `m_bStopped` to `TRUE`. This allows existing clients to finish their work without cutting them off in the middle of a method, but no new activations can be made. The Visual Basic client that we'll use to test the service a little later in the chapter will get the following run-time error the next time it tries to create an object:

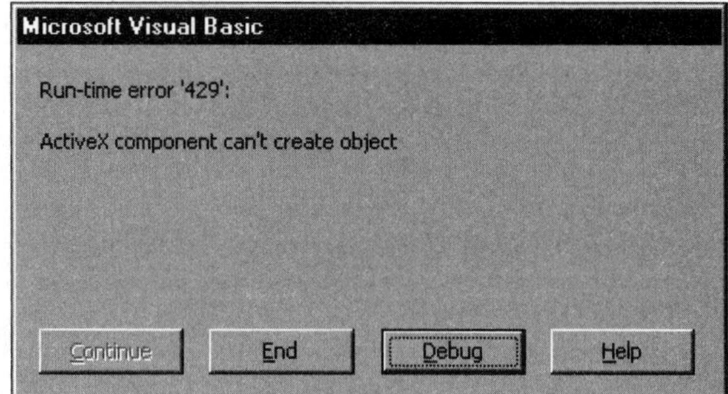

With the class objects suspended, I go into a short loop while waiting for clients to finish their work. This involves waiting for some maximum amount of cycles while all the clients return their handles to the free handle pool. When this happens, I break the loop. After a while, I exit anyway.

In the final portion of the function, I actually revoke the class objects. Then I close all of the connection handles properly, using `DeallocateResources()`. After leaving `Run()`, it's a short trip back out to `STOPPED` state and service exit.

Pause/Continue Semantics

The changes to the `Handler()` function are pretty much what you would expect. For pause and continue, I simply implemented a Boolean member variable called `m_bPaused` that gets atomically set to `TRUE` on a `PAUSE`, and to `FALSE` on `CONTINUE`. The `CQuartermaster::GetFreeResource()` call checks to make sure that this variable is not set before handing out a session to a requester.

```
inline void CServiceModule::Handler(DWORD dwOpcode)
{
   if(m_dwRequestedControl == dwOpcode)
      return;

   switch(dwOpcode)
   {
   case SERVICE_CONTROL_STOP:
      SetServiceStatus(SERVICE_STOP_PENDING, 1, 5000);
      SetEvent(m_hStopEvent);
      break;

   case SERVICE_CONTROL_PAUSE:
      // Pause pending
      SetServiceStatus(SERVICE_PAUSE_PENDING, 1, 5000);

      // Keep new objects from being dished out
      CoSuspendClassObjects();

      // Gets checked in CQuartermaster::GetFreeResource()
      // to keep *existing* objects from getting a handle
      InterlockedExchange((long*)&m_bPaused, (long)TRUE);

      // Paused
      SetServiceStatus(SERVICE_PAUSED);
      break;

   case SERVICE_CONTROL_CONTINUE:
      SetServiceStatus(SERVICE_CONTINUE_PENDING, 1, 5000);
      InterlockedExchange((long*)&m_bPaused, (long)FALSE);
      CoResumeClassObjects();
      SetServiceStatus(SERVICE_RUNNING);
      break;

   case SERVICE_CONTROL_INTERROGATE:
      ::SetServiceStatus(m_hServiceStatus, &m_status);
      break;
```

```
        case SERVICE_CONTROL_SHUTDOWN:
            SetEvent(m_hStopEvent);
            break;

        default:
            m_pEl->LogEvent(BUSOBJ_GENERIC_ERROR, _T("Bad service request"));
            return;
        }
        m_dwRequestedControl = dwOpcode;
    }
```

The modified version of `GetFreeResource()` is shown below:

```
    DWORD CQuartermaster::GetFreeResource(const RHANDLE** poutHandle)
    {
        // Function does *not* find a handle *known* to be valid. It is up to the
        // client to check handle validity and retry if necessary.
        const RHANDLE* pHandle = 0;

        if(_Module.m_bPaused || _Module.m_bStopped)
            return BUSOBJ_SERVICE_STOPPED_PAUSED;

        // Wait on the semaphore. I can block for a short time if no handles left.
        if(WaitForSingleObject(m_hSem, m_dwWaitForHandleTime) == WAIT_OBJECT_0)
        {
            // Get the handle and give it out
            pHandle = m_pFreeList->Pop();
            if(pHandle)
            {
                // Mark time and busy
                m_pResources->SetBusy(pHandle->pos);
                *poutHandle = pHandle;
                return 0;
            }
        }

        *poutHandle = NULL;
        return BUSOBJ_NOSESSIONS_AVAILABLE;
    }
```

Finally in the `Handler()` function, I also used a `CoSuspendClassObjects()` call to keep any clients from being able to create an `Author` object while the service is paused; a call to `CoResumeClassObjects()` allows it to continue when the service resumes its function.

GetAuthorList Code

The single method on the `IAuthor` interface for calling the ODBC database and wrapping up the result set into a `VARIANT` array for returning to the client is relatively straightforward – it's mostly ODBC grunge and allocating array structures for `VARIANT`s. The first thing to do is to obtain a free ODBC connection handle from the Quartermaster.

```
STDMETHODIMP CAuthor::GetAuthorList(long nContract, VARIANT * pDataArray)
{
   const RHANDLE* pRH = 0;
   DWORD dwErr = _Module.m_pQM->GetFreeResource(&pRH);
   if(dwErr != 0)
      return dwErr;

   SQLHDBC hdbc = pRH->handle;
```

The next stage is to get the statement handle and format the structures to create the `VARIANT` array that we'll need to package up the results of the query and send them back as a `VARIANT` to the calling client.

```
   // Do the work
   SQLRETURN rc;
   SQLHSTMT hstmt = NULL;

   // Allocate statement handle
   rc = SQLAllocHandle(SQL_HANDLE_STMT, hdbc, &hstmt);

   // Allocations for variant array
   long theDim[2];
   long count = 0;
   const int INITROWS = 5;                        // Batch size for resizing
   const int numcols = 7;

   // Set up array
   // Create the array
   SAFEARRAYBOUND sabound[2];
   sabound[0].cElements = numcols;
   sabound[0].lLbound = 1;
   sabound[1].cElements = INITROWS;
   sabound[1].lLbound = 1;

   int currows = INITROWS;
   VariantInit(pDataArray);
   pDataArray->vt = VT_VARIANT | VT_ARRAY;        // Means variant array
   pDataArray->parray = SafeArrayCreate(VT_VARIANT, 2, sabound);
```

Next, we begin setting up the necessary structures for making the ODBC calls to the databases. I simply create a bunch of character arrays and integers to store the column values in, and create constants to set the length of each string. I also bind the one parameter to the query (`Contract` = 0 or `Contract` = 1), the value of which is passed into the method by the calling client.

```
   SQLSMALLINT Contract;
   SQLINTEGER ContractInd = 0;
   UCHAR szSQL[100] = "select au_lname, au_fname, phone, address,
                      city, state, zip from authors where contract=?\0";
```

```
SQLPrepare(hstmt, szSQL , SQL_NTS);
SQLBindParameter(hstmt, 1, SQL_PARAM_INPUT, SQL_C_SSHORT, SQL_BIT,
                           0, 0, &Contract, 0, &ContractInd);

Contract = (short)nContract;

rc = SQLExecute(hstmt);

const int LNAMELEN = 41;
const int FNAMELEN = 21;
const int PHONELEN = 13;
const int ADDRLEN = 41;
const int CITYLEN = 21;
const int STATELEN = 3;
const int ZIPLEN = 6;

SQLCHAR szLName[LNAMELEN];
SQLCHAR szFName[FNAMELEN];
SQLCHAR szPhone[PHONELEN];
SQLCHAR szAddress[ADDRLEN];
SQLCHAR szCity[CITYLEN];
SQLCHAR szState[STATELEN];
SQLCHAR szZip[ZIPLEN];

SQLINTEGER cbLName, cbFName, cbPhone, cbAddress, cbCity, cbState, cbZip;
```

Next, I enumerate through the result set, fetching each row and getting the data from each column.

```
if(rc == SQL_SUCCESS)
{
   while(true)
   {
      rc = SQLFetch(hstmt);
      if(rc == SQL_ERROR)
         break;

      if(rc == SQL_SUCCESS || rc == SQL_SUCCESS_WITH_INFO)
      {
         count++;
         if(count > currows)
         {
            // Resize the array by INITROWS
            SAFEARRAYBOUND sabound2[1];
            sabound2[0].cElements = currows + INITROWS;
            sabound2[0].lLbound = 1;

            // Tricky; the new bound only describes the dimension you can
            //  change, not all new dimensions
            SafeArrayRedim(pDataArray->parray, sabound2);
            currows += INITROWS;
         }
```

```
            SQLGetData(hstmt, 1, SQL_C_CHAR, szLName, LNAMELEN, &cbLName);
            SQLGetData(hstmt, 2, SQL_C_CHAR, szFName, FNAMELEN, &cbFName);
            SQLGetData(hstmt, 3, SQL_C_CHAR, szPhone, PHONELEN, &cbPhone);
            SQLGetData(hstmt, 4, SQL_C_CHAR, szAddress, ADDRLEN, &cbAddress);
            SQLGetData(hstmt, 5, SQL_C_CHAR, szCity, CITYLEN, &cbCity);
            SQLGetData(hstmt, 6, SQL_C_CHAR, szState, STATELEN, &cbState);
            SQLGetData(hstmt, 7, SQL_C_CHAR, szZip, ZIPLEN, &cbZip);
```

I set the different elements in the `VARIANT` array equal to the values I just obtained from the data set columns.

```
            // Set the value in each row
            theDim[1] = count;                       // Row dimension value

            theDim[0] = 1;                           // Column dimension value
            CComVariant vC1((CHAR*)szLName);
            SafeArrayPutElement(pDataArray->parray, theDim, &vC1);

            theDim[0] = 2;
            CComVariant vC2((CHAR*)szFName);
            SafeArrayPutElement(pDataArray->parray, theDim, &vC2);

            theDim[0] = 3;
            CComVariant vC3((CHAR*)szPhone);
            SafeArrayPutElement(pDataArray->parray, theDim, &vC3);

            theDim[0] = 4;
            CComVariant vC4((CHAR*)szAddress);
            SafeArrayPutElement(pDataArray->parray, theDim, &vC4);

            theDim[0] = 5;
            CComVariant vC5((CHAR*)szCity);
            SafeArrayPutElement(pDataArray->parray, theDim, &vC5);

            theDim[0] = 6;
            CComVariant vC6((CHAR*)szState);
            SafeArrayPutElement(pDataArray->parray, theDim, &vC6);

            theDim[0] = 7;
            CComVariant vC7((CHAR*)szZip);
            SafeArrayPutElement(pDataArray->parray, theDim, &vC7);
         }
         else
            break;
      }
   }
```

Finally, I close the statement handle and release the ODBC resource I had checked out from the Quartermaster. Then, I fix up the array to its proper size and return.

```
    // Close
    SQLFreeHandle(SQL_HANDLE_STMT, hstmt);

    // Return the handle to the pool
    _Module.m_pQM->ReleaseResource(pRH);

    // Redimension the array to its actual size
    SAFEARRAYBOUND sabound2[1];
    sabound2[0].cElements = count;
    sabound2[0].lLbound = 1;
    SafeArrayRedim(pDataArray->parray, sabound2);

    return S_OK;
}
```

Running the Service

To test the service, you can build and launch this tiny Visual Basic test program:

```
Private Sub Command1_Click()

Dim x%
For x = 1 To CInt(Text2.Text)
   Dim o As Object
   Set o = CreateObject("BusObject.Author.1")
   List1.Clear

   Dim va As Variant
   va = o.GetAuthorList(CLng(Text1.Text))

   Dim I As Integer
   Dim j As Integer
   Dim row$

   For j = LBound(va, 2) To UBound(va, 2)
      row$ = ""
      For I = LBound(va, 1) To UBound(va, 1)
         row$ = row$ + CStr(va(I, j)) + Chr$(9)
      Next I
      List1.AddItem row$
   Next j
   DoEvents
   Set o = Nothing
Next x
End Sub

Private Sub Form_Load()
   Me.Show
'  Command1_Click
End Sub
```

The interface I created for the program is shown below; you can probably deduce from the code that the two edit boxes are called (from left to right) `Text1` and `Text2`, the **Get List** button is `Command1`, and the list box is `List1`:

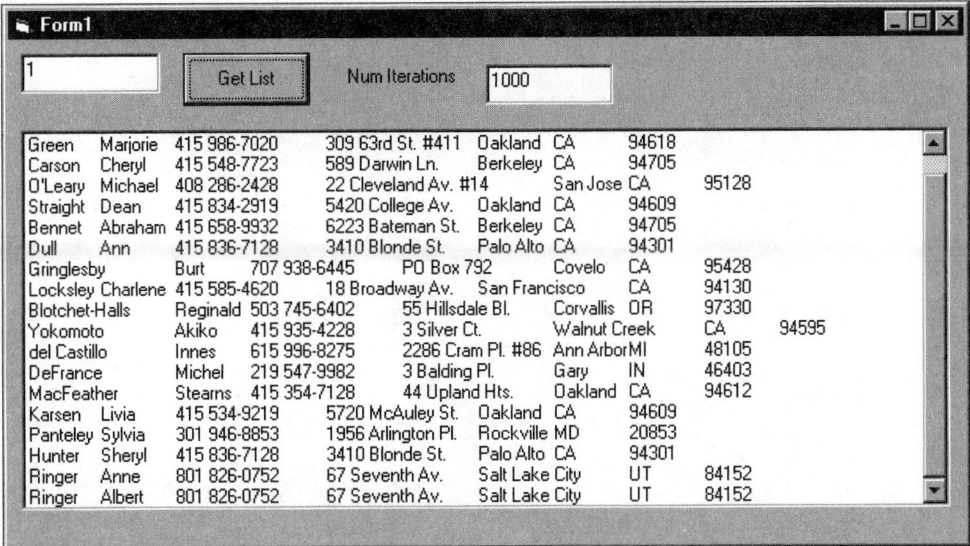

The application shows the output result set in a (rather poorly formatted) list box. There's a text box where you can change the argument that is passed to `GetAuthorList()` (1 or 0 for contracted/non-contracted), and a place to type the number of iterations you want. When you click the **Get List** button, the object will be instantiated, the method run, and the object released, the number of times requested in the **Iterations** text box. Don't worry if the service isn't started; the COM SCM will start it for you when you push the button.

Final Statements about the Service

All in all, I'm pleased with the performance of the service. I ran about 15 instances of the Visual Basic client, each running 1000 iterations of object creation, method invocation, and unpacking the returned variant data. Even though it had *all* the software on it, my dual 233MHz Pentium II machine it remained relatively untaxed, as you can see. The performance statistics averaged at around 30-35% processor utilization, most of which was probably the GUI processing required for showing the list in each of the client windows. The one peak you see was when I opened Microsoft Word and pasted in the screenshot!

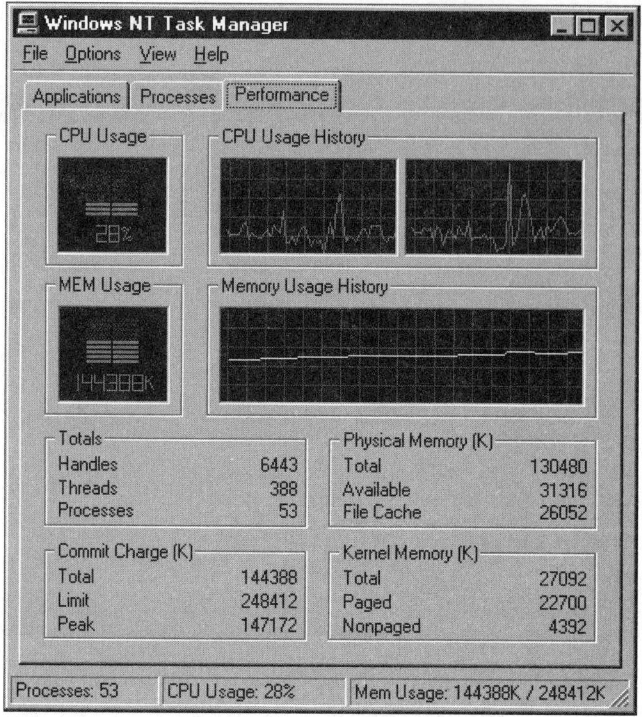

Of course, this is a rather rough and dirty look at performance. In the next chapter, when we'll talk about debugging and profiling your code, we'll take a much harder look at service performance.

Using COM in a Service

For the most part, using COM components from inside a service is just the same as using COM from inside any executable. The main difference is that because the consumer is a service, it *always* has at least two threads, and if it's built to handle multiple clients there are probably many more. Therefore, special care needs to be taken in choosing and using the threading model for the consumer and for the provider.

MTA Objects Using STA Objects

We've talked in some detail about the consequences of the using the different threading models. Deep down inside, you know that you want your services to handle incoming client requests with objects hosted in an MTA. But what happens when you need to use *someone else's* in-process DLL as a component in your service? Imagine, for example, that your server exposes the `IFoo` interface, but that in order for your objects to do their work, they need to use a third-party server DLL (say, Microsoft's ActiveX Data Objects (ADO)) that only supports the apartment (STA) model. What are the consequences?

As you might expect, this is a far from happy situation. Creating an instance of an STA component in an MTA apartment means that COM will create an STA behind the scenes, and access to the STA from the MTA will be through a proxy. Each method request will have to be marshaled over to the STA, and the results will be marshaled back. Performance of the third-party object while being accessed through a proxy will be many, many times slower than if it were resident in the same apartment.

So, what's the solution? Should you host your own objects from an STA to avoid marshaling? Perhaps, but now access to your objects (and to all the other objects in the apartment) from the outside will be serialized through a message queue – performance with only a couple of clients might be better, but with many simultaneous clients it could be quite a bit worse. How about creating multiple STAs? This may help if you're exposing many different objects, but you can only have as many apartments as you have class objects to begin with.

To tell the truth, there isn't really a good answer to this problem. The best recommendation I can make is to use Microsoft Transaction Server (MTS) to host the components, if it's feasible to do so, because that has mechanisms to make STA model components work more efficiently. On the other hand, MTS components are hosted out-of-process themselves, in their own server package, so you incur the cost of marshaling anyway.

Short of using MTS, I guess my preference would be to put up with the cost of MTA to STA marshaling in a high-usage environment, or to put everything in as many STAs as you have objects in an environment with fewer simultaneous clients. Where the break-even point is for your application can only be determined by performance testing.

Using a DCOM Server from a Service

If your service needs to use a *DCOM* server, the issues are pretty straightforward: security, security, and performance. First, if the DCOM server (of which your service is a client) is off-host, then you cannot use the LocalSystem account as the security principal for the service – no outbound RPCs will be allowed. If the other server is on the same machine, then you're fine.

Next, if you *are* using a 'real' account as the security context for the service in order to get off host, that account has to have the appropriate launch and access permissions on the remote DCOM server. Security may need to be configured with `DCOMCnfg` to get the remote server ready to use.

Lastly, remember that the cost of marshaling soon starts to add up. The more out-of-process calls you need to make in order to complete work for a client of one of your objects, the faster the associated performance penalties multiply. This is not a recommendation that you shouldn't do it, but you must always take account of consequences like these when you're laying out the component architecture.

An MTS Component used from a Service

As a kind of final twist of the COM knife, I have a small sample for you to download from the web site. The `MQMonMTS` project is a version of the Agent pattern from Chapter 6, but with a couple of differences thrown in:

- Instead of being able to handle only one message at a time, processing it, and then moving on to the next, this service can handle multiple messages on multiple worker threads.
- The project uses a Visual Basic component called `MQMTSObject` to look up information in a SQL Server database. This component is hosted inside MTS. The component returns a result that's then packaged up by the service into a response message and sent back to the client.

The actual work the sample does is fairly trivial. On receipt of a MSMQ message into the queue, the service processes the message by determining its type, retrieving a parameter value from the message body, and then calling an MTS component written in Visual Basic to run a query against the SQL Server `pubs` database. When the component has completed the query, it sends back the result to the service, which then packages it up and sends it to the response queue specified in the original request message.

If you request a message of 'type 1', then you'll be asking the service to retrieve the store number with the fewest sales *above* the numeric threshold that you type into the box. If you select a message of 'type 2', you'll receive the store number with highest sales *below* the entered threshold. You can imagine that this might be a fairly difficult request if the service were accessing many databases connected by a corporate WAN and consolidating information.

Making the Sample Work

To use the sample, you'll need to do several things. Before you start, though, you need access to several technologies:

- MTS 2.0 from the Windows NT Option Pack
- A SQL Server with the `pubs` database installed
- An MSMQ queue of some sort (independent or dependent, at least)

Now, let's get ready to run the sample.

- Build the service from the source code you've downloaded.
- Install it by running `MQMonMTS.exe -install` from the command line.
- Install a system DSN for SQL Server to the `pubs` database. Call it `MQMTS`.
- Bring up the `MQMTSObject` Visual Basic project. If the user ID and password you need are different from `sa\pw`, then change them and build the DLL.
- Install the component into a package in MTS. Consult the MTS documentation if you need help.
- Start the `MQMonMTS` service.

Code

Let's take a look at the code. As we do so, I'll rely on the fact that you are (or can quickly become) familiar with the material from the earlier chapter – I just want to mention the differences between the two applications. We will be examining code from the `CQService.cpp` file exclusively.

Message Retriever

The function which retrieves messages, `CQueueService::RetrieveMessage()`, has changed slightly. Look below:

```
void CQueueService::RetrieveMessage()
{
   // Rest of the function as before, and omitted for brevity
   // ...

   while(m_bStop == FALSE)
   {
      HRESULT hr = MQReceiveMessage(m_hQueue, 10000, MQ_ACTION_RECEIVE,
                                    pMsgp, pov, NULL, NULL, NULL);

      if(SUCCEEDED(hr))
      {
         if(hr == MQ_INFORMATION_OPERATION_PENDING)
            WaitForSingleObject(pov->hEvent, INFINITE);

         int count = 0;

         if(paVar[0].ulVal == AGENT_REQUEST_1 ||
               paVar[0].ulVal == AGENT_REQUEST_2)
         {
            count++;

            // Get hold of thread and give it new work to do
            LPVOID mem = CoTaskMemAlloc(256);
            _tcscpy((LPTSTR)mem, paVar[3].pwszVal);

            TCHAR szTemp[BODY_LEN] = {0};
            memcpy(szTemp, paVar[1].caub.pElems, paVar[1].caub.cElems);

            UINT threshold = _ttoi(szTemp);

            DWORD type = (paVar[0].ulVal == AGENT_REQUEST_1) ?
                                         TH_TYPE1 : TH_TYPE2;
            PostThreadMessage(m_dwWorkerID[count % NUMWORKERS], type,
                              (WPARAM)mem, (LPARAM)threshold);

            paVar[0].ulVal = 0;        // Clear Type
```

```
                // Must clear out buffer for next read. MQ won't clear it.
                memset(paVar[1].caub.pElems, 0, paVar[1].caub.cElems);
            }
        }
        else
        {
            ErrorHandler(_T("MQReceiveMessage"));
            break;
        }
    }

    CloseHandle(pov->hEvent);
    delete pov;
    delete paVar[3].pwszVal;
    delete paVar[1].caub.pElems;
    delete [] paPropid;
    delete [] paVar;
    delete pMsgp;
}
```

Instead of processing the message inline, as I did in the earlier version, I instead delegate the processing work out to one of several (currently, it's set for four) worker threads. Since the threads are all using apartment model Visual Basic components, each thread is an STA and has a message queue, and I can communicate with them using user-defined window messages.

The first thing I do is to copy the format name string for the message's response queue into a memory area; I'm going to use the pointer to this area as the `WPARAM` for the window message. The receiving thread will decipher it and use it as the destination queue for the return message it will send. Then, I grab the threshold value from the message body and pass it as the `LPARAM` in the message. I'll use this value to send off to the MTS component to run the query. After sending the message, I return to the top of loop and wait for the next message. Notice that I keep a count and decide which of the available worker threads I post the work message to in a round-robin fashion.

Worker Thread Function

The other interesting (new) thing about the service is the worker thread function, shown below:

```
DWORD CQueueService::TFuncType(LPVOID lpParameter)
{
    CoInitializeEx(NULL, COINIT_APARTMENTTHREADED);

    MSG msg;
    LPVOID mem = 0;
    LPTSTR szFN = 0;
    TCHAR szLabel[40] = {0};
    TCHAR szMsg[75] = {0};
    int storeid = 0;
    while(GetMessage(&msg, NULL, 0, 0) > 0)
    {
        // Crack the message params
        if(msg.message == TH_TYPE1)
        {
```

```
        _Type1Ptr pT1(__uuidof(Type1));
        _tcscpy(szLabel, _T("Least Sales Over Threshold"));

        mem = (LPVOID)msg.wParam;
        szFN = (LPTSTR)mem;

        storeid = pT1->GetLowestSales(msg.lParam);
        pT1 = NULL;

        wsprintf(szMsg, _T("The store with the least sales above the
              threshold of %lu is store# %d"), msg.lParam, storeid);
     }
     else if(msg.message == TH_TYPE2)
     {
        _Type2Ptr pT2(__uuidof(Type2));
        _tcscpy(szLabel, _T("Highest Sales Under Threshold"));

        mem = (LPVOID)msg.wParam;
        szFN = (LPTSTR)mem;

        storeid = pT2->GetHighestSales(msg.lParam);
        pT2 = NULL;

        wsprintf(szMsg, _T("The store with the highest sales below the
                threshold of %lu is store# %d"), msg.lParam, storeid);
     }

     m_pThis2->SendMessage(szFN, szLabel, szMsg);

     // Free the memory allocated to pass the response queue format name
     CoTaskMemFree(mem);
  }

  CoUninitialize();
  return 0;
}
```

This function initializes itself as an STA and then launches into its message loop. If either of the messages it receives are work request messages, it unpacks the message `LPARAM` and sends it off as the threshold parameter to the MTS component. The results of that component's work are formatted into a message string and passed on to `SendMessage()`, which sends a message to the response queue's format name, specified in the window message's `WPARAM`.

The COM syntax I'm using to call the MTS object's methods is down to the fact that I'm using the `#import` directive, native to the Visual C++ 5.0 compiler, to import a component's type library and build a header I can use to call methods conveniently. The following call is located at the top of the file; the reason for it will be clearer once we've created our MTS object in the next section but one:

```
#import "D:\MQMTSObject\AgentMonMTSObject.dll" no_namespace
```

Run

Lastly, note that since my threads use message loops, I can use messages to tell them when the service has been requested to stop. The `Run()` function shows this technique:

```
void CQueueService::Run()
{
   SetStatus(SERVICE_RUNNING, 0, 0, SERVICE_ACCEPT_STOP);

   RetrieveMessage();                              // Loops until m_bStop is set

   // Tell the workers to quit
   for(int i = 0 ; i < NUMWORKERS ; i++)
   {
      PostThreadMessage(m_dwWorkerID[i], WM_QUIT, 0, 0);
   }

   WaitForMultipleObjects(NUMWORKERS, m_hWorkers, TRUE, 2000);

   // Stopped, so exit
   SetStatus(SERVICE_STOP_PENDING, 2, 5000);
}
```

MTS Object

There isn't too much to say about the MTS object that was built in Visual Basic – it is very simple. Each message type is actually implemented as two different objects in the same component; here's the code for the first of those:

```
Const DSN = "DSN=MQMTS;uid=sa;pwd=pw"
Public Function GetLowestSales(ByVal LowQuantity As Integer) As Integer

On Error GoTo eh
   Dim cn As New ADODB.Connection
   Dim rs As New ADODB.Recordset
   Dim sql$
   sql = "select stor_id, SUM(qty) total from sales group by " _
      & "stor_id, qty having SUM(qty)>" & LowQuantity & " order by total asc"

   cn.Open DSN
   Set rs = cn.Execute(sql, adCmdText)
   If Not rs.EOF Then
      GetLowestSales = rs("stor_id")
   Else
      GetLowestSales = 0
   End If
   rs.Close
   cn.Close

   GetObjectContext().SetComplete

Exit Function
```

```
eh:
   GetLowestSales = 0
   GetObjectContext().SetAbort
End Function
```

You can see that the component properly notifies MTS when the object instance can be recycled by calling `SetComplete()`.

Running the Test Client

Launch the corresponding version of the `MSMQClient` application, from the Wrox web site to try out the service; this is a slightly different version of the client from the one in the previous chapter. Use a number between 0 and 75 in the Threshold text box to get interesting results. If you click on the Asynch message receive box, you'll start to see messages pump back in as you receive them.

To pump up the volume, enter higher number in the Iterations text boxes to the right of the buttons. You can also run multiple clients, but be aware that the retrieval of the response messages from different clients will be mixed, since I made no effort to separate the response queues of multiple clients.

Summary

Let me wind up this chapter by recapping and summarizing a few of the major (and minor) issues relating to services and COM.

- RPCSS is a mandatory dependency for any COM service
- COM services must expose their class objects as 'multiple use'. Single use class objects would be useless!
- You must ensure that the service's 'log on as' account is the same as the APPID's `RunAs` parameter. Furthermore, if the service is running as LocalSystem, COM requires that the APPID *must not have* a `RunAs` value
- Watch out for DCOM through firewalls
- Use DNS in a round-robin fashion to provide for a better distribution of clients across multiple service instances
- Host your COM objects in MTAs

If you take heed of these instructions and suggestions, you should find that you're able to marry COM and services effectively. In fact, when synchronous communication is required, COM is my preferred method for dealing with communication between services and their clients.

10

Debugging and Tuning

If debugging a service were simply a matter of setting a few breakpoints and hitting *F5*, like you would for a normal executable, there wouldn't be much to talk about on the topic. We've all used Visual C++'s interactive debugger, and by now we're probably experts at doing so. Unfortunately, that experience is not going to be much help here.

The first problem, as you already know, is that you can't run a service simply by running the executable that houses it. Running a service requires interacting with the SCM and launching it using `StartService()`. The second problem is that even if you've solved the first one, the service runs under a different security context – usually the LocalSystem account. As a consequence, many of the normal feedback mechanisms you might be tempted to use, such as console window output, simply don't work because they're not directed to the desktop of the interactive user – that is, you the developer.

In this chapter, I'll show you a number of different techniques that you can use to work around these problems, and then focus on some more general issues that can help to keep you out of trouble in the first place. Later on, I'll discuss some of the profiling tools that you can use to tune the service (or any application, for that matter) for maximum performance.

Debugging Techniques

To be honest, debugging a service really isn't *that* much more trouble than debugging a regular Win32 executable, as long as you know the right buttons to push – that is, if you know how to set up your development environment to make debugging work.

The first thing to do is to make sure that whatever interactive account you are logged on under has the SE_DEBUG_NAME (debug programs) right. All members of the local Administrators group have this privilege. If you're developing a service, you're probably a member of Administrators already, but you should keep this point in mind if you need to debug a service running on a remote machine.

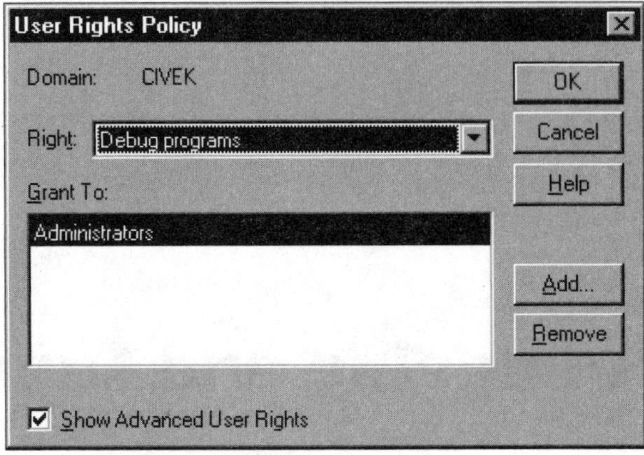

Prying into a Running Service

Sometimes, you just need to get into a service that's already functioning to troubleshoot a minor bug. This is one of the easiest debugging problems, because it doesn't require that you customize the development environment or your machine in any special way. You simply use the ability of Visual C++ to step into and debug a running process.

To perform this task, select the Build | Start Debug | Attach to Process... menu item in Visual C++. When you do that, you'll be presented with the following dialog:

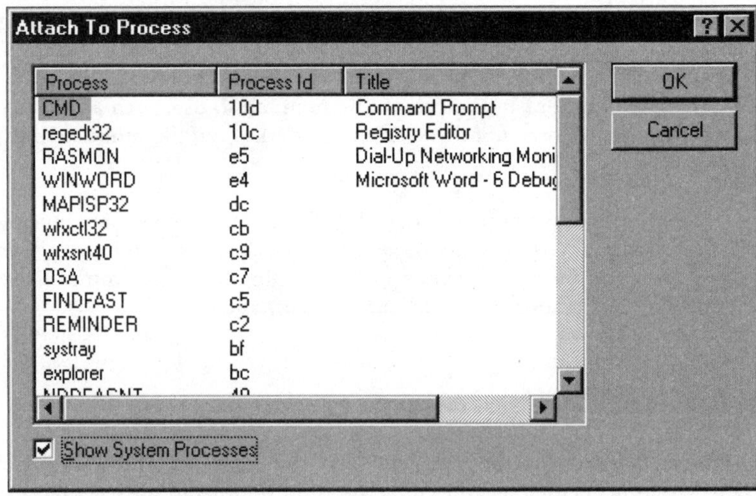

You'll need to check the Show System Processes box at the bottom in order to be able to see the module that contains your service; this checkbox allows you to see processes running in the system context. Highlight the name of the executable that houses your service, then hit OK.

Developer Studio will immediately attach itself to the process. To go into debug mode, select the Debug | Break menu item. The debugger will stop on the very next line of code in the service that it possibly can – this is usually somewhere in the middle of some assembly language code. If you're an assembler buff, you'll know what to do from here. If not, you just need to hit *F10* a few times to single-step through assembly statements until you get to one of the lines of code you can recognize (helpfully intertwined into the disassembly window, so you can tell where you are). Then you can use the call stack to view the source code window where the break occurred, and then set your breakpoints or single step from there.

Using Task Manager

The other method of worming your way into a running process is to use the Windows NT Task Manager's process pane to find the name of the module you want, and then right click on it. Next, select the Debug item from the context menu. This will bring up the default debugger for the current Windows NT installation (usually Visual C++ if it's installed), or whatever debugger the current module is set up to launch when debugged (I'll show you how to do this in the next section). Then you can just proceed as above, by selecting Debug | Break to break into the module.

Of course, this *doesn't* give you the ability to set a breakpoint on a particular line of code before the service starts, and then to start the service and have it stop on the breakpoint. In other words, the only way to really use this debugging technique is if the function you are debugging is not on the main execution path of the running service. If the place you want to debug is in the 'initialization' or 'run' segments of the service, there's no way to stop it with a breakpoint before the function runs. You'd have to have pretty fast hands to start a service and then break into it during its initialization phase using this technique!

Setting Breakpoints Before the Service Starts

Instead of the above, what you may need to do is set breakpoints and have the service step into debug mode when it hits one. To do this, you must use the registry to attach a debugger to your module name. The example below assumes you want to use the Visual C++ debugger, but you're completely free to substitute it with your favorite.

- In the registry path `HKEY_LOCAL_MACHINE\SOFTWARE\Microsoft\Windows NT\CurrentVersion`, create a subkey called `Image File Executable Options`. (This subkey may already exist.)
- Beneath that key, create a key with the same name as the executable that houses the service you want to debug. If the service is housed in `myservices.exe`, then create a key with exactly that name.
- Beneath the module name key, create a value of type `REG_SZ` named `Debugger`, with a string that's the fully qualified path to the debugger. On my machine, this would be `d:\devstudio\sharedide\bin\msdev.exe`.
- Your service is now ready to be debugged using calls to `DebugBreak()`.

Alternatively, you can just set up `msdev.exe` as your default debugger for all modules. By default, this sets itself up as the default debugger for the system, but if that's not true in the case of your machine, you can use the `HKEY_LOCAL_MACHINE\SOFTWARE\Microsoft\Windows NT\CurrentVersion\AeDebug` registry key to set it up that way.

The key contains two values: `Auto` and `Debugger`. `Auto` can be set to either 0 or 1. If it is set to "0", the system will generate the usual popup message box that states that an exception has occurred and gives you the choice of either terminating the application by pressing OK, or debugging it by choosing Cancel. If the `Auto` value is set to "1", then the system dispenses with the dialog box and simply launches right into the debugger specified in the `Debugger` value. When Visual C++ is installed, it changes the `Debugger` value to the path name of `msdev.exe`.

Invoking the Debugger

Now you can use the `DebugBreak()` Win32 API function in your code to invoke the debugger. Simply put a call to `DebugBreak()` anywhere you would normally use a red dot breakpoint from the interactive debugger. When it's encountered at runtime, the function causes a breakpoint exception that launches the debugger.

It wouldn't feel right if everything were as easy as it looks, and of course this method of debugging has its own set of annoyances. Every time you want to change the locations of breakpoints, you have to move the calls to `DebugBreak()` around in the code, and then rebuild the application. Then, you have to go out to the command line and start the service, hit Cancel when the exception box pops up (spawning a new instance of Visual C++), and so on. It's just not as easy or as much fun as using *F5* to start debugging straight from the editor.

A Quick Demonstration

We can look at this in action by placing a call to `DebugBreak()` in the Business Object project from Chapter 9. A reasonably good first place to put it would be right before the `_Module::Start()` call in `_tWinMain()`, like so:

```
   _Module.m_bService = false;
   if(lRes == ERROR_SUCCESS)
      _Module.m_bService = true;

   lRes = _Module.ReadParameters();
   if(lRes != ERROR_SUCCESS)
      return lRes;

   DebugBreak();
   _Module.Start();

   // When we get here, the service has been stopped
   return _Module.m_status.dwWin32ExitCode;
}
```

Now, when you attempt to start the service from the Services applet, you quickly hit the exception breakpoint, as shown here:

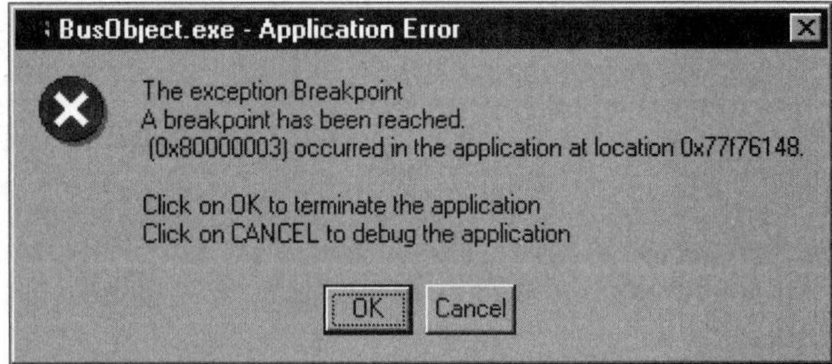

Click the Cancel button and a new instance of the debugger will launch, putting you right into the thick of some assembly code:

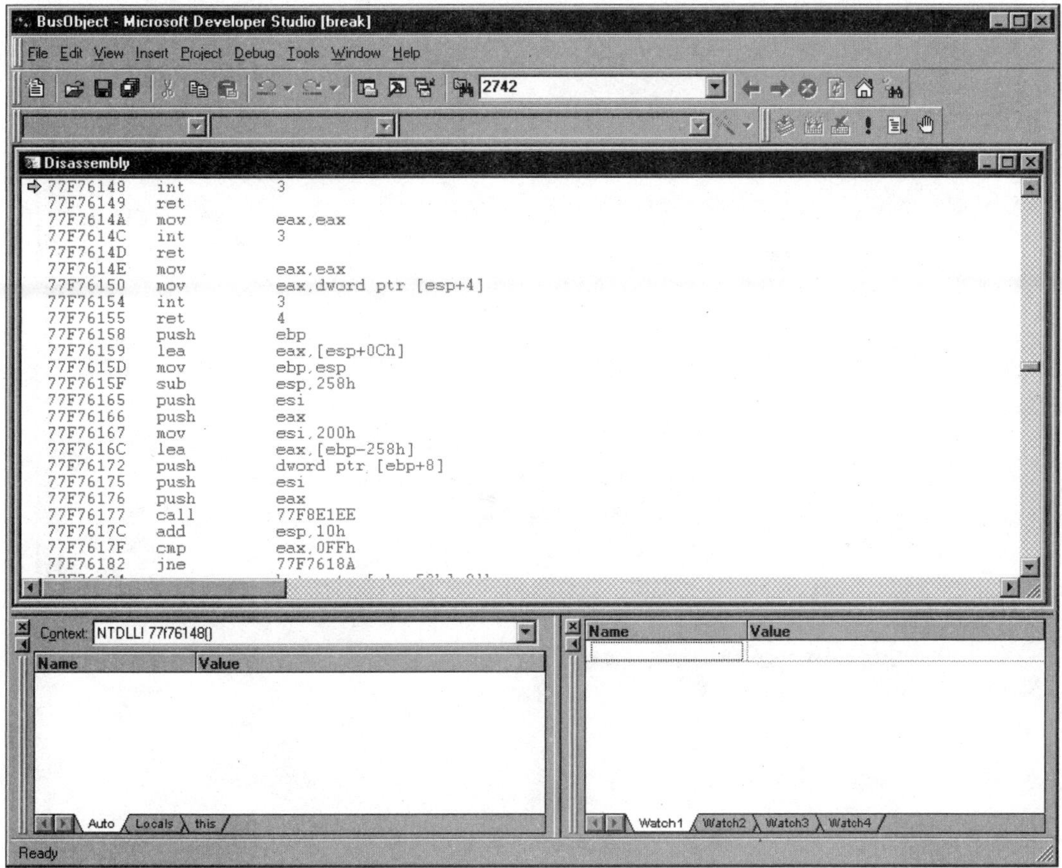

When you hit *F10* a couple of times, you'll start to recognize where you are. You can select the function you want to step into using the Context dropdown:

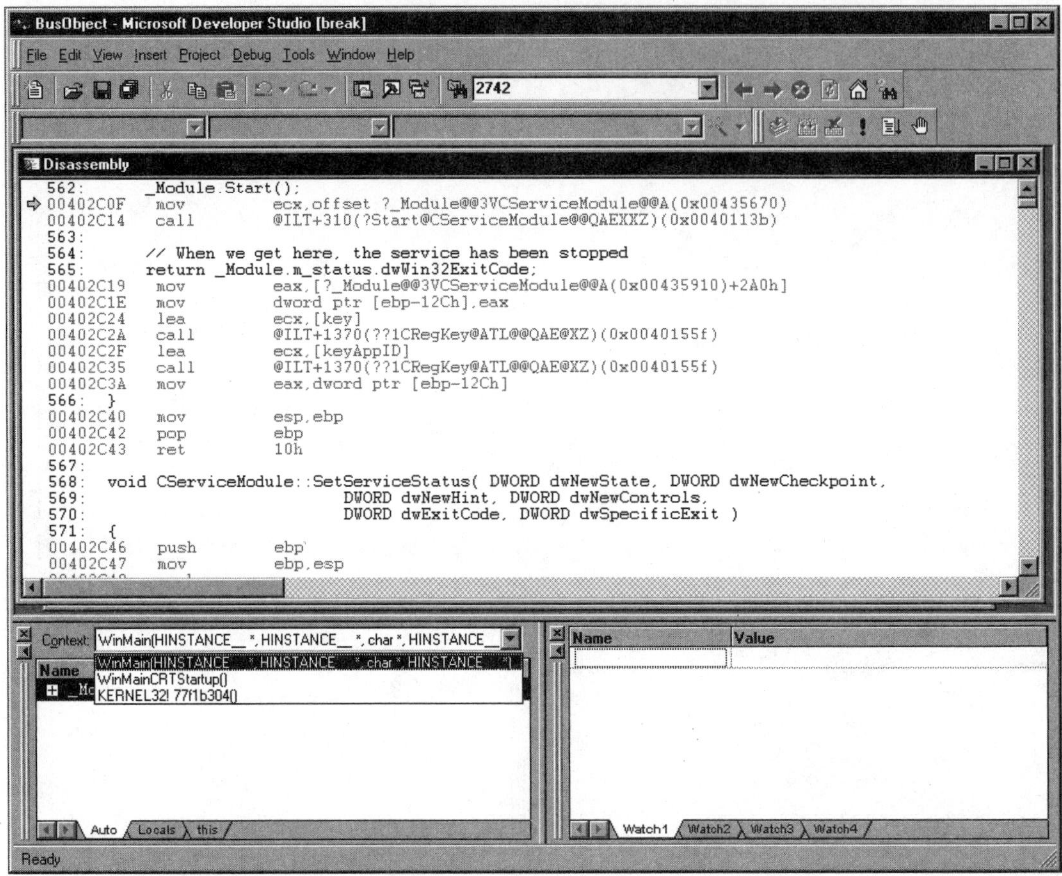

Once you select a function from here, you'll be placed into the familiar source file that the function lives in.

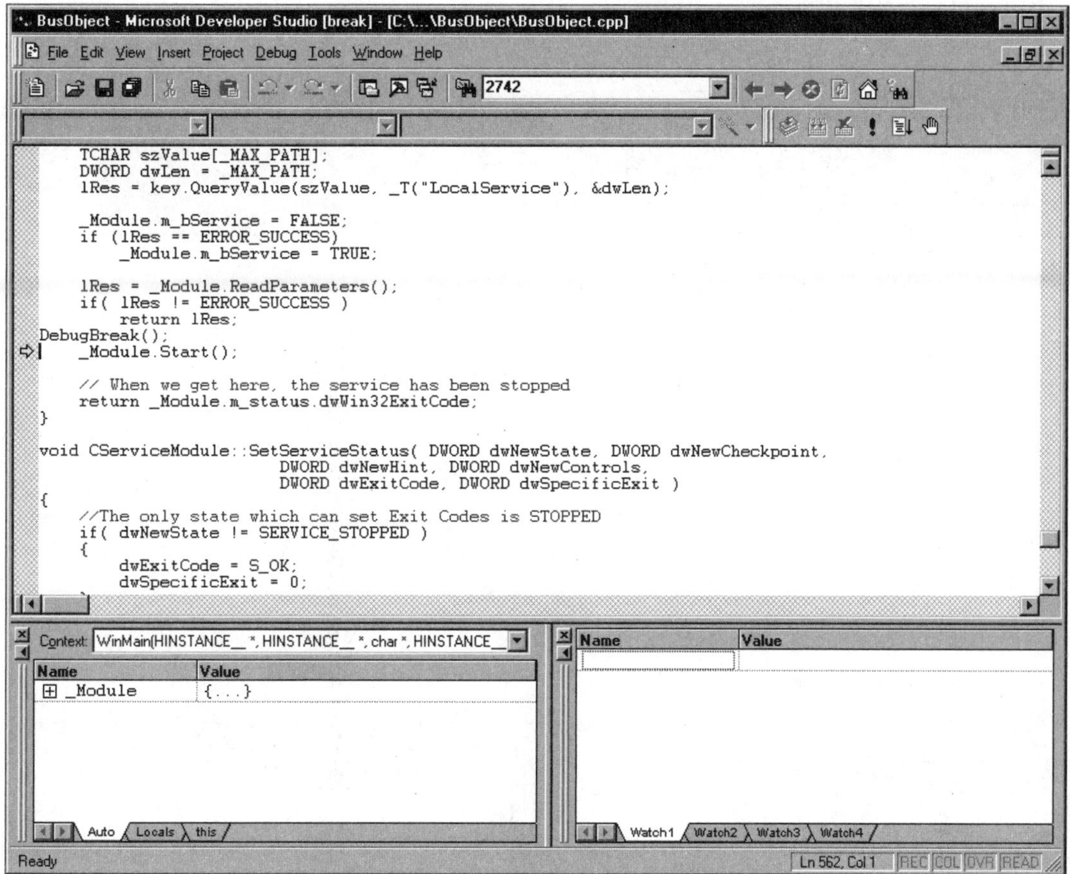
BusObject - Microsoft Developer Studio [break] - [C:\...\BusObject\BusObject.cpp]
File Edit View Insert Project Debug Tools Window Help
2742
TCHAR szValue[_MAX_PATH];
DWORD dwLen = _MAX_PATH;
lRes = key.QueryValue(szValue, _T("LocalService"), &dwLen);
_Module.m_bService = FALSE;
if (lRes == ERROR_SUCCESS)
_Module.m_bService = TRUE;
lRes = _Module.ReadParameters();
if(lRes != ERROR_SUCCESS)
return lRes;
DebugBreak();
_Module.Start();
// When we get here, the service has been stopped
return _Module.m_status.dwWin32ExitCode;
}
void CServiceModule::SetServiceStatus(DWORD dwNewState, DWORD dwNewCheckpoint,
DWORD dwNewHint, DWORD dwNewControls,
DWORD dwExitCode, DWORD dwSpecificExit)
{
//The only state which can set Exit Codes is STOPPED
if(dwNewState != SERVICE_STOPPED)
{
dwExitCode = S_OK;
dwSpecificExit = 0;
Context: WinMain(HINSTANCE__ *, HINSTANCE__ *, char *, HINSTANCE__
Name
Value
_Module
{...}
Auto
Locals
this
Name
Value
Watch1
Watch2
Watch3
Watch4
Ready
Ln 562, Col 1
REC
COL
OVR
READ

Now, you can use *F10*, *F11*, set breakpoints, and do whatever you are used to doing when debugging. You can also load other source files in the project, set a breakpoint, and then allow execution to run to that breakpoint. For instance, if you wanted to step into the debugger when a client called the `IAuthor::GetAuthorList()` method, just set a breakpoint there, like so, and then press *F5* to let the project run:

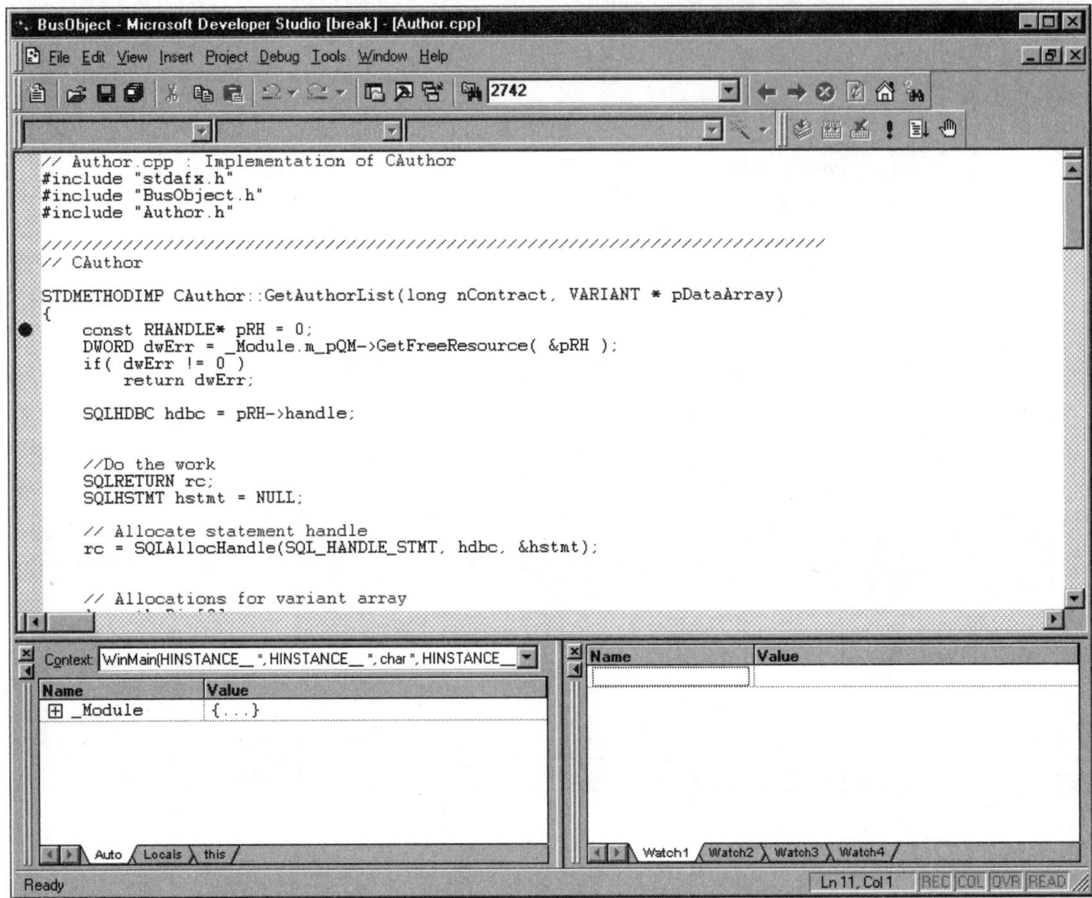

If a client calls the method, the debugger window will immediately pop up at the breakpoint, allowing you do debug the method call in action.

When you've finished, and you close the workspace, save your interactive debug environment each time. Then, next time you debug the service it will reload the old workspace with all your breakpoints intact and source files loaded.

DebugBreak and Structured Exception Handling

When you're using `DebugBreak()` to cause an exception in your service so that it can be debugged, be aware that, if the function that calls `DebugBreak()` is nested inside a structured exception handling framework that wraps unhandled exceptions, things won't work in quite the way you expected. Instead of getting an exception dialog box that allows you to click Cancel to spawn the debugger, your service will halt on the breakpoint but never give you the option of spawning the debugger.

This happens because the `DebugBreak()` call is really an `EXCEPTION_BREAKPOINT` exception. If a generic exception handler traps it, the exception message gets quashed; the only time that the dialog is raised is when the exception goes unhandled. There are a couple of ways around this problem:

- You can use a special preprocessor symbol to omit selectively the exception handler that's wrapping the `DebugBreak()` call. When debugging is needed, just build with the preprocessor symbol defined. For instance:

```
#ifndef _DEBUGBREAK
   __try
   {
#endif

      // Some code

#ifndef _DEBUGBREAK
   }
   __except(EXCEPTION_EXECUTE_HANDLER)
   {
      // Handler
   }
#endif
```

- A second option is to fool the system into thinking that the exception is not being handled, so the message box appears. You can do that by wrapping the `DebugBreak()` call in its own structured exception handling block, giving the *inner* block the chance to handle the call. The trick is to use the Win32 API function `UnhandledExceptionFilter()` to tell the system that the call was unhandled and that it should therefore display the 'unhandled exception' message box:

```
#ifdef _DEBUGBREAK

   __try
   {
      DebugBreak();
   }
   __except(UnhandledExceptionFilter(GetExceptionInformation()))
   {
      // Do nothing
   }

#endif
```

DebugBreak and Non-LocalSystem Accounts

The `DebugBreak()` method has another little hitch. If the 'log on as' account for the service is not the LocalSystem account but a member of the local Administrators group, the following error will pop up when you hit Cancel to enter the debugger:

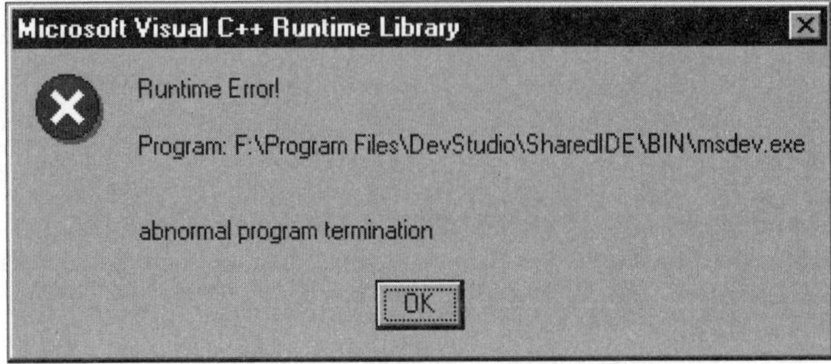

If the 'log on as' account is *not* a member of the local Administrators group (but still isn't LocalSystem), the message will be different, although it indicates the same problem:

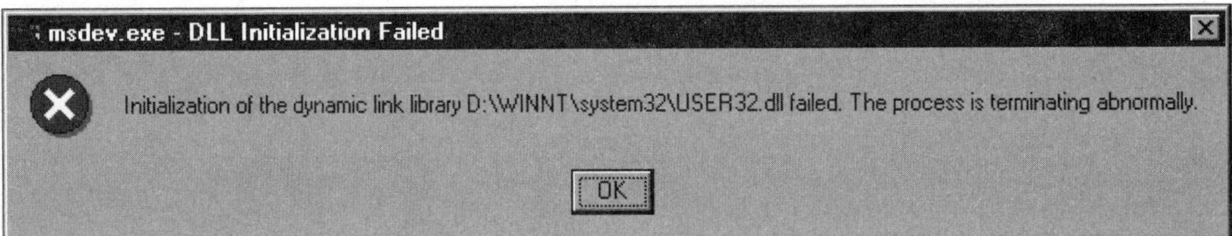

This should look familiar to you from the Chapter 7 – the problem here is that the account you're running the service under doesn't have access to the interactive user's window station and desktop. Incidentally, this will happen even if the interactive and 'log on as' accounts are the *same* account, because the two logon sessions get separate window stations. To solve *this* problem, you can do one of two things:

- Do your debugging while the service is running under the context of the LocalSystem account, and then switch to the real 'log on as' account when the problem is solved.
- If the problem the service is having is actually related to the account it is being run under, and it's necessary to debug the service while it is running under that account, you can run the following short program. It applies a null DACL to the interactive window station and desktop (`winsta0\\default`). Running this program before debugging will set the DACL for the duration of the user logon, and reset it after log off. Be aware that your screensaver will not work after you do this.

```
#include <windows.h>

int main()
{
   HDESK hdesk = NULL;
   HWINSTA hwinsta = NULL;
   SECURITY_DESCRIPTOR sd;
   SECURITY_INFORMATION si = DACL_SECURITY_INFORMATION;
```

```
    __try
    {
       // Open the window station and desktop
       hwinsta = OpenWindowStation("winsta0", FALSE, WRITE_DAC);
       if (hwinsta == NULL)
          __leave;

       hdesk = OpenDesktop("default", 0, FALSE,
                     WRITE_DAC | DESKTOP_WRITEOBJECTS | DESKTOP_READOBJECTS);
       if (hdesk == NULL)
          __leave;

       // Create a security descriptor with a NULL DACL
       if(!InitializeSecurityDescriptor(&sd, SECURITY_DESCRIPTOR_REVISION))
          __leave;

       if(!SetSecurityDescriptorDacl(&sd, TRUE, (PACL)NULL, FALSE))
          __leave;

       // Set the security descriptors on the winstation and desktop
       //  to the new one you just created
       if(!SetUserObjectSecurity(hwinsta, &si, &sd))
          __leave;

       if(!SetUserObjectSecurity(hdesk, &si, &sd))
          __leave;
    }
    __finally                 // Close the handles on error or as normal flow
    {
       if(hdesk != NULL)
          CloseDesktop(hdesk);
       if(hwinsta != NULL)
          CloseWindowStation(hwinsta);
    }
    return 0;
}
```

Other Debugging Strategies

When it come to debugging a service during development, there are a couple of other techniques you might want to consider. In this section, I will discuss some of the overall strategies that can help make debugging a service a little bit easier. I *won't* go into general debugging techniques, for which every experienced programmer has his or her own preference.

Write the Base Portions of your Code Before Creating a Service

In order to work around some of the annoyances of having to debug the service by starting it outside of the interactive debugger, you can choose another technique. Write the basic functionality of the service as a good old executable server, troubleshoot and debug the code, and then move the whole architecture into the service infrastructure. Of course, how well this technique works varies according to what your service is doing; sometimes, it's very the act of trying to put in proper SCM control handling that turns a working executable server into an ugly beast with lots of thread synchronization and communication problems.

Adding the service-specific stuff at the end of the development process usually works best for simpler services, but you should be wary of unwittingly introducing the race conditions or thread communication problems we discussed at the end Chapter 2 by adding service code as an 'afterthought'. Furthermore, if you want to use the C++ service class from Chapter 4, then merging the code from the two sources might take a while anyway. In summary, and as so often, this technique can sometimes work well, while at other times it may be more trouble than it's worth.

Use a Switch to Start the Service as a Regular Application

The second overall strategy is to structure the code so that by using a special command-line switch, the service can be started either as an executable server or as a service. For instance, in the main loop of the code, you might select different code paths based on the switch. You might also create an additional project configuration, say Executable Server, which has different settings and `#define` statements so that service infrastructure code is excluded from this build type. The advantage of the special build is that checking for the switch doesn't weigh down your production code too much.

This technique has similar drawbacks to the previous strategy, although it does at least allow you quickly to isolate problems in the logic of the server from problems in the service code itself, and to debug the server logic without too much trouble. On the downside, it's sometimes a bit hard to extricate the service infrastructure and the synchronization mechanisms from the real processing logic. It takes a bit of up-front planning, but it may be worth the extra work if you can do it without overburdening the performance of the main service code.

ATL Debugging

The default implementation provided for services by Microsoft's Active Template Library provides most of the necessary infrastructure for COM services to be started as COM servers if you desire it. However, you need to be careful about a couple of things if you intend to write the service so that it can be started both ways.

First, keep any 'real' initialization code (that's needed for both servers and services) out of `ServiceMain()` – `ServiceMain()` is skipped if the executable is started as a COM server. Second, only perform status updates *outside* of the `Run()` function. Since this is really a hard rule to follow if the service does anything interesting besides serving up COM objects, you can conditionally bracket the calls to `SetServiceStatus()` so that they are not called if the process wasn't started as a service.

Using the Event Log

One of the most useful ideas I can give you is to use the event log to track problems with API calls and your own functions. If the return code on a function is an error, jump out to the error handler, call `GetLastError()`, and format a message string to output what happened to the event log. Being conscientious about doing this can save lots of time tracking down problems in the long run – especially security issues, which always tend to happen at installation ("Well, it ran on *my* machine!").

For instance, you could use a variation of the following function to send Win32 errors to the event log, which is taken from the classes we developed in Chapter 4:

```
// Generic error handler that gathers the last error, looks up the
// description string, and optionally prints the string to the event log and/
// and/or raises an exception to stop the service
DWORD CService::ErrorHandler(const TCHAR* psz, bool bPrintEvent,
                                        bool bRaiseException, DWORD dwErr)
{
   LPVOID lpvMsgBuf;
   TCHAR sz[512 + 50];                    // Max message len + pre-string

   if(dwErr != 0)
   {
      if(!FormatMessage(
        FORMAT_MESSAGE_FROM_SYSTEM | FORMAT_MESSAGE_ALLOCATE_BUFFER,
        0, dwErr,
        MAKELANGID(LANG_NEUTRAL, SUBLANG_DEFAULT), (LPTSTR)&lpvMsgBuf, 0, 0))
      {
         wsprintf(sz, _T("%s failed: Unknown error %lu"), psz, dwErr);
      }
      else
      {
         wsprintf(sz, _T("%s failed: %s"), psz, (LPTSTR)lpvMsgBuf);
      }

      LocalFree(lpvMsgBuf);
   }
   else
   {
      // This is a custom error that is application-specific
      wsprintf(sz, _T("%s\n"), psz);
   }

#ifdef _DEBUG
   OutputDebugString(sz);
#endif

   if(bPrintEvent)
      PrintEvent(sz);

   if(bRaiseException)
      RaiseException( dwErr, EXCEPTION_NONCONTINUABLE, 0, 0 );

   return dwErr;
}
```

If you require it, this function even raises an exception to stop execution and invoke your exception handler. You might call it like so:

```
   m_hServiceStatus = RegisterServiceCtrlHandler(m_szName, lpHandlerProc);
   if(!m_hServiceStatus)
   {
      ErrorHandler(_T("RegisterServiceCtrlHandler"));
      return FALSE;
   }
```

OutputDebugString and DBMON

Sometimes, it can be handy simply to send a trace of what's happening in the service to an output window, rather than to the event log. To do that, use the `OutputDebugString()` function. (You saw this technique in Chapter 8; the DbMon output below is from the Quartermaster sample):

```
VOID OutputDebugString(
                LPCTSTR lpOutputString    // Pointer to string to be displayed
);
```

This function simply accepts any string to be printed to the system debug window. If the service is running in debug mode inside a Visual C++ 5.0 debug session, it causes messages to be printed to the output window. However, the debug messages can also be read from DbMon, which is a handy tool for monitoring debug messages that's shipped with the Platform SDK. It allows you to read the output without launching the debugger and stepping into the service. DbMon provides a simple console window where the messages are displayed:

```
DbMon - D:\DEV\MSSDK\BIN\winnt\dbmon.exe
296: Handle Allocated------------------------------->Handle: 5834368
296: Handle Allocated------------------------------->Handle: 5838464
296: Handle Allocated------------------------------->Handle: 5839056
296: Handle Allocated------------------------------->Handle: 5842560
296: Handle Allocated------------------------------->Handle: 5843152
296: Handle Allocated------------------------------->Handle: 5846656
296: Handle Allocated------------------------------->Handle: 5847248
296: Handle Allocated------------------------------->Handle: 5850752
296: Handle Allocated------------------------------->Handle: 5851344
296: Handle Allocated------------------------------->Handle: 5854848
296: Allocations were increased---------------------------->10
296: Handle Dellocated------------------------------>Handle: 5834368
296: Handle Dellocated------------------------------>Handle: 5838464
296: Handle Dellocated------------------------------>Handle: 5839056
296: Handle Dellocated------------------------------>Handle: 5842560
296: Handle Dellocated------------------------------>Handle: 5843152
296: Handle Dellocated------------------------------>Handle: 5846656
296: Handle Dellocated------------------------------>Handle: 5847248
296: Handle Dellocated------------------------------>Handle: 5850752
296: Handle Dellocated------------------------------>Handle: 5851344
296: Handle Dellocated------------------------------>Handle: 5854848
```

This function will do work whether the application is in debug mode or not, so it's usually a good idea to surround your calls to `OutputDebugString()` with `#ifdef _DEBUG` statements to compile out the code when building for release. However, it can be useful to be able to 'trace' the application when the release build is running on a customer's machine, so you may wish to provide a command-line parameter that allows an administrator to start the service in 'verbose' mode. This would enable debug strings to be output to the window when (and only when) more detailed information was desired.

MessageBox

To show a message box from a service, even though it is running in a different window station from the interactive user, call the `MessageBox()` function, specifying the `MB_SERVICE_NOTIFICATION` flag. This will display a message box in the current desktop, whether or not there is a user logged on at the moment. However, making this call stops *all* activity in the service, so it should only be used for debugging, and certainly not for a production service.

Debugging Thread Routines

Debugging multithreaded applications can be incredibly difficult, at best. Because of the rapid context switches between breakpoints, it can be particularly hard to step through a worker thread routine that several threads are using at once – the debugger will cycle among the multiple threads that are using the same function. Furthermore, the very act of debugging changes the balance of the ordering of context switches, timings, and so forth. If your problem is a race condition, simply examining the problem in the debugger will probably solve it! When you go back to a test run with no breakpoints, the problem crops up again. The Visual C++ debugger has one relatively simple tool to try to help you debug multithreaded apps: the Debug | Threads... window, which is only available when the application is stopped at a breakpoint. It shows the currently running threads and their IDs, as well as the names of the functions they are currently in, if available.

The screenshot below shows the threads running in the Business Object service from the previous chapter. At the time of this snapshot, there are six threads. The main thread is in `CServiceModule::Start()`, waiting for the control dispatcher to release it. The `ServiceMain()` thread is cranking along in `CServiceModule::ServiceMain()`. The two worker threads – the allocator and the dead session poller – are both alive in the `_threadstartex` threads. The other two threads are unknown, but they were probably created by the ODBC driver manager to manage the open connections.

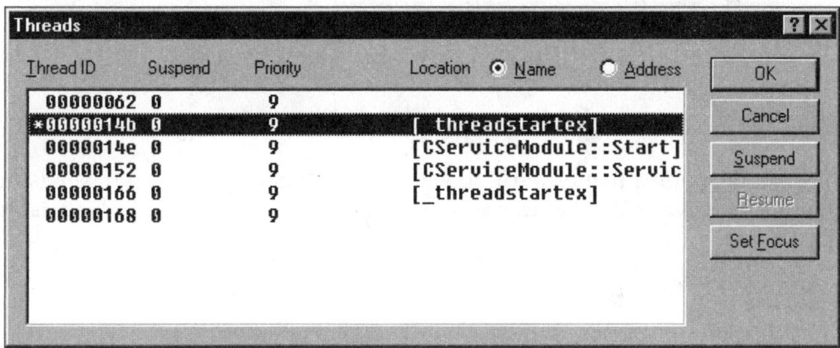

One nice feature of this tool is that threads can be suspended from execution to help slow down context switches while you are stepping through. Simply suspend all threads that you are not interested in looking at, and the cycling will stop. The focus of the debugger can also be switched to other threads to help get you back into the right execution context (the thread with the asterisk is the one with the current debugging focus). This is handy when you launch the debugger on a running service and don't exactly know where you jumped into the code. Remember, though, that debugging a service using this technique actually changes its behavior, and it may be difficult to duplicate the errors you are seeing in non-debug mode in the debugger. That's one of the things that make debugging multithreaded applications so difficult.

Another useful way to debug complex threading interactions is to use a logging technique. You can use `OutputDebugString()` to show the activities of individual threads, and the order they occurred in. Alternatively, you can use stream output functions to write the information to a file. This usually works pretty well, because the debug version of the C runtime serializes calls to I/O functions, to make sure that only one function can call them at a time – the output is therefore in order. The drawback is that these serialization mechanisms themselves take time, and can change the behavior of the routine you're trying to debug.

As a final word on this topic, it is sometimes difficult to know when different threads are changing the values of certain member or global variables. Visual C++'s Breakpoints window can help you here – simply select Edit | Breakpoints... and switch to the Data tab. Then, enter the expression or variable you want to break on if it changes:

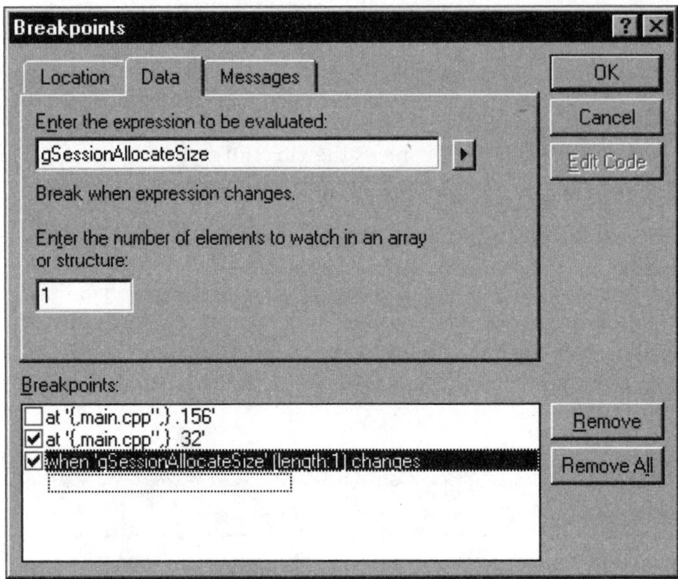

This little technique can give you a handy warning when your memory is getting trashed and you don't know by whom. You can also specify raw addresses and cast to the type of the variable you want to watch, like so:

```
DW(0x0041a6a0)
```

Using this technique is faster because it uses the hardware registers instead of doing a software evaluation.

Stopping a Dead Service

Sometimes during development and debugging, you will get a service into a state such that it cannot be stopped. You don't have to reboot! The command line `kill` directive is ideal for such situations. If your service is housed in `myservice.exe`, for example, then just issue '`kill myservice.exe`'. Remember to use the executable name, not the service name.

The other alternative is to run the 'special' version of `Taskmgr.exe` that I showed you in Chapter 7. This version has the `SE_DEBUG_NAME` privilege enabled for the process, so that the End Process command inside the task manager actually works.

Other Miscellaneous Tips

A few other tips you might find handy:

- Install the `.dbg` symbol files, which are very helpful when you're debugging and need to step into a Windows API call. They are usually installed using an icon provided by the SDK or Visual C++ itself, and they're shipped with the operating system or service pack version you are using. Unfortunately, because of the rapid changes in certain software for Windows NT, they can be very difficult to keep up to date. Many system DLLs are changed much more frequently than with a new service pack, and new debug symbols are not usually shipped with them. The hallmark of an incorrect debug symbol version is the message, "No matching symbolic information found," which appears when the debugger loads a DLL.
- If you're *really* serious, you can install the **checked build** of Windows NT. Essentially, this is NT compiled with the `_DEBUG` symbol, and it's available with MSDN. The checked build contains all of the `ASSERT`s and has debug information built in, with the inevitable result that it's substantially larger and slower than the 'normal' version. It is used primarily by device driver developers.
- You can set breakpoints inside a system call by specifying the function to break on in the Breakpoints dialog. If the function you want to break on is a `__stdcall` function, simply preface the function name with an underscore, and add `@nn` onto the end. (*nn* is the number of parameters multiplied by four; if any of the parameters are `WORD`s, just multiply those by two.) If the call type is `__cdecl`, leave out the `@nn`.

> *If you have trouble figuring a function out, you can also look for the proper name by using* `Dumpbin.exe` *on the module. Look up the parameters to the call in the Windows API documentation.*

- To debug the initialization routine of an auto-start service properly, you may need to change your load time to demand-start. If the problem goes away when you do so, you probably have a load-ordering group or dependency problem. Re-think the services the problematic service depends on to discover the problem.
- A variety of other applications you already know about are also available to help you debug, including PView, PWalk, Spy++, and so on.
- The Dependency Walker is a handy SDK tool that gives you a tree view of all the DLL dependencies an executable has, and all the functions the executable calls from each dependency. It also shows a great deal of handy information about the DLL itself, such as the load address, version and so forth. It is useful for debugging load address problems and DLL dependency version, problems (you think the executable is using one version of a DLL, but it is really using another).

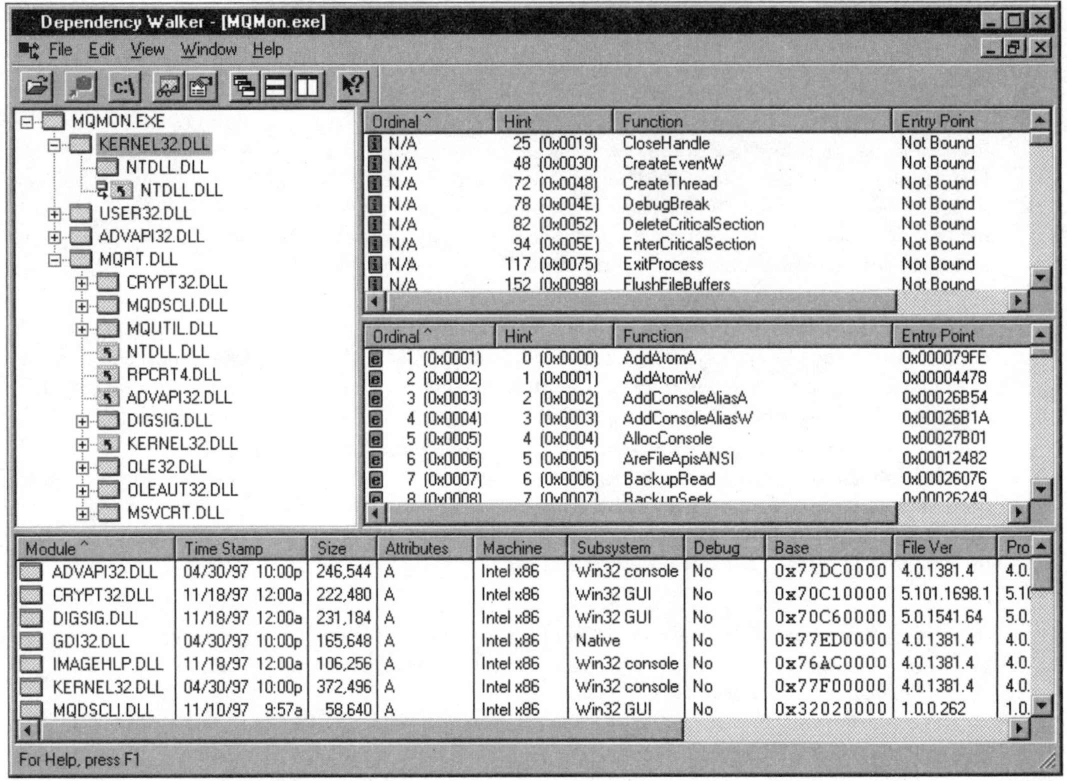

I've given you a number of tools and techniques that will help you to debug services and (hopefully) to write services with fewer bugs in to begin with. I think that the best tip I can give you going forward is to *single-step through your code in debug mode*, even if there is nothing wrong with it that you know of. You'll catch more problems by doing that than you could ever imagine. In a service, the way to do this is to put a `DebugBreak()` call into the execution path early, and just start single-stepping from there. Do this at least once for the whole project and for any major code changes.

Performance Tuning

Tuning your service for maximum performance is every bit as important as making sure that it is bug-free. Often, the best way to tune a service is to get feedback on *exactly* what the code is doing, and how long each thing that it does takes. The Win32 SDK and the NT Resource Kit provide a variety of profiling and tuning tools that can help you to understand what your code is really up to. Then, you can use the feedback to make adjustments and optimize those areas that are least efficient.

Tuning the Code

Let's start, though, with the code. When optimizing code, it's important to know what you are tuning *for*. It's usually the case that you're forced to make a trade-off between being more concerned about execution speed, or memory efficiency. These are not always mutually exclusive, but often one is achieved at the expense of the other, at least in terms of the code that you write. Your mission as a software designer is to decide which of these is more important before trying to tune at all. In fact, I would argue that the best time to decide about memory versus speed is when you are still in the design phases of the project. The decisions you make there will not only influence how you tune; they will affect you long *before* tuning by directing your choice of underlying algorithms and architectural strategies.

Think about the question, and commit your decision to paper. If you are on a large project, everyone should know what the strategy is, and be aware of its ramifications. When discussing the trade-offs, don't accept criteria like, "It should be as fast as possible," or, "It should use as little memory as possible." (Or worse, both!) These are non-statements. Have specific numbers in mind, like, "Service 500 requests per second," or, "Use a working set of only 18K." Then, if you're not meeting the parameters that were agreed upon, you can tune to meet your design goals.

Software development is too difficult and too time-consuming for you to be able to tune your programs to the edges of possibility, but there is nothing wrong with using profiling tools to expose and repair misuses of system resources, even if the component is functioning within specifications. Here, though, are some techniques that you can employ before resorting to those tools.

Use Fast Algorithms

This goes without saying, I suppose, but it emphasizes the point: The greatest performance gains or losses are going to come from your algorithms, not from optimizing tools. The nice thing about the *profiling* tools you'll see in the next section is that they will help you to find those poor algorithms and fix them. Choose fast algorithms to begin with, and performance will almost always be within a few percent of what you needed. Choose slow algorithms, and nothing can help you.

Optimizers

While many people have questioned the quality of code that optimizers produce, it is generally much better than the code that the non-optimized (debug) build would spit out. The commonest complaint from programmers is that the optimizer 'broke' code that was already tested and functioning correctly.

First of all, it is very rare for the 'optimize for size' option ever to break anything that wasn't already broken. If you are careful to unit-test your algorithms and build at Visual C++'s warning level 4, you will seldom (if ever) have a problem. Speed optimizations are a slightly different story: occasionally, I've heard of circumstances where the compiler *has* been over-aggressive and introduced bugs. These sometimes have to do with optimizations that keep temporary copies of variables in registers that may get changed by other threads. This can happen in situations where pointers to memory locations are passed to functions, and then the function uses the pointer multiple times – the optimizer generates assembly code that only reads the value once and never reads it again. If another thread changes value of the memory location being pointed to, the value might not get updated from the perspective of the optimized function.

If the desired effect is that the value should never seem to change in mid-stream, you can wrap the function that causes the *read* operation with a critical section, or you can make a temporary copy. On the other hand, it may be that the function in question is called from inside a loop in a thread function. In this case, you probably *want* to know about variable changes, and you can use the C++ `volatile` keyword to tell the compiler not to optimize a particular variable by keeping temporary copies of it.

Presuming you're able to 'fix' your code so that optimizations will work, the question now is which kind to use. Strangely, both of the optimizations that the compiler produces are very similar – a size optimization is aimed at cutting down the number of assembly instructions which, consequently, usually trims down execution time as well. (Contrast this to your own 'algorithmic' design decisions, which affect things at a higher level: "Do I cache this recordset from the database, or re-read it each time?")

The big difference is that the compiler usually optimizes for speed alone by making intrinsic functions inline, which means that instead of calling out to particular functions, it will insert the function source code right in the middle of your calling function. However, if the increased code size pushes it over a 4kb page boundary, this 'improvement' can actually be more costly than not doing it – be careful that your 'speed' optimization doesn't turn out to be slower than the 'size' optimization!

Incremental Linking and Debug Information

Before shipping, you'll want to turn off **incremental linking** on the release build. Incremental linking works by inserting `INT 3` instructions at various points inside the executable to make extra space for inserting changes. On a re-link, any changes are just inserted into the padded areas, but this convenience can fatten up your executable size by more than 30%. (The size of `Quartermaster.exe` went from 30kb to 55kb with incremental linking turned on.) There is simply no need to ship a file full of padding.

In a similar vein, debug information (if it is used with a release build) should be kept in a PDB file, since it stores the debug information separately and doesn't load down the file with extra information. The only extra overhead in the executable is then a simple filename pointer to the PDB file.

Rebasing DLLs

To improve the load time of your service executable, it is always a good idea to **rebase** the dependent DLLs so that they don't conflict and end up having to be relocated dynamically by the Win32 loader. You can do this either by using the `/BASE:`*`nnnn`* switch when you base your own DLLs, to change them to an unused address, or by using the Rebase utility. Rebase takes a list of the files that are in a project and figures out where they should all load so that they do not conflict with other DLLs in the process. Usually, rebasing is done as a build step *after* the link step. Take a look at the SDK documentation for Rebase for more information.

Tuning Tools

In this section, we'll examine some of the different tools that are available to help applications run faster and more efficiently. As it turns out, there are a whole host of different tools and gadgets that give detailed information about applications while they're running. Most of these tools are categorized as **profilers**, or tools that give you information about:

- How long an application takes to run a function
- The number of times a function was called
- The percentage of **function coverage**, or the overall percentage of code that was hit when the application ran

We'll also look briefly at the NT Performance Monitor and examine how to use it to expose resource bottlenecks in the system. Throughout this section, I'll use the Quartermaster example from Chapter 8 as a guinea pig. Most of the tools we will use are installed by the January '98 version of the Platform SDK, so if you haven't installed that yet, you will need to do so in order to work along with the book.

The Visual C++ Profiler

The Profiler is a handy tool that's available from within Visual C++. In fact, Visual C++ just wraps up the command line interface available in the PREP, Profile and PLIST tools (Microsoft's command-line preparation, run, post-run, and formatted output tools for doing code profiling), automating the run cycle, and formatting the results into a special pane in the Output window.

To use the Profiler:

- Go to the Project | Settings... dialog and then to the Link tab. Select General in the dropdown and check the Enable profiling box. You may also want to check the Generate mapfile box while you're in there (you'll see why very shortly).
- Check the Generate debug info box on the same tab. (This enables you to do line-by-line profiling as well.)
- Select the Build | Profile... item from the menu. The following dialog box will appear:

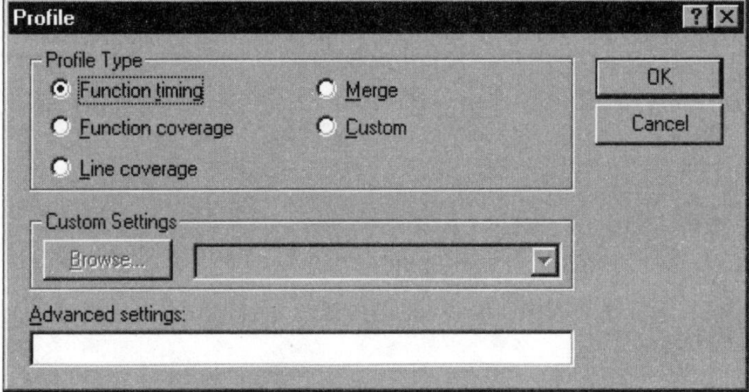

From here, you can select several options:

- Function timing. Outputs function times and counts for specified functions.
- Function coverage. Outputs degree of code coverage in specified functions.
- Line coverage. Profiles each line, with counts, and shows code coverage (That is, the percentage of code that was 'covered' by the profiling run. Usually this will be a number between 75-100%, depending on what activity you were profiling and the amount of error-handling code you have.)

- Merge. Advanced. Allows merging of the results of several runs into one output sample.
- Custom. Allows you to use a custom setting file, written as a batch, to drive the profiler.
- Advanced settings. This box allows you to specify any of the PREP command line options as additional settings. The PREP options are shown below:

```
Command Prompt
Microsoft (R) PREP Version 1.30.7022
Copyright (c) Microsoft Corp 1991-1997. All rights reserved.

PREP [options] [module-names]

options:

/EXC     Exclude function/source/obj/lib from profile
/EXCALL  Exclude everything from profile
/FC      Profile by function with counts
/FT      Profile by function with times and counts
/FV      Profile by function with coverage
/INC     Include function/source/obj/lib in profile
/HELP    Display PREP usage
/IO      <filename> Read a PBO file
/IT      <filename> Read a PBT file
/LC      Profile by line with counts
/CB      <number> Calibrate overhead
/LV      Profile by line with coverage
/M       <filename> Merge PBT and PBO file
/NOLOGO  Suppress copyright message
/OI      <filename> Write a PBI file
/OM      Store modified EXE/DLL in external file
/OT      <filename> Write a PBT file
/SF      <function> Start profile with function
/?       Display PREP usage
/AT      Collect attribution data
/STACK   <number> Set attributed stack depth

D:\Data\Book\Code\Chapter 12\Pooler\Release>_
```

For instance, you can use the `/INC` option to specify particular files or source code lines to profile, so to specify all the source lines in a particular module, specify the OBJ file as:

```
/EXCALL /INC pooler.obj
```

Alternatively, the following options will profile the lines 0-50:

```
/EXCALL /INC pooler.cpp(0-50)
```

Running the Visual C++ Profiler actually executes a series of commands, like so:

- A PREP (phase I) call, to set up the profiling run and specify which files to run against, etc.
- Profile, to execute the profiling session.
- PREP (phase II), which assembles the results.
- PLIST, to display the results from the output (`.pbt`) file.

Profiler has a great many other options, which are best discovered by exploring the documentation.

Tips on Using Profiler

Usually, it is not very helpful just to do a function profile of an entire application run. The information that gets returned is too bulky and too difficult to sort through. A better approach is often to profile specific functions, to see whether they are giving the degree of performance expected. Choose the place you think a bottleneck might be occurring and start from there.

To do that, you need to use the `/SF` 'advanced' setting. It allows you to profile a specific function by specifying its name. Be aware, though, that you can't simply use the C function name when you're compiling a C++ program, and this is where the mapfile that I recommended you to build comes in handy. Open the `.map` file, find the mangled name of the function and specify it as the parameter, as shown below:

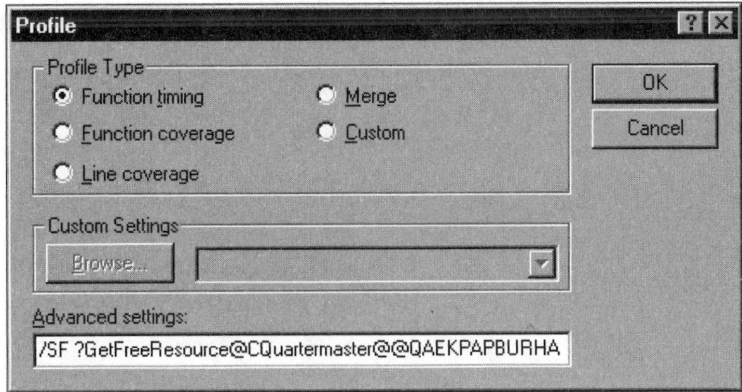

To make best use of this tool, you should know that, while the line profiling and line counting features work fine in a multithreaded environment, timing functions can be problematic when the application is multithreaded. Generally, avoid trying to profile functions that might cut across multiple threads, because these functions' processing may be interrupted, producing hard-to-interpret results. Another reason is that functions profiled from the main thread when most of the work occurs in worker threads do not have the proper degree of timing granularity. A better idea is to try to profile a *single* thread's work at a time, at the very most. This is possible by using the `/SF` flag and specifying the thread's starting function, and including *all* the program's functions.

Incidentally, there is a macro called `Profiler.xlm` available in the `Vc\Bin` directory that you can use to do more sophisticated reporting in Excel based on the contents of the PBT file produced.

Profiling a Service

Now that I've explained a few of the niceties of profiling, it's time for an admission: profiling an NT service while it's actually running as such is a bit more trouble than profiling the executable alone. This is a good reason to check your algorithms out in a standard executable *before* building a service wrapper around them, if possible. However, if you do need to profile a running service, you can do it like so:

- ❑ Add a couple of new system environment variables:

```
__ProfilePBI=<full path of executable>
__ProfilePBO=<full path of executable>
```

- ❑ Make sure that `Profile.dll` is in the path.
- ❑ Build the executable with profiling turned on in the linker settings.
- ❑ Figure out where to profile *from.* If the work you are profiling occurs in `ServiceMain()`, you'll need to specify `ServiceMain` in the command below. Otherwise, specify the name of the worker thread.
- ❑ Run the PREP command to create an EXE modified for profiling, like so:

```
PREP /om /ft /sf <name of the thread function to time>
```

- ❑ Copy `MySvc._xe` to `MySvc.exe`.
- ❑ Run the service and stop it when timing is complete.
- ❑ Run the following commands to prepare the output file (`MySvc.pbt`):

```
PREP /m MYSVC
PLIST MYSVC
```

FIOSAP

One of the more interesting profiling tools available is **FIOSAP**, the File I/O and Synchronization Profiler, which looks *specifically* at synchronization and file I/O calls. It is particularly useful in services, because it tabulates all the activity going on in all of the synchronization objects. This tool will show timings per call type, number of calls, and average time spent per call.

FIOSAP works by routing each call that normally requires `Kernel32.dll` through a different library known as `Fernel32.dll`. This allows the profiler to track statistics on the time spent in each call. To activate the FIOSAP profiler, make the following command in the directory in which the executable to be profiled is located:

```
apf32cvt fernel32 <appname>.exe
```

To undo the operation, use

```
apf32cvt undo <appname>.exe
```

Each command is only good for a particular build of the executable, so if you build, use FIOSAP, then build again, you'll have to reset using the first command again. When the executable is deleted and rebuilt, the mapping to `fernel32.dll` goes away.

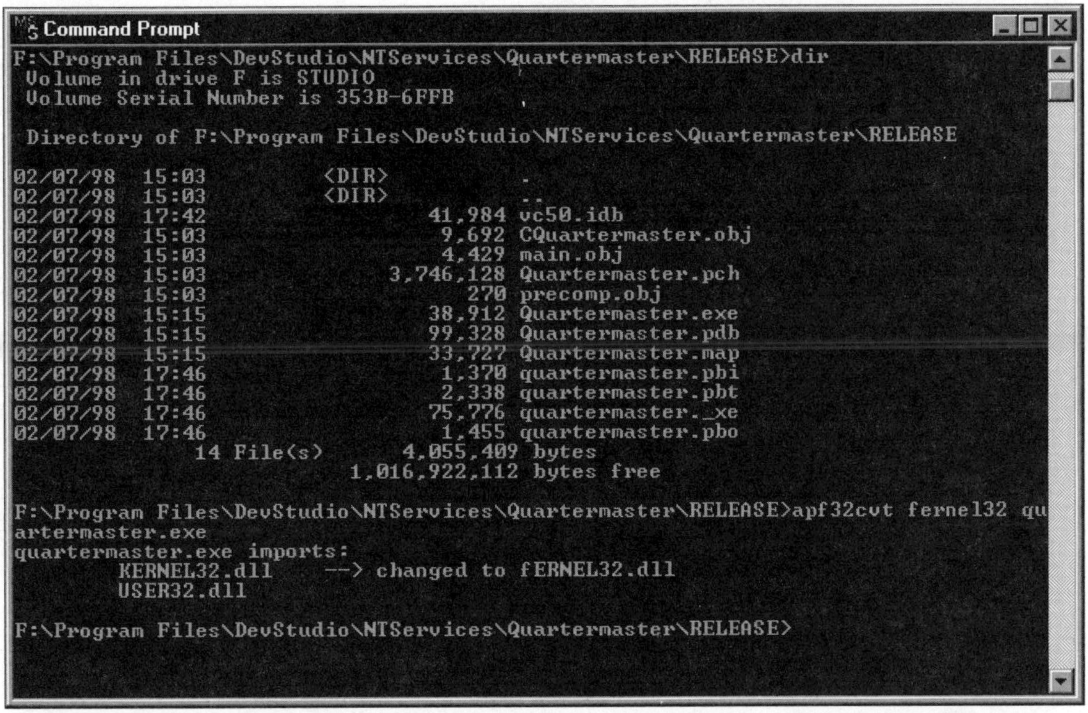

```
Command Prompt
F:\Program Files\DevStudio\NTServices\Quartermaster\RELEASE>dir
 Volume in drive F is STUDIO
 Volume Serial Number is 353B-6FFB

 Directory of F:\Program Files\DevStudio\NTServices\Quartermaster\RELEASE

02/07/98  15:03         <DIR>          .
02/07/98  15:03         <DIR>          ..
02/07/98  17:42                 41,984 vc50.idb
02/07/98  15:03                  9,692 CQuartermaster.obj
02/07/98  15:03                  4,429 main.obj
02/07/98  15:03              3,746,128 Quartermaster.pch
02/07/98  15:03                    270 precomp.obj
02/07/98  15:15                 38,912 Quartermaster.exe
02/07/98  15:15                 99,328 Quartermaster.pdb
02/07/98  15:15                 33,727 Quartermaster.map
02/07/98  17:46                  1,370 quartermaster.pbi
02/07/98  17:46                  2,338 quartermaster.pbt
02/07/98  17:46                 75,776 quartermaster._xe
02/07/98  17:46                  1,455 quartermaster.pbo
              14 File(s)      4,055,409 bytes
                          1,016,922,112 bytes free

F:\Program Files\DevStudio\NTServices\Quartermaster\RELEASE>apf32cvt fernel32 qu
artermaster.exe
quartermaster.exe imports:
        KERNEL32.dll    --> changed to fERNEL32.dll
        USER32.dll

F:\Program Files\DevStudio\NTServices\Quartermaster\RELEASE>
```

When the application terminates, a file called `fernel32.end` is created in the directory where the executable is located. It's a simple text file with formatted output containing timings and other information about what the application did when it made calls to various synchronization objects. An example of the output is shown below; I ran the profile that generated this file from the Quartermaster example in Chapter 8.

```
                  SYNCHRONIZATION PROFILER OUTPUT
                (Note: All times are in microseconds)


 1. Event Profiler

------------------------------------------------------------------------------
-
Event:            Type: Manual Reset
--------------------+----------+----------+----------+-----------------------
-
    Operation       |  Total   |Number of | Average  |Successful
       Name         |  Time    |operations|  Time    | Waits
--------------------+----------+----------+----------+----------
Overall             |     79934|       464|       172|         -
Create              |        38|         1|        38|         -
Set                 |        17|         1|        17|         -
Wait                |4387779010|       462|   9497357|         2.
   Single           |4387779010|       462|   9497357|         2.


------------------------------------------------------------------------------
-
Statistics for all event activity  (Number of handles used: 1)
--------------------+----------+----------+----------+-----------------------
-
    Operation       |  Total   |Number of | Average  |Successful
       Name         |  Time    |operations|  Time    | Waits
--------------------+----------+----------+----------+----------
Overall             |     79934|       464|       172|         -
Create              |        38|         1|        38|         -
Set                 |        17|         1|        17|         -
Wait                |4387779010|       462|   9497357|         2.
   Single           |4387779010|       462|   9497357|         2.
```

```
2. Semaphore Profiler

------------------------------------------------------------------------------
-
Semaphore:                 Max Count: 255
-------------------+----------+----------+----------+-----------------------
-
     Operation       |  Total    |Number of | Average   |Successful
        Name         |   Time    |operations|   Time    |  Waits
-------------------+----------+----------+----------+----------
Overall              |      1009|     14993|          0|          -
Create               |        45|         1|         45|          -
Release              |8590014710|      7494|    1146252|          -
Wait                 |3.86766e10|      7497|    5158950|      7497.
   Single            |3.86766e10|      7497|    5158950|      7497.
Close                |        11|         1|         11|          -


------------------------------------------------------------------------------
-
Statistics for all semaphore activity  (Number of handles used: 1)
-------------------+----------+----------+----------+-----------------------
-
     Operation       |  Total    |Number of | Average   |Successful
        Name         |   Time    |operations|   Time    |  Waits
-------------------+----------+----------+----------+----------
Overall              |      1009|     14993|          0|          -
Create               |        45|         1|         45|          -
Release              |8590014710|      7494|    1146252|          -
Wait                 |3.86766e10|      7497|    5158950|      7497.
   Single            |3.86766e10|      7497|    5158950|      7497.
Close                |        11|         1|         11|          -
```

Notice that for each synchronization object, there is a table showing how much time was spent in each operation on the object. In the case of the semaphore, that means creating, releasing, waiting for, and closing it. The table also shows the raw number of calls to each function, and the average time per call. Finally, it shows how many successful waits occurred. The objects are listed by name, if they were given names when created (I chose not to). There is also a summary table for each *type* of object that was tracked.

> *Unfortunately, since critical sections are not kernel objects, no timings for critical sections are available using FIOSAP.*

The nice thing about FIOSAP is that you can even use it on a running service. Simply set up the call, then start the service. When you have completed the testing, stop the service and the summary file will be created. It is one of the few profilers that you can use on your service while it is actually working in service mode. It also provides very useful information on where the service might be having performance problems because of contention for resources.

Interpreting the Results

If you are unfamiliar with what the Quartermaster does, or you could use a reminder, now may be the time to take a quick glance at Chapter 8 to understand what is going on.

In profiling the Quartermaster, I had a couple of things in mind: First, I wanted to make sure that the data structures used inside the allocation mechanism would not bottleneck under a very high load (several thousand transactions per second). So, I was interested in raw performance. I was also interested in seeing what impact changing the number of available resources would have on allocation and the wait times involved. To determine these things, I profiled with no 'check-out' time (`HANDLEALLOCCOST = 0`), and with two different 'available resource' numbers.

The sample figures above were generated in a simulation that contained 25 client threads, each of which ran 300 iterations of the function. It was given 20 resources to start off with, and each resource was 'held' by each client for 250 milliseconds. The handle re-allocation mechanism (the ability to create more handles on the fly when the handle count equals zero) was left intact and functioning, and the simulation took around one-and-a-half minutes to run. You can see that the Quartermaster served these clients fairly well; each semaphore wait was successful.

The second test run that I performed was radically different from the first. It had the same 25 client threads running 300 iterations, and the resource handles were held on to for 250ms each time. However, this time I allowed only *2* resources and turned *off* the dynamic reallocation mechanism. The same test run took almost 15 minutes to complete, and FIOSAP produced the following output:

```
2. Semaphore Profiler
--------------------------------------------------------------------------------
-
Semaphore:                    Max Count: 255
--------------------+----------+---------+----------+------------------------
-
     Operation       |  Total   |Number of | Average  |Successful
        Name         |   Time   |operations|   Time   |  Waits
--------------------+----------+----------+----------+----------
Overall              |   2000002|     11142|       179|         -
Create               |        35|         1|        35|         -
Release              |     92444|      3652|        25|         -
Wait                 |2.71781e10|      7488|   3629554|     3657.
   Single            |2.71781e10|      7488|   3629554|     3657.
Close                |        11|         1|        11|         -
```

You can see the rather predictable results. There were only 3,657 successful waits out of 7,488 attempts. Most of the waits for the semaphore (set for a maximum of two seconds) timed out, and would have returned an error to the caller.

For the third test run, I kept all variables the same as for the second run, except that I assumed there was no real cost associated with work done on the handle. I did this to test whether the allocation data structures themselves (rather than the fact that each client holds a resource for a relatively long period) were the bottleneck. The parameters were as follows:

```
NUMCLIENTS = 25
NUMSTARTRESOURCES = 2
SLEEP = 0
NUMALLOC = 300
```

This scenario took roughly one second to run, and the following FIOSAP results were generated:

```
-------------------------------------------------------------------------------
-
Semaphore:                   Max Count: 255
--------------------+----------+----------+----------+----------------------
-
     Operation       |  Total   |Number of | Average  |Successful
        Name         |   Time   |operations|   Time   |  Waits
--------------------+----------+----------+----------+----------
Overall              |2147483910|     15003|    143136|         -
Create               |        68|         1|        68|         -
Release              |5.28570e10|      7501|   7046660|         -
Wait                 |7.75390e10|      7500|  10338544|     7500.
   Single            |7.75390e10|      7500|  10338544|     7500.
Close                |2147483661|         1|2147483661|         -
```

As you can see, all the waits were successful, even under this highly-loaded scenario. This validates the assumption that the primary reason for bottlenecking in the Quartermaster will be that the clients are checking out resource handles for proportionally long periods of time, rather than that the allocation mechanism is not fast enough.

ApiMon

The ApiMon tool has a similar use to the FIOSAP profiler, but it counts and times the calls that an application makes to various system API functions. It also has a nice graphical interface that allows you to view the final analysis as a list, and to sort on different columns. You use the tool by opening ApiMon, and then loading an executable. Next, press the start button, and the application will run. As it runs, you can watch the timings and counts for the various API calls go by in the window. Another pane shows the DLLs upon which the executable is dependent.

Scenarios

To illustrate the use of ApiMon, I've included screenshots of several scenarios that show the results of changing various parameters. Once again, I've used the Quartermaster application as my guinea pig, but make sure that you undo the mapping to `fernel32.dll` before you try this example. The first of these test runs is the same as the third of the FIOSAP samples above – 300 iterations on 25 client threads, with no work done on the handles. The output window is below, sorted by the Time column:

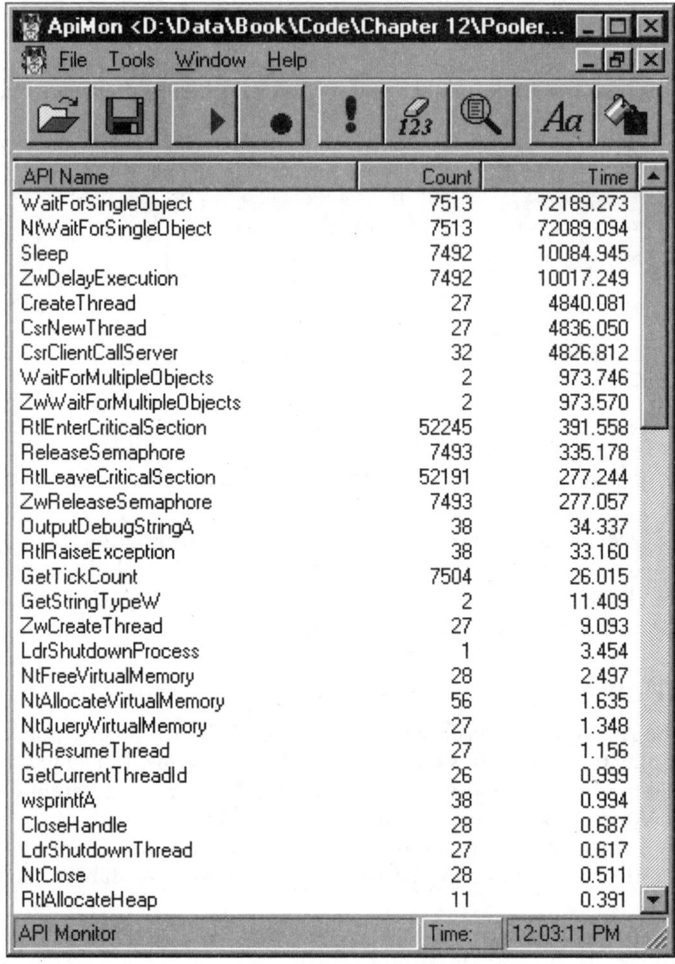

API Name	Count	Time
WaitForSingleObject	7513	72189.273
NtWaitForSingleObject	7513	72089.094
Sleep	7492	10084.945
ZwDelayExecution	7492	10017.249
CreateThread	27	4840.081
CsrNewThread	27	4836.050
CsrClientCallServer	32	4826.812
WaitForMultipleObjects	2	973.746
ZwWaitForMultipleObjects	2	973.570
RtlEnterCriticalSection	52245	391.558
ReleaseSemaphore	7493	335.178
RtlLeaveCriticalSection	52191	277.244
ZwReleaseSemaphore	7493	277.057
OutputDebugStringA	38	34.337
RtlRaiseException	38	33.160
GetTickCount	7504	26.015
GetStringTypeW	2	11.409
ZwCreateThread	27	9.093
LdrShutdownProcess	1	3.454
NtFreeVirtualMemory	28	2.497
NtAllocateVirtualMemory	56	1.635
NtQueryVirtualMemory	27	1.348
NtResumeThread	27	1.156
GetCurrentThreadId	26	0.999
wsprintfA	38	0.994
CloseHandle	28	0.687
LdrShutdownThread	27	0.617
NtClose	28	0.511
RtlAllocateHeap	11	0.391

You can see that most of the application's time is spent in single object wait operations. At the very top of the list is the operation in which a client waits for the semaphore before grabbing a free handle. (I know that because that's the only single object wait call I make in `Quartermaster.exe`!)

The next scenario involves 25 clients being checked out for a 250ms period, for 100 iterations each. As you can see from the output, there was a lot more waiting going on, for a much longer period of time. Clients were simply bottlenecked here, waiting for other clients to give back the handles:

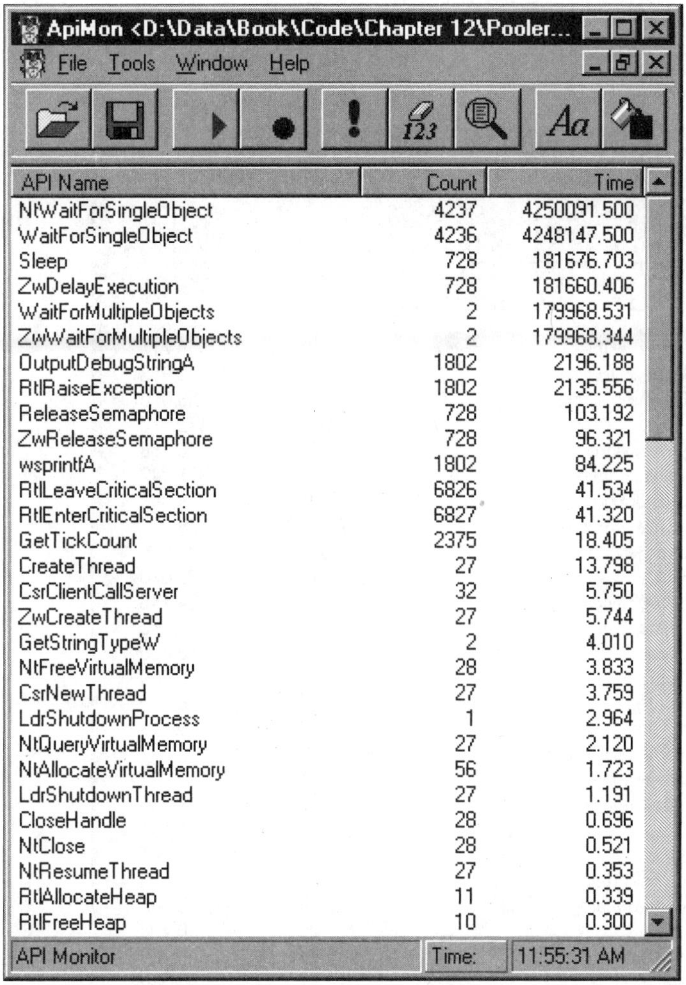

ApiMon <D:\Data\Book\Code\Chapter 12\Pooler...

File Tools Window Help

API Name	Count	Time
NtWaitForSingleObject	4237	4250091.500
WaitForSingleObject	4236	4248147.500
Sleep	728	181676.703
ZwDelayExecution	728	181660.406
WaitForMultipleObjects	2	179968.531
ZwWaitForMultipleObjects	2	179968.344
OutputDebugStringA	1802	2196.188
RtlRaiseException	1802	2135.556
ReleaseSemaphore	728	103.192
ZwReleaseSemaphore	728	96.321
wsprintfA	1802	84.225
RtlLeaveCriticalSection	6826	41.534
RtlEnterCriticalSection	6827	41.320
GetTickCount	2375	18.405
CreateThread	27	13.798
CsrClientCallServer	32	5.750
ZwCreateThread	27	5.744
GetStringTypeW	2	4.010
NtFreeVirtualMemory	28	3.833
CsrNewThread	27	3.759
LdrShutdownProcess	1	2.964
NtQueryVirtualMemory	27	2.120
NtAllocateVirtualMemory	56	1.723
LdrShutdownThread	27	1.191
CloseHandle	28	0.696
NtClose	28	0.521
NtResumeThread	27	0.353
RtlAllocateHeap	11	0.339
RtlFreeHeap	10	0.300

API Monitor | Time: | 11:55:31 AM

The parameters for the third and final run were the same as those for scenario 1: 25 clients, no work time, and 300 iterations. However, instead of a standard critical section, a spin count critical section `InitializeCriticalSectionAndSpinCount()` was used. As you can see, not only is this radically faster in terms of wait times, but also it's *noticeably* quicker to the naked eye – by at least a second or two.

My evaluation is that the critical sections on the heavily burdened internal data structures are *not* changing to mutexes on each call (the way they would do if the critical section blocked), and so less time is spent waiting for the data structures to free up. This translates into less time waiting for a lock on the semaphore.

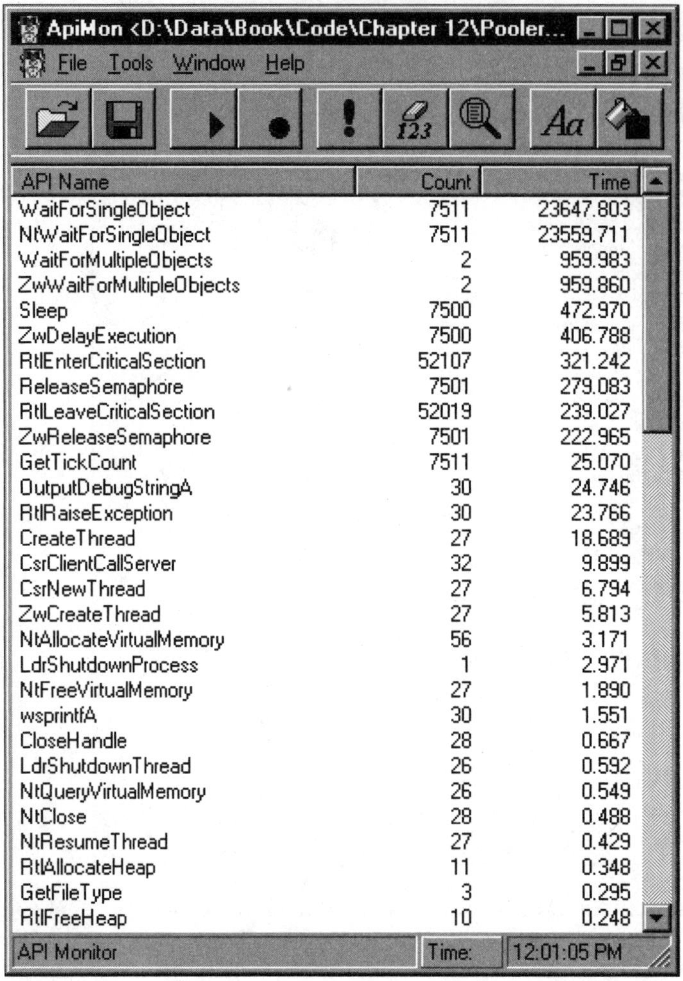

ApiMon <D:\Data\Book\Code\Chapter 12\Pooler...

File Tools Window Help

API Name	Count	Time
WaitForSingleObject	7511	23647.803
NtWaitForSingleObject	7511	23559.711
WaitForMultipleObjects	2	959.983
ZwWaitForMultipleObjects	2	959.860
Sleep	7500	472.970
ZwDelayExecution	7500	406.788
RtlEnterCriticalSection	52107	321.242
ReleaseSemaphore	7501	279.083
RtlLeaveCriticalSection	52019	239.027
ZwReleaseSemaphore	7501	222.965
GetTickCount	7511	25.070
OutputDebugStringA	30	24.746
RtlRaiseException	30	23.766
CreateThread	27	18.689
CsrClientCallServer	32	9.899
CsrNewThread	27	6.794
ZwCreateThread	27	5.813
NtAllocateVirtualMemory	56	3.171
LdrShutdownProcess	1	2.971
NtFreeVirtualMemory	27	1.890
wsprintfA	30	1.551
CloseHandle	28	0.667
LdrShutdownThread	26	0.592
NtQueryVirtualMemory	26	0.549
NtClose	28	0.488
NtResumeThread	27	0.429
RtlAllocateHeap	11	0.348
GetFileType	3	0.295
RtlFreeHeap	10	0.248

API Monitor | Time: | 12:01:05 PM

I present this example not to prove to you that the spin count critical section is faster than an 'ordinary' one, but to show you how having real timings on real function calls can have a big effect on how well you can tune the service. The only drawback to ApiMon (apart from the fact that you have to restart it each time you want to run another profile) is that you can't use it on a running service. Because of this, critical data structures that need tuning should be profiled separately, outside the service – possibly using custom loading infrastructures to pound against them (like the Quartermaster has).

The Performance Monitor (PerfMon)

The performance monitor is a rich tool that allows you to view and chart *any* counter or other feedback metric exposed by *any* process on the system. I'm not even going to attempt to describe all the functionality of the tool here; I just want to show you how to analyze your service in a couple of areas that are easy to understand. After that, you'll be on your own to explore it at your leisure. The Windows NT Resource Kit includes complete documentation on using the tool and on the meanings of each of the standard counters.

Working Set

The first of the two areas I would like to explore is the **working set**. I chose this because it demonstrates one of the areas where your service can be tuned not only to improve its performance, but also to use fewer precious system resources, thereby making more resources available to other applications.

The working set of a process is the physical memory assigned to it by the operating system. It contains the code and data pages most recently referenced by the process. Whenever a process needs code or data pages that are not in the working set, a **page fault** occurs, causing the system to load the pages from virtual memory. The larger the working set requirement (the more data and code pages required to run a process during 'normal' operation), the less likely that the system will keep all the code and data pages for the process in memory. In turn, this means that there will be proportionally more page faults will occur.

When memory is not a scarce resource on the system, the memory manager leaves older pages in the working set when new pages are loaded, increasing the size of the working set. As free memory becomes scarcer (when it falls below a certain threshold), the memory manager will move older pages out of the working sets and perform page replacement. Under these circumstances, a process can incur many expensive page faults, substantially slowing its operation.

An efficient application's working set can shrink (within reason), without causing an excessive number of page faults. Generally speaking, the more you can arrange for data to be stored in the sequence that it is used, the smaller the working set can be – pages that are needed together tend to be loaded together.

Let's examine the PerfMon counters necessary for looking at the working set of our Quartermaster application. We will chart the following:

- The process's working set
- The number of page faults per second in the process
- The number of free bytes available in memory

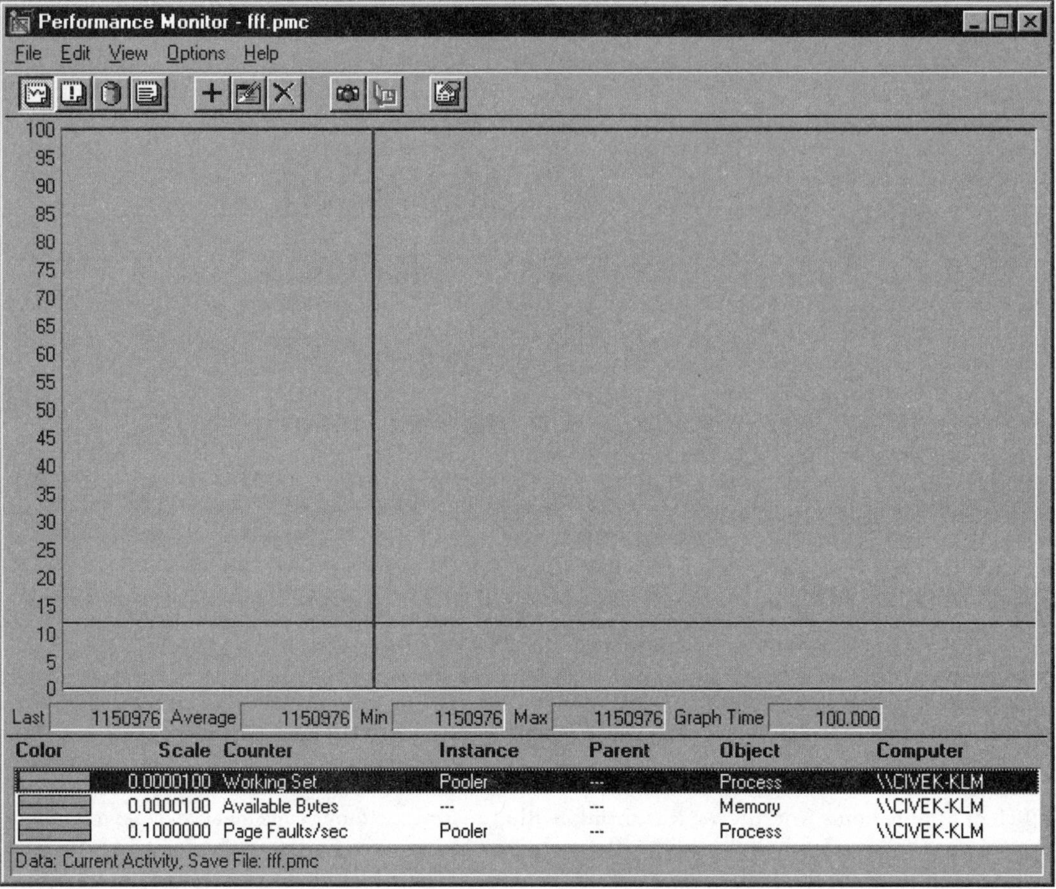

The PerfMon counter above shows that working set is relatively small, though not extremely so, at about 1Mb. Because the system is not heavily loaded (it's a 128Mb system), there is really no page faulting going on at all. I then stressed the system memory by opening about twenty other applications and recorded the following PerfMon results:

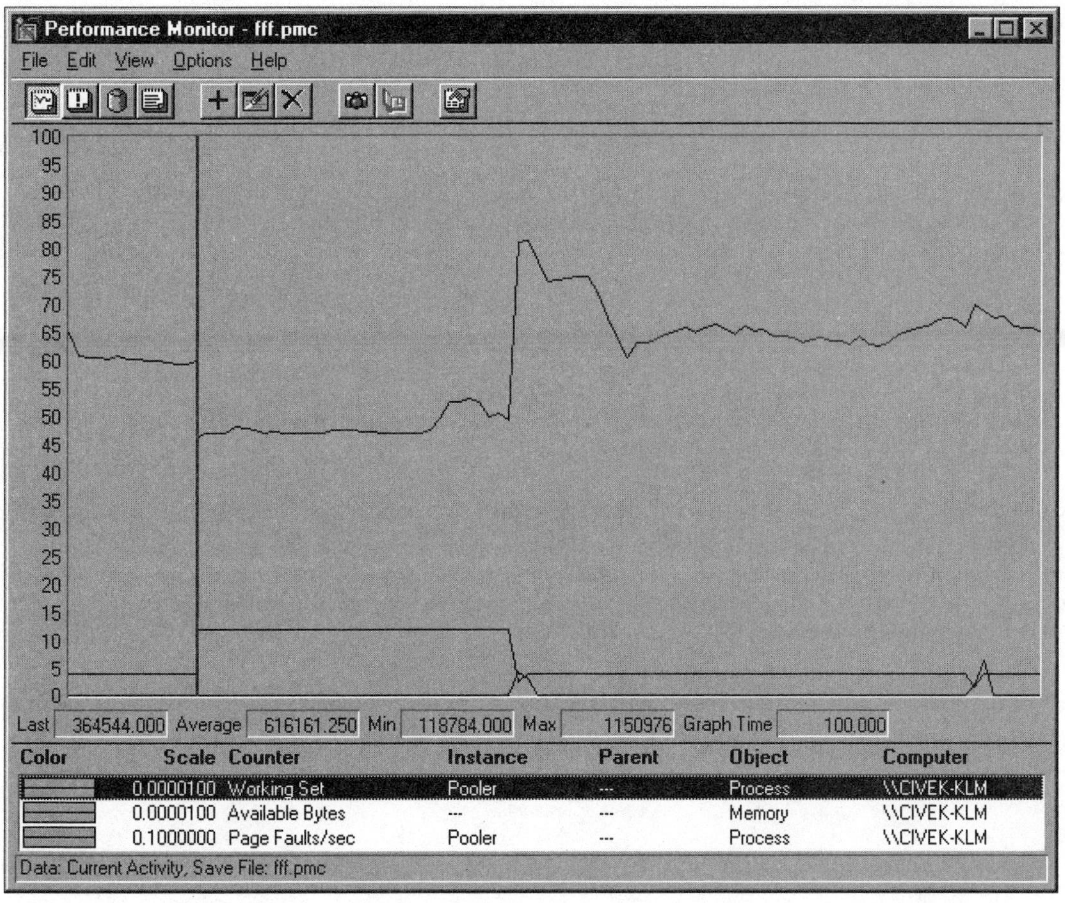

You can see that when memory requirements increased (as demonstrated by the top trace), the working set shrank, as shown by the downward spike in the middle trace at around the center of the chart. At the same time, the number of page faults increased, indicated by the upward spike at the same point in the bottom trace. Later on, at the far right of the screen, the system attempted to shrink the working set some more, but was greeted by a sharp rise in the rate of page faults, which it countered by growing the working set again. After that, the process hummed along with no more page faults, so it would appear that 364,544 bytes seems to be a ballpark estimate of a minimal working set size.

It is difficult to say what constitutes a 'good' working set for your service, because it mostly depends on the sizes of internal data structures, code size, and so forth. For guidance, try to compare the working set size for your service to that of a known entity, such as SQL Server. The way it's configured on my machine, SQL Server uses about 8Mb of working set. If, for instance, you wrote a service on the scale of the Ping Monitor in Chapter 4 and determined that its working set was 30Mb, then you'd probably draw the conclusion that tuning was needed!

If, having discovered the size of the working set, you feel that it needs some tuning, you can use the **Working Set Tuner** that's available with the SDK. (This comprises several applications whose names begin with `Wst`, stored in the `bin\winnt` directory). This tool attempts to tune your EXE file by rearranging the functions in the executable image so that they appear in an order that reflects which ones are used together most often. By placing these functions close to one another, code page paging is reduced.

The tuner does this by analyzing the application and tracking how often, and in what order, various functions are used. It then figures out an ordering sequence based on the statistics. You have to be sure to construct your usage scenario carefully, because the order in which you call the functions will determine the ordering of the pages in the working set. Choose your most common usage scenario, and perform it realistically. In a service like the Business Object, the scenario is fairly straightforward: start the service and let it instantiate COM objects for clients. A GUI application would be much more difficult to model.

Setting up the tuner for a run test is a several-step process. Instead of reprinting those steps here, I'll refer you to the SDK documentation for precise usage.

Processor Usage

The second metric I want to measure is the load of the service or application on the processor. If the service uses too much processor time, it is probably hogging cycles from other applications. We want our services to be efficient! The way to track processor usage is to chart the following items; the results are shown in the screenshot:

- The system's processor queue length. This shows the number of threads that are waiting on work to be done by the processor. Queues indicate that the processor is bottlenecked.
- The percentage of processor time being taken by a process.
- The 'thread count' counter, just as a baseline to make sure that things were working properly.

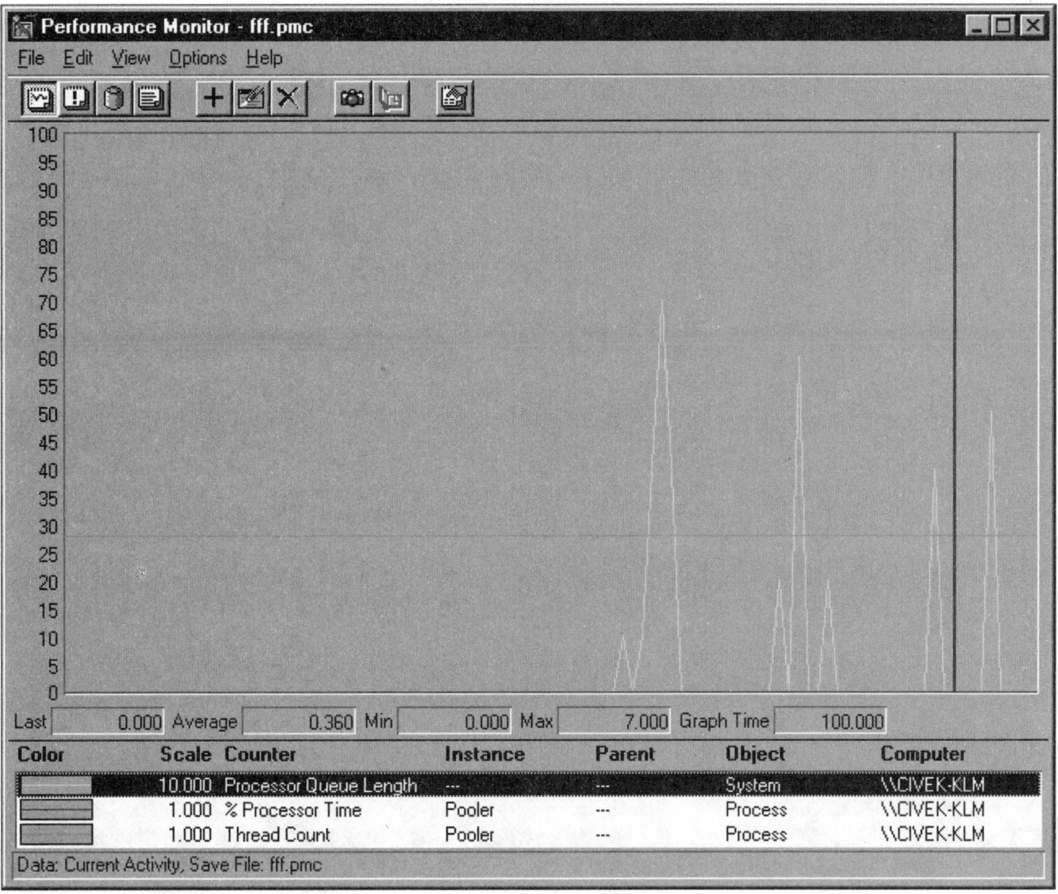

This paints a clear picture. Even with a substantial thread count (the flat line in the middle), the service is using an insignificantly small percentage of processor time (the flat line at the bottom). The queue length spikes that you can see occurred when I opened another instance of PerfMon and switched tasks between several different applications.

The next chart tells a very different story. This time, I ran 30,000 iterations on 25 client threads with 5 initial sessions and *no* `SLEEP` time. The application took about 30 seconds to complete its test run:

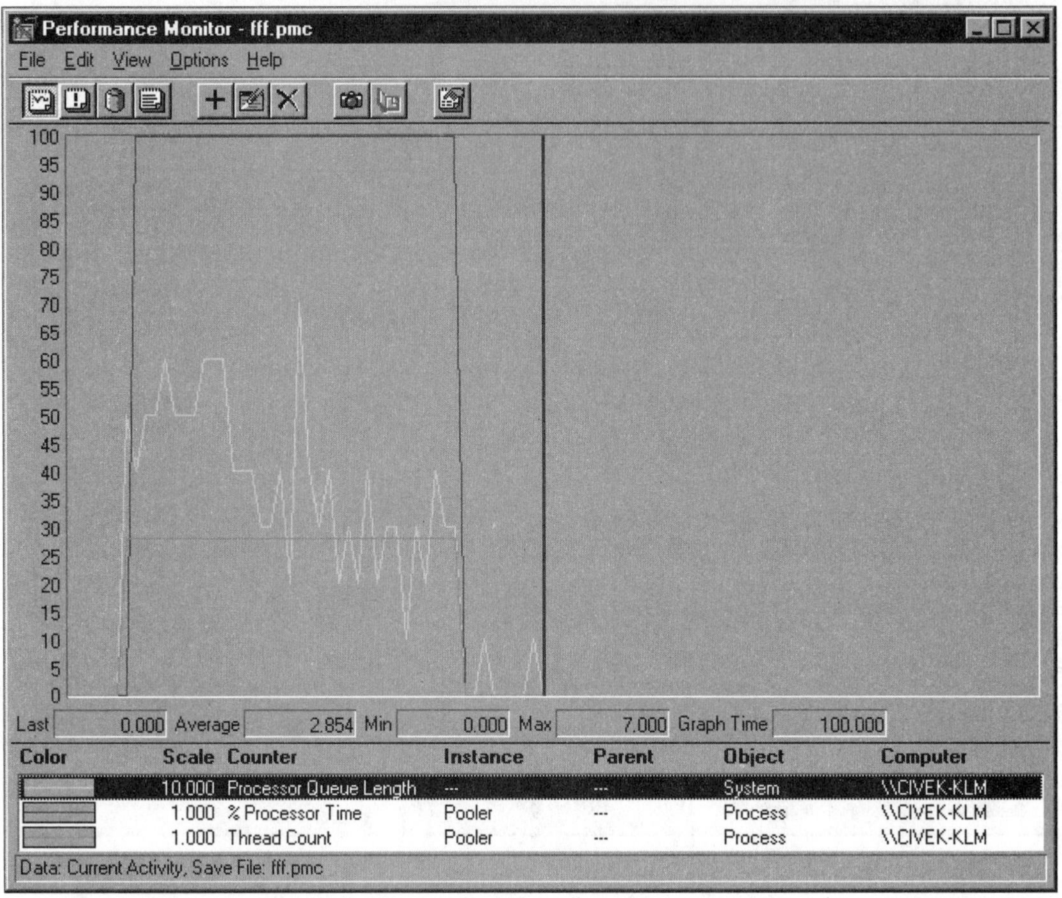

As you can see, the process ate up all the processor time for the duration of its execution, and this is entirely due to the fact that there was no wait state between calls. The length of the queue also built up substantially. If you introduce even a 1-millisecond sleep time between calls, utilization of the processor drops back to virtually zero.

It's very tough to state any general rules about what might be tunable in your service if, after checking the results from PerfMon, it seems as though it's hogging the processor. The problem truly could be any variety of things, but 'busy loops' (while loops that run and run, perhaps waiting on a flag to get set, with no `Wait()` call in them) should certainly be avoided if possible. Alternatively, you may have too many worker threads in your service, loading down the processor with excessive context switching. If you identify that the service uses too much CPU time, you might try to home in on the culprit by using the Thread | % Processor Time counter to narrow the high usage down to fewer threads in the service. By knowing that, it may be easier to find the offending code.

Again, I show this as an example of how to use the tools to help you find problems in your applications, rather than to prove anything significant about the test subject. If your application used different resources, such as file handles or network pipes or sockets, you would want to do PerfMon statistics on those counters as well as the ones examined here.

Summary

In this chapter, we've reviewed the tools and strategies that you can use to debug and tune your services. While being, of necessity, quite discursive, the usefulness of these techniques in improving the performance of the Quartermaster service should be obvious.

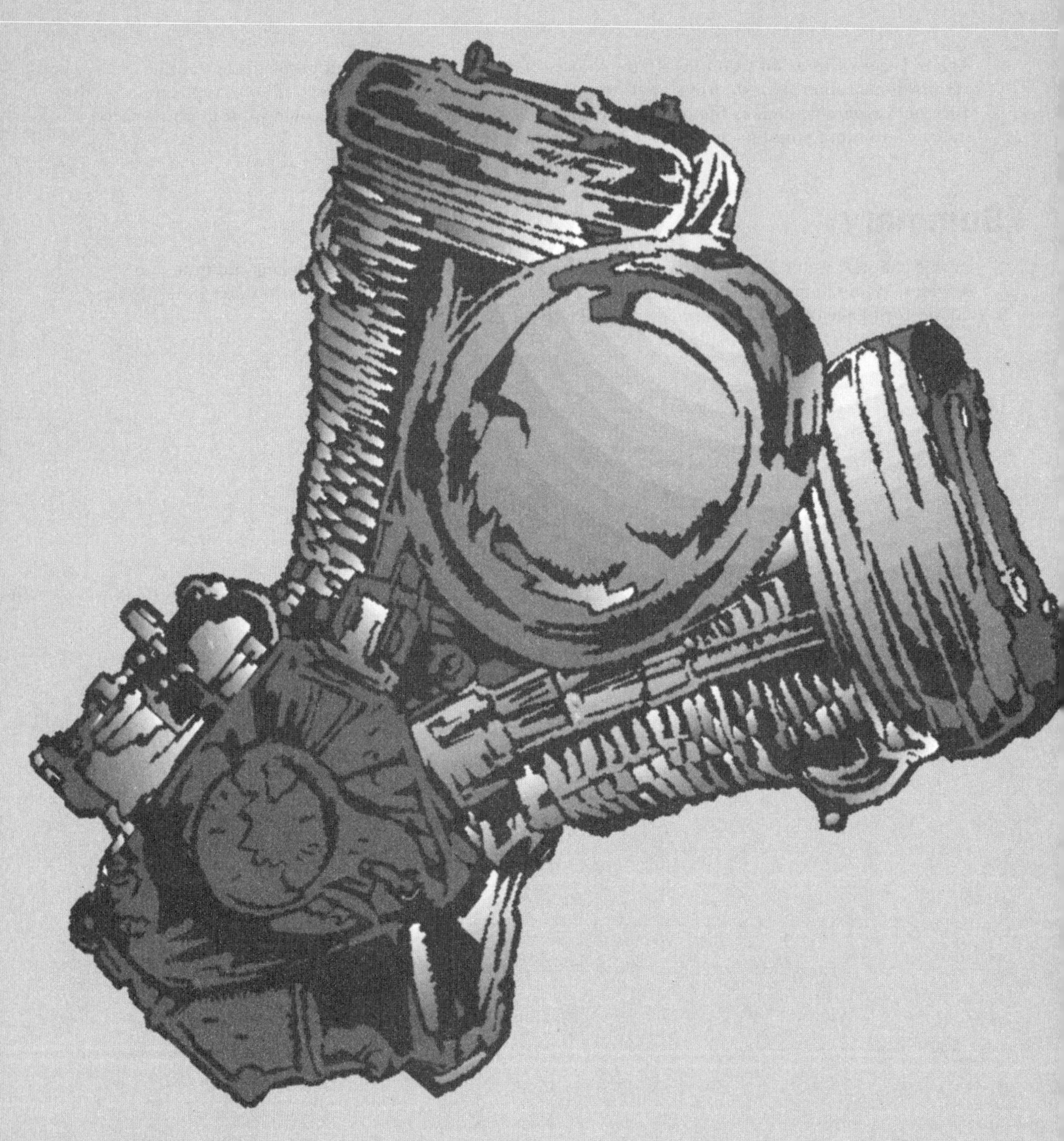

11

Administration Tools for Services

The next stop on our journey of discovery is the administration tool: a professional service should have a professional way to administer itself. That means that it should be part of one of the mainstream administration tools for NT – either a **control panel applet** or an **MMC Console Snap-In**. If you locate your service's administration tool in one of these places, then system administrators will know exactly where to look for the tool when they need to administer the service. You *could* write your administration tool as a stand-alone application, but this is less desirable – in order to use it, system administrators would have to know not only that it exists in the first place, but also where to look for it. Writing your administration program to one of the standard interfaces ensures that it resides firmly in the mainstream.

Having just sung their praises, however, I have to admit that even control panel applets are becoming slightly 'out of vogue'. Microsoft Management Console (MMC) is the new trend in administration tools, because it allows administrators to create a custom 'command console' that contains exactly the tools they need. There are only a couple of mainstream administration tools that are MMC snap-ins right now, but they will begin to crop up in real volume when NT 5.0 is released. MMC is the recommended interface for administration tools in the new version of Windows NT.

Control Panel Applets

All right, so control panel applets might be considered an older technology, but they can't be beaten for simplicity. Writing control panel applets is really, really easy: they're just DLLs with a different extension – CPL – that are located in the `Winnt\system32` directory. Whenever the user opens the control panel, any DLLs in the `system32` directory with the extension `.cpl` are loaded and queried for certain configuration information.

Applet Architecture

The key to the way control panel applets connect to the control panel is in the `CPlApplet()` callback function, which is exported by applet DLLs. Whenever the control panel executable loads the CPL, it immediately looks for this exported function so that it can call back into the DLL with requests. Essentially, this function is the routing mechanism for all the requests that the control panel makes of the applet.

When the control panel first loads an applet, it sends a `CPL_NEWINQUIRE` message, to which the applet responds by providing its icon, its name, and its description. Later, when a user opens the applet by double clicking on it, it is sent the `CPL_DBLCLICK` message, to which it responds by displaying its dialog or property page. Finally, when the control panel is exiting, it first sends the `CPL_STOP` message to each applet, then the `CPL_EXIT` message, right before it calls `FreeLibrary()` on the CPL. The applet and the executable containing it get the chance to respond to both, as outlined in the more detailed chart of messages below.

CPlApplet

The `CPlApplet()` function must have this signature:

```
LONG APIENTRY CPlApplet(HWND hwndCPl,
                        UINT uMsg,
                        LONG lParam1,
                        LONG lParam2)
```

As you can see by the parameter names, the function is influenced by Windows messaging, although it doesn't really have anything to do with window messages. When the control panel wishes to request that the applet do something, it sends its window handle, a message request, and a couple of other parameters. The first of these (`lParam1`) is always the applet number, while the second is applet-specific data that doesn't have much use under most circumstances, but which can be used to pass specific information *from* the applet *to* the control panel in its response to the `CPL_NEWINQUIRE` message. That data value is then passed back to the applet in subsequent messages, such as `CPL_DBLCLICK`.

To process a message, the applet simply switches on the message type and does the work. The message types that a control panel applet must be able to handle (and their associated structures) are defined in the `cpl.h` header file.

Each CPL file can expose multiple control panel applets; the same file can contain multiple icons, each with different dialogs, etc. You will quickly notice from the list below that the semantics of the messages are designed to handle exactly such scenarios – as I said earlier, the applet number from which the control panel is requesting action is always sent in the `lParam1` of the message, when appropriate. The chart below lists all the possible messages and how they work.

Control Panel Message	Description
CPL_INIT	Sent to indicate that CPlApplet() was found. Return TRUE or FALSE to tell the control panel to proceed.
CPL_GETCOUNT	Retrieves the number of applets that will be displayed by this CPL.
CPL_INQUIRE	Handles an inquiry by the control panel. lParam1 is the applet number to register, which will be a value from 0 to (CPL_GETCOUNT - 1). The applet should fill in the CPLINFO structure that was passed in the lParam2 parameter with information about the name and icon that the applet uses. This will be cached at runtime, and possibly across different control panel sessions.
CPL_SELECT	No longer used. Just return 1.
CPL_DBLCLK	Occurs when the applet is double-clicked. The usual response to this message is for the applet to show its dialog box or user interface. lParam1 is the number of the applet that was selected. lParam2 is the applet's lData value, which is just a long data variable that the applet can use for anything it likes.
CPL_STOP	Sent to each registered applet when the control panel is exiting. Applet-specific cleanup should be done here. lParam1 is the applet number, and lParam2 is the applet's lData value.
CPL_EXIT	Sent just before the control panel calls FreeLibrary(). Non applet-specific cleanup should be done here.
CPL_NEWINQUIRE	The same as CPL_INQUIRE, except that it handles a new inquiry. Therefore, the lParam2 parameter is a pointer to a NEWCPLINFO structure, which contains additional data such as the help context and help file name. The applet should respond to both messages.
CPL_STARTWPARMS	Used when the applet is started by RunDLL(), and therefore might have parameters. Should show the dialog box, like CPL_DBLCLK, except it may need to handle additional initialization. Only used in NT 4.0+.

CControlPanel Class

In keeping with my efforts elsewhere in this book, and to assist in your quest to create control panel applets, I have developed a class called `CControlPanel` that implements handlers for all the messages listed above. To be honest, the class itself is really very simple. It implements `CPlApplet()` as a static member function so that it can be exported as a callback. In turn, `CPlApplet()` calls a variety of members to do the work for each message. As it stands, however, the class does not take great pains to deal with the case where your CPL file contains multiple applets, so if you find yourself in this relatively unusual situation, you'll need to do some customizing of your own. (To begin with, you'll need to change the `CPL_GETCOUNT` handler and check the value of `lParam1` in `DBLCLICK`, `NEWINQUIRE`, and `INQUIRE`.) The complete class definition for `CControlPanel` is shown below; I put it in a file called `CPanel.h`:

```
#include <cpl.h>                                         // Control panel definitions

class CControlPanel
{
public:
   LONG OnInquire(UINT uAppNum, CPLINFO* pInfo);
   CControlPanel();
   virtual ~CControlPanel();

   // Event handlers
   virtual LONG OnDblclk(HWND hwndCPl, UINT uAppNum, LONG lData);
   virtual LONG OnExit();
   virtual LONG OnGetCount();
   virtual LONG OnInit();
   virtual LONG OnNewInquire(UINT uAppNum, NEWCPLINFO* pInfo);
   virtual LONG OnStop(UINT uAppNum, LONG lData);

   // Static member functions (callbacks)
   static LONG APIENTRY CPlApplet(HWND hwndCPl, UINT uMsg,
                                  LONG lParam1, LONG lParam2);

   // Static data
   static CControlPanel* m_pThis;
};
```

Let's start going through the implementation. First of all, notice that `CPlApplet()` (below) just delegates out to member functions, passing them the parameters they require depending on what they do. The other interesting aspect is that it makes a call to `AFX_MANAGE_STATE()`, which should tip you off that I'm using MFC for this applet – I want to use all of MFC's nifty tools for property sheets and pages, and dialog data exchange.

```
#include "CPanel.h"

// Static data
CControlPanel* CControlPanel::m_pThis = NULL; // CplApplet is static because
                                              //  it is a DLL entry point
```

```
CControlPanel::CControlPanel()
{
   m_pThis = this;
}

CControlPanel::~CControlPanel()
{
}

////////////////////////////////////////////////////////////////////////////
/
// Callback function
LONG APIENTRY CControlPanel::CPlApplet(HWND hwndCPl,
                                       UINT uMsg,
                                       LONG lParam1,
                                       LONG lParam2)
{
   // Avoids state problems in MFC extensions using shared MFC libs
   AFX_MANAGE_STATE(AfxGetStaticModuleState());

   CControlPanel* pCtrl = m_pThis;
   ASSERT(pCtrl);

   switch(uMsg)
   {
   case CPL_DBLCLK:
      return pCtrl->OnDblclk(hwndCPl, lParam1, lParam2);

   case CPL_EXIT:
      return pCtrl->OnExit();

   case CPL_GETCOUNT:
      return pCtrl->OnGetCount();

   case CPL_INIT:
      return pCtrl->OnInit();

   case CPL_NEWINQUIRE:
      return pCtrl->OnNewInquire(lParam1, (NEWCPLINFO*)lParam2);

   case CPL_INQUIRE:
      return pCtrl->OnInquire(lParam1, (CPLINFO*)lParam2);

   case CPL_SELECT:
      return 1;                                // Message no longer used

   case CPL_STOP:
      return pCtrl->OnStop(lParam1, lParam2);

   case CPL_STARTWPARMS:
      return pCtrl->OnDblclk(hwndCPl, lParam1, lParam2);
   }

   return 1;
}
```

Next, let's look at the OnNewInquire() function, which handles CPL_NEWINQUIRE messages.

```
///////////////////////////////////////////////////////////////////////////////
/
// Default command handlers

LONG CControlPanel::OnNewInquire(UINT uAppNum, NEWCPLINFO* pInfo)
{
   // Fill in the data
   pInfo->dwSize = sizeof(NEWCPLINFO);
   pInfo->dwFlags = 0;
   pInfo->dwHelpContext = 0;
   pInfo->lData = 0;

   HINSTANCE h = AfxGetResourceHandle();
   pInfo->hIcon = LoadIcon(h, MAKEINTRESOURCE(IDI_ICON));
   LoadString(h, IDS_CPLNAME, pInfo->szName,
                                    sizeof(pInfo->szName) / sizeof(TCHAR));
   LoadString(h, IDS_CPLINFOSTRING, pInfo->szInfo,
                                    sizeof(pInfo->szInfo) / sizeof(TCHAR));

   strcpy(pInfo->szHelpFile, "");
   return 0;
}
```

This function just initializes the NEWCPLINFO structure that was passed to it with the proper data. The most important members are the icon handle and the strings that name the icon and show the description in the status area of the control panel window; these are loaded from resources in the applet. This function can be used as-is, provided that you create an icon resource and string resources with the same names as the ones it uses.

OnInquire(), shown below, handles a similar task but with a more limited set of information. It merely assigns the resource IDs for the same resources to members of the CPLINFO structure. The control panel will use this structure to cache the visible portions of the applet.

```
LONG CControlPanel::OnInquire(UINT uAppNum, CPLINFO* pInfo)
{
   pInfo->idIcon = IDI_ICON;
   pInfo->idName = IDS_CPLNAME;
   pInfo->idInfo = IDS_CPLINFOSTRING;
   pInfo->lData = 0;

   return 0;
}
```

The work of showing the user interface for the applet is contained within OnDblclk(). This version of the function instantiates two property page dialogs and a property sheet, and shows them modally. If you use the CControlPanel class in your own applet, you will need to customize this function, or else derive a class from CControlPanel and override it.

```
LONG CControlPanel::OnDblclk(HWND hwndCPl, UINT uAppNum, LONG lData)
{
   CPropPage1 page1;
   CPropPage2 page2;

   CCplPropSheet sheet(IDS_PSHEETTITLE);

   sheet.AddPage(&page1);
   sheet.AddPage(&page2);

   sheet.DoModal();

   return 0;
}
```

The remaining functions just return whatever values are appropriate to their message type, outlined in the chart above; they can of course be overridden or changed if you desire:

```
LONG CControlPanel::OnExit()
{
   return 0;                                          // OK
}

LONG CControlPanel::OnGetCount()
{
   return 1;                                          // Only one applet
}

LONG CControlPanel::OnInit()
{
   return 1;                                          // TRUE
}

LONG CControlPanel::OnStop(UINT uAppNum, LONG lData)
{
   return 1;                                          // Not handled
}
```

Steps for Creating an Applet

We're going to create a control panel applet for the Business Object sample we put together in Chapter 9. Again, I want to use MFC for this, so this is MFC-specific. If you have trouble with any of the steps, read on or take a look at the `BusObjCpl` project that's contained in the source code you can download for this book.

1. Create a new project of type MFC AppWizard (dll).

2. On the next panel, select Regular DLL using shared MFC DLL.

3. Create the icon you wish to display as the icon for your control panel applet. Name it `IDI_ICON`.

4. Change the output file name and location for the DLL to have a `.cpl` extension, and to be placed in the `system32` directory.

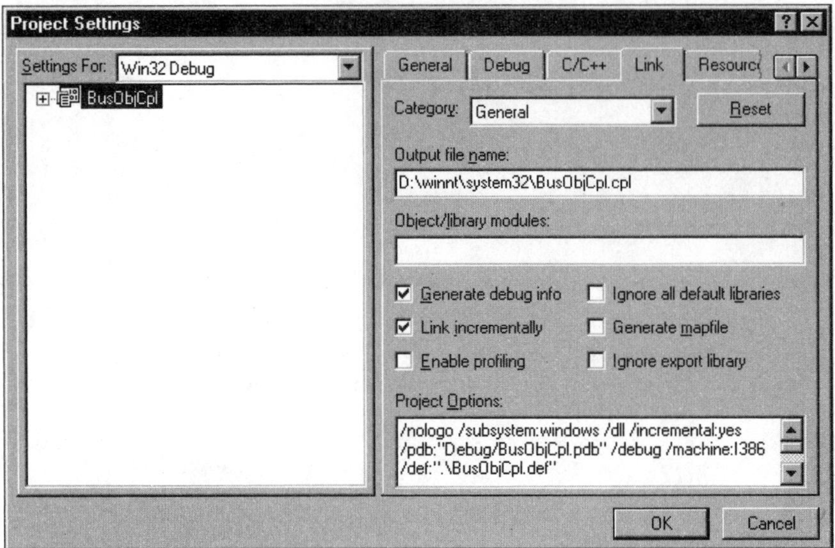

5. Add the `CPanel.h` and `CPanel.cpp` files (all the code for which is shown above) to the project. Add `#include` statements for `StdAfx.h` and your main project's `.h` file to the top of `CPanel.cpp`.

6. Add two string resources. One should be called `IDS_CPLNAME`, and contain the name you want the icon to have when the control panel opens (I used Business Object Service). The other should be called `IDS_CPLINFOSTRING`, and contain a longer description of what the applet does (Business Object Service Parameters Configuration). This will be shown in the status bar of the control panel's main window.

7. To fit in with the above implementation of `OnDblclk()`, I created two dialog resources called `IDD_PAGE_SERVER` and `IDD_PAGE_PARAMS`, and hooked them up to property page classes called `CPropPage1` and `CPropPage2` respectively. The first of these will be used to get and set registry information about the SQL Server machine, and looks like this:

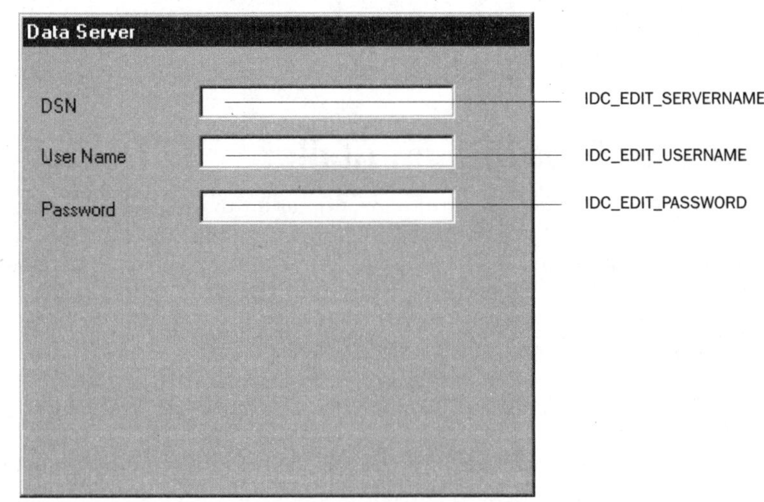

The second property page will deal with the settings of the Quartermaster itself, saving them and retrieving them to and from the registry:

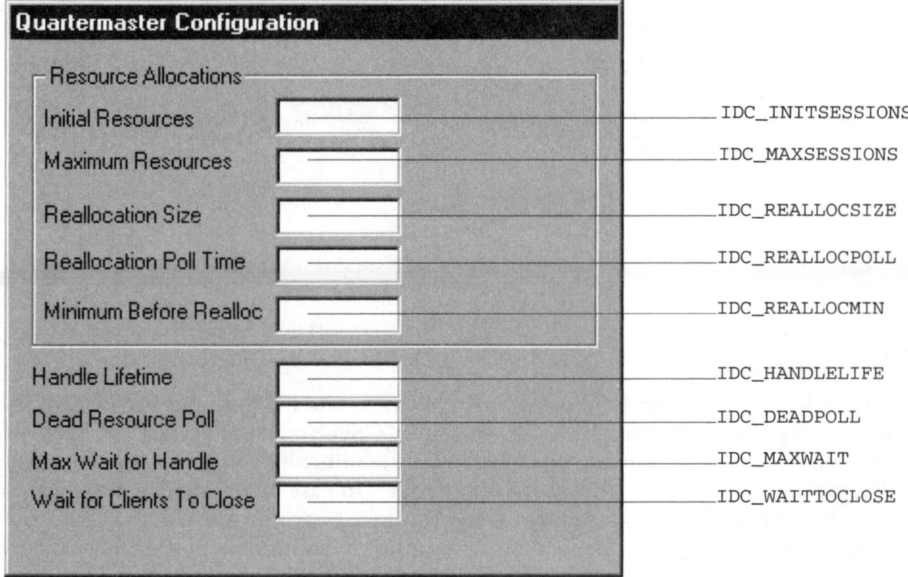

Finally in this section, add a property sheet class called `CCplPropSheet` to the project, and then add a resource string called `IDS_PSHEETTITLE` to the string table, which should contain the title of the property sheet (Business Object Service Configuration).

8. The property sheet and property page classes need to be available in `CPanel.cpp`, so add `#include` directives for `CplPropSheet.h`, `PropPage1.h` and `PropPage2.h` to the top of the file.

The last two steps have detailed a process that was particular to this implementation, but it's not hard to see how you could change `OnDblclk()` *to perform a different task – it could just call the* `DoModal()` *function of an ordinary dialog, for example.*

9. Add the `CplApplet()` DLL export to the `.def` file for the DLL, like so:

```
EXPORTS
    ; Explicit exports can go here
    CPlApplet
```

This needs to be exported through the `.def` file so that it is not mangled by the `__stdcall` export style.

10. Finally, add a member variable of type `CControlPanel` to the `C[My]App` class. This ensures that an instance of the class is created when the DLL is loaded:

```
#include "CPanel.h"

/////////////////////////////////////////////////////////////////////////////
// CBusObjCplApp
// See BusObjCpl.cpp for the implementation of this class
//

class CBusObjCplApp : public CWinApp
{
public:
   CBusObjCplApp();
   CControlPanel m_panel;
```

Adding Functionality

Now we can put some code behind the property pages we created above, and I'll be using the dialog class for the first page as the centerpiece of the example. Once you've seen the code here, you should be able to manage the second page on your own with little difficulty. (I figured that life was too short to do pretty much the same things twice just for a sample.) In case of any doubts, the source code on the Wrox web site is complete in this respect. Anyway, the `CPropPage1::OnInitDialog()` function takes on the responsibility for loading the data from the registry by calling a function called `ReadRegistry()`:

```
BOOL CPropPage1::OnInitDialog()
{
   ReadRegistry();
   CPropertyPage::OnInitDialog();

   return TRUE;  // return TRUE unless you set the focus to a control
                 // EXCEPTION: OCX Property Pages should return FALSE
}
```

In this series of calls, the parameters are first read from the registry into the property page class's member variables. The base class implementation of `OnInitDialog()` calls `DoDataExchange()`, which transfers the data from the members into the dialog controls. This is all pretty standard MFC stuff, and `ReadRegistry()` is just a bunch of registry-reading code, much like the `ReadParameters()` function from Chapter 9:

```
void CPropPage1::ReadRegistry()
{
   HKEY hkey;
   CHAR szKey[256];
   CHAR psz[100] = {0};
   CHAR psz2[100] = {0};
```

```
    strcpy(szKey, "SOFTWARE\\WroxBook\\BusObject\\Parameters\0");
    long lres = RegOpenKeyEx(HKEY_LOCAL_MACHINE, szKey, 0,
                                                  KEY_ALL_ACCESS, &hkey);
    if(lres != ERROR_SUCCESS)
    {
       // Generate message - service not installed
       AfxMessageBox(
             "Registry Open Failed. The service is not installed properly.");
       return;
    }

    DWORD dwSize = 0;
    DWORD dwType = 0;
    CHAR sz[25] = {0};

    // Read each value
    // Server
    dwSize = 25;
    strcpy(psz, "Server");
    lres = RegQueryValueEx(hkey, psz, NULL, &dwType, (BYTE*)sz, &dwSize);
    if(lres != ERROR_SUCCESS)
       goto RegReadError;
    m_szServer = sz;

    // User
    dwSize = 25;
    strcpy(psz, "User");
    lres = RegQueryValueEx(hkey, psz, NULL, &dwType, (BYTE*)sz, &dwSize);
    if(lres != ERROR_SUCCESS)
       goto RegReadError;
    m_szUserName = sz;

    // Password
    dwSize = 25;
    strcpy(psz, "Password");
    lres = RegQueryValueEx(hkey, psz, NULL, &dwType, (BYTE*)sz, &dwSize);
    if(lres != ERROR_SUCCESS)
       goto RegReadError;
    m_szPassword = sz;

    // Finished with key
    RegCloseKey(hkey);
    return;

RegReadError:
    wsprintf(psz2, "Value query on '%s' failed with code %lu", psz, lres);
    AfxMessageBox(psz2);
    RegCloseKey(hkey);
}
```

As you can see, I have tied the three edit controls to `CString` member variables called `m_szServer`, `m_szUserName`, and `m_szPassword`. I have also added MFC control handlers for the `EN_CHANGE` notification to each of the edit controls in the property page. All the handlers map to a single function, `OnChangeEdit()`, which in turn calls a function to mark the dialog as 'dirty'.

```
void CPropPage1::OnChangeEdit()
{
   SetModified(TRUE);
}
```

A 'dirty' dialog means that the Apply button on the property sheet is enabled, so that the user can make incremental changes without closing the property sheet. The default `OnApply()` handler makes a call to `UpdateData()`, so that the dialog data exchange mechanism knows that when the Apply button is clicked, it should initiate the *reverse* data exchange, which means that data from the controls should be written back to the class's members.

The `DoDataExchange()` function handles data transfer from members to controls, and vice versa, depending on which direction the data needs to move:

```
void CPropPage1::DoDataExchange(CDataExchange* pDX)
{
   CPropertyPage::DoDataExchange(pDX);
   //{{AFX_DATA_MAP(CPropPage1)
   DDX_Text(pDX, IDC_EDIT_PASSWORD, m_szPassword);
   DDV_MaxChars(pDX, m_szPassword, 25);
   DDX_Text(pDX, IDC_EDIT_SERVERNAME, m_szServer);
   DDV_MaxChars(pDX, m_szServer, 25);
   DDX_Text(pDX, IDC_EDIT_USERNAME, m_szUserName);
   DDV_MaxChars(pDX, m_szUserName, 25);
   //}}AFX_DATA_MAP

   if(pDX->m_bSaveAndValidate == TRUE)
   {
      UpdateRegistry();
    SendControlMessage();  //Sends custom message to handler for the service
   }
}
```

Most of this is MFC stuff, but I inserted a special mechanism at the end to check to see whether the update is in the 'dialog controls to class member data' direction. If it is, that tells me that changes were made to the data and that the registry should therefore be updated. Unsurprisingly, the `UpdateRegistry()` function is extremely similar to `ReadRegistry()`, differing only in that it writes rather than reads entries:

```
   DWORD dwSize = 0;
   DWORD dwType = REG_SZ;
   char sz[25] = {0};
```

```
    // Write each value
    dwSize = 25;
    strcpy(psz, "Server");
    strcpy(sz, m_szServer.GetBuffer(25));
    lres = RegSetValueEx(hkey, psz, NULL, dwType, (BYTE*)sz, dwSize);
    if(lres != ERROR_SUCCESS)
       goto RegReadError;

    dwSize = 25;
    strcpy(psz, "User");
    strcpy(sz, m_szUserName.GetBuffer(25));
    lres = RegSetValueEx(hkey, psz, NULL, dwType, (BYTE*)sz, dwSize);
    if(lres != ERROR_SUCCESS)
       goto RegReadError;

    dwSize = 25;
    strcpy(psz, "Password");
    strcpy(sz, m_szPassword.GetBuffer(25));
    lres = RegSetValueEx(hkey, psz, NULL, dwType, (BYTE*)sz, dwSize);
    if(lres != ERROR_SUCCESS)
       goto RegReadError;
```

Sending a Control Message

That leads us at last to the most interesting part of this applet: the `SendControlMessage()` function. Since this is a functioning (and probably running) service, a mechanism is needed to tell the service that changes to its registry parameters have taken place. Changes to the parameters could drastically affect what the service is doing, and it may be necessary to change particular parameters without cutting off existing clients by stopping the service or otherwise making it unavailable.

A good mechanism for doing this is to use the SCM to send a 'custom' control message to the service's handler. Long, long ago, I said you that can send your own, personalized handler message to any service. Provided that the service knows the message is coming, it is able to respond. If you wondered at the time what that would be good for, here's one use. I'll send a message called `SERVICE_CONTROL_UPDATEFROMREGISTRY` to the service from my administration applet to let the service know that changes to its parameters have occurred. Then the service can do what it wants to handle that message – it can ignore it, or wait until it is idle to process it.

The function I use in the administration program is called `SendControlMessage()`, and it just opens the SCM and the service, and sends the message using a `ControlService()` call (don't forget the `#include` for `WinSvc.h`!):

```
void CPropPage1::SendControlMessage()
{
    SERVICE_STATUS ss;
    const DWORD SERVICE_CONTROL_UPDATEFROMREGISTRY = 129;
    char szService[10] = "BusObject";
```

```
    SC_HANDLE hSCM = OpenSCManager(NULL, NULL,
                          SC_MANAGER_CONNECT | SC_MANAGER_QUERY_LOCK_STATUS);
    if(hSCM == NULL)
    {
       AfxMessageBox("Couldn't open service manager");
       return;
    }

    SC_HANDLE hService = OpenService(hSCM, szService,
                                          SERVICE_USER_DEFINED_CONTROL);
    if(hService == NULL)
    {
       CloseServiceHandle(hSCM);
       AfxMessageBox("Couldn't open service to notify of registry changes");
       return;
    }

    ControlService(hService, SERVICE_CONTROL_UPDATEFROMREGISTRY, &ss);
    CloseServiceHandle(hService);
    CloseServiceHandle(hSCM);
}
```

Easy as pi. Now, on the service side, you can just implement an additional handler `case` to trap for the new message and do the work of re-reading its parameters from the registry, or at least re-reading those parameters it can adjust while it is running. That new control handler might look something like this:

```
    case SERVICE_CONTROL_UPDATEFROMREGISTRY:
       DoSomethingToUpdateRegParams();
       SetServiceStatus(m_hServiceStatus, &m_status);
       break;
```

Of course, you'll need `#defines` for the same value for the custom message in both administration program and service. Remember that the value for the message must be between 128 and 255, and that the `hService` handle must have `SERVICE_USER_DEFINED_CONTROL` access rights.

Running the Applet

When you build the sample and bring up the control panel, you'll notice that there is now an icon for the new applet:

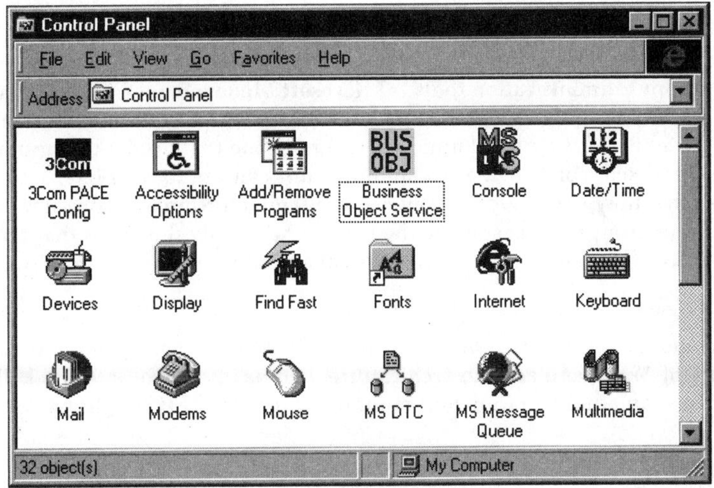

I know: it's a lame icon, but it gets the point across. Double-click it, and you'll get the following property sheet:

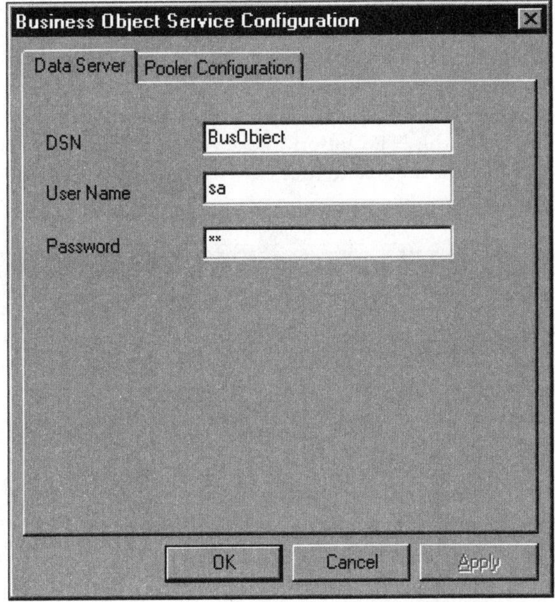

This simple but effective interface allows you to change any of the registry parameters for the Business Object service. Any time you change any of the parameters, the Apply button is enabled. At that point, hitting Apply or OK will write the parameters to the registry.

MMC Snap-ins

The real trend in 'snappy' administration tools is **Microsoft Management Console**. In developing MMC, Microsoft was responding to the demands of their enterprise customers' system administrators, who were looking for an easier way to administer systems – one that used a task-grouping approach. MMC provides a centralized 'console' that an administrator can use to plug in exactly those administration tools that they need, so that they can use them all from a single view. This means that different administration groups can customize the console with only the views that *they* want for *their* particular administrative function. For example, IIS 4.0 and MTS are both administered from MMC snap-ins.

MMC is very open-ended, and has a great variety of possibilities. What I want to do in this chapter is provide an overview of MMC and snap-in architecture, and its important interfaces. I'll also show you an example of how an administration and monitoring tool in MMC might be developed.

MMC Overview

Essentially, the MMC console interface is an executable that acts as a host for COM in-process servers. The MMC console itself is merely a container, or shell, that acts as a context frame for hosting in-process servers called **snap-ins**. Each console configuration can be persisted to disk, saving details of which snap-ins were loaded into it at the time and any other information about its context that the snap-in wants to persist. The console window itself is saved to a file with a `.msc` extension. Users can totally change the context of what they are viewing simply by loading a different `.msc` file into the console's main window.

Once you've installed MMC from the NT Option Pack, you can start it up with Start | Run... | MMC. The screenshot below shows the main console loaded with an empty console window. There are no snap-ins currently added to the console:

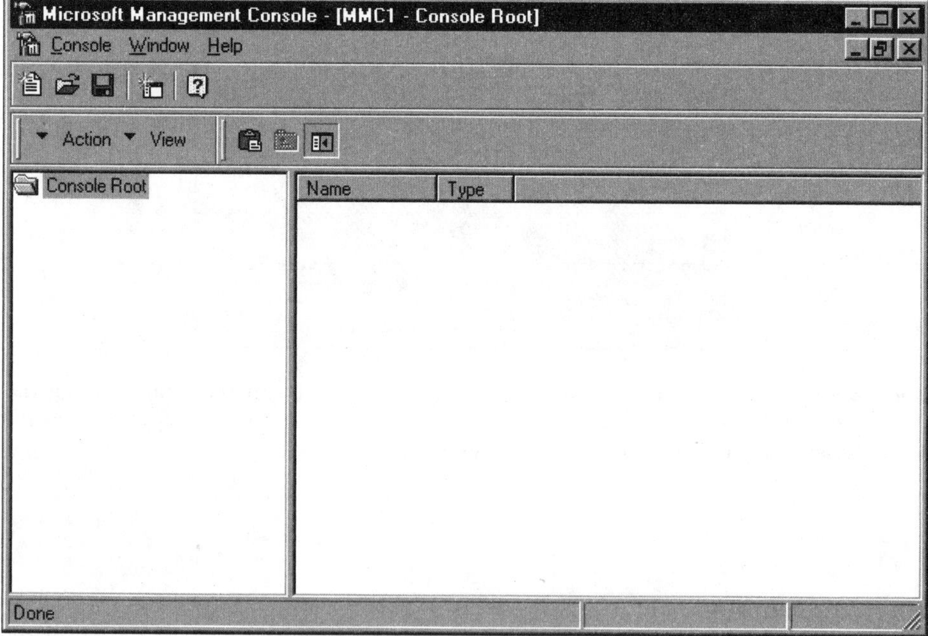

Once a snap-in or two has been loaded into the console, notice that the individual snap-ins are loaded beneath the Console Root node:

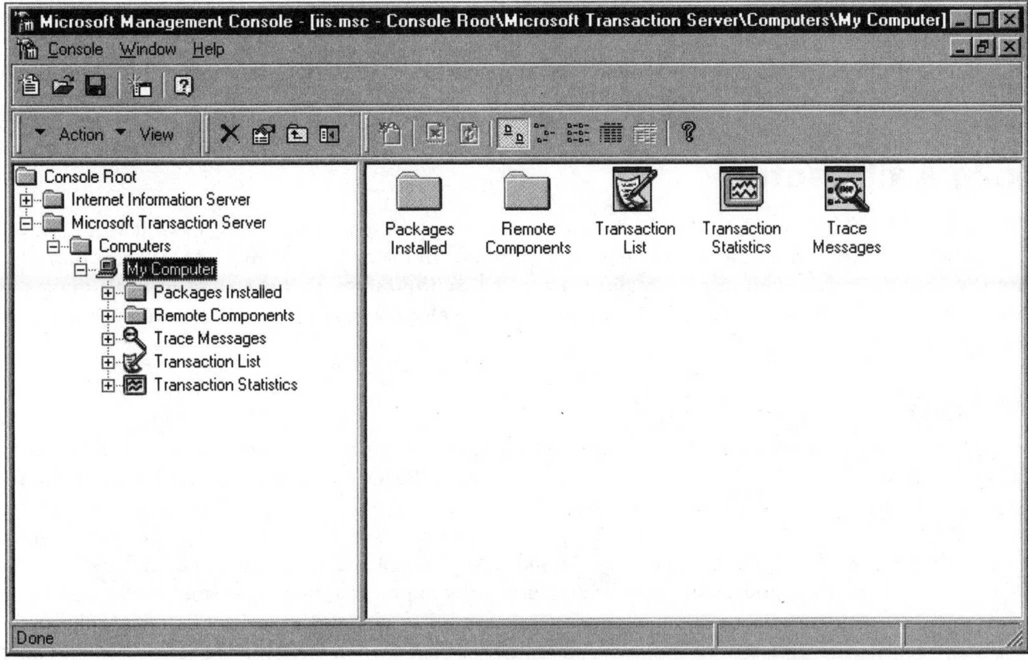

In the screenshot above, you can see that two snap-ins have been loaded – one for IIS 4.0, and one for MTS. To add a new snap-in to the console window, simply choose Console | Add/Remove Snap-in... from the menu. You will then get a dialog like this one:

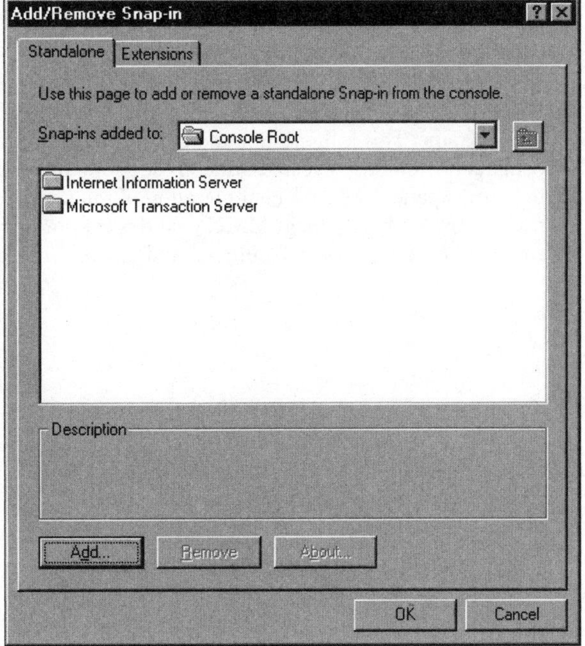

Select the Add... button, and you'll see a list of all the possible **standalone snap-ins** you have installed on your system. These work independently; and a single tool is usually aimed at an entire product. An **extension snap-in**, on the other hand, is used to extend the functionality of an existing standalone snap-in. This might be used if a third party wrote an extension to an existing product, and wanted to add additional management interfaces to the existing product. Microsoft Site Server 3.0 does just such a thing to extend the interface for IIS 4.0.

Snap-in Architecture

MMC uses a lot of different COM interfaces to string everything together and make it work. In fact, the number of interfaces that a snap-in has to implement in order to work with MMC can be rather daunting, and there are even more interfaces exposed by the *console* that the snap-in itself makes use of to do its work. This can all make for a very sticky development effort, so let's start by getting our heads around a few concepts.

Terminology

First of all, I'll define a few terms for you that will make it easier to understand the architectural issues related to the COM interfaces we'll be dealing with. Refer to the screen shot below, which maps the terminology to an actual snap-in.

- **Scope pane.** This is the left-hand pane in the MMC console window. Each item in the scope pane is referred to as a **node**, and the collective hierarchy of items in the scope pane is referred to as a **namespace**. In familiar fashion, a node is represented as a label next to a folder icon (unless you customize the icon, as we'll see later); the folder is closed when the node is not selected and open when it is. It is the responsibility of a snap-in to add the appropriate nodes and their descriptions to the scope pane.A user can expand different nodes in the namespace tree by double-clicking an item in the scope pane, or by clicking the + icon next to the node. At this point, any **sub-containers** (other nodes beneath a node) within the node become visible, because each node is responsible for enumerating the sub-containers that it owns.
- **Results pane.** This is the right-hand pane in the console window. The results pane shows the data contained within the selected node in the scope pane. If the scope pane item is a container, then the results pane displays an enumeration of the items contained in it. In general, the results pane can be absolutely anything; MMC includes support for a standard list view, with columns and rows, or you can pull everything out and display your own custom view or control.

- **Static Node.** This is a type of node that is present for as long as the snap-in providing it is loaded. The first time a static node is accessed, MMC creates an instance of the snap-in COM server. Furthermore, each static node in the console window has a different instance of the COM server.
- **Enumerated Node.** Every static node can have its own tree of enumerated nodes, and it's up to the snap-in to show and rebuild these nodes in each view. These enumerated nodes are not persisted by MMC to the `.msc` file. Furthermore, enumerated nodes can only have other enumerated nodes as their children, never static nodes.

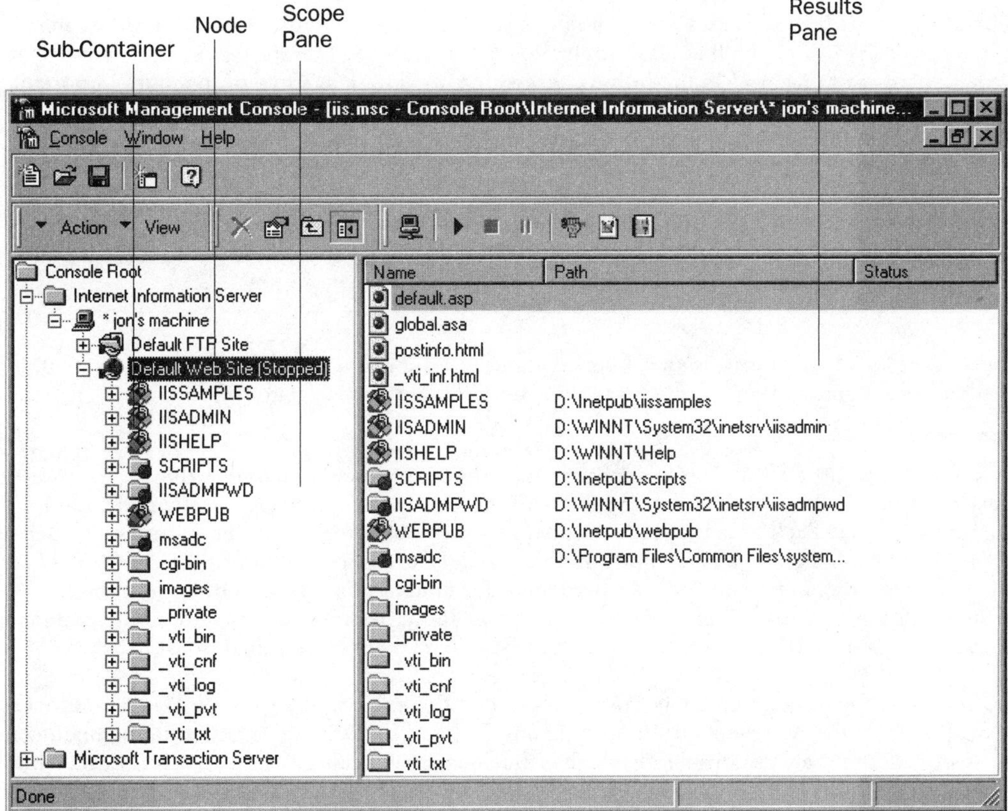

Interfaces Implemented by the Snap-in

The interfaces defined by MMC can be divided into those interfaces that the snap-in has to implement, and those that the console implements and allows the snap-in to use. The interfaces in the first of these two categories are:

```
IComponent          IComponentData      IExtendPropertySheet IExtendContextMenu
IExtendControlBar IResultDataCompare ISnapinAbout            IResultOwnerData
IDataObject
```

Depending on the features you want, you may not need to use or implement all of these interfaces in your snap-in. Typically, you'll at least implement `IComponent`, `IComponentData`, and sometimes `IExtendPropertySheet`. In the following sections, we'll look at some of the more important interfaces in more detail, and there are some in the list above that I won't even discuss. If you need more information about a particular interface, you should consult the SDK documentation.

> **Each of the interfaces above is defined in the `mmc.idl` file, which you should import into your own project's IDL file. Your project files should also `#include "mmc.h"`, and link to `mmc.lib`.**

The coverage of these interfaces that I'll provide now will be at a fairly general level. We will look at detailed implementations of the methods later, in the sample code section.

IComponentData

A snap-in that wants a new node to appear in the namespace must implement the `IComponentData` interface. You can think of this as doing the work necessary for managing a static node and its enumerated nodes. Each time that the console processes a user request in the scope pane (such as a mouse click on a node), it calls methods on this interface to perform actions, like showing the associated information for the node. In particular, for enumerating the sub-items for a node, the console calls the `IComponentData::Notify()` method, passing it the type of notification message, the most common of which is `MMCN_EXPAND`. I bet you can guess what that does!

The `IComponentData` interface is MMC's main point of entry into a snap-in. When you first select the snap-in from the Add/Remove Snap-in dialog box and hit OK, it gets added to the main console. The act of adding it to the console means that the console will call `CoCreateInstance()` on the object, and then call its `IComponentData::Initialize()` method, whose responsibilities are many. First, it must create the root node (the top-level static node) for the snap-in. When the method is called, the console passes an interface pointer to itself, so that the snap-in can manipulate the console and call the *console's* methods when it needs to. `Initialize()` also sets up the image list containing the icons for the various enumerated nodes.

It's up to the snap-in to do the work of defining and displaying the sub-items for a node. To show the node objects in the namespace, it has to get hold of a pointer to the `IConsoleNameSpace` interface, which is implemented by the console manager. Once you have this interface pointer, you can call `InsertItem()` and `DeleteItem()` to add and remove items from the scope pane – you create a `SCOPEDATAITEM` structure for each item that you want to add, and then pass the structure to the `InsertItem()` method.

`IComponentData::Destroy()` is called when the snap-in is removed from the console. It should release any interface pointers to the console that were saved in the member data for the object instance.

IComponent

You can think of `IComponent` as the interface that implements all of the necessary functions for managing items in the results pane. The methods of `IComponent` are very similar to those of `IComponentData`, except that they apply to individual items in the *results* pane, rather than to items in the *scope* pane.

Like its partner in `IComponentData`, the `Initialize()` method provides an entry point into the snap-in. It receives an `IConsole` interface pointer that it can use to manipulate the console. Typically, you'll use this to obtain and save the interface pointer to the results pane's header control, and to the `IResultData` interface you'll use later to manipulate the data items in the pane itself.

The `Notify()` function is called by the console when an event has occurred as a result of a user action. The function can receive any of several messages from the console, but the most important ones are `MMCN_SHOW`, `MMCN_REFRESH`, and `MMCN_SELECT`. The usual response to the `SHOW` message, which happens the first time that a scope pane item is clicked, is to set up the results pane with a set of column headings. In response to `REFRESH` you re-obtain the underlying data values for the items you are displaying, and then redisplay them. In the handler for the `SELECT` message, you typically enable whatever special verbs might be relevant to the items in the scope pane that are selected, so that the right-click context menu displays the proper actions.

Once again, the `Destroy()` method is called when the snap-in is being unloaded, and should be used to release all interfaces to the console.

The last important `IComponent` method is `GetDisplayInfo()`, which is called once for each column in each data item in the results pane. In this method, you obtain the value for the column in the selected item that you are displaying, and write it to the results pane by reassigning the `str` member of the `RESULTDATAITEM` structure that is passed as an argument. If that sounds a little confusing, don't worry – I'll say more about this mechanism later on.

IExtendContextMenu

An interface that a snap-in can, but does not necessarily, implement is `IExtendContextMenu`. This interface is used when the snap-in needs to add a custom command to the right-click context menu for a node in the scope pane. The node registers its need to have a special context menu by calling `AddPrimaryExtensionItems()` on the `IContextMenuProvider` interface pointer owned by the object that implements `IComponentData`. The `IExtendContextMenu` interface itself implements `AddMenuItems()` to tell the context provider what menu items to add, and the `Command()` method to handle the calls to the menu items when they come in.

IDataObject

`IDataObject` is a standard COM interface for passing data around, particularly to the clipboard. In snap-ins, it is used as a standard way to pass information back and forth between the snap-in and the console. The only method that really needs to be implemented by the snap-in is `GetDataHere()`.

Every node in the scope pane has a particular node type, and each node type must register several clipboard formats to be used in the data transfer between snap-in and console. These are listed in the table below:

Clipboard Format	Description
CCF_NODETYPE	The node type's GUID in CLSID form
CCF_SZNODETYPE	The node type's GUID in string form
CCF_DISPLAY_NAME	The default snap-in name to be displayed in the Add box, and in the console as the root node
CCF_SNAPIN_CLASSID	The CLSID of the snap-in's `ComponentData` coclass

A node type is defined by the individual snap-in using a standard COM GUID. The GUID has no significance to COM in this scenario, but it is a useful way to avoid collisions in node types across multiple objects.

These clipboard formats must be registered using a call to `RegisterClipboardFormat()`, as shown:

```
UINT cfDisplayName = RegisterClipboardFormat(CCF_DISPLAY_NAME)
```

You're probably wondering what this has to do with `IDataObject::GetDataHere()`. Well, the console sends a request for specific information by calling this method for a specific node, and requesting whichever `CCF_` format type it desires. The snap-in's implementation then packages up the requested data 'answer' into a stream object and sends it back to the console.

Whenever the snap-in is picked from the list in the Add/Remove Snap-in dialog box, MMC has called `GetDataHere()` to retrieve the display name for the snap-in's root node. This keeps MMC from having to call `IComponentData::Initialize()` before the user has decided whether to instantiate the object or not.

MMC-provided Interfaces

Now we turn to the MMC-provided interfaces that the snap-in can use to call back into MMC functionality. There are a great many of these (listed below), but only a couple that we'll actually need to use:

```
IConsole                   IConsoleNameSpace          IConsoleVerb
IContextMenuCallback       IContextMenuProvider       IControlbar
IHeaderCtrl                IImageList                 IMenuButton
IPropertySheetCallback     IPropertySheetProvider     IResultData
                           IToolbar
```

IConsole

`IConsole` is the snap-in's interface to the management console. Whenever the console creates an instance of the object that implements `IComponentData`, it passes its `IConsole` interface pointer to the `IComponentData::Initialize()` function. It also passes this interface pointer to `IComponent` by similar means. These snap-in implemented interfaces use the `IConsole` pointer to obtain pointers to *other* interfaces they need to do their work, such as `IHeaderCtrl`, `IResultData`, and `IConsoleNameSpace`. Typically, the implementation on the snap-in side will save these pointers in class members for use in various functions later on.

IResultData

`IResultData` allows a user to manipulate items and the view style associated with the standard results pane. `IResultData` has methods very similar to those of `IConsoleNameSpace`, including `InsertItem()` and `DeleteItem()`, which are used by the snap-in to add items into the results pane. The interface also has several other methods that give snap-ins the ability to manipulate and sort the items in the data list.

Items are added to the list by setting up a `RESULTDATAITEM` structure and then passing it to `InsertItem()`. Later, when the time comes to display the data in each column, that `RESULTDATAITEM` is passed to the `IComponent::GetDisplayInfo()` method, where it gets set by the snap-in's implementation.

IHeaderCtrl

This interface gives you access to change the number and labels of the columns in the default results view pane. To add a column, simply use `InsertColumn()`. The sample later in the chapter will demonstrate how to use this interface.

IImageList

This interface allows the snap-in to insert the icons that will be used to depict items in the results or scope panes. Use `ImageListSetIcon()` to set an icon in an image list, or `ImageListSetStrip()` to set a *strip* of icons in an image list.

IConsoleVerb

You use `IConsoleVerb` to set the active verbs in the context menu for a particular `IComponent` object being shown in the results pane. You'd usually do this in response to the `MMCN_SELECT` message being sent to the `IComponent::Notify()` function.

The PoolerMMC Snap-in

All of those interfaces were probably a lot to take in. If you don't quite get it yet, don't worry: I've got an example that you can use to get your head around the implementation of the various snap-in-side interfaces.

Once again, the sample that I created was for the Business Object service that we built in Chapter 9. Unlike the control panel applet you saw earlier in the chapter, this snap-in allows you not merely to manipulate registry entries, but to examine actively the total number of connections, and the remaining free connections. It also allows you to drill down and examine the individual connections themselves – their ODBC handle values, and whether they are busy or free.

First, let's take a look at what the snap-in needs to be able to do. We want it to be able to administer any machine in the domain, so we need the facility to add a computer name to the nodes in the namespace, so that we can monitor a particular computer. If I select the Pooler SnapIn node in the scope pane, I want to be able to see a quick summary of all the connected computers as a list in the results pane. The information to be displayed about each *computer* in the results pane will be the number of total resources, and the number of resources remaining. Furthermore, we should be able to select any computer node (sub-container) in the scope pane and see a list of its handles in the results pane. For each computer, there will be a single list item for every resource handle that the service is managing. The columns in that list will be the handle name, its resource array position, its raw handle value, and its state – that is, 'in use' or 'free'.

In developing this snap-in, I took my cue from the DISK systems management sample in the Platform SDK. Unfortunately, there are very few examples of MMC code around, and the documentation in the library is still considered to be 'beta'. In my implementation, I didn't do everything I could have done, and those things that I did do could probably use more refinement. Keep an eye on the Wrox web site for changes and improvements.

Modified Business Object Service

In order to make the snap-in work, the first thing I had to do was somehow export the data from the Business Object service that I wanted to be able to see in the snap-in. To do that, I added an object that exposed the `IPoolAdminData` interface. This interface has two methods: `GetPoolInfo()`, which returns an array of data about each connection, and `GetUsageStats()`, which returns the numbers of available and free connections in the service. The two methods are shown below:

```
STDMETHODIMP CPoolAdminData::GetPoolInfo(VARIANT* paVariant)
{
   RHANDLEHEADER* pTemp = 0;
   bool bTemp = 0;
   long tmpHandle = 0;

   CResourceArray* pArray = _Module.m_pQM->GetResourceArray();
   int count = pArray->GetCount();

   // Allocations for variant array
   long theDim[2];
   const int numcols = 3;

   // Set up Array
   // Create the array
   SAFEARRAYBOUND sabound[2];
   sabound[0].cElements = numcols;
   sabound[0].lLbound = 1;
   sabound[1].cElements = count;
   sabound[1].lLbound = 0;

   VariantInit(paVariant);
   paVariant->vt = VT_VARIANT | VT_ARRAY;
   paVariant->parray = SafeArrayCreate(VT_VARIANT, 2, sabound);
   for(int pos = 0 ; pos < count ; pos++)
   {
      pTemp = pArray->m_pHandles[pos];
      if(pTemp)
```

```
        {
            // Poke in the position and busy state
            bTemp = pTemp->bFree;
            // Access the RHANDLE and get handle value
            tmpHandle = (long)pTemp->pRH->handle;

            theDim[1] = pos;                         // Row dimension value

            theDim[0] = 1;                           // Position
            CComVariant vC1(pos);
            SafeArrayPutElement(paVariant->parray, theDim, &vC1);

            theDim[0] = 2;                           // Handle
            CComVariant vC2(tmpHandle);
            SafeArrayPutElement(paVariant->parray, theDim, &vC2);

            theDim[0] = 3;                           // Busy
            CComVariant vC3(bTemp);
            SafeArrayPutElement(paVariant->parray, theDim, &vC3);
        }
    }

    return S_OK;
}

STDMETHODIMP CPoolAdminData::GetUsageStats(long* pConnections,
                                           long* pRemaining)
{
    *pConnections = _Module.m_pQM->GetNumResources();
    *pRemaining = _Module.m_pQM->FreeResourcesLeft();
    return S_OK;
}
```

I also had to tweak the `CQuarterMaster` class, because some of the variables that I needed to access in order to obtain administration information were private. To solve this, I added a public function to return the pointer to the handle array, so that it could be walked and its contents dumped.

```
    CResourceArray* GetResourceArray() {return m_pResources;}
```

This modified version of the Business Object service is available in the source code for this chapter.

PoolerMMC Code

Now, let's begin marching through the code for the snap-in sample itself. Since it supports views in both the scope pane and the results pane, it implements both the `IComponentData` and the `IComponent` interfaces. It also, of course, implements `IDataObject`, since that's how the snap-in and the console share data. Finally, the New | Computer item on the context menu for the root node is a context menu extension, and thus requires the `IExtendContextMenu` interface. In this section, we'll look at these four interfaces, as well as a custom class called `CEntry` that's used to manage every node entry that appears in the scope and results panes.

*This sample requires a considerable quantity of code, and for that reason I have restricted discussion here to the more important aspects – there are some minor functions and member variables that aren't included in the listings. The techniques involved, though, are explained in full, and you can get the complete project from the Wrox web site (*http://www.wrox.com*).*

General Information

First, you need some general information. This sample was created using ATL 2.1. It is a COM server DLL that exposes objects supporting the STA (apartment) model. The coclasses that implement the interfaces support the bare interfaces as imported from `mmc.idl`, and they are custom interfaces, not dual ones. For instance, take a look at the class that implements `IExtendContextMenu`:

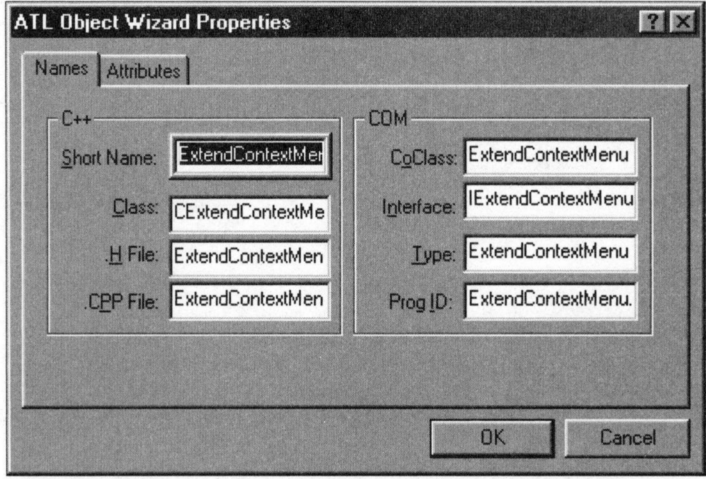

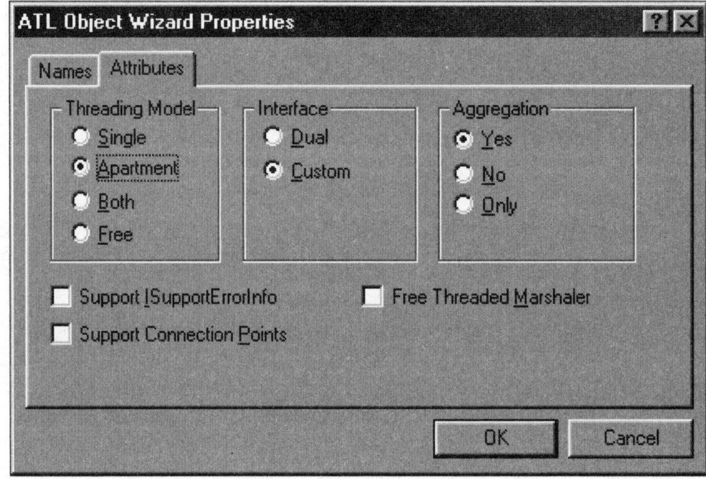

Once you have added this and the other three coclasses (`Component`, `ComponentData`, and `DataObject`) in this way, you should go to the IDL file and *remove* the interface definitions for the interfaces that were just put in by the Wizard. The definitions of these interfaces will be imported from the `mmc.idl` file that you `import` at the top of the IDL file, just below `ocidl.idl`.

Furthermore, the DLL should be built in Unicode mode, and you must add `MMC.lib` to the list of link libraries for all configurations. Finally, I should point out that I haven't included much in the way of COM error checking in this sample, simply to keep down the volume of code. In real life, you should do the right thing and check errors more diligently!

CDataObject

First, let's look at the implementation of `CDataObject`, which implements `IDataObject` for the snap-in. Remember that `IDataObject::GetDataHere()` is the method most likely to be called first (before even `IComponentData::Initialize()`), in order to obtain the display name for the snap-in when you are adding it to the current console window. Now, the only method of `IDataObject` that this class actually implements is `GetDataHere()`; the other eight methods of `IDataObject` (which you can find in `ObjIDL.idl`) just return `E_NOTIMPL`. `GetDataHere()` is shown below:

```
STDMETHODIMP CDataObject::GetDataHere(LPFORMATETC lpFormatEtc,
                                              LPSTGMEDIUM lpMedium)
{
   IStream* pStream;
   CreateStreamOnHGlobal(lpMedium->hGlobal, FALSE, &pStream);
   CLIPFORMAT cf = lpFormatEtc->cfFormat;
   if(cf == s_DisplayName)
      pStream->Write(L"Pooler SnapIn", sizeof(L"Pooler SnapIn"), NULL);
   else if(cf == s_NodeType)
   {
      LPENTRY lpEntry = (LPENTRY)m_cookie;
      int tier = lpEntry->GetTier();
      switch(tier)
      {
      case -1:
         pStream->Write(&UUIDRootNode, sizeof(UUID), NULL);
         break;

      case 0:
         pStream->Write(&UUIDCompNode, sizeof(UUID), NULL);
         break;

      case 1:
         pStream->Write(&UUIDArrayNode, sizeof(UUID), NULL);
         break;
      }
   }
   else if(cf == s_SnapinClsid)
     pStream->Write(&CLSID_ComponentData, sizeof(CLSID_ComponentData),NULL);

   pStream->Release();
   return S_OK;
}
```

The function figures out what was requested (display name, node type, or snap-in CLSID) and then pops that information into the stream. In the first case, it writes the display name you saw in the Add/Remove Snap-in dialog to the stream. If the console wants the CLSID, it returns the ID of the ComponentData coclass.

If the console asks for the node type, the function returns the type depending on what 'tier' the node is in the namespace hierarchy. If it is the root node, then the tier is –1, if it's the computer node, the tier is 0, and if it is the handle array node, then the tier is 1. The call to GetTier() on the CEntry object tells you what level the node is at, which it does by obtaining a 'cookie' value out of the CDataObject object, and using that as a pointer to a CEntry object that holds all the special, snap-in defined information about the node. You will see this kind of mechanism time and time again, and I'll re-explain it, so don't worry if it hasn't quite gelled yet.

In case you were wondering, all of the clipboard formats being tested against here were registered in the CDataObject constructor:

```
CDataObject()
{
   s_DisplayName = RegisterClipboardFormat(CCF_DISPLAY_NAME);
   s_NodeType    = RegisterClipboardFormat(CCF_NODETYPE);
   s_SnapinClsid = RegisterClipboardFormat(CCF_SNAPIN_CLASSID);
   m_cookie = 0;
}
```

In order to create a mechanism whereby that cookie could be stored in the data object on a per-node basis, I added an additional interface to the CDataObject class that allows the getting and setting of the cookie value; I called it IPoolerMMCDataObject. The interface has two methods: a get_Cookie() property, and a put_Cookie() property. An additional interface was used in this scenario because extending a standard interface such as IDataObject simply by adding additional methods to it is not legitimate COM technique, even though it would have been convenient here. The methods just do this:

```
STDMETHODIMP CDataObject::get_Cookie(long* pVal)
{
   *pVal = m_cookie;
   return S_OK;
}

STDMETHODIMP CDataObject::put_Cookie(long newval)
{
   m_cookie = newval;
   return S_OK;
}
```

The very first time through, though, you can be sure that the console is just calling for the display name for the node. The other format types won't be requested until after IComponentData::Initialize().

CComponentData

Now let's move on to the next important class, `CComponentData`, which implements the `IComponentData` interface. As I've explained, the console creates an instance of the object that implements this interface, which has seven methods, as soon as you expand the snap-in's root node for the first time. It then calls the `Initialize()` method, implemented below:

```
STDMETHODIMP CComponentData::Initialize(LPUNKNOWN pUnknown)
{
   m_pRoot = new CEntry();

   pUnknown->QueryInterface(IID_IConsoleNameSpace,
                            (void**)(&m_pConsoleNameSpace));
   pUnknown->QueryInterface(IID_IContextMenuProvider,
                            (void**)(&m_pContextMenuProvider));
   CComObject<CExtendContextMenu>* pExtendContextMenu;
   CComObject<CExtendContextMenu>::CreateInstance(&pExtendContextMenu);

   pExtendContextMenu->QueryInterface(IID_IExtendContextMenu,
                                      (void**)&m_pExtendContextMenu);

   IPoolerMMCExtendContextMenu* pMyExtendContextMenu;
   pExtendContextMenu->QueryInterface(IID_IPoolerMMCExtendContextMenu,
                                      (void**)&pMyExtendContextMenu);

   pMyExtendContextMenu->put_Console(pUnknown);
   pMyExtendContextMenu->Release();

   LPCONSOLE lpConsole;
   pUnknown->QueryInterface(IID_IConsole, (void**)(&lpConsole));

   LPIMAGELIST lpImageScope;
   lpConsole->QueryScopeImageList(&lpImageScope);

   HINSTANCE hInst = _Module.GetModuleInstance();
   HBITMAP hBmp16 = LoadBitmap(hInst, MAKEINTRESOURCE (IDB_BITMAP1));
   HBITMAP hBmp32 = LoadBitmap(hInst, MAKEINTRESOURCE (IDB_BITMAP2));

   lpImageScope->ImageListSetStrip((LONG*)hBmp16, (LONG*)hBmp32, 0,
        RGB(0,255,0));

   lpConsole->Release();
   return S_OK;
}
```

This method does a good number of things, most of which are to do with setup. First, it creates an instance of the CEntry object that manages the information about the root node. It also uses the IConsole pointer to save pointers to the console's IContextMenuProvider and IConsoleNameSpace interfaces as class member data. Next, it creates an instance of its own object that implements IExtendContextMenu and saves a pointer to it. It also obtains a pointer to a special, home-grown interface called IPoolerMMCExtendContextMenu, which is used to save the pointer to the console on behalf of the class that implements the context menu extension. Finally, Initialize() does some work to set up the images that will be shown next to the nodes in the scope pane.

The next thing that happens is that the console calls QueryDataObject() in order to obtain the data object that's associated with the particular node in the namespace. In this case, the node is the root node:

```
STDMETHODIMP CComponentData::QueryDataObject(long              cookie,
                                             DATA_OBJECT_TYPES type,
                                             LPDATAOBJECT*     ppDataObject)
{
   CComObject<CDataObject>* pDataObject;
   CComObject<CDataObject>::CreateInstance(&pDataObject);
   IPoolerMMCDataObject* pPoolObject;
   pDataObject->QueryInterface(IID_IPoolerMMCDataObject,
                               (void**)&pPoolObject);

   if(cookie)
      pPoolObject->put_Cookie(cookie);
   else
      pPoolObject->put_Cookie((long)m_pRoot);

   *ppDataObject = pDataObject;

   if(m_pContextMenuProvider)
      m_pContextMenuProvider->AddPrimaryExtensionItems(m_pExtendContextMenu,
                                                       pDataObject);
   return S_OK;
}
```

The implementation here is straightforward. First, we *create* a data object on behalf of the node. Later on in the function, we assign a pointer to that object to the [out] parameter.

The cookie is simply a long tag value managed by the console to mark individual nodes uniquely in the namespace. If the cookie value coming in is non-zero (which it won't be at this stage, because we are dealing with the root node), then we stick the cookie value into the data object. This mechanism will be important for later, enumerated nodes, as it serves as the mechanism whereby the data object is linked up to the cookie managed by the console. Finally, we hook up our context menu extension, implemented in CExtendContextMenu, to the provider for the node. We'll look at this class in the next section.

The next important method in the CComponentData class is Notify(). If you remember, Notify() handles messages from the console indicating that a node should be expanded:

```
STDMETHODIMP CComponentData::Notify(LPDATAOBJECT lpDataObject,
                               MMC_NOTIFY_TYPE event, long arg, long param)
{
   if(event != MMCN_EXPAND)
      return S_OK;
   SCOPEDATAITEM sdi;
   memset(&sdi, 0, sizeof(SCOPEDATAITEM));
   sdi.mask = SDI_STR | SDI_PARAM | SDI_IMAGE | SDI_OPENIMAGE | SDI_PARENT;
   sdi.relativeID = (HSCOPEITEM)param;
   sdi.displayname = MMC_CALLBACK;

   IPoolerMMCDataObject* pPoolObject;
   lpDataObject->QueryInterface(IID_IPoolerMMCDataObject,
                                  (void**)&pPoolObject);
   long cookie;
   pPoolObject->get_Cookie(&cookie);
   pPoolObject->Release();

   LPENTRY lpEntry;
   if(cookie)
      lpEntry = (LPENTRY)cookie;
   else
      lpEntry = m_pRoot;

   lpEntry->SetScope((HSCOPEITEM)param);

   // Only add to scope pane at computer level, not connection level
   if(lpEntry->GetTier() == -1)
   {
      int count = lpEntry->GetSubCount();
      for(int pos = 0 ; pos < count ; pos++)
      {
         LPENTRY lpSubItem = lpEntry->GetSubEntry(pos);
         sdi.lParam = (LPARAM)lpSubItem;
         sdi.nImage = 0;
         sdi.nOpenImage = 1;

         m_pConsoleNameSpace->InsertItem(&sdi);
      }
   }
   return S_OK;
}
```

The `Notify()` member does quite a bit of work. To begin, it sets up a `SCOPEDATAITEM` structure for each item that's going to be displayed in the scope pane when the node is expanded. That structure has a few important members, including `mask`, which allows you to specify what types of data members in the structure will be filled with information, and `displayname`, which is marked as `MMC_CALLBACK`. This means that the console should actually use the callback function `IComponentData::GetDisplayInfo()` to obtain the display name for the item when it needs to show it, rather than relying on a hard-coded `displayname` value. We'll have a look at that function in a few moments.

Next, `Notify()` takes the data object pointer that was passed in as an argument, and uses it to obtain the cookie that's associated with the data object that was also passed to it. That cookie, as you remember, is just a pointer to a `CEntry` object that contains data about the item being displayed.

The function can now check which tier the actual node being expanded is on. If it's the root node, then `Notify()` asks the `CEntry` object that holds information about it to enumerate its sub-nodes, which will make up the 'computer' node level. It then assigns the rest of the members in the `SCOPEDATAITEM` structure, including the `lparam` member, which can hold user-defined data and in this case holds the pointer to the `CEntry` object that represents the sub-item being enumerated. It also assigns which images in the image map apply to the 'closed' and 'open' state for the node. Finally, `Notify()` uses the `InsertItem()` method of the `IConsoleNameSpace` interface to put the object in the scope pane.

> **Note that if the node is at the 'computer' level, it does not enumerate sub-items into the scope pane. This is because I don't really want the individual connections to come up in the scope pane – there is no deeper level to drill to.**

A moment ago I mentioned the `GetDisplayInfo()` member function. The console calls this method each time it needs to show information about the items in the scope pane.

```
STDMETHODIMP CComponentData::GetDisplayInfo(LPSCOPEDATAITEM pItem)
{
   LPENTRY lpEntry = (LPENTRY)pItem->lParam;
   pItem->displayname = lpEntry->GetName();
   return S_OK;
}
```

This simply uses the `lparam` of the `SCOPEDATAITEM` that was passed in to obtain the pointer to the underlying `CEntry` object that holds data about the node. It then calls the `GetName()` member function, and assigns that string to the `displayname` member of the structure.

Apart from `Destroy()`, which just performs some cleanup of interfaces and dynamic variables, the last `IComponentData` interface method that the sample actually implements is `CreateComponent()`, which gets called by the console when the `CComponent` object for displaying in the *results* pane needs to be created by the snap-in. This typically happens when you select an item in the scope pane, and the rest of its associated information comes up in the results pane:

```
STDMETHODIMP CComponentData::CreateComponent(LPCOMPONENT* ppComponent)
{
   CComObject<CComponent>* pComponent;
   CComObject<CComponent>::CreateInstance(&pComponent);

   *ppComponent = pComponent;
   return S_OK;
}
```

All this does – all it has to do – is create an instance of the `CComponent` class and pass the pointer back to the console.

CExtendContextMenu

Next up, let's have a look at the context menu extension class. You may remember that this was set up in the `IComponentData::QueryDataObject()` method for each node that supports a special context menu. In this case, only the root node extends the context menu, and does so by adding a menu option that allows you to add a new computer.

My implementation of `AddMenuItems()` is shown below, and it's one of only two methods defined by the `IExtendContextMenu` interface. It is responsible for actually putting the menu items into the extended menu, and attaching a command ID to the item.

```
STDMETHODIMP CExtendContextMenu::AddMenuItems(LPDATAOBJECT pDataObject,
                    LPCONTEXTMENUCALLBACK pCallback, long* pInsertionAllowed)
{
   IPoolerMMCDataObject* pPoolObject;
   pDataObject->QueryInterface(IID_IPoolerMMCDataObject,
                                                    (void**)&pPoolObject);

   long cookie;
   pPoolObject->get_Cookie(&cookie);
   pPoolObject->Release();

   LPENTRY lpEntry = (LPENTRY)cookie;
   if(!lpEntry)
      return S_OK;

   int tier = lpEntry->GetTier();

   CONTEXTMENUITEM cmi;
   memset(&cmi, 0, sizeof (CONTEXTMENUITEM));

   if((*pInsertionAllowed & CCM_INSERTIONALLOWED_NEW) && (tier == -1))
   {
      cmi.strName = L"Computer";
      cmi.lCommandID = 0x1;
      cmi.lInsertionPointID = CCM_INSERTIONPOINTID_PRIMARY_NEW;

      pCallback->AddItem(&cmi);
   }
   return S_OK;
}
```

This simple function goes through the usual process of obtaining the pointer to the `CEntry` object and then finding out which of the three 'tiers' of nodes it is in. If the tier is the root node, then it adds a **Computer** entry underneath the **New...** item on the context menu. It sets the string name and the command ID of the entry, and then uses the `IContextMenuCallback` pointer that was passed in to add it to the context menu.

When a user actually *selects* one of the menu items from the context menu extension, the console calls into the interface's second method, `Command()`, to notify the snap-in that a menu item has been selected. That function simply needs to invoke the proper function to do the work that implements the command:

```
STDMETHODIMP CExtendContextMenu::Command(long lCommandID,
                                          LPDATAOBJECT pDataObject)
{
   switch(lCommandID)
   {
   case 0x01:
      DoTheNew(pDataObject);
      break;
   }

   return S_OK;
}
```

The function receives the command ID that was set up in `AddMenuItems()`, and it can simply switch on this value. It also receives a pointer to the node's data object, which it can use to tell exactly upon which node of a group of enumerated nodes it needs to act. I simply delegate out to a private helper function called `DoTheNew()` to take the appropriate actions.

```
void CExtendContextMenu::DoTheNew(LPDATAOBJECT pDataObject)
{
   if(!m_pConsoleNameSpace)
      return;

   CComputer dlg;
   if(dlg.DoModal() == IDCANCEL)
      return;

   long cookie;
   IPoolerMMCDataObject* pPoolObject;

   pDataObject->QueryInterface(IID_IPoolerMMCDataObject,
                               (void**)&pPoolObject);
   pPoolObject->get_Cookie(&cookie);
   pPoolObject->Release();

   LPENTRY lpEntry = (LPENTRY)cookie;
   LPENTRY lpSubEntry = lpEntry->AddSubEntry(dlg.m_szComputer);

   SCOPEDATAITEM sdi;
   memset(&sdi, 0, sizeof(SCOPEDATAITEM));

   sdi.mask = SDI_STR | SDI_PARAM | SDI_IMAGE | SDI_OPENIMAGE | SDI_PARENT;
   sdi.lParam = (LPARAM)lpSubEntry;
   sdi.relativeID = lpEntry->GetScope();
   sdi.displayname = MMC_CALLBACK;
```

```
        sdi.nImage = 0;
        sdi.nOpenImage = 1;

        m_pConsoleNameSpace->InsertItem(&sdi);
        lpSubEntry->SetScope(sdi.ID);
    }
```

`DoTheNew()` takes on the burden of bringing up a dialog box so that users can enter the name of the computer on which they want to make a connection to the Business Object service. I won't reprint the simple code for the dialog box here, but it sets a member variable called `m_szComputer`, and the dialog itself looks something like this:

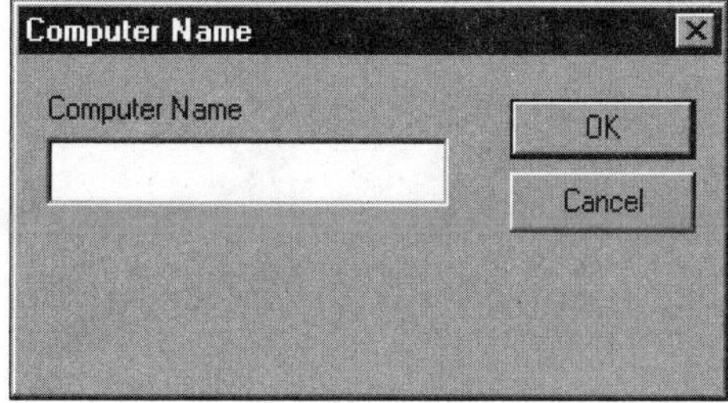

Once the dialog has been dismissed (and not just cancelled), the function uses the `pDataObject` pointer to obtain the cookie and get the pointer to the `CEntry` object that was selected. In this case, it is the root node. It then adds a sub-entry to the object for the computer that was attached, and sets up a `SCOPEDATAITEM` structure in order to insert the new node into the namespace.

CEntry Class

OK, we've come this far, and we simply can't put off talking about `CEntry` any longer. `CEntry` is the class that the snap-in uses to manage *all* the data related to individual nodes in the scope pane *and* the results pane. The `CEntry` class holds such things as the name of the node, and any other data that gets displayed when a node is selected into the results pane. It also holds the current tier number, who its parent is, and an array of pointers to any items it enumerates. Thus, the root node holds an array of pointers to all computer nodes, and each computer node holds an array of pointers to all connection nodes.

First, let's look at what happens in the construction of the `CEntry` object, which differs depending on what type of node (which tier) the object represents.

```
CEntry::CEntry()
{
    m_nTier = -1;
    m_pParent = 0;
    m_nSubCount = 0;
    m_pSubEntries = NULL;
    m_hScope = NULL;

    wcscpy(m_szName, L"Root");

    m_nPos = 0;
    m_Handle = NULL;
    m_bFree = FALSE;
    m_lConnections = 0;
    m_lRemaining = 0;
}
```

For the root node, the constructor is trivial. It just sets up the variables, and sets the `m_nTier` member to –1. At this point, it has no sub-entries (until a computer is added) and no parent. Don't be fooled by this simplicity, though – the constructor for the 'computer' (tier-0) node is a bit more complicated.

```
// Constructor for tier 0
CEntry::CEntry(LPOLESTR szName, int nTier, LPENTRY lpParent)
{
   m_nTier = nTier;
   m_nSubCount = 0;
   m_pParent = lpParent;

   wcscpy(m_szName, szName);

   RefreshConnectionData();
   LoadSubEntries();
}
```

This constructor requires that its tier be passed in, as well as a pointer to its parent's (the root's) data object. It also requires its own name (that is, the name of the computer you're connecting to) as an argument. The constructor then calls a function that connects to the Business Object service on the requested computer, and retrieves the information about the number of total and free database handles. This function, `RefreshConnectionData()`, is fairly straightforward:

```
void CEntry::RefreshConnectionData()
{
   COSERVERINFO serverInfo;
   memset(&serverInfo, 0, sizeof(COSERVERINFO));
   serverInfo.pwszName = m_szName;

   MULTI_QI qis[1];
   memset(qis, 0, sizeof(MULTI_QI));

   qis[0].pIID = &IID_IPoolAdminData;
   HRESULT hr = CoCreateInstanceEx(CLSID_PoolAdminData,
                                   NULL,
                                   CLSCTX_LOCAL_SERVER,
                                   &serverInfo,
                                   1,
                                   qis);

   if(FAILED(hr))
      return;

   IPoolAdminData* piPoolAdmin = (IPoolAdminData*)qis[0].pItf;

   long lConnections = 0;
   long lRemaining = 0;

   hr = piPoolAdmin->GetUsageStats(&lConnections, &lRemaining);
   if(FAILED(hr))
      return;
```

```
    m_lConnections = lConnections;
    m_lRemaining = lRemaining;

    piPoolAdmin->Release();
}
```

What this function does is to create an instance of the `PoolAdminData` object we added to the Business Object service and call `GetUsageStats()` on it. It then assigns the returned parameters of those functions to local member variables. Relatively straightforward COM stuff.

Returning to the `CEntry` constructor, the next function to be called is `LoadSubEntries()`. This function again connects to the Business Object service to grab the individual connection data for all the connections the service is holding on to.

```
void CEntry::LoadSubEntries()
{
    // Attach to server and query for variant array
    COSERVERINFO serverInfo;
    memset(&serverInfo, 0, sizeof(COSERVERINFO));
    serverInfo.pwszName = m_szName;

    MULTI_QI qis[1];
    memset(qis, 0, sizeof (MULTI_QI));

    qis[0].pIID = &IID_IPoolAdminData;
    HRESULT hr = CoCreateInstanceEx(CLSID_PoolAdminData,
                                    NULL,
                                    CLSCTX_LOCAL_SERVER,
                                    &serverInfo,
                                    1,
                                    qis);

    if(FAILED(hr))
        return;

    IPoolAdminData* piPoolAdmin = (IPoolAdminData*)qis[0].pItf;

    // Return the data into a variant array
    VARIANT var;
    VariantInit(&var);
    hr = piPoolAdmin->GetPoolInfo(&var);
    if(FAILED(hr))
        return;

    // March through array and attach to sub items
    long rowLower=0;
    long rowUpper=0;
    long thedim[2];

    SAFEARRAY* psa = var.parray;
    hr = SafeArrayGetLBound(psa, 2, &rowLower);
    hr = SafeArrayGetUBound(psa, 2, &rowUpper);
```

```
    for(int i = rowLower ; i <= rowUpper ; i++)
    {
       thedim[1] = i;

       thedim[0] = 1;
       CComVariant vPos;
       hr = SafeArrayGetElement(psa, thedim, &vPos);

       CComVariant vHandle;
       thedim[0] = 2;
       hr = SafeArrayGetElement(psa, thedim, &vHandle);

       CComVariant vFree;
       thedim[0] = 3;
       hr = SafeArrayGetElement(psa, thedim, &vFree);

       AddSubEntry(vPos.lVal, vHandle.lVal, vFree.boolVal);
    }

    piPoolAdmin->Release();
}
```

This function has to do a little bit more work, because the `IPoolAdminData` interface method `GetPoolInfo()` returns a variant array containing the connection data. `LoadSubEntries()` walks the variant array and calls `AddSubEntry()` for each row in it, passing in the columns as parameters. Each call to `AddSubEntry()` creates a new third-tier (tier-1) `CEntry` object that contains all the data about the connection.

```
// Overloaded for adding handle map items (tier 1)
LPENTRY CEntry::AddSubEntry(int pos, long handle, BOOL bFree)
{
   LPENTRY pEntry = new CEntry(pos, handle, bFree, m_nTier + 1, this);
   LPENTRY* pSub = new LPENTRY[m_nSubCount + 1];

   // Copy array
   if(m_nSubCount)
   {
      memcpy(pSub, m_pSubEntries, m_nSubCount * sizeof(LPENTRY));
      for(int n = 0 ; n < m_nSubCount ; delete m_pSubEntries[n++])
         ;
      delete [] m_pSubEntries;
   }

   m_pSubEntries = pSub;
   m_pSubEntries[m_nSubCount++] = pEntry;

   return pEntry;
}
```

All this function does is call the overloaded constructor for creating objects of the third-tier type. It then expands the array of sub-entries contained in the `m_pSubEntries` class member, and reassigns the counts.

Next, let's look at the constructor for the third-tier `CEntry` objects. It's actually quite simple, just assigning the passed-in parameters that originally came back from the variant array to the member data for the object:

```
// Constructor for list items
CEntry::CEntry(int pos, long handle, BOOL bFree, int nTier, LPENTRY lpParent)
{
   if(nTier != 1)
      return;

   m_nTier = nTier;
   m_pParent = lpParent;
   m_nSubCount = 0;
   m_pSubEntries = NULL;
   m_hScope = NULL;

   OLECHAR sz[25];
   wsprintf(sz, L"Handle #%d", pos);
   wcscpy(m_szName, sz);

   m_nPos = pos;
   m_Handle = handle;
   m_bFree = bFree;
   m_lConnections = 0;
   m_lRemaining = 0;
}
```

There are really only a couple of other `CEntry` class member functions worthy of mention. One is the `RefreshSubEntries()` function, which essentially dumps the object's sub-entries array and reloads it by reconnecting to the Business Object service. This function is used when the object selects the **Refresh** menu item on the node in the scope pane.

```
void CEntry::RefreshSubEntries()
{
   if(m_nTier == 0)
   {
      for(int n = 0 ; n < m_nSubCount ; delete m_pSubEntries[n++])
         ;
      delete [] m_pSubEntries;
      m_pSubEntries = NULL;
      m_nSubCount = 0;
      LoadSubEntries();
   }
   else if(m_nTier == -1)
   {
      for(int i = 0 ; i < m_nSubCount ; i++)
      {
         m_pSubEntries[i]->RefreshConnectionData();
      }
   }
}
```

The other members in the class just return the data in different member variables. For instance, take a look at `GetState()`, which returns the value of the `m_bFree` data member to the caller as an OLE string.

```
LPOLESTR CEntry::GetState()
{
   LPOLESTR sz = new OLECHAR[5];
   if(m_bFree)
      wsprintf(sz, L"Free");
   else
      wsprintf(sz, L"Used");

   return sz;
}
```

In the next section, you'll see that `IComponent` uses these discrete member access functions to gather the values of columns in the rows of the results pane.

To be honest, the `CEntry` class is a bit of a quick fix. A cleaner solution might have been to develop `CEntry` as a base class, and then to derive individual classes from it, each with their own overrides for functions like `AddSubItems()` and the constructor. This would eliminate the need to overload these functions in order to handle the different data types, and allow each derived class to contain *only* the data members it needs, without having some used and some unused data members. The architecture would be cleaner, although it would make passing around pointers to these objects more difficult because of typecasting issues. In your implementation of a snap-in, you could solve the problem in a different way – you might simply keep an array of the members of each node type.

CComponent

The final class in the sample that I want to talk about is `CComponent`, the snap-in's implementation of the `IComponent` interface. As you already know, this interface is very similar to `IComponentData`; the first thing that gets called on a new instance is the `Initialize()` function:

```
STDMETHODIMP CComponent::Initialize(LPCONSOLE lpConsole)
{
   lpConsole->QueryInterface(IID_IHeaderCtrl, (void**)&m_pHeaderCtrl);

   m_pConsole = lpConsole;
   lpConsole->SetHeader(m_pHeaderCtrl);

   lpConsole->QueryInterface(IID_IResultData, (void**)&m_pResultData);

   lpConsole->QueryConsoleVerb(&m_pConsoleVerb);
   lpConsole->QueryResultImageList(&m_pImageResult);

   HINSTANCE hInst = _Module.GetModuleInstance();
   m_hBmp16 = LoadBitmap(hInst, MAKEINTRESOURCE(IDB_BITMAP1));
   m_hBmp32 = LoadBitmap(hInst, MAKEINTRESOURCE(IDB_BITMAP2));

   return S_OK;
}
```

Unsurprisingly, this function does similar things to `IComponentData::Initialize()`. It uses the `IConsole` pointer that's passed in to obtain several interface pointers – to the results pane's header control, to the `IResultData` interface, and to the context verbs. It also loads in the bitmap resource for items in the results pane.

The next major thing to happen is that the individual component receives a notification message from the console that the user needs something done. The console calls in on the `Notify()` function, passing in the message type and the data object pointer for the item.

```
STDMETHODIMP CComponent::Notify(LPDATAOBJECT lpDataObject,
                                 MMC_NOTIFY_TYPE event, long arg, long param)
{
   switch(event)
   {
   case MMCN_ACTIVATE:
      break;
   case MMCN_DBLCLICK:
      break;
   case MMCN_COLUMN_CLICK:
      break;

   case MMCN_ADD_IMAGES:
      AddImages(lpDataObject);
      break;

   case MMCN_SELECT:
      Select(lpDataObject, arg);
      break;

   case MMCN_REFRESH:
      Refresh(lpDataObject);
      Show(lpDataObject);
      break;
   case MMCN_SHOW:
      Show(lpDataObject);
      break;
   }

   return S_OK;
}
```

To handle these messages, which the snap-in can choose to deal with or not, the `CComponent` class just calls local member functions to do the work. If the item in question is being selected, the `Select()` function is called:

```
void CComponent::Select(LPDATAOBJECT lpDataObject, long arg)
{
   BOOL bScope = LOWORD(arg);
   BOOL bSelect = HIWORD(arg);
```

```
    if(!bScope || !bSelect)
        return;
    IPoolerMMCDataObject* pPoolObject;
    lpDataObject->QueryInterface(IID_IPoolerMMCDataObject,
                                        (void**)&pPoolObject);

    long cookie;
    pPoolObject->get_Cookie(&cookie);
    pPoolObject->Release();

    // Enable the refresh verb on scope pane components
    if(cookie)
        m_pConsoleVerb->SetVerbState(MMC_VERB_REFRESH, ENABLED, TRUE);
}
```

`Select()` first checks to confirm that the item being selected is in the scope pane. If it is, then it enables the Refresh verb on the context menu for that item.

If the snap-in is notified that an object is being shown for the first time, it receives the `MMCN_SHOW` message. The typical response to this notification is to set up the results pane to display the list of items of which the node being shown is the parent. For our purposes, if the node being shown is the root node, then the results pane gets set up to show each item in the tier *beneath* that node – that is, the computer nodes. If it is the computer node, then the results pane is set up to show the individual connection entries:

```
void CComponent::Show(LPDATAOBJECT lpDataObject)
{
    long cookie;
    IPoolerMMCDataObject* pPoolObject;
    lpDataObject->QueryInterface(IID_IPoolerMMCDataObject,
                                        (void**)&pPoolObject);
    pPoolObject->get_Cookie(&cookie);
    pPoolObject->Release();

    LPENTRY lpEntry = (LPENTRY)cookie;

    if(!lpEntry)
        return;

    int tier = lpEntry->GetTier();

    switch(tier)
    {
    case -1:
        m_pHeaderCtrl->InsertColumn(0, L"Name", 0, 100);
        m_pHeaderCtrl->InsertColumn(1, L"Total Connections", 0, 100);
        m_pHeaderCtrl->InsertColumn(2, L"Remaining Connections", 0, 100);
        break;
```

```
        case 0:
            m_pHeaderCtrl->InsertColumn(0, L"Name", 0, 100);
            m_pHeaderCtrl->InsertColumn(1, L"Position", 0, 60);
            m_pHeaderCtrl->InsertColumn(2, L"Handle", 0, 100);
            m_pHeaderCtrl->InsertColumn(3, L"State", 0, 75);
            m_pResultData->DeleteAllRsltItems();

            RESULTDATAITEM rdi;
            memset(&rdi, 0, sizeof(RESULTDATAITEM));
            rdi.mask = RDI_STR | RDI_IMAGE | RDI_PARAM;
            rdi.nImage = 2;
            rdi.str = MMC_CALLBACK;

            int nSub = lpEntry->GetSubCount();
            for (int sub = 0 ; sub < nSub ; sub++)
            {
                LPENTRY lpSubItem = lpEntry->GetSubEntry(sub);
                rdi.lParam = (LPARAM)lpSubItem;
                m_pResultData->InsertItem(&rdi);
            }
            break;
        }
    }
```

This function handles its work by first finding out the level of the object being shown, in the usual way: it obtains the cookie from the data object. Depending on the tier the object is on, `Show()` then sets up the columns in the header control for the results pane.

Once this relatively simple operation is out of the way, however, the issues become a bit subtler. If the sub-entries for a node are already displayed in the scope pane, then there is no more work to be done – the console handles the process of showing scope pane items in the results pane beneath the columns that you set up. However, if the items you want to display are *not* already scope data items, then you have to do the work of adding them to the results pane yourself. In the code above, items in the third-tier – the individual database connection information – are not shown in the scope pane, so they have to be added by you, through the `IResultData` interface. Using that is a lot like using the `IConsoleNameSpace` interface for adding scope-pane items: simply set up a `RESULTDATAITEM` structure and fill it with the information you want. Then, using `IResultData::InsertItem()`, insert one item for each sub-entry on the node.

This mechanism uses the same callback system as `SCOPEDATAITEM` does. When the console actually needs to show the individual items in the results pane, it makes one call to `GetDisplayInfo()` for each column in the results list, for each item:

```
STDMETHODIMP CComponent::GetDisplayInfo(RESULTDATAITEM* pResultDataItem)
{
    LPENTRY lpEntry = (LPENTRY)pResultDataItem->lParam;

    if(!lpEntry)
        return E_FAIL;
```

```
    if(pResultDataItem->str)
        delete [] pResultDataItem->str;

    int nTier = lpEntry->GetTier();

    switch(nTier)
    {
    // For computer level
    case 0:
        switch(pResultDataItem->nCol)
        {
        case 0:
            pResultDataItem->str = lpEntry->GetName();
            pResultDataItem->nImage = 0;
            break;
        case 1:
            pResultDataItem->str = lpEntry->GetConnections();
            break;
        case 2:
            pResultDataItem->str = lpEntry->GetRemaining();
            break;
        }
        break;

    // For Connections
    case 1:
        switch(pResultDataItem->nCol)
        {
        case 0:
            pResultDataItem->str = lpEntry->GetName();
            pResultDataItem->nImage = 2;
            break;
        case 1:
            pResultDataItem->str = lpEntry->GetPos();
            break;
        case 2:
            pResultDataItem->str = lpEntry->GetHandle();
            break;
        case 3:
            pResultDataItem->str = lpEntry->GetState();
            break;
        }
        break;

    }
    return S_OK;
}
```

This implementation simply determines which item is being shown (through the `CEntry` pointer stored in the `RESULTDATAITEM` structure's `lParam`), and then switches on the item and the column to show. After that, it reassigns the `str` member of the structure to equal the string representation of whatever member data for the entry the snap-in needs to show.

The last item I want to discuss in `CComponent` is the `Refresh()` method, which is a private function that handles the work necessary when the user selects the **Refresh** menu item – the message handler calls it from the `Notify()` function. To do its work, it simply calls the `RefreshSubEntries()` method on the `CEntry` object for the selected node.

```
void CComponent::Refresh(LPDATAOBJECT lpDataObject)
{
   long cookie;
   IPoolerMMCDataObject* pPoolObject;
   lpDataObject->QueryInterface(IID_IPoolerMMCDataObject,
                                (void**)&pPoolObject);
   pPoolObject->get_Cookie(&cookie);
   pPoolObject->Release();

   LPENTRY lpEntry = (LPENTRY)cookie;
   lpEntry->RefreshSubEntries();
}
```

Registry Entries

That's it for the interfaces! The last thing I want to look at here is the code to configure the proper registry entries for the snap-in, which sets up the snap-in name and the CLSID for the `ComponentData` coclass. The `Register()` function (below) is simply called from `DllRegisterServer()`, and there's a matching call to `Unregister()` from `DllUnregisterServer()`.

```
void Register()
{
   HKEY hMmcParentKey;
   RegOpenKey(HKEY_LOCAL_MACHINE,
           L"Software\\Microsoft\\MMC\\SnapIns", &hMmcParentKey);

   HKEY hObjMonParentKey;
   RegCreateKey(
         hMmcParentKey,
         L"{C8FF6D1B-F7C9-11D1-846A-0020AF05ED45}", // ComponentData coclass
         &hObjMonParentKey);

   RegSetValueEx(hObjMonParentKey,
              L"NameString", 0, REG_SZ,
              (LPBYTE)L"Pooler SnapIn", sizeof(L"Pooler SnapIn"));

   RegSetValueEx(
     hObjMonParentKey,
     L"NodeType", 0, REG_SZ,
   (LPBYTE)L"{A2AF0D5A-F7E6-11d1-846A-0020AF05ED45}", // Root Node Type UUID
     sizeof(L"{A2AF0D5A-F7E6-11d1-846A-0020AF05ED45}"));

   HKEY hStandAloneKey;
   RegCreateKey(hObjMonParentKey, L"StandAlone", &hStandAloneKey);
   RegCloseKey(hStandAloneKey);
```

```
    HKEY hNodeTypesKey;
    RegCreateKey(hObjMonParentKey, L"NodeTypes", &hNodeTypesKey);

    HKEY hNodeKey;
    RegCreateKey(hNodeTypesKey,
                 L"{A2AF0D5A-F7E6-11d1-846A-0020AF05ED45}",
                 &hNodeKey);

    RegSetValueEx(hNodeKey,
                  NULL, 0, REG_SZ,
                  (LPBYTE)L"Root Node",
                  sizeof(L"Root Node"));

    RegCloseKey(hNodeKey);
    RegCloseKey(hNodeTypesKey);
    RegCloseKey(hObjMonParentKey);
    RegCloseKey(hMmcParentKey);
}
```

Running the Sample

First, build the project. It should be automatically registered on the system as a snap-in. Then open MMC, and make sure that the amended Business Object service is started.

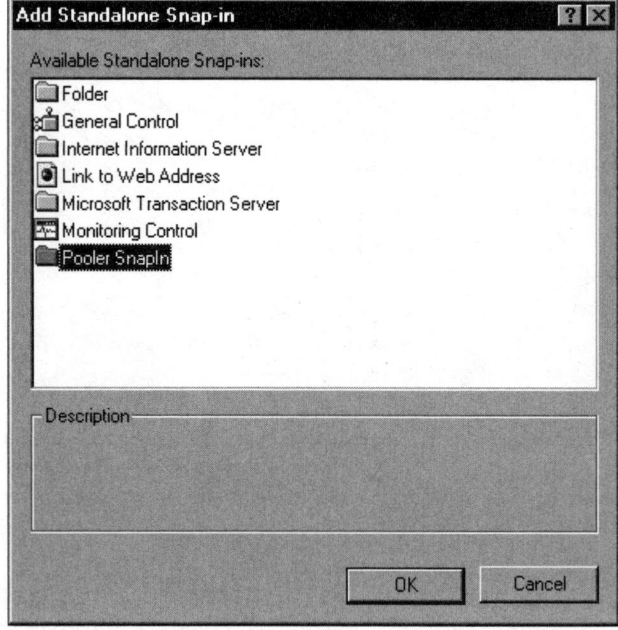

To try it out for yourself, simply add an instance of the Pooler SnapIn to the console, then right click on the main node and click New | Computer. The dialog box will appear in which you can specify the name of the machine that has the instance of the Business Object service you want to monitor.

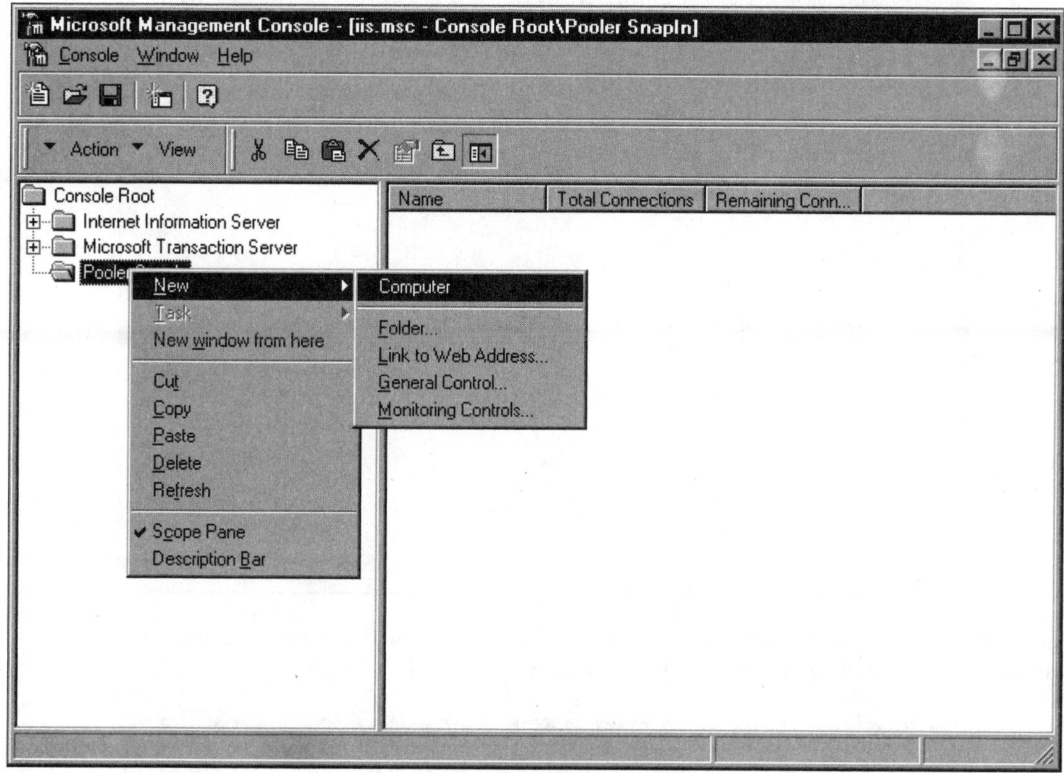

This sample allows you to view the information that it's configured to gather about any number of instances of the service, and on various machines. To monitor an additional system, you just have to add a new computer to the root node when you start the console.

You should now see a display something like the screenshots below. Notice that some of the handles are free and some are used. To achieve this load, I ran a few instances of the BusObjClient application to load down the system a bit, then selected Refresh from the context menu a few times until I got a decent picture of the load; you can do the same as you experiment.

At the top node level, summary information is displayed for each computer.

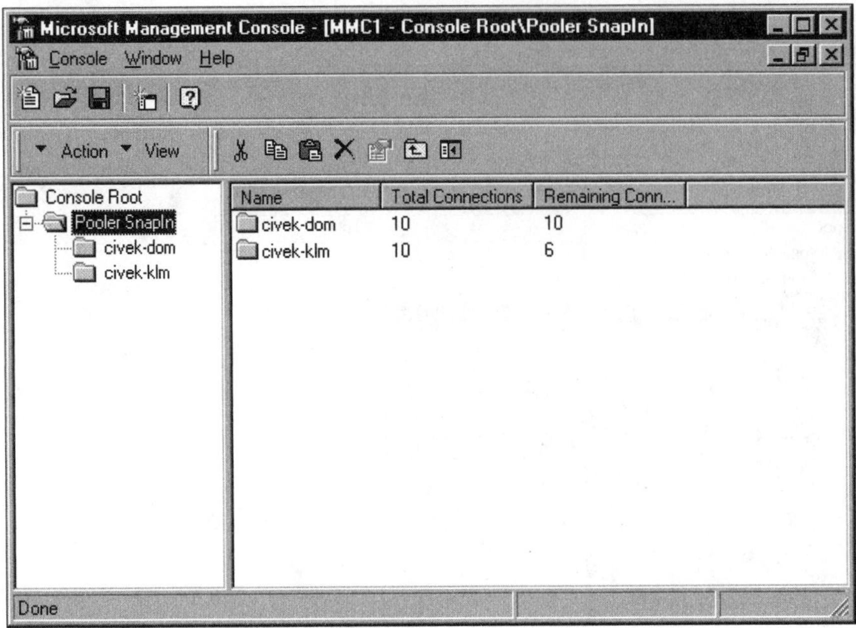

And, at the computer node level, the res ults pane is populated with information about each individual handle being managed by that running instance of the service.

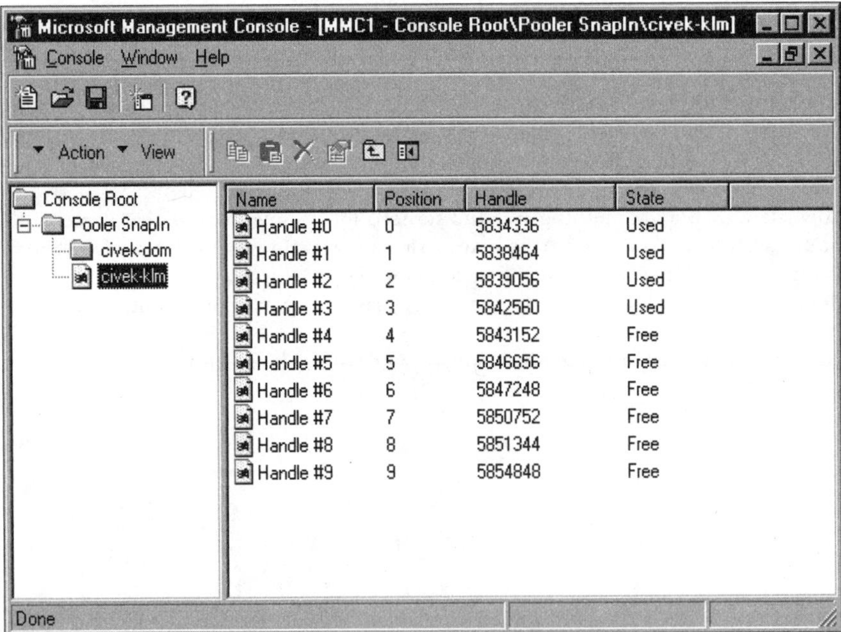

Conclusions, Disclaimers, and Limitations

A couple of final comments on this MMC sample:

- Typically, some of the node levels would be persisted to the `.msc` file, allowing the user to save configuration information. In our example, you would probably want to store the computer names, so that the user doesn't have to set up connections again each time. To do it, you'll need to add support for `IPersistStorage` to the `CComponentData` object.
- I didn't implement a property page dialog for manipulating the registry settings, but you could do it as an additional exercise, if you desire. To do so, you'd just need to add support for a dialog box and a context menu extension for Properties on the 'computer' node type. You should also add support for the custom handler message back to the service, as we did in the control panel applet.

All in all, I consider MMC to be a fairly elegant, powerful, sometimes complex mechanism for building robust administration applications for your services. There's a lot of work to do, but the results can be impressive.

Summary

In this chapter, we`ve looked at the two main administration APIs. Between them, they give a high degree of control to administrators of your service. Along with the use of event log, they are an important aspect of professional service implementation.

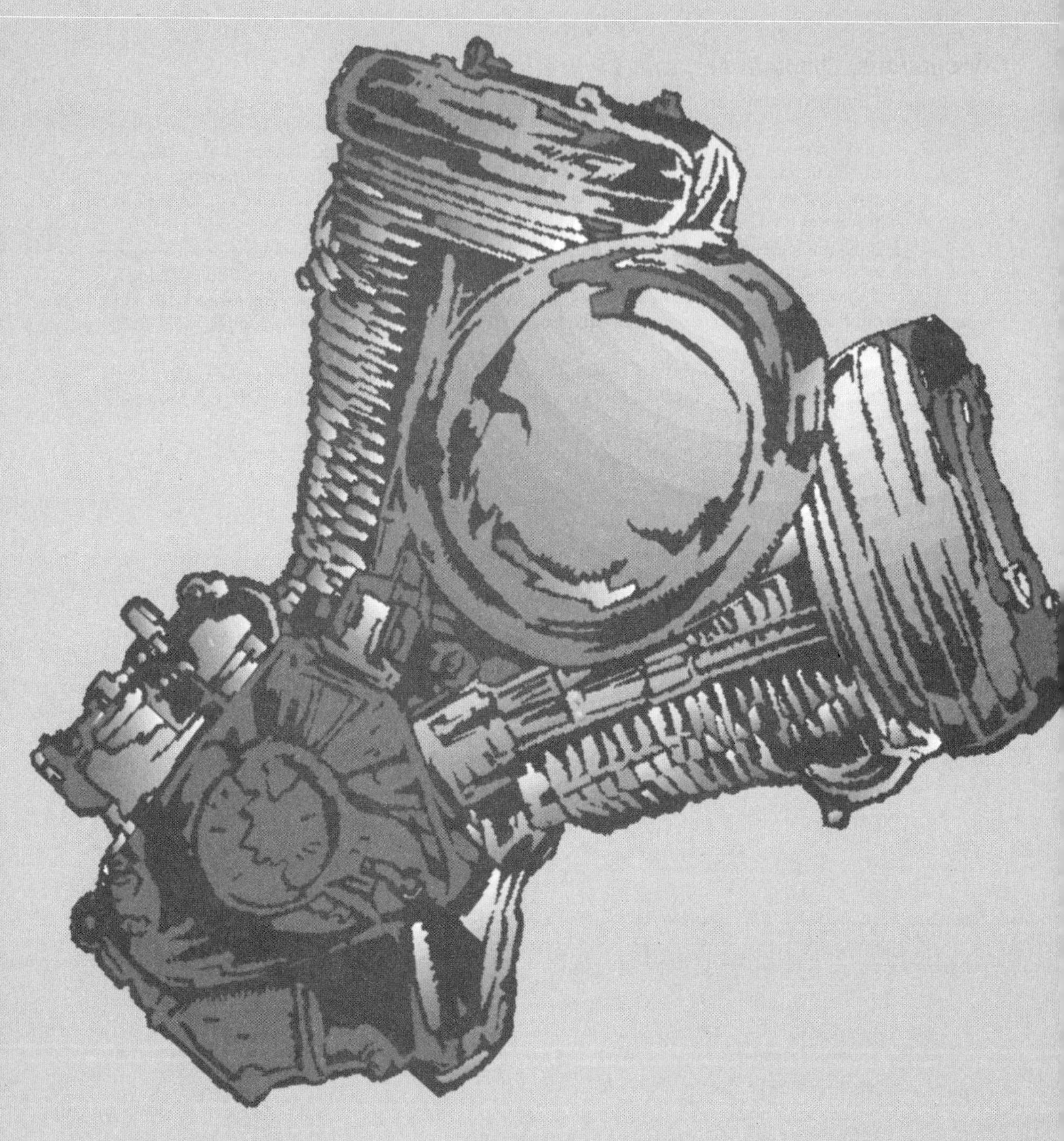

12

Service Design Recap

In this final chapter, I want to accomplish a couple of things. First, I want to supply you with a process, or method, that you can go through when designing a service that will help you uncover the majority of the architectural issues that need considering. Second, I will discuss some of the miscellaneous issues that don't really fit anywhere else, such as creating 'service-like' applications in the Windows 95 operating system.

Service Design Checklist

Let's start out with an overview of the service design considerations checklist that I'm going to present:

- ❑ What is the usage pattern?
- ❑ What triggers action?
- ❑ How will the service communicate?
- ❑ What types of clients will it communicate with?
- ❑ Security:
  - ❑ What account will the service run under?
    - ❑ Is access to remote resources required?
  - ❑ How will the service protect access to resources:
    - ❑ Impersonation?
    - ❑ Do its own access check calls?
    - ❑ Call `LogonUser()`?
    - ❑ How will the service protect its own data?
    - ❑ Is data encryption needed?
    - ❑ Are security audits needed?

- What do control requests mean to the service?
- When will the service start?
- How will the service be administered:
  - What tool will administer it?
  - What will be 'administerable'?
  - Who will be able to administer it?
  - Will it expose performance counter data?
- How will the service be installed?
- What events will be logged?
- What threading model will it use?
- Will the service present a user interface?
- Other considerations:
  - Should more than one service go in the process?
  - Does the service need parameters?
  - What other services does the service depend on?
- Why *not* use a service?

What is the Usage Pattern?

This very first question is helpful in focusing your attention on what the service *does*. Throughout this book, I've presented different usage patterns that sample the major rôles a service can fit into, and it's highly likely that the service you're writing fits one or more of these patterns. If you can discern the pattern or patterns that it fits, you are well on your way to understanding a great many of the major design issues for the service you're writing.

For the sake of clarity (and memory), here are those patterns again:

Pattern	Description
Monitor	Watches a resource and notifies when something happens
Agent	Takes an action on behalf of someone in an automated way
Quartermaster	Pre-allocates expensive or hard-to-obtain resources and hands them out to clients in an efficient way, saving time for the client and strain on the resource.
Business Object	Serves to house components that encapsulate business logic.
Switchboard	Serves as a 'hub' to connect clients to the 'required' resource server – the one that's least busy or that has the correct files or data set, perhaps. A rarer pattern.

Clearly, you already have a pretty good idea of what the service is going to do – if you didn't, you wouldn't be writing it. However, if you can frame the design in terms of identifying the usage patterns (and you'll find that most services fit into at least one of the patterns above), then you can do some quick architectural work in your head.

For example, think about the Business Object sample from Chapter 9. In fact, despite its name, this is a *combination* of the Quartermaster and Business Object patterns, because not only does it hand out objects that encapsulate business logic to clients, but it also does its work with 'pooled' ODBC connections. Right away, this knowledge tells you that you need a global mechanism to handle the 'pooler' portion, and probably a set of COM objects to do the requested work. Already the architecture is starting to take shape in your head.

What Triggers Action?

Considering services as usage patterns also helps you to answer another important question: "What triggers the service to do something?" Think about it. Most of the time, a service just sits there and doesn't do much. What wakes it up and makes it take action?

In the **Monitor** pattern, it is usually either the fact that a fixed amount of time for a run cycle has elapsed, or there has been notification by a resource on a callback that something has happened to that resource. That means the service has to run on a timer loop, or watch a callback mechanism.

In the case of the **Agent**, the service either goes out on a time schedule to gather some resources (data, files, or results of calculations), or it reacts to a user request and then comes back asynchronously when it's done.

The **Quartermaster** usually gets forced into action when a client asks for one of its resources. However, it may also do things of its own accord, to 'tune' its utilization of resources. During periods of heavy load, it could keep an eye on its own state and pump up the number of resources it pre-allocates. In periods of lighter load, it may relax a little and de-allocate some of those resources.

The **Business Object** typically acts on behalf of a client request. When the client wants some work done, the service creates an instance of the Business Object and does the work. This object may in turn have interactions with other resources resident inside the service.

The **Switchboard** watches a set of resources or resource servers. When a client wants to be connected to one of the watched resources, the Switchboard reacts by handing out a connection or resource name that can best handle the request. It bases its decision on whatever criteria it is watching for in the resource servers.

If you're really concentrating hard, you'll have noticed that examining the thing that triggers action will start to give you an idea of what the service's main run loop is going to look like. Will it work on a timer, or react to an incoming network call, or both? This in turn clues you in to what the different control operations (start, stop, pause, and continue) are going to mean semantically to the service.

How will the Service Communicate?

If the service fits one of the patterns that does work directly on request of a client, then you must decide what mechanism the service will use to communicate with the client. We've discussed some of these mechanisms within the pages of this book, but there are others to choose from as well. Personally, I prefer to use the 'new' technologies, such as COM/DCOM or MSMQ, to communicate between client process and server process. I have found that these technologies work well for a high percentage of service scenarios.

Under some circumstances, though, you may wish to use one of the other networking technologies, such as named pipes, sockets, or even straight RPC (rather than DCOM). Of these three, sockets are probably the most common, as they have applications in Internet scenarios in which you might need custom socket services to handle Internet client requests. In these situations, it is more difficult to use DCOM and virtually impossible to use MSMQ because of security and other concerns.

Note that this question remains relevant even when the service is of the Monitor pattern and therefore has no 'clients' *per se*. How will the service let interested parties, such as system administrators, know about the results of its monitoring activity? By posting events to the event log? By posting log entries to a private log? By using an MMC snap-in, or a custom application, or performance monitor counters? The answer to these questions affects design a lot.

What Types of Clients will it Communicate With?

As an extension to the previous question, you will probably want to consider the *types* of clients that the service will be communicating with. Will they be VB apps running on Windows 95, NT server processes, other NT services, or web clients? Sometimes, these considerations can change the design picture radically. For instance, the level of authentication you can achieve when using DCOM with Windows 95 clients may alter your security architecture to a considerable degree.

Security

The next high-level design topic to consider is security. Within this subject, there are several issues to consider:

- What account will the service run under?
  - Is access to remote resources required?
- How will the service protect access to resources:
  - Impersonation?
  - Do its own access check calls?
  - Call `LogonUser()`?
- How will the service protect its own data?
- Is data encryption needed?
- Are security audits needed?

Let's take a look at these questions and consider them in a bit more detail.

What Account will the Service Run Under?

As you'll remember, this is a fairly important consideration, and its solution is dictated by a whole host of other issues. The most important of these is what *other* resources the service needs to access, both on its own machine and on remote machines. If the service needs extensive access to resources on *remote* machines, then a 'logon as' account that's a domain account may be necessary. On the other hand, if the service needs extensive access to resources on the *local* machine, there is no better account than LocalSystem, because it has almost total access to the machine's resources.

If the service needs lots of access locally *and* needs access to remote resources that differ by client, then you may wish to use LocalSystem as the 'logon as' account and do `LogonUser()` calls to get a primary token for the client, and then make the remote access. If you need access locally and the remote access is more general (that is, not client-specific), you may wish to use a special domain account and be sure to grant explicit access to the local resources you need.

As a final consideration, remember that every service with a non-LocalSystem 'logon as' account requires its own window station, and those are scarce resources that run out quickly. Furthermore, if you want to interact with the logged-on user directly (heavens forbid!), LocalSystem is really the only choice.

My general rule of thumb is to assume that LocalSystem will do the trick, unless I have some convincing reason to believe otherwise.

How will the Service Protect Access to Resources?

The next question to answer concerns the security mechanism that the service will use to authorize the use of resources. The first option is for the service to impersonate the calling client, and then access the resources. This gives the operating system the opportunity to call `AccessCheck()` itself, to validate that the client has the right to do what it is asking to do. This works perfectly well for resources on the same machine as the service. If the service needs to access a resource on a different machine, then impersonation doesn't work and the service will have to fall back on `LogonUser()` to imitate the client.

Second, the service can call `AccessCheck()` itself on the secured resource, and then if the check passes muster it can access the resource under the service's principal. This method is used less often; most of the time, allowing NT to do the access check is adequate.

Finally, if the service does not access local or remote resources, or if security on those resources is not considered to be an issue (it could be that Everyone has access to them anyway), you might choose to ignore resource security altogether and do no validation of the client.

How will the Service Protect its Own Data?

Sometimes, a service will create its own private data that is not really a securable system resource. This private information might be a data structure that contains the results of a query, for instance, that the service holds in a cache. It may want certain clients to access the structure and others not to. In such cases, the service can create its own private objects, assign them rights with DACLs, and then call `AccessCheck()` on them to make sure that the calling client has the rights it should. This is a pretty elegant solution to securing private data structures or private objects, should you need to do so.

Is Data Encryption Needed?

Another question you will want to ask yourself is whether the information that moves back and forth between client and service needs to be encrypted. For instance, a service that moves credit card numbers back and forth to clients probably requires some sort of packet-level encryption. You will need to decide which functions (perhaps all of them) require that wire-level encryption. Be aware, though, that encryption can be slow. It should only be used if the information to protect is truly valuable, and in those specific areas where that information is moved from place to place.

If you decide that you need encryption, you'll need to select a networking mechanism that supports it. That means using DCOM, RPC, SSL, or MSMQ encrypted messages to move data back and forth. Alternatively, you might choose to move data on a file-by-file basis and encrypt the file itself with some other mechanism (like the CryptoAPI), and then move it with standard networking mechanisms.

Are Security Audits Needed?

Lastly, you'll want to consider whether the service requires auditing and audit alarms. Do you just *have* to know when a client tries an incorrect password? Do you need a log of *every* client who accesses that private data object? NT can audit just about anything, so try to choose exactly what you need carefully. Remember, too, that all auditing has overhead associated with it, so don't get carried away.

What do Control Requests Mean to the Service?

Another issue that you need to consider very early in the design process is what the various control messages – stop, pause, continue – mean to the service. Everybody knows that 'stop' should close down the service process, but what it does *before* closing down the process can differ radically by service. For instance, should the service stop accepting new requests? Almost definitely. Should the service let existing clients finish their immediate work before closing? Maybe – it depends on what that work is, and how long it will take.

In fact, this decision depends almost entirely on the granularity of the requests that clients might make. If the clients make quick calls to interface methods on relatively stateless COM objects hosted in the service, they should probably be allowed to finish. If client requests entail multiple calls to objects that do have state, then probably the service shouldn't wait for the interface pointers to free up.

What about pause/continue semantics? Should a pause request prevent clients from issuing new requests, but maintain their state? Should it keep new clients from connecting? Should it keep a Monitor-style service from iterating through its timing loop? Should it clear the service's cache of any data structures it might be holding? I can't tell you the *answers* to these questions; the point is that it's up to you to decide, and you should do so *before* you start writing code for the service.

When will the Service Start?

Does the service need to start when the machine boots up, or can it start on the first request from a client? The deciding factor here is how long the setup for that first client request will be. If starting the service and connecting to the required resources takes only a few seconds, and the client calls might be few and far between, it may be OK to let the first client start it (presuming it's a COM service). On the other hand, if the resources it needs are expensive, it may be better to let the service start at boot time so they're ready for the first client. In other words, it's a question of time-to-start and the amount of use the service gets.

As a rule, services that fit the Monitor and Agent patterns will be auto-start services. This is because they typically do background work independent of client requests. You don't want the administrator to have to remember to start them!

How will the Service be Administered?

This major subject area breaks down into several sub-topics:

- What tool will administer it?
- What will be 'administerable'?
- Who will be able to administer it?
- Will it expose performance counter data?

What Tool will Administer it?

Your choice here is between a custom application, a control panel applet, or an MMC snap-in. In an ideal world, I'd pick the snap-in, since that fits best with NT's long-term direction in administration applications. However, snap-ins can be difficult to learn to program, and development time or a different administration security model may constrain you to using one of the other options.

What will be Administerable?

A bigger issue is that of the *kind* of information the administration tool will show. It certainly needs to be able to change any of the configuration information stored in the registry (and *all* configuration information needs to be in the registry, so the service can be configured remotely), but what else it does depends on the service. In the previous chapter, we created an MMC snap-in that was able to view the states of the various resource handles in the Quartermaster sample in real time. You may wish to show something different, or indeed nothing at all. If you *do* need to show information like this, be sure to plan the entry points to the service so that the snap-in or other administration application can get to the information it needs quickly and with low overhead.

Who will be Able to Administer it?

Under Windows NT, only members of the Administrators group, power users, or the LocalSystem account can stop and start services by default. If you need a different group of people to be able to do it, you must change the service DACL with a call to `SetServiceObjectSecurity()`.

Will it Expose Performance Counter Data?

We didn't discuss the development of performance counter DLLs in this book, but for some types of services, the information they provide can be very important. If this is the case for your service, decide *exactly* what those counters will be early on, so that you can track them inside the service with efficient data structures. There's nothing worse than designing a whole service, and then deciding to add performance counters for information that you don't code for, or that's very inefficient to obtain. On the other hand, don't make the service itself inefficient just so that you get easy access to counter data – find a healthy way to satisfy both needs. You'll also need a good mechanism to move those counters out to the memory file to share them with the service's performance DLL.

For information about adding performance counters to your projects, you could do worse than take a look in the online help under Platform SDK\Windows Base Services\General Library\Performance Data Helper\Adding Performance Counters.

How will the Service be Installed?

Another issue to consider is the installation mechanism for the service. Will you install it with a command-line parameter like the `-service` flag provided by the ATL service implementation, or should you write your own installation package? That mostly depends on whether the service is 'commercial grade' or not. Typically, when people buy services, they expect them to have an installation package. For in-house services, the answer really depends on how many supporting files, DLLs, and executables come with the service, and how much additional registry configuration and so forth might be necessary. The greater these dependencies, the better it usually is to ship an installation program with the service. Also, if installing the service requires the user to answer questions about configuration information for it, an installation package is necessary.

What Events will be Logged?

This question really boils down to, "What events will be interesting to the system administrator?" Typically, in a released service, relatively few events should be logged. The administrator should be notified only when certain exception conditions that affect the performance of the service occur, or when a critical error causes the service process to terminate. You don't have to be an absolute minimalist and log nothing at all, but as the saying goes, "No news is good news." If everything is working, keep the log chatter to a minimum. If it's not, be as loquacious as you need to be to help out the administrator.

Furthermore, 'cascading' event information should be avoided if possible. For example, if your service is running out of disk space to do work for a client request, should you really post an event to the log with *every* request, notifying the administrator that the system is almost out of space? Once is almost certainly enough. We've all seen services that get into an error state and post an event to the log every few milliseconds until the log is out of space; if you can, you should try not to do this.

Sometimes, though, it *is* helpful to be able to see a lot more information about what's going on inside a service. For instance, to solve a real-time problem at a customer site, you might need a 'diagnostic' run that logs much more information about what the service is doing. Simply starting the service with an additional parameter might enable this behavior. If you do need such functionality, decide what you need to log on all levels, and plan it into the code as you're writing the service.

On the occasions when a service requires an 'activity' log that shows the outcomes of serviced requests, attempts at access, etc., an alternative to high-volume logging to the event log is to create your own logging mechanism. The format of a log file that might be used for this purpose could be anything you want, but a decent choice is to output a simple text file in standard HTML format. This keeps the logging structures simple and lightweight, and allows a variety of viewers to read the log.

What Threading Model will it Use?

This section is not so much the answer to a question, as a group of design considerations to remember. When you write NT services, multiple threads are a given, so choosing a high performance model to get work done is also essential.

Choosing a Threading Model

Depending on which networking mechanism you use to communicate between client and server, the threading model you use is more or less of an issue. If you're using RPC or DCOM, then the threading model is pretty much handled for you beneath the covers. RPC handles the size and mechanics of the thread pool for servicing client requests, so you have very few responsibilities in this area. About your only responsibility for DCOM is to choose the threading model that the objects you are hosting will be contained in. As we saw in Chapter 9, when you're programming services the model should almost always be a multithreaded apartment (MTA). If you choose that, and protect your class members and shared code in the way I described, you'll get a way of handling many simultaneous requests with good performance, virtually for free.

Some network communication mechanisms, on the other hand, require you to do more work. Sockets, for example, and MSMQ require you to roll your own model in which multiple client requests (or multiple messages) can be processed simultaneously. Therefore, you have to implement a model in order for work to get done. As in any situation, you have several choices:

- **A process per client.** Actually, you really *don't* have this choice for services. Furthermore, it would be stupid on NT – it's really a UNIX thing to do. I just mention it for the sake of completeness, and unless you are only prototyping or testing, never do it on NT.
- **Single thread, single client at a time.** The simplest model, and the one with the worst performance. The process has a single run loop that accepts a single connection, does the work it asks, and then returns to the top of the loop. Such a model could not take advantage of having multiple processors; it wouldn't scale at all.
- **Single thread, multiple clients.** The service maintains and selects between multiple connections on a single thread. In the sockets API, this type of model is handled by the `select()` function. This is a poorly performing and poorly scalable model, and high-performance services that employ sockets should never use it.
- **A thread per client.** In this model, you create a thread for each incoming client request. This model performs quite well for small numbers of clients, but scales poorly for larger and larger numbers of simultaneous requests. This is because a growing number of threads in the process tax the system due to too much context switching.
- **Worker threads.** For many types of service, this is the most scaleable of the models. In it, the service creates a pool of worker threads. An additional thread monitors the incoming requests and assigns the work to one of the worker threads. When a worker thread is done, it is returned to the pool to await further work, which is usually done synchronously in this model. This model performs better and is more scaleable than the thread-per-client model for large numbers of clients, but performs less well for smaller numbers of clients. Different people have different formulas, but the one I use is below:

  Number of worker threads = Number of processors * 2 + 1

  As a general rule, you should have at least as many threads doing work for clients as you have processors, provided that those threads can actually do work independently of one another. The formula above works well for me in most cases.
- **Worker threads with Asynchronous I/O.** This model is only appropriate to services that deal with file handles. In it, I/O is done asynchronously, so a single thread can initiate multiple I/O requests *without* waiting for them to return. This is known as **overlapped I/O**, and for services to which it is appropriate, it is the most highly scalable model of all.

Helpfully, both sockets' and MSMQ's programming motif is native NT file handles, so asynchronous I/O using overlapped I/O is possible. Furthermore, it is possible to use I/O completion ports as a mechanism to help coordinate the work between worker threads.

Which of the available models you choose depends on what the service is doing, and on what kind of client load you expect.

Other Design Issues

It is important that when a service has no work to do, it should be truly idle. It should consume as few resources as possible, keeping memory, CPU, and I/O low by not having many timers or busy loops, and by keeping miscellaneous housekeeping activity to a minimum.

Writing good multithreaded applications is difficult, even for people who are proficient at it and have lots of experience. The best general rule that I can give you is to try to reduce the surface area between threads as much as possible. In other words, keep globals and class members as few as possible, and know that when you touch them, you need to protect them with synchronization mechanisms. If you think about what different threads will be touching what parts of your classes and objects as you're coding, you'll find that knowing what to protect becomes much easier.

By the way, you *have* to test your multithreaded code on a symmetric multiprocessing (SMP) machine. You just have to. There is no way you'll find all the problems in your service until you do so. Just as an example, your service can actually run *slower* on an SMP system if it has highly contentious critical sections, because now, multiple processors are simultaneously contending for the section and causing it to block. If you discover that during testing, you can change the locking design.

Will the Service Present a User Interface?

Please say that it won't! All communication with the user should be through a separate mechanism, such as a separate application or the Event Log. If the service must have a user interface, it must run under the LocalSystem account, or perform manipulations to open the interactive window station.

Other Considerations

Other things you might want to consider:

- **Should more than one service go in the process?** Sometimes, two parts of a service really are separate, and you need the ability to start and stop them separately. However, they may still need to share global data structures, or it could just make sense to put them both in the same process to reduce overhead. If so, multiple services in the same process may be just the ticket.
- **Does the service need parameters?** Will the service need any start-up parameters, such as an adjustable diagnostic logging level, or will the service executable need any command-line parameters?
- **What other services does the service depend on?** Typically, this is not too important until installation time, but you'll want to make sure that the service dependencies are done right, especially for auto-start services.

Why *not* Use a Service?

You now have a pretty good idea about how to begin designing a service if you need one, but when *shouldn't* you use a service? Here are a few situations in which your application should not be a service:

- It needs a GUI, or its main work is user interface work
- Use by clients is few and far between, and it doesn't do any work when a client isn't calling into it
- It doesn't have heavy startup cost
- It doesn't need to keep any type of process state between calls
- It doesn't do any background processing independent of user requests

As a rule, if the proposed service doesn't fit into one of the design patterns I've mentioned in this book, its work could quite probably be done just as well by an application or a COM server.

Microsoft Transaction Server

Under some situations, MTS can be a good substitute for writing a service. MTS allows COM DLL servers to be run in their own process space by using the MTS surrogate. MTS packages can be configured to live for several minutes (or forever) even after the client call that launched the package is over. In a sense, then, the server can 'live on' beyond the last client call, much like a demand-start COM service would.

Furthermore, the COM servers resident inside an MTS package can use a resource manager known as the SPM (shared property manager) to keep state for the package even while there are no clients. And, in situations where the resource(s) being used by the COM server has resource dispensers for MTS, these resources are pooled by MTS. So, for instance, the ODBC connections used by different COM DLLs inside a package can be pooled and shared. Under some circumstances, this functionality is exactly what you need to keep from having to write a service.

Lastly, it is also possible to write custom resource dispensers to dole out resources from a pool, much like the Quartermaster pattern from Chapter 8 does. These dispensers can then be plugged into MTS and used to pool resources to any MTS component.

Ways Around Writing Real Services

The preceding discussion notwithstanding, sometimes you just don't need a high performance service, or one with total flexibility, or one with all the bells and whistles. Occasionally, all you need is an executable that *looks* like a service, and gets started by the operating system at boot time. Perhaps you need something that runs on Windows 95, or you like to write VB code instead of C++, but you still want your application to be run like a service. In this section, I'll talk about two topics that can get you started in writing services that require a little less investment in time and energy. (I can do that now that you've read the whole book!)

Windows 95 'Fake' Services

If you need to create a process that runs under Windows 95 but acts like a service, the issues are not really that hard. There are just a few things to look out for because Windows 95 is more limited in certain areas than Windows NT is.

No ServiceMain

The main area of limitation is that Windows 95 has none of the service API – no SCM, no service installation APIs, no nothing. That means that to the casual observer, a Windows 95 server application looks exactly like a regular console application. In other words, it starts from `main()` just as any other application does.

No Service Control Handler

There is no service control handler under Windows 95, so the stop semantics and proper shutdown have to be handled with a **Ctrl-Break handler**. This means that the user must issue a stop command manually, in the console window. To register the *Ctrl-Break* handler with the system, use the following API call:

```
SetConsoleCtrlHandler(W95Handler, TRUE);
```

In this call, `W95Handler` is the name of the function that gets called by the operating system when *Ctrl+Break* is pressed. As you might expect, the function has a similar set of semantics to `Handler()` for services, accepting a parameter that is the type of control command. `W95Handler()` might look something like this:

```
BOOL WINAPI W95Handler(DWORD dwControlType)
{
   switch(dwControlType)
   {
   case CTRL_C_EVENT:
      break;

   case CTRL_BREAK_EVENT:
      break;

   case CTRL_CLOSE_EVENT:
      break;

   case CTRL_LOGOFF_EVENT:
      break;

   case CTRL_SHUTDOWN_EVENT:
      break;
   }

   return TRUE;
}
```

For each `case`, you would do whatever was relevant. That might mean posting a 'quit' message to a thread, or any one of a number of other things.

Registry Entries for AutoLoad

There is no service installation API, so to make a process start automatically when the system boots, you must add its executable name to the registry. Simply add a string value whose name is whatever you want to name the 'service', and whose data is the path and command line that it takes to run the executable. Add that value to the following path:

```
HKEY_LOCAL_MACHINE\SOFTWARE\Microsoft\Windows\CurrentVersion\RunServices
```

Other Differences

There are a host of technologies you can't use under Windows 95, including Unicode, the extensive security API set, and the Event Log. You'll have to find substitutes or workarounds for all of these missing features.

NT Service ActiveX Control

Since Visual Basic applications have difficulty with the programming model for NT services, a tool was created in the form of an ActiveX control to help VB applications call the service API functions. The control is known as **NTSRVOCX**. To use it, simply drop the control onto the main form for the proposed VB service.

The control works by translating control events from the operating system into VB events, and by wrapping `ServiceMain()`. This keeps VB from having to deal with the pointers to functions that the service API requires. The control also has support for event logging and service installation.

The tool is very handy for writing services in VB, but you should be aware that the services it creates have only a single thread, and are really not acceptable for high-performance work. Still, if you need something that will only handle a few clients and needs to be written quickly, this tool may be for you. Check out the article *NT Service: An OLE Control for Creating Windows NT Services in Visual Basic* in the MSDN Library for more details, including where you can obtain **NTSRVOCX**.

Conclusion

In this capstone chapter, I have reiterated and re-framed many of the issues from the preceding chapters into a full-blown design checklist. Hopefully, this list will help you start your own service design work. Good luck!

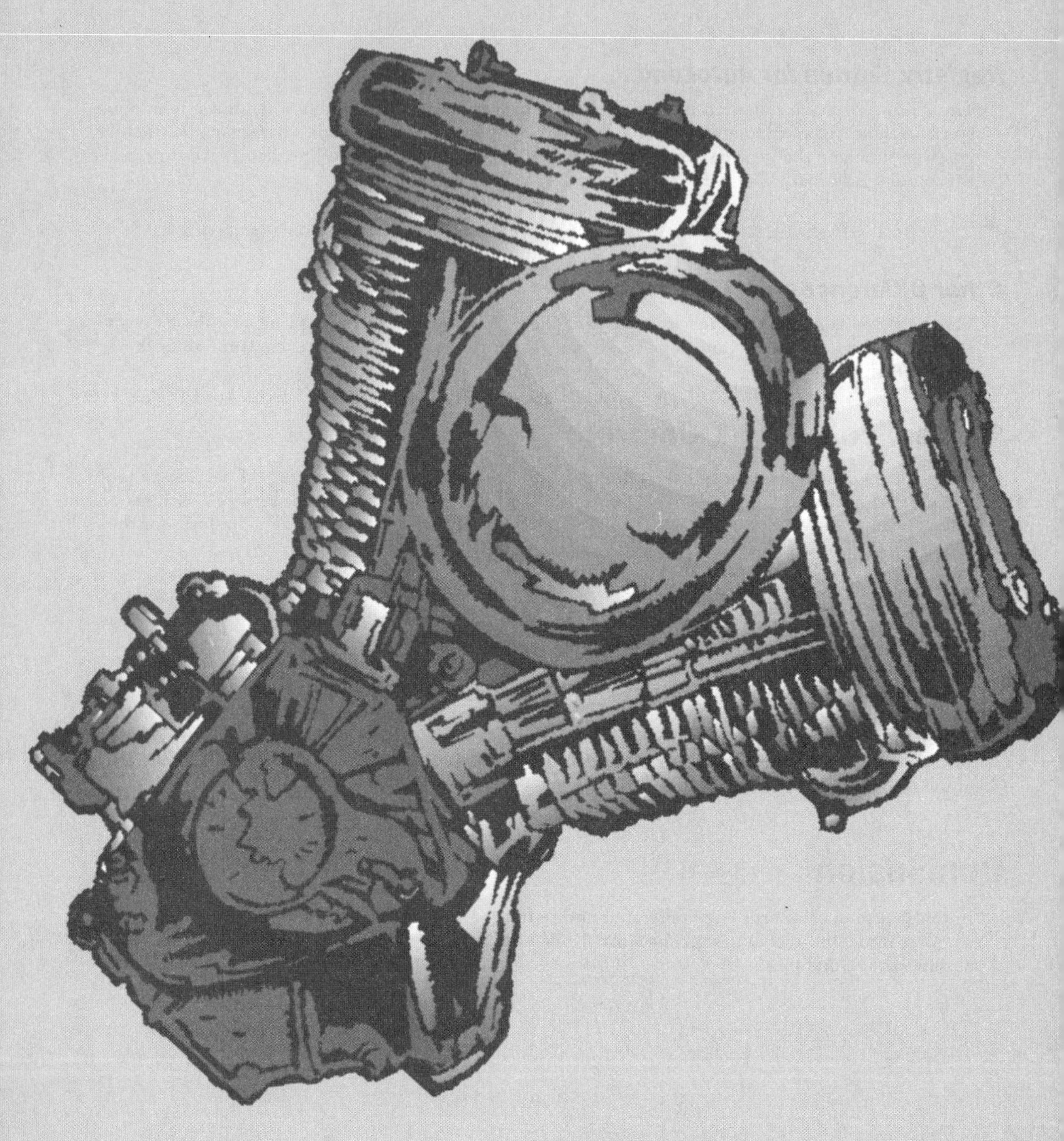

Index

Symbols

A

D

E

J

K

L

O

S

V

W